CHILD DEVELOPMENT

McGRAW-HILL SERIES IN PSYCHOLOGY

Consulting Editors
Norman Garmezy
Lyle V. Jones

SIXTH EDITION

McGRAW-HILL BOOK COMPANY
New York St. Louis San Francisco Auckland Bogotá Düsseldorf Johannesburg London

CHILD DEVELOPMENT

ELIZABETH B. HURLOCK

Madrid Mexico Montreal New Delhi Panama Paris São Paulo Singapore Sydney Tokyo Toronto

This book was set in Helvetica by Progressive
Typographers.
The editors were Richard R. Wright and David Dunham;
the designer was Joan E. O'Connor;
the production supervisor was Leroy A. Young.
New drawings were done by
J & R Services, Inc.
Von Hoffmann Press, Inc., was printer and binder.

Our special thanks to the children of the Glen Rock, New Jersey,
Public Schools and to their art teacher, Sandy Wright,
for the chapter-opening artwork.

Cover   Chris Johnson, age 7
Title Page   Jennifer Rudnitsky, age 9
Chapter 1   David Alport, age 9
        2   Kristen Van Vliet, age 8
        3   Gail Richman, age 12
        4   Donna Shields, age 8
        5   Lauren Heller, age 5
        6   Nancy Alessi, age 10
        7   Andrew Tuite, age 8
        8   Sally Ann Fortescue, age 10
        9   Cindy DeLucia, age 8
       10   Lori Campora, age 9
       11   Carolyn Marra, age 9
       12   Natalie Cvijanovich, age 9
       13   Karen Soderlund, age 9
       14   Christine Colosimo, age 10
       15   Mary Jane Slump, age 9
       16   Karen Bloom, age 11
       17   Jay Banta, age 6
       18   David Rosenstein, age 12

CHILD DEVELOPMENT

1234567890 VHVH 783210987
Library of Congress Cataloging in Publication Data

Hurlock, Elizabeth Bergner, date
    Child development.

    (McGraw-Hill series in psychology)
    Includes bibliographies and index.
    1. Child psychology. I. Title.
BF721.H8 1978   155.4   77-24365
ISBN 0-07-031427-6

To my daughter,
Gail McKnight Beckman

CONTENTS

PREFACE

The purpose of revising a textbook is to make it a better teaching tool for instructors and a better, more interesting learning tool for students. In this sixth edition of *Child Development,* which first appeared in 1942, attempts have been made to reach these objectives by the following changes and additions.

First, because of favorable reactions to the boxes used to highlight important facts in the previous edition, more boxes are used in this edition. These boxes should help instructors and students gain quick insight into the most important facts presented in each chapter.

Second, at the end of each chapter a section has been added to stress the important hazards in the area of development covered in the chapter. This section is designed to serve two purposes: to emphasize that all development is subject to variations and distortions that are hazardous to children's personal and social adjustments and to show that, with foreknowledge, many of these variations and distortions can be prevented or minimized.

Third, the bibliographies, given at the end of each chapter, have been updated by omitting many of the older studies to provide space for the newer ones in the same areas. Instructors and students will thus have at their disposal the latest sources of research material, most of which give references to the older studies in their bibliographies.

Fourth, fewer graphs from research studies have been used than in the earlier editions of this book. The justification for this is that, unless the studies from which these graphs have been taken are reported in detail, the graphs will lose much of their meaning. In their place, more cartoons and line drawings have

been added. It is hoped that they will make the material of each chapter more meaningful and easier to remember.

Fifth, while all revisions update old material, this revision has added material from research areas that are somewhat off the beaten track and have not yet appeared in many of the textbooks in child development. This material includes children's interests in names and the effects of names on their personal and social adjustments; the effects of attractiveness and clothes on children; the sources of happiness in childhood; and the importance of sex-role development. Because of the present trend toward changing the traditional sex roles of the two sexes, a new chapter devoted to sex-role development has been added.

Sixth, because of the important role theories about different areas of development have played in spurring research in those areas, a brief discussion of some of the most influential theories has been added. In each case, an attempt has been made to show what the theory has contributed to an understanding of children's development.

Seventh, to eliminate the distraction to readers of constant reference in the text to sources from which the material has been taken, relatively few references are given throughout the chapters. When they are given, they are used mainly for three purposes: to indicate the source of a quotation, to indicate the source or sources of evidence for what might be regarded as a controversial statement, and to show the sources from which material for the boxes has been taken.

All the references listed in the bibliographies at the end of each chapter have been used directly for sources of material in that chapter and indirectly have influenced my thinking about the material presented. I want to acknowledge my indebtedness to the authors of the books and journals I have used as sources for this book.

I also want to express my gratitude to my professional colleagues who have read the manuscript for this revision, and for their many helpful criticisms and suggestions, most of which I have used. Their help has been invaluable to me in making this revision. To each of the reviewers of the manuscript, I say, "Thank you very much."

Elizabeth B. Hurlock

CHILD DEVELOPMENT

CHAPTER 1

SCIENTIFIC STUDIES OF CHILD DEVELOPMENT

Long before there were attempts to make scientific studies of children, traditional beliefs were used as guidelines by parents and teachers for the rearing of children. In spite of the fact that there is little evidence that these traditional beliefs are accurate or even partially accurate, many are widely held today, just as they were in the past.

Why is this so? The best general answer is that not enough scientific evidence exists to prove that they are not true. Until recently, scientists have not been motivated to examine traditional beliefs critically and to subject them to the same carefully controlled research procedures that they use in other areas of research.

Lack of motivation to make such studies can be explained in two ways. *First,* children were regarded as miniature adults. Since adults are easier to study, scientists concentrated on them and assumed that what was learned could then be applied to an understanding of children. *Second,* traditional beliefs provided ready-made guidelines for the training of children, and it was taken for granted that they were adequate for use both in the home and in the school.

Early Interest in Studying Children

Lack of widespread motivation to study children does not mean that they were entirely neglected. Rather, it means that the vast majority of early studies came not from an interest in children themselves or in their development but primarily from an interest in the best means of educating them to be useful citizens. One of the first persons to study children as individuals was John Amos Comenius, the famous Slavic educational reformer of the seventeenth century. Comenius strongly felt that children should be studied not as embryonic adults but in their essential child nature so as to understand their capacities and know how to deal with them.

Following the pioneer work of Comenius, two definite trends appeared in the study of children: (1) philosophical treatises on education in which children were studied only indirectly, and (2) direct daily observations of children in which they were studied at first hand.

Among the educational reformers who indirectly contributed valuable information about children and their capacities were Locke, of England; Rousseau, of France; Pestalozzi, of Switzerland; and Herbart and Froebel, of Germany.

Direct observations proved to be far more fruitful than philosophical treatises, however, because they focused attention on the child. Educational and pediatric literature of the sixteenth and seventeenth centuries refers to such present-day problems as breast-feeding, feeding the poor eater, and emotional care of the child during illness (67). The first scientific record of the development of a young child, published in 1774, was based on the observational notes Pestalozzi made of his 3½-year-old son. Several years later, Tiedemann, of Germany, kept biographical records of the development of his children during the early years of their lives. The best-known and most thorough of the early American studies was Millicent Shinn's *Biography of a Baby,* based on her observations of her niece from birth through the first year of life. This appeared in 1900 and was modeled along the lines of the German baby biographies (76).

Interest in scientific studies of children was given great impetus by the work of G. Stanley Hall, of Clark University. Beginning with his study of children's concepts, reported in 1891 in his *Contents of Children's Minds on Entering School,* Hall emphasized that children are not miniature adults (31). Hall's students adopted this point of view, and soon many psychologists and educators became interested in studying children, without reference to education. Because of the interest Hall stimulated, he is often referred to as the "father of the child study movement." Since Hall's original work, thousands of studies of almost every phase of child development have appeared.

Few of the early studies of children employed scientific methodology. Most, for example, used questionnaires, introspective or retrospective reports, or spasmodic rather than continuous observations of the same child. As J. B. Watson pointed out, early in this century (87):

Would you believe the most astonishing truth that *no well trained man or woman has ever watched the complete and daily development of a single child from its birth to its third year? Plants and animals we know about because we have studied them, but the human child until very recently has been a mystery.*

Because of their poor methodology, the early studies of children contributed little to our knowledge of how children develop or how they change from one age level to another. The science of child development has changed. As Sears has pointed out, "The last half century has seen enormous growth in child psychology, both as part of the general science of psychology and as one segment of child development. Theory has grown more sophisticated, methods have become more precise, the whole quality of the science has become infinitely better" (74).

Child Psychology versus Child Development

The early scientific studies of children, concentrated on specific areas of child behavior, such as speech, emotions, or play interests and activities. The name given to this new branch of psychological research was "child psychology"—a label which suggested that interest was centered on the psychological phenomena of the preschool and school-age child.

In time, it became apparent that studying different areas of child behavior at different age levels would not be enough. It would not add to our understanding of how behavioral characteristics change as children grow older and of what causes them to change. So interest began to shift. The name "child psychology" was changed to "child development" to emphasize that the focus was now on the *pattern* of the child's development rather than certain aspects of development (69).

There are four ways in which child development differs from child psychology. *First,* child psychology focuses more on the content or products of development while child development focuses more on the process itself. For example, while both may study speech, in child psychology more emphasis is placed on children's vocabularies and what they say. In child development, however, the emphasis is on how children learn to speak, the characteristic pattern of their learning to speak, and conditions that cause variations in this pattern.

Second, child development puts more emphasis on the roles played by environment and experience than child psychology does. This, of course, does not mean that the child psychologist ignores the roles played by environment and experience but, rather, that less emphasis is placed on them than by the developmental psychologist.

Third, child psychology has one major objective: to study the different areas of child behavior. Child development, however, has six objectives: to find out what are the characteristic age changes in appearance, behavior, interests, and goals from one developmental period to another; to find out when these changes

occur; to find out under what conditions these changes occur; to find out how these changes influence the child's behavior; to find out whether or not these changes can be predicted; and, finally, to find out whether these changes are individual or characteristic of all children.

Fourth, instead of concentrating on preschool and school-age children, as was true of the early studies of the child psychologist, the developmental child psychologist has extended the area of study in both directions, down to the newborn infant and up to the pubescent child. Since reports from medical research have emphasized the lasting effects on the child of the prenatal environment, child development now extends back to the moment of conception.

This shift in interest and goals has meant that far more research is needed. Child development is a broader field than child psychology. And, because scientific studies of children are of relatively recent origin and require many years of investigation to produce valid evidence, it is not surprising that our knowledge of the psychological phenomena characteristic of the childhood years is far from complete.

There are three major reasons for the gaps that now exist in our knowledge of how children develop. *First,* scientists have been more strongly motivated to study practical problems that affect the child's personal and social adjustments, such as those relating to unfavorable self-concepts and those conditions that contribute to social acceptance and leadership roles, than to study more theoretical problems, such as conceptual development or whether personality and intelligence are consistent or subject to change. *Second,* it is harder to study some areas of development than others. As a result, they have received less attention from researchers. It is more difficult, for example, to study the content of children's daydreams than the characteristic patterns of temper tantrums. *Third,* to date there have been so few longitudinal studies that it is difficult to trace the pattern of development over a long enough period of time to give a complete picture of the characteristic pattern for any area of development. The importance of the longitudinal method will be discussed in more detail later in this chapter.

In some instances, our picture of certain aspects of development and of age changes over a relatively short span is fairly well-rounded. In other instances, the picture is only beginning to take shape. With further research, the gaps will be filled in. Until then, it will be necessary to say, "So far as our present knowledge goes, all evidence points to this conclusion, but as further evidence is accumulated, our present knowledge may be radically changed.''

Spurs to Studying Children

The early studies of children, like those being made today, were inspired by a number of motives. Of those that have acted as spurs to scientific research, four have had the greatest impact: the solution of a practical problem, the desire to test traditional beliefs to see if they are accurate and, thus, reliable guidelines to use in guiding the child's development, theories about how and why children develop, and a desire to test further the evidence gained from scientific studies of children.

Solution of a Practical Problem

The first spur to studying children scientifically is the desire to deal with a practical problem relating to children. Just as early investigations of children were designed primarily to find answers to the practical problem of how the child could best be educated, so scientists today want answers that will enable them to resolve the practical problems relating to child behavior and child rearing that parents, teachers, and others who are responsible for children face.

The newborn infant, for example, has been studied to discover which behavior traits are hereditary, which must be taught, and when they can best be taught. The problem of discipline—an almost universal problem in the home and school—has been subjected to extensive research to discover what is the best way to discipline children not only from the point of view of their immediate behavior but also from the point of view of their attitudes toward people in authority and their ability and willingness to assume responsibility for their own conduct as they grow older.

Because many underachievers in school—those whose academic achievements fall below their tested abilities—have been reported to dislike school, the practical problem of removing this dislike has led to studies of lack of peer acceptance and its causes—one of the most commonly reported causes of dislike of school. The practical problems of the effects of television watching, adjustments of children of working mothers, and causes of deterioration in family relationships as children grow older have all motivated research studies of children.

Traditional Beliefs

In recent years, traditional beliefs have been a second spur to scientific studies of children. Scientists have begun to examine critically many traditional beliefs which have, for centuries, served as guidelines for the training of children. As scientific evidence accumulates, it has become increasingly apparent that many of the traditional beliefs are not in keeping with findings from scientific research. This has served as a spur to further inquiry.

Traditional beliefs about sex differences and masculine superiority, for example, have motivated as many or more scientific investigations than any other traditional beliefs. Maccoby and Jacklin spent three years reviewing and interpreting research studies related to sex differences in over 2,000 books and articles in this area (51). And these studies are continuing at an unabated rate.

Theories about Child Development

A third spur that has motivated scientific studies of children has been a desire to substantiate or refute prevailing theories about the child's development. As Liebert et al. have pointed out (49):

> Theories guide research into areas which might not otherwise attract interest or that might otherwise seem too complicated to handle. Like a prospector's map of a secret treasure, they lead us to expect substantial yields in areas that would otherwise seem to have little promise.

Most of these theories were based not on speculation but on clinical, laboratory, or field studies of groups of children. Because, more often than not, the groups used for these studies were relatively small and homogeneous and because the results were not compared with those obtained from control groups, scientists wanted more proof of their validity before accepting them. This desire led to studies using larger and more heterogeneous groups to see if the theories still held true.

The theory of the constancy of the intelligence quotient (IQ), for example, has motivated long-term studies of the development of intelligence (7, 35). Maslow's theory of personality has motivated many scientists to study creativity and its causes (53).

While theories about different areas of the child's

development are myriad, some have had a more wide-spread influence on scientific research than others. Rank's theory of the birth trauma has led to innumerable studies of the effects of birth on the child's future development (68). Freud's theory about the importance of the child's early experiences has motivated many studies of how the important foundations of the child's future development are laid and what effects they have on this development (27).

Theories holding that development passes through stages, each with predictable characteristics that are normal for that stage, have been numerous and have inspired extensive research. Some of these theories emphasize predictable stages of all areas of the child's development while others are limited to specific areas of development.

Gesell and his coworkers, Ames and Ilg, not only claimed that the child's development advances by stages but also that some of these stages are characterized by "equilibrium," when the child is "in focus" and thus easy to live with and manage, while others are characterized by "disequilibrium," when being "out of focus" made the child hard to live with and manage (3). Erikson likewise theorized from his studies of children that everyone passes through predictable stages in ego-development and that these stages are not limited to childhood but extend to old age (18, 25).

Numerous other theories have been developed on certain stages of development. The theories of Kohlberg and Piaget have, however, led to the greatest amount of research. Kohlberg's theory of moral development contends that the child's moral development passes through three stages (44). Piaget has proposed four stages in cognitive development. He also maintains that there are stages in the development of language, of animistic thinking, and of reasoning (65, 66).

The theories that have had the greatest impact on scientific research are those related to the relative importance of heredity and environment. Shortly after the turn of this century, some of the theories concentrated on the fact that the newborn infant is "gene-controlled" and could scarcely be changed at all by environmental influences. There were equally strong proponents of the importance of environment as expressed in such early social-learning theories as those of Dewey, Thorndike, and Watson (89).

Since these early theories appeared, the controversy has continued to rage, with some theories stressing the importance of heredity and others stressing the importance of environment. These have given impetus to many studies in different areas of the child's development, studies which, today, bring out facts to substantiate the belief that development is due not to the maturation of hereditary potentials alone or to environmental forces alone but to an interaction of both. This means that, as Kohlberg, Piaget, and other theorists have contended, while the foundations for the pattern of development are hereditary in origin, the pattern that these hereditary potentials will take is subject to control by environmental forces. Piaget's theory, for example, stresses the importance of maturation, experience with the environment, training, and cultural norms (65, 66).

Many of these theories will be discussed more fully later in connection with the topics to which they are related. It will then become apparent that their influence on research in these areas has led to an increased knowledge of the pattern of development in these areas.

Testing Evidence from Scientific Studies

The fourth important spur to scientific studies of children has come from a desire to test evidence as it flows from different research centers. Valuable as theories are as sources of motivation to future research, they cause confusion and dissatisfaction when they disagree, as in the case of the nature-nurture controversy.

However, this confusion and dissatisfaction is not without value. It leads to still further research by motivating scientists to probe further to obtain additional information. They want to know, for example, what is responsible for the patterns of behavior that have been reported to be typical for children of different ages. Is it due to the maturation of hereditary potentials, as the proponents of heredity claim, or is it primarily the result of social learning and experiences, as the proponents of the theories of social learning claim (28, 61)?

Scientists are also anxious to know under what conditions these patterns of behavior can be expected to manifest themselves. For example, why are temper tantrums more frequent among preschool children, and why do they become less frequent and less intense as children grow older?

As evidence piles up from scientific studies, scientists are motivated to study problems of practical importance in the child's life. In the case of racial differences in intellectual ability which have a marked influence on the school achievements of children, there is a strong motivation to find out whether these differences in intellectual ability are due to heredity or whether they are environmental in origin (35).

The more evidence there is, as scientific studies multiply, the more contradiction there is likely to be. Under such conditions, scientists are motivated to more research to resolve these contradictions. As Jensen has pointed out, in speaking of the present-day evidence from the vast number of scientific studies related to the nature-nurture controversy, "The evidence we now have does not support the environmentalist theory, which, until recently, has been accepted as scientifically established." Instead, he goes on to say, the issue is "an open question, calling for further scientific study" (34).

Obstacles to Scientific Studies of Children

In spite of the attempts to make scientific studies of children, there are obstacles to such studies that sometimes are almost insurmountable. Even worse, they make it hazardous to accept as final the evidence coming from these studies and to use this evidence as the basis for guidelines for the training of children.

Because of these obstacles, scientific studies of children have been more limited in number and scope than they otherwise would have been and the results of these studies are often incomplete and conflicting. They are sometimes actually inaccurate. If, for example, children are hesitant to tell what frightens them to avoid being regarded as "fraidy cats" and if they try to hide their fears in real-life situations to avoid being unfavorably judged by their peers and other members of the social group, the results of studies of children's fears may fail to include many fears which are severe and widely experienced by children of the age groups studied.

Scientists encounter many obstacles in their attempts to study children. Some of these, however, are especially common. They are: traditional beliefs about children, securing children for scientific research, finding suitable and scientifically accurate methods for studying children, controlling the accuracy of the material obtained, both in the laboratory and outside the laboratory setting, establishing rapport with children, and ethical aspects of research with children.

Traditional Beliefs

The first obstacle to scientific research using children as subjects comes from the widespread acceptance of traditional beliefs. These beliefs set up roadblocks to scientific research in a number of ways, three of the most common and most serious of which are explained in Box 1–1.

Throughout this book, different traditional beliefs will be discussed in the chapters related to the subject matter areas with which these beliefs are identified. At that time, scientifically determined evidence will be given to show whether these traditional beliefs are true, partly true, or false. In addition, an attempt will be made to explain why and how they are damaging to the child.

BOX 1–1

HOW TRADITIONAL BELIEFS OBSTRUCT SCIENTIFIC STUDIES

EARLY ENDORSEMENT BY SCIENTISTS
Many traditional beliefs gained support from their early endorsement by scientists. When early and scanty findings agreed with the traditional beliefs, scientists gave their stamp of approval to these beliefs. This tended to discourage further research.

INERTIA ON THE PART OF SCIENTISTS
When a traditional belief has been accepted for many generations, it is surrounded by a halo of infallibility that even scientists often hesitate to penetrate. They justify this by relegating the traditional beliefs to future study and turn their attention to areas about which there are few, if any, traditional beliefs.

SKEPTICISM ON THE PART OF RESEARCHERS
When research studies present conflicting evidence about a traditional belief, not only the layman but also the scientist tends to become skeptical. This may act as a spur to greater effort and further research, or it may encourage the scientist to label the findings of research that contradict the traditional belief as a "new-fangled idea."

Securing Children for Scientific Research

The second major obstacle to scientists who wish to study children is the difficulty they encounter in securing children for their studies. Getting large and unselected groups of children for scientific research has long been a troublesome problem. This is especially true when the scientist wants to study newborn infants. While today most babies are born in hospitals and, as a result, could be readily available for scientific studies, this cannot be done without parental consent. This consent is often withheld by parents who believe that newborn babies are "too delicate" to be studied and that, by doing so, some permanent damage may result.

Even today there are serious obstacles to studying school-age children. Although many school administrators willingly cooperate with the scientist, this has not solved the problem completely. School children themselves are often reluctant to cooperate. They feel that they are being treated like guinea pigs or that testing is a waste of their time. Even more serious is the limitation placed on what can be studied. School authorities often will not permit research on a "touchy" subject, such as sex, religion, or parent-child and sibling relationships.

Finding Suitable and Scientifically Accurate Methods

A third obstacle to the scientific study of children is finding methods that not only will be suitable for use with children of different ages but will also be scientifically accurate and yield valid results. The problem of methodology in the study of children has always been a thorny one. Many approaches have been abandoned because they proved to be too complicated or because they lacked reliability. For example, baby biographies and questionnaires are seldom used today because they are too difficult to control for accuracy.

Actually, *no one method or measuring technique is suitable for all age levels or for all forms of behavior.* Entirely different methods must be used for studying children who cannot verbalize their thoughts and for those whose speech is well developed. Different measuring techniques must be used for children who cannot read and write and for those who can. Sociometric techniques (techniques to measure social

acceptance in a group) are valuable, for example, in studies of social development, but they are inadequate and inappropriate for studies of language or motor development. As a result of this obstacle, accumulation of information about child development has been slow as well as spotty.

LABORATORY VERSUS FIELD STUDIES. In the early days of scientific psychological research, most studies were made in the laboratory, where conditions that affect the pattern of a subject's behavior can be carefully controlled. It soon became apparent, however, that the laboratory setting itself made children apprehensive. Was the behavior they displayed in the laboratory situation a true picture of their everyday behavior or only a picture of how they behaved in a laboratory?

To eliminate this obstacle to accurate research, some scientists began making studies in the child's natural habitat of the home, school, and playground. These studies—called "field studies"—showed that results obtained in the field did not always agree with those from the lab. Consequently, more and more field studies have been made—studies of anger, discipline, and conversation in the home, of social behavior in school and in the neighborhood, of reactions to school (as school phobias), and a host of other behavior patterns. These will be discussed in detail in subsequent chapters.

An experiment by Fawl will serve to show why many psychologists have become skeptical about the results of laboratory studies of children. Fawl compared the results of a laboratory study of frustration made by Barker, Dembo, and Lewin, where the psychologist acted to produce an artificial state of frustration in the child, with the results of a field study in which the psychologist observed and reported children's reactions to frustrating situations in real-life settings. The results obtained from the two studies were quite different (26). Unquestionably, the field-study approach yielded a more accurate appraisal of children's characteristic reactions to frustrating situations.

This does not mean that laboratory studies should be abandoned. Nor does it mean that field studies are universally believed to be superior. Field studies can seldom match laboratory studies in controlling conditions that might affect the subject's reactions. (5).

CROSS-SECTIONAL VERSUS LONGITUDINAL APPROACH. Information from questionnaires, observations, retrospective reports, etc., can be combined with data from other studies to give a composite picture of child development. This is known as the *normative cross-sectional approach* because the norms for different areas of development are obtained by studying many groups over a short period. When the groups are made up of representative samplings of the population, environmental influences are, to a large extent, ruled out, and the normative pattern of development can then be observed (13, 58).

The *longitudinal approach* to studying child development consists of reexamining the same children at intervals throughout the childhood and adolescent years. Box 1–2 gives an evaluation of the cross-sectional and longitudinal methods of studying children.

Some of the most important longitudinal studies to date have been the Berkeley Longitudinal Studies which studied the child's total development over a span of years (7, 24, 48): those of intellectual development by Bayley, Oden, Owens, and Terman and Oden (7, 59, 62, 81): studies of the long-term effects of age of sexual maturing on social behavior and personality by Ames, Jones, and Jones and Mussen (4, 36, 39): studies of the persistence of personality characteristics from childhood into adulthood and old age by Bühler, Erikson, Kagan and Moss, Peck and Havig-hurst, Smith and others (13, 25, 42, 63, 79): and studies of the long-term effects of child-training methods on personality and behavior by Bronson, Kagan, Mac-farlane et al., Schachter et al., and Watson (12, 40, 52, 73, 87).

HUMAN VERSUS ANIMAL SUBJECTS. A further methodological obstacle in the study of children is that methods which have proved to be highly reliable and harmless in studies of animals cannot be used on human beings because of the fear of possible psychological damage. From a scientific as well as from a practical angle, for example, it is important to know how much of a child's development will occur of its own accord and how much will depend on the child's experiences. In studies of the hereditary endowment of animals, the animals can be deprived of learning opportunities. They can be isolated from other members of their species or kept in cages so that they have no opportunities to imitate acts characteristically found in their species. Then, should the behavior appear, it could logically be concluded that it was a hereditary trait.

This method, known as the *method of isolation,* has been used with human subjects but was quickly abandoned. The reason for this is not only the practical difficulty of gaining parental consent for such studies,

---

BOX 1–2

EVALUATION OF CROSS-SECTIONAL AND LONGITUDINAL APPROACHES

CROSS-SECTIONAL APPROACH
ADVANTAGES
- Time-saving
- Gives a picture of typical characteristics at different ages
- Relatively inexpensive to carry out
- Can be carried out by one experimenter

DISADVANTAGES
- Gives only an approximate representation of the developmental process
- Does not take into consideration variations within age groups
- Does not take into consideration cultural or environmental changes over time

LONGITUDINAL APPROACH
ADVANTAGES
- Permits analysis of development of each child
- Permits study of growth increments
- Gives an opportunity to analyze relationships between maturational and experiential processes
- Gives an opportunity to study effects of cultural and environmental changes on behavior and personality

DISADVANTAGES
- Generally requires follow-up study by new experimenter, owing to length of time covered
- Expensive to carry out
- Data are extensive and cumbersome to handle
- Difficult to maintain original sample of subjects
- Must often fill in gaps by retrospective reports

but the strong objections, raised by parents and others, that isolation is unfair to children and might damage them so severely that they would never again be "normal."

Controlling Accuracy of Data

The fourth major obstacle scientists have encountered in their studies of the child's development is the difficulty of ensuring the accuracy of the material they obtain from their studies. Regardless of whether the studies are made in the laboratory or in a field setting and regardless of what method is used, this obstacle hampers research, leaves gaps in our knowledge, and often makes experimenters doubt the validity of their findings. Box 1–3 gives some of the most common conditions that make it difficult for experimenters to obtain accurate data about children.

Controlling the accuracy of data is more difficult under some conditions than others. In field studies, for example, obtaining accurate data is more difficult than in a laboratory situation. Similarly, some areas of the child's behavior can be more accurately observed than others. It is easier to observe the hand and arm movements the baby makes when picking up a small object than it is to get accurate data about cooing and babbling sounds.

When it is necessary to rely on reports of observations made by parents and teachers, who have an excellent opportunity to observe children in natural settings but who have infrequently had training in laboratory procedures, accuracy of the data obtained is especially difficult to achieve. If, for example, the scientist wants information about temper tantrums to supplement information about anger in young children, the scientist must usually call on parents for this information. Few children have temper tantrums away from home because they have discovered the unfavorable social reactions to these tantrums. As a result, they have learned to reserve them for home.

Accuracy of data is almost impossible to achieve when the observer has a biased attitude toward the child. This is especially likely to exist when parents are called on to give data about the child's behavior. As Yarrow et al. have explained: "Generally the subject matter is not neutral for the respondent; he has investments of various kinds in the experiences about which he is asked to report" (92).

Establishing Rapport with Children

A fifth obstacle to scientific studies of children is the difficulty of establishing rapport with one's subjects. If accurate data are to be obtained, children must speak and act naturally. They must not show off or put up a front to impress the observer, and they must not be intimidated by the observer or by the strangeness of the setting.

The importance of good rapport was discovered in the early days of intelligence testing. Testers were advised to inform the children that they wanted to "play games" with them, and to take time to establish a friendly relationship before beginning the test. Only then could they hope to get an accurate picture of the child's intellectual abilities.

What is true of the testing situation is even more true of the experimental situation, especially if it is that of the laboratory. Children must be made to feel at home in the new environment and with the experimenter if they are to react in their characteristic, normal manner. This takes time, but it increases the accuracy of the results.

No one can predict with accuracy who will make a good experimenter for studies in the area of child development and who will not. The reason for this is that good child-experimenter rapport depends not only on the child's attitude toward the experimenter but also on the experimenter's attitude toward the child as a person and toward children as a group. Other things equal, both men and women experimenters are more successful if they have had experience with children as surrogate parents during their own childhood or as camp counselors, teachers, or parents. Even with such experience, if they regard children as "subjects" rather than "people," the establishment of rapport will be slow and difficult. Children quickly sense a cold, impersonal attitude and react to it with fear or resentment.

Ethical Aspects of Research with Children

The sixth obstacle scientists are encountering in their studies of children concerns the ethical aspects of the techniques they use and the areas of development they investigate. In the early days of research with children, some experimenters questioned whether the techniques they were using were likely to damage the

REASONS FOR DIFFICULTIES IN OBTAINING ACCURATE DATA ABOUT CHILDREN

- It is impossible to observe everything a child does or says and make accurate records of what goes on.
- Most children do not behave in the same way when they are alone or with other children and when they know they are being observed by adults.
- Data reported by parents and teachers is often inaccurate because they lack training in what to observe and what to report.
- The perceptiveness of the observers determines what they observe and what they will later report.
- Giving or withholding material is influenced by the observer's own ideas of the significance of certain aspects of what has been observed.
- The observer's emotional reaction to the child's behavior at the time the observation is made tends to distort the later report.
- There is a tendency to forget what the child did or said unless reports are made immediately after the observation. Figure 1–1 shows how parents forget facts about their children in two months or less time.
- There may be a deliberate distortion by the observer to show the child or the parent in a favorable light.

Figure 1–1 Inaccuracies in parental reports about their children. (*Adapted from L. C. Robbins: The accuracy of parental recall of aspects of child development and child rearing practices.* Journal of Abnormal and Social Psychology, *1963, 66, 261–270. Used by permission.*)

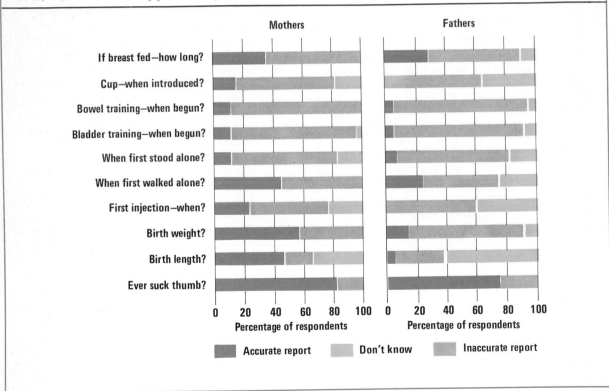

child's development. The late R. S. Woodworth, for example, in a desire to find out if motor control comes from maturation, from learning, or from a combination of both, deprived one of his children from having opportunities to learn motor control by making it impossible to move the arms, legs, and trunk. He did this by pinning crib covers tightly over the baby's body. Before the baby was a year old, Woodworth abandoned this study on the grounds that it might have permanent effects of an unfavorable kind on the baby's later motor development.

With each passing year, the ethical aspect of research with children has become more and more a focal point of interest and concern. This interest and concern has been heightened by popular interest in the legal rights of children and by the increasing widespread parental abuse of children.

Psychologists of today are taking a hard, critical look at some of the widely accepted practices in research studies of children to see if they violate the rights of children and, if they do, to devise new practices that will be fairer to children. Some of the questions that are being asked today relate to the following techniques and aspects of research with children.

Do scientists, who are usually complete strangers to the children they are studying, have any more right to observe them from behind a one-way screen without the children's awareness that they are being observed than adults have of "peeking in" on complete strangers without their being aware of the fact that they are being observed?

Do scientists have any more right to tape record conversations children have with their peers without informing them that this is being done than government officials have to wiretap and tape record the supposedly confidential conversations adults have with other adults?

Is it fair to children for graduate students or professors to take up a school class to give them tests or questionnaires that are totally unrelated to their studies to enable these researchers to gather data for doctoral dissertations, journal articles, or books that will increase their chances for promotion but will, in no way, benefit the children whose time they have used?

Should children not be asked if they wish to participate in a research project rather than treating them as human guinea pigs or as a captive audience in a classroom?

Before children are old enough to understand what participation in a research study means, should their parents not be informed of the type of study that is being made, the purpose of the study, and the techniques to be used and their consent gained, preferably in writing, before the study is made? It should not be assumed that children, placed in a preschool or a child-care center by their parents, are automatically available as subjects for any research study a graduate student or an established scientist wishes to make.

Since children tend to be suggestible and gullible, owing to their inexperience and to their respect for those in authority, is it right to suggest attitudes and values that may be contradictory to those their parents are trying to teach them? For example, is it fair to children, in an attempt to gain information about family relationships, to ask them questions that suggest that they have or should have a preference for one parent or that they have or should have an antagonistic attitude toward a sibling or a grandparent?

These are just a few of the many questions that are being asked, discussed, and critically examined by psychologists, sociologists, doctors, and other scientists who are interested in research related to children's development. The important aspect of this questioning is not the area of research that is being investigated but rather the fundamental principle of what scientists should or should not do in their research investigations to ensure children the same rights that are taken for granted in research studies of adolescents and adults.

Overcoming Obstacles to Scientific Studies of Children

Obstacles to scientific studies of children have resulted in a paucity or absence of scientific evidence about some areas of the child's development. This has had two serious consequences. *First*, it may, and often does, distort the picture of normal development. For example, difficulties in finding satisfactory techniques to discover how well developed the different sensory capacities of the newborn are and to determine whether newborn infants are capable of learning encourage acceptance of the traditional belief that the newborn infant is a completely helpless individual—a picture that may, in time, prove incorrect.

Second, lack of scientifically accurate information

encourages the continued acceptance of traditional beliefs with their damaging effects to further scientific research. Until, for example, there is adequate scientific evidence to refute the traditional belief that females are inferior to males, intellectually as well as physically, and that the greater emotionality of females stems from gonadal differences related to their reproductive capacities, traditional beliefs about sex differences and their causes will persist.

Difficult as it has been, great strides have been made in the scientist's attempts to overcome the obstacles to studying the child's development. Some of these attempts have met with total success, some with only marginal success, and some have proved failures. For example, attempts to measure intelligence during the first two years of life by infant intelligence scales, have, to date, proved unsuccessful (48, 82). How each obstacle has been tackled and with what success will be discussed in the following pages.

Overcoming Acceptance of Traditional Beliefs

Overcoming the widespread acceptance of traditional beliefs as guidelines for child-rearing has, to date, met with only marginal success. The reason for this, as Naffziger and Naffziger have pointed out is that "myths die hard" and many still have "plenty of bounce in them" (57).

There are two conditions standing in the way of removal of traditional beliefs as obstacles to scientific research. *First,* all traditional beliefs are not faulty. Some have elements of truth in them but are not completely true. However, the false part is rarely stressed, thus encouraging the continued complete acceptance of them as true because of the *element* of truth they contain. For example, the traditional belief, expressed in the saying, "Sticks and stones will hurt my bones but words will never harm me," is true except for the word, "never." If the words are derogatory, they will harm the person psychologically even though they do no physical harm, as sticks and stones do.

Second, until adequate scientific information can be accumulated to prove conclusively that a traditional belief is true or false, scientists hesitate to make judgments about it, even if they do not give it their stamp of approval. Those who hold the belief are likely to interpret this lack of scientific refutation as the stamp of scientific approval.

Ways of Obtaining Children for Research Studies

Day-care centers, nursery schools, kindergartens, health and mental health clinics give the scientist of today an excellent opportunity to study children of the preschool age. Parents bring their children to these centers for training, for free medical care, and for guidance in overcoming behavior problems. In return, they permit the children to be studied and tested at regular intervals.

The problem of studying newborn infants is gradually waning as parents become convinced that study will not harm the newborn infant. Furthermore, many scientists study their own newborn infants. This, however, is not necessarily a satisfactory solution to the problem because, on the whole, such infants are representative of a limited group, not of the population at large.

The problems related to securing school-age children for scientific studies are still largely unresolved. This is especially true of the problem of studying "touchy" subjects—religion, racial differences, and sex—and of gaining the cooperation of the children themselves.

Overcoming Methodological Obstacles

Better success has been achieved in coping with this obstacle than with the two just described. Yet, methodological obstacles have forced scientists to postpone the studying of many important areas of child behavior. They are, in part, responsible for the gaps in our knowledge of how and why children develop as they do.

Today, whenever possible, animal subjects are being replaced by human subjects. For example, in an attempt to find out how much of a child's development comes from maturation of hereditary potentials and how much depends on the child's opportunities and encouragement to learn, the "method of isolation," used so successfully with animal subjects, has been replaced by the "genetic study of large groups method."

The fundamental principle of the genetic study is that when environmental factors are controlled by having many different racial, socioeconomic, religious, intellectual, and physical factors represented in the group, environmental influences are ruled out;

any similarity in the developmental patterns of children in the group may then be regarded as "nature's work."

Other attempts to improve the methodology used to study children have included making more longitudinal studies and improving the methods that have proved applicable to the areas of child behavior to be studied. Introspective reports have been, to a large extent, discarded. Testing procedures have been improved and, when field studies are made, there are attempts to control the conditions under which these studies are made in much the same way as they are controlled in the laboratory.

The difficulty of finding suitable methods of studying children has been met, in part, by borrowing methods used in related fields of research—mainly medicine, sociology, and experimental psychology. Since many of these methods were devised for use with adolescents or adults, however, they must be modified before they can be applied to the study of children.

Increasing Accuracy of Data

To increase the accuracy of observation, cameras, television, and other electronic devices have been used to record children's movements and speech. By photographing children in action and studying the pictures in slow motion, observers can see all parts of the body in motion. The film can be rerun if any movement is missed in one observation. An advantage of this method is that it eliminates the temptation on the part of observers to interpret what they are observing. In a rerun, they see the child's activity in a more objective manner than they might while actually observing the child.

To overcome the obstacle to studying speech and prespeech sounds, marked refinements have been made in the early techniques used. Ostwald and Peltzman, for example, suspended a sensitive microphone from 6 to 12 centimeters above the infant's mouth. In this way it was possible to get accurate recordings of early prespeech sounds (60). Figure 1-2 shows how the cries of newborn infants have been recorded.

Because accuracy of observation is especially difficult in field studies, whenever possible electronic recording devices are used to get a permanent picture of the child's behavior and a recording of the child's speech. Tape recorders have been used successfully

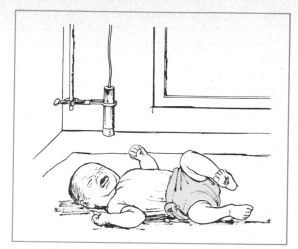

Figure 1–2 A method of recording the cries of the newborn infant. (*Adapted from P. F. Ostwald and P. Peltzman: The cry of the human infant. Scientific American, 1974, 230 (3), 84–90. Copyright © (1974) by Scientific American, Inc. All rights reserved. Used by permission.*)

in studies of what children talk about when alone, away from the watchful eyes and listening ears of parents, teachers, or experimenters, and what they say to family members at the dinner table or to the dentist when having their teeth cleaned (23). Allen and Evans, for example, reported that by setting up a "dentist's office" in the laboratory and by using different electronic devices to record the speech and behavior of children who came for dental check-ups, they could make accurate records of children's speech and behavior without their being aware of it. Even though an arrangement of this kind may greatly increase the accuracy of observations, it is much too complicated and expensive to be widely used (1).

To improve observations, Gesell, many years ago, suggested that this methodological obstacle could be eliminated by using a one-way screen which would permit scientists to observe children without their realizing it (29). This has been done with success and with improvements in the technique ever since. The major drawback to this technique, however, is that children beyond the 3-year age level find ways to explore behind the screen and soon discover that it is a device for watching them. Then its usefulness is limited. To date, no satisfactory way has been found to cope with this problem.

When scientists find it necessary to use data from reports made by parents and teachers, they give parents and teachers training in what to observe and what to report in the hopes that this will increase the accuracy of the data. However, such training *does not guarantee* effective control. To avoid the effects of biased attitudes on the part of observers, clinicians sometimes use retrospections of earlier experiences. This, they contend, helps the observer to see a situation in the perspective of time and, as a result, the observer will be less likely to distort the observations. This is especially applicable to studies of parent-child relationships where annoyances of the moment can readily color the parents' reports (91). On the other hand, it subjects the facts reported to the effects of forgetfulness on the parents' part—a problem that can be overcome only if parental memories are accurate and if some record of the observations has been kept (70). Refer to Figure 1–1 which shows the effects of forgetting on parental reports.

Improving Rapport with Children

To be able to achieve the rapport necessary for scientific studies of children, some future researchers are learning useful techniques in training laboratories for developmental psychology. They are advised, for example, to call themselves Miss, Mrs., or Mr. rather than Dr. So-and-So, a label children associate with persons who examine their bodies or "stick them with needles." They are advised to make the children feel at ease by showing them the lab and demonstrating some of the apparatus. Above all, they are advised to answer all questions or even to suggest questions that the children might be afraid to ask themselves (46, 56, 88).

Establishment of Ethical Standards for Research

One of the thorniest problems in overcoming obstacles in the way of research with children is, at the present time, still unsolved—the problem of the rights of children. As concern grows, it is inevitable that, sooner or later, a code of ethics for research with children will be formulated. Specially appointed committees composed of members of the American Psychological Association whose area of interest is developmental psychology will do this work.

An approved and accepted code of ethics could then serve as guidelines for studies of children. It will point out to researchers what they should or should not do so as to protect the rights of children, just as there are guidelines for research using animal, adolescent, or adult subjects. Until these guidelines are formulated into a code of ethics, researchers will have to depend on their own judgments about their fairness to the children they are using as their research subjects.

How Much Headway Have Scientists Made?

There is no question that scientific research in different areas of child development has made great strides since the early studies of G. Stanley Hall at the turn of this century. There is also no question that improvements in methodology used in these studies will increase rather than decrease as more and more scientists become involved in this research.

However, in spite of the headway that has been made, the study of child development is hampered to a certain extent by gaps in our knowledge of different developmental processes. In some instances, only the beginnings of the processes have been carefully explored; in others, only the terminal states. In very few is the picture complete.

Even more serious than the gaps themselves is the tendency of some writers to fill them in with material drawn from studies of adults or adolescents. There have, for example, been many studies of adolescent gangs but very few of children's gangs. Consequently, some people assume that since some adolescent gangs are delinquent, children's gangs are also delinquent. Studies of children's gangs show that this assumption is false; children's gangs do not conform to the adolescent pattern but to a pattern of their own (77).

In discussing what has been responsible for the "steep and thorny way to a science of behavior," Skinner has given the following explanation which is just as applicable to studies of children as to those of other age levels (78):

Why has it been so difficult to be scientific about human behavior? Why have methods that have been so prodigiously successful almost everywhere else failed so ignominiously in this one field? Is it because human nature presents unusual obstacles to a science? No doubt it has, but I think we are beginning to see how these obstacles may be overcome. The problem, I submit, is digression. We have been drawn off the straight and narrow path, and the word *diversion* serves me well by suggesting not only digression but dalliance.

In this "steep and thorny way to a science of behavior," as Skinner has labeled it, developmental psychologists cannot rightly be accused of "dalliance," if by "dalliance" he means wasting time or not giving serious thought or attention to research in this area. All one has to do is to examine the large number of research reports in scientific journals or the books on different areas of child development that are constantly appearing to realize that this term does not apply to psychologists and other scientists whose primary interest is focused on children's development.

On the other hand, there is evidence that "digression" does exist. Before one area of development is fully explored and resolved, research attention often shifts to another area. There are two possible explanations. Many psychologists concentrate their research efforts on areas that are primarily interesting to them instead of concentrating their efforts on areas that may be of greater importance at that time. Or, they may be diverted from research in one area to another area that is, at the moment, attracting attention in scientific journals, instead of steadfastly pursuing their original research to the point of conclusive results.

While diversion of research pursuits may open up new areas of interest in children's development and produce knowledge about these areas, it leaves gaps in other areas of knowledge that have not yet been fully explored. In time, these gaps will unquestionably be closed. Until this happens, knowledge about children's development will continue to be incomplete.

Chapter Highlights

1   Long before there were scientific studies of children, traditional beliefs were used as guidelines for the rearing of children.

2   Early interest in studying children was concentrated on how to educate them to be useful citizens.

3   G. Stanley Hall has been called the "father of the child study movement" more because he stimulated an interest in scientific studies of children than because he used methods which, today, would be considered good scientific procedures.

4   Child psychology differs from child development because the former concentrates on different psychological phenomena while the latter concentrates on the pattern of development of these phenomena.

5   There are four major spurs to studying children scientifically; the solution of some practical problem, an attempt to prove or disprove the traditional beliefs which have served as guidelines for rearing children, theories about different areas of child development, and testing evidence from scientific studies.

6   Obstacles to scientific studies of children have resulted in many gaps in our knowledge of how children grow and develop.

7   Traditional beliefs have been obstacles to scientific studies of children for three reasons: they are sometimes endorsed by scientists, they are often surrounded by a halo of infallibility which even scientists hesitate to penetrate, and when research studies provide evidence that conflicts with traditional beliefs it sometimes leads to skepticism on the part of the researcher.

8   The difficulty of obtaining children of different ages for scientific research has been a roadblock to these studies.

9   Finding suitable and scientifically accurate methods for studying children has been difficult because no one method is adequate for investigation of all areas of the child's development.

10   Longitudinal studies provide the most accurate information about development, but they are difficult and costly to make.

11   Accuracy of data obtained from studies of children is a major problem because of the many difficulties involved in studying children in both laboratory and field settings and because of the necessity of getting some important information from such untrained observers as parents.

12   Unless good rapport can be established with chil-

dren, the data obtained by experimenters will be biased. This is a serious obstacle in both laboratory and field studies.

13 There are two serious consequences of obstacles to scientific studies of children; first, they tend to distort the picture of normal development and, second, they encourage the continued acceptance of traditional beliefs about children.

14 Obtaining children for research studies is an especially difficult obstacle to overcome partly because

children, as they grow older, resent being studied and partly because school authorities refuse to give researchers permission to study "touchy" subjects, such as sex, religion, or family relationships.

15 With the introduction of electronic devices and by training experimenters to work with children, some of the methodological difficulties encountered in early studies of children have been partly overcome. Thus the accuracy of the data obtained from these studies has increased.

Bibliography

1 Allen, B. P., and R. I. Evans. Video tape recording in social psychological research: An illustrative study in podontia. *Psychological Reports*, 1968, *23*, 1115–1119.

2 Altus, W. D. Birth order and its sequelae. *Science*, 1966, *151*, 44–49.

3 Ames, L. B., and F. L. Ilg. The developmental point of view with special reference to the principle of reciprocal neuromotor interweaving. *Journal of Genetic Psychology*, 1964, *105*, 195–209.

4 Ames, R. Physical maturing among boys as related to adult social behavior. *California Journal of Educational Research*, 1957, *8*, 69–75.

5 Barker, R. G. Exploration in ecological psychology. *American Psychologist*, 1965, *20*, 1–14.

6 Baugh, J. R., G. R. Pascal, and T. B. Cottrell. Relationship of reported memories of early experiences with parents on interview behavior. *Journal of Consulting and Clinical Psychology*, 1970, *35*, 23–29.

7 Bayley, N. The life span as a frame of reference in psychological research. In D. C. Charles and W. R. Looft (eds.), *Readings in psychological development through life*. New York: Holt, Rinehart & Winston, 1973. Pp. 5–17.

8 Bell, R. Q., G. M. Weller, and M. F. Waldrop. Newborn and preschooler: Organization of behavior and relations between periods. *Monographs of the Society for Research in Child Development*, 1971, *36* (1 and 2).

9 Bijou, S. W. Ages, stages and the naturalization of human development. *American Psychologist*, 1968, *23*, 419–427.

10 Blum, S. H., and L. H. Blum. Do's and dont's: An informal study of some prevailing superstitions. *Psychological Reports*, 1974, *35*, 567–571.

11 Bronfenbrenner, U. Developmental research, public policy and the ecology of childhood. *Child Development*, 1974, *45*, 1–5.

12 Bronson, W. C. Central orientations: A study of behavior organization from childhood to adolescence. *Child Development*, 1966, *37*, 125–155.

13 Buhler, C. The course of human life as a psychological problem. *Human Development*, 1968, *11*, 184–200.

14 Burton, R. V. Validity of retrospective reports assessed by the multitrait–multimethod analysis. *Developmental Psychology Monographs*, 1970, *3* (2), part 2.

15 Cable, M. *The little darlings: A history of child rearing in America*. New York: Scribners, 1975.

16 Charlesworth, W. R. Developmental psychology: Does it offer anything distinctive? In W. R. Looft (ed.), *Developmental psychology: A book of readings*. Hinsdale, Ill.: Dryden Press, 1972. Pp. 3–22.

17 Cohler, B. J. The role of retrospective accounts in the study of intergenerational attitudes. *Merrill-Palmer Quarterly*, 1972, *18*, 59–60.

18 Coles, R. *Erik H. Erikson: The growth of his work*. Boston: Little, Brown, 1970.

19 Cooke, S., and T. Cooke. Implications of child development theories for pre-school programing. *Education*, 1973, *94*, 112–116.

20 Cotler, S., and D. J. Shoemaker. The accuracy of Mothers' reports. *Journal of Genetic Psychology*, 1969, *114*, 97–107.

21 Cronbach, L. J. Five decades of public controversy over mental testing. *American Psychologist*, 1975, *30*, 1–14.

22 Dennis, W. (ed.) *Historical readings in developmental psychology*. New York: Appleton-Century-Crofts, 1972.

23 Dreger, R. M. Spontaneous conversation and story-telling of children in a naturalistic setting. *Journal of Psychology*, 1955, *40*, 163–180.

24 Eichorn, D. H. The Berkeley longitudinal studies: Continuities and correlates of behavior. *Canadian Journal of Behavioral Science*, 1973, *5*, 297–320.

25 Erikson, E. H. *Childhood and society*, rev. ed. New York: Norton, 1964.

26 Fawl, C. L. Disturbances experienced by children in their natural habitat. In R. G. Barker (ed.), *The stream of behavior*. New York: Appleton-Century-Crofts, 1963. Pp. 99–126.

27 Freud, S. *The standard edition of the complete psychological works of Sigmund Freud*. London: Hogarth Press, 1953–1962, 21 vols.

28 Furth, H. G. Piaget, IQ and the nature-nurture controversy. *Human Development*, 1973, *16*, 61–73.

29 Gesell, A. How science studies the child. *Scientific Monthly*, 1932, *34*, 265–267.

30 Gottfried, N. W., and B. Seay. An observational technique for preschool children. *Journal of Genetic Psychology*, 1973, *122*, 263–268.

31 Hall, G. S. The contents of children's minds on entering school. *Pedagogical Seminary*, 1891, *1*, 139–173.

32 Harris, S. L. Influence of the interviewer: A note for the nonresearcher. *Family Coordinator*, 1971, *20*, 149–150.

33 James, W. *The principles of psychology*. New York: Holt, 1890.

34 Jensen, A. The differences are real. *Psychology Today*, 1973, 7 (7), 80–86.

35 Jensen, A. R. How much can we boost IQ and scholastic achievement? *Harvard Educational Review*, 1969, 39, 1–123.

36 Jones, M. C. Psychological correlates of somatic development. *Child Development*, 1965, 36, 899–911.

37 Jones, M. C. A report on three growth studies at the University of California. In D. C. Charles and W. R. Looft (eds.), *Readings in psychological development through life*. New York: Holt, Rinehart & Winston, 1973. Pp. 18–29.

38 Jones, M. C., N. Bayley, J. W. Macfarlane and M. P. Honzik (eds.). *The course of human development. Selected papers from The Longitudinal Studies, Institute of Human Development, The University of California, Berkeley*. Waltham, Mass.: Xerox College Publications, 1971.

39 Jones, M. C. and P. H. Mussen. Self-conceptions, motivations, and interpersonal attitudes of early- and late-maturing girls. *Child Development*, 1958, 29, 491–501.

40 Kagan, J. American longitudinal research on psychological development. *Child Development*, 1964, 35, 1–32.

41 Kagan, J. Future of child development research. *Human Biology* 1972, 44, 277–287.

42 Kagan, J., and H. A. Moss. *Birth to maturity: A study in psychological development*. New York: Wiley, 1962.

43 Kessen, W., L. S. Hendry, and A. M. Leutzendorf. Measurement of movement in the human newborn: A new technique. *Child Development*, 1961, 32, 95–105.

44 Kohlberg, L. The development of children's orientations toward a moral order. I. Sequence in the development of moral thought. *Vita Humana, Basel*, 1963, 6, 11–33.

45 Kuhlen, R. G. Age and intelligence: The significance of cultural change in longitudinal versus cross-sectional findings. In D. C. Charles and W. R. Looft (eds.), *Readings in psychological development through life*. New York: Holt, Rinehart & Winston, 1973. Pp. 273–282.

46 Landreth, C. Child laboratories on university campuses. *Child Development*, 1964, 35, 989–992.

47 Lefrancois, G. R. Jean Piaget's developmental model: Equilibrium-through-adaptation. In W. R. Looft (ed.), *Developmental psychology: A book of readings*. Hinsdale, Ill.,: Dryden Press, 1972. Pp. 297–307.

48 Lewis, M. Infant intelligence tests: Their use and misuse. *Human Development*, 1973, 16, 108–118.

49 Liebert, R. M., R. W. Poulos and G. D. Strauss. *Developmental psychology*. Englewood Cliffs, N. J.: Prentice-Hall, 1974.

50 Looft, W. R. Perceptions across the life span of important informational sources for children and adolescents. *Journal of Psychology*, 1971, 78, 207–211.

51 Maccoby, E. E., and C. N. Jacklin. Myth, reality and shades of gray: What we know and don't know about sex differences. *Psychology Today*, 1974, 8 (7), 109–112.

52 Macfarlane, J. W., L. Allen, and M. P. Honzik. *A developmental study of the behavior problems of normal children between twenty-one months and fourteen years*. Berkeley, Calif.: University of California Press, 1954.

53 Maslow, A. H. *Motivation and personality*. New York: Harper & Row, 1954.

54 McCarthy, D. *The McCarthy Scale of Children's Abilities*. New York; Psychological Corporation, 1975.

55 McCullers, J. C. G. Stanley Hall's conception of mental development and some indications of its influence on developmental psychology. *American Psychologist*, 1969, 24, 1109–1114.

56 Nadelman, L. Training laboratories in developmental psychology. *Psychological Reports*, 1968, 23, 923–931.

57 Naffziger, C. C., and K. Naffziger. Development of sex role stereotypes. *Family Coordinator*, 1974, 23, 251–258.

58 Neugarten, B. L. Continuities and discontinuities of psychological issues into adult life. *Human Development*, 1969, 12, 121–130.

59 Oden, M. H. The fulfillment of promise: 40-year follow-up of the Terman gifted group. *Genetic Psychology Monographs*, 1968, 77, 3–93.

60 Ostwald, P. F., and P. Peltzman. The cry of the human infant. *Scientific American*, 1974, 230 (3), 84–90.

61 Overton, W. F. On the assumptive base of the nature-nurture controversy; Additive versus interactive conceptions. *Human Development*, 1973, 16, 74–89.

62 Owens, W. A. Age and mental abilities: A second adult follow-up. *Journal of Educational Psychology*, 1966, 57, 311–325.

63 Peck, R., and R. J. Havighurst. *The psychology of character development*. New York: Wiley, 1962.

64 Phillips, D. C., and M. E. Kelley. Hierarchial theories of development in education and psychology. *Harvard Educational Review*, 1975, 45, 351–375.

65 Piaget, J. *Science of education and the psychology of the child*. New York: Orion Press, 1970.

66 Piaget, J. *Psychology and epistemology*. New York: Grossman, 1971.

67 Pratt, K. J. Motivation and learning in medieval writings. *American Psychologist*, 1962, 17, 496–500.

68 Rank, O. *The trauma of birth*. New York: Harcourt, Brace, 1929.

69 Reese, H. W., and L. P. Lipsitt. *Experimental child psychology*. New York: Academic Press, 1970.

70 Robbins, L. C. The accuracy of parental recall of aspects of child development and child rearing practices. *Journal of Abnormal and Social Psychology*, 1963, 66, 261–270.

71 Rosenkrantz, A. L., and V. Van de Riet. The influence of prior contact between child subjects and adult experimenters on subsequent child performance. *Journal of Genetic Psychology*, 1974, 124, 79–90.

72 Rosenthal, T. L., R. W. Henderson, A. Hobson, and M. Hart. Social strata and perception of magical and folk-medical child-care practices. *Journal of Social Psychology*, 1969, 77, 3–13.

73 Schachter, F. F, A. Cooper, and R. Gordet. A method for assessing personality development for follow-up evaluations of the preschool child. *Monographs of the Society for Research in Child Development*, 1968, 33 (3).

74 Sears, R. R. Child development since the 40's. *APA Division on Developmental Psychology Newsletter*, Feb., 1976. Pp. 50–52.

75 Senn, M. J. E. Insights on the child development movement. *Monographs of the Society for Research in Child Development*, 1975, no. 161.

76 Shinn, M. W. *The biography of a baby.* New York: Macmillan, 1900.

77 Siegel, A. E. Current issues in research on early development. *Human Development,* 1969, *12,* 86–92.

78 Skinner, B. F. The steep and thorny way to a science of behavior. *American Psychologist,* 1975, *30,* 42–49.

79 Smith, M. E. A comparison of certain personality traits as related to the same individuals in childhood and fifty years later. *Child Development,* 1952, *23,* 159–180.

80 Stone, J. L., and J. Church. Some representative theoretical orientations in developmental psychology. In W. R. Looft (ed.), *Developmental psychology: A book of readings.* Hinsdale, Ill.: Dryden Press, 1972. Pp. 35–59.

81 Terman, L. M., and M. H. Oden. *The gifted group at mid-life: Follow-up of the superior child.* Stanford, Calif.: Stanford University Press, 1959. Vol. 5.

82 Thomas, H. Psychological assessment instruments for use with human infants. *Merrill-Palmer Quarterly,* 1970, *16,* 179–223.

83 Thorndike, E. L. *Human learning.* New York: Century Company, 1931.

84 Tizard, J. New trends in developmental psychology. *British Journal of Educational Psychology,* 1970, *40,* 1–7.

85 Tulkin, S. R., and J. Kagan. Mother-child interaction in the first year of life. *Child Development,* 1972, *43,* 31–41.

86 Van den Daele, L. D. A cook's tour of development. *Journal of Genetic Psychology,* 1976, *128,* 137–143.

87 Watson, J. B. *Psychological care of infant and child.* New York: W. W. Norton, 1928.

88 Westerburg, L. H. Child development laboratory: A preview of parenting. *Journal of Home Economics,* 1974, *66,* 25–27.

89 White, S. H. The learning-maturation controversy: Hall to Hull. *Merrill-Palmer Quarterly,* 1968, *14,* 187–196.

90 Whiting, B. B. Folk wisdom and child rearing. *Merrill-Palmer Quarterly,* 1974, *20,* 9–19.

91 Yarrow, M. R. Problems of methods in parent-child research. *Child Development,* 1963, *34,* 215–226.

92 Yarrow, M. R., J. D. Campbell, and R. V. Burton. Recollections of childhood: A study of the retrospective method. *Monographs of the Society for Research in Child Development,* 1970, *35* (5).

CHAPTER 2

CHAPTER 2

PRINCIPLES OF DEVELOPMENT

Developmental psychologists realize that an accurate picture of the developmental pattern is fundamental to an understanding of children. They also recognize that knowledge of what causes variations in development is essential to an understanding of each individual child.

Knowing what the developmental pattern is like has scientific as well as practical value. These values are:

First, knowledge of the pattern of human development helps developmental psychologists to know what to expect of children, at approximately what ages to expect different patterns of behavior to appear, and when these patterns will normally be replaced by more mature patterns. This is important because if too much is expected at a given age, children are likely to develop feelings of inadequacy if they do not live up to the standards their parents and teachers set for them. If, on the other hand, too little is expected of them, they are deprived of incentives to develop their potentials. Equally serious, they often build up resentments toward those who underestimate their capacities.

Second, knowing what to expect enables developmental psychologists to set up guidelines in the form of height-weight scales, age-weight scales, age-height scales, mental-age scales, and social- or emotional-development scales. Since the pattern of development for all normal children is approximately the same, it is then possible to evaluate each child in terms of the norm for that child's age. If development is typical, it means that the child is making normal adjustments to social expectations. Should, on the other hand, there be deviations from the normal pattern, this may be regarded as a danger signal of poor personal, emotional, or social adjustments. Steps can then be taken to discover the cause of the deviation and to remedy it. Should the deviation be the result of lack of opportunities to learn, for example, the child can then be given learning opportunities and encouragement to use these opportunities.

Third, since successful development requires guidance, knowing the developmental pattern enables parents and teachers to guide the child's learning at appropriate times. A baby who is ready to learn to walk must be given opportunities to practice walking and encouragement to keep on trying until the walking skill has been mastered. Lack of opportunity and encouragement may delay normal development.

Fourth, knowing what the normal developmental pattern is makes it possible for parents and teachers to prepare children ahead of time for the changes that will take place in their bodies, their interests, or their

Figure 2–1 Preparation for what will be expected in new situations helps to relieve the tensions all changes give rise to. (*Adapted from Ralph Dunagin: "Dunagin's People." Field Newspaper Syndicate, August 22, 1975. Used by permission.*)

behavior. For example, children can be prepared for what will be expected of them when they enter school. While this psychological preparation will not eliminate all tensions that come from such a radical adjustment, it will go a long way toward minimizing them. See Figure 2–1.

In the remaining pages of this chapter, the 10 fundamental facts about development—usually called the "principles of development"—will be discussed and an attempt will be made to show their implications. As new and more extensive studies of children are made, it is possible that new principles will emerge from these studies.

I. Development Involves Change

Many people use the terms "growth" and "development" interchangeably. In reality they are different, though they are inseparable; neither takes place alone. Growth refers to *quantitative* changes—increases in size and structure. Not only does the child become larger physically, but the size and structure of the internal organs and the brain increase. As a result of the growth of the brain, the child has a greater capacity for learning, for remembering, and for reasoning. The child grows mentally as well as physically.

Development, by contrast, refers to *qualitative* and quantitative changes. It may be defined as a progressive series of orderly, coherent changes. "Progressive" signifies that the changes are directional, that they lead forward rather than backward. "Orderly" and "coherent" suggest that there is a definite relationship between the changes taking place and those that preceded or will follow them (4, 6, 72). Neugarten has explained how changes in development affect people as they grow older (61):

> *People change, whether for good or for bad, as a result of the accumulation of experience. As events are registered in the organism, individuals invariably abstract from the traces of those experiences and they create more encompassing as well as more refined categories for the interpretation of new events. The mental filing system not only grows larger, but it is reorganized over time, with infinitely more cross references. . . . Adults are not only much more complex than children, but they are more different one from another, and increasingly different as they move from youth to extreme old age.*

The Goal of Developmental Changes

The goal of developmental changes is self-realization or the achievement of genetic potentials. This Maslow has labeled "self-actualization"—the striving to be the best person possible, both physically and mentally. It is the urge to do what one is fitted to do (57). To be happy and well-adjusted, a person must be given an opportunity to fulfill this urge.

However, whether the person will achieve this goal will depend on what obstacles are encountered and how successful the person is in overcoming these obstacles. Obstacles may be environmental, such as growing up in an environment where children are deprived of educational and cultural opportunities; or they may be from within the person, such as a fear of attempting to do what they are capable of doing because of social criticism. Many potentially creative children, for example, fail to achieve the creativity they are capable of because of early social criticism of their creative endeavors.

Box 2–1 gives some suggestions to aid children to achieve self-realization. Note that some of these aids are environmental while others are personal.

Types of Change in Development

The human being is never static. From the moment of conception to the time of death, the person is undergoing changes. As Piaget has explained, structures are "far from being static and given from the start." He goes on to explain that, instead of being static, a maturing organism undergoes continued and progressive changes in response to experiential conditions and these changes result in a complex network of interaction (67).

At every age, some of the changes that occur during the developmental process are just beginning, some are at their peak, and some are in the process of decline. These changes may be divided into four major categories, each of which is explained in Box 2–2.

While some of the changes that occur in development are antagonistic in the sense that they occur in opposition to each other, others are interrelated. Two *antagonistic* processes take place simultaneously—growth or evolution and atrophy (wasting away) or involution. In the early years of life, growth predominates, though atrophic changes occur as early as embryonic life. In the later years of life, the reverse is true.

Interrelated changes may be seen in the changes in size and proportions. Increase in body size, for example, is accompanied by modifications of the composition of the body. Gain in weight in babyhood, it has been found, comes not from increase in fat tissue alone but also from increase in neural, bone, and glandular tissue. In childhood, the gain comes principally from bone and muscle tissue. In adulthood, the gain is from an accumulation of fat tissue.

Interrelated changes are apparent also in the men-
tal characteristics of the child. The young child's emotions, for example, lack gradations; violent temper outbursts may have no relation to the intensity of the frustrating situation. With increased intelligence and experience, the child is able to control anger responses to meet the approved standards of the social group.

Children's Attitudes toward Change

As adulthood progresses, many men and women dread change whether it be failing eyesight or the accumulation of middle-age fat that proclaims to the world that they are growing old or the added responsibilities that age brings. By contrast, children tend to

---

BOX 2–2

TYPES OF CHANGE

CHANGES IN SIZE
These include *physical* changes in height, weight, circumference, and internal organs, and *mental* changes in memory, reasoning, perception, and creative imagination.

CHANGES IN PROPORTIONS
As may be seen in Figure 2–2, children are not miniature adults in their physical proportions. Nor are they mentally miniature adults. Their imaginative capacity is better developed than their reasoning capacity, while the reverse is true of adults.

DISAPPEARANCE OF OLD FEATURES
When certain physical features, such as the thymus gland after puberty and baby hair and teeth, lose their usefulness, they gradually atrophy, as do some psychological and behavioral traits—babyish locomotion and speech and fantastic extensions of the imagination.

ACQUISITION OF NEW FEATURES
Some new physical and mental features develop from maturation and some develop from learning and experience. New physical features include second teeth and primary and secondary sex characteristics; new mental features include interest in sex, moral standards, and religious beliefs.

Figure 2–2 The body proportions of the newborn infant and adult. (*After Stratz, from K. Bühler: Mental development of the child. Harcourt Brace Jovanovich, 1930. Used by permission.*)

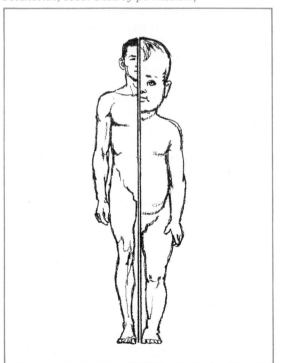

welcome each change because it brings them closer to the privileges and freedom they associate with being "grown up."

That children's attitudes toward change are, for the most part, favorable is also apparent from studies of happiness. Retrospective reports, in which adults looked back and tried to recall how they felt about their lives at different ages, have revealed that their outstanding memories were related to their first new experiences, each of which was a symbol of progress toward maturity.

Whether the individual child's attitudes toward change are generally favorable or unfavorable depends upon many factors. *First,* children's awareness of the change. As babies become more autonomous, they begin to resent being waited on. Pubescent children, aware of the awkwardness that normally accompanies rapid growth, feel self-conscious and embarrassed instead of self-confident as they were earlier when slow growth enabled them to have better control over bodily movements.

Second, how the change affects their behavior. If the change enables children to be more independent of adult help or if it gives them added strength and speed so that they can take part in the play activities they associate with older children, they will welcome the change.

Third, social attitudes toward the change affect children just as they do adults. Most parents, for example, encourage their children to "grow up" as soon as possible. When children live up to parental expectations, they are praised; when they fall below these expectations, they are reproved for not "acting their age."

Fourth, social attitudes are influenced, to some extent at least, by how the change affects the child's appearance. As a cuddly baby becomes a spindly preadolescent and as teeth fall out, giving the face a comical, if not homely look, the child may be less appealing to adults. If so, they are likely to show it in their treatment of the child.

Fifth, cultural attitudes affect the way people treat children as a result of changes in their appearance and behavior. Attitudes are, for the most part, more favorable toward babies and young children than toward older children. Just as "everyone loves a baby," so many people dread the prepubescent stage when children tend to become glum, moody, surly, and difficult to live or work with. Even peers may regard the prepubescent as a "pest" and old friendships often break as a result. Under such conditions, it is unlikely that chil-

dren will have favorable attitudes toward many of the changes that puberty brings.

II. Early Development Is More Critical Than Later Development

Long before scientific studies of children were made, it was an accepted fact that the early years are critical in the child's development. This was expressed in the old Chinese proverb, "As the twig is bent, so the tree's inclined." In a more poetic way, Milton expressed the same fact when he wrote, "The childhood shows the man, as morning shows the day."

The first important scientific clue of the significance of the early years came from Freud's studies of personality maladjustment. Such maladjustments, Freud found, could be traced to unfavorable childhood experiences (32). More recent studies have substantiated Freud. From clinical studies of children from birth to maturity, Erikson has concluded that "childhood is the scene of man's beginning as man, the place where our particular virtues and vices slowly but clearly develop and make themselves felt." He has further explained that babyhood is a time of "basic trust"—the individual learns to view the world as safe, reliable, and nurturing; or a time of "basic distrust"—the individual learns to view the world as full of threat, unpredictability, and treachery.

Which the child will learn, Erikson explained, will depend on how parents gratify the child's needs for food, attention, and love. Once learned, these attitudes will color the individual's perceptions of people and situations throughout life (31).

The histories of maladjusted children from preschool years into high school or college have revealed that most of them were so poorly adjusted as young children that they never belonged to any group or had many friends. In addition, many suffered from speech, academic, and enuretic difficulties and were regarded by their families as "problem" children (27, 35, 75). From studies of the life histories of delinquents, Glueck concluded that potential delinquents could be identified as early as two or three years of age by their antisocial behavior (38).

The persistence of early patterns of behavior has been demonstrated by studies in several areas of development. In attitudes and values and in preferred leisure activities, people change little as life progresses, even when marked cultural changes are taking place (14, 16). Studies of creative adults have revealed that, as children, they showed an interest in imaginative and creative play and in different forms of artistic expression (40).

Studies of personality have likewise revealed that early patterns persist relatively unchanged as time goes on. The first five years of the child's school experience, for example, has been called the "critical period" in the development of the achievement drive. The reason for this, Sontag and Kagan have pointed out, is that "High levels of achievement behavior at that age are highly correlated with achievement behavior in adulthood" (77). Adults who, as children, were afraid of ridicule, punishment, or other unpleasant

experiences, had negative self-concepts characterized by self-derogation (52). Results of such studies have justified this conclusion by Bijou (9):

> Most child psychologists have said that the preschool years, from about ages 2 to 5, are among the most important, if not *the* most important, of all the stages of development, and a functional analysis of that stage strongly points to the same conclusion. It is unquestionably the period during which the foundations are laid for the complex behavioral structures that are built in a child's lifetime.

White, after years of research involving children during the preschool years, contends that the first two years are critical in setting the pattern for personal and

---

BOX 2–3

CONDITIONS AFFECTING EARLY FOUNDATIONS

FAVORABLE INTERPERSONAL RELATIONSHIPS
Favorable relationships with people, especially with family members, will encourage the child to develop outgoing tendencies and to become other-oriented—a characteristic that leads to good personal and social adjustments.

EMOTIONAL STATES
Emotional deprivation, resulting from rejection by family members or separation from parents, often leads to personality disorders. Emotional satisfaction, by contrast, encourages healthy personality development.

CHILD-TRAINING METHODS*
Children brought up by permissive parents tend, as they grow older, to lack a sense of responsibility, to have poor emotional control, and to become underachievers in

whatever they undertake. Those brought up by democratic or even slightly authoritarian parents make better personal and social adjustments.

EARLY ROLE-PLAYING
The firstborn child, who is, for example, often expected to assume responsibilities in the home and to take care of younger children, may have greater self-confidence than later-born siblings but may also have a tendency to develop a lifelong habit of bossiness.

CHILDHOOD FAMILY STRUCTURE
The child who comes from a large family tends to become authoritarian in attitudes and behavior, while coming from a divorced or separated family makes the child anxious, distrustful, and somewhat rigid.

ENVIRONMENTAL STIMULATION
A stimulating environment is one that encourages the development of the child's hereditary potentials. Talking to a baby or showing a preschooler pictures in story books encourages interest in learning words and a desire to learn to read. A stimulating environment encourages good physical and mental development, while an unstimulating environment causes the child's development to fall below its potential.

---

* While the meaning of different child-training methods will be explained in detail and evaluated in the chapters of moral development and family relationships, a brief explanation of their meanings is essential now because they will be referred to in the earlier chapters. The terms, "authoritarian," "democratic," and "permissive" are used in the traditional sense. "Authoritarian child training" refers to training designed to mold children's behavior to conform to standards set by those in authority. This is done by threats or use of punishment. "Democratic child training" puts emphasis on the educational aspect of training children to conform to standards through explanation of why conformity is necessary. It permits children

to express their opinions about rules and modifications of rules are made if children's reasons for doing so seem valid. "Permissive child training" is actually not training because it permits children to act as they wish and to learn, from the consequences of their acts, what approved behavior is. Within each of these major categories, there are variations from strict to lenient.

social adjustment. According to him, "Providing a rich social life for a 12-to-15 month-old child is the best thing you can do to guarantee a good mind" (90).

Conditions Affecting Early Foundations

The environment in which children live during the early formative years of life has a strong impact on their hereditary potentials. Of the many environmental factors, six can be singled out as especially important and as almost universal in their effects (5, 15, 50, 73, 90). These are listed and explained in Box 2–3.

Because foundations for attitudes and behavior patterns are laid early, when the environment is limited almost exclusively to the home and when the child's most constant social contacts are with family members, these foundations are "home grown."

Even as children grow older and spend increasingly more time with members of the peer group, in the neighborhood and school, the influence of the home on the early foundations will still be apparent. By that time, the foundations will be so firmly established that any changes that do occur will be minimal.

Why Early Foundations Are Important

As evidence piles up to show that early foundations tend to be persistent and to influence the child's attitudes and behavior throughout life, it becomes increasingly apparent why early foundations are important. There are four lines of evidence to substantiate this claim.

First, since learning and experience play increasingly dominant roles in development as children grow older, they can be directed into channels that will lead to good adjustment. Basically, this task must be handled by the family, though the larger social group can provide a culture in which children can fulfill their potentials.

Allowing children to grow up, doing what they want when they want, is obviously unfair to them. Children are too inexperienced to know what the social group expects of them. How, for example, can children know that mispronunciations and grammatical mistakes will create the impression that they are ignorant? How can they know that aggressive attacks on playmates will create more enemies than friends?

Guidance is most needed in the early stages of learning when the foundations are being laid. If children are put on the right track at first and encouraged to remain there until they become accustomed to it or realize why it is best, they will be less likely to get on the wrong track later.

Second, because early foundations quickly develop into habitual patterns, they will have a lifelong influence on children's personal and social adjustments. Many years ago James warned of this habituation when he said, "Could the young but realize how quickly they will become mere walking bundles of habits, they would give more heed to their conduct while still in the plastic stage" (45).

Third, contrary to popular belief, children do not outgrow undesirable traits as they grow older. Instead, as was stressed earlier, patterns of attitudes and behavior, established early in life, tend to persist regardless of whether they are good or bad, beneficial or harmful to the child's adjustments.

Fourth, because it is sometimes desirable to make changes in what has been learned, the sooner the changes are made, the easier it is for children and, consequently, the more cooperative they are in making the changes.

In spite of the fact that early foundations are difficult to change, they can be, and often are, changed. There are three conditions that facilitate such change. First, when children receive guidance and help in making the changes, second, when the significant people in their lives treat them in a different way, and third, when the children themselves have a strong motivation to make the changes.

III. Development Is the Product of Maturation and Learning

One of the oldest controversies in the world of science concerns the relative importance of heredity and environment in determining the physical and mental characteristics of the developing child. Despite wide scientific and practical interest in this problem, valid evidence is still far from adequate to solve it to everyone's satisfaction. As was pointed out in Chapter I, no completely acceptable method has been found to isolate the influence of heredity from that of environment. There is always the possibility of psychological damage to the children used as subjects for scientific experimentation.

The evidence seems to indicate that the development of physical and mental traits comes partly from an intrinsic maturing of those traits and partly from exercise and effort on the part of the individual. Which plays the more important role is still a matter of conjecture (46, 91).

Meaning of "Maturation"

Intrinsic maturing—*maturation*—is the unfolding of characteristics potentially present in the individual that come from the individual's genetic endowment. In *phylogenetic* functions—functions common to the race—such as creeping, crawling, sitting, and walking, development comes from maturation. Training, per se, is of little advantage. Controlling the environment in such a way as to reduce opportunities to practice may, on the other hand, retard development.

By contrast, in *ontogenetic* functions—functions specific to the individual—such as swimming, ball throwing, riding bicycles or writing, training is essential. Without such training, development will not take place. No hereditary tendency can mature fully, however, without environmental support.

Meaning of Learning

Learning is development that comes from exercise and effort. Through learning, children acquire competence in using their hereditary resources. They must, however, have opportunities to learn. A child with superior neuromuscular organization, for example, may have a high aptitude for musical performance. But, if deprived of opportunities for practice and systematic training, the child will not develop this hereditary potential.

Some learning comes from practice or the mere repetition of an act. This, in time, brings about a change in the person's behavior. Such learning may consist of *imitation,* in which the person consciously copies what others do. Or it may consist of *identification,* in which the person attempts to adopt the attitudes, values, motives, and behavior of admired and loved persons.

Learning may come from *training*—selected, directed, and purposive activity. In training, children are directed in their behavior by adults or older children who attempt to mold their behavior into patterns that will contribute to their welfare and be acceptable to the social group.

Interaction of Maturation and Learning

Development during the prenatal period comes mainly from maturation and is very little dependent upon activity. There is evidence, however, that fetal activity is related to the development of certain motor performances in early postnatal life (76). Infants who were highly active as fetuses, for example, acquire skills at an earlier age than those who were less active.

Postnatal maturation and learning are closely interrelated; one influences the other. There is a high correlation between gross physical development and the ability to manipulate the parts of the body that have grown. Development thus depends on the interaction of this hereditary endowment and the social and cultural forces of the environment (17).

A number of significant facts of both practical and theoretical value come from the present evidence of the interrelationship of maturation and learning. These are listed and briefly explained in Box 2–4.

Some of these facts are so important that they require further explanation. There is evidence that maturation does set limits to what a person can do or become. This limitation may occur when environmental influences during intrauterine or postnatal life reduce the genetic potentials for development or it may come from the quality of the genetic inheritance.

In the early days of child psychology, there was a tendency to accept the popular belief that a person can do or become whatever he wants, as long as he is willing to work hard and is given the opportunity. J. B. Watson, for example, maintained that he could train any normal infant to become any kind of specialist he wished—doctor, lawyer, artist, or even beggar and thief—regardless of the child's talents, abilities, tendencies, and racial origin (88). This early overemphasis on the influence of learning has gradually been abandoned. Studies of intelligence, aptitudes, and physical growth have revealed differences in ability which are, to a large extent, immune to environmental influences (14, 46, 67, 82). The inability to educate mentally defective children as normal children are educated is a practical illustration of the limiting effects of heredity.

Deprivation of learning opportunities, due to poverty, parental rejection, institutionalization, or other

EFFECTS OF THE MATURATION– LEARNING INTERRELATIONSHIP

VARIATIONS IN PATTERN OF DEVELOPMENT
The different environmental influences children experience affect the pattern of their development. Were human development due to maturation alone, as in some animal species, individuality would be reduced to a minimum.

MATURATION SETS LIMITS TO DEVELOPMENT
Because of limitations in the hereditary endowment of the child, development cannot go beyond a certain point even when learning is encouraged.

MATURATIONAL LIMITS ARE RARELY REACHED
When children reach a temporary plateau in their development, they often conclude that they have reached their limits. As a result, they put forth little effort to learn and remain on the plateau instead of advancing to higher levels.

DEPRIVATION OF LEARNING OPPORTUNITIES LIMITS DEVELOPMENT
When the environment limits opportunities for learning, children will be unable to reach their hereditary potentials.

STIMULATION IS ESSENTIAL FOR FULL DEVELOPMENT
For full development of hereditary potentials, children's innate capacities must be stimulated or encouraged to develop, especially at the time they normally develop.

EFFECTIVENESS OF LEARNING DEPENDS ON PROPER TIMING
Regardless of how much effort children put into learning, they cannot learn until they are developmentally ready to learn.

conditions, may prevent children from developing their hereditary potentials (2, 18). This is especially true of intellectual development. Studies of institutionalized children have revealed that this environmental deprivation affects their ability to conceptualize, results in limited vocabularies, and causes them to be distractible to the point where they are unable to integrate their experiences (79, 92).

By contrast, stimulation fosters the development of hereditary potentials. This is especially important during the early months of life before babies can walk and do things for themselves (90). Even as children grow older, they need environmental stimulation to make them alert and responsive, both physically and mentally. The more children are talked to, for example, the sooner and better they will be able to talk and the larger their vocabularies (49, 84).

While stimulation to the development of genetic potentials usually comes from the environment, it may also come from within. When, for example, children set goals for themselves, they will do all they can to reach these goals. This often means that they will have to draw upon all their resources and use them to a maximum, especially when the goals are unrealistically high. Self-stimulation can be as powerful as outer stimulation though the former is less common in early childhood than the latter. Only after children have learned how important achievements are to social recognition have they the motivation to aspire to high goals.

Importance of Readiness to Learn

Regardless of how much stimulation children receive, they cannot learn until they are developmentally ready to do so. This means that the necessary physical and mental foundations must be present before new abilities can be built on them. While structure and function parallel each other in childhood, structure actually precedes function. This is true for motor skills, mental skills, and sexual behavior (24, 35).

If children are not ready to learn, teaching may be a waste of time and effort. It may lead to resistant behavior which militates against successful learning, such as learning of bad habits or not wanting to learn. If, on the other hand, children are maturationally ready to learn but are not permitted or encouraged to do so, they may lose interest. Later, when parents and teachers decide that the time has come for them to learn, they may be unwilling to put forth the necessary effort.

Havighurst has referred to maturational readiness as the "teachable moment." As he explained, "When the body is ripe, and society requires it, and the self is ready to achieve a certain task, the teachable moment has come. Efforts at teaching which would have been largely wasted if they had come earlier give gratifying results when they come at the *teachable moment,* when the task should be learned" (39).

How, one may ask, can adults know when a child has

with certain traits appearing at fixed intervals. The same orderly pattern is evident in postnatal development, though the individual rate of development may vary more in the postnatal period than in the prenatal.

Genetic studies of children over a period of years have demonstrated that behavioral development, too, follows a pattern and that this pattern is relatively little influenced by experience (59, 63).

Some Predictable Patterns

From the many evidences of an orderly, predictable pattern in *physical development,* in both prenatal and postnatal life, have come two laws of the directional sequence of development: the *cephalocaudal law* and the *proximodistal law.* According to the cephalocaudal law, development spreads over the body from head to foot. This means that improvements in structure and function come first in the head region, then in the trunk, and last in the leg region. According to the proximodistal law, development proceeds from near to far—outward from the central axis of the body toward the extremities. In the fetus, the head and trunk are fairly well developed before the rudimentary limb buds appear. Gradually, the arm buds lengthen and then develop into the hands and fingers. Functionally, babies can use their arms before their hands and can use their hands as a unit before they can control the movements of the fingers (86). The laws of developmental direction are illustrated in Figure 2–3. The arrows on this figure show the pattern of development.

Longitudinal studies of *intelligence* have revealed that the pattern of mental development is as predictable as the pattern of physical development. The results of several longitudinal studies covering different segments of the life-span from birth to 50 years show that the major part of mental growth comes when the body is developing most rapidly, during the first 16 to 18 years (65, 71). There is also a predictable pattern for development of the different intellectual functions, such as memory and reasoning, that constitute general intelligence. Follow-up studies over a period of 40 years led Oden to conclude that "with few exceptions the superior child becomes the superior adult. . . . The Terman study has shown that the great majority of gifted children do indeed live up to their abilities" (63).

Genetic studies of babies from birth to 5 years have shown that all young children follow a general *behav-*

reached the "teachable moment"? Three practical and easily applied criteria are generally used by psychologists to indicate the child's state of readiness. These are shown in Box 2–5.

To ensure an accurate picture of the child's readiness, all three criteria should be applied. An interest, for example, may be merely transitory—a whim—resulting from a desire to imitate an older sibling or playmate. If a general interest is sustained for some time, this is a better indication of readiness than a strong interest that is transitory. Parental or peer pressures may cause a child to sustain an interest long enough to justify the conclusion that the teachable moment has been reached. Application of the third criterion—progress with practice—may show, however, that the child has not yet reached the point where there can be any benefit from learning opportunities. When interest wanes quickly or when the child seems to make no appreciable improvement, in spite of continued practice, there is reason to question whether the teachable moment has arrived.

IV. The Developmental Pattern Is Predictable

Every species, whether animal or human, follows a pattern of development peculiar to that species. In prenatal development, there is a genetic sequence,

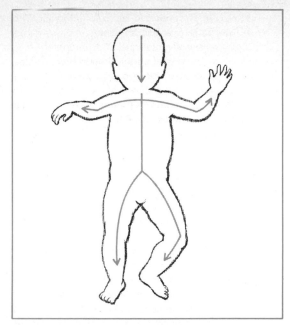

Figure 2–3 The laws of developmental direction.
(*Adapted from E. L. Vincent and P. C. Martin:*
Human psychological development. *Ronald, 1961.*
Used by permission.)

ioral pattern. *Specific areas* of development likewise follow predictable patterns. These include different aspects of motor development, emotional behavior, speech, social behavior, concept development, goals, interests, and identification with others. All these patterns will be discussed in subsequent chapters.

Conditions That Affect the Developmental Pattern

The pattern of development can be interfered with, either temporarily or permanently, by environmental or physical conditions. This interference may take the form of delaying or accelerating the speed with which the pattern of development normally occurs, or it may alter the pattern.

Present evidence based on longitudinal studies shows that when the pattern of physical growth is temporarily upset by such environmental conditions as malnutrition, illness, season of the year, or severe emotional stress, there will be a period of "catch-up"

growth after the conditions are removed or ameliorated. Then the child will return to the pattern followed earlier, before the interference occurred (78).

The pattern of physical development may be altered permanently by unfavorable environmental conditions before or after birth. Deficiency of thyroid activity during the prenatal period, for example, stunts both physical and mental growth, thus producing a "cretin" or deformed idiot. Calcium deficiency during the prenatal and early postnatal months results in rickets—a disease in which the bones do not harden normally—thus resulting in carious teeth, a flat chest, crooked legs or back, or deformed pelvis.

Interference with the pattern of mental development when there are unfavorable conditions in the prenatal and early postnatal environments are equally as marked as in the pattern of physical development. Severe malnutrition at this time not only results in smaller head circumference and lower cognitive ability but it also affects personality by making children apathetic (21, 26, 81). Even after nutritional rehabilitation, a lag in cognitive ability has been reported (12). Blindness from birth causes babies and young children to lack the curiosity normal for their ages not only because they cannot see that things are new and different but also because they are held back from exploring by fear. This lack of curiosity also affects the pattern of their motor development (1).

The pattern of development may also be retarded by psychological conditions. Emotional deprivation, due to parental rejection, loss of a parent, or institutionalization, for example, may retard both the physical and psychological patterns of development (27, 84). How emotional deprivation affects physical and psychological development will be explained in detail in the chapter on emotional development. However, as Tulkin has warned, a lag in development may be due to differences in values, not to environmental deprivation. A culture, for example, that values cooperation will not encourage children to be competitive and, as a result, in a culture that values competition, they may be judged as "deprived" and appear to lag behind their peers in social development (83).

Stimulation of physical and mental development, as was pointed out earlier, affects the predictable pattern of development by accelerating it. Good health, encouragement, and opportunities to learn, plus a strong motivation on the child's part, will speed up development in all areas.

Importance of Predicting Development

Time consuming and difficult as it is to determine whether a predictable pattern of development exists and what factors may interfere with this pattern, most child psychologists consider such information vital. This is true not only from a theoretical but also from a practical angle.

Theoretically, such information is important because it serves as a foundation for the study of development in different areas. If, for example, there were not a predictable pattern in the child's motor or speech development, it would be impossible to formulate principles about these areas of development. The practical implications of this knowledge are summarized in Box 2–6.

BOX 2–6

PRACTICAL SIGNIFICANCE OF
PREDICTING DEVELOPMENT

MATURE SIZE
It is possible to predict at a fairly early age what the child's adult physique will be.

EDUCATIONAL PLANNING
Educational plans can be based on the child's early intellectual aptitudes.

PREPARATION FOR NEXT STAGE
At every stage of development, the child can be prepared for the next stage.

VOCATIONAL PLANNING
Early physical, intellectual, and personality development give clues as to what the child may be able to do vocationally in adulthood. These clues can be used by parents and teachers for planning the training for the child's future vocation.

ADOPTION
Since early patterns of physical and mental development are predictive of later development, they can be used as an aid in selecting babies for adoption.

V. The Developmental Pattern Has Predictable Characteristics

Not only is the developmental pattern predictable but also it has certain common and predictable characteristics. This holds true for the pattern of mental as well as physical development.

Studies of development have shown that there are a number of predictable characteristics, five of which are described and their significance explained below.

Similarity in Developmental Patterns

All children follow a similar developmental pattern with one stage leading to the next. Babies stand before they walk, for example, and draw circles before squares. In no instance is this order normally reversed.

Furthermore, the general pattern is not altered by individual variations in the speed of development. Children who are born prematurely may lag behind in development for about a year, but after that, they usually catch up to the norm for full-term babies and follow their developmental pattern at about the same rate. Very bright and very dull children likewise follow the same developmental sequence as those of average intelligence. However, those who are very bright develop at a more rapid rate than those who are average while very dull children develop at a slower rate.

Development Proceeds from General to Specific Responses

In mental as well as in motor responses, general activity always precedes specific activity. The fetus moves its whole body but is incapable of making specific responses. So it is in early postnatal life. Babies wave their arms in general, random movements before they are capable of such specific responses as reaching for an object held before them.

Similarly, in emotional behavior babies first respond to strange and unusual objects with a general fear. Later, their fears become more specific and are characterized by different types of behavior, such as crying, turning away and hiding, or standing their ground and pretending not to be afraid.

Development Is Continuous

Development is continuous from the moment of conception to death but it occurs at different rates—sometimes slowly and sometimes rapidly. As Piechowski has emphasized, "Development does not occur at an even pace. There are periods of great intensity and disequilibrium . . . and there are periods of equilibrium. Development achieves a plateau and this may occur at any level or between levels" (68).

Furthermore, developmental changes do not always go forward in a straight line. They sometimes go backward, as when a jealous child regresses to babyish ways of doing things in the hopes of winning the parental attention enjoyed earlier. However, in the end, these changes lead forward (10).

Since development is continuous, what happens at one stage influences the following stage. Unhealthy attitudes about self or about relationships with others during the early years, for example, are rarely eliminated completely. They are reflected in the individual's outlook on life even in middle and old age. "Basic trust" or "basic distrust," developed during the babyhood years, Erikson found, persist throughout life and color the person's reactions to people and to life situations (31).

Different Areas Develop at Different Rates

While the development of different physical and mental traits is continuous, it is never uniform for the entire organism. If the body is to attain its adult proportions, inequalities in rate must occur. The feet, hands, and nose, for example, reach maximum development early in adolescence, while the lower parts of the face and the shoulders develop more slowly (26). Refer to Figure 2–1 for a graphic illustration of the differences in body proportions of a newborn infant and an adult. Figure 2–4 shows the pattern of development for four different parts of the body.

Measurements of intellectual capacities reveal that they, like physical traits, develop at different rates and reach maturity at different ages. Creative imagination, for example, develops rapidly in childhood and reaches its peak early in adolescence. Reasoning, on the other hand, develops more slowly. Rote memory and memory for concrete objects and facts develop more quickly than memory for abstract, theoretical material (7, 71).

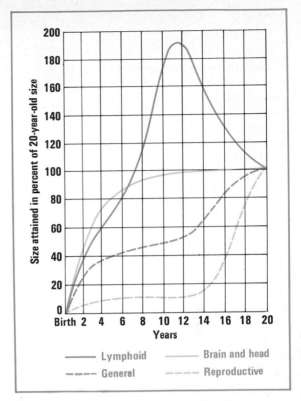

Figure 2–4 Patterns of development for different parts of the body. (*Adapted from D. B. Coursin: Nutrition and brain development in infants.* Merrill-Palmer Quarterly, *1972,* 18, *177–202. Used by permission.*)

Variations in the rate of development of different physical and mental traits, especially when pronounced, lead to many adjustment problems. The "superior-immature" child, whose intellectual development outpaces physical, social, or emotional development, will be out of step with both contemporaries and older children. Similarly, the fact that some parts of the body reach their mature size earlier than others accounts in part at least for the awkwardness and self-consciousness of the young adolescent.

There Is Correlation in Development

There is a widely held traditional belief that nature compensates for inadequacies in one area by greater development in other areas. The girl who is "beautiful

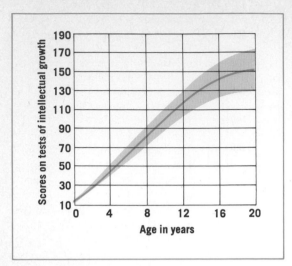

Figure 2–5 The pattern of intellectual development from birth to 20 years. The shaded area shows the normal deviations at different age levels. (*Adapted from N. Bayley: On the growth of intelligence.* American Psychologist, *1955, 10, 805–818. Used by permission.*)

but dumb'' and the boy who is ''brainy but a physical weakling'' are stereotypes of this belief. The belief has not been validated by experimental studies. Terman and Oden concluded, on the basis of genetic studies, that ''desirable traits tend to go together. No negative correlations were found between intelligence and size, strength, physical well-being, or emotional stability'' (80).

When physical development is rapid, so is mental development, Just as physical development is marked by changes in body proportions as well as by increase in size, so mental development is characterized by different rates of growth for memory, reasoning, association, and other mental abilities. The typical curve of mental growth, as shown in Figure 2–5, displays the same pattern as that of physical development which will be described in detail in the chapter on physical development.

VI. There Are Individual Differences in Development

Although the pattern of development is similar for all children, all children follow the predictable pattern in

their own way and at their own rate. Some children develop in a smooth, gradual, step-by-step fashion, while others move in spurts. Some show slight swings, while others show wide ones. All children do not, thererfore, reach the same point of development at the same age.

Causes of Differences

Dobzhansky has said, ''Every person is indeed biologically and genetically different from every other'' (29). In addition, no two people have identical environmental influences, even identical twins. This means that individual differences are caused by both internal and external conditions. As a result, the pattern of development will be different for every child, even though it is similar in its major aspects to the pattern followed by other children.

Physical development, for example, depends partly on hereditary potentials and partly on such environmental factors as food, general health, sunlight, fresh air, climate, emotions, and physical exertion. *Intellectual development* is affected by such factors as inherent capacity, the emotional climate, whether one is encouraged to pursue intellectual activities, whether one has a strong intellectual drive, and whether one has opportunities for experiences and learning. *Personality development* is influenced by genetic factors as well as by attitudes and social relationships, both in the home and outside.

There is evidence that physical and mental differences exist between the sexes and in children of different racial backgrounds. These differences are due in part to hereditary factors and, in part, to environmental factors. Of the two, there is evidence that the environmental factors play a more dominant role in producing the differences that do the hereditary factors (36, 53).

Consistency Within Patterns

Even though the rate of development varies among children, all children display a certain consistency of development. This means that children follow a pattern that is characteristically theirs, controlled by their unique combination of hereditary endowment and environmental factors.

Studies reveal that children who are tall at one age

are tall at other ages, while those who are short remain short (86). Growth curves of the mental age of bright, average, and dull children show a similar consistency. Children with accelerated mental growth continue to be accelerated. Those who are mentally deficient rarely catch up, but are likely to become more and more retarded as they grow older (65).

Retests of the intelligence of children from birth to maturity reveal a strong underlying consistency. Figure 2–6 shows curves for five boys and five girls, from 1 month to 25 years. They are relatively similar at first, but around 6 years of age, individual differences begin to appear. The early similarity may not actually be as great as it appears: Tests for the early years may not be as diagnostic of differences as those for the older age levels (7).

Practical Significance of Individual Differences

Valuable as it is, from a theoretical angle, to know that children follow a developmental pattern that differs, even though only in minor details, from the pattern followed by other children, the practical value of such knowledge far outweighs its theoretical value. The reason for this is that parents and teachers tend to think of children of the same age as being alike and, consequently, expect similar behavior from them or they expect that what "works" with one child will automatically "work" with another child.

Of the many practical values of knowing that the developmental pattern differs for all children, the four most important of these are explained in Box 2–7.

Figure 2–6 Individual differences in the intellectual development of 5 boys and 5 girls. (*Adapted from N. Bayley: On the growth of intelligence.* American Psychologist, *1955,* 10, *805–818. Used by permission.*)

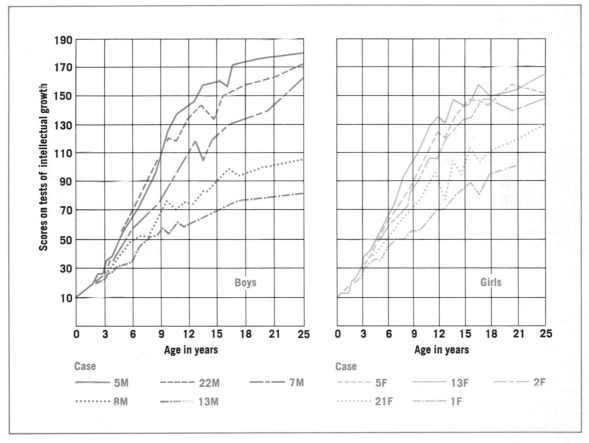

VALUES OF KNOWING THAT CHILDREN DEVELOP DIFFERENTLY

DIFFERENT EXPECTATIONS

All children of the same age cannot be expected to behave in the same way. A child who comes from a culturally deprived environment cannot be expected to learn to read as early as a child of the same ability whose parents put high value on education and encourage the child to be interested in reading.

BASIS OF INDIVIDUALITY

The child who is different from members of the group, provided the difference is not so great as to be conspicuous, will be interesting to other children and will be able to contribute something different to the group activities.

CHILD-REARING MUST BE INDIVIDUALIZED

One child may respond favorably to authoritarian control because it gives a feeling of security while another child will respond with antagonism and resentment.

PREDICTION IS DIFFICULT

Even when it is known how the *average* person reacts in a given situation, it is never possible to predict how a specific person will react. One person, for example, may find a joke "hilariously funny" while another person finds the same joke "boring" or "stupid".

VII. There Are Periods in the Developmental Pattern

Even though development is continuous, there is evidence that at different ages certain traits stand out more conspicuously than others because their development is taking place at a more rapid rate. It is possible, therefore, to mark off major periods, characterized by a specific kind of development which overshadows all others. Owing to individual variations, the age limits for these periods can be only roughly predicted. Bijou has suggested that the periods be marked off not by age but by biological events and changes in the individual's behavior (8).

The five major developmental periods in childhood begin with the moment of conception and end when the child becomes sexually mature. These periods,

with their characteristic forms of development and *approximate* ages, are shown in Box 2–8.

Periods of Equilibrium and Disequilibrium

In the developmental pattern, some periods are characterized by "equilibrium" and others by "disequilibrium." In the former, the child is making good adjustments and is easy to live with. In the latter, adjustments appear to be disrupted by conditions within or by environmental factors; there are tensions, indecisions, insecurities, and other behavior problems. As a result, the child is difficult to live with.

Figure 2–7 shows the periods of equilibrium and disequilibrium between the ages of 18 months and 6 years. Between 6 years and the onset of puberty, equilibrium prevails. A new period of disequilibrium occurs, however, as childhood draws to a close, during the time of the puberty changes.

Just as there are predictable ages of equilibrium and disequilibrium, so there are predictable patterns of

Figure 2–7 Ages of equilibrium and disequilibrium during the early years of life. (*Adapted from L. B. Ames and F. L. Ilg: The developmental point of view with special reference to the principle of reciprocal neuromotor interweaving.* Journal of Genetic Psychology, *1964,* 105, *195–209. Used by permission.*)

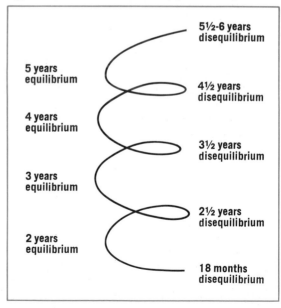

behavior at these ages. During periods of disequilibrium, children seem to be making an effort to snap the old bonds. "Good" children are suddenly "bad." They have difficulties in eating and sleeping and in adapting to people and life in general. By contrast, during periods of equilibrium, children are "in focus" and show signs of good adjustment. They not only adapt better to people and environmental demands but they are happier and more relaxed (3).

Boys and girls develop at different rates, and their periods of equilibrium and disequilibrium occur at slightly different ages. This is especially true as childhood draws to a close, because girls begin their puberty changes approximately a year earlier than boys. Within each sex group there are also differences between early and late maturers.

Normal versus "Problem" Behavior

During every period of development, some normal patterns of behavior are regarded as "problem" behavior by parents, teachers, and other adults because they do not conform to adult standards. Young children, for example, who take things belonging to others or who tell "tall tales" have not yet reached a point in their mental development that enables them to understand the difference between "mine and thine" or between reality and the product of imagination.

These patterns of so-called "problem" behavior arise because of the adjustments the child must make to new demands and new environmental conditions. The more demands and the greater the changes in the environment, the more adjustment problems the child will encounter. During phases of disequilibrium, a constellation of environmental pressures and biological changes affects the child's behavior. At puberty, for example, social expectations to "act like an adult" coincide with the adjustments the child must make to the physical and physiological changes puberty gives rise to.

Parents and teachers often regard normal behavior that interferes with the efficient running of the home or school as problem behavior. When they do this, they are likely to develop in the child unfavorable attitudes toward them and toward the situation in which the behavior occurs. The result is that many children then develop real problem behavior, such as lying, sneakiness, or destructiveness, as a way of getting their revenge.

Most forms of real problem behavior are normal for

a younger age. Children may cling to immature behavior because they have not yet learned to meet their needs in a more mature manner or because they derive less satisfaction from mature behavior. Children who revert to infantile behavior when they are jealous derive satisfaction from the attention their helplessness brings. If they persist in this pattern, it is symptomatic of some disturbance in their social relationships

PRINCIPLES OF DEVELOPMENT

and may be regarded as true problem behavior. Stealing, for example, will be tolerated in preschool children, but in an older child or adolescent it will be regarded as "delinquent" behavior.

The fact that certain forms of behavior are normal for certain ages does not make them acceptable. Nor does it mean that they should be tolerated without any effort to change them. If, for example, children have enough motor coordination to grab another child's toys, they have enough motor coordination to offer the other child one of their toys in exchange.

No form of problem behavior should be overlooked on the grounds that it is "typical" and that children will "outgrow" it. They may, but the chances are just as great that they will not. Instead, behavior that is not typically found at the child's age or maturity level is a danger signal of possible future trouble. As such, attempts should be made to remedy it before it has developed into a habitual method of adjustment.

Practical Significance of Developmental Periods

In spite of the differences noted above, all children normally pass through the different periods of development at approximately the same ages. Therefore, child training and provisions for learning are planned to fit into the pattern most characteristic of children of a given cultural group. Further, the cultural group expects each child to master the developmental tasks it sets for these stages.

A slight variation from the norm can generally be compensated for with help from parents and teachers. When deviations are great, special provisions must be made. Otherwise, the child will be too out of step to profit from the learning experiences provided.

When the developmental pattern is normal, one period prepares children for, and leads them successfully into, the next. In social development, for example, preschool children are expected to learn to make social adjustments to age-mates. If they are deprived of the necessary learning opportunities, they will be unready for the gang age of later childhood—a time when children's play is unsupervised by adults and when all children are expected to know how to get along reasonably well with their age-mates.

Retardation in an area that is dominant at a given age is likely to interfere with development in related areas. It has been found, for example, that children who are unpopular are deprived of opportunities to become socialized. Cut off from social contacts with age-mates, such children are likewise deprived of opportunities to develop motor skills, communications skills, and emotional control. As a result, the whole developmental pattern is affected.

VIII. There Are Social Expectations for Every Developmental Period

In every cultural group, experience has shown that people learn certain behavior patterns and certain skills more easily and more successfully at some ages than at others. The group then comes to expect each individual to perform according to this timetable of development.

People of all ages are well aware of these "social expectations." Even young children know, from what people say to them and ask them to do, that certain things are expected of them. They soon realize, from the approval or disapproval of their behavior, that these social expectations largely determine the pattern of their learning.

Social expectations are known as "developmental tasks" (39, 95). Havighurst has defined a developmental task as a "task which arises at or about a certain period in the life of an individual, successful achievement of which leads to his happiness and success with later tasks, while failure leads to unhappiness in the individual, disapproval by society, and difficulty with later tasks." Some developmental tasks arise mainly as a result of physical maturation (learning to walk); others are developed mainly from the cultural pressures of society (learning to read or learning appropriate sex roles); still others grow out of the personal values and aspirations of the individual (choosing and preparing for a vocation). Most developmental tasks arise from all three of these forces working together (39). The major developmental tasks for childhood are shown in Box 2–9.

In a culture that is relatively static, developmental tasks remain much the same one generation after another. In a changing culture, however, the new generation must perform new developmental tasks, while some of the old tasks will become less important or be eliminated. In a culture that changes from hand labor to machine labor, for example, learning hand skills becomes less important than learning to operate machines.

HAVIGHURST'S DEVELOPMENTAL TASKS FOR CHILDHOOD

BIRTH TO 6 YEARS
- Learning to walk
- Learning to take solid foods
- Learning to talk
- Learning to control the elimination of body wastes
- Learning sex differences and sexual modesty
- Achieving physiological stability
- Forming simple concepts of social and physical reality
- Learning to relate oneself emotionally to parents, siblings, and other people
- Learning to distinguish right and wrong and developing a conscience

6 TO 12 YEARS
- Learning physical skills necessary for ordinary games
- Building wholesome attitudes toward oneself as a growing organism
- Learning to get along with age-mates
- Learning an appropriate masculine or feminine sex role
- Developing fundamental skills in reading, writing, and calculating
- Developing concepts necessary for everyday living
- Developing conscience, morality, and a scale of values
- Achieving personal independence
- Developing attitudes toward social groups and institutions

Purposes of Developmental Tasks

Developmental tasks serve three very useful purposes. *First,* they act as guidelines to help parents and teachers to know what children should learn at a given age. If, for example, children are to make good adjustments to school, they must have mastered the tasks needed to be independent of teacher help, such as putting on or taking off outer garments, and they must know how to play the games other children in the neighborhood play.

Second, developmental tasks serve as motivating forces for children to learn what the social group expects them to learn at that age. Children quickly learn that social acceptance depends on their being able to do what their age-mates do. The stronger their desire for social acceptance, the greater will be their motivation to learn to do what their age-mates do.

Third, developmental tasks tell parents and teachers what will be expected of children in the immediate and remote future. As such, they alert them to the necessity of preparing children to meet these new expectations. When children begin to play with their age-mates, it alerts parents, for example, to the importance of teaching them how to play the games and sports that are popular among the older children of the neighborhood so that their children will be ready to play them when playing with age-mates becomes an important play activity for their children.

Factors Influencing Mastery of Developmental Tasks

A number of factors influence the mastery of developmental tasks; some act as obstacles to this mastery and some aid it. Some of these factors are controllable, as in the case of opportunities to learn. Others, as is true of body build and intelligence, are either not controllable or are controllable only within narrow limits.

Box 2–10 gives listings of factors that aid and factors that hinder the mastery of developmental tasks during the childhood years. Note that the factors that aid the mastery are almost the opposite of those that prove to be obstacles.

Importance of Mastering Developmental Tasks

In spite of the importance of mastering the developmental tasks appropriate for the child's age and level of development, not all children do so. This failure has three serious consequences. *First,* it makes the child feel inferior, and this leads to unhappiness. *Second,* it results in social disapproval, which is often accompanied by social rejection. The child is considered immature and babyish. *Third,* it makes the mastery of new developmental tasks difficult. Each year, the child

Some of these hazards are environmental in origin while others originate from within. Regardless of their origin, hazards can and do affect the physical, psychological, and social adjustments the child is attempting to make. As a result, they change the developmental pattern by producing a plateau in which no forward movement occurs or they cause a regression to a lower stage. When this happens, the child encounters adjustment problems and is said to be "poorly adjusted" or "immature."

Importance of Forewarning of Hazards

Forewarning of potential hazards associated with different areas of development is important because it enables those who are responsible for guiding the child's development—mainly parents and teachers—to be ready to cope with the causes of these hazards and, equally important, to take steps to ward them off. Knowing, for example, that lack of supervision is likely to lead to childhood accidents, parents who cannot assume responsibility for supervising their children can put them in nursery schools, kindergartens, or day-care centers where adequate supervision will be provided.

Similarly, knowing that during the early stages of learning to talk almost all children begin to stutter or slur when they become excited, parents can ward off this speech hazard by keeping the environment from being too stimulating and by calming their children when they become excited.

In each of the following chapters of this book, the common hazards associated with the areas of development under discussion will be described in a section at the end of the chapter. This will serve not only to highlight these hazards but also to emphasize that the normal pattern of development, described in the chapter, is often altered because of individual hazards arising from the child's genetic endowment or environment.

will lag further and further behind because the necessary foundations on which to build will not be present.

By contrast, children who are precocious in mastering the developmental tasks set by the social group are rewarded by social approval and self-approval. Both of these contribute to happiness. Social approval, in addition, puts children in line for leadership roles because they are judged by their age-mates to be superior in skills and general maturity. Self-approval contributes to self-confidence and provides a strong motivation to live up to social and self-expectations.

IX. Every Area of Development Has Potential Hazards

Even when the developmental pattern is progressing normally, there are likely to be, at every age, hazards in some areas of development that interfere with this normal pattern. As Erikson has explained, "The struggles that inevitably characterize all growth can generate utterly reliable talents as well as intractable 'problems'" (31).

X. Happiness Varies at Different Periods in Development

According to tradition, childhood is the happiest period of life. This tradition has been reinforced by another, that childhood should be a happy, carefree time to guarantee good adjustment to adult life. There is ample evidence today to show that neither of these beliefs is totally true and that, for many children, they are actually false.

Studies of childhood happiness have revealed that, for some children, childhood is a happy age while, for others, it is an unhappy age. Retrospective reports by adults of happiness at different ages have produced similar results.

Some adults remember their childhood days as the happiest in their lives. On the other hand, retrospective reports of some adults have emphasized both that unhappy memories overshadow the happy and that they have no desire to return to childhood (23, 51, 54, 56, 85).

Difficulties in Studying Happiness

Unquestionably one of the biggest gaps in scientific information about how children develop relates to happiness at different periods during the childhood years. This gap does not come from lack of interest or from the belief that the role of happiness in the child's life is too unimportant to warrant scientific study.

Instead, lack of information is due to two conditions. *First,* "happiness" is a nebulous term which, to date, has different meanings for different people. Just as in the early days of research in personality development there was no agreement as to what the term personality meant, so today there is no agreement as to what "happiness" means. To some, it is synonymous with joy while others accept the standard dictionary definition that happiness is a state of well-being or contentment—a condition dominated by pleasurable satisfaction. Commenting on this matter, Campbell has said (19):

It would appear that we have come to the point where we must stop using the word happiness indiscriminately to refer to any aspect of experience we regard as positive and begin to work seriously on the problem of identifying the major dimensions of the experience of well-being, developing instruments to measure them, analyzing their relationships to each other, and building time series that make possible the study of the nature of the change.

Second, happiness is a subjective experience and, as such, it is difficult to measure it by standard objective procedures. Instead, introspective and retrospective reports must be relied upon to get the information.

Since the early days of psychological research, it has been widely accepted that introspection and retrospection are far from scientifically approved methods for research. Only when their results can be checked by objective techniques can much reliance be placed on their findings.

It has also been widely agreed since the early days of psychological research that children, especially during the preschool years, are incapable of using introspective and retrospective techniques partly because they lack the linguistic facility to express their thoughts and feelings in words and partly because they are mentally too immature to separate important facts from unimportant. Even as children approach adolescence it is questionable whether much reliance can be placed on their introspections; probably even less can be placed on their retrospections.

Because of the methodological difficulties of studying happiness in children, an attempt will be made to present facts about happiness based not on children's reports alone but mainly on such objective evidence as their behavior, their speech, their emotions and their facial expressions. Inadequate as such data are, they give a clue to when and under what conditions happiness can be expected to occur.

Happiness or lack of it has such a great impact on children's personal and social adjustments that to understand these adjustments one must understand how they are influenced by this difficult-to-study and still scientifically undefined term called "happiness" or well-being (19).

Periods of Happiness and Unhappiness

The results of the various studies of happiness have shown that some ages are, predictably, happier than others. *Babyhood* is, for the most part, one of the happiest periods in the life-span. This is because almost everyone—adults and children—find the helplessness of babies appealing and they try to make babies happy. Some babies, however, are unwanted, neglected, and mistreated. For them, babyhood can be a very unhappy age.

Typically, the second year of life is less happy than the first. During this year, babies are often fretful and irritable when teething, and this makes them less appealing. They dislike being babied, and in showing their independence, become resistant and hard to handle. They resent being frustrated in what they want to do by disciplinary techniques that may include slaps and spanks. Finally, many babies are made unhappy during the second year of life by the arrival of a new sibling who becomes the center of parental attention.

Because the environment of *young children* is primarily limited to the home, their happiness is largely determined by how family members treat them. If, for example, siblings refuse to play with them because they cannot keep up the pace set by siblings or if parents show greater interest in other siblings than in them, they will feel unloved and unwanted.

Many factors contribute to happiness in *late childhood*. As a result, it is one of the happiest periods of the life-span. One of the most important conditions that contribute to happiness at this age is that older children have more choice in their environments than they had when they were preschoolers. If they are unhappy at home, they can spend more and more time at school, on the playground, or in the homes of age-mates where the home climate is more favorable than in their own homes. In addition, they are usually healthier than they were earlier and this enables them to do what they want to do. Once they have mastered the adjustment problems of elementary school, there will be only minor adjustments in their school lives until they reach the junior high school age of puberty. And, because the circle of acquaintances school provides for them is broad, they can select from this group those who are most congenial.

Puberty is such an unhappy period for many children that they try to escape from life either by spending their time in a daydream world or by talking about or even threatening suicide. Many conditions are responsible for unhappiness at this period. Rapid growth and change during puberty lead to fatigue, which predisposes pubescents to grumpiness. This, in turn, makes them less appealing to family members, teachers, and age-mates. Even a happy home climate is likely to become frictional unless parents and siblings understand that the pubescent is not up to par physically and make allowance for unsocial behavior. In retrospect, most adults regard puberty as the most unhappy period they have lived through.

Within each major developmental period, there are times of equilibrium and of disequilibrium. The periods of equilibrium are, on the whole, far happier than periods of disequilibrium. This is because, as was explained earlier, periods of disequilibrium are times when children are "out of focus" and tend, as a result, to make poor personal and social adjustments.

Essentials of Happiness

From the analysis of happiness and unhappiness at different times during the childhood years, as described above, it should be obvious that three essentials stand out. They are often called the "three A's of happiness" and are acceptance, affection, and achievement.

Acceptance means not only acceptance by others but also acceptance of self. However, they normally go hand-in-hand. Children who are accepted by others find it easy to like and accept themselves. They thus become well-adjusted people who are popular with both age-mates and adults.

Children who are accepted can count on *affection*—the second "A of happiness." The more accepted children are by others, the more affection they will receive from them. However, to receive affection, children must, in turn, show affection. Unless they do so, their acceptance by others will be reduced and, in turn, the amount of affection they receive from them.

The third "A of happiness" is *achievement*. For children to be happy, their achievement must be in an area regarded as important to the members of the social

Figure 2–8 Successful achievement in an activity that is important to a child at that time contributes to happiness. (*Adapted from Bil Keane: "The Family Circus." Register and Tribune Syndicate, October 2, 1974. Used by permission.*)

"I'm the best one in the class in buttoning."

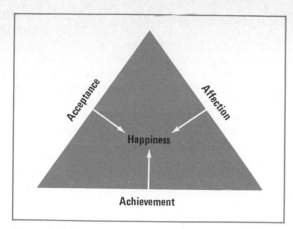

Figure 2–9 Interrelationship of the "Three A's of Happiness."

group with which they are identified. If, for example, being a good ball player is important to the group, the child who is regarded as a good ball player will be happy. How achievement in a task valued by the group affects the child's happiness is illustrated in Figure 2–8.

In addition, children's happiness depends on their reaching the goals they set for themselves. One of the biggest obstacles to happiness in childhood is the setting of unrealistically high goals. If children are encouraged by parents, teachers, or peers to do things they are not developmentally ready to do, they are bound to meet with failure. As a result, they become dissatisfied with themselves and feel that others regard them as failures. Only when goals are realistic in the sense that children have the capacity to reach them can they have the achievements that are essential to self-acceptance as well as acceptance by others (74).

Not one of these three essentials will, alone, bring happiness. If children are to experience the state of well-being and contentment that constitutes happiness, they must experience all three of them. Their interrelationship is shown in Figure 2–9.

Significance of Happiness

Unhappiness plays havoc with children's personal and social adjustments. This is because it affects their patterns of development and, as a result, they fall below their capacities in whatever they undertake. When this happens, self-dissatisfaction and unhappiness increase and the damage to personal and social adjustments, in turn, is increased. A vicious circle of unhappiness and maladjustment is then set in motion.

Because of this effect, there is justification for saying that the traditional belief that childhood should be a happy age is correct, though the emphasis on achieving adult happiness through a carefree childhood is open to serious doubt. Why this is true will be explained in more detail in Chapter 18 on personality.

By contrast, happiness does have a pervading influence on children's development and on the type of adjustments they make. It affects their attitudes, behavior, and personalities. Many studies have been made of happy and unhappy children at different ages to determine how they adjust to life and how their behavior measures up to their potentials (19, 51, 54, 56). Some of the ways in which happiness affects children's characteristic patterns of adjustment are given in Box 2–11. Note that the effects of happiness are, in most

---

BOX 2–11

HOW HAPPINESS AFFECTS CHILDHOOD ADJUSTMENT

- Happy children are normally *healthy and energetic.* Unhappiness saps their strength and energy and lowers their general physical well-being.
- Happy children turn their energies into *purposeful activities,* while unhappy children dissipate their energies in brooding, daydreaming, and self-pity.
- Happiness improves children's *looks* by giving them a cheerful expression. People react positively to cheerfulness and negatively to the "whipped-dog" expression characteristic of an unhappy child.
- Happiness supplies a strong *motivation* to do things, while unhappiness stifles motivation.
- Happy children *accept frustrations* more calmly and try to understand the reasons for frustrations. Unhappy children react with temper outbursts, and this militates against their learning why frustrations exist.
- Happiness *encourages social contacts* and participation in social activities. Unhappiness encourages children to be withdrawn and self-oriented.
- With repetition, *happiness becomes a habit.* In the same way, unhappiness can develop into a habit.
- A happy childhood does not guarantee adult success, but it *lays the foundation for success,* while unhappiness lays the foundation for failure.

cases, the opposite of the effects of unhappiness. Note, also, how happiness contributes to good personal and social adjustments while unhappiness tends to lead to maladjustments. Why this is true will be explained in the discussion of maladjustments in the chapter on personality development.

Chapter Highlights

1   Knowledge of the developmental pattern is important for scientific reasons because it helps developmental psychologists to know at approximately what ages to expect different patterns of behavior and to use these to set up guidelines. For practical reasons it is important because it emphasizes the necessity for guidance and stimulation if the child's full potentials are to be reached and it enables parents and teachers to prepare children ahead for what will be expected of them at given ages.

2   Research studies have provided evidence for 10 fundamental facts about principles of development during the childhood years. As research continues, more principles may emerge.

3   The first principle of development is that development involves changes, the goal of which is self-realization or the achievement of hereditary potentials.

4   Children's attitudes toward change are influenced by their awareness of these changes, how they affect children's behavior, social attitudes toward these changes, how they affect children's appearance, and how the social group reacts to children when these changes occur.

5   The second principle of development is that early development is more critical than later development. Because early foundations are greatly influenced by learning and experience, if they are harmful to a child's personal and social adjustments, they can be changed before they settle into habitual patterns.

6   The third principle of development emphasizes the fact that development comes from the interaction of maturation and learning, with maturation setting limits to the development.

7   The fourth principle of development is that the pattern of development is predictable, though this predictable pattern can be delayed or accelerated by conditions within the prenatal and postnatal environments.

8   The fifth principle of development is that the developmental pattern has certain predictable characteristics, the most important of which are that there is similarity in the developmental pattern for all children; development proceeds from general to specific responses; development is continuous; different areas develop at different rates; and there is correlation in development.

9   The sixth principle of development is that there are individual differences in development due partly to hereditary influences and partly to environmental conditions. This is true both for physical and psychological development.

10   The practical significance of knowing that there are individual differences in development is that it emphasizes the importance of training children according to their individual needs and of not expecting the same behavior in all children.

11   The seventh principle of development is that there are periods in the developmental pattern which are labeled the prenatal period, infancy, babyhood, early childhood, late childhood, and puberty. Within these periods there are times of equilibrium and disequilibrium and behavior patterns that are normal and those that are carry-overs from an earlier period—usually called "problem" behavior.

12   The eighth principle of development is that there are social expectations for every developmental period. These social expectations are in the form of developmental tasks which enable parents and teachers to know at what ages children are capable of mastering the different patterns of behavior necessary to make good adjustments.

13   The ninth principle of development is that every area of development has potential hazards—physical and psychological—which may alter the pattern of development.

14   The tenth principle of development is that happiness varies at different periods in the developmental pattern. The first year of life is usually the happiest and puberty is usually the most unhappy.

15 Difficult as it is to get scientifically accurate information about happiness, it is important to do so because happiness, which has such a profound effect on children's adjustment, is, within limits, controllable.

Bibliography

1 Adelson, E., and S. Fraiberg. Gross motor development in infants blind from birth. *Child Development,* 1974, *45,* 114–126.

2 Allen, G., and K. D. Pettigrew. Heritability of IQ by social class: evidence inconclusive. *Science,* 1973, *182,* 1042–1044.

3 Ames, L. B., and F. L. Ilg. The developmental point of view with special reference to the principle of reciprocal neuromotor interweaving. *Journal of Genetic Psychology,* 1964, *105,* 195–209.

4 Anderson, J. E. Dynamics of development: System in process. In J. Eliot (ed.), *Human development and cognitive processes.* New York: Holt, Rinehart & Winston, 1971. Pp. 38–55.

5 Baker, G. P. The effective use of nursery school on affective and cognitive development of disadvantaged and nondisadvantaged children. *Developmental Psychology,* 1973, *9,* 140.

6 Baumrind, D. From each according to her ability. *School Review,* 1972, *80,* 161–197.

7 Bayley, N. Development of mental abilities. In P. H. Mussen (ed.), *Carmichael's manual of child psychology,* 3d ed. New York: Wiley, 1970. Vol. 1, Pp. 1163–1209.

8 Bijou, S. W. Ages, stages, and the naturalization of human development. *American Psychologist,* 1968, *23,* 419–427.

9 Bijou, S. W. Development in the preschool years: A functional analysis. *American Psychologist,* 1975, *30,* 829–837.

10 Bower, T. G. R. Repetition in human development. *Merrill-Palmer Quarterly,* 1974, *20,* 303–318.

11 Boyd, R. D., and R. N. Koskela. A test of Erikson's theory of ego-stage development by means of a self-report instrument. *Journal of Experimental Education,* 1970, *38,* 1–14.

12 Brockman, L. M., and H. N. Ricciuti. Severe protein-calorie malnutrition and cognitive development in infancy and early childhood. *Developmental Psychology,* 1971, *4,* 312–319.

13 Bronfenbrenner, U. *Influences on human development.* New York: Holt, Rinehart & Winston, 1972.

14 Bronson, W. C. Central orientations: A study of behavior organization from childhood to adolescence. *Child Development,* 1966, *37,* 125–155.

15 Bronson, W. C. Mother-toddler interaction: A perspective on studying the development of competence. *Merrill-Palmer Quarterly* 1974, *20,* 275–301.

16 Brooks, J. B., and D. M. Elliott. Prediction of psychological development at age thirty from leisure time activities and satisfactions in childhood. *Human Development,* 1971, *14,* 51–61.

17 Bühler, C. The course of human life as a psychological problem. In W. R. Looft (ed.), *Developmental psychology: A book of readings.* Hinsdale, Ill.: Dryden Press, 1972. Pp. 68–84.

18 Caldwell, B. M. The effects of psychological deprivation on human development in infancy. *Merrill-Palmer Quarterly,* 1970, *16,* 260–277.

19 Campbell, A. Subjective measures of well-being. *American Psychologist,* 1976, *31,* 117–124.

20 Chalmers, D. K., and M. E. Rosenbaum. Learning by observation versus learning by doing. *Journal of Educational Psychology,* 1974, *66,* 216–224.

21 Chase, H. P., and H. P. Martin. Malnutrition and child development. *New England Journal of Medicine,* 1970, *282,* 933–939.

22 Chilman, C. S. Families in development at mid-stage in the family life cycle. *Family Coordinator,* 1968, *17,* 297–312.

23 Chiriboga, D., and M. F. Lowenthal. Psychological correlates of perceived well-being. *Proceedings of the Annual Convention of APA,* 1971, *6,* 603–604.

24 Church, J. *Understanding your child from birth to three: A guide to your child's psychological development.* New York: Random House, 1973.

25 Clarke, A. D. B. Consistency and variability in the growth of human characteristics. *Developmental Medicine and Child Neurology,* 1972, *14,* 668–683.

26 Coursin, D. B. Nutrition and brain development in infants. *Merrill-Palmer Quarterly,* 1972, *18,* 177–202.

27 Crumley, F. E., and R. S. Blumenthal. Children's reactions to temporary loss of the father. *American Journal of Psychiatry,* 1973, *130,* 778–782.

28 Denney, N. W. Evidence for developmental changes in categorization criteria for children and adults. *Human Development,* 1974, *17,* 41–53.

29 Dobzhansky, T. Differences are not deficits. *Psychology Today,* 1973, *7* (7), 96–101.

30 Douglass, J. H. The child, the father of the man. *Family Coordinator,* 1969, *18,* 3–8.

31 Erikson, E. H. *Childhood and society,* rev. ed. New York: Norton, 1964.

32 Freud, S. *The standard edition of the complete psychological works of Sigmund Freud.* London: Hogarth, 1953–1962. 21 vols.

33 Furth, H. G. On language and knowing in Piaget's developmental theory. *Human Development,* 1970, *13,* 241–257.

34 Gagné, R. M. Contributions of learning to human development. In J. Eliot (ed.), *Human development and cognitive processes.* New York: Holt, Rinehart & Winston, 1971. Pp. 111–128.

35 Gagné, R. M. Developmental readiness. In D. C. Charles and W. R. Looft (eds.), *Readings in psychological development through life.* New York: Holt, Rinehart & Winston, 1973. Pp. 139–146.

36 Garai, J. E. Sex differences in mental health. *Genetic Psychology Monographs,* 1970, *81,* 123–142.

37 Glavin, J. P. Persistence of behavior disorders in children. *Exceptional Children,* 1972, *38,* 367–376.

38 Glueck, E. Identification of potential delinquents at age 2–3 years. *International Journal of Social Psychiatry,* 1966, *12,* 5–16.

39 Havighurst, R. J. *Developmental*

Tasks and Education, 3d ed. New York: McKay, 1972.

40 Helson, R. Childhood interest clusters related to creativity in women. *Journal of Consulting Psychology,* 1965, *29,* 352–361.

41 Hirsch, J. Behavior-genetic analysis and biosocial consequences. In W. R. Looft (ed.), *Developmental psychology: A book of readings.* Hinsdale, Ill.: Dryden Press, 1972. Pp. 99–118.

42 Honzik, M. P. Environmental correlates of mental growth: Prediction from the family setting at 21 months. *Child Development,* 1967, *38,* 337–364.

43 Horowitz, F. D. Infant learning and development: Retrospect and prospect. In J. Eliot (ed.), *Human development and cognitive processes.* New York: Holt, Rinehart & Winston, 1971. Pp. 96–110.

44 Hunt, J. McV., and G. E. Kirk. Criterion-referenced tests of school readiness: A paradigm with illustrations. *Genetic Psychology Monographs,* 1974, *90,* 143–182.

45 James, W. *Talks to teachers on psychology.* New York: Holt, 1899.

46 Jensen, A. R. How much can we boost IQ and scholastic achievement? *Harvard Educational Review,* 1969, *39,* 1–123.

47 Jensen, A. R. The meaning of heritability in the behavioral sciences. *Educational Psychologist,* 1975, *1,* 171–183.

48 Jones, M. C., N. Bayley, J. W. Macfarlane, and M. P. Honzik (eds.), *The course of human development: Selected papers from the Longitudinal Studies, Institute of Human Development, University of California, Berkeley.* Waltham, Mass.: Xerox College Publications, 1971.

49 Jones, P. A. Home environment and the development of verbal ability. *Child Development,* 1972, *43,* 1081–1086.

50 Jordon, T. E., and S. D. Spaner. Biological and ecological influences on development at 72 months of age. *Human Development,* 1970, *13,* 178–187.

51 Kaplan, H. B., and A. D. Pokorny. Age-related correlates of self-derogation: Report of childhood experiences. *British Journal of Psychiatry,* 1970, *117,* 533–534.

52 Kaplan, H. B., and A. D. Pokorny. Sex-related correlates of adult self-derogation: Report of childhood experiences. *Developmental Psychology,* 1972, *6,* 536.

53 Kaufman, A. S., and N. L. Kaufman. Black-white differences at ages 2½–8½ on the McCarthy Scales of Children's Abilities. *Journal of School Psychology,* 1973, *11,* 196–206.

54 Kreitler, H., and S. Kreitler. Unhappy memories of the happy past: Studies in cognitive dissonance. *British Journal of Psychology,* 1968, *59,* 157–166.

55 Lefrancois, G. R. Jean Piaget's developmental model: Equilibrium through adaptation. In W. R. Looft (ed.), *Developmental psychology: A book of readings.* Hinsdale, Ill.: Dryden Press, 1972. Pp. 297–307.

56 Linn, M. W. Perceptions of childhood: Present functioning and past events. *Journal of Gerontology,* 1973, *28,* 202–206.

57 Maslow, A. H. *Motivation and personality.* New York: Harper & Row, 1954.

58 Minton, J. H. The impact of Sesame Street on readiness. *Sociology of Education,* 1975, *48,* 141–151.

59 Mischel, W. Continuity and change in personality. *American Psychologist,* 1969, *24,* 1012–1018.

60 Montagu, A. *The direction of human development,* rev. ed., New York: Hawthorn, 1970.

61 Neugarten, B. L., J. W. Moore, and discontinuities of psychological issues into adult life. *Human Development,* 1969, *12,* 121–130.

62 Neugarten, B. L., J. W. Moore, and J. C. Lowe. Norms, age constraints, and adult socialization. In B. L. Neugarten (ed.), *Middle age and aging: A reader in social psychology.* Chicago, Ill.: University of Chicago Press, 1968. Pp. 22–28.

63 Oden, M. H. The fulfillment of promise: 40-year follow-up of the Terman gifted group. *Genetic Psychology Monographs,* 1968, *77,* 3–93.

64 Osofsky, J. D., and B. Danzger. Relationships between neonatal characteristics and mother-infant interaction. *Developmental Psychology,* 1974, *10,* 124–130.

65 Owens, W. A. Age and mental abilities: A second adult follow-up. *Journal of Educational Psychology,* 1966, *57,* 311–325.

66 Phillips, D. C., and M. E. Kelly. Hierarchial theories of development in education and psychology. *Harvard Educational Review,* 1975, *45,* 351–375.

67 Piaget, J. *Psychology and epistemology.* New York: Grossman, 1971.

68 Piechowski, M. M. A theoretical and empirical approach to the study of development. *Genetic Psychology Monographs,* 1975, *92,* 231–297.

69 Powell, L. F. The effect of extra stimulation and maternal involvement on the development of low-birth-weight infants and on maternal behavior. *Child Development,* 1974, *45,* 106–113.

70 Scarr-Salapatek, S., and M. L. Williams. The effects of early stimulation on low-birth-weight infants. *Child Development,* 1973, *44,* 94–101.

71 Schaie, K. W. Age changes and age differences. In W. R. Looft (ed.), *Developmental psychology: A book of readings.* Hinsdale, Ill.: Dryden Press, 1972. Pp. 60–67.

72 Schneirla, T. C. The concept of development in comparative psychology. In J. Eliot (ed.), *Human development and cognitive processes.* New York: Holt, Rinehart & Winston, 1971. Pp. 55–78.

73 Schooler, C. Childhood family structure and adult characteristics. *Sociometry,* 1972, *35,* 255–269.

74 Shaver, B., and J. Freedman. The pursuit of happiness. *Psychology Today,* 1976, *10* (3), 26–32, 75.

75 Smith, A. C., G. L. Flick, G. S. Ferriss, and A. H. Sellmann. Prediction of developmental outcome at seven years from prenatal, perinatal, and postnatal events. *Child Development,* 1972, *43,* 495–507.

76 Sontag, L. W. Implications of infant behavior and environment for adult personalities. *New York Academy of Science,* 1966, *132,* 782–786.

77 Sontag, L. W., and J. Kagan. The emergence of intellectual achievement motives. *American Journal of Orthopsychiatry,* 1963, *33,* 532–534.

78 Tanner, J. M. Growing up. *Scientific American,* 1973, *229* (3), 35–43.

79 Taylor, A. Institutionalized infants' concept formation ability. *American Journal of Orthopsychiatry,* 1968, *38,* 110–115.

80 Terman, L. M., and M. H. Oden. *The gifted child at mid-life: Thirty-five year follow-up of the superior child.* Stanford, Calif.: Stanford University Press, 1959.

Terry, R. L. Parental assimilation by children with and without behavioral problems. *Journal of Genetic Psychology,* 1973, *122,* 55–61.

82 Tizard, J. Early malnutrition, growth and mental development in man. *British Medical Bulletin,* 1974, *30,* 169–174.

83 Tulkin, S. R. An analysis of the concept of cultural deprivation. *Developmental Psychology,* 1972, *6,* 326–339.

84 Tulkin, S. R., and J. Kagan. Mother-child interaction in the first year of life. *Child Development,* 1972, *43,* 31–41.

85 Unger, H. E. The feeling of happiness. *Psychiatry,* 1970, *7,* 27–33.

86 Vincent, E. L., and P. C. Martin. *Human psychological development.* New York: Ronald, 1961.

87 Wachs, T. D., and P. Cucinotta. The effects of enriched neonatal experiences upon later cognitive functioning. *Developmental Psychology,* 1971, *5,* 542.

88 Watson, J. B. *Behaviorism.* New York: People's Institute, 1925.

89 Werner, E. E., M. P. Honzik, and R. S. Smith. Prediction of intelligence and achievement at ten years from twenty months pediatric and psychologic examinations. *Child Development,* 1968, *39,* 1063–1075.

90 White, B. L. Exploring the origins of human competence. *APA Monitor,* 1976, *7* (4), 4–5.

91 White, S. H. The learning-maturation controversy: Hall to Hull. *Merrill-Palmer Quarterly,* 1968, *14,* 187–196.

92 Willerman, L., S. H. Broman, and M. Fiedler. Infant development, preschool IQ and social class. *Child Development,* 1970, *41,* 69–77.

93 Woods, M. B. The unsupervised child of the working mother. *Developmental Psychology,* 1972, *6,* 14–25.

94 Yarrow, L. J., J. L. Rubenstein, F. A. Pedersen, and J. J. Jankowski. Dimensions of early stimulation and their differential effects on infant development. *Merrill-Palmer Quarterly,* 1972, *18,* 205–218.

95 Zaccaria, J. S. Developmental tasks: Implications for the goal of guidance. *Personnel and Guidance Journal,* 1965, *44,* 372–375.

96 Zender, M. E., and B. F. Zender. Vygotsky's view about age polarization of child development. *Human Development,* 1974, *17,* 24–40.

CHAPTER 3

FOUNDATIONS OF THE DEVELOP- MENTAL PATTERN

In the early days of scientific research in child development, most studies started with the newborn infant, ignoring the prenatal period. The justification for this was that development during uterine life was physical and, consequently, could contribute little to a psychological understanding of development.

Today, it is recognized that what happens before birth is essential to a complete understanding of what happens after birth. Just as coming into a play or movie after it has started makes it difficult to understand what was responsible for the action taking place, so starting a study of the human being after birth eliminates an understanding of what is responsible for the developmental state present at birth.

In recent years, scientific research has shown that there are a number of important developmental patterns occurring at this time which make the prenatal period not only a distinctive period in the life-span but also a very important one. Box 3–1 shows four of the most significant characteristics of the prenatal period, each of which affects the child's later development so greatly that lack of this knowledge would seriously impair a person's understanding of the pattern of postnatal development.

Scientific Interest in Prenatal Development

Early interest in prenatal development centered around the origin of life rather than on the development of the unborn child. In ancient times, there was a great deal of speculation about how a new human being comes into existence.

In prehistoric and early historic times, there is evidence that people did not associate sexual intercourse with the birth of a baby. As a result, many theories of a mystical sort grew up to explain birth.

The Greek philosophers and physicians, on the other hand, knew that sexual intercourse *always preceded* the birth of a baby though they did not know exactly how this led to the production of a new life. On the basis of the knowledge they had, they evolved the theory that the woman was the receptive soil in which the seed from the male was planted.

It was not until the seventeenth century that the woman's contribution to fertilization was recognized. During that period de Graaf, a Dutch physician, suggested that the woman supplied an egg. A few years later, a Dutch spectaclemaker, van Leeuwenhoek, reported that "little animals," or what are now known as *sperm cells,* were found in the male semen. These, he contended, were the male contribution to the new human being (9). Figure 3–1 shows two early concepts of the sperm.

Gradually, in addition to the interest in the origin of life, there developed strong interests in other areas. The most important of these were; *first,* the role played by heredity in determining the child's future development; *second,* what role, if any, prenatal influences play; *third,* what is responsible for determining the sex of the child and how it can be controlled and predicted; *fourth,* the effect of multiple births on development; *fifth,* how ordinal position affects the child; and *sixth,* how attitudes of significant people toward the child-to-be are developed, when they are developed, how persistent they are, and how they affect the child's personal and social adjustments.

BOX 3–1

IMPORTANT CHARACTERISTICS
OF THE PRENATAL PERIOD

HEREDITARY ENDOWMENT
The hereditary endowment, which serves as the foundation for later development, is fixed at this time. This is true not only of physical and mental traits but also of the individual's sex.

RAPID GROWTH AND DEVELOPMENT
Proportionally greater growth and development occur at this time than at any other time in the entire life-span. During the 9 months before birth, the individual grows from a microscopically small germ cell to an infant of approximately 7 pounds in weight and 20 inches in length. It has been estimated that weight during this time increases 11 million times. In addition, all the bodily features of the human being are formed.

CONDITIONS IN PRENATAL ENVIRONMENT
Favorable conditions in the mother's body foster the development of hereditary potentials while unfavorable conditions can stunt their development or distort the pattern of future development.

ATTITUDES OF SIGNIFICANT PEOPLE
Attitudes of people who are significant in the child's life, especially family members, are formed at this time and have a marked effect on their treatment of the child during the early, formative years of life.

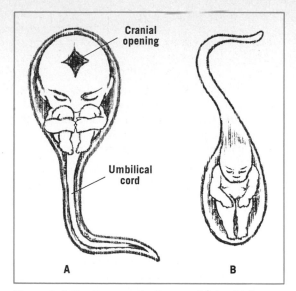

Figure 3–1 The homunculus (or manikin), which early scientists believed was contained in the sperm. After drawings by (a) Hartsoeker, 1694 and (b) Dalempatius, 1699. (*Adapted from A. Scheinfeld: The new you and heredity. Lippincott, 1961. Used by permission.*)

In spite of the scientific interest in the development that takes place before birth, there are still gaps in the information about it. There are a number of reasons for these gaps. Much of the information about factors that influence prenatal development must come from medical research. Psychologists must, therefore, wait until this information is available. For example, medical information about the effect of maternal use of drugs, especially marajuana and heroin, on the unborn child's development is still so new that its full impact will not be known until there is time to make further studies.

The problem of getting subjects to study is a major obstacle to research. While twins are numerous enough to make adequate study of the effect on development of being a twin on the child's personal and social adjustments, larger numbers of multiple births are so infrequent and the chances of survival so slim that studying them has been almost impossible.

Interest in the effects of sex and ordinal position has been strong for several decades. However, interest in the persistent effects of sex and ordinal position on children's development is of relatively recent origin.

Until there is time to make longitudinal studies to see if these effects are transitory or persistent, our knowledge of these important factors will be limited and fragmentary.

The methodological problems of studying attitudes are still only partially solved. While headway is being made, the problems still exist. As a result, knowledge about the effects of attitudes of significant people toward the child-to-be is still far from adequate. Furthermore, because interest in the effects of attitudes of significant people toward the child on the child's development is one of the newest focal points of scientific research, there simply has not been time to get information about how long the influence of these attitudes will persist.

How Life Begins

Life begins at the moment of conception—the time when a female reproductive cell, the *ovum* (plural, *ova*), is fertilized by a male reproductive cell, the *spermatozoon* (plural, *spermatozoa*). This is approximately 280 days before birth. The major differences between the male and female reproductive cells are listed in Box 3–2.

Before life can begin, the male and female reproductive cells must go through several preparatory processes. In the case of the female cells, there are three preparatory processes—maturation, ovulation, and fertilization—and in the case of the male cells, there are two preparatory processes—maturation and fertilization.

Maturation of Reproductive Cells

The maturation of the reproductive cells, the first preparatory process, is important in determining what the hereditary endowment of the newly created person will be. It consists of chromosome reduction through cell division.

Within each sex cell, whether the spermatozoon—the male cell—or the ovum—the female cell—there are 23 pairs of *chromosomes* before the maturational process takes place. Chromosomes are threadlike particles within each of which are strings of microscopically small particles, the *genes*. The genes are the physical substances passed on from parent to offspring; they are the carriers of hereditary traits.

During the maturational process, the chromosomes

**MAJOR DIFFERENCES BETWEEN
OVUM AND SPERMATOZOON**

OVUM

- Developed in the female gonads—the ovaries.
- One of the largest cells of the body—approximately 0.1 millimeter in diameter.
- Round.
- Contains yolk to nourish new individual after fertilization.
- No means of locomotion within itself; locomotion depends on contractions of surrounding tissues.
- While hundreds of thousands of ova are stored in the ovaries, normally only one ripens and is released every menstrual cycle of approximately 28 days.
- Every mature ovum contains 23 matched chromosomes.

SPERMATOZOON

- Developed in the male gonads—the testes.
- One of the smallest cells of the body—approximately 0.05 millimeter in diameter.
- Elongated, with a fine, hairlike tail.
- Contains no yolk, thus accounting for its small size.
- Moves by lashing tail.
- Several hundred million spermatozoa develop every 4 or 5 days.
- One-half of all mature spermatozoa contain 23 matched chromosomes: the other half contain 22 matched and 1 unmatched.

Since there is no specific scientific knowledge of how the pairs of chromosomes of either the ovum or the spermatozoon divide during the maturational process, it is assumed that division is largely a matter of chance. In one cell, for example, after division has occurred, there may be 20 chromosomes from the female and 3 from the male, or 8 from the female and 15 from the male, or any other combination. For that reason, when one cell combines with another in fertilization it is possible and probable that more traits will be inherited from one side of the family than from the other. This explains the "skipping of a generation" in a given trait.

It has been estimated that there are 16,777,216 possible arrangements of chromosome combination (67). Under such conditions, it is understandable why children of the same family are often so different. Only in the case of identical twins do children of the same family have the same genetic makeup. Since the combination of chromosomes is a matter of chance, one cannot predict with any degree of accuracy what the physical and mental characteristics of an unborn child will be.

Ovulation of the Female Reproductive Cell

The second preparatory process necessary for the beginning of life is ovulation. It is limited to the female reproductive cell, the ovum.

Ovulation is the process of escape of one mature ovum during the menstrual cycle. In the case of multiple births that are nonidentical, two or more mature ova are released from the follicles of one or both ovaries. To date, no one knows why this happens. It is believed, but not yet medically proved, that the two ovaries alternate in producing one ripe ovum during each menstrual cycle.

Once released from one of the follicles of an ovary, the mature ovum finds its way to the open end of the Fallopian tube nearest the ovary from which it was released. After it enters the tube, the ovum is propelled along the length of the tube by a combination of agents consisting of cilia or hairlike cells which line the tube, fluids composed of estrogen from the ovarian follicles and a mucus from the lining of the tube, and rhythmic contractions of the walls of the tube.

If the length of the menstrual cycle is normal—approximately 28 days—ovulation occurs between the

of each cell arrange themselves into pairs on opposite sides of the cell's nucleus, with each pair containing one chromosome from the mother and one from the father. When the pairs separate, one chromosome goes to one of the newly formed cells, and its mate goes to the other. The two cells thus formed split again, but this time lengthwise, so that one-half of the original number of chromosomes is retained.

This means that after the maturational process has been completed, there are four mature cells of each sex; each mature sex cell contains 23 chromosomes. In the case of the sperm cells, each one of the four mature cells that came from the original cell is capable of fertilizing an ovum. In the ovum, on the other hand, only one—the part that retains most of the yolk—is capable of being fertilized; the other three cells, the *polar bodies,* are absorbed and secreted.

fifth and the twenty-third days of the cycle with the average on the eleventh day. However, there are marked variations in ovulation among different women and in the same woman from time to time.

Fertilization

The third preparatory process to the beginning of a new individual is the fertilization of the ovum by a spermatozoon. In normal fertilization, the ovum is in one of the Fallopian tubes, on its way from the ovary to the uterus. As a result of coitus, spermatozoa in large numbers are deposited from the male at the mouth of the uterus and make their way toward the Fallopian tubes. They are attracted to the ovum by a strong hormonal force which draws them into the tube. After one sperm cell enters the ovum, the surface of the ovum is so changed that no other sperm can enter it. Thus fertilization is completed when union with one sperm has occurred.

When the sperm cell penetrates the wall of the ovum, the nuclei from the two cells approach each other. There is a breakdown in the membrane surrounding each, and the two nuclei merge. The new cell thus formed has 23 pairs of chromosomes, one-half of which have come from the male and one-half from the female cell.

From the two parents, the child receives a *new* combination of parental genes. This combination is made up of the genes the parents themselves received from their parents, and they, in turn, from their parents. Some of the chromosomes which the child receives from each parent may come from either or both grandparents on that parent's side of the family. As a result, a child may have many traits in common with one or both of the parents; the child may also resemble one of the grandparents or great-grandparents.

Importance of Fertilization

The time of conception can be regarded as one of the most important in a person's life. The reason for this is that four very important conditions which have a great impact, both directly and indirectly, on the newly created individual's future development are determined at that time.

Box 3–3 gives a list of these important conditions and explains briefly why they are important. Because of the far-reaching and long-lasting effects they have

on the individual's development, they will be explained in more detail in the following sections.

Hereditary Endowment

The first important condition occuring at the time of conception, when the ovum is fertilized by the spermatozoon, is the determination of the newly created individual's hereditary endowment. When the sperm unites with the ovum, everything the newly conceived individual will ever inherit from parents, grandparents, and other more remote ancestors is set. It has been estimated that there are between 40,000 and 60,000 genes in the chromosomes in the mature male cell and a similar number in a mature ovum. This means that the newly created baby's hereditary endowment contains between 80,000 and 120,000 genes, each of which carries potentials for physical and mental traits (67). The transmission of genetic inheritance is illustrated in Figure 3–2.

Chance determines which of a vast number of possible combinations of characteristics the baby will

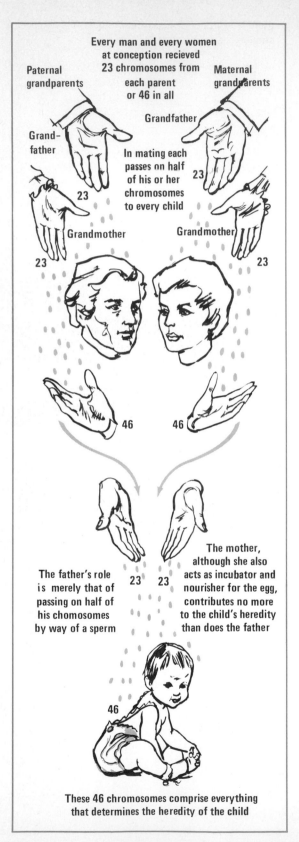

Every man and every women at conception recieved 23 chromosomes from each parent or 46 in all

Paternal grandparents

Maternal grandparents

Grandfather

Grandfather

In mating each passes on half of his or her chromosomes to every child

23

23

Grandmother

Grandmother

23

23

46

46

The father's role is merely that of passing on half of his chomosomes by way of a sperm

23

23

The mother, although she also acts as incubator and nourisher for the egg, contributes no more to the child's heredity than does the father

46

These 46 chromosomes comprise everything that determines the heredity of the child

inherit. As is true of chromosome combinations from parents, it is entirely a matter of chance how many chromosomes from different ancestors on the maternal or paternal side will be passed down to a child. To produce a given kind of person, a particular ovum must unite with a particular sperm. It has been estimated that the probability that this particular union will occur is but 1 in 300,000,000,000,000 (67).

After conception, nothing can be done to add to, or subtract from, the individual's hereditary endowment. If, however, the mother establishes a favorable prenatal environment through good physical health and healthy attitudes, the chances of a favorable development of the genes her unborn child *already has* will be greatly increased.

Some inherited characteristics, such as eye color and skin texture, are relatively immune to environmental influences. Most inherited characteristics, however, are markedly influenced by environment. As was explained in the discussion of the relationship between maturation and learning in the preceding chapter, favorable environmental conditions, including the stimulation of hereditary potentials, encourage the full development of hereditary potentials while unfavorable environmental conditions stifle this development.

Sex Determination

The second important condition determined at the time of conception is whether the child will be male or female. For centuries, parents have tried to predict and control the sex of their unborn children. And, for centuries, there have been beliefs about how this could be done.

How accurate are the predictions and how much control can parents exert? These practical problems have motivated research in the hopes of finding answers to these questions. What is known to date will be presented below.

PREDICTION OF SEX   Modern scientific techniques for predicting the unborn child's sex have included the *heartbeat test,* which maintains that a male fetus has a slower heartbeat than a female; the *smear test* to determine the amount of the estrogenic and androgenic hormones present; the *saliva test* to see if the mother's saliva contains a chemical substance associated with a masculine fetus; and the *amniotic fluid test*—"am-

Figure 3–2 The hereditary process. (*Adapted from A. Scheinfeld:* The new you and heredity. *Lippincott, 1961. Used by permission.*)

niocentesis." Amniocentesis is a medical technique of extracting a sample of amniotic fluid from the uterus. Examination of the cells in this fluid has proved 100 percent accurate in predicting the sex of the unborn fetus—the only test to date that can claim such a record of accuracy (54, 67).

However, up until now, amniocentesis has been reserved for diagnosis of possible birth defects in overage pregnant women who are more likely to have mongoloid babies (babies with severe mental deficiency and slightly distorted head and slanting eyes) than are younger women, and for those whose family histories suggest that they are high-risk parents. Only indirectly is this method used for determination of sex. While dangers to the fetus are reported to be nil, most doctors will not use this test for sex determination alone.

CONTROL OF SEX   Discovery of the sex chromosomes has shown that the factors that actually determine sex are internal and that the sex of the child is fixed at the time of fertilization. Of the chromosomes provided by the mature spermatozoon, one differs in character and structure from the others. This is true also of the chromosomes provided by the mature ovum. These different chromosomes are the *sex chromosomes*. They are of two kinds: The larger is the X chromosome, and the smaller—about one-third the size of the X chromosome—is the Y chromosome. One-half of all mature spermatozoa carry the X chromosome, and the other half carry the Y. By contrast, all mature ova carry the X chromosome.

Thus, in any fertilized ovum, there is always an X chromosome from the ovum and either an X or a Y chromosome from the spermatozoon. If the spermatozoon that unites with the ovum is of the Y-bearing type, the result will be an XY sex chromosome combination; this always results in a male offspring. Should an X-bearing spermatozoon unite with the ovum, the result will be an XX sex chromosome combination; this always produces a female offspring. Figure 3–3 shows how male and female offspring are determined.

While attempts have been made to control the chemical condition of the woman's reproductive apparatus to make it favorable to those sperm cells that will produce an offspring of the desired sex, only very limited success has been reported to date. Until this can be done, there is no known way to influence the combination of the ovum with a sperm that will produce a child of the desired sex. Consequently, at the present time,

there is evidence that sex determination is a matter of chance.

EFFECTS OF SEX ON DEVELOPMENT   The child's sex affects development both directly and indirectly. The direct effects occur both before and after birth, while the indirect effects occur only after birth.

Figure 3–3 How sex is determined. (*Adapted from A. Scheinfeld:* The new you and heredity. *Lippincott, 1961. Used by permission.*)

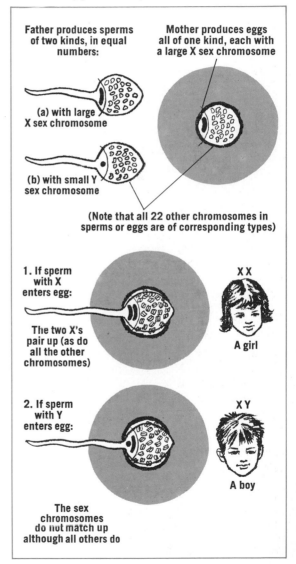

The *direct* effects of sex on development come from hormonal conditions. Throughout the childhood years, the sex organs of boys and girls produce sex hormones in small quantities. These sex hormones differ in quantity but not in type. Both sexes produce *androgen,* the male hormone, and *estrogen,* the female hormone. Males produce more androgen, and females more estrogen. It is the predominance of the sex hormone appropriate for their sex that is responsible for the differences in physical and psychological development of boys and girls. If this balance is upset, variations result. Boys who are castrated, for example, become "feminine" in appearance and behavior, while girls whose ovaries are removed because of a diseased condition become "masculine" (54, 60, 62, 67).

The *indirect* effects of sex on development come from environmental conditions. From the time children are born, strong social pressures are put on them to conform to the culturally approved patterns for their sexes. Throughout the childhood years, both boys and girls are molded—first by the family, later by the peer and school groups, and still later by the community group—into a pattern the group considers appropriate for the child's sex. This matter will be discussed in detail in the chapter on the development of sex roles.

Number of Offspring

The third important condition determined at the time of conception is whether the birth will be single or multiple. The term "multiple birth" refers to the birth of two or more babies within a few hours or days; twins, triplets, quadruplets, and quintuplets. "Singletons" are children who are born alone. They may have siblings—brothers and sisters—but a period of 9 months or more separate their births from those of their siblings.

Meredith has reported that twins occur once in every 80 births, triplets once in every 9,000 births, and quadruplets once in every 570,000 births (49). There are no statistics for larger numbers of multiple births because they are extremely rare.

Multiple births have been reported to occur more often among blacks than among whites and more often among whites than among members of the yellow race. Maternal age has little effect on multiple births coming from the division of one egg. Up to the age of 38 years, however, women show a definite tendency to have twins from two eggs, after which age there is a rapid decline in the tendency. The probability of later multiple maternity is ten times greater for a woman who has produced children of multiple birth than for a woman who has not. Contrary to popular belief, there is no evidence that twins run in families, nor is there any evidence of weather or seasonal effects on multiple birth (54, 66, 67). There is some evidence that taking fertility drugs to facilitate pregancy is responsible for multiple birth of large numbers, but this is occasional rather than universal.

Scientific investigations to determine the effect of multiple birth on child development have been numerous in the case of twins but few for those of larger number. This is not because of lack of interest in triplets, quadruplets, or quintuplets but rather because they are far less frequent; often one or more will die at birth or shortly afterward, and as a result, their postnatal environment is similar to that of twins. What is known about the effect of multiple births on development is presented below.

TWINS   There are two distinctly different types of twins. *Identical,* or uniovular, twins come from a single ovum fertilized by a single sperm; *nonidentical*—biovular, or fraternal—twins are the product of two ova fertilized simultaneously. It is estimated that one-fourth of all twins are of the one-egg type. Figure 3–4 shows how the two types of twins develop.

When one ovum is fertilized by one spermatozoon, it occasionally happens that, at the time of the first division of the cell, the new cells separate instead of remaining together. Why this separation occurs, no one knows for certain, but there is some evidence that it is the result of hormonal disturbances. There is also the belief—as yet unproved—that the egg has an inherent tendency to divide. Whatever its cause, if a separation occurs before the reduction division, during the maturational process, two separate eggs will result. Twins formed from such divided eggs are called "identical"; they have exactly the same assortment of genes.

Because of their identical hereditary endowment, identical twins resemble each other very closely in all their hereditary traits. They have the closest degree of kinship possible for two distinctly separated individuals and they are always of the same sex.

Occasionally, two ova develop simultaneously and are fertilized at the same time. The individuals who develop from these two ova are "nonidentical"—often called fraternal—twins. The name "nonidentical" suggests lack of similarity in the physical and mental makeup of the twins. When the chromosomes of the

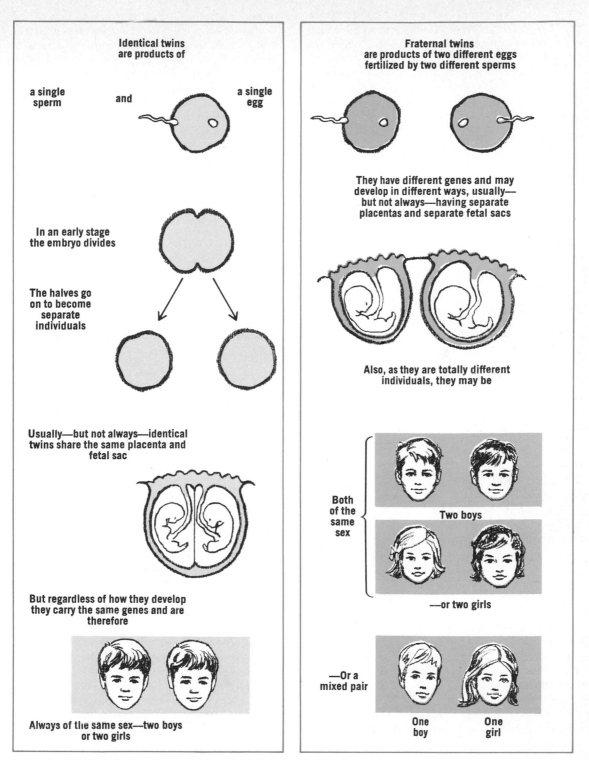

Identical twins are products of

a single sperm and a single egg

In an early stage the embryo divides

The halves go on to become separate individuals

Usually—but not always—identical twins share the same placenta and fetal sac

But regardless of how they develop they carry the same genes and are therefore

Always of the same sex—two boys or two girls

Fraternal twins are products of two different eggs fertilized by two different sperms

They have different genes and may develop in different ways, usually—but not always—having separate placentas and separate fetal sacs

Also, as they are totally different individuals, they may be

Both of the same sex

Two boys

—or two girls

—Or a mixed pair

One boy   One girl

Figure 3–4 The two types of twins. (*Adapted from A. Scheinfeld:* The new you and heredity. *Lippincott, 1961. Used by permission.*)

two ova divide, the grouping is not likely to be the same for both. One ovum may receive a preponderance of chromosomes from the maternal grandfather, and the other from the maternal grandmother. In addition, the ova are fertilized by individual spermatozoa, each with its own assortment of chromosomes. Nonidentical twins may be of the same sex or of opposite sexes. Nonidentical twins are not really twins;

COMMON CHARACTERISTICS OF TWINS

DEVELOPMENTAL LAG
Twins tend to lag in their physical, motor, intellectual, and speech development during the first 6 years of life and then catch up, at least partially, to the norm. This lag is due to many factors, mainly prematurity, parental overprotectiveness, and mutual dependency. Figure 3–5 shows the lag in motor and speech development.

PHYSICAL DEVELOPMENT
Because twins are usually premature, they tend to be below the norm in size for several years and sometimes suffer from brain damage or other defects.

INTELLECTUAL DEVELOPMENT
Mental similarities, as revealed by intelligence tests and educational achievement, are much more striking in identical than in nonidentical twins.

SPECIAL ABILITIES
In special abilities, such as musical or athletic ability, similarities between identical twins are common. These similarities may be due more to environmental conditions than to heredity.

SOCIAL BEHAVIOR
During the preschool years, twins are competitive for adult attention, copy each other, and show similar feelings about others. They have few interactions with others during the preschool years but these increase as they grow older.

PERSONALITY DEVELOPMENT
Mutual dependency prevents the development of individuality. Rivalries and antagonisms, however, leave their mark, and one twin, usually the larger and stronger, becomes dominant, thus developing the personality pattern of a leader while the other twin develops a follower personality pattern.

BEHAVIOR PROBLEMS
Behavior problems have been reported to be more common among twins than among singletons of the same ages. However, it has also been suggested that this difference is due to the way twins are treated at home and outside the home. Behavior problems have also been reported to be more common among nonidentical than among identical twins, though, to date, no explanation based on conclusive evidence has been given for this difference.

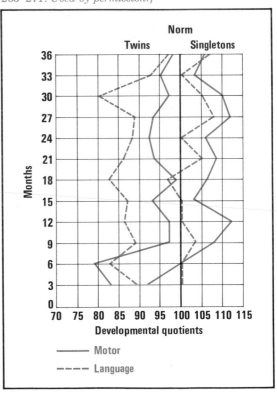

Figure 3–5 Developmental lag in motor and language development among twins during the first 3 years of postnatal life. (*Adapted from R. J. Dales: Motor and language development of twins during the first three years.* Journal of Genetic Psychology, *1969,* 114, *263–271. Used by permission.*)

---

rather, they are the result of simultaneous pregnancies.

Many studies have been made of twins to determine how similar they are in physical and mental makeup, how they differ from ordinary siblings, and how long their similarities persist. In general, these studies reveal that twins are more likely than singletons to miscarry, to be born ahead of schedule, to suffer from birth injuries, or to be stillborn. These studies have also shown some of the characteristics commonly found in twins, the most important of which are listed and briefly explained in Box 3–4.

TRIPLETS Triplets may be of three types: (1) identical, in that all three have come from the same fertilized ovum; (2) two identical and one sibling; and (3) three siblings, each having come from a separate fertilized ovum. A few sets of triplets have been studied extensively to determine what their physical and mental characteristics are.

Physically, there is a lag in tempo of development between triplets and singletons. The eruption of the first tooth, for example, comes a month later than for twins. In *developmental traits,* such as sitting alone, standing alone, and walking, there is a lag. Triplets are also slower in saying their *first words* and in *forming sentences* (31, 66).

Mental development, as measured by intelligence tests, likewise shows a lag. Among older triplets, however, the lag is less pronounced, suggesting that it may affect only the early development. Tests of *emotional* and *personality development* have indicated that triplets behave socially and temperamentally like single-born children of the same age and have interests and attitudes normal for their sex (29, 38).

QUADRUPLETS Studies of quadruplets are exceedingly limited. A study of one set of 12-year-old quadruplets showed them to be emotionally immature, dependent on adults, and unable to conform to social expectations. They also had difficulty in thinking independently and tended to project the blame for their acts on others. In this set of quadruplets, two of whom were boys and two girls, one of the boys assumed the leadership role. Some of their retardation in social and emotional behavior may have been due to the fact that they came from a poor home setting marked by divorce and spent some of their time in foster homes (69).

QUINTUPLETS One of the most authoritative reports of the famous Dionne quintuplets is that of Blatz. According to Blatz, the quintuplets did not begin to walk until they were about 15 months old. They used gesture language, as is true of twins, and did not catch up to single children until about the fifth year. At the age of 3 years, they had a vocabulary of 110 words, which is retarded for singletons of that age. Intelligence tests were given only until the quintuplets were about 3½ years old. These tests showed them to be backward as compared with norms for single children (7).

DEVELOPMENTAL DIFFERENCES OF SINGLETONS AND MULTIPLE BIRTHS Whether the child is a singleton or one of multiple birth will have a marked influence on development both before and after birth. Identical children of multiple birth have similar physical and mental potentials. Consequently, it is inevitable that they will have less individuality—even if they have markedly different postnatal environments—than children of nonidentical multiple births or singletons. These differences are traceable to three important influences:

First, the prenatal environment of children of multiple birth differs in important respects from that of singletons. Children of multiple birth are usually crowded into a space nature intended for only one. As a result, one child in the set may be in a less favorable position than the others. The significance of this crowding will be discussed in the section on fetal activity. Children of multiple birth are often born prematurely because the uterus is incapable of further expansion as the fetuses grow larger. This is not always true, of course, but physical or psychological handicaps are more common among children of multiple birth than among singletons (37, 66, 79, 87).

Second, the postnatal environment of children of multiple birth is also quite different from that of singletons. Children of multiple birth must share parental time and attention. If one child is weaker, he is likely to get the lion's share; thus, his sibling may feel that the parents are playing favorites. In addition, the weaker child is likely to develop a "follower" personality pattern, while the stronger learns to play the role of leader. Furthermore, sibling rivalries and competition, animosities, and resentments are heightened if a child feels that the parents are showing favoritism. The weaker child may develop feelings of inadequacy and martyrdom. The stronger child may feel discriminated against. In spite of such unfavorable sibling relationships, affectional relationships become stronger as children of multiple birth grow older, as is true also of singletons (10, 37, 80).

Because tradition holds that children who shared the same prenatal environment should share the same postnatal environment, children of multiple birth are thrown together constantly. They are expected to play together, share the same toys and friends, and dress alike, whether or not they are of the same sex. This stifles the development of individuality.

Third, parental attitudes toward multiple births, reflected in parental behavior, indirectly affects the child's development. This matter will be discussed in detail later in the section devoted to a discussion of the influence of attitudes on prenatal and postnatal development.

Ordinal Position in the Family

The child's position in a sequence of siblings is the fourth condition, determined at the time of conception, which has a profound influence on later development. Forer has explained the importance of ordinal position in this way (24):

> When we are born into a family unit or brought into it through adoption or as a stepchild, we take a certain place in the family hierarchy. We become *only* child, *oldest* child, *middle* child or *youngest* child. The first and most obvious effect of taking a certain position in the family is the relationship we have with respect to the people already there. . . . The place in the family establishes for the child a specific role to be played within the family group. It influences him to develop attitudes toward himself and toward other people and helps him to develop specific patterns of behavior.

FACTORS INFLUENCING THE EFFECT OF ORDINAL POSITION Scientific studies of ordinal position have revealed that environmental influences play a more important role than heredity in determining the differences that have been found in children of different ordinal positions in a family. For example, while there appears to be a decline in some abilities, especially intellectual abilities and achievements, there is evidence that this decline is due more to environmental factors than to heredity (68, 91, 92). Of the many environmental factors that determine the influence of or-

dinal position, the five that seem to be most important, from present evidence, are:

First, cultural attitudes toward ordinal position. In cultures where the firstborn is regarded as the heir to authority, power, and wealth, parents brought up in these cultures will be influenced in the treatment of their children.

Second, attitudes of significant people. How family members regard different ordinal positions influence children's attitudes toward them and, in turn, their behavior. When younger children look up to firstborns, they use them as models and pacesetters.

Third, role expectations. If firstborns are expected to act as models for younger siblings, and to take care of them, it affects firstborns' attitudes toward themselves and their behavior. Figure 3–6 shows how some firstborns feel about being expected to be models for younger siblings.

Fourth, early treatment. Regardless of ordinal position, children who are the center of attention during the early months of life often become anxious and resentful when replaced by a younger sibling.

Figure 3–6 Many firstborns resent parental expectations that they serve as models for younger siblings. (*Adapted from Bil Keane: "The Family Circus."* Register and Tribune Syndicate, *October 11, 1974. Used by permission.*)

"You're lucky PJ — you don't have to be a good example to ANYBODY!"

Fifth, stimulation of innate abilities. Parents normally have more time to devote to the stimulation of children's innate abilities in the case of firstborns and last-borns than in those who come between (2, 5, 6, 24, 63, 93).

CHARACTERISTICS OF CHILDREN OF DIFFERENT ORDINAL POSITIONS   Because of environmental conditions, children of different ordinal positions have been found to have certain characteristics in common, though these are, by no means, universal. In the case of lastborns, for example, characteristics they develop will be greatly influenced by whether family members regard them as "adorable dolls" or as "pests."

Studies have revealed that there are certain syndromes or clusters of traits that are characteristically found among children of different birth order. There is no evidence whatever that the traits are hereditary and much evidence that they are the product of the way children have been treated during the early, formative years by people who are significant to them. Box 3–5 gives the typical syndromes of children of different ordinal positions. (2, 6, 35, 41, 58, 68, 92).

As Box 3–5 indicates, no ordinal position can be regarded as best. Firstborns have more guidance and help in their development than later-born children. Altus has commented that "the dice are loaded in favor of the first-born" (2). Because of parental pressures on them to achieve, they usually achieve more than later-born siblings. In addition, firstborns usually conform more closely to social expectations and, as a result, they tend to be better accepted and more likely to play leadership roles. If later-borns were given the same guidance and attention as firstborns, they would probably achieve as much and be as well accepted socially (41, 57).

LONG-TERM EFFECTS OF ORDINAL POSITION   Because attitudes, treatment, and roles assigned to children of different ordinal positions in the family are not likely to change, their effects become persistent and influence the personal and social adjustments children of different ordinal position make as they grow older.

Studies of persistent effects of ordinal position have been limited in number. However, those that have been made show that ordinal-position effects are persistent enough to justify the claim that ordinal position

BOX 3–5

TYPICAL ORDINAL-POSITION SYNDROMES

THE FIRSTBORN CHILD
Uncertainty, mistrustfulness, insecurity, shrewdness, stinginess, dependency, responsibility, authoritarianism, jealousy, conservatism, lack of dominance and aggressiveness, suggestibility, excitability, sensitiveness, timidity, introversion, strong achievement drive, need for affilliation, petulant, spoiled, and prone to behavior disorders

THE SECOND CHILD
Independence, aggressiveness, extroversion, funloving, gregarious, adventuresome, dependable, well adjusted

THE MIDDLE CHILD
Aggressiveness, easily distracted, craves demonstrations of affection, jealousy, plagued by feelings of parental neglect, inferiority, and inadequacy, and prone to behavior disorders

THE LAST CHILD
Secure, confident, spontaneous, good-natured, generous, spoiled, immature, extroverted, ability to empathize, feelings of inadequacy and inferiority, resentments against older siblings, envy and jealousy, irresponsible, and happy.

is, indeed, one of the most important conditions occurring at the time of conception.

For example, even though there is no evidence that firstborns are less healthy than their later-born siblings, they tend to be more health-conscious and concerned and to consult doctors more often than their later-born siblings, even when they become adults. They also tend to be more cautious and take fewer risks (58, 82).

Ordinal position in a childhood family has been found to have an important influence on adult marital adjustments. This is because adults learned to play certain roles in their childhood homes and continue to play those roles after marriage. The best marital adjustments have been reported to occur when husbands were the oldest brothers with younger sisters and when wives were younger sisters with older brothers. When, on the other hand, husbands were younger brothers of older sisters and wives the older sisters of younger brothers, there is likely to be a frictional relationship because wives try to "boss" their husbands as they did their younger brothers. If both husband and wife were firstborns, there is likely to be a highly frictional relationship with each trying to dominate the other (28).

Ordinal position has also been found to affect divorce. Firstborn men, who learned to assume responsibilities when they were young, tend to have a low divorce rate while firstborn women, who often were given the responsibility for the care of younger siblings and, as a result, learned to be "bossy," have a high divorce rate (26, 78).

Timetable of Prenatal Development

As soon as an ovum is fertilized by a spermatozoon, development begins. Growth—in the short period of 9 calendar months—from a single cell, microscopically

small, to a baby of about two hundred billion cells is phenomenal. Equally phenomenal is the change from a single cell with no power of its own to a child composed of bones, muscles, skin, internal organs, and a nervous system—all ready to function at or even before birth.

Studies of animals and human beings show that development follows a pattern, not only in the formation of the different parts of the body but in their functioning as well. At no time is the developing organism a miniature adult in body proportions. Figure 3–7 shows the different body proportions in the early prenatal stages. Because the pattern is orderly and predictable, it is possible to give a "timetable" of the development of structures and functions.

It is customary for the layman to think of pregnancy in terms of 9 *calendar months*. By contrast, scientists use as their measuring rod *lunar months* of 28 days each. These coincide with the periods of the female menstrual cycle. While the total length of the prenatal period, when measured in calendar months, is several days less than when lunar months are used, few babies

Figure 3–7 The development of body form during the prenatal period. (*Adapted from P. C. Martin and E. L. Vincent:* Human development. *Ronald, 1960. Used by permission.*)

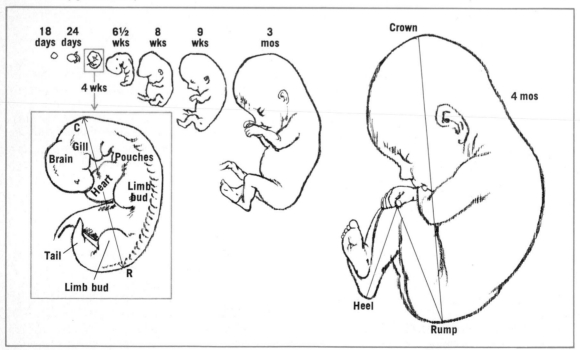

are born exactly 280 days after the time of conception.

The 10 lunar months of the prenatal period may be marked off into three subdivisions, each characterized by a particular phase of development. These are the *period of the ovum,* the *period of the embryo,* and the *period of the fetus.* Box 3–6 lists the highlights of each of these developmental periods.

Conditions Affecting Prenatal Development

The environment in which the child lives before birth—the mother's uterus—determines whether the fetus will follow nature's timetable. Normally, conditions within the uterus are ideal for the development of a healthy child. *Marked* variations may spell trouble. Any injurious agent introduced through the placental bloodstream can disturb the uterine environment. If introduced at a critical time in the developmental timetable, it can temporarily or permanently change the pattern.

Experimental studies of animal and human subjects have positively identified certain conditions in the prenatal environment that affect development. Other conditions are suspected of being influential, but the evidence is as yet inconclusive. These conditions are listed in Box 3–7.

Attitudes of Significant People

While maternal health, nutrition, age, and the other factors discussed above are, unquestionably, the major influences in determining how the fertilized ovum will develop, *indirect* influences in the form of attitudes of significant people in the unborn child's life are too important to be ignored. The attitudes developed at this time are important because they serve as the bases for maternal attitudes toward the child after birth, toward the role of parent, and toward the child-training methods used during the early, formative years of life. What is true of maternal attitudes is likewise true of paternal attitudes and, to a lesser extent, of the attitudes of siblings and other family members.

How much influence the attitudes of significant people in the unborn child's life will have on attitudes of

---

BOX 3–6

HIGHLIGHTS OF TIMETABLE
FOR PRENATAL DEVELOPMENT

PERIOD OF THE OVUM
(Conception to End of the Second Week)
- Practically unchanged in size because of lack of outside source of nourishment.
- Rapid internal development.
- Implantation in uterine wall about 10 days after fertilization.
- With implantation, the ovum becomes a parasite.

PERIOD OF THE EMBRYO
(End of the Second Week to End of the Second Lunar Month)
- All important external and internal features start to develop and function.
- Sex organs well enough developed to distinguish sex of embryo.
- By end of period, embryo measures 1½ to 2 inches in length and weighs about 1 ounce.
- Growth in the head region is proportionally much greater than in the rest of the body. See Figure 3–7.
- Accessory apparatus—placenta, umbilical cord, and amniotic sac—develops.

PERIOD OF THE FETUS
(End of Second Lunar Month to Birth)
- External and internal features continue growth and development.
- Growth follows the laws of developmental direction. Refer to Figure 2–3.
- Internal organs assume nearly adult positions by fifth lunar month.
- Nerve cells, present since the third week, increase rapidly in number during the second, third, and fourth months.
- Age of viability reached by sixth or seventh month.
- Fetal activity (e.g., kicking, squirming) begins between second and third months.

---

family members will depend partly on how close their relationship is with family members (and consequently how much influence they have over their attitudes) and partly on how many and how close their contacts are with the child in the early, formative years of postnatal life. The mother-to-be's attitude, for example, can be greatly influenced by the attitude of a close, personal friend. If this friend is happy in her maternal role, her influence on the mother-to-be's attitude will be very different than it would be if she found the maternal role boring and frustrating and constantly complained about the work and privations this role entailed.

Parental Attitudes

Most attitudes toward children and toward parenthood originate in the childhood experiences of the parents-to-be and crystallize when pregnancy is confirmed. Many women, from the time when they played with dolls, have looked forward to having children of their own, and have developed *definite* ideas of what they want their children to be like. Men are generally too concerned about their vocations to give much thought to parenthood during their childhood and youth. They do, however, have *general* ideas of what parenthood will mean to them.

Parents' attitudes toward their children are influenced by their concept of the role of parenthood. Some people romanticize parenthood; some view it realistically. Some view it favorably; others, unfavorably. These attitudes have emotional accompaniments ranging from joy to fear, anger, and disgust. No two parents-to-be have had the same childhood experiences or the same experiences during pregnancy, and it is understandable that their attitudes should be different. Some of the factors responsible for variations in attitudes, however, are almost universally operative. The most important of these factors are given in Box 3–8.

Sibling Attitudes

Sibling attitudes are usually formed during the prenatal period and are well established by the time the baby is born. How siblings feel about a new baby in the family will depend largely on their ages and other interests. If they are still young when the new baby arrives, they may resent having to share their parents with the newcomer. By contrast, older children have friends and interests outside the home. So long as the new baby does not interfere with the pattern of their lives, their attitudes will be favorable. They may even find the baby more fun to play with than their toys.

Adolescents, especially girls, often have an unfavorable attitude toward a new baby in the family. They are embarrassed about their mothers' pregnancy and are often called on to help take care of the baby. Their social lives may be curtailed somewhat, and, as a result, jealousy and resentment develop.

BOX 3–8

FACTORS INFLUENCING PARENTAL ATTITUDES

DESIRE TO HAVE CHILDREN
Some people want many children, others want a few or none. Some feel that a marriage is incomplete without children and others feel that children are an obstacle to vocational success or upward mobility.

PHYSICAL STATE DURING PREGNANCY
If the mother-to-be feels well and has few discomforts even when discomforts are common, she will likely have a more favorable attitude than the mother-to-be who has many discomforts.

EMOTIONAL STATE DURING PREGNANCY
For many women, pregnancy is a time of depression, anxiety, and worry about childbirth, having a deformed child, or her adequacy for motherhood; for others, it is a time of joyful anticipation.

MATERNAL DREAMS AND FANTASIES
The fears, doubts, and anxieties mothers-to-be experience are often intensified by dreams and fantasies just as are the happy emotional states.

EARLY EXPERIENCES WITH CHILDREN
Parents-to-be who were expected to assume responsibilities for the care of younger siblings in their youth tend to have less favorable attitudes toward having children than those who never had these experiences.

ATTITUDES AND EXPERIENCES OF FRIENDS
Friends who have had unfavorable experiences in their homes and who are unhappy in their parental roles can and do influence the attitudes of parents-to-be unfavorably.

CONCEPT OF A "DREAM CHILD"
If parents have a highly romanticized concept of the child-to-be, it is likely to lead to disappointment and resentment when the child does not conform to this concept. Figure 3–8 shows the typical discrepancy between a mother's dream child and her real child.

SOCIAL CLASS OF PARENTS
Many adults from the lower classes tend to regard parenthood as the "inevitable payment for sex relations" while those from middle and upper classes regard it as the "fulfillment" of marriage.

ECONOMIC STATUS OF FAMILY
If financial conditions are strained, parental attitudes toward the arrival of a child are likely to be adversely affected.

AGE OF PARENTS
Older parents, in general, welcome their parental roles more wholeheartedly than younger parents.

MATERNAL INTERESTS AND ASPIRATIONS
Women whose major aspirations are to be good mothers have more favorable attitudes toward their children-to-be than women whose interests center mainly on social or vocational activities.

MASS MEDIA
Different mass media—books, magazines, movies, radio and television—tend to present a romanticized picture of children and of parenthood. Women, as a rule, tend to be more influenced by these media than men.

Dream child

Real child

Figure 3–8 "Dream child" versus real child.

Attitudes of Other Significant People

Attitudes of other significant people in a baby-to-be's life—grandparents, uncles, aunts, cousins, and close personal friends of the parents—are important both directly and indirectly. *Directly,* they are important because, once formed, they are likely to be persistent and affect the way they treat the child during the early, formative years when the child's social horizons are limited mainly to family members and close friends of the parents.

Indirectly, their attitudes are important through the effect they have on attitudes of parents and siblings. If, for example, the maternal or paternal grandparents-to-be are happy about the prospects of having a grandchild, they will communicate to the parents-to-be far more favorable attitudes toward the expected child than they would if they showed annoyance at the prospect of being considered "old" because they are grandparents or if they told the parents-to-be that they were "foolish" to start a family before they were on their feet both vocationally and economically.

Persistence of Attitudes

Attitudes of significant people, whether favorable or unfavorable, are unlikely to change radically. They do change somewhat, however. For example, studies of maternal attitudes during pregnancy and again after the birth of the baby report that mothers who had a rejectant attitude toward their unborn children become more acceptant after the children's birth. This shift may have been due primarily to a *repression* of their attitudes, owing to a feeling of guilt, rather than to an actual change in attitudes (17, 18, 65).

Similarly, while attitudes toward the role of parenthood may change after the child is born, the fundamental elements of these attitudes persist. Favorable attitudes based on romantic ideas may deteriorate after the child is born or when the helplessness of the baby gives way to the growing independence of the toddler. If there is more work and personal privation than the parent had anticipated, the mother may suddenly feel victimized. On the other hand, unfavorable attitudes may give way to favorable attitudes when the parent experiences the satisfactions of parenthood.

There are two reasons why attitudes, formed during the prenatal period, tend to be persistent. *First,* they are usually emotionally toned and, like all emotionally toned attitudes, they are difficult to change. A sibling's attitude toward the impending arrival of a new baby in the family, for example, is not likely to be neutral. Instead, it will be tinged with pleasure or annoyance.

Second, people usually have what they consider to be valid and justified reasons for their attitudes. A grandmother-to-be, for example, may feel that her daughter is bored with her marriage and ready to get a divorce. However, as the grandmother-to-be sees it, having a baby will add excitement and joy to the marriage, thus saving her daughter from a trip to the divorce courts.

Hazards during the Prenatal Period

During the prenatal period, there are many hazards, often more serious and far-reaching in their effects than most people realize. These hazards are both physical and psychological.

Because the physical hazards are easier to recognize and study than the psychological, they have received more research attention. However, this does not mean that psychological hazards are less important than physical hazards. In fact, they are sometimes more important than the physical hazards, first, because they intensify the physical hazards and, second, because their effects are often more persistent than the physical hazards. As a result, they affect postnatal as well as prenatal development.

Physical Hazards

Scientific studies have revealed that there are a number of physical hazards, some more serious, more persistent, and more far-reaching in their effects than others. These studies have also revealed that each period during prenatal development has certain potential hazards associated with it. These potential hazards are given in Box 3–9.

Several of these potential hazards are so serious that they justify further explanation as to their causes and effects. Others, equally serious, will be discussed in the following chapter. As scientific research in this area continues, it is possible that other potential hazards of equal seriousness will be revealed. However, what is known at the present time about potential physical hazards is reported below.

BOX 3–9

POTENTIAL PHYSICAL HAZARDS OF DIFFERENT PRENATAL PERIODS

PERIOD OF THE OVUM
- The possibility that the fertilized ovum will die of starvation before it becomes implanted in the uterine wall due to the time needed to pass down the Fallopian tube.
- Lack of preparation of the uterine wall to receive the fertilized ovum due to an imbalance between the mother's pituitary gland and ovaries.
- Attachment of the fertilized ovum to the wall of the Fallopian tube—a "tubal pregnancy"—resulting in lack of nourishment or space for growth.
- Attachment of the fertilized ovum to a small area of fibroid tissue in the uterine wall which would prevent it from receiving nourishment.

PERIOD OF THE EMBRYO
- Miscarriages or "spontaneous abortions" due to unfavorable conditions in the maternal environment such as malnutrition, glandular disorders, emotional stress, etc., which may cause the embryo to be dislodged from its place in the uterine wall.
- Developmental irregularities which are more likely to occur now than during the period of the fetus.

PERIOD OF THE FETUS
- Possibility of miscarriage up to the fifth lunar month, especially at times when the woman's menstrual period would normally occur.
- Premature birth with its complications and possibility of death.
- Postmature birth with its complications and possibility of death.
- Complications of delivery resulting from postmaturity of the fetus, unfavorable position of the fetus in the uterus, and glandular imbalance due to maternal stress.
- Developmental irregularities caused by conditions similar to those of the period of the embryo may retard the development of the fetus or affect the development of fetal features, especially the brain.

DEVELOPMENTAL IRREGULARITIES Developmental irregularities are distortions of the normal pattern of development of different physical features. Scientific studies of the *causes* of developmental irregularities justify two important conclusions; first, the irregularities may be due to defective genes, but they are far more likely to be due to environmental disturbances in the uterus; and, second, the irregularities may result from environmental disturbances which occur at the same time as the formation of a particular organ.

Some of the most common and most serious environmental disturbances in the uterus are pronounced and prolonged *maternal malnutrition* which may lead to mental deficiency or some physical abnormality, such as rickets, epilepsy, or cerebral palsy (11, 15, 21, 34, 55); *endocrine disorders* (sometimes caused by an hereditary condition but more often by advanced maternal age when glandular balance is upset by the menopausal changes of the later thirties or early forties) which may lead to "cretinism"—a deformed body accompanied by subnormal intelligence—"microcephaly"—mental deficiency accompanied by a small, pointed skull—or "mongolism"—mental deficiency accompanied by slanting eyes, a broad, short skull, and other characteristics (45, 54, 67); *chronic alcoholism; excessive maternal smoking; excessive use of drugs; severe, prolonged and wasting diseases,* such as diabetes and tuberculosis; and a host of other conditions not yet fully explored (48, 49, 85, 86).

For example, until recently, it was believed that smoking on the mother's part had only minimal effect on her developing child. Today, medical research has found that excessive smoking—not determined by the number of cigarettes smoked but by the effects on the mother-to-be, such as nervousness, wakefulness, and irregular heartbeat—not only affects the fetal heart and circulatory system but that the effects persist after birth (32, 48, 49, 67). In a follow-up study of children whose mothers smoked excessively during pregnancy, Goldstein found that by the time the children were 7 years old they were not only shorter and less well developed than the mean for their ages but they were also less well adjusted socially and read less well than children of the same age born to nonsmoking or moderately smoking mothers (27). Figure 3–9 shows how different amounts of smoking during pregnancy affected the height of a group of children at 7 years of age.

Medical research has not yet reached the point where there is conclusive evidence about the effects of drugs on the prenatal environment. What evidence there is at the present time suggests that drugs taken for pleasure—marajuana, heroin, and cocaine, for example—are harmful if used persistently and excessively, while drugs taken for therapeutic purposes—aspirin, tranquilizers, laxatives, etc.—may or may not be harmful. That is why, as was mentioned in Box 3–7, it is urged that all pregnant women consult their doctors before taking *any* drugs, even an aspirin for a cold or headache.

Whether or not unfavorable environmental conditions will result in developmental irregularities depends on when they occur. If they occur at the same time as the formation of an organ, developmental irregularities are far more likely to result than if these unfavorable conditions occur after the organ has been formed. This means that the time when the unfavorable environmental condition is introduced, rather than the unfavorable condition itself, is the determining influence.

The first 3 months of prenatal life are the critical developmental period. During the period of the embryo, all the structures of the body are being formed. From the eighth week on—the period of the fetus—the structures whose foundations were laid during the period of the embryo are being completed. However, even though the first trimester is the most critical period in prenatal life, this does not mean that all possibility of damage from an unfavorable environment ends then. Unfavorable prenatal conditions rarely produce developmental irregularities when they occur *before* a certain part of the body has started to develop or

Figure 3–9 The relationship of maternal smoking during pregnancy and the height of children up to 7 years of age: mean scores for a group of boys and girls. (*Adapted from H. Goldstein: Factors influencing the height of seven-year-old children: Results of the National Child Development Study.* Human Biology, *1971, 43, 92–111. Reprinted by permission of the Wayne State University Press.*)

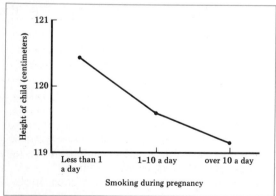

after it has formed. The critical time is *when* it is being formed.

Rubella, or German measles, for example, is a mild childhood disease, but if contracted by the mother *during the first 3 or 4 months of pregnancy,* it can produce such defects as cataracts, deafness, anomalies in the structure of the heart, defective teeth, microcephaly, and mental deficiency in the child. If contracted after the fifth month of pregnancy, it has little or no effect on the unborn child because the parts of the body affected by this disease are already formed (54, 67).

Similarly, *thalidomide,* taken during the early 1960's for morning sickness, nervousness, or sleeplessness, has no damaging effect on the unborn child if used after the first trimester of pregnancy. If taken during the first trimester, it may cause malformation of the limbs—phocomelia—in which the long bones of the arms and legs fail to grow. In addition, it may cause strawberry marks to appear on the child's face (76). These defects are shown in Figure 3–10.

Prolonged emotional stress during the early part of pregnancy may cause hyperactivity of the mother's adrenal glands, thus releasing an increased supply of the hormone *hydrocortisone.* If this happens during the early part of pregnancy, it is likely to cause physical irregularities and may also cause mental retardation. If, on the other hand, it occurs in the latter part of pregnancy, during the period of the fetus, it may not only cause mental retardation, because the brain continues to develop rapidly at this time, but it may also result in premature birth, difficult labor, and stillbirth (17, 23, 46, 73).

The *effects* of developmental irregularities are widespread and numerous. Some of the effects of an unfavorable prenatal environment may not become apparent for many months, or even years, after birth. Under such conditions, it is often assumed that the defect was caused by a postnatal condition. It is commonly assumed, for example, that rickets results from a dietary deficiency in postnatal life, while, in reality, there is medical evidence that rickets occurs in babies who were born prematurely and were thus deprived of the mineralization that normally takes place in the latter part of the period of the fetus (54, 67).

Similarly, epilepsy, cerebral palsy, or mental deficiency may not become apparent until babyhood or the early years of childhood. Since there are, for example, no adequate tests for measuring mental retardation in the newborn infant, mental deficiency re-

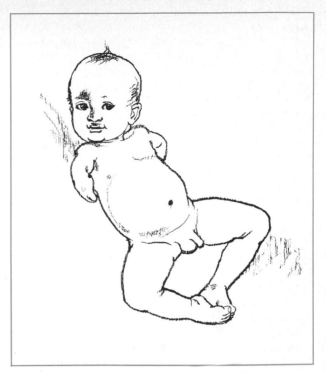

Figure 3–10 Effects of thalidomide. Deformity of infant is typical: useless short arms and hands, characteristic strawberry marks on face and forehead. *(Adapted from H. B. Taussig: The thalidomide syndrome.* Scientific American, *1962,* 207(2), *29–35.* (Copyright © (1962) by Scientific American, Inc. All rights reserved. Used by permission.)

sulting from prolonged or severe malnutrition during the prenatal period may not be apparent until the child begins to have difficulties in school. Again, the defect may be incorrectly attributed to unfavorable postnatal conditions (13, 40).

Regardless of when developmental irregularities become apparent, they can and often do affect the whole course of a child's life. Blindness or deafness, for example, is a major handicap. Furthermore, physical defects affect children's self-concepts and thus influence their personalities. Whether children will grow up to be personally and socially well adjusted will depend, to some extent, upon whether or not they come into the world in sound physical condition.

Family relationships—not only parent-child relationships but also relationships between husband and wife and between siblings—are influenced by developmental irregularities and by what parents *believe* to be the cause of them. The traditional belief, for example, that the mother is primarily responsible for any developmental irregularity that appears in her baby, whether it is a small birthmark or a serious mental or physical deficiency, often leads to feelings of guilt on her part and an unhealthy overprotective or overindulgent attitude toward the baby. Such an attitude will affect the child's whole future. The belief that the mother is responsible may also lead to friction between the parents. The effect of a handicapped child on family relationships will be discussed in more detail in the chapter on family relationships.

Because of the long-term and serious effects of developmental irregularities on the child as well as on members of the child's family, some doctors and hospital clinics today are advising pregnant women who are overage—35 years or older—or whose family history or that of the husband suggests they might be "high-risk" parents to submit to the medical procedure known as "amniocentesis," a procedure which, as was explained in the discussion of predicting sex during the prenatal period, consists of extracting a sample of amniotic fluid from the uterus and testing it to see if there is any evidence of chromosomal abnormalities or other signs of possible developmental irregularities. This is usually done during the first 20 weeks of pregnancy.

Should this test show that there is definite evidence of a developmental irregularity that can affect the future life of the unborn child, parents-to-be are told what these effects will be and what their responsibilities in the care of such a child will entail. For example, are parents prepared financially, emotionally, and in other ways to care for a mongoloid child without slighting the care they normally would give to their other children?

It then becomes the responsibility of the parents-to-be to decide whether they want the pregnancy to continue and face the responsibilities of caring for a child whose chances of being normal are almost nil or whether they want an abortion as the best solution for the child as well as for the entire family. After years of research to discover the long-term effects of maternal stress during pregnancy on children, Ferraira has concluded that the "psychiatric and social implications of these observations suggest a sober reappraisal of the current attitudes toward the unwanted pregnancy" (23).

MISCARRIAGES   If the fertilized ovum is defective, the chances are that nature will eliminate it by a miscarriage or by a stillbirth. However, not all miscarriages or stillbirths result from defective ova, but more than a chance percentage of them do. A miscarriage due to a defective fertilized ovum generally occurs early in the prenatal period. When, on the other hand, the fertilized ovum is normal but the environment in which it is developing is abnormal, the miscarriage usually comes later, most often between the tenth and eleventh weeks following conception. The most hazardous times for miscarriages, as was pointed out earlier, is at the time of the month when the mother's menstrual period normally occurs (54, 67).

Just because miscarriages cannot affect the child-to-be does not mean that they are not a serious hazard. This hazard comes from the effects they have on the parents, on husband-wife relationships, and on any future children the parents may have. If, for example, a woman accepts the traditional belief that miscarriages come from some imprudent act on the part of the mother-to-be, such as taking too strenuous exercise or keeping too late hours, she will feel guilty about her acts and feel that she was responsible for the death of her unborn child. A man who accepts this traditional belief is likely to feel resentful toward his wife for what he believes was responsible for the death of the child he had anticipated having and to accuse her of doing "foolish" things or of not being "careful" during her pregnancy.

In a subsequent pregnancy, the woman who has suffered from a miscarriage is likely to be anxious and apprehensive about a possible repetition of her former miscarriage. Her anxiety and apprehension may then bring about the emotional stress which, unless kept under control, may result in glandular imbalance, a condition which, as was stressed earlier, may be responsible for developmental irregularities, miscarriages, stillbirths or childbirth complications. Thus, a child-to-be suffers a severe penalty for the miscarriage of a former child.

MULTIPLE BIRTHS   Normally, the prenatal environment is more hazardous for children of multiple birth than for singletons. During the prenatal period, they must share a space in the uterus designed for a singleton. As a result of this crowding, they are prevented from making the movements of the different parts of the body that are essential for normal fetal development. Consequently, they are usually smaller and weaker than singletons. The larger the number of multiple births, the greater the crowding and the greater the obstacles to normal growth and development (30, 84).

Equally serious is the possibility of premature births. When the combined size of multiple births reaches that of a singleton, toward the end of the period of the fetus, the uterine walls are usually unable to expand further and the fetuses are than expelled from their prenatal environment before they are ready to live independently in the world outside the mother's body. As will be explained in detail in the following chapter, prematurity is hazardous partly because of the increased risk of developmental irregularities and birth injuries and partly because infant mortality and stillbirths are more common than among fetuses born at full term.

Because multiple births are more common among blacks than among whites, as was pointed out earlier, the higher incidents of stillbirths and of infant mortality may, in part, be explained in this way. It is also, in part, responsible for the higher incidence of developmental irregularities among blacks than among whites (54, 66, 67).

The physical hazards of multiple births are intensified by the psychological hazard of unfavorable attitudes on the part of significant people, especially parents and siblings, toward children of multiple birth. While not all parents and siblings, by any means, have unfavorable attitudes toward children of multiple birth, they tend to be more unfavorable than favorable during the early, formative years of life for reasons to be explained in the following section on psychological hazards.

Psychological Hazards

As is true of physical hazards, psychological hazards are serious because their effects tend to be persistent and, as a result, influence development after birth as well as before birth. Because of the relatively recent scientific interest in psychological hazards, less is known about them than about physical hazards. What is known to date is presented here in the form of three hazards: traditional beliefs about prenatal influences, maternal stress, and unfavorable attitudes on the part of significant people.

TRADITIONAL BELIEFS ABOUT PRENATAL INFLUENCES Traditional beliefs about prenatal influences may be regarded as hazardous not because of their effects on the developing child during the prenatal period but because of their effects on the attitudes and treatment children receive during the early, formative years of their lives from significant people who hold these beliefs.

If, for example, parents accept the traditional belief that the mother-to-be can mark her unborn child by her thoughts, emotions, and actions, it may lead to resentments toward the mother on the part of the father if the child does not come up to his expectations. Figure 3–11 shows how the acceptance of this belief can affect a man's attitude toward his wife. Acceptance of the traditional belief, expressed in the old American Indian saying, "Papoose double make heap trouble," will affect parents' attitudes toward the work load, sibling problems, and other conditions multiple births often give rise to in a family (66).

MATERNAL STRESS Stress—a persistent form of heightened emotionality involving such unpleasant emotions as fear, anger, or grief—may come from many causes. In maternal stress, it may be the result of not wanting the child-to-be, feelings of inadequacy about performing the maternal role successfully, or

Figure 3–11 Acceptance of the traditional belief that the mother's behavior during pregnancy will affect the child's development often leads to husband-wife conflicts. (*Drawn by Art Gates*. Atlanta Journal and Constitution, *Oct. 28, 1973. Used by permission.*)

"I warned Janet about eating all of those sour pickles!"

dreams and fantasies about having a defective child. Or, it may come from conditions only indirectly related to the child, such as poor material health, concern about family finances, overwork in the home and the care of older children, or a strained husband-wife relationship.

The reason that maternal stress is hazardous to prenatal development is that it upsets the normal functioning of the maternal endocrine system. This results in a hyperactive state of the thyroid and adrenal glands—the glands of the endocrine system that prepare the body for increased activity during an emotional state. These endocrine secretions are then transmitted to the prenatal environment in the uterus and result in a condition in that environment that affects the developing child. *How* this affects the developing child and when the effects are most pronounced and most serious has been explained in the discussion of timing of unfavorable environmental conditions in the section on developmental irregularities under the heading of *physical hazards*.

If, as was pointed out earlier, the heightened emotional state of the mother-to-be is only temporary, the effect on the prenatal environment will likewise be only temporary. In the case of the fetus, for example, it will result in a temporary increase in fetal activity and fetal heartbeat. In maternal stress, on the other hand, the heightened emotional state is persistent, though it will vary in intensity from time to time. It is this persistence of the glandular upsets that is responsible for the hazardous nature of maternal stress.

Because the conditions that give rise to maternal stress are more likely to persist than to change, stress that develops during the prenatal period tends to persist after childbirth. The infant who was made hyperactive by maternal stress during the prenatal period or who suffers from some developmental irregularity must make the adjustments to postnatal life which even newborn infants who have been spared the effects of maternal stress find difficult. What these adjustments are will be explained in the following chapter, together with the reasons for the difficulties that accompany these adjustments. In addition, their adjustments to postnatal life are intensified by the effects of maternal stress which is communicated to them by the way the mother takes care of them. Under such conditions, adjustments to postnatal life tend to be poor.

Babies who make poor adjustments to postnatal life not only affect the mother-child relationship but they also affect relationships with other family members. As "difficult" babies, they will be less warmly received in the family than they would be if they were calmer and made quicker and better adjustments. As they grow older, they will sense the unfavorable feelings of parents and other family members toward them. As a result of feeling unloved and rejected, they may show below average physical development, hyperactivity, difficulties in mastering motor skills and speech, learning problems, and poor personal and social adjustments (17, 73, 74, 84).

UNFAVORABLE ATTITUDES ON THE PART OF SIGNIFICANT PEOPLE   Like maternal stress, unfavorable attitudes toward children on the part of people who play important roles in their lives can and do affect postnatal development as well as development during the prenatal period. Some of these unfavorable attitudes are held by relatives, siblings, neighbors, and friends of the family, but for the most part they are parental attitudes. The most common of these unfavorable parental attitudes are listed and briefly explained in Box 3–10.

At first glance, some of these attitudes, such as wanting a child of a particular kind or of a particular sex, may not seem unfavorable, but they are because they are unrealistic. As there is no known way to control the sex or hereditary endowment of children, there is no known way to guarantee that children will have the characteristics their parents or other significant people want them to have. If parents have set their hearts on having children with these characteristics, they may be bitterly disappointed and resentful toward the children if the children do not come up to their hopes and expectations.

The reason that unfavorable attitudes toward unborn children on the part of significant people are hazardous to prenatal development is that they usually lead to maternal stress with its unfavorable effects on the prenatal environment, as described before. An unwed mother-to-be, for example, is likely to experience stress from the time she becomes aware of her pregnancy. This stress may come from fear of the personal and social consequences of her socially unapproved pregnancy, concern about the source of income for childbirth and the care of the baby, or fear of how family members and friends will treat her when they learn of her pregnancy. Stress may be heightened by anger and resentment against the father of her child who cannot or will not marry her. As her pregnancy

BOX 3-10

UNFAVORABLE ATTITUDES
TOWARD AN UNBORN CHILD

NOT WANTING THE CHILD
Some family members may not want the child for reasons they regard as valid. When parents intend to have a child, the child is always wanted. If, on the other hand, they did not intend to have a child, the child is sometimes wanted and sometimes unwanted, especially if the desired family size has been reached.

NOT WANTING A CHILD AT THAT TIME
If the child is conceived at a time that the parents regard as "inconvenient" because the child will interfere with their educational, vocational, or social plans, because it is shortly after marriage or the birth of another child, or because of economic problems in the family, the husband often blames the wife for being "careless" and she feels guilty about not preventing the unwanted pregnancy.

NOT WANTING CHILDREN OF MULTIPLE BIRTH
When parents or relatives regard multiple birth as "animallike" or accept the traditional belief that children of multiple birth will never be like "normal" people, family members may develop unfavorable attitudes when the doctor informs the pregnant woman that she will have twins, triplets, or other multiple births.

STRONG DESIRE FOR A CHILD OF A GIVEN SEX
Many family members and relatives have a strong preference for the sex of the child-to-be. If the child is not of the sex they wanted, their disappointment often leads to a rejectant attitude.

STRONG DESIRE FOR A PARTICULAR TYPE OF CHILD
Parents and other family members may have definite concepts of what the child-to-be should be like—their "dream child." *Very* few children match this dream child in looks, abilities, or personality. The further the real child deviates from the romanticized version, the more unfavorable will be the attitudes toward that child.

WANTING TO HAVE A MISCARRIAGE OR ABORTION
When a child is unwanted, parents may secretly hope for a miscarriage or they may contemplate an abortion. If the child-to-be's life is ended by a miscarriage or an abortion, they may feel guilty and carry over an unhealthy attitude toward subsequent children. If a miscarriage or abortion fails, they are likely to express their guilt in overprotectiveness of the child as a form of compensation.

SCORN FOR THE CHILD
Relatives, neighbors, or friends of the family may develop attitudes of scorn if the child is illegitimate, the product of an interracial or interfaith marriage, or if there is some stigma associated with the mother's or father's side of the family, such as insanity, chronic alcoholism, drug addiction, or a penal record. These unfavorable social attitudes, expressed in the treatment the child receives from outsiders, may make the parents overprotective of the child as a form of compensation, or it may make them rejectant.

continues, unfavorable attitudes on the part of family members, relatives, neighbors, and friends will increase the stress she experiences.

The consequences of unfavorable attitudes toward unborn children on their postnatal development may be equally as serious and often more far-reaching than the effects on their prenatal development. If, for example, a woman has an unfavorable attitude toward children of multiple birth, as explained in Box 3-10, this attitude is likely to persist and color her treatment of her children after they are born. A woman who has an unfavorable attitude toward twins is likely to feel "victimized" by the extra work needed to care for two or more helpless babies simultaneously while taking care of a home and possible other children. As a result, her unfavorable attitude toward them, developed before their birth, will be intensified, as expressed anonymously in the jingle quoted by Scheinfeld (66):

The Joy (?) of Twins

Drudgery that's double or more
Laundering till your hands are sore;
Tangle of lines with soggy things drying,
Day and night chorus of yelling and crying,
Endless chores and no end of expenses.
Worries that drive you out of your senses,

Everyone bothering you with questions,
Everyone giving you crazy suggestions,
Husband complaining you're no kind of wife,
Everything mixed up in your life.
If I knew whom to blame for twins, I'd sue 'em.
Those who want twins are welcome to 'em.

Sooner or later, the children will sense what the mother's attitude toward them is; this will not only affect their relationships with her but may also spread to other family members as the children sense their attitudes.

If unfavorable attitudes on the part of significant people were only transitory, they would have little effect on children's postnatal adjustments. However, so long as they persist, they make the normal adjustments to postnatal life even more difficult than they usually are. Fortunately, unfavorable attitudes often do become less unfavorable or may even become favorable as children grow older. Parents, for example, who had set their hearts on having a son may, as time passes, warmly welcome the daughter they at first did not want. Similarly, a mother of twins who felt victimized by the extra work twins caused in the early years of life, may be even more acceptant of them than of her other children when she realizes how congenial they are and how little sibling rivalry and jealousy they experience as compared with their siblings who are singletons.

Chapter Highlights

1 Scientific research has revealed that there are four very important happenings before birth: establishment of the hereditary endowment; rapid growth and development; conditions in the prenatal environment that influence the pattern of development; and the development of attitudes of significant people toward the unborn child.

2 Early scientific interest in the prenatal period centered on the origin of life; later interest centered on the roles played by heredity and prenatal influences, conditions responsible for sex determination, and the effects of sex, multiple births, and attitudes of significant people on the pattern of prenatal development.

3 Before a new life can begin, the male and female reproductive cells—the spermatozoa and ova—go through preparatory processes known as maturation, ovulation, and fertilization.

4 The four important conditions determined when the ovum is fertilized by a sperm cell are determination of the hereditary endowment, the sex of the newly created individual, the number of offspring, and the ordinal position of the newly created person in the family. Each of these four conditions plays an important role in the individual's development before and after birth.

5 Once established at the time of fertilization of the ovum by the sperm cell, the newly created individual's hereditary endowment is fixed, though achievement of the full development of hereditary potentials may not occur if environmental conditions are unfavorable.

6 At the time of conception, the sex of the newly created individual is determined by the type of sperm cell that unites with the ovum. At the present time there is no completely accurate way to predict or control the child's sex.

7 Whether the newly created individual will be a singleton or one of multiple births—a condition determined at the time of conception—is important because of effects of differences in the prenatal and postnatal environments and of parental attitudes.

8 The ordinal position of the child in the family, determined at the time of conception, affects the child's development because of attitudes of parents and other significant people in the child's life and because of the roles children of different ordinal positions are expected to play.

9 The prenatal period is divided into three subdivisions—the period of the ovum, the period of the embryo, and the period of the fetus—during each of which a predictable pattern of development is followed by all individuals.

10 Scientific studies of development during the prenatal period have shown that the normal pattern of development is greatly influenced by many factors, all of which affect the environment in the mother's body in which the child is developing.

11 Attitudes of significant people toward the child-to-be, formed during the prenatal period, are important because they tend to be persistent and to affect the way in which the child is treated during the childhood years.

12   There are many potential hazards to normal development during the prenatal period, some of which are physical and some psychological.

13   The most common and most serious of the potential physical hazards during the prenatal period are developmental irregularities, miscarriages, and multiple births.

14   The most common and most serious of the potential psychological hazards during the prenatal period are traditional beliefs about prenatal influences, maternal stress, and unfavorable attitudes of significant people toward the child-to-be.

15   Unfavorable attitudes of significant people may be considered the most serious potential psychological hazard to a child's personal and social adjustments because they tend to be persistent even though they are often expressed in camouflaged forms, such as overprotectiveness and indulgence.

Bibliography

1   Allen, M. G., M. Pollin, and A. Hoffer. Parental, birth, and infancy factors in infant twin development. *American Journal of Psychiatry,* 1971, *127,* 1597–1604.

2   Altus, W. D. Birth order and its sequelae. *Science,* 1966, *151,* 44–49.

3   Babson, S. G., and D. S. Phillips. Growth and development of twins dissimilar in size at birth. *New England Journal of Medicine,* 1973, *289,* 937–940.

4   Bakwin, H. Body-weight regulation in twins. *Developmental Medicine and Child Neurology,* 1973, *15,* 178–183.

5   Belmont, L., and F. A. Marolla. Birth order, family size, and intelligence. *Science,* 1973, *182,* 1096–1101.

6   Bigner, J. J. Second borns' discrimination of sibling role concepts. *Developmental Psychology,* 1974, *10,* 564–573.

7   Blatz, W. E. *The five sisters.* New York: Morrow, 1938.

8   Bracken, M. B., M. Hachamovitch, and G. Grossman. The decision to abort and psychological sequelae. *Journal of Nervous and Mental Disease,* 1974, *158,* 154–162.

9   Brody, J. E. 1976 marks tricentennial of the discovery of the sperm. *The New York Times, Dec. 20, 1975.*

10   Brooks, J., and M. Lewis. Attachment behavior in thirteen-month-old opposite-sex twins. *Child Development,* 1974, *45,* 213–247.

11   Burn, J., J. A. Birkbeck, and D. F. Roberts. Early fetal brain growth. *Human Biology,* 1975, *47,* 511–522.

12   Burnard, G. Birth order and autobiography. *Journal of Individual Psychology,* 1973, *29,* 35–38.

13   Chess, S. The influence of defect on development in children with congenital rubella. *Merrill-Palmer Quarterly,* 1974, *20,* 255–274.

14   Copans, S. A. Human prenatal effects: Methodological problems and some suggested solutions. *Merrill-Palmer Quarterly,* 1974, *20,* 43–52.

15   Coursin, D. B. Nutrition and brain development in infants. *Merrill-Palmer Quarterly,* 1972, *18,* 177–202.

16   Dales, R. G. Motor and language development of twins during the first three years. *Journal of Genetic Psychology,* 1969, *114,* 263–271.

17   Davids, A. A research design for studying maternal emotionality before childbirth and after social interaction with the child. *Merrill-Palmer Quarterly,* 1968, *14,* 345–354.

18   Doty, B. A. Relationships among attitudes of pregnancy and other maternal characteristics. *Journal of Genetic Psychology,* 1967, *111,* 203–217.

19   Edwards, D. DeA., and J. S. Edwards. Fetal movements: Development and time course. *Science,* 1970, *169,* 95–97.

20   Farquahar, J. W. Prognosis for babies born to diabetic mothers in Edinburgh. *Archives of Disease in Childhood,* 1969, *44,* 36–47.

21   Felig, P., and V. Lynch. Starvation in human pregnancy: Hypoglycemia, hypoinsulinemia and hyperketonemia. *Science,* 1970, *170,* 990–992.

22   Ferdon, N. K. Chromosomal abnormalities and antisocial behavior. *Journal of Genetic Psychology,* 1971, *118,* 281–292.

23   Ferreira, A. J. Emotional factors in prenatal environment. *Journal of Nervous and Mental Disease,* 1965, *141,* 108–118.

24   Forer, L. H. *Birth order and life roles.* Springfield, Ill.: Charles C Thomas, 1969.

25   Gillman, R. D. The dreams of pregnant women and maternal adaptation. *American Journal of Orthopsychiatry,* 1968, *38,* 688–692.

26   Glick, P. C., and A. J. Norton. Frequency, duration and probability of marriage and divorce. *Journal of Marriage and the Family,* 1971, *33,* 307–317.

27   Goldstein, H. Factors influencing the height of seven-year-old children: Results from the National Child Development Study. *Human Biology,* 1971, *43,* 92–111.

28   Hall, E. Ordinal position and success in engagement and marriage. *Journal of Individual Psychology,* 1965, *21,* 154–158.

29   Heath, H. A. Three eight-year-olds. *Child Development,* 1967, *38,* 753–764.

30   Howard, R. G., and A. M. Brown. Twinning: A marker for biological insults. *Child Development,* 1970, *41,* 519–530.

31   Howard, R. W. The developmental history of a group of triplets. *Journal of Genetic Psychology,* 1947, *70,* 191–204.

32   Hytten, F. E. Smoking in pregnancy. *Developmental Medicine and Child Neurology,* 1973, *15,* 355–357.

33   Joesting, J., and R. Joesting. Birth order and desired family size. *Journal of Individual Psychology,* 1973, *29,* 34.

34 Kaplan, B. J. Malnutrition and mental deficiency. *Psychological Bulletin*, 1972, *78*, 321–334.

35 Karabenick, S. A. On the relation between personality and birth order. *Psychological Reports*, 1971, *28*, 258.

36 Kennelly, J. H., R. Jerauld, H. Wolfe, D. Chesler, N. C. Kreger, W. McAlpine, M. Steffa, and M. H. Klaus. Maternal behavior one year after early and extended postpartum contact. *Developmental Medicine and Child Neurology*, 1974, *16*, 172–179.

37 Koch, H. L. *Twins and twin relations*. Chicago, Ill.: University of Chicago Press, 1966.

38 Langsley, D. G., T. P. Burton, M. Griswold, H. Walzer, and R. B. Spinka. Schizophrenia in triplets: A family study. *American Journal of Psychiatry*, 1963, *120*, 528–532.

39 Lunneborg, B. Expectant fathers. *Child and Family*, 1969, *8*, 265–278.

40 Lyle, J. G. Certain antenatal, perinatal and developmental variables and reading retardation in middle-class boys. *Child Development*, 1970, *41*, 481–491.

41 MacDonald, A. P. Manifestations of differential levels of socialization by birth order. *Developmental Psychology*, 1969, *1*, 485–492.

42 Matheny, A. P. Twins: Concordance for Piagetian-equivalent items derived from the Bayley Mental Test. *Developmental Psychology*, 1975, *11*, 224–227.

43 Matheny, A. P., and A. M. Brown. Activity, motor coordination and attention differences in twins. *Perceptual and Motor Skills*, 1971, *32*, 151–158.

44 Matheny, A. P., and A. M. Brown. The behavior of twins: Effects of birth weight and birth sequence. *Child Development*, 1971, *42*, 251–257.

45 McClearn, G. E. Genetic influences on behavior and development. In P. H. Mussen (ed.), *Carmichael's manual of child psychology*, 3d ed. New York: Wiley, 1970. Vol. 1, pp. 39–76.

46 McDonald, R. L. The role of emotional factors in obstetric complications: A review. *Psychosomatic Medicine*, 1968, *30*, 222–237.

47 McGurk, H., and M. Lewis. Birth order: A phenomenon in search of an explanation. *Developmental Psychology*, 1972, *7*, 366.

48 Meredith, H. V. Relation between tobacco smoking of pregnant women and body size of their progeny: A compilation and synthesis of published studies. *Human Biology*, 1975, *47*, 451–472.

49 Meredith, H. V. Somatic changes during human prenatal life. *Child Development*, 1975, *46*, 603–610.

50 Meyerowitz, J. H. Satisfaction during pregnancy. *Journal of Marriage and the Family*, 1970, *32*, 38–42.

51 Miller, H. C., and K. Hassanein. Fetal malnutrition in white newborn infants: Maternal factors. *Pediatrics*, 1973, *52*, 504–512.

52 Miller, W. B. Relationship between the intendedness of conception and the wantedness of pregnancy. *Journal of Nervous and Mental Disease*, 1974, *159*, 396–406.

53 Mittler, P. Biological and social aspects of language development in twins. *Developmental Medicine and Child Neurology*, 1970, *12*, 741–757.

54 Montagu, A. *The direction of human development*. New York: Hawthorn, 1970.

55 Naeye, R. L., W. Blanc, and C. Paul. Effects of maternal nutrition on the human fetus. *Pediatrics*, 1973, *52*, 370–371.

56 Neale, A. V. The placenta: Historiae fides III. *Developmental Medicine and Child Neurology*, 1970, *12*, 79–86.

57 Neetz, J. M. Birth order and leadership in the elementary school: A cross-cultural study. *Journal of Social Psychology*, 1974, *92*, 143–144.

58 Nisbet, R. E. Birth order and participation in dangerous sports. *Journal of Personality and Social Psychology*, 1968, *8*, 351–353.

59 Ounsted, M. Fetal growth and mental ability. *Developmental Medicine and Child Neurology*, 1970, *12*, 79–86.

60 Page, E. W., C. A. Villee, and D. B. Villee. *Human reproduction: The core concent of obstetrics, gynecology, and perinatal medicine*. Philadelphia: Saunders, 1972.

61 Paluszny, M., and R. Gibson. Twin interactions in a normal nursery school. *American Journal of Psychiatry*, 1974, *131*, 293–296.

62 Reid, D. E., K. J. Ryan, and K. Benirschke (eds.), *Principles and management of human reproduction*. Philadelphia: Saunders, 1972.

63 Rosenblatt, P. C., and E. L. Skoogberg. Birth order in cross-cultural perspectives. *Developmental Psychology*, 1974, *10*, 48–54.

64 Scarr, S. Environmental bias in twin studies. *Eugenics Quarterly*, 1968, *15*, 34–40.

65 Schaefer, E. S., and N. Bayley. Consistency of maternal behavior from infancy to preadolescence. *Journal of Abnormal and Social Psychology*, 1960, *61*, 1–6.

66 Scheinfeld, A. *Twins and supertwins*. Philadelphia: Lippincott, 1967.

67 Scheinfeld, A. *Heredity in humans*, rev. ed. Philadelphia: Lippincott, 1971.

68 Schooler, C. Birth order effects: Not here, not now. *Psychological Bulletin*, 1972, *78*, 161–175.

69 Scott, E. M. Psychological examination of quadruplets. *Psychological Reports*, 1960, *6*, 281–282.

70 Senay, E. C., and S. Wexler. Fantasies about the fetus in wanted and unwanted pregnancies. *Journal of Youth and Adolescence*, 1972, *1*, 333–337.

71 Singer, E. Adult orientations of first and later children. *Sociometry*, 1971, *34*, 328–345.

72 Skovholt, T., E. Moore, and F. Wellman. Birth order and academic behavior in first grade. *Psychological Reports*, 1973, *32*, 395–398.

73 Sontag, L. W. Implication of fetal behavior and environment for adult personalities. *Annals of the New York Academy of Science*, 1966, *134*, 782–786.

74 Stewart, M. A. Hyperactive children. *Scientific American*, 1970, *222* (4), 94–98.

75 Stone, L. J., H. T. Smith, and L. B. Murphy (eds.). *The competent infant: Research and commentary*. New York. Basic Books, 1975.

76 Taussig, H. B. The thalidomide syndrome. *Scientific American*, 1962, *207* (2), 29–35.

77 Toman, W., and E. Toman. Sibling positions of a sample of distinguished persons. *Perceptual and Motor Skills*, 1970, *31*, 825–826.

78 U. S. News & World Report article: Who stays married longer? Oct. 30, 1972, p. 39.

79 Van Den Daele, L. D. Natal influence and twin differences. *Journal of Genetic Psychology*, 1974, *124*, 41–60.

80 Very, P. S., and N. P. Van Hine. Effects of birth order upon personality development of twins. *Journal of Genetic Psychology*, 1969, *114*, 93–95.

81 Vockell, E. L., and B. Bennett. Birth order, sex of siblings and incidence of learning disabilities. *Exceptional Children,* 1972, *39,* 162–164.

82 Weiner, H. Birth order and illness behavior. *Journal of Individual Psychology,* 1973, *29,* 173–175.

83 Werner, E. E. From birth to latency: Behavior differences in a multiracial group of twins. *Child Development,* 1973, *44,* 438–444.

84 Willerman, L. Activity level and hyperactivity in twins. *Child Development,* 1973, *44,* 288–293.

85 Williamson, D. A. J. A syndrome of congenital malformations possibly due to maternal diabetes. *Develop-*

mental Medicine and Child Neurology, 1970, *12,* 145–152.

86 Wilson, G. S., M. M. Desmond, and W. M. Verniaud. Early development of infants of heroin-addicted mothers. *American Journal of Diseases of Children,* 1973, *126,* 457–462.

87 Wilson, R. S. Twins: Mental development in the preschool years. *Developmental Psychology,* 1974, *10,* 580–588.

88 Wilson, R. S. Twins: Patterns of cognitive development as measured on the Wechsler Preschool and Primary Scale of Intelligence. *Developmental Psychology,* 1975, *11,* 126–134.

89 Wilson, R. S., and E. B. Harpring. Mental and motor development in infant twins. *Developmental Psychology,* 1972, *7,* 277–287.

90 Winestine, M. C. Twinship and psychological differentiation. *Journal of the American Academy of Child Psychiatry,* 1968, *8,* 436–455.

91 Zajonc, R. B. Dumber by the dozen. *Psychology Today,* 1975, *8* (8) 37–43.

92 Zajonc, R. B. Family configuration and intelligence. *Science,* 1976, *192,* 227–236.

93 Zajonc, R. B., and G. B. Markus. Birth order and intellectual development. *Psychological Review,* 1975, *82,* 74–88.

CHAPTER 4

EFFECTS OF BIRTH
ON DEVELOPMENT

Birth is not the beginning of life. Instead, it is merely an interruption in the developmental pattern that began at the time of conception. It is the time when the individual must make a transition from the internal environment of the mother's uterus to the world outside the mother's body. In so doing, the individual must adjust from being a parasite, completely dependent on the mother for survival, to being independent.

The time when the transition is being made—the perinatal experience—and the necessary adjustments to it is known as "infancy"—a term suggesting complete helplessness. Although the time needed to bring about the change in locale from the mother's body to the world outside is seldom more than 48 hours even in a difficult birth, the time needed to adjust to the change is relatively long. Most infants require at least 2 weeks and those whose birth has been difficult or premature require proportionally more time.

Infancy is divided into two periods, the *period of the partunate* and the *period of the neonate*. The period of the partunate refers to the time when the birth process is actually taking place, and the period of the neonate—derived from the Greek word, *neos,* meaning "new" and the past participle of the Latin verb, *nascor,* meaning "born"—is the adjustment period to the changes brought about by birth. The length and characteristics of each of these subperiods are shown in Box 4–1.

BOX 4–1

SUBDIVISIONS OF INFANCY

PERIOD OF THE PARTUNATE
- This period covers the first 15 or 30 minutes after birth.
- With the cutting of the umbilical cord, the infant becomes a separate, distinct, and independent individual.

PERIOD OF THE NEONATE
- This period covers the remainder of the infancy period.
- According to medical criteria, it ends with the falling off of the umbilical cord, about 2 weeks after birth.
- According to psychological criteria, it ends with the regaining of lost birth weight and indications of a resumption of development.
- Adjustments essential to a life free from the protection of the intrauterine environment are successfully made.

During the time when adjustments to the postnatal environment are being made, no marked changes in development occur. It may, therefore, be regarded as a "plateau" in development—a time when development comes to a temporary standstill or may even show signs of regression.

Because most of infancy is devoted to making adjustments to postnatal life, infancy is often called the "period of the newborn" or the period of the neonate. The newly born child is known as an "infant," a "newborn," or a "neonate."

Scientific Interest in Birth

Long before philosophical, medical, or psychological studies of birth were made, there were many traditional beliefs about it. These traditional beliefs centered on such aspects of birth as the best day of the week or season of the year for birth, the effects of birth on the child, both in infancy and throughout life, the effects of prematurity, and ways to control the hazards of birth to mother and child.

Philosophers and scientists stressed the traumatic effects of birth. The birth cry, for example, has long been interpreted as the infant's expression of rage at being dislodged from the safety and comfort of the womb and suddenly thrown out into a cold and unfriendly world. Kant (1724–1804) called the birth cry a "cry of wrath at the catastrophe of birth" (47).

Among the early American psychologists, William James (1842–1910) suggested that the birth experience was so traumatic that it left the child in a state of shock. The child experienced the world as a "big, blooming, buzzing confusion" (45). More recently, members of the psychoanalytic school have suggested that there is a psychic *trauma* resulting from the rupture of the fetal relations with the mother. These suggestions were formulated into a theory of the effects of birth on the personality development of the child—Otto Rank's theory of the birth trauma. According to this theory, the shock of birth creates a reservoir of anxiety which is a disturbing influence throughout life. Because birth is the first danger the child experiences, it provides the model for all later anxieties. (75).

Since the time of the early Greek physicians in the fourth and fifth centuries B.C., medical science has been interested in birth. This interest, however, was concentrated mainly on how to ease the pain of childbirth for the mother, how to ensure the safety of mother and child during childbirth, and how to keep the prematurely-born child alive. There was little or no interest in how birth affects the development of the child.

In recent decades, interest has changed. Some of our most important information about the effects of birth on postnatal development, the effects of post- and prematurity on development, the state of development present at birth—as measured by such medical instruments as the Apgar Test—and the potential hazards of different types of birth has come from medical research.

Psychological studies of birth are of relatively recent origin as compared with medical studies. These studies began to appear around the middle of the present century and are, today, a major focus of scientific research. The focal point of interest in these studies has been concentrated on how birth affects the child's postnatal development, drawing on medical studies of types of birth, conditions in the prenatal environment, and other factors that influence development both before and after birth. Another focal point of interest has been prematurity and its immediate as well as its long-term effects on the child's development.

As a result of this psychological interest in birth, it has become apparent that birth, like conception, is a significant time in the individual's life—too significant to be overlooked by those interested in studying the child's development as was true in the early days of child psychology. The important findings of the psychological studies related to birth will be presented in the remaining pages of this chapter, grouped together in the following areas: adjustments to postnatal life; the effects of different kinds of birth and factors related to them on postnatal development; the influence of time of birth; the level of development present at birth; and the physical and psychological hazards of birth.

Some of the areas listed above have been extensively studied while in others there are gaps in our knowledge at the present time. These gaps are not due to lack of interest or to the belief that they are unimportant but rather to difficulties involved in making the studies. This is especially true of studies of the state of development of the different sense organs at birth. For example, at the present time, there is no known adequate way to test color vision in newborn infants. Consequently, knowledge about this must come indirectly from studies of the state of development of the rods and cones in the eyes of infants who died at birth or shortly afterwards (73).

Adjustments to Postnatal Life

Because of the vast differences between the internal and external environments, infants must make radical and rapid adjustments. If they do not make them and make them quickly, their lives will be threatened. There are four major adjustments every infant must make. They are listed and explained in Box 4–2.

A change in any accustomed pattern of life is upsetting. Consequently, adjusting to this change requires

---

BOX 4–2

MAJOR ADJUSTMENTS
NECESSITATED BY BIRTH

ADJUSTMENT TO TEMPERATURE CHANGES
In the sac in the mother's uterus, the temperature is constantly around 100°F. In the postnatal environment, it will be between 68 and 70°F. and will vary, especially after the infant leaves the hospital nursery.

ADJUSTMENT TO BREATHING
Before birth, oxygen comes from the placenta through the umbilical cord. When the cord is cut, after birth, the infant must inhale and exhale air. The birth cry normally comes when breathing begins and thus serves to inflate the lungs. At first, breathing is imperfect and irregular. The infant yawns, gasps, sneezes, and coughs in an effort to regulate the amount of air needed. If the infant is unable to do so, oxygen must be administered to help establish normal breathing.

ADJUSTMENT TO TAKING NOURISHMENT
Since the reflex activities of sucking and swallowing are often imperfectly developed at birth, the infant is frequently unable to get the nourishment needed and thus loses weight. This is in direct contrast to the situation in the prenatal environment, where the fetus received constant nourishment through the umbilical cord.

ADJUSTMENT TO ELIMINATION
Within a few minutes or hours after birth, the excretory organs begin to function, eliminating waste products from the body which formerly were eliminated through the umbilical cord and the maternal placenta.

time and effort. The adjustment to such a radical change as that from an internal to an external environment is especially difficult. That infancy is a time of radical and difficult adjustments is shown by three important lines of evidence: loss of weight, disorganization of behavior, and mortality.

The *first* indication of the adjustment difficulties all infants encounter is loss of weight. After birth, infants normally lose weight for approximately a week. They may lose only a few ounces or they may lose a pound or more. As they become adjusted to the new environment outside the mother's body and to the changes that are essential for survival, they begin to regain the lost weight.

By the end of the second week of life, most infants are back to their normal birth weight or may even show a slight weight gain. As a general rule, heavy infants lose more and lose for a longer time than light infants. Firstborn infants generally lose less than those born later. Infants born in the summer and autumn regain their birth weight sooner than those born in the winter and spring (62, 70, 76).

The *second* indication of the difficulty newborn infants encounter in adjusting to postnatal life is a disorganized pattern of behavior. All infants experience a state of relative disorganization after birth. Their behavior suggests that they have been stunned by the experience. Ordinarily, pulse and respiration rates are irregular. The infant urinates and defecates frequently, wheezes, and regurgitates food (27).

There are two major causes for this disorganized behavior. First, all infants, even those born normally, suffer some disturbance of the cranial circulation. This disturbance is the result of the severe pressure on the head during the birth process. Deficient mechanisms for maintaining body homeostasis owing to the underdeveloped autonomic nervous system at birth is the second cause. How inability to maintain body homeostasis affects the infant's behavior will be explained in detail later, in the discussion of the helplessness of the infant.

Some infants require much more time than others to recover from the stunned state that leads to disorganization. On the average, they need about a week—approximately the time needed to start to regain the lost birth weight. Infants who lose much weight and regain it slowly are likely to take longer to achieve organized behavior.

The *third* and most important evidence of the difficulty newborn infants experience in their adjustment to postnatal life is the infant mortality rate. While the percentages of stillbirths—deaths at or immediately after birth—and deaths during infancy have been declining, owing to improved prenatal, childbirth, and postnatal care, the death toll is still high. Because infant mortality is one of the most serious hazards of infancy, it will be discussed in detail in this chapter in connection with a discussion of the hazards of infancy.

How Birth Affects Postnatal Development

Because no two human beings have the same kind of prenatal environment or the same birth experiences, it is to be expected that birth will affect the postnatal development of one individual differently than it would affect the postnatal development of another individual. Psychological and medical studies have borne out this expectation. They have also produced evidence, from the many studies that have been made in this area of research, to show what conditions are responsible for the effects of birth on postnatal development. These conditions are discussed below.

Type of Birth

The first condition associated with birth that affects postnatal development is type of birth. In general, there are five different types of birth. These are explained in Box 4–3. Two of the five types, natural or spontaneous birth and breech birth, are illustrated in Figure 4–1.

Infants born spontaneously usually adjust more quickly and more successfully to their new environment than those who experience long and difficult labor where instruments or surgical delivery have to be used. Even in natural childbirth, however, maternal tension, resulting from fear of childbirth or from not wanting the child, will complicate the birth process and make the infant's adjustment to postnatal life more difficult.

Infants born by caesarean section are generally the quietest, crying less than those born spontaneously or with the use of instruments, and expending less energy in random movements of the body. Unless they are brain-damaged, as a result of difficulty in establishing respiration, they normally make better and quicker adjustments to postnatal life than those born in any other way (2, 8, 52, 76).

Medication of the Mother

The second condition associated with birth that affects the infant's postnatal adjustment is the medication of the mother before and during childbirth. Studies of the effects of medication of the mother to relieve the pain of childbirth have revealed that the more medication given the mother, the longer and more difficult the infant's adjustment to postnatal life. The disorganization of behavior immediately after birth, for example, lasted 3 to 4 days, as compared with 1 to 2 days for infants whose mothers had very light medication or none at all. The effects on the infant, however, varied according to the type, amount, and timing of the medication. An inhalent anesthesia, for example, had a more transient effect than premedication, such as barbiturates (27, 54).

Medication has also been reported to affect breast feeding, especially during the first 5 days after birth. In addition, it has been found that infants whose mothers had heavy medication lost more weight and took a longer time to regain it than those whose mothers had less medication (2).

Prenatal Environment

The third condition associated with birth that affects postnatal adjustment is the type of prenatal environment the infant had. Any condition in the prenatal environment that keeps the fetus from developing according to the normal timetable will result in more difficulties at birth and in postnatal adjustment than are usually experienced. That is why, for example, the mortality rate is higher among infants whose mothers suffer from severe malnutrition or drug addiction. Intense and prolonged emotional disturbances of the mother during the last months of pregnancy, as was explained in the preceding chapter, are especially damaging. Many childbirth complications have been traced to these sources (16, 21, 91, 104).

The effects of unfavorable prenatal conditions usually persist after birth, and they manifest themselves in various adjustment difficulties, such as feeding problems, gastrointestinal dysfunction, sleep problems, hyperactivity, and general irritability (24, 56, 99). In commenting on maternal stress during the

---

BOX 4–3

TYPES OF BIRTH

NATURAL OR SPONTANEOUS BIRTH
Spontaneous birth is usually referred to as "natural" childbirth because it occurs without outside aid and with a minimum of or no medication of the mother. In this type of birth, the position of the fetus in the mother's uterus and the size of the fetus make it possible for the fetus to emerge headfirst. After the head, one shoulder and then the other appear as the fetal body rotates slowly in the birth canal. Next the arms emerge, one at a time, and finally the legs. See Figure 4–1(a).

INSTRUMENT BIRTH
If the fetus is too large to emerge from the mother's body spontaneously or if its position in the uterus is such that it makes normal birth impossible, surgical instruments must be used to aid in delivery.

BREECH BIRTH
The fetal buttocks appear first, followed by the legs, the arms, and finally the head. If the position of the fetus cannot be changed before the birth process begins, instruments must be used to aid the delivery. See Figure 4–1(b).

TRANSVERSE-PRESENTATION BIRTH
The fetus lies crosswise in the mother's uterus. If this position cannot be changed before the birth process begins, instruments must be used to aid delivery.

CAESAREAN-SECTION BIRTH
When the fetal body becomes too large to pass through the birth canal without a prolonged and difficult labor, even when instruments are used, the fetus is delivered surgically by making a slit in the maternal abdominal wall.

---

prenatal period on the infant's postnatal development, Sontag has explained (91):

> To all intents and purposes, a newborn infant with such a background is a neurotic infant when he is born—the result of an unsatisfactory fetal environment. In this instance, he does not have to wait until childhood for a bad home situation or other cause to make him neurotic. It was done for him before he even saw the light of day.

EFFECTS OF BIRTH ON DEVELOPMENT

(a)

(b)

Figure 4–1. In a natural or spontaneous birth (a) the infant emerges from the mother's body headfirst while in a breech birth (b) the buttocks emerge first and the head last. (*Adapted from N. J. Eastman and L. M. Hellman:* Williams obstetrics, *13th ed. Appleton-Century-Crofts, 1966. Used by permission.*)

Length of the Gestation Period

The fourth condition associated with birth that affects postnatal development is the length of the gestation period. Even though the *average* length of the gestation period is 38 weeks or 266 days, very few infants arrive exactly on schedule. Meredith has reported that the gestation period varies from 36 to 40 weeks for 70 percent of all infants and from 34 to 42 weeks for 98 percent of all infants (62).

Those whose arrival is late are called "postmatures" and those whose arrival is early are called "prematures" or for short, "premies." Infants are called postmature if born two or more weeks late and premature if they arrive two or more weeks ahead of schedule. However, as it is often impossible to tell just when conception occurred, more accurate criteria are used.

As a rough indication of *postmaturity,* 21 or more inches in length and 8 or more pounds in weight are used as criteria. Postmature infants are seldom over 10 pounds in weight and 11 or more pounds are rare (62).

Because *prematurity* is far more common and more hazardous to later development than postmaturity, more specific criteria are used. In addition to the length of the gestation period, body size is added. Body size is calculated in terms of the weight-length ratio. When infants weigh 5½ pounds or less and are

less than 19 inches in length, they are called premature. Should the head circumference be less than 12.87 inches and the crown-rump length less than 12.48 inches, this is additional proof of prematurity. Because body size is, to some extent, influenced by heredity—with small women, on the average, having smaller babies than large women—additional criteria are being used, such as the nutritional status of the infant, ossification, and neurological assessment (19, 62, 98).

Unless damaged before or during birth, the postmature infant adjusts more quickly and more successfully to the postnatal environment than does the full-term infant. By contrast, premature infants usually experience difficulty in adjusting to their postnatal environment, even if they have not been damaged before or during birth. What these difficulties are will be discussed in detail in the section dealing with hazards resulting from birth.

Postnatal Care

The fifth condition associated with birth that affects the infant's postnatal adjustments is the type of care received in the early days following birth. After 9 months in the stable environment of the uterus, the fetus is suddenly thrust into an environment which is not only different, but highly variable.

In days when babies were born at home, the mother or a mother substitute was a constant source of aid in making these adjustments. With childbirth in hospitals, a stable source of aid is less common. While it is true that newborn infants usually remain in the hospital environment for only 4 to 6 days before going home, these are the critical days in learning to adjust to the postnatal environment. Even though most normal, healthy, full-term infants suffer no serious or lasting effects from the impersonal and unstable care they receive in hospital nurseries, there is evidence that it delays their adjustment to postnatal life (24, 76).

Infants who receive individual attention and handling in addition to the routine care of the hospital nursery are more alert, more active, and tend to be more responsive to external stimuli than those who fail to receive this stimulation. Furthermore, they regain their lost weight sooner and the dazed state which normally follows birth disappears more rapidly (25, 56, 99, 103).

Figure 4–2. Percentage of mothers with rooming-in experience who were able to interpret the meaning of the infant's cry as compared with mothers who had the conventional hospital experience. (*Adapted from M. Greenberg, I. Rosenberg, and J. Lind: First mothers' rooming-in with their newborns: Its impact upon the mother.* American Journal of Orthopsychiatry, *1973, 43, 783–788. Used by permission.*)

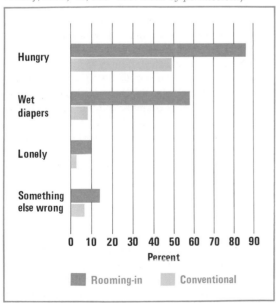

Recognizing the importance of individual and stable attention to postnatal adjustments, some hospitals are using the "rooming-in" plan—having a crib beside the mother's bed so she can take care of the infant's needs. This has proved to be especially important in handling the crying problem—a problem that baffles many mothers of firstborns. Figure 4–2 shows the percentage of mothers who claimed they understood the meaning of different cries by the time they were ready to take their infants home as compared with mothers who had not had the rooming-in experience (37). When the mother understands the infant's cry and reacts to it appropriately, the infant cries less and makes better adjustments to the postnatal environment. (13).

Parental Attitudes

The sixth condition associated with birth that affects adjustment to postnatal life is parental attitudes. When parental attitudes are favorable, the parent-child relationship is relaxed. This aids the infant's adjustments to the new conditions of the postnatal environment.

A relaxed mother, for example, produces more milk than a tense one, thus helping the infant adjust to the new method of taking nourishment which birth has necessitated. Unfavorable parental attitudes, by contrast, make for a highly emotionally-toned parent-infant relationship. This slows down the infant's adjustments to eating and sleeping and encourages excessive crying, which further interferes with the adjustments the infant must make to the postnatal environment.

Box 4–4 gives some of the conditions responsible for parental attitudes toward a newborn infant. Some of these conditions affect the attitudes either of the mother or the father while others affect the attitudes of both parents.

Influence of Time of Birth on Development

Scientific interest in the question, "Is there a 'best time' to be born?" has produced a great deal of reliable information. Most of this is contradictory to the traditional beliefs that have prevailed for generations.

There is no evidence that it is better to be *born on one day of the week* than on another. The old belief that being *born under certain stars* would fix one's destiny

CONDITIONS ASSOCIATED WITH BIRTH THAT AFFECT PARENTAL ATTITUDES

THE MOTHER'S CHILDBIRTH EXPERIENCE
When birth gives the mother a minimum of discomfort, her attitude will be more favorable than when labor is prolonged and difficult.

THE MOTHER'S PHYSICAL CONDITION AFTER CHILDBIRTH
Women who are physically exhausted after childbirth have far less favorable attitudes toward their infants than those who recover quickly.

PREPARATION FOR PARENTHOOD
The more preparation parents have for their parental roles, the more relaxed they will be when they bring the infant home from the hospital and take over its care.

PARENTAL EXPECTATIONS
When the infant is of the desired sex and attractive looking, parental attitudes will be far more favorable than when the infant is not of the desired sex and fails to conform to the parents' "dream child" concept.

THE INFANT'S POSTNATAL ADJUSTMENTS
The infant who adjusts quickly and satisfactorily to the postnatal environment encourages more favorable parental attitudes than the one whose adjustments are slow and unsatisfactory.

PARENTAL RESENTMENTS AGAINST WORK AND PRIVATIONS
If care of the infant in the home requires more work, more expense, more sleepless nights, and more privations than parents had anticipated, it may lead to resentments toward the infant.

CONCERN ABOUT NORMALITY
If the doctor is concerned about the infant's difficulties in adjusting to postnatal life and if the infant is kept in the hospital longer than the usual time, parents become anxious, concerned, and unhappy. They wonder if the infant will ever be a physically and mentally normal person.

CONCERN ABOUT SURVIVAL
Concern about survival, especially in difficult and premature births, is heightened when the infant must be given special and intensive care in the hospital and is not released from the hospital for days or weeks after the usual release time. This leads to parental concern about ability to care for the infant in the home.

---

has likewise not been substantiated. There is some evidence that more births occur during the fall and new moon stages of the lunar cycle but there is no evidence—at least to date—that this has any effect whatsoever on the pattern of the child's development (61).

Studies of the relationship of season of year and *mental abilities* have shown that the effects of the season of birth are exceedingly slight. Spring and summer babies are no brighter than autumn and winter babies. Nor is the *school performance* of children born in one season superior to that of children born in other seasons (50, 59). Studies of eminent men have likewise failed to support the belief that people born in certain months or seasons are brighter and will, as a result, achieve greater *success*. Some studies have shown that more outstanding men were born in the fall than in the spring, while other studies claim other "best seasons" (67).

According to tradition, the individual's *personality* is affected by the season of birth. Children born during the "cheerful seasons" of the year—spring and summer—will, for example, be gay, outgoing, and cheerful—"extroverts"—while those born in the "gloomy" fall and winter months will, by contrast, be "introverts"—dour and gloomy. While few scientific investigations have been made to test these traditional beliefs, some studies have reported that children born in the spring, summer, and autumn months are decidedly more sociable than those born in the winter months. Other studies have found that season of birth has no effect on personality (5, 42).

Neonatal deaths are reported to be most common in June and July (5). Figure 4–3 shows the common causes and peak periods of neonatal deaths. To date, no satisfactory explanation has been given for these variations.

Level of Development Present at Birth

To understand postnatal development, one must know what the status of the child is when life outside the mother's body begins. The characteristics of the neonate can be divided into three categories: *appearance, helplessness,* and *individuality.* Newborn infants show distinct individual differences, and their differences tend to become greater as they adjust to postnatal life. Consequently, the description given will be of a typical or "average" newborn infant, not of any specific infant. Furthermore, the description applies to the normal full-term infant whose development before birth has covered approximately 270 days.

Appearance

The first characteristic of the "average" newborn is appearance. The *weight* of the average newborn infant is 7.5 pounds and the *length* is 19.5 inches. Weight ranges from 3 to 16 pounds and length from 17 to 21

inches. Male infants are generally slightly larger than female infants, but the differences are not so great between the sexes as within each sex group (62). Variations in birth size depend on many factors, the most important of which are shown in Box 4–5.

The *physical proportions* of the infant differ greatly from those of the adult, as may be seen in Figure 2–2. In the infant, the head is about one-fourth the entire body length, while in the adult, it is one-seventh. The greatest difference between the adult head size and the infant head size is in the area above the eyes, the cranial region. In the infant, the ratio between the cranium and face is 8:1, while in the adult it is 1:2. Often, the infant's head is slightly—and temporarily—misshapen (8).

The infant's face appears to be broad and short be-

Figure 4–3. Relative infant death rate for broad causes of death by month. (*Adapted from U.S. Department of Health, Education, and Welfare:* Vital Statistics of the United States, *1970.*)

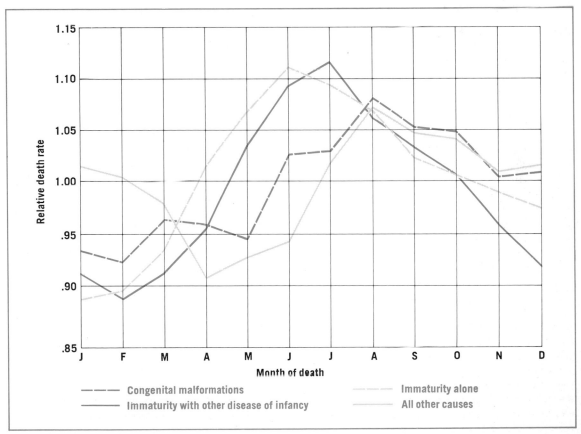

EFFECTS OF BIRTH ON DEVELOPMENT

The muscles of the newborn are small, soft, and uncontrolled, with those of the legs and neck less developed than those of the arms and hands. The bones are soft and flexible. The flesh is firm and elastic, while the skin is soft and often blotchy, especially in the head region. Sometimes a soft, downy growth of hair is found on the body, mostly on the back, but this soon disappears (62, 72).

Helplessness

The second characteristic of a "typical" newborn infant is helplessness. *All* newborn infants are helpless. This is due to the undeveloped state of the body and nervous system. There are five important areas in which this lack of development plays an important role in contributing to the helplessness of the newborn. They are: inability to maintain homeostasis; inability to control motor activity; inability to communicate; undeveloped state of the sense organs; and inability to learn. Each of these will be discussed below.

INABILITY TO MAINTAIN HOMEOSTASIS   The first condition that contributes to the newborn infant's helplessness is inability to maintain homeostasis—the tendency of an organism to maintain within itself relatively stable conditions of temperature, chemical composition, or the like by means of its own regulatory mechanism.

In the prenatal environment, homeostasis was maintained for the fetus by the mother's homeostasis. After birth, the infant's body must take over this responsibility. This a newborn infant is unable to do because of the undeveloped state of the autonomic nervous system which controls body homeostasis.

Studies of the physiological functions of the newborn infant have shown how unstable they are. The *basal pulse rate* ranges, for example, from 130 to 150 beats per minute at birth and then drops to an average of 117 beats several days later. This compares with the average adult basal rate of 70 beats per minute. The *respiration rate* during the first week of life is 35 to 45 breathing movements per minute, compared with 18 at adulthood. *The body temperature* is higher and more variable in a healthy infant than in an adult (76, 82, 94).

Sucking and *swallowing,* though possible at birth, are not well developed. At first, the infant sucks in small bursts of three or four sucks, often choking when attempting to swallow. Because the stomach

cause of lack of teeth, the undeveloped jaws, and the flat nose. The arms, legs, and trunk are small in relation to the head. The abdominal region of the trunk is large and bulging, while the shoulders are narrow, just the opposite of adult proportions. The hands and feet are miniature—much too small for the rest of the body.

Typically, white babies have bluish-gray eyes, and nonwhite babies have dark brown eyes. Gradually the eyes change to whatever the permanent color will be. Though almost mature in size, they move uncontrolled in a meaningless fashion. The neck is so short that it scarcely exists, and the skin covering it lies in deep folds or creases. A heavy growth of fine-textured hair often covers the head.

and intestines have different rates of emptying and because the infant has difficulty sucking and swallowing, *defecation* and *regurgitation* are frequent, and wheezing and colic are common. *Voidings* are variable in time and amount.

Perhaps in no area of body function is lack of homeostasis more marked than in *sleep*. Typically, the infant's sleep is broken by short waking periods caused by pain, hunger, and internal sources of discomfort. The infant sleeps lightly, can be wakened easily, and then falls to sleep easily (4, 10, 29, 34).

INABILITY TO CONTROL MOTOR ACTIVITY   The second condition that contributes to the helplessness of the newborn infant is inability to control body movements. To be independent, a person must be capable of voluntary activity—activity controlled by conscious desire. Newborn infants are incapable of this kind of activity. Even though they are more or less in constant motion, they have no control over the movements they make.

Studies of the movements made by newborn infants have shown that they can be divided roughly into two categories: mass activity and specific activities. These two types of activity and their characteristics are explained in Box 4–6. In spite of the fact that all movements made by the newborn infant, even the reflexes present at birth, are random and uncoordinated, they are important because they are the basis from which the highly coordinated movements of the child will eventually develop as a result of learning and maturation.

There are wide and stable differences from one infant to another not only in general body movements but also in some specific movements, such as hand-mouth contacting and head turning (102). In the same infant there are also patterns and variations. For example, infants who are most active before birth are also most active after birth. There are variations in activity, however, at different times of the day, with the peak coming in the early morning and the quietest period at noon. Activity is greatest during crying, hunger, pain, and general bodily discomfort and least when the infant is asleep, is sucking, or has just been fed.

Environmental conditions also influence neonatal activity. Light and auditory stimuli, for example, increase the amount of activity, as do excessive clothing and coverings. Complicated deliveries result in decreased activity during the early days of postnatal life.

BOX 4–6

CATEGORIES OF INFANT ACTIVITY

MASS ACTIVITY
When one part of the body is stimulated, the whole body responds, though most profoundly in the area stimulated. Mass activity is greatest in the trunk and legs and least in the head. It is highly uncoordinated and diffuse and results in a great expenditure of energy. Normally, mass activity increases in frequency as the infant adjusts to the postnatal environment.

SPECIFIC ACTIVITY
There are two types of specific activity: reflexes and general responses. The first *reflexes* to make their appearance are those which have distinct survival value—heart action, breathing, sneezing, and the digestive reflexes. The others can be aroused within a few hours or days after birth. *General responses* involve larger portions of the body than reflexes, such as random arm and hand movements, prancing, stretching and kicking of the legs, and head turning. Like mass activity, general responses increase in frequency shortly after birth.

And, finally, variations in activity may be caused by differences in tension due to the kinds of treatment newborn infants receive (51, 91).

INABILITY TO COMMUNICATE   Lack of ability to communicate needs and wants to others is the third condition that contributes to the helplessness of newborn infants. Owing to the uncoordinated state of the body, infants cannot speak or point or use other gestures. The best they can do is cry as a way of communicating with others.

As Ostwald and Peltzman have pointed out, the first sounds the infant makes after birth—the "birth sounds" are "usually combinations of gasping, coughing, and efforts to breathe as the newborn struggles to adapt to his new environment" (69). These are quickly followed by crying—the "birth cry"—which is purely reflexive and is caused by air being drawn rapidly over the vocal cords, thus setting up vibrations in them. Like the first sounds the infant makes, the birth cry is affected by the kind of anesthetic drug given to the mother during labor and childbirth and by how quickly the umbilical cord is clamped after delivery (69).

The birth cry serves two purposes: to supply the blood with sufficient oxygen and to inflate the lungs, thus making breathing possible. Once the lungs are inflated and breathing begins, crying comes from internal and external stimulation and is part of the pattern of generalized behavior characteristic of the newborn infant. Most crying during infancy occurs when the infant is hungry, in pain, or in a state of discomfort.

During the first 24 hours after birth, the infant's cry may have different meanings, which can be determined from the pitch, intensity, and continuity of the cry. In general discomfort, for example, the cry is at first monotonous in pitch, staccato-like, and intermittent; then gradually, unless some relief is given, the cry becomes more insistent. Pain is characterized by a cry which rises in pitch. If pain is accompanied by increasing physical weakness, piercing tones give way to low moans. While variations in the tonal quality and intensity of crying increase its value as a form of communication, only persons familiar with an infant's cries can be expected to know what they mean. That is why, as was pointed out earlier, mothers who have an opportunity to be with their babies in the hospital, because of the "rooming-in" plan, are able to know what their cries mean better than mothers who have the conventional hospital experience.

Body activity generally begins when the infant starts to cry. In vigorous crying, every part of the body is thrown into action. This is shown in Figure 4–4 and also in Figure 1–2. The crying infant squirms, kicks, rolls the body, turns the head from side to side, and

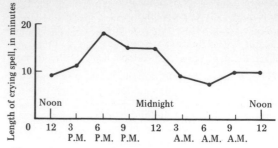

Figure 4–5. The characteristic 24-hour pattern of crying during the first 10 days of life. (*Adapted from J. Bernal: Crying during the first 10 days of life, and maternal responses.* Developmental Medicine and Child Neurology, *1972,* 14, *362–372. Used by permission.*)

flexes and extends the arms, legs, fingers, and toes. This activity is a signal that the infant needs attention. It thus serves as a form of communication.

Studies of crying during the period of the newborn have revealed marked differences in the amount of crying and in the conditions under which crying occurs. During the first 9 days of postnatal life, the duration of crying lessens and the intervals between cries become shorter and less variable. The more intense the stimulus, the louder and longer the cries. Most crying occurs between 6 P.M. and midnight, as may be seen in Figure 4–5. However, this pattern varies from infant to infant and is influenced to a marked extent by how the mother reacts to the infant's cries (13, 52, 89).

In addition to crying, the infant is capable of producing another type of vocalization, usually called "explosive sounds." They take many forms—whimpers, whistle-tones, whines, gurgling, and coughing noises, and sounds not unlike heavy breathing. These are often referred to as "hums" or "coos" and are most common when the infant is relaxed or at the breast (69).

Explosive sounds are uttered without intent and without meaning: they occur purely by chance whenever there is a contraction of the vocal muscles. They are not a form of communication as crying is because infants are not trying to let others know their needs or wants, as in crying.

Furthermore, since these sounds are low in pitch and weak, as compared with cries, they are often regarded as unimportant and are ignored by parents or those who take care of the infant. In the long run,

Figure 4–4. Crying in the newborn infant is accompanied by mass activity. (*Adapted from* Heredity and Prenatal Development, *a McGraw-Hill Text-Film.*)

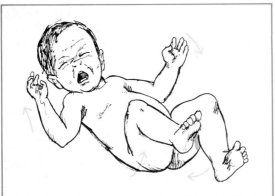

however, explosive sounds are far more important than cries. The reason for this is that the explosive sounds are gradually strengthened and, during the second half of the first year of life, develop into babbling. In time, speech develops from babbling, not from crying.

UNDEVELOPED STATE OF THE SENSE ORGANS A fourth condition contributing to the helplessness of the newborn infant is the undeveloped state of the sense organs. This is especially true of the sense organs that are most important to independent behavior—the eyes and the ears.

Studying sensitivity in the newborn infant is far more difficult than is usually recognized. Because of these difficulties, present-day evidence about the state of development of the newborn infant's sense organs may not be completely accurate. It is quite possible that newborn infants have a greater capacity for sensory discrimination than current studies show. This is especially applicable to vision and hearing—the two areas where fear of possible damage to the delicate sense organs has been a serious obstacle to experimental research (48).

What scientific evidence is available today shows that, at birth, the sense organs are ready to function but some are more highly developed than others. Box 4–7 describes the developmental status of the dif-

---

BOX 4–7

SENSE ORGAN DEVELOPMENT OF THE NEWBORN

SMELL
The cells for smell, at the upper interior part of the nose, are well developed at birth. That the infant's smell is keen is shown by crying, head turning, and attempts to withdraw from unpleasant stimuli and by sucking in response to pleasant stimuli.

TASTE
The cells for taste, located on the surface of the tongue, are well developed at birth and are as numerous as they will be later in life. Because of the well-developed sense of smell, which supplements taste reactions, the infant can distinguish between pleasant and unpleasant taste stimuli. This is shown by crying and squirming when unpleasant stimuli—sour, salty and bitter—are placed on the tongue and by relaxing the body and sucking when pleasant stimuli—sweet—are presented.

ORGANIC SENSITIVITIES
Hunger and thirst are well developed at birth. Hunger contractions of the stomach, which produce a painful sensation in the abdominal region, occur within the first day of life.

SKIN SENSITIVITIES
The sense organs for touch, temperature, and pressure are well developed at birth and lie close to the surface of the skin. Sensitivity to *cold* is more highly developed than to *heat*. Sensitivity to *touch* and *pressure* is greater in the face region, especially the lips, than in the trunk, thighs, and arms. Sensitivity to *pain* is slow in developing and is adversely affected by maternal medication during childbirth. Pain responses develop earlier in the anterior than in the posterior end of the body. The pain threshold normally drops during the first 4 days in postnatal life.

VISION
The cones in the retina are small and poorly developed, suggesting that neonates are color blind. The rods are better developed but are limited to a small area surrounding the fovea, thus restricting the visual field. The black-and-white vision of the infant is blurred because the muscles that control eye movement are too small and weak to enable both eyes to focus on the same object simultaneously. Optic nystagmus—the ability to follow a moving object and then move the eyes backwards—appears during the first week of life. Infants can follow moving stimuli horizontally before vertically. There is also evidence that infants respond to differences in brightness.

HEARING
Hearing is the least developed of all the senses at birth. There are two reasons: *First,* owing to the stoppage of the middle ear with amniotic fluid, sound waves cannot penetrate to the sense cells in the inner ear, and the infant is unable to hear for several hours or days after birth. *Second,* the sense cells in the inner ear are still only partially developed. Low-frequency sounds are more effective in soothing crying and stopping nonnutritive sucking than are high-frequency sounds. Most infants can discriminate the location of sound within the first 3 to 4 days of life. They also respond more to the human voice than to other sounds, such as the ringing of a bell. Continuous sounds have a more soothing effect than noncontinuous.

ferent sense organs at birth and the development that takes place during the period of infancy.

INABILITY TO LEARN The fifth condition contributing to the helplessness of the newborn child is inability to learn. Studies of learning among neonates indicate that even the simplest form of learning—conditioning or learning by association—is often too complex for an infant. For the most part, studies show that, with the possible exception of conditioning in feeding situations, conditioned responses are difficult to elicit and, when they do appear, they are unstable and of little permanent value (32, 83, 92).

Considering the undeveloped state of the fetal brain and autonomic nervous system, it is equally unlikely that an infant can experience any specific emotion—fear, anger, or anxiety—profoundly enough for it to have a lasting influence on personality.

Individuality

The third characteristic of the "average" newborn infant is individuality. No two newborn infants are exactly alike in appearance or behavior. Each starts life with an individuality that will manifest itself more and more as the hereditary potentials unfold.

Individuality is even apparent in twins. A longitudinal study of twins found that individuality was caused, in part, by differences in birth weight. The smaller twin experienced more adjustment difficulties, and these were reflected in sleeping and feeding problems, temper tantrums, and irritability. As a result, the twins developed markedly different personality patterns (85).

CAUSES OF INDIVIDUALITY Some people claim that individuality is the product of hereditary differences, others that heredity plays only a minor role while environment plays a major role, and still others that the roles of heredity and environment are approximately equal. Scientific studies of the causes of individuality present at birth have shown that both heredity and environment are responsible for the differences between infants with environment playing a more extensive and, hence, more important role than heredity (51, 78, 91, 100). The most important causes of individuality at birth are listed and explained in Box 4–8.

AREAS OF INDIVIDUALITY Studies of newborn infants report individual differences in a number of areas of development. The most important findings of these studies will be reported below.

In *appearance,* the only thing that all newborn infants have in common is their smallness and top-heaviness. Some are chubby and cherubic in appearance, while others look wizened and senile. Not all newborn infants feel the same when they are held. As Stone and Church have remarked, some are "compactly and comfortably curled, like a kitten, others sprawl like a bundle of loosely joined sticks, still others hold themselves tense and stiff" (93).

Newborn infants vary greatly in their ability to *maintain homeostasis.* This contributes to individuality in adjustment, especially in response to food, patterns of sleep, crying, motor activities, and need for attention. Some infants, for example, are able to take nourishment and keep it down from the very beginning, with the result that they lose little of their birth weight. Others have difficulty adjusting to sucking and swallowing and, consequently, may lose a frightening amount of weight.

Individuality is even more strikingly illustrated in *motor activity.* Some infants show slow, poorly developed reflex responses, while others have reflexes similar in form—though slower in rate—to those of older children. Marked variations also occur in mass activity, with some infants in constant motion, even in sleep, while others are relatively placid.

Newborn infants differ greatly in *distractibility.* Some are distracted by noises or any other change in their environments and others seem to ignore these changes. While most infants adjust successfully to *changes in pattern of living,* necessitated by the change from the intrauterine environment to the world outside the mother's body, some do so more slowly than others and some so slowly that their lives are endangered. There are also differences in the state of development of the *sense organs* at birth. Some infants hear more acutely and are more sensitive to pain than others.

There is no area in which individuality expresses itself as forcefully as in *crying.* This is greatly influenced by the infant's birth experience. In a quick, explosive delivery, for example, the cry is sharp and deep; in premature births or when the infant is in poor condition, the cry is like a little moan. Prolonged labor, resulting in the exhaustion of the infant, generally causes a weak, short, intermittent cry. Infants damaged prenatally or at birth have cries that differ in pitch, volume, rhythm, and accentual character from those of normal infants (69).

The amount of crying as well as the tonal quality is an individual characteristic. Some infants are "good as gold," crying only infrequently and for short intervals. Others seem to be angry or frustrated all the time, crying incessantly and at the top of their lungs. Some are easily distracted from crying by being picked up or talked to while others continue to cry, regardless of what is done to distract them.

Hazards Associated with Birth

As is true of the prenatal period, there are certain physical and psychological hazards that are commonly associated with birth. Some of these hazards are due to the birth process itself and some to the adjustment the infant must make to a new pattern of life necessitated by birth. Some of the hazards are physical, some are psychological, and some are both physical and psychological. In the case of prematurity, for example, there are serious physical hazards involved in the birth process and in the physical adjustments immediately after birth. There are also psychological hazards in the form of unfavorable parental attitudes as the premature child grows older.

Physical Hazards

Medical science has, for years, studied the hazards related to birth in the hopes of preventing these hazards or, at least, of reducing their effects on the infant's later life. Because of this medical interest, there is more information available about physical hazards than about psychological hazards which, until recently, were regarded as of minor importance.

In the following sections, a brief report will be made of what is known today about the causes and consequences of the most common physical hazards associated with birth and the adjustment to the postnatal environment immediately after birth.

THE BIRTH PROCESS Since the beginning of time, the birth process has been regarded as hazardous for both mother and child. All studies, both medical and psychological, have shown that this is true. While a spontaneous birth may have few hazards associated with it, a difficult birth or one requiring the use of instruments or surgery may result in temporary or permanent brain damage. How this will affect the infant's adjustments after birth or for many years to come will be discussed in the section related to birth damage.

BOX 4–8

CONDITIONS CONTRIBUTING TO INDIVIDUALITY IN NEWBORNS

AGE AT BIRTH
How old infants are at birth depends on whether they are full-term, postmature, or premature. Appearance and developmental level are affected by age.

INHERITED CHARACTERISTICS
Except for identical multiple births, no two individuals inherit exactly the same physical and mental characteristics and, as a result, they will not be alike.

PRENATAL CONDITIONS
Even in multiple births, the conditions of the prenatal environment differ depending on which fetus gets a favored position in the uterine sac.

TYPE OF BIRTH
Infants delivered by caesarean section tend to be less active and to cry less than those born spontaneously or delivered with the aid of instruments. There is little evidence that the amount of activity or crying is influenced by the length of labor.

MEDICATION OF MOTHER
Infants whose mothers had been heavily medicated to relieve childbirth pain show greater disorganization of behavior at birth and for several days after birth than those whose mothers received little or no medication.

BRAIN DAMAGE
Infants whose brains were damaged during the prenatal period or during birth have different appearances, behavior, and developmental levels than those who suffered no brain damage.

POSTNATAL CARE
Infants who receive individualized care, either from rooming-in with their mothers or from special nurses, are more alert, cry less, and show less disorganized behavior than those who receive only routine hospital care.

PARENTAL ATTITUDES AND EXPECTATIONS
Parents who feel insecure in their roles or expect the infant to be too delicate and helpless to be handled, fail to stimulate the infant or are so nervous and anxious that they make the infant nervous and tense.

Multiple birth and precipitate labor are especially hazardous. There are three reasons for the hazardous nature of *multiple births*. First, infants of multiple birth are usually smaller and weaker at birth than singletons, and this adds to the adjustment problems every infant faces. Second, they are usually premature and this adds to their adjustment problems, as will be explained in the section related to prematurity. Third, because of prematurity, they are more subject to birth damage, especially damage to their brains, than are singletons who are more likely to be born at full term than to be premature (85).

Precipitate labor—labor lasting less than two hours—is hazardous because it causes difficulties in establishing respiration. As a result, the infant is introduced to oxygen too suddenly and is not yet ready to start to breathe. How much brain damage will result will depend on how quickly the infant can establish respiration (76).

Medication of the mother during labor and the birth process, as was pointed out earlier, can be and often is hazardous because it slows down the birth process and often requires the use of instruments. These conditions may lead to temporary or permanent brain damage.

INFANT MORTALITY Any time during the period of infancy may be regarded as critical for survival. The *most* critical time is the day of birth, and the next most critical is the second and third days after birth. With each passing day, the infant's chances for survival increase (31, 42, 62).

The most common causes of infant mortality are prematurity, congenital debility, malformation, injury at birth, pneumonia, influenza, diarrhea, and deficiency of oxygen resulting either from the excessive use of drugs to relieve the pains of childbirth or from having the umbilical cord tighten around the fetal neck during the birth process. Some of these conditions detrimentally affect the prenatal environment, some are related to the birth process, and some come from an unfavorable postnatal environment (57, 62, 66).

A number of factors influence the mortality rate during the neonatal period. *Sex differences* exist, with more boys dying than girls, even when they have the same birth weight. *Racial differences* are marked, with nonwhites showing a higher mortality rate than whites. Women who experience *stressful pregnancies* have more difficulties in childbirth, and their babies are more likely to be born dead, to die shortly after birth, or to have some congenital malformation.

The economic level of the family is a factor of influence, with the highest mortality rate occurring in families of the lowest economic levels. The poor prenatal diet of mothers in the low economic groups contributes to the high neonatal mortality rate. The longer the *gestation period,* the lower the mortality rate in the neonatal period. There is a tendency for mortality to increase with increasing *birth order. Maternal age* likewise affects infant mortality. Women under 25 years and over 40 have more stillbirths and more infants dying shortly after birth than do mothers between these ages. And, finally, mortality varies with the *size* of the infant. The smaller the infant, the greater the risk of mortality (6, 9, 44, 57, 62).

POSTMATURITY Even though postmaturity is far less common today than in the past, due to the fact that doctors use medical techniques to induce labor when X-rays of the fetus show that it is becoming proportionally too large to pass down the mother's birth canal without the aid of instruments, it is still a potential hazard. This hazard is less often mortality than brain damage.

If the fetal body, especially the head, becomes so large that the fetus must be delivered by instruments or by caesarean section, there is always the possibility that brain damage will occur from pressure on the fetal head during an instrument birth or from lack of oxygen during a caesarean birth due to difficulties in establishing respiration—a characteristic of this type of birth. These hazards will be discussed more fully in connection with the discussion of brain damage as a physical hazard. Thus, it is apparent that postmaturity per se is not hazardous but rather the conditions of birth that postmaturity gives rise to.

Studies of the later development of children who were postmature at birth and, as a result, experienced difficult births, have shown that they not only experienced many neonatal adjustment problems but also problems of schooling and of social and personal adjustments as they grew older. They are often retarded in their intellectual development, are slow in learning to read, and require special schooling. Many are so poorly adjusted personally and socially that they find themselves without playmates as young children and with few friends as they grow older. These conditions, it must be recognized, come from brain damage, not from postmaturity per se (40, 58, 91).

PREMATURITY It has been reported that approximately 7 of every 100 babies born in the United States every year are premature. Some, of course, are more premature than others (62, 65, 85).

Prematurity is most likely to occur among firstborn children, and this accounts partially for the higher mortality rate among the firstborn. It is most common among infants of the lower socioeconomic classes and is more common among nonwhites than whites. Small women are more likely to give birth prematurely than larger women. Prematurity occurs more often in multiple births than in singletons. The larger the number of infants in a multiple birth, the greater the chances of prematurity and the greater the prematurity.

One complication about knowing just how many newborn infants are premature, what their state of development at birth is, and how prematurity affects their postnatal development is that many researchers use low birth weight as their criterion of prematurity and do not take into consideration the other criteria—gestation age, body length, etc., as described earlier. Unless this distinction is made, it is difficult to know exactly how prematurity affects development (19).

Medical science has not yet pinpointed the exact *cause* or causes. It has found strong evidence that a number of conditions either cause or contribute to prematurity: uterine crowding in multiple births and unfavorable prenatal environments due to maternal malnutrition and illness at critical times in pregnancy. There is even stronger medical evidence that prematurity comes from a glandular imbalance in the mother's body. This imbalance is often caused by prolonged emotional stress (62, 65, 85, 91).

Excessive drinking and smoking are common among women who give birth prematurely. People who smoke excessively often suffer from emotional stress. Smoking, like drinking, acts as a psychological pain-killer, helping them to forget, at least temporarily, the stress-inducing conditions. Consequently, it seems likely that heavy smoking is only an outward sign of stress. As stated above, intense stress produces a glandular imbalance which leads to premature labor (19, 91).

To date, no studies have been made of the relationship of excessive drinking to prematurity. Excessive drinking, like excessive smoking, is probably a *contributing factor* to prematurity. Future studies may substantiate this.

While many prematurely born children do not, in the long run, suffer from the effects of prematurity, others do. The most common *dangers* of prematurity are diffi-

culties in adjusting to postnatal life, especially establishing respiration, brain damage due to the undeveloped state of the skull to protect the brain during the birth process, and early deaths (19, 25, 64).

For the most part, scientific studies indicate that many of the unfavorable effects of prematurity, during infancy and as children grow older, are the result of unfavorable parental attitudes, often colored by acceptance of the traditional belief that *all* premature children are destined to be handicapped. Some of the reported effects of prematurity are based on studies in which the sole criterion of prematurity was low birth weight, ignoring the possibility that low birth weight might be due to conditions other than prematurity.

The studies reveal that the developmental status of children born prematurely is generally below normal for the first 5 or 6 months of life. After that, the retardation becomes less and less until the age of 2 years, by which time the gap between full-term and prematurely born children is usually closed.

When the starting point for measuring development is taken as conception, rather than birth, less difference is noted between full-term and premature infants even in the early months of life. A specific example will illustrate this point. An infant born 2 months prematurely will, when 2 months old, be more mature than a full-term infant who has just been born. Both have had 9 months of development. For the former, 7 months have been *in utero* and 2 outside; for the latter, 9 months have been *in utero*. When the premature infant is judged by norms for a 2-month-old full-term infant, the premature is at a decided disadvantage because the full-term infant has had 11 months for development since conception as compared with 9 months for the premature. On the other hand, if *age from conception* is considered, the premature will compare favorably with the full-term infant.

Studies of the effects of prematurity in different areas of development show that the behavior patterns of the prematurely born infant are similar to those of the full-term infant, though the former lags behind for a while. How much lag there is depends largely upon birth weight, *unless* the baby was injured in birth. Babies who weigh under 4 pounds at birth will be retarded by a month or more during the first 18 months of their lives; those weighing 4 to 5 pounds at birth will catch up to the norm for their ages by the time they are 9 or 10 months old (19, 23, 25, 33, 40, 80). Figure 4–6 shows a comparison of premature and full-term infants up to 3 years of age in different areas of develop-

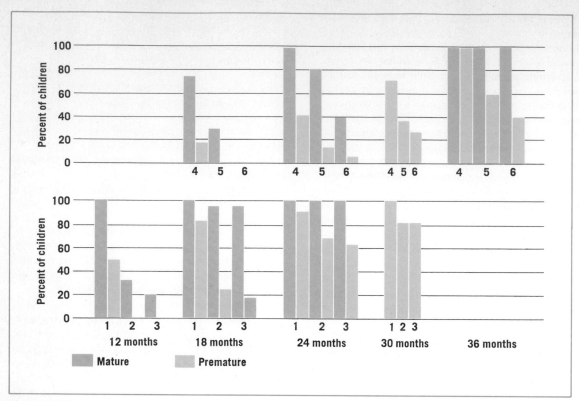

Figure 4–6. Milestones of development in premature and mature children: (1) sitting, (2) standing, (3) walking, (4) single words, (5) phrases, (6) sentences. (*Adapted from C. M. Drillien: A longitudinal study of the growth and development of prematurely and maturely born children. Part VI. Physical development in age period 2 to 4 years.* Archives of Disease in Childhood, *1961, 36, 1–70.* Used by permission.)

ment. In Box 4–9 are listed some of the common effects of prematurity on later development.

There is evidence that some of the developmental lag that is common among children born prematurely could be overcome, partially at least, if they were given more stimulation, especially in the early days of postnatal life. Prematurely born infants who were subjected to stroking, even while in their isolettes in the hospital, have been reported to be more active, to regain lost birth weight faster, and to be healthier than those who lacked this stimulation (90). As soon as premature infants can be removed from their isolettes, if they are stimulated by being held, rocked, and played with, they overcome much of the developmental lag

that is characteristic of prematures who are not brain damaged (74, 84).

BRAIN DAMAGE   Medical science has found that there are two "great killers" during the birth process. The term "killer" does not necessarily mean that the infant will die. It means, in the broader sense, that the infant's chances for a normal development are "killed." Even those infants who do not die as a result of brain damage may be so harmed that their hereditary potentials will never be reached. This may not be apparent for months or even years after birth.

The *first* great killer is brain damage caused by pressure on the fetal head during the birth process. As the fetal body passes down the birth canal, there is certain to be some compression of the brain, especially if the fetal head is large. Under normal conditions, nature provides for this by adequately covering the brain tissue with a partially formed skull; however, the infant's head may be misshapen or marked where the forceps have been applied during birth. These birth scars normally clear up in a short time. The pressure generally has no permanent effect on the brain tissue, though most newborn infants are stunned for a day or more.

When birth is long and difficult, the pressure on the brain is increased. It may be great enough to cause hemorrhages in and around the brain. The effects of the hemorrhages may be temporary or permanent, depending mainly on their severity. The area of the brain that is damaged is also important. If the left hemisphere is damaged, for example, it is likely to affect speech.

The *second* great killer at the time of birth is brain damage caused by anoxia—an interruption of the oxygen supply to the brain. The extent of the brain damage will depend on the severity of the oxygen deprivation. Damage may be temporary or permanent. A total lack of oxygen will kill the brain cells in 18 seconds. A longer deprivation can kill the infant.

Most cases of anoxia occur during the birth process. Difficulties may arise before birth, however. They may

---

BOX 4–9

COMMON EFFECTS OF PREMATURITY ON LATER DEVELOPMENT

PHYSICAL DEVELOPMENT
Premature infants are slower to reach the growth spurt characteristic of the early months of life, but by the end of the first year they have almost caught up to the norm for full-term infants.

HEALTH
In their first year, prematures have more illnesses, especially respiratory and nasopharyngeal disturbances. As they grow older, they suffer slightly more from such physical defects as malnutrition, dwarfism, and obesity. The most serious defect associated with prematurity is eye damage resulting from anoxia.

MOTOR CONTROL
Prematures sit, stand, and walk at a later age than full-term infants with the greatest retardation in those who were smallest at birth. As young children, they are less graceful in their movements.

INTELLIGENCE
More cases of serious mental deficiency are found among prematures than in the general population. For the most part, mental defects are found among those who suffered from cerebral hemorrhages at or immediately after birth.

SPEECH
Prematurely born children use baby talk longer and have more speech defects than full-term children. Stuttering is the most common speech defect.

SENSORY BEHAVIOR
Premature infants are highly sensitive to sounds and noises. As they grow older, they are easily distracted by noises and are very sensitive to colors and moving objects.

EMOTIONAL BEHAVIOR
Some prematures are "gentle babies," but most are shy, petulant, irascible, and negativistic. *Nervous traits,* such as finger-sucking and nail-biting, and *behavior disorders,* such as temper outbursts and a tendency to cry frequently, are more common among prematures.

SOCIAL ADJUSTMENTS
In general, prematurely born children make better adjustments in the early years of life than later. As infants, they tend to be shy, closely attached to their parents, and more dependent than full-term infants of the same age. In the preschool and early elementary school years, they show more forms of problem behavior, especially feeding difficulties.

DEVIANT BEHAVIOR
Hyperkinetic, disorganized behavior, nervous mannerisms, and accident-proneness are especially common among prematures who have suffered brain damage at birth.

be caused by the premature separation of the placenta, which cuts off the oxygen supply to the fetal bloodstream, or by abnormalities in circulation which interfere with the fetal supply of nutritional substances and oxygen (35).

The possibility of brain damage varies according to the type of birth. In a breech birth, for example, there is always the possibility of anoxia—the possibility that before the head emerges, the fetus will be cut off from the oxygen supply from the mother's body that the fetus has been receiving through the umbilical cord and that this will either damage or kill the fetal brain cells. Since epilepsy is most common among children delivered in breech birth, this disorder is believed to be the result of damage to brain cells caused by oxygen deprivation. A transverse presentation inevitably necessitates the use of instruments, and these may, if applied to the fetal head, cause brain injury.

The infant delivered by caesarean section is less likely to suffer brain injury due to pressure on the fetal head than one delivered by a long, difficult birth requiring the use of instruments. Many infants delivered by caesarean section, however, have difficulty in establishing respiration and, as a result, their brains may be damaged by oxygen deprivation. Precipitate labor, as was pointed out earlier, is very likely to have deleterious effects on later development. The reason for this is that it introduces the infant to oxygen too suddenly, thus causing anoxia because the infant is not yet ready to establish respiration through the use of the lungs (35, 58).

Studies of the *effects* of brain damage on postnatal development have revealed that brain damage is not necessarily shown in any one pattern of behavior. Some brain-damaged infants are hyperactive, irritable, and sensitive to any mild stimulation. Their behavior tends to be more disorganized than is normal for that age. Others show diminished general activity and are placid and apathetic. When brain damage is severe enough to show hemorrhaging, mental deficiency, cerebral palsy, and other complications are common (4, 13, 25, 66).

Long-term effects of brain damage on postnatal development have also been found. It has been reported that some children who have difficulties in learning to read experienced brain damage during birth (58). But there are many causes of reading difficulties, and brain damage is only one of them. Instrumental delivery has been reported to affect the intellectual level and the personalities of children as they grow older. Among the traits reported as more common among those born with the aid of instruments are general hyperactivity, restlessness, speech defects, and poor concentration. Whether these were caused by the birth experience, by the attitudes of parents, or by some other factor or factors is unknown (35, 40, 52, 91).

Because brain damage is a hazard to good personal and social adjustments as children grow older, not just a hazard during the infancy period, medical science has been trying to find ways to keep it to a minimum and eventually to eliminate it completely. Improved medical techniques used in childbirth have helped to eliminate brain damage caused by pressure on the fetal head during the birth process. X-rays taken toward the end of pregnancy have been used to diagnose the possibility of a difficult birth which will necessitate the use of instruments for delivery. When this diagnosis suggests that an instrument birth will be necessary, many doctors decide in favor of a caesarean-section birth.

Coping with the problem of brain damage from anoxia has not been so successful to date. Consequently, many doctors regard brain damage from anoxia to be a greater hazard than damage from pressure.

At the present time, medical science is experimenting with a technique to monitor oxygen intake. This is used during the birth process and immediately after birth to determine if there is adequate oxygen to prevent brain damage. If not, oxygen can be administered in the *right amount* to prevent other complications, such as blindness, which is known to occur when too much oxygen is given to infants for too long a time. This problem is associated with extremely low birth-weight infants whose prematurity has made it impossible for them to establish normal respiration.

To date, the problem of preventing anoxia is showing signs of being solved. If the present medical research proves as successful as the results indicate, a time may come when the hazard of brain damage will be reduced to a minimum.

Psychological Hazards

Because scientific interest in the psychological hazards that accompany birth have been relatively recent in origin, far less is known about them than about physical hazards. Enough is known now, however, to justify saying that, even though this information is limited, the psychological hazards are in the long run often more serious and far-reaching in their effects than the physical hazards.

There are six conditions associated with birth that are now known to give rise to psychological hazards. They are: the plateau in development that normally occurs immediately after birth; the developmental lag which is characteristic of infants who are unhealthy or of multiple birth, the helplessness of the newborn infant, the individuality of all newborn infants, "new parent blues," and the name given to the infant at the time of birth.

PLATEAU IN DEVELOPMENT While a plateau in development is normal immediately after birth, many parents become concerned because they believe there must be something seriously wrong to make their infants lose weight and to have difficulty in keeping down what little nourishment they take. This concern is especially common among parents of firstborns.

If the plateau lasts for only a few days, parental concern gradually gives way to confidence that all is well. However, there are many cases where the plateau lasts for a week or even longer, during which time the infant seems to lose an alarming amount of weight and to be less healthy than immediately after birth. Should the doctor recommend that the infant remain in the hospital longer than originally planned, this heightens parental concern about the infant's well-being.

Once this concern develops, it has two serious effects. First, it makes parents believe that the infant is delicate and, as a result, needs extra attention and care—a belief that fosters overprotectiveness with its tendency to deprive the child of opportunities to become independent even when developmentally ready to do so. Second, it makes parents question their ability to take care of the infant after release from the hospital. This makes them anxious and nervous, a condition that the infant senses and reacts to with nervousness and tension that interferes with eating and sleeping—two essentials to good postnatal adjustment.

DEVELOPMENTAL LAG Developmental lag means physical and mental development below the norm for the individual's age. Developmental lag may appear during infancy, or it may not appear until several months after birth. When development falls below the norm, or when parents judge the child's development in terms of the development of older children in the family or children of relatives and friends, they are concerned about the child's normality.

Concern is almost universal in the case of prematurely born infants. Because their development is below the norm at birth, they must usually be kept in the hospital, often with special care, for weeks or months after birth. Even after they are sent home from the hospital, their developmental lag is of concern to their parents. This, as was explained earlier, is due to the fact that prematurely born children are usually judged in terms of their age since birth rather than in terms of their age since conception.

After several years, when prematurely born children have caught up to the norms for full-term children, some parents, in an attempt to close the gap between them and their age-mates, push them to do more than they may be ready to do at that time. At the same time, parents often continue to be overprotective. This merely prolongs the unfavorable environmental conditions that do so much psychological damage. Being pushed always makes children nervous. In addition, they feel that their parents are being unfair because one minute they are doing things for them and the next minute they are criticizing them for not doing things for themselves. Feelings of inadequacy, lack of self-confidence, resentments, and antagonisms are the inevitable results.

HELPLESSNESS Because the helplessness and dependency of newborn infants are appealing and because they make infants easy to take care of and manage, some parents get into the habit of waiting on their children hand and foot. This habit, once established, tends to persist long after infancy has passed and long after children need or want so much help. Sometimes a mother continues to wait on her child simply because of selfish possessiveness or because she thinks that is what a "good mother" should do. Some mothers are motivated by the satisfaction they get from feeling "indispensable."

Whatever the reason for such parental behavior, it is damaging to children's development. It deprives them of opportunities to learn things that other children of their age are learning. Failure to master the developmental tasks appropriate for their age means that they will make poor social adjustments and this will lead to poor personal adjustments.

Furthermore, children resent being frustrated in their attempts to learn to be independent. The more they are frustrated, the more angry, resentful, and negativistic they become. Because parents often cannot understand this behavior and feel that their children are unappreciative of all they have done for them, the parent-child relationship deteriorates.

INDIVIDUALITY There is a widespread tendency among adults as well as children to regard anyone who is different as either inferior or abnormal in some respect. Many parents set up standards of what a newborn's behavior and appearance should be and then judge their own infant by these standards.

For example, many parents expect a second- or later-born infant to look and behave as they *remember* their firstborn looked and behaved when it was an infant. Other parents steep themselves in "baby-care" information and, from this source, learn norms for infants at birth and in the adjustment period following birth. Whether their standards come from their own experiences or from norms in mass media, they use them as measuring rods for the newly born infant.

If the infant conforms to these standards, parents feel that all is well. Should the infant be ahead of their standards, they tend to be smugly satisfied that the infant is superior. On the other hand, if the infant falls below these standards, they become panicky and are convinced that all is not well.

A newborn's crying, for example, is, to most parents, a signal that something is wrong. They compare the infant's cries with their memories of cries of their earlier-born children or of other infants in the hospital nursery. If the infant cries more and more loudly than others, or if the cries are weak and gasping, parents inevitably conclude that something is the matter.

When infants refuse to nurse or when they regurgitate what nourishment they take, mothers tend to wonder if their milk or the formula given in a bottle is "right" for them. And, it does not ease parental concern to be told by other parents how easily and quickly their infants have adjusted to the feeding situation.

"NEW PARENT BLUES" Few parents escape experiencing "new parent blues." These are states of depression of mild or pronounced intensity that come from a constellation of causes. In the case of new *mothers*, they come partly from the new mother's physical condition—exhaustion from the ordeal of childbirth, glandular changes resulting from pregnancy, sleepless nights due to the care and nursing of the infant, and fatigue caused by work in the home and care of other children in the family—and partly from con-

cerns about adequacy to perform the role of mother satisfactorily, resentments against the privations, work, and interference with the normal pattern of her life, and disappointments if the infant does not come up to her hopes and expectations in appearance or adjustments to postnatal life.

While "new parent blues" in *fathers* are less influenced by physical causes than is true of mothers, men often experience a temporary state of exhaustion after the strain of concern about their wives before and during the childbirth experience and the worry about financial matters if complications arise in connection with birth. Exhaustion may be intensified and prolonged by sleepless nights after the infant is brought home from the hospital. In addition, realization of how parenthood will change the pattern of their lives and affect their plans for the future, how it will affect the husband-wife relationship, and how adequate they will be to assume new responsibilities as fathers all add to the "new parent blues" few new fathers escape.

"New parent blues" are not limited to first children. While they may not be as long and as severe with later-born children, they are still very common. In most cases, the depressive state characteristic of "new parent blues" begins just before or just after parents take their newborn child home from the hospital and assume responsibility for its care. If the infant is a source of concern or of disappointment, this depressive state may begin immediately after the infant's birth. How long it will last will depend on conditions in the home and in the lives of the parents.

If, for example, the infant makes quick adjustments to postnatal life and is easy to take care of, the depressive state characteristic of "new parent blues" will last for a much shorter time than if the infant cries a great deal, has difficulty in nursing, and regurgitates an alarming amount of milk. When "new parent blues" come mainly from unfavorable attitudes, how long they will last will be dependent on the persistence of these attitudes. Parental disappointment and shock, for example, about the homeliness or actual ugliness of the infant's appearance immediately after birth may change to pride as the infant's appearance improves, often even before release from the hospital. The father's resentment against the infant because of his wife's preoccupation with its care may change to paternal pride if he becomes engrossed in the infant's care and, later, with its training.

While they last, "new parent blues" are hazards to the infant's adjustment to postnatal life because they make parents tense, nervous, and even rejectant in their attitudes. These unfavorable states are reflected in the care the infant receives. Because much of the care of an infant is assumed by the mother, after the infant is released from the hospital, "new mother blues" are especially harmful. However, "new father blues" are also serious because they tend to intensify the mother's depressive state. Sensing, for example, that her husband is disappointed because the infant is not of the sex he desired tends to increase her disappointment and thus intensify her depressive state.

Because "new parent blues" can and do play havoc with the infant's adjustments to postnatal life, three approaches are being used today to cut down on the severity and length of these depressive states. *First,* parents-to-be, especially if they are "first" parents, are urged by their doctors to attend prenatal courses in the hospitals to learn how to take care of newborn infants, to learn about the birth process and what possible complications may arise that they must be prepared, both financially and psychologically, to cope with, and to become familiar with the characteristics of a newborn infant, especially appearance, helplessness, individuality and possible adjustment difficulties.

Second, many hospitals offer the rooming-in plan explained earlier and urge women to take advantage of it to increase their feelings of adequacy for assuming the responsibility of care of the infant after leaving the hospital. *Third,* many doctors advise parents-to-be to make arrangements for outside help from relatives, nurses, or houseworkers until the new mother has regained her strength and is ready to assume full responsibility for the infant's care in addition to other home responsibilities.

NAMES In a culture like the American culture, it is customary for parents-to-be to select names for their children even before they are born. Sometimes girls decide on the names they will give to their future children and bestow these names on their dolls. Some boys decide on names for their future sons, usually selecting the name of an athletic hero. Not knowing ahead of time whether the child-to-be will be a boy or a girl, parents are usually prepared with a name for a child of either sex.

It is also customary to give the infant a name immediately after birth. This name is then registered on the birth certificate, thus legally establishing it as the child's name. Although it is possible to change names legally if, as children grow older, they dislike their

EFFECTS OF BIRTH ON DEVELOPMENT

names or feel that their names are handicaps to them, there is usually such strong opposition from family members that the change is never made.

Because changing a name is so difficult, names given to infants at the time of birth can be and often are *potential hazards*. They do not become *real* hazards unless, as time goes on, children feel that their names are a constant source of embarrassment or humiliation to them. These feelings come from the way members of the social group, especially of the peer group, react to them because of their names.

There are a number of types of names that are *potential* psychological hazards to good personal and social adjustments, some of the most common of which are given and the reasons for their hazardous nature explained in Box 4–10.

No one can predict how infants will feel about their names as they grow older and how their names will affect their adjustments to life. Consequently, parents should not consider their own preferences when selecting names for their children. Instead, they should give serious thought to how the names they select may and can affect their children as they grow older. Just because a mother-to-be, for example, has always disliked having a common name like "Mary" or "Jane" does not guarantee that her daughter will like an unusual name, such as "Araminta" or "Eulalia."

Allen et al. made this point when they warned that an "unfortunate selection" of a name for the child may "doom him to recurring embarrassment or even unhappiness" not only in childhood but throughout life (3). McDavid and Harari sounded a similar warning when they said a "parent might appropriately think twice before naming his offspring for Great Aunt Sophronia" (60).

Chapter Highlights

1 Infancy, which extends from birth to approximately the end of the second week of life, is divided into two subperiods—the period of the partunate and the period of the neonate.

2 Early medical interest in birth began with the Greek physicians in the fourth and fifth centuries B.C., but psychological interest did not develop until the middle of the present century.

3 There are four major adjustments all newborn infants must make immediately after birth—adjustments to temperature changes, to breathing, to taking nourishment, and to elimination.

4 That adjustment to postnatal life is difficult has been substantiated by three lines of evidence—loss of weight, disorganization of behavior, and mortality.

5 How much effect birth will have on postnatal development depends on type of birth, medication of the mother before and during childbirth, conditions in the prenatal environment, length of the gestation period, postnatal care, and parental attitudes.

6 Parental attitudes are very important because they influence the treatment infants receive during the critical period of adjustment to postnatal life.

7 Scientific interest in the influence of time of birth on development has produced little evidence to substantiate the traditional beliefs about the "best" times to be born.

8 All newborn infants are top-heavy, and many are homely because of their facial and bodily disproportions.

9 Helplessness during infancy comes from inability to maintain homeostasis, to control motor activity, to communicate in a meaningful way, to experience clearly and distinctly the most important sensations, and to learn new patterns of behavior.

10 Individuality in appearance and behavior at birth comes partly from heredity and partly from environmental experiences before, during, and after birth.

11 Physical hazards during infancy have received more scientific attention than psychological hazards though the latter tend to have a more persistent effect on development than the former.

12 While birth has always been recognized as a hazardous experience, certain types of birth are more hazardous than others.

13 The most serious physical hazards associated with birth are infant mortality, postmaturity, prematurity, and brain damage.

14 There are six conditions associated with birth that are now known to give rise to psychological hazards:

the neonatal plateau, developmental lag, helplessness of the newborn infant, individuality in appearance and behavior, unfavorable attitudes of significant people toward the infant, and the name given to the infant shortly after birth.

15 Of the psychological hazards, information available at the present time points to the fact that the infant's helplessness, "new parent blues," and names are the most serious because their effects are most persistent.

Bibliography

1 Albott, W. L., and J. L. Bruning. Given names: A neglected social variable. *Psychological Record,* 1970, *20,* 527–533.

2 Aleksandrowicz, M. K. The effect of pain relieving drugs administered during labor and delivery on the behavior of the newborn. *Merrill-Palmer Quarterly,* 1974, *20,* 121–140.

3 Allen, L., L. Brown, L. Dickinson, and K. C. Pratt. The relation of first name preference to the frequency in the culture. *Journal of Social Psychology,* 1941, *14,* 279–293.

4 Ashton, R. The state variable in neonatal research: A review. *Merrill-Palmer Quarterly,* 1973, *19,* 3–20.

5 Bailar, J. C., and J. Gurian. The medical significance of date of birth. *Eugenics Quarterly,* 1967, *14,* 89–102.

6 Baird, D. Perinatal mortality. *Developmental Medicine and Child Neurology,* 1970, *12,* 358–369.

7 Barten, S., B. Birns, and J. Ronch. Individual differences in the pursuit behavior of neonates. *Child Development,* 1971, *42,* 313–319.

8 Baum, J. D., and D. Searls. Head shape and size of newborn infants. *Developmental Medicine and Child Neurology,* 1971, *13,* 572–573.

9 Behrman, R. E. Fetal and neonatal mortality in white middle class infants. *American Journal of Diseases of Children,* 1971, *121,* 486–489.

10 Bell, R. Q., and R. A. Haaf. Prevalence of newborn waking states to some motor and appellative responses. *Child Development,* 1971, *42,* 69–77.

11 Bell, R. Q., G. M. Weller, and M. F. Waldrop. Newborn and pre-schooler: Organization of behavior and relations between periods. *Monographs of the Society for Research in Child Development,* 1971, *36,* nos. 1 and 2.

12 Berg, W. K., C. D. Adkinson, and B. D. Strock. Duration and frequency of periods of alertness in neonates. *Developmental Psychology,* 1973, *9,* 434.

13 Bernal, J. Crying during the first 10 days of life, and maternal responses. *Developmental Medicine and Child Neurology,* 1972, *14,* 362–372.

14 Birns, B., and M. Golden. Prediction of intellectual performance at 3 years from infant tests and personality measures. *Merrill-Palmer Quarterly,* 1972, *18,* 53–58.

15 Brazelton, T. B. Effect of maternal expectations on early infant behavior. *Early Child Development and Care,* 1973, *2,* 259–273.

16 Brockman, L. M., and H. N. Ricciuti. Severe protein-calorie malnutrition and cognitive development in infancy and early childhood. *Developmental Psychology,* 1971, *4,* 312–319.

17 Buchanan, B. A., and J. L. Bruning. Connotative meanings of first names and nicknames on three dimensions. *Journal of Social Psychology,* 1971, *85,* 143–144.

18 Busse, T. V., and C. Love. The effect of first names on conflicted decisions: An experimental study. *Journal of Psychology* 1973, *84,* 253–256.

19 Caputo, C. V., and W. Mandell. Consequences of low birth weight. *Developmental Psychology,* 1970, *3,* 363–383.

20 Condon, W. S., and L. W. Sander. Neonate movement as synchronized with adult speech: Interactional participation and language acquisition. *Science,* 1974, *183,* 99–101.

21 Coursin, D. B. Nutrition and brain development in infants. *Merrill-Palmer Quarterly,* 1972, *18,* 177–202.

22 Cronenwett, L. R., and L. L. Newmark. Fathers' responses to childbirth. *Nursing Research,* 1974, *23,* 210–217.

23 Cruise, M. O. A longitudinal study of the growth of low birth weight infants: 1. Velocity and distance growth, birth to 3 years. *Pediatrics,* 1973, *51,* 620–628.

24 Davids, A., and R. H. Holden. Consistency of maternal attitudes and personality from pregnancy to eight months following childbirth. *Developmental Psychology,* 1970, *2,* 364–366.

25 Davies, P. A., and J. P. M. Tizard. Very low birth weight and subsequent neurological defect (with special reference to spastic diplegia). *Developmental Medicine and Child Neurology,* 1975, *17,* 3–17.

26 Desor, J. A., O. Maller, and R. E. Turner. Taste in acceptance of sugars by human infants. *Journal of Comparative and Physiological Psychology,* 1973, *84,* 496–501.

27 DeSouza, S. W., R. W. Joln, B. Richards, and R. D. G. Milner. Fetal distress and birth scores in newborn infants. *Archives of Disease in Childhood,* 1975, *50,* 920–926.

28 Eastman, N. J., and L. M. Hellman. *Williams obstetrics,* 13th ed. New York: Appleton-Century-Crofts, 1966.

29 Emde, R. N., T. J. Gaensbauer, and B. H. Suzuki. Quiet sleep and indices of maturation in the newborn. *Perceptual and Motor Skills,* 1973, *36,* 633–634.

30 Engen, T., L. P. Lipsitt, and M. B. Peck. Ability of newborn infants to discriminate sapid substances. *Developmental Psychology,* 1974, *10,* 741–744.

31 Falkner, F. Infant mortality—an urgent national problem. *Children,* 1970, *17* (3), 83–87.

32 Fitzgerald, H. E., and S. W. Porges. A decade of infant conditioning and

learning research. *Merrill-Palmer Quarterly,* 1971, *17,* 79–119.

33 Francis-Williams, J., and P. A. Davies. Very low birth weight and later intelligence. *Developmental Medicine and Child Neurology,* 1974, *16,* 709–728.

34 Gaensbauer, T. J., and R. N. Emde. Wakefulness and feeding in human newborns. *Archives of General Psychiatry,* 1973, *28,* 894–897.

35 Gottfried, A. W. Intellectual consequences of perinatal anoxia. *Psychological Bulletin,* 1973, *80,* 231–242.

36 Greenberg, M., and N. Morris. Engrossment: The newborn's impact upon the father. *American Journal of Orthopsychiatry,* 1974, *44,* 520–531.

37 Greenberg, M., I. Rosenberg, and J. Lind. First mothers' rooming-in with their newborns: Its impact upon the mother. *American Journal of Orthopsychiatry,* 1973, *43,* 783–788.

38 Hammond, J. Hearing and response in the newborn. *Developmental Medicine and Child Neurology,* 1970, *12,* 3–5.

39 Harari, J., and J. W. McDavis. Name stereotypes and teachers' expectations. *Journal of Educational Psychology,* 1973, *65,* 222–225.

40 Hardy, J. B. Birth weight and subsequent physical and intellectual development. *New England Journal of Medicine,* 1973, *289,* 973–974.

41 Hartman, A. A., R. C. Nicolay, and J. Hurley. Unique personal names as a social adjustment factor. *Journal of Social Psychology,* 1968, *75,* 107–110.

42 Hillman, R. W., P. Slater, and M. J. Nelson. Season of birth, parental age, menarchial age and body form: Some inter-relationships in young women. *Human Biology,* 1970, *42,* 570–580.

43 Howard, R. G., and A. M. Brown. Twinning: A marker for biological insults. *Child Development,* 1970, *41,* 519–530.

44 Hunt, E. Infant mortality trends and maternal and infant care. *Children,* 1970, *17*(3) 88–90.

45 James, W. *The principles of psychology.* New York: Holt, 1890.

46 Johnson, P. A., and J. R. Staffieri. Stereotypic affective properties of personal names and somatotypes in children. *Developmental Psychology,* 1971, *5,* 176.

47 Kant, I. *Critique of practical reason and other works on the theory of ethics,* 6th ed. London: Longmans, 1963.

48 Kearsley, R. B. The newborn's response to auditory stimuli: A demonstration of orienting and defensive behavior. *Child Development,* 1973, *44,* 582–590.

49 Kennell, J. H., R. Jerauld, H. Wolfe, D. Chesler, N. G. Kreger, W. McAlpine, M. Steffa, and M. H. Klaus. Maternal behavior one year after early and extended postpartum contact. *Developmental Medicine and Child Neurology,* 1974, *16,* 172–179.

50 Kerr, A. S. Month of birth, age, and early school performance. *Educational Research,* 1973, *15,* 232–234.

51 Kessen, W., M. H. Haith, and P. H. Salapatek. Human infancy: A bibliography and guide. In P. H. Mussen (ed.), *Carmichael's manual of child psychology,* 3d ed. New York: Wiley, 1970. Vol. 1, pp. 287–445.

52 Korner, A. F. Sex differences in newborns with special reference to differences in the organization of oral behavior. *Journal of Child Psychology and Psychiatry and Allied Disciplines,* 1973, *14,* 19–29.

53 Korner, A. F., and E. B. Thoman. The relative efficacy of contact and vestibular-proprioceptive stimulation in soothing neonates. *Child Development,* 1972, *43,* 443–453.

54 Kraemer, H. C., A. F. Korner, and E. B. Thoman. Methodological considerations in evaluating the influence of drugs used during labor and delivery on the behavior of the newborn. *Developmental Psychology,* 1972, *6,* 128–134.

55 Lamper, C., and C. Eisdorfer. Prestimulus activity level and responsivity in the neonate. *Child Development,* 1971, *42,* 465–473.

56 Lewis, M. State as an infant-environment interaction: An analysis of mother-infant interaction as a function of sex. *Merrill-Palmer Quarterly,* 1972, *18,* 95–121.

57 Lubchenco, L. O., D. T. Searls, and J. V. Brazie. Neonatal mortality rate: Relationship to birth weight and gestational age. *Journal of Pediatrics,* 1972, *81,* 814–822.

58 Lyle, J. G. Certain antenatal, perinatal and developmental variables and reading retardation in middle-class boys. *Child Development,* 1970, *41,* 481–491.

59 Martindale, C., and F. W. Black. Season of birth and intelligence. *Journal of Genetic Psychology,* 1970, *117,* 137–138.

60 McDavid, J. W., and H. Harari. Stereotyping of names and popularity in grade-school children. *Child Development,* 1966, *37,* 453–459.

61 McDonald, R. L. Lunar and seasonal variations in obstetric factors. *Journal of Genetic Psychology,* 1966, *108,* 81–87.

62 Meredith, H. V. Somatic changes during human postnatal life. *Child Development,* 1975, *46,* 603–610.

63 Meyerowitz, J. H. Satisfaction during pregnancy. *Journal of Marriage and the Family,* 1970, *32,* 38–42.

64 Michaelis, R., A. H. Parmelee, E. Stern, and A. Haber. Activity states in premature and term infants. *Developmental Psychobiology,* 1973, *6,* 209–215.

65 Montagu, A. *The direction of human development,* rev. ed. New York: Hawthorn, 1970.

66 Natelson, S. E., and M. P. Sayers. The fate of children sustaining severe head trauma during birth. *Pediatrics,* 1973, *51,* 169–174.

67 Orme, J. E. Ability and season of birth. *British Journal of Psychology,* 1965, *56,* 471–475.

68 Osofsky, J. D., and B. Danzger. Relationships between neonatal characteristics and mother-infant interaction. *Developmental Psychology,* 1974, *10,* 124–130.

69 Ostwald, P. F., and P. Peltzman. The cry of the human infant. *Scientific American,* 1974, *230* (3), 84–90.

70 Page, E. W., C. A. Villee, and D. B. Villee. *Human reproduction: The core content of obstetrics, gynecology and perinatal medicine.* Philadelphia: Saunders, 1972.

71 Paige, K. E., and J. M. Paige. The politics of birth practices: A strategic analysis. *American Sociological Review,* 1973, *38,* 663–677.

72 Palti, H., and B. Adler. Anthrometric

measurements of the newborn, sex differences and correlations between measurements. *Human Biology*, 1975, *47*, 523–530.

73 Peeples, D. R., and D. Y. Teller. Color vision and brightness discrimination in two-month-old human infants. *Science*, 1975, *189*, 1102–1103.

74 Powell, L. F. The effect of extra stimulation and maternal involvement on the development of low-birth-weight infants and on maternal behavior. *Child Development*, 1974, *45*, 106–113.

75 Rank, O. *The trauma of birth*, New York: Harcourt, Brace & World, 1929.

76 Reid, D. E., K. J. Ryan, and K. Benirschke (eds.) *Principles and management of human reproduction*. Philadelphia: Saunders, 1972.

77 Rich, E. C., R. E. Marshall, and J. J. Volpe. The normal neonatal response to pin prick. *Developmental Medicine and Child Neurology*, 1974, *16*, 432–434.

78 Richman, N. Individual differences at birth. *Developmental Medicine and Child Neurology*, 1972, *14*, 400–402.

79 Rosenblith, J. F. Relations between neonatal behaviors and those at eight months. *Developmental Psychology*, 1974, *10*, 779–792.

80 Rubin, R. A., C. Rosenblatt, and B. Balow. Psychological and educational sequelae of prematurity. *Pediatrics*, 1973, *52*, 352–363.

81 Sagi, A., and M. L. Hoffman. Empathic distress in the newborn. *Developmental Psychology*, 1976, *12*, 175–176.

82 Salk, L. The role of the heartbeat in the relations between mother and infant. *Scientific American*, 1973, *228* (5), 24–29.

83 Sameroff, A. J. Can conditioned responses be established in the newborn infant: 1971? *Developmental Psychology*, 1971, *5*, 1–12.

84 Scarr-Salapatek, S., and M. L. Williams. The effects of early stimula-

tion on low-birth-weight infants. *Child Development*, 1973, *44*, 94–101.

85 Scheinfeld, A. *Twins and supertwins*. Philadelphia: Lippincott, 1967.

86 Schonberg, W. B., and M. Murphy. The relationship between the uniqueness of a given name and personality. *Journal of Social Psychology*, 1974, *93*, 147–148.

87 Self, P. A., D. D. Horowitz, and L. Y. Paden. Olfaction in newborn infants. *Developmental Psychology*, 1972, *7*, 349–363.

88 Sigman, M., C. B. Kopp, A. H. Parmelee, and W. E. Jeffrey. Visual attention and neurological organization in neonates. *Child Development*, 1973, *44*, 461–466.

89 Simner, M. L. Newborn's response to the cry of another infant. *Developmental Psychology*, 1971, *5*, 136–150.

90 Solkoff, N., S. Yaffe, D. Weintraub, and B. Blase. Effects of handling on the subsequent developments of premature infants. *Developmental Psychology*, 1969, *1*, 765–768.

91 Sontag, L. W. Implications of infant behavior and environment for adult personalities. *Annals of the New York Academy of Sciences*, 1966, *132*, 782–786.

92 Sostek, A. M., A. J. Sameroff, and A. J. Sostek. Evidence for the unconditionability of the Babkin reflex in newborns. *Child Development*, 1972, *43*, 509–519.

93 Stone, L. J., and J. Church. *Childhood and adolescence: A psychology of the growing person*, 3d ed. New York: Random House, 1973.

94 Stone, L. J., H. T. Smith, and L. B. Murphy (eds.). *The competent infant: Research and commentary*. New York: Basic Books, 1975.

95 Stratton, P. M., and K. Connolly. Discrimination by newborns of the intensity, frequency and temporal characteristics of auditory stimuli. *British Journal of Psychology*, 1973, *64*, 219–232.

96 Tanner, J. M. Growing up. *Scientific American*, 1973, *229*(3), 35–43.

97 Tantermannová, M. Smiling in infants. *Child Development*, 1973, *44*, 701–704.

98 Taub, H. B., D. V. Caputo, and K. M. Goldstein. Toward a modification of the indices of neonatal prematurity. *Perceptual and Motor Skills*, 1975, *40*, 43–48.

99 Thoman, E. B., P. H. Leiderman, and J. Polsen. Neonate-mother interaction during breast feeding. *Developmental Psychology*, 1972, *6*, 110–118.

100 Thomas, A., S. Chess, and H. G. Birch. The origin of personality. *Scientific American*, 1970, *223* (2), 102–109.

101 Turkewitz, G., H. G. Birch, and K. K. Cooper. Responsiveness to simple and complex auditory stimuli in the human newborn. *Developmental Psychology*, 1972, *5*, 7–19.

102 Turkewitz, G., and S. Creighton. Changes in lateral differentiation of head posture in the human neonate. *Developmental Psychobiology*, 1975, *8*, 85–89.

103 Wachs, T. D., and P. Cucinotta. The effects of enriched neonatal experiences upon later cognitive functioning. *Developmental Psychology*, 1971, *5*, 542.

104 Wilson, G. S., M. M. Desmond, and W. M. Verniaud. Early development of infants of heroin-addicted mothers. *American Journal of Diseases of Children*, 1973, *126*, 457–462.

105 Yang, R. K., and T. C. Douthitt. Newborn responses to threshold tactile stimulation. *Child Development*, 1974, *45*, 237–242.

106 Yarrow, L. J., J. L. Rubenstein, F. A. Pedersen, and J. J. Jankowski. Dimensions of early stimulation and their differential effects on infant development. *Merrill-Palmer Quarterly*, 1972, *18*, 205–218.

107 Zelazo, P. R., N. A. Zelazo, and S. Kolb. "Walking" in the newborn. *Science*, 1972, *176*, 314–315.

CHAPTER 5

PHYSICAL DEVELOPMENT

To get a complete picture of children's development, it is essential to know how they develop physically as well as psychologically. The reason for this is that physical development influences children's behavior both directly and indirectly. *Directly,* physical development determines what children can do. If, for example, children are well developed for their ages, they will be able to compete on equal terms with their peers in games and sports. If not, they will be handicapped in competition with them and may be excluded from the peer group.

Indirectly, physical development influences attitudes toward self and others. These, in turn, are reflected in the kind of adjustments children make. Children who are markedly overweight, for example, soon discover that they cannot keep up to the pace set by their thinner age-mates. This often leads to feelings of personal inadequacy. If, in addition, their age-mates refuse to play with them because they are "too slow" or ridicule them because they are "fatties," feelings of martyrdom will be added to feelings of inadequacy. These feelings will play havoc with children's developing personalities.

Trying to give a complete picture of a child's physical development in one chapter would be impossible. Therefore, only those aspects of physical development that have an influence on the child's personal and social adjustments will be touched upon in this chapter. In discussing each, an explanation will be given as to how it affects the child's personal and social adjustments.

BOX 5–1

COMMON EFFECTS OF GROWTH CYCLES

ADJUSTMENT DIFFICULTIES
During periods of rapid growth, the constant need to make new adjustments can be emotionally disturbing. During periods of slow growth, adjustments are much easier.

ENERGY LEVEL
Rapid growth is energy-consuming with the result that children are easily fatigued. This makes them moody and irritable. A slow growth cycle leaves more energy for play and other activities. Children are then more cheerful and easier to live with.

NUTRITIONAL NEEDS
Nutritional requirements are greatest during periods of rapid growth—the first 2 or 3 months of life and at puberty. Children who are not getting enough nourishment of the right kind for their growth needs become tired and irritable. They show little interest in schoolwork or play and generally make poor social adjustments.

MAINTENANCE OF HOMEOSTASIS
During periods of slow growth, the body normally can maintain homeostasis. During rapid growth, homeostasis is disturbed; this is reflected in a finicky appetite, general fatigue, irritablity, and unsocial behavior.

AWKWARDNESS
Rapid growth is almost always accompanied by awkwardness. Children who formerly had good coordination become clumsy and seem to stumble over their own feet. When growth slows down, the awkwardness is replaced by good motor coordination.

Physical Growth Cycles

The term "cycles" means that physical growth does not occur at a regular rate but rather in periods, phases, or "waves" of different velocities, sometimes rapidly and sometimes slowly. If, for example, growth in weight continued at the same rate as during the first year of life, when it normally triples, it would mean that a person who weighed 7 pounds at birth would, at the age of 11 years, weigh 1,240,029 pounds.

Growth cycles are orderly and predictable, though the tempo varies from child to child, with some children growing at a slow rate and others at a normal or rapid rate. However, each child is fairly consistent, showing a constant tendency toward earliness or lateness in reaching critical points in development.

Growth cycles are psychologically as well as physically important because they inevitably affect the child's behavior. Box 5–1 lists the effects that are most common and most difficult to adjust to.

Major Growth Cycles

Studies of growth have shown that there are four distinct periods, two characterized by slow growth and two by rapid growth. During the prenatal period and for the first 6 months of postnatal life, growth is at a rapid rate. By the end of the first postnatal year, growth begins to slow down and is followed by a period of slow and relatively even growth up to the time of puberty, or sexual maturing. This may begin at any time between the eighth and twelfth years.

From then until 15 or 16 years there is rapid growth—usually called the "puberty growth spurt." This is followed by a period of fairly abrupt tapering off to the time of maturity. The height attained in this fourth growth cycle is maintained until old age, but there may be an increase in weight (58, 81).

Variations in Growth Cycles

In spite of the fact that growth cycles are orderly and predictable, they are subject to variations. As Johnston et al. have pointed out, "The time clock which governs the developmental process in children is an individual one" (36).

A number of factors determine whether that time clock will run fast, slow, or at a moderate rate. Children with a Negro *racial* background tend to grow at a slower rate than those with a white background. This difference may, however, be due to differences in nutrition and general health (44, 52, 54).

Genetic *body size* and *build* also influence rates of growth with those of large, heavy builds growing faster

than those of small and slight build. They usually reach the puberty growth spurt sooner than children of smaller builds (81). Good *health* and *nutrition,* especially during the early growth period, speed up the growth cycles while poor health and nutrition slow them down (52). Children who are *immunized* against disease during the early growth period continue to grow faster than those who have not been immunized because they suffer from fewer diseases and are generally healthier (90).

Placid children tend to grow faster than those who experience *emotional tension,* though tension has a greater effect on weight than on height (19). There are *seasonal* variations in growth with July to mid-December most favorable for growth in weight and April to mid-August for growth in height (55).

Children of *multiple birth* tend to grow at a slower rate than singletons. This is especially true of those who are smallest at birth. Even in a pair of twins, the smaller one at birth grows more slowly than the larger one (4, 5).

The most pronounced variations are due to *sex,* with boys growing faster than girls at certain ages and girls faster than boys at other ages. From about 9 to 10 to 13 or 14 years of age, for example, girls are taller and heav-

Figure 5–1. Changes in body size and proportions of one boy and one girl observed between the ages of 15 months and 18 years. (*Adapted from N. Bayley: Individual patterns of development.* Child Development, *1956, 27, 45–74. Used by permission.*)

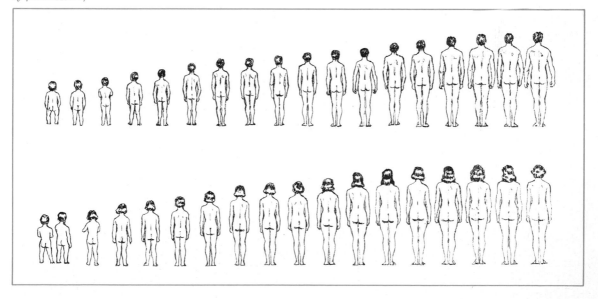

ier than boys because of their early pubertal development. Variability within the sex group is usually greater among boys, though variability in growth rates for both sexes increases with age (6, 34, 44, 58, 71). Characteristic patterns of growth for the two sexes are shown in Figure 5–1.

Body Size

Body size is controlled by hereditary and environmental influences. The *hereditary* control comes from the growth hormone secreted by the anterior lobe of the pituitary gland—a small gland located at the base of the brain. If growth is to proceed normally, the hormone must be produced in the right amounts and at the right times. If too little is produced, growth ceases earlier than normal. If too much is produced, overgrowth results.

Whether the growth hormone will be produced in the right amounts and at the right times depends not upon the pituitary gland alone but also upon the thyroid glands and gonads. At puberty, for example, the hormones produced in the gonads—*estrogen* in the female and *androgen* in the male—act as retarding influences on growth. These hormones stimulate the deposition of calcium, which causes the bones to harden and bring about the closure of the epiphyses of the bones. When this happens, growth is gradually brought to a halt.

Environmental control of body size comes from conditions in the prenatal environment as well as conditions in the postnatal environment. As was explained earlier (see pages 68–69 and Figure 3–9), malnutrition, excessive smoking, maternal stress, and many other conditions that affect the prenatal environment affect the size of the infant, and this effect continues to influence the child's ultimate size. Many conditions in the postnatal environment likewise affect the size of the child and are responsible for the variations in size among children of the same age that are apparent as childhood progresses. Refer to Box 5–2 for some of the most common of these environmental conditions that affect body size in childhood, as well as those that are hereditary in nature.

Body size is measured in terms of height and weight. While height and weight follow similar patterns of development—with slow gains in one paralleled by slow gains in the other, and vice versa—the total growth in height from birth to maturity is less than the total growth in weight. The total increase in height is approximately 3½-fold and the total increase in weight is approximately 20-fold (44). Increases in the body size for boys and girls at different ages are shown in Figure 5–1.

Height

Children of the same age vary greatly in height, but the pattern of growth is similar for all. Expressed in terms of averages, the pattern gives a picture of the growth of the typical child. The neonate measures between 17 and 21 inches. For 2 years, height increases rapidly. At 4 months, the baby measures 23 to 24 inches; at 8 months, 26 to 28 inches; and at 1 year, 28 to 30 inches. At 2 years, the child is 32 to 34 inches tall, and by 5 years, birth height has doubled. Then there is a slow gain of approximately 3 inches annually until the onset of the puberty growth spurt.

At 11 years of age, when the average American girl begins her puberty growth spurt, she is 58 inches tall. By the time she is sexually mature, at 13 years, she is 63 inches tall, and at 18 years, when her growth in height is complete, she measures 66 inches.

Boys begin the puberty growth spurt approximately a year later than girls. So the average American boy is from ½ to 1 inch shorter than the average girl at 13 years of age. From then on, however, boys grow more rapidly than girls and continue to grow approximately a year longer. At maturity they are taller than girls. At 13, the average boy measures 62 inches. A year later, when he becomes sexually mature, he measures 65 inches; at 18 years, he measures 69.5 inches. Between 18 and 20, he may add another half inch or even an inch (58,81). The difference in height between the sexes after the puberty growth spurt is shown in Figure 5–2.

Weight

While the average newborn weighs between 6 and 8 pounds, some weigh only 3 or 4 pounds, and some few nearly 16. The pattern of increase, however, is much the same for all. By the end of the first month, the average baby not only has regained the weight lost after birth but has begun to show a weight increase. At 4 months, the baby has doubled its birth weight and, at the end of the first year, trebled it. During the second and third years, the child gains from 3 to 5 pounds annually. The pattern of weight gain is shown in Figure 5–3.

After the third year, gains in weight are even slower, until the onset of puberty. At 5 years, the typical child weighs approximately five times birth weight, and at the onset of puberty weighs between 80 and 90 pounds. By the age of 15, the average girl weighs 126.5 pounds. The average weight for boys at 12 years, when they begin their puberty growth spurt, is 96 pounds and, at 16, when the spurt is nearly complete, 142 pounds (44, 54, 81).

Between 10 and 12 years, at or near the onset of the growth spurt, many children have a *puberty fat period*. Sometimes this period lasts for 2 years, until the child becomes sexually mature. Part of the fat comes from hormone dislocations, which occur with the onset of sexual maturing, and part from overeating, which is stimulated by rapid physical growth. The pubescent child is not fat all over. Rather, fat accumulates over the abdomen, around the nipples, in the hips and thighs, and in the neck, jaws, and cheeks. These are conspicuous areas, and the child has a "fat look" (58, 71, 81, 82).

In babyhood, most of the weight gain comes from an increase in fat tissue, owing to the high content of fat in milk, the chief component of the baby's diet. As childhood progresses, body weight comes more from bone and muscle tissue than from fat tissue. In the

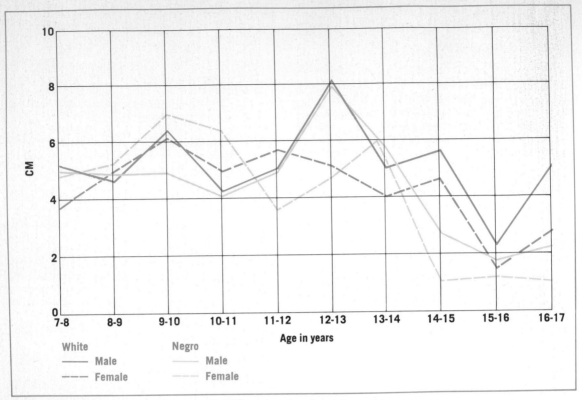

Figure 5–2. Growth in height during late childhood and early adolescence. Note the slow rate of growth in childhood and the rapid rate at puberty. (*Adapted from W. M. Krogman: Growth of head, face, trunk, and limbs in Philadelphia white and Negro children of elementary and high school age.* Monographs of the Society for Research in Child Development, *1970, 35, no. 3. Used by permission.*)

latter part of childhood, for example, fat tissue is responsible for only 21 to 29 percent of total weight.

During puberty, the bones of the body increase in length. Shortly afterward, they begin to harden, or ossify, and the muscle tissue begins to increase. Both add to the child's weight. In the latter part of childhood, the muscles make up approximately one-fourth of the body weight. At sexual maturity, they make up approximately 45 percent of total weight (58, 71, 82).

Psychological Significance of Body Size

The psychological importance of body size to children depends on how others, especially peers, react to their size. Most children are not body-size conscious except when there is a marked deviation from the norm. Being slightly shorter than other children does not affect children's popularity. However, because of the prestige and respect associated with tallness, being slightly taller than other members of the peer group is a social asset (34, 46, 71).

While peer reactions to their body size play a more important role than adult reactions, children are not unaffected by adult reactions. However, if parents are concerned about their children's being too short or too thin and if they constantly urge them to eat more than they want so that they will "grow bigger," children are likely to become concerned and wonder if there is something wrong with them.

Because deviations in weight are far more common than deviations in height, they have a greater psychological impact on the child than do deviations in height. Most often deviations in weight are on the plus side. The majority of excessively fat children become aware, even before they enter school, of how others feel about their obesity. They know that adults feel sorry for them and that peers regard them as slow and clumsy. Obese children often develop severe feelings of personal inadequacy. They may compensate by eating even more than before, thus becoming fatter and even less acceptable to their peers.

Body Proportions

The proportions of the neonate's body are quite different from those of the adult's body. Refer to Figure 2–2. Growth, therefore, results not only in an increase in size but, of equal importance, in changes in body proportions. While not all parts of the body attain mature proportions at the same time, all, on the whole, have done so by the time the individual is 16 or 17 years old. Figure 5–4 shows changes in body proportions and the ages at which these changes usually occur.

In general, changes in proportions follow the laws of developmental direction (discussed in Chapter 2). The changes are relatively slight during the first half year of postnatal life. From then until puberty, head growth is slow, limb growth rapid, and trunk growth intermediate. The brain and facial features attain maturity in size and development before the organs and features of the trunk and limbs.

Conditions Responsible for Changes in Body Proportions

Changes in body proportions are due to *asynchronous growth,* or "split growth" (80). This means that the different parts of the body have their own periods of rapid and slow growth and that each reaches its mature size

Figure 5–3. Growth in weight during late childhood and early adolescence. (*Adapted from W. M. Krogman: Growth of head, face, trunk, and limbs in Philadelphia white and Negro children of elementary and high school age.* Monographs of the Society for Research in Child Development, *1970, 35, no. 3. Used by permission.*)

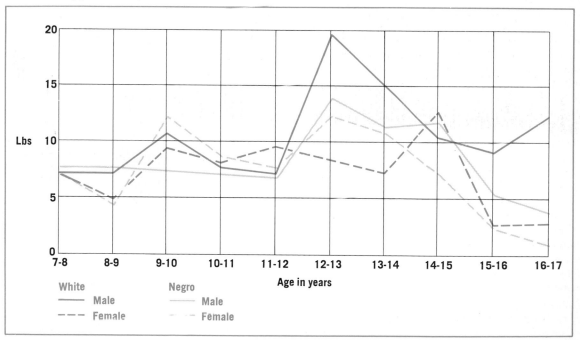

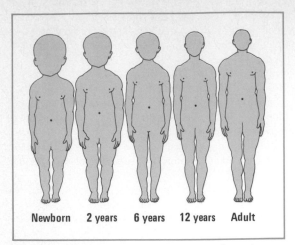

Figure 5–4. Changes in body proportions from birth to adulthood. (*Adapted from H. Nash: Ascription of maturity to human figure drawings by preschool children.* Journal of Genetic Psychology, *1973,* 122, *319–328. Used by permission.*)

Newborn   2 years   6 years   12 years   Adult

at its own time. Growth in all parts of the body, however, is continuous and concurrent. A child's brain, for example, does not stop growing while the muscles, lungs, and bones are growing.

Growth curves for height and weight show that, except during the first year of life, children grow more rapidly in height than in weight. To express this relationship, Krogman has suggested a simple rule: "Children grow tall before they grow heavy" (44). In the latter part of childhood, the extremities grow faster than the trunk, and the child seems to be all arms and legs.

Asynchrony is especially apparent when different regions of the body are compared. The adult head, for example, is twice its birth size; the trunk is three times its birth size; and the arms and legs are, respectively, four and five times their birth length. The muscles, bones, lungs, and genitals increase approximately twenty times in size during the growth years, while the eyes, brain, and some other organs which are relatively more developed at birth increase much less. The eyeball completes most of its growth during the first 5 years of life and the brain during the first 10. The heart and some other internal organs require more than 20 years to complete their growth.

Variations in Changes in Body Proportions

Even though there is an orderly and predictable pattern for the changes that take place in body proportions throughout the growth years, there are variations in this pattern. That is why children become increasingly dissimilar in appearance with each passing year. Newborn infants, for example, have very similar body proportions. They all have large heads, small arms and legs, and trunks that are baglike in shape. By the time they reach adulthood, when their growth has been completed, they differ not only in size but also in body proportions. Some have large heads for their bodies and some small heads; some are long-legged and some short-legged.

In spite of the variations, children as well as adults can be divided roughly into three general types of body build, determined by the relative proportions of the different parts of their bodies. These three types of body build are the *endomorphic* build which tends to be round and fat; the *mesomorphic* build which tends to be heavy, hard, and rectangular; and the *ectomorphic* build which tends to be long and slender. Very few children, as is true of adults, conform completely to these types of body build though most show a tendency to have body builds with the characteristic features of one of the three types. Figure 5–5 shows the

Figure 5–5. Types of body build in children.

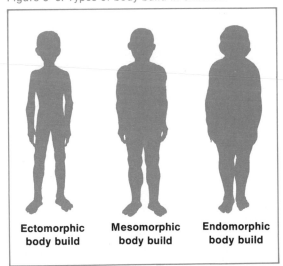

Ectomorphic   Mesomorphic   Endomorphic
body build   body build   body build

typical body build of the endomorph, the mesomorph, and the ectomorph.

There are only slight *sex* differences in body build during the early years of childhood. As children approach the age when puberty changes occur, in the closing years of childhood, sex differences begin to be more and more apparent. Boys, as a group, show a greater tendency to have mesomorphic builds than girls while girls tend to have either ectomorphic or endomorphic builds. Within each sex group, however, there are variations even when the puberty changes have taken place. Some boys have endomorphic or ectomorphic builds, just as some girls have mesomorphic builds.

Racial differences in body build are not only greater than sex differences but they begin to appear earlier. Studies of the body builds of white and black children, for example, have shown that they not only differ as groups, in height and weight, but also in body proportions. These differences begin to appear during the second year of life (52, 54).

From a nationwide survey of white and black children, 6 through 11 years, Malina et al. have concluded (54):

The major anthrometric differences between Negro and white children are differences in the proportions of the trunk and limbs. Negro children, on the average, have shorter trunks, more slender hips and chests, longer lower extremities (especially longer lower legs), and longer upper extremities (especially longer forearms and hands) than white children. White children, conversely, tend to have longer, thicker trunks, wider hips, and shorter lower and upper extremities than Negro children.

Consequences of Changes in Body Proportions

The changes in the body proportions that take place during the growth years have a marked influence on children's behavior, their personalities, and the reactions of other people toward them—reactions that affect their attitudes toward themselves. Of the many consequences of the changes in body proportions throughout the childhood years, five are almost universal. They affect children both directly and indirectly. These five consequences are explained in Box 5 3.

BOX 5–3

IMPORTANT CONSEQUENCES OF CHANGES IN BODY PROPORTIONS

AWKWARDNESS
When body proportions change, especially when the change is rapid, children temporarily lose control over their bodies. This is especially true at puberty when the short, childish hand suddenly becomes large and the small feet of childhood are replaced by the large feet of an adult.

ATTRACTIVENESS
Because attractiveness is judged by adult standards, most children create the impression of being homely. Too large teeth for a small nose and lips create the impression that the face is homely while long, spindly arms and legs give children a coltlike appearance.

SOCIAL ATTITUDES
Children who are unattractive looking because of facial or bodily disproportions elicit less favorable reactions from others, especially adults, than they would if their faces and bodies were less disproportionate. These unfavorable reactions are often interpreted by children to mean social rejection.

CONCERN ABOUT BODY DISPROPORTIONS
Sensing unfavorable social attitudes toward their homeliness and awkwardness, children become concerned about their body disproportions. This is especially true during the early part of puberty when body disproportions are normally at their peak. Children are also concerned when their body disproportions differ from those of their age-mates, as is true of early and late maturers.

MATURITY STATUS
Children who are overweight create the impression that they are younger than they actually are because fat gives them a "babyish" look. Lean, long-legged children create the impression that they are older than they actually are and, as a result, more is expected of them than they may be developmentally capable of. When people respond to children as exceptionally mature or immature, it is likely to influence children's self-concepts.

Bones

Bone development consists of growth in bone size, change in the number of bones, and change in their composition. It follows the same general trend as growth in size; that is, bone development is most rapid during the first year of life, then relatively slow up to the time of puberty, and then once again more rapid.

Bones grow in length at the ends, the *epiphyses,* where a strip of cartilage separates the bone shaft, or *diaphysis,* from other bony masses. The original cartilage at the epiphyses is gradually converted into bone, and as long as the epiphysis and the diaphysis do not fuse, the bone will continue to grow. Stimulation by the sex hormone at puberty is responsible for the fusion of the two portions and, ultimately, the limitation of growth. Bones grow in width by adding new bone tissue at their outer edges (36, 44, 71, 81).

Ossification

Ossification, or hardening of the bones, is mainly postnatal, beginning in the early part of the first year and ending during puberty. The process begins at the "ossification center" in the cartilage and gradually spreads throughout the bone. When the process is finished, each bone has its characteristic shape.

Ossification proceeds at different rates for different parts of the body. The fontanels, or "soft spots" of the cranium, for example, are closed in over 50 percent of all babies by the age of 18 months and in nearly all by 2 years. Ossification of the long bones of the legs, on the other hand, does not occur until puberty.

Ossification is largely dependent upon the secretion of a hormone from the thyroid glands. A deficiency of this hormone will delay ossification. There is also a close relationship between ossification and nutrition. A dietary deficiency may mean inadequate mineralization and delayed ossification. The child may then have bowed legs and other skeletal deformities because the bones are not hard enough to withstand the pressure from the weight of the body (26, 49, 54, 71).

Importance of Ossification

Because the bones of babies are soft, they can be easily deformed. The shape of the head, for example, can be flattened if babies spend most of their sleep time on their backs, or the chest can be flattened if they sleep too long on their stomachs. Even in the elementary school years, bone deformities can result from too short shoes or from sitting in a cramped position at a school desk.

Psychologically, ossification is important because it affects children's appearances and this is one of the important bases on which others judge them. Should their heads become flattened, for example, because they were permitted to sleep mainly on their backs during babyhood, they may be judged as less attractive than their facial features would justify.

Furthermore, because bones in childhood are less subject to fractures or breaks than they will be after ossification, the physical and psychological hazards of accidents are less serious than they will be later. These hazards are discussed in detail under the heading "Hazards in Physical Development."

Muscles and Fat

Besides the weight contributed by the bones, increase in body weight comes mainly from *muscle* and *adipose,* or fatty, *tissue.* In the early years of childhood, adipose tissue develops more rapidly than muscle. From the ages of 12 to 15 in girls and 15 to 16 in boys, there is a marked increase in muscle tissue. What proportion of the child's body weight will come from muscle and what from adipose tissue will depend largely upon body type.

Children who tend toward *endomorphy* have more soft adipose tissue than muscular tissue. Those who tend toward *mesomorphy* have a predominance of muscle and connective tissue. And those who incline toward *ectomorphy* do not have a predominance of either: the muscles are slender, and the adipose tissue is minimal.

At birth, *muscle* fibers are present, but undeveloped. After birth, they change in size, shape, and composition. The muscle fibers grow in length, breadth, and thickness. At maturity, the muscles are at least five times as thick as at birth.

For the average person, muscle weight increases fortyfold from birth to maturity. Up to 5 years of age, the muscles grow in proportion to the increase in body weight. Then, from 5 to 6 years, comes a rapid spurt in muscle growth, at which time the child's weight gain is approximately 75 percent muscle weight. After this, muscle growth slows, to be followed by a marked spurt at puberty.

Children who have broad, thick muscles have superior physical strength; those with smaller muscles are usually more agile and show better coordination in skilled activities. Some children have muscles that fatigue easily; others have muscles that show great endurance (26, 36, 81).

The amount of *adipose* tissue children have depends not only on their hereditary endowments and body builds but also on their eating habits. It is also related to their ages. There are three critical periods of fat cell development. The first comes during the last 3 months of prenatal life; the second during the first 2 to 3 years of postnatal life; and the third, between 11 and 13 years—the "puberty fat period." Overeating or a diet high in carbohydrates at these critical ages will result in a too rapid development of fat cells. Once formed, they are there forever and make reducing difficult if not impossible (29, 36, 44).

Among children over 13 years of age, sex differences in the amount of adipose tissue become increasingly great. Differences are also associated with socioeconomic status. Children from the upper socioeconomic groups tend to have greater amounts of muscle and of subcutaneous fat from 8 through 11 years of age, and they tend to be heavier than children from lower socioeconomic groups (30, 36).

Effects of Fat-Muscle Ratio

The relative amounts of adipose tissue and muscles affect children both directly and indirectly. *Directly,* they influence the type and quality of children's behavior. Children with a predominance of muscle tissue have the physique to excel in sports and games. This raises their prestige in the eyes of their peers. By contrast, excessively fat children tend to be poor in sports and to be be excluded from peer activities.

The *indirect* effect of the fat-muscle ratio comes from children's reactions to their body builds. This is greatly influenced by knowledge of how others react to different body builds. As early as kindergarten age, it has been reported that many children realize that a mesomorphic build is more favorably judged than an ectomorphic or an endomorphic build. In fact, they learn that there is a cultural aversion to a child who is a "chubby"—a fact that they have learned from comments others make about fat children and from the way fat children are treated by their peers (40, 47, 77). Even a preschooler who tends to be chubby develops

a strong motivation to develop a mesomorphic build with big muscles.

By the time they are 7 or 8, most children can type themselves (77). They are also aware of the popular stereotypes associated with different body builds. For example, they know that a fat person is thought of as lazy and stupid, that the thin and lanky person is regarded as a "brain," and that the muscular person is assumed to be an athlete (9, 41, 46).

Teeth

The growth of teeth is a continuous process from the third prenatal month, when the teeth begin to form in the jaw, until 21 to 25 years of age, when the last of the permanent teeth, the wisdom teeth, reach their full size. During this time, the child develops two sets of teeth—the baby or temporary teeth and the permanent teeth.

Ordinarily, the first *temporary* tooth cuts through the baby's gum between the sixth and eighth months, but the time of eruption depends upon health, heredity, nutrition before and after birth, race, sex, and other factors. By 9 months, the average baby has three teeth. Between 2 and 2$\frac{1}{2}$ years of age, most young children have all 20 of their baby teeth.

The *sequence* of eruption of the temporary teeth is more important than the age of eruption. The lower teeth, as a rule, appear before the upper. Irregularity in the sequence of eruption is likely to throw the jaws out of position and result in malocclusion, or poor alignment of the teeth. This may permanently affect the shape of the lower part of the face and cause the permanent teeth to be out of line.

After the temporary teeth have erupted, much activity goes on inside the gums as the *permanent* teeth begin to calcify. The order of calcifying is the same as the later order of eruption. On the average, the child at 6 years of age has 1 or 2 permanent teeth; at 10 years, 14 to 16; and at 13 years, 27 or 28. The last four of the permanent teeth, the wisdom teeth, erupt between the ages of 17 and 25 years, if they appear at all.

Psychological Importance of Teeth

Most people think only of the health factor of teeth—preventing them from becoming carious or so decayed that they must be removed. Some parents are

PSYCHOLOGICAL SIGNIFICANCE OF TEETH

EFFECT ON EMOTIONS
The physical discomfort accompanying the cutting of temporary teeth is partially responsible for the heightened emotionality characteristic of the second and third years of life. This is true also of permanent teeth that erupt in areas of the gums where there were no temporary teeth.

DISTURBANCE IN BODY EQUILIBRIUM
Pain and discomfort from teething and poisons thrown into the blood stream from carious teeth upset body equilibrium. This is often responsible for retardation in normal growth and for eating, sleeping, and other behavior problems.

INSIGNIA OF MATURITY
Permanent teeth are psychologically important as an indication to others that children are leaving babyhood behind and are reaching a new level of maturity.

EFFECT ON APPEARANCE
If the child pulls out a loose baby tooth—hoping to speed up the insignia of maturity in this way—the interval before the permanent tooth erupts may be long enough for the gum to shrink and cause the permanent tooth to come in crooked. This may not disturb young children but it will when they reach the appearance–conscious age of adolescence. In addition, small baby teeth, side by side with large permanent teeth, give the child's face a comical look.

EFFECT ON SPEECH
Before the permanent teeth erupt, there is normally a gap where the baby teeth have fallen out. Few children go through this transition without lisping—the softening of harsh sounds. If the period of transition is lengthened by premature pulling of baby teeth, the longer the period of lisping and the greater the likelihood that it will persist even when the permanent teeth erupt.

also fail to realize that teeth are likely to have a long-lasting impact on children's behavior and on their self-concepts. Box 5–4 explains what forms this impact takes.

Development of the Nervous System

The growth of the nervous system is very rapid before birth and in the first 3 to 4 years after birth. Growth during the prenatal period consists primarily of an increase in the number and size of *nerve cells*. Later growth consists primarily of the development of immature cells present at birth. After the age of 3 or 4, growth of the nervous system proceeds at a relatively slow rate.

At birth, brain weight is one-eighth of total weight; at 10 years, one-eighteenth; at 15 years, one-thirtieth; and at maturity, one-fortieth. This pattern is characteristic of the growth of both the *cerebrum* and the *cerebellum*. The rate of gain in weight of both is greatest during the first 2 years of life. The cerebellum, which plays an important role in body balance and postural control, triples its weight during the first year of postnatal life. By the eighth year, the brain is nearly mature in size, but the development of intercerebral association tracts and the building up of gray matter are hardly complete. Growth is thus internal and cannot be measured in terms of size or weight (26, 81).

Growth and development of the brain and nervous system affect all aspects of the child's development. The areas in which the effects are most pronounced are explained in Box 5–5.

Puberty Changes

Before childhood comes to an end, the physical changes that transform a child into a sexually mature adult begin. The time of these changes is *puberty*—from the Latin word *pubertas*, meaning "age of manhood." Contrary to popular belief, the transformation is not quick or easy. It takes, on the average, from 2 to 4 years. Approximately one-half of puberty overlaps the last part of childhood, and approximately one-half overlaps the early part of adolescence. These two parts of puberty are called "preadolescence" and "early adolescence." In preadolescence, the child is not, strictly speaking, a child, nor is he an adolescent.

concerned if the teeth are so crooked as to make the child homely or if the upper and lower jaws are so out of line that it will distort the lower part of the child's face or lead to digestive disturbance because of inability to chew food properly.

Few people think of the psychological significance of teeth. They fail to realize that children's teeth are important to them for other than physical reasons. They

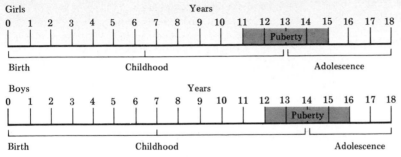

Figure 5–6. Puberty overlaps the end of childhood and the beginning of adolescence.

He is often referred to as a "pubescent child." Figure 5–6 shows the overlap of puberty, childhood, and adolescence.

When the sex organs begin to function, childhood comes to an end and adolescence begins. Girls become sexually mature at about 13 years, when the first menstruation—the *menarche*—occurs. From 11 to 13, many physical changes take place. After the menarche, other changes occur, and those begun earlier are completed. Boys reach sexual maturity—as indicated by the first nocturnal emission—at an average age of 14 years. Puberty changes begin between the ages of 12 and 14 in boys and are completed by 16 or 17 (53, 82).

Cause of Puberty Changes

Until the turn of the century, the cause of puberty changes was a mystery. Today it is known that they are caused by an increase in the activity of two glands of the endocrine system, the pituitary gland and the gonads. The *pituitary* gland, located at the base of the brain, produces two hormones closely associated with puberty changes: the *growth hormone,* which is responsible for growth in body size, and the *gonadotropic*—or "gonad-stimulating"—*hormone,* which stimulates the gonads to greater activity. Shortly before puberty begins, there is a gradual increase in the production of these two hormones; the increase becomes greater as puberty progresses. The whole process is controlled by the endocrine changes which are initiated by the *hypothalmus,* centered in the middle of the brain, which is known as the "trigger-mechanism" for puberty (82).

While the *gonads,* or sex glands, are present and active at birth, their activity is increased at puberty by the gonadotropic hormone from the pituitary gland. This

---

BOX 5–5

SOME IMPORTANT EFFECTS OF NEUROLOGICAL DEVELOPMENT

EFFECT ON BODY PROPORTIONS
The rapid growth in the size of the brain during the early years is one of the causes of the top-heavy look of the young child. Top-heaviness is further accentuated as the child's trunk and extremities elongate and become slender. Spindly, top-heavy children are far less appealing to others than they were when they were chubby babies. This affects the way others treat them.

EFFECT ON LOOKS
Because the face remains small and the features undeveloped until puberty, the brain region of the head becomes increasingly too large for the rest of the body. Furthermore, as permanent teeth come through the gums, this adds to the unattractiveness of the child's face. The "pretty" baby becomes a homely child.

EFFECT ON HELPLESSNESS
Because the cerebrum is responsible for control of mental functions and the cerebellum for postural control and balance, rapid growth in both of these areas of the brain makes it possible for the baby to shift from a state of complete helplessness to relative independence within the first 2 years of postnatal life. This matter will be discussed in detail in the following chapter.

EFFECT ON MENTAL CAPACITIES
With rapid growth and development of the cortical tissues of the cerebrum come rapid changes in mental abilities. The abilities to remember, to attach meanings to people and objects, and to reason show marked increases with every passing year throughout childhood. This enables the child to make better personal and social adjustments.

MAJOR PHYSICAL CHANGES AT PUBERTY

CHANGES IN BODY SIZE

Growth rate increases suddenly about 2 years before sexual maturing. In the year preceding sexual maturing—the "apex" of the puberty growth spurt—the child may grow 4 to 6 inches and gain 10 to 20 pounds. After sexual maturity, growth continues, but at a slower pace. During the entire 4-year growth spurt, height increases about 25 percent and weight almost doubles. Boys continue to grow more rapidly than girls, reaching their adult size at about 19 or 20, as compared with 18 for girls.

CHANGES IN BODY PROPORTIONS

The body disproportions characteristic of the child increase in certain areas and decrease in others. Not until puberty is completed will all parts of the body be mature, and hence in adult proportions. Changes occur inside the body as well as on the surface. In childhood, for example, the heart is small, while the veins and arteries are large. After puberty, the reverse is true.

PRIMARY SEX CHARACTERISTICS

The sex organs—the primary sex characteristics—are small and functionally immature in childhood. At the onset of puberty they begin to enlarge. Ordinarily, the *testes* are ready to function at the age of 14. The *ovaries* begin to function at the menarche—the first menstrual period—about age 13. Other parts of the female reproductive apparatus develop more slowly and are not ready for childbearing for several months or a year or more. This interval is the period of "adolescent sterility."

SECONDARY SEX CHARACTERISTICS

The secondary sex characteristics are those physical features which distinguish the male from the female body. They are indirectly related to reproduction in that they make members of one sex attractive to members of the other. They develop concurrently with the primary sex characteristics and reach maturity during the first year or two of adolescence. They include the growth of hair on the face and body, the development of the female breasts and hips, the change in voice, increased muscular development, and the change in skin texture.

results in marked physical as well as psychological and behavioral changes in the child. Shortly after sexual maturity, hormones from the gonads stop the activity of the growth hormone; this ends physical growth. A proper balance in the interrelationship between the pituitary gland and the gonads leads to normal physical development. An imbalance, on the other hand, results in deviations.

During puberty, the entire body goes through a metamorphosis, both externally and internally, in structure as well as in function. For the most part, the changes follow a predictable timetable. The changes are most rapid and most pronounced during the early part of puberty. In Box 5–6 are shown the important physical changes that occur during puberty.

Variations in Age of Puberty

Not all children experience puberty at the same time, nor do they complete it at the same rate. These variations are responsible for many of the emotional, social, and personality problems characteristically associated with puberty.

Children who begin the transformation process a year or more ahead of the normal time for their sex group are "early maturers"; those who begin a year or more later are "late maturers." They are popularly known as "early bloomers" and "late bloomers." Some children seem to complete their puberty changes at lightning speed: they are called "rapid maturers." Others, who take more than the normal time, are "slow maturers."

There is some evidence that early and rapid maturing—and late and slow maturing—go hand in hand. The time as well as the speed of maturing is controlled by the endocrine glands. An active pituitary gland accelerates the process, just as a less active pituitary slows it down and sets it into motion at a later age (37, 72, 87).

The evidence that early and rapid maturing go hand in hand does not seem to apply universally. Children with endomorphic builds take longer to complete puberty than those of ectomorphic or mesomorphic builds. Among boys, it has been found that the fatter the child the slower the rate of maturing (65, 81). The late-maturing child who matures rapidly has rather abrupt spurts of growth, whereas slow-maturing and early-maturing children grow at a more even rate and have less organic imbalance. In the late maturer, growth tends to be irregular and asymmetrical, with growth of the internal organs and some parts of the body lagging behind growth in stature (3, 6).

Adult size and shape are also influenced by the age and rate of maturing. The effect on the adult stature is shown in Figure 5–7.

Consequences of Puberty Changes

Physical changes are always accompanied by changes in behavior and attitudes. In addition, there are usually concerns about these changes on the part of the person whose body is changing as well as on the part of significant people in the person's life.

In puberty, the changes are so pronounced that the established pattern of life is disturbed. Children feel uncertain, insecure, and confused. Their behavior is often unpredictable and unsocial. For that reason, puberty is sometimes referred to as the "negative phase." As the tempo of growth slows down and the body changes are completed, both attitudes and behavior gradually become more equable.

The period of most rapid growth and the most difficult part of the negative phase come at the end of childhood. While some of the effects persist into early adolescence, they wane rapidly. In girls, the worst part of the negative phase is over by the time of the menarche.

While puberty affects children differently, certain *outward expressions* of tension are almost universal. These include restlessness, moodiness, withdrawal from family and friends, irritability, rebellion against authority, assertion of independence, critical attacks on others, disinclination to work at home or in school, and a generalized state of unhappiness.

As a result of glandular changes and changes in the size and position of the internal organs, the pubescent child suffers at times from such physical disturbances as digestive upset, finicky appetite, headache, backache, and a general feeling of wretchedness. These disturbances are more common in girls, though few boys escape them completely. They do not predispose the pubescent child to behave in a socially acceptable way. Many children at this time become anemic, owing to poor eating habits more often than to marked changes in blood chemistry. Anemia leads to listlessness and predisposes the child to emotional tension.

Pubescent children have innumerable *concerns* relating to the changes taking place in their bodies. These concerns fall into two major categories, concerns about normality and concerns about sex-appropriateness. If pubescent children differ in any way from their age-mates, they wonder if they are normal. If, for example, they deviate, even slightly in time or rate of maturing, this becomes a major concern to them. Rapid or early maturers worry about becoming abnormally tall adults while slow or late

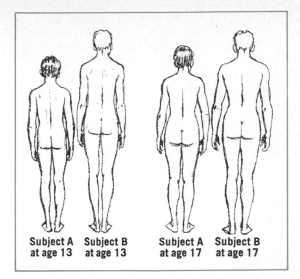

Figure 5–7. Influence of age of maturing on body build. Note the differences in body build for the physically retarded boy (A) and the physically accelerated boy (B) at both ages. (*Adapted from N. Bayley: Individual patterns of development. Child Development, 1956, 27, 45–74. Used by permission.*)

maturers worry about whether they will be abnormally short adults or remain sexually undeveloped.

In addition to being concerned about the normality of their changing bodies, pubescent children often become concerned about no longer enjoying the interests and activities that were formerly so important to them and which continue to be important to their age-mates who lag behind them in sexual maturing. On the other hand, if they lag behind their age-mates in interests and activities—showing little interest in what their age-mates find enjoyable—they wonder if they will ever turn into adults.

Concerns about sex-appropriateness are also common during puberty. By the time they reach puberty, children have a definite concept of what is sex-appropriate in appearance. These concepts are based on movies, comics, television programs, or people in real life they admire. When they fail to come up to the standards they set for sex appropriateness, they are concerned about being sex inappropriate in appearance for the rest of their lives.

One of the most important consequences of puberty changes is their *long-term effect* on the child's interests, attitudes, behavior, and personality. If the unfavorable behavior and attitudes, characteristic of pubescent children, disappeared when homeostasis was restored, they would not be serious. Studies have revealed, however, that the undesirable traits and behavior patterns tend to persist, rather than disappear, with the passage of time and often grow worse (2, 23, 37). This matter will be discussed in detail in the chapter on social development.

The most persistent unfavorable effect of puberty comes from deviations in the age of sexual maturing. Deviant sexual development affects boys and girls differently, both at puberty and afterward. For boys, early maturing is socially advantageous, while for girls, it is not. Superior height, weight, and strength add to a boy's athletic ability and give him prestige in the eyes of peers of both sexes. By comparison, the early-maturing girl may acquire the reputation of being "boy-crazy." This affects her social adjustments then as well as later. The late-maturing girl escapes these social problems, while the late-maturing boy is deprived of the sources of recognition and prestige that come from being a good athlete (3, 24, 27, 65).

Hazards in Physical Development

Studies of hazards in physical development have all emphasized the psychological significance of these hazards. The reason for this is that, in most cases, the psychological repercussions are as severe and often more long-lasting than the physical effects.

Some of the physical hazards of childhood have psychological as well as physical causes. In the case of upsets in body homeostasis, for example, the cause may be physical, as illness or glandular imbalance, or it may be psychological, due to living in an emotionally charged environment or trying to come up to unrealistic parental expectations.

A survey of the most common hazards arising from the child's physical development will be discussed below. In each case the psychological repercussions will be stressed to show how these hazards affect the child's personal and social adjustments not only during childhood but often into the adult years.

Mortality

Death is more of a potential hazard during the first year of life than it is as the child grows older. Because the first two weeks after birth are especially hazard-ous, it is not surprising that two-thirds of all deaths during the first year of life occur during the month following birth. After that there is a rapid decrease in the mortality rate.

Deaths during the first year of life are more often caused by serious illness than by accidents while the reverse is true during the second year. The reason that this is true is that during the first year of life babies can be better protected from accidents than they can when they begin to creep, crawl, walk and explore their environment; further, medical protection against serious illness prevents many deaths from illness during the second year. One of the serious hazards of the first year of life is "crib deaths" which take the lives of apparently normal, healthy babies for reasons still unexplained by the medical profession.

During the preschool years, serious illness is far less common today than in the past due to the use of "wonder drugs" and immunization against such childhood diseases as polio, measles, whooping cough, and mumps, which formerly added to the mortality rate at this age. As a result, more young children die from accidents than from illness.

Deaths due to accidents decline when children approach puberty partly because older children learn to be more cautious and partly because the pubescent child, feeling under par, tends to be too inactive and too self-preoccupied to engage in play that is likely to lead to accidents. Furthermore, while not feeling up to par physically, the pubescent child infrequently has an illness serious enough to lead to death (18, 70, 74).

Illness

Certain illnesses are regarded as "typical" for certain ages. During babyhood, respiratory and gastrointestinal diseases are frequent and sometimes fatal. From 3 to 6 or 8 years the commonly called "children's diseases"—polio, measles, mumps, rubella (German measles), whooping cough, chicken pox, and even diptheria and scarlet fever—are frequent among those who have not been inoculated as a protection against these diseases. Children at this time also suffer from digestive disturbances and colds of minor or major severity.

Normally, from then to the onset of puberty there is a "healthy age." This is especially true of children living in states that require inoculations for children's diseases before school entrance. In the early part of puberty, before sexual maturing has occurred, poor health is characteristic though serious illness is infrequent (18, 24, 70, 85).

ILLNESS-PRONE CHILDREN Some children are illness-prone in the sense that they seem to have more than their share of illness and tend to be sicker, when they are ill, than other children. Studies reveal that the cause may be physical or psychological. Children who had a poor prenatal *environment* or whose birth was difficult have the most trouble adjusting to postnatal life. Children whose nutrition is good, before and after birth, tend to be healthier and less illness-prone. Birth order is said to be related to illness-proneness, with firstborn children less subject to illness than those born later. This is not because firstborns are healthier but rather because they receive more parental care and attention which helps to cut down on the frequency and severity of their illnesses. Children who have been immunized early in life are less likely to be illness-prone than those who are not immunized (18, 85, 90).

Unfavorable *psychological* factors appear to predispose a child to illness. Young babies who are nervous and high-strung have great difficulty adjusting to postnatal life; they are more likely to experience feeding difficulties and digestive disturbances than calm babies. Young children brought up by authoritarian child-training methods tend to be more nervous and sickly than those brought up by more democratic methods. If children are deprived of "mothering" during the early years of life, they are likely to have more illnesses then and as they grow older than children whose home life had been emotionally more favorable (14, 57, 70).

IMAGINARY ILLNESS All children at some time or other complain of "not feeling well" in order to escape an unpleasant duty or avoid punishment. How well developed imaginary invalidism—or psychosomatic illness—is in childhood has not yet been determined. It occurs more frequently during adolescence than during childhood.

When parents, but especially mothers, are anxious and concerned about their children's health, they encourage children to imagine that they are not feeling well. The more parents talk to their children about their health and the more they warn them to "be careful" to avoid getting sick, the more likely children are to wonder if they are not sick (70). Figure 5–8 shows how many mothers, in a nationwide survey, rate

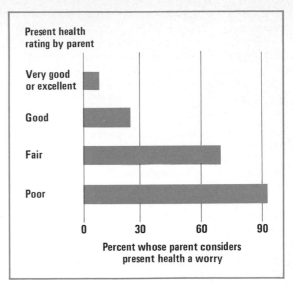

Figure 5–8. Percentages of school-age children in a nationwide survey whose parents worry about their children's health based on parental ratings of the children's health. (*Adapted from J. Roberts:* Examination and health history findings among children and youths, 6-17 years: United States. *Health Resources Administration, National Center for Health Statistics, 1973. Used by permission.*)

their children's health as "poor" or "fair" and how few as "good" or "very good."

EFFECTS OF ILLNESS Regardless of whether an illness is physical or psychological in origin, it brings changes in development, behavior, attitudes, and personality. The illness itself may be chronic or transitory, mild or intense. It may be brief or prolonged. How severe and how lasting the effects will be depends largely on the child's attitudes.

Studies of children of different ages have revealed many specific effects of illness on development and on the type of personal and social adjustments the child makes. The most important of these effects are shown in Box 5–7.

Physical Defects

Physical defects may be hereditary, or they may result from an unfavorable prenatal environment or an injury during birth. Some are caused by illness or accident. A

COMMON EFFECTS OF ILLNESS

PHYSICAL GROWTH AND DEVELOPMENT
Ordinary illnesses seldom have a permanent effect upon growth, but a long and severe illness may stunt the child's growth, if it coincides with a period of rapid development. Most illnesses are accompanied by a temporary loss of weight.

AFTEREFFECTS OF ILLNESS
Because of inactivity during illness, the muscles lose some of their tone and are easily fatigued. Some illnesses have permanent effects, such as damaged heart following rheumatic fever.

HEIGHTENED EMOTIONALITY
Illness always upsets homeostasis. This makes children irritable and more subject than usual to anxieties and temper tantrums.

SOCIAL BEHAVIOR
Children who are segregated from the peer group during a long illness fail to learn patterns of social behavior at the time their peers are learning them. If they are pampered at home, they may develop unhealthy attitudes about their own importance.

LIMITATION ON ACTIVITIES
Illness and recuperation require that activities be restricted. This is frustrating to children. If, in addition, children are unsure of their status in the peer group, they will worry about the effect of their absence on peer relationships.

SCHOOLWORK
Even when sick children receive help from parents and teachers, their schoolwork usually suffers from absence from school. This is likely to contribute to their dislike for school.

BEHAVIOR DIFFICULTIES
Illness is often the starting point for social-adjustment problems such as finicky eating and other behavior difficulties. Many children become so accustomed to special attention that they are aggressive and demanding after they recover. This will affect their relationships with the peer group.

PERSONALITY DISTURBANCES
Allergies, asthma, and diabetes are especially damaging to personality because they are chronic. They often lead to emotional and dependency problems. Even temporary illness, if severe, may cause personality disturbances.

---

few defects, such as stuttering and slurring, are psychosomatic, mental, or emotional in origin. This subject will be discussed in detail in the chapter on speech development. Some are "phantom handicaps"—imaginary defects. Children imagine they are handicapped and as a result, are excused from doing the things they do not want to do.

Children suffer from many physical defects, some of which are common and some uncommon. Among the defects reported are dental caries, visual and auditory impairments, orthopedic disabilities, central-nervous-system disorders, heart disturbances, speech defects, harelips, cleft palates, facial or bodily birthmarks, abnormalities of physique (such as webbed fingers, cross-eyes, hunchbacks, a sixth finger, or malformed ears) and scars or contractures resulting from burns. Some of these can be covered up, and some become progressively worse with time (14, 18, 33).

EFFECTS OF PHYSICAL DEFECTS How children react to their physical defects determines what effect their defects will have on their personal and social adjust-

ments. Some children—relatively few—try to compensate for their defects by achieving success in an area which is not affected by their defects. A lame child, for example, who is unable to participate in games and sports with peers, may try to win a place in the peer group by success in card games or other sedentary forms of play that are popular with the peer group.

Most children who are handicapped in some way or other by their physical defects develop feelings of inadequacy and inferiority and many, in addition, develop martyr complexes. The repercussions of physical defects are felt in many areas, the most common and most serious of which are described in Box 5–8.

Even though most children are psychologically damaged by physical handicaps, the extent of the psychological damage varies and depends on a number of factors, six of which are especially common.

First, the severity of the defect influences children's attitudes toward the defect. The better the defect can be camouflaged, the less children will have to revise their body images and the less psychologically harmful the defect will be.

Second, the time when the defect occurs will influence the child's adjustment to it. Should the defect be present at birth or occur shortly after birth, the child will make better adjustments to it than if it occurs later.

Third, the degree of restriction of activity will greatly influence the effect the defect has on the child. The child who is blind or crippled, for example, will be more restricted than the child who is deaf or suffers from a facial disfigurement.

Fourth, if people feel sorry for children with physical defects, they will pity themselves and develop feelings of martyrdom. If, on the other hand, people are sympathetic, as is true when the defect is readily apparent, children will develop healthier and more acceptant attitudes.

Fifth, children's attitudes toward their defects will influence the effect it has on them. Some children recognize and accept their defects, though most try to convince themselves that they are not different from other children. Many feel guilty about their disabilities, especially if they resulted from engaging in forbidden activities or ones that they were warned against.

Sixth, the degree to which children feel that they are different from other children affects their attitudes toward themselves. The more they recognize that they are different, the more psychologically damaging the effect will be.

That few children do adjust successfully to their disabilities is shown by the large number of poorly adjusted handicapped adults—most of whom were handicapped children. In studies of adults with physical handicaps who seek employment or rehabilitation, it has been found that many have emotional problems that may interfere with occupational success. Often their emotional problems trace back to childhood years. They also make poor social adjustments, shunning outside social activities and spending their time reading, watching television, and doing things with family members (10, 18, 33).

Malnutrition

Malnutrition may be caused by poverty but it more often stems from faulty eating habits due to parental ignorance about what constitutes good nutrition, food likes and dislikes resulting from rebellion against the authoritarian "clean plate" training of childhood, and snacking between meals when with their peers or when watching television. Emotional stress also keeps the child from getting proper nutrition from even the most balanced diet.

BOX 5–8

AREAS OF INFLUENCE OF PHYSICAL DEFECTS

DEVELOPMENTAL STATUS
The developmental status of children suffering from physical defects is usually below that of physically normal children. Since handicapped children tend to be overprotected, they are deprived of learning opportunities and are not motivated to do things for themselves.

SCHOOL ACHIEVEMENT
The physically handicapped child is often an underachiever in school. The child with poor vision, for example, may not be able to see the blackboard or may have difficulty in seeing printed words in books. Physical handicaps also affect children's school achievements indirectly by making them feel excluded from their classmates' activities. This often leads to a dislike for school and lack of motivation to do good work.

PLAY SKILLS
Physical defects often prevent children from acquiring the skills needed for play. As a result, they are forced to play alone when they want to play with other children. This not only deprives them of social contacts but it makes them feel rejected.

SOCIAL ADJUSTMENTS
Since physically handicapped children have fewer opportunities to learn how to get along with others than do those who are physically normal, they usually make poorer social adjustments and behave in a less socially acceptable way than those who are not handicapped. Many children with physical handicaps are doomed to social isolation. Usually they are ignored rather than actively disliked.

PERSONALITY PATTERN
It is not uncommon for children with physical handicaps to develop unfavorable personality patterns. They tend to be withdrawn and unsocial and to develop inferiority or martyr complexes. This sometimes leads to aggressiveness and impulsiveness, both of which have further unfavorable effects on their personalities.

ADJUSTMENT PROBLEMS
Physically handicapped children are faced with adjustment problems characteristic of their ages and level of development *in addition* to those arising from their handicaps. Thus they tend to be less well adjusted than other children of the same ages.

BOX 5–9

EFFECTS OF MALNUTRITION

BODY BUILD

Malnutrition may stunt growth in height and result in either an endomorphic or an ectomorphic body type. The greater the malnutrition, the more pronounced the body type.

ENERGY LEVEL

Children suffering from severe and prolonged malnutrition tend to be listless and apathetic, preferring sedentary play to the active play healthy children engage in. This tendency is pronounced at puberty when malnutrition often causes anemia.

HEALTH

Children who suffer from malnutrition are more susceptible to diseases of all kinds in childhood than are children who are well nourished.

HEIGHTENED EMOTIONALITY

While heightened emotionality—or greater emotionality than is normal for the age and level of development—may be environmental in origin, it may result from malnutrition or it is accentuated by malnutrition.

PERSONALITY

Children who are suffering from malnutrition tend to be depressed, irritable, undependable, unpredictable, and nervous.

INTELLIGENCE

If malnutrition occurs in the early years of life, it affects the development of the brain cells and thus lowers the intellectual capacities of the child. If it occurs later, it affects the child's learning abilities.

APPEARANCE

A child who is suffering from malnutrition looks unhealthy The skin has a pasty look, the eyes are lusterless, the flesh is either flabby or drawn, the shoulders are rounded, the legs tend to be bowed, the teeth are carious, and the gums have a grayish look and may have pus sacs.

Malnutrition is especially serious during the very early years of life when the brain cells are developing. As a result of malnutrition at this time, brain functioning may be permanently impaired (12, 75, 87). As Coursin has pointed out, "Malnutrition may produce structural and metabolic derangements in the central nervous system that can limit its capabilities and performance" (16).

There is evidence that there is a correlation between height in babyhood and adulthood. Babies who suffer from malnutrition, which stunts growth, will under such circumstances be shorter adults than they would have been, had their nutrition been better during this critical period in growth (52). Even when the diet is improved as children grow older, they still tend to lag behind the norm in height. This is true also of intellectual development (54).

EFFECTS OF MALNUTRITION According to tradition, a child who is chubby is well nourished and, thus, "healthy," while a child who is skinny is undernourished and, thus, "unhealthy." Medical evidence today shows that neither claim is true. Chubby and skinny children are both suffering from malnutrition and neither is healthy (16, 18, 75). Medical science has also shown how malnutrition affects children and how widespread these effects are. Some of the most important effects of malnutrition in childhood are given in Box 5–9.

Not only do the effects of malnutrition prove harmful to the individual's development during the childhood years but there is evidence that the harmful effects persist into adult life. Children who are overweight because of overeating and an unbalanced diet with too many carbohydrates tend to have diabetes, high blood pressure, and heart disease as they grow older. In addition, they tend to be depressed and unhappy, thus affecting their personality patterns unfavorably (52, 87, 89).

Disturbances in Homeostasis

Body homeostasis can be upset by unfavorable physical or psychological conditions. *Glandular disturbances,* which normally occur at times of rapid physical growth and development, are almost universal during the puberty period. These disturbances persist until growth slows down.

Any *illness,* even though minor and temporary, can likewise disturb homeostasis. A prolonged and serious illness is especially damaging and requires a long period of recuperation before homeostasis is restored.

Psychological causes are primarily *emotional* in origin. Any emotion, no matter how transient and mild it may be, upsets homeostasis because of the glandular changes that accompany it. Prolonged and persistent emotionality, as in the case of stress, is accompanied by glandular upsets which play havoc with homeostasis.

Many children, as will be pointed out in the chapter on emotional development, experience more or less constant stress because they live in an environment in which there is too much pressure to live up to adult standards or expectations, because they are in constant association with nervous, tense, and emotional people, or because they are constantly thwarted in doing what they want to do. Authoritarian child training is also a source of stress for the child (14, 18, 24, 26).

EFFECTS OF DISTURBANCES IN HOMEOSTASIS When homeostasis is upset, it disturbs the normal pattern of physical growth and development, and it affects the normal pattern of behavior. While an occasional disturbance in homeostasis will have little effect on growth, constant disturbances, as in the case of stress, retard growth and the onset of puberty (50).

Disturbances in homeostasis likewise play havoc with the blood pressure level of the child. If blood pressure is constantly raised above the normal level, the child becomes nervous, irritable, and tense. This affects the patterns of eating and sleeping and control over the organs of elimination. When the patterns of eating and sleeping are upset, for example, the child will become excessively fat or thin and when control over the organs of elimination is upset, the child is likely to suffer from enuresis (7, 66, 78).

Disturbances in homeostasis result in awkwardness, clumsiness, distractibility, and a tendency toward hyperactivity. Under such conditions, children are unable to concentrate on what they are doing and, as a result, work below their abilities in school. In games and sports with age-mates, such children are awkward and clumsy because of nervous tension. As a result, they make poor personal and social adjustments and this affects the degree of social acceptance they are able to achieve. Many children who are rejected or ignored by their age-mates suffer from the effects of disturbances in homeostasis which are expressed in patterns of behavior that annoy others (79).

Accidents

Some accidents are minor—cuts, bruises, and falls—while others are more serious and more lasting in their effects. Figure 5–9 shows the most common types of accidents among school-age children, as

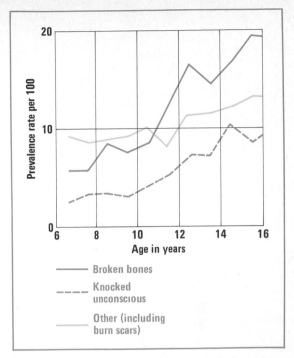

Figure 5–9. Most serious accidental injuries at different ages, based on a nationwide survey of American children. (*Adapted from J. Roberts:* Examination and health history findings among children and youths. *Health Resources Administration, National Center for Health Statistics, 1973. Used by permission.*)

based on a nationwide survey. Note the rapid increase in number of serious accidents, especially broken bones, as children approach the adolescent years. Figure 5–10 shows the parts of the body most often injured in childhood accidents.

Studies of childhood accidents have revealed that there are many conditions contributing to accidents during the childhood years (35, 70, 76, 91). Box 5–10 lists and briefly explains the conditions that contribute to accidents in children.

Just as some children are illness-prone, so some are accident-prone in the sense that they have more accidents for their age and level of development than other children. There are many conditions that contribute to accident-proneness. Among these, the most common are too little supervision, permissive training which fails to establish rules and permits children to do as they please, awkwardness and clumsiness due to poor motor coordination, hyperactivity which encourages

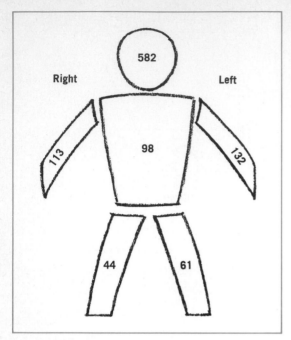

Right   Left

582

113   98   132

44   61

Figure 5–10. Parts of the body most often injured per 1,000 nonfatal childhood accidents reported to the Bureau of Child Health, New York City. In several cases more than one part of the body was injured in the same accident. (*Adapted from H. Jacobziner: Accidents—a major child health problem.* Journal of Pediatrics, *1955,* 46, *419–436. Used by permission.*)

children to do things impulsively without thinking of the consequences, lack of emotional control which not only encourages children to act impulsively but which also prevents them from thinking of the consequences of the acts they impulsively decide to carry out, and rebellion against authoritarian discipline or parental overprotectiveness (76, 79).

EFFECTS OF ACCIDENTS   Accidents cause both physical and psychological damage. Even a minor accident may leave a *physical* scar. A small cut on the face, for example, may leave a scar which will make the child very self-conscious when the appearance-conscious years of adolescence are reached. More serious accidents may maim the child for life or bring about death.

While many accidents leave no physical scars, all accidents leave *psychological scars.* Furthermore, the psychological scars tend to be more far-reaching and persistent than the physical scars.

Even a minor accident is a source of embarrassment to children. They are afraid that people will think them clumsy or careless, and they dread the teasings or scolding they often receive after an accident. Furthermore, they dread the possibility of repeating the accident. This intimidates them, makes them feel insecure, and makes them wonder if there is something wrong with them, especially if they have more accidents than their siblings and age-mates. These feelings tend to make children overcautious and afraid to take chances or face new situations. In time, these feelings may lead to a generalized anxiety which will make them timid, retiring, and self-effacing in any situation involving new tasks or new people. If accidents occur when children do something they have been warned not to do or have been forbidden to do, feelings of guilt, along with other psychological scars, intensify their already unfavorable attitudes.

The attitudes of significant people—especially parents and peers—will determine the extent of the psychological damage accidents bring. If parents are sympathetic, for example, and try to convince the children who have had accidents that they were not to blame, they will be spared the humiliation of feeling that there is something the matter with them. If, on the other hand, parents emphasize the naughtiness of the acts that led to the accidents and the inconvenience and expense the accidents have caused them, this will intensify children's feelings of guilt and shame and thus intensify the psychological scars of the accidents.

Deviant Body Builds

Children may deviate from their age-mates in body build by being taller or shorter, thinner or fatter, or less sex-appropriate in appearance than them. If these deviations are minor, they will not be readily apparent to others. Consequently, they will have little influence on the judgments others make of these children or in the way they treat them.

On the other hand, deviations that are major do become noticeable. As a result, they are hazards to children's personal and social adjustments. When, for example, children under 6 years of age are 20 percent or more over the ideal weight for their ages and when children over 6 years of age are 30 percent or more above the ideals for those ages, children are conspicuous and are regarded as "obese" (64).

Deviations in body build are especially common at puberty due to differences in age of sexual maturing.

BOX 5–10

CONDITIONS CONTRIBUTING TO CHILDHOOD ACCIDENTS

AGE
About two-thirds of all childhood accidents occur before age 9. Ages 2 and 3 are the most vulnerable, with 5 and 6 next. The years from 5 to 14 are the most dangerous for fatal accidents.

SEX
Boys at all ages have more accidents than girls, and this tendency increases as they grow older. Four out of ten boys suffer some sort of accidental injury as compared with two of every ten girls. Between 10 and 14 years, boys have nearly three times as many accidents as girls.

PERSONALITY
Bright, alert, adventuresome children have more accidents than their less bright, less curious age-mates. Children who are resentful because they are thwarted by strict discipline or feel that they have been unfairly treated by parents, teachers, or peers are especially accident-prone. Boys who have feelings of inadequacy because of sex-inappropriate builds often try to compensate by being daring, and this may lead to accidents.

ORDINAL POSITION
Firstborn children tend to have fewer accidents than their siblings, partly because they receive more supervision, partly because they are trained to be more cautious, and partly because they tend to have less self-confidence and are thus somewhat timid.

TIME OF DAY
Among all children, more accidents occur during the afternoon and evening than during the morning. The high-hazard time for young children is from 3 to 6 P.M., when the mother is busy and cannot supervise them carefully and when they are tired, fretful, and quarrelsome. Among older children, the high-hazard time is between 7 and 8 P.M.

TIME OF WEEK
The high-hazard days for children's accidents are Thursday through Saturday. The safest day is Sunday, when adults have more leisure time to supervise children.

WEATHER CONDITIONS
Childhood accidents rise in rainy and stormy weather. In winter, for example, housebound children become bored. If boredom leads to rambunctiousness, accidents often follow.

PLACE
Older children have more accidents outside the home while younger children have more accidents in the home or yard.

Early maturers, for example, are not only larger than average maturers of the same age but their bodies look more like those of adults than like those of children. This makes early maturers conspicuous among their age-mates.

EFFECTS OF DEVIANT BODY BUILDS There are two conditions under which deviant body build becomes a psychological hazard. *First,* children must realize that their bodies differ from those of their age-mates. During the preschool years, most children realize that their bodies deviate in height and weight from the bodies of their age-mates but realization of deviation in sex appropriateness does not usually come until early in the elementary school years. Boys, for example, who show an increasing tendency toward ectomorphy or endomorphy begin to compare their bodies with those of a mesomorphic boy who is admired by the peer group. They then become aware of the fact that their bodies deviate from this admired pattern.

Second, before deviant body builds can become psychological hazards, children must be aware, from comments by others, from the nicknames others use for them, or by the treatment they receive from others that social attitudes toward them are unfavorable. Overweight children, for example, become aware of unfavorable social attitudes when they are nicknamed "Chubby" or "Fatso." When their peers make derogatory comments, as "You're too fat to run," or when parents constantly criticize them for eating anything that might increase their weight, they become well aware of unfavorable social attitudes.

Box 5–11 gives a list of some of the common ways children with deviant body builds have been reported

Homeliness

After the first two years of life, there is a tendency for children to lose their babyish attractiveness and appeal and to become gradually homelier and homelier. This tendency reaches its high point as childhood draws to a close and the puberty changes begin to take place.

Just as judging children's behavior in terms of adult standards is unfair to them, so it is unfair to judge their attractiveness by adult standards of beauty. This, however, is usually done. As a result, children are judged as "homely."

There are certain characteristics of appearance, normal for a child's age and level of development, that do not conform to adult standards. Consequently, judgments of the child's looks are unfavorable.

For example, all children have facial disproportions due to lips that are small and slitlike, eyes that are too large, and a small, flat-on-the-face nose. As baby teeth are gradually replaced by permanent teeth, small teeth remain side by side with large teeth and often there are gaps with no teeth at all. Then there is the sacklike body with spindly arms and legs and hair that is often unmanageable and greasy, especially as the child approaches puberty. All these are normal conditions and are more or less universal, though varying in degrees of intensity of homeliness.

An important condition that contributes to homeliness during the childhood years is absence of the camoutflages adolescents and adults use to cover up unattractive physical features and improve attractive features. The three important sources of camouflage used by adolescents and adults are clothes, hair styling, and beauty airs.

Instead of wanting to wear *clothes* that will improve their looks, children want to wear clothes in their favorite colors and in styles like their friends wear, regardless of whether or not they are suited to them. A boy with red hair, for example, may insist on wearing red jackets or sweaters because he "likes red" and regards red as a sex-appropriate color. A girl may insist upon wearing dresses with ruffles because all her friends wear ruffles. This may make her chubby body look even chubbier than it is, but it gives her the satisfaction of knowing that her clothes are like her friends' clothes.

Then, too, there is the problem of hand-me-down clothes to contend with. Most parents buy clothes that they hope will enhance the attractiveness of the child

to react to others and the ways in which their behavior has been affected by their body builds (20, 41, 47, 49, 64, 77). Not all children, of course, react in the same way, though few escape some of the patterns of behavior listed in this box.

for whom they are bought. However, when these clothes are passed down to the next child in the family, they may be all wrong in color and style for that child. As a result, they contribute to the new wearer's homeliness.

Sooner or later, most adolescents and adults discover that *hair styling* can do wonders to improve their facial features. As a result, they individualize the way they wear their hair, trying, at the same time, to conform to the prevailing styles. Just as children want their clothes to be as nearly like those of their age-mates as possible. so they insist upon wearing their hair just like their age-mates wear theirs, regardless of whether the style is becoming to them or not.

Few children use any *beauty aids* to camouflage their unattractive features or improve their good features. It is unusual, for example, for children to use rouge or lipstick to improve their coloring, and even fewer use hair rinses to enhance the color of their hair or have permanent waves to improve the straight, stringy, unmanageable hair of childhood.

EFFECTS OF HOMELINESS As is true of deviant body builds, homeliness does not become a hazard to children's personal and social adjustments until they become aware of the fact that people regard them as homely and until they realize that people have unfavorable attitudes toward them because they are homely. Because most of their age-mates are homely also, unfavorable attitudes come more from adults than from peers.

Realization that attractiveness is an asset and that homeliness can be and often is a liability comes as early as the preschool years. As one preschooler put it, "People like you better if you are pretty" while another observed, "You're nice to pretty people" (20).

The hazardous nature of homeliness has been shown by studies of the effects of homeliness on children's personal and social adjustments and by the favorable effects of attractiveness on these adjustments. Some of the results of these studies will serve to show in what ways attractiveness and homeliness affect children.

First, attractiveness affects first impressions favorably. An attractive child creates a better first impression on others than does an unattractive child and this facilitates the child's acceptance (22).

Second, even though homeliness may not be as great a hazard to peer relationships as to relationships with adults, attractiveness is an asset. As Clifford and Wal-

ster have pointed out, "Attractive children have a sizeable advantage over unattractive ones" (13).

Third, children who are attractive tend to be better liked and to have more friends than children who are homely. Popularity encourages children to try to improve their appearance while social isolation encourages them to neglect their appearance (22, 41).

Fourth, homeliness makes a child less appealing to others than attractiveness. As a result, people tend to be more critical and less tolerant of a homely child's behavior than they are of similar behavior in a more attractive child (21, 45). Berscheid et al. have commented, "We treat beautiful people differently from the way we treat homely ones, and denying this truth will not make a person's looks less important" (8).

Fifth, there is a tendency for some teachers to think of homely children as less bright and less able than attractive children. As a result, homely children must work harder than attractive children to get grades that show their real abilities (1, 13, 68).

Sixth, homely children resent the treatment they receive from others, especially adults, and this has an unfavorable effect on their personalities. They feel unloved, unwanted, and rejected, thus laying the basis for a martyr complex (21, 60).

Seventh, feelings of resentment about the treatment they receive encourage children to behave in an unsocial way. This may lead to the development of problem behavior (1).

Eighth, if children feel that the teacher is less favorable to them than to their more attractive classmates, they develop a dislike for school and tend to become underachievers (1).

Because of the favorable effects of attractiveness and the unfavorable effects of homeliness, as shown by the studies above, Mathes and Kahn's comments about the importance of attractiveness in childhood are worthy of serious consideration. As they say (56):

In a social exchange, physical attractiveness is a positive input and can be used to obtain a variety of good outcomes for its possessor. One of the most frequently obtained outcomes is liking. Attractive people are liked more as friends . . . and receive more positive evaluations from others . . . and empathy . . . than unattractive people. . . . As a result of the many good outcomes obtained by attractive people, it seems likely that they are happier and better adjusted than unattractive people. It is also probable that the liking received from others is reflected in a high self-esteem.

By contrast the seriousness of homeliness has been stressed by Krebs and Adinolfi (42):

The most tragic aspect of the effect of physical unattractiveness is its potential to initiate a sequence of circular reactions. Physical unattractiveness evokes unfavorable trait attribution which mediates social avoidance. Social avoidance preserves the initial impression by reducing the probability of exposure to disconfirming information; and it perpetuates it by depriving the physically unattractive of the feedback necessary to develop socially effective personalities.

Chapter Highlights

1 It is important to know how children develop physically because physical development influences children's behavior directly by determining what they can do and indirectly by influencing their attitudes toward self and others, thus affecting the kind of personal and social adjustments they make.

2 Throughout the growth years, there are four cycles of growth, two of which are characterized by slow growth and development and two by rapid growth and development. Cycles of growth affect adjustment difficulties, energy level, maintenance of homeostasis, and degree of awkwardness.

3 Body size, which is controlled partly by heredity and partly by environmental conditions before and after birth, is measured in terms of height and weight, both of which follow predictable patterns.

4 The psychological significance of body size comes from the way others—both adults and peers—react to it.

5 Because not all parts of the body grow at the same rate, body proportions do not reach their mature level until the body completes its growth early in the adolescent years. Body disproportions lead to such consequences as awkwardness, unattractiveness, judgments of maturity status, concern about disproportions, and favorable or unfavorable attitudes toward children.

6 As body proportions change, children's bodies begin to take on the characteristics of endomorphic, ectomorphic, and mesomorphic body builds.

7 The development of bones is psychologically significant because ossification affects the seriousness of accidents involving broken bones and the attractiveness of the shape of the child's head.

8 The fat-muscle ratio directly affects the quality of children's behavior and, indirectly, children's reactions to their body builds.

9 There are five psychologically significant facts about teeth: they have an effect on emotionality, they can disturb body equilibrium, they serve as insignia of maturity, and they affect the child's appearance and speech.

10 Growth and development of the nervous system have their greatest effects on children's body proportions, their looks, the degree of helplessness they experience, and their intellectual capacity.

11 Puberty changes, which occur as childhood draws to a close and require about 4 years to complete, include changes in size and proportions and the development of primary and secondary sex characteristics.

12 Puberty changes lead to changes in behavior and concerns about normality and sex-appropriateness, some of which have only temporary effects while others have persistent effects.

13 Because hazards in physical development have psychological as well as physical effects, their importance to children's personal and social adjustments has led to the extensive scientific research to determine what these effects are and how temporary or persistent they are.

14 Among the many hazards in physical development, those that are now known to be most common are mortality, illness, physical defects, malnutrition, disturbances in homeostasis, accidents, deviant body builds, and homeliness.

15 The psychological significance of hazards in physical development comes from the fact that hazards not only affect children's behavior but they also affect attitudes of significant people toward children and the way they treat children who are experiencing these hazards.

Bibliography

1 Adams, G. R., and J. C. La Voie. The effect of students' sex, conduct, and facial attractiveness on teacher expectancy. *Education,* 1974, *95,* 76–83.

2 Adams, P. L. Puberty as a biosocial turning point. *Psychosomatics,* 1969, *10,* 343–349.

3 Anderson, D. L., G. W. Thompson, and F. Popovich. Adolescent variation in weight, height, and mandibular length of 111 females. *Human Biology,* 1975, *47,* 309–319.

4 Babson, S. G., and D. S. Phillips. Growth and development of twins dissimilar in size at birth. *New England Journal of Medicine,* 1973, *289,* 937–940.

5 Bakwin, H. Body-weight regulation in twins. *Developmental Medicine and Child Neurology,* 1973, *15,* 178–183.

6 Bayley, N. Research in child development: A longitudinal perspective. *Merrill-Palmer Quarterly,* 1965, *11,* 183–208.

7 Bernstein, P., R. Emde, and J. Campos. REM sleep in four month infants under home and laboratory conditions. *Psychosomatic Medicine,* 1973, *35,* 322–329.

8 Berscheid, E., E. Walster, and G. Bohrnstedt. The happy American body: A survey report. *Psychology Today,* 1973, 7(6), 119–131.

9 Biller, H. B., and L. J. Borstelmann. Masculine development: An integrative review. *Merrill-Palmer Quarterly,* 1967, *13,* 253–294.

10 Brockman, L. M., and H. N. Ricciuti. Severe protein-calorie malnutrition and cognitive development in infancy and early childhood. *Developmental Psychology,* 1971, *4,* 312–319.

11 Carron, A. V., and D. A. Bailey. Strength development in boys from 10 through 16 years. *Monographs of the Society for Research in Child Development,* 1974, No. 157.

12 Chase, H. P., and H. P. Martin. Undernutrition and child development. *New England Journal of Medicine,* 1970, *282,* 933–939.

13 Clifford, M. M., and E. Walster. The effect of physical attractiveness on teacher expectations. *Sociology of Education,* 1973, *46,* 248–258.

14 Coddington, R. D. The significance of life events as etiologic factors in the diseases of children. II. A study of a normal population. *Psychosomatic Research,* 1972, *16,* 205–213.

15 Compton, M. H. Body build, clothing and delinquent behavior. *Journal of Home Economics,* 1967, *49,* 655–659.

16 Coursin, D. B. Nutrition and brain development in infants. *Merrill-Palmer Quarterly,* 1972, *18,* 177–202.

17 Cross, J. F., and J. Cross. Age, sex, race and the perception of facial beauty. *Developmental Psychology,* 1971, *3,* 433–439.

18 Cruickshank, W. M., and G. O. Johnson. (eds.) *Education of exceptional children and youth,* 3d ed. Englewood Cliffs, N.J.: Prentice-Hall, 1975.

19 De Wign, J. F. Parameters of changing metabolism during growth from 8 to 18, related to physique and body composition. *Child Development Abstracts,* 1970, *44,* no. 3.

20 Dion, K. K. Young children's stereotyping of facial attractiveness. *Developmental Psychology,* 1973, *9,* 183–188.

21 Dion, K. K. Children's physical attractiveness and sex as determinants of adult punitiveness. *Developmental Psychology,* 1974, *10,* 772–778.

22 Dion, K. K., and E. Berscheid. Physical attractiveness and peer perception among children. *Sociometry,* 1974, *37,* 1–12.

23 Dreyer, A. S., V. Hulac, and D. Rigler. Differential adjustment to pubescence and cognitive style patterns. *Developmental Psychology* 1971, *4,* 456–462.

24 Dunbar, F. Homeostasis during puberty. *American Journal of Psychiatry,* 1858, *114,* 673–682.

25 Dwyer, J., and J. Mayer. Psychological effects of variations in physical appearance during adolescence. *Adolescence,* 1968–1969, *3,* 353–380.

26 Eichorn, D. H. Physiological development. In P. H. Mussen (ed.), *Carmichael's manual of child psychology,* 3d ed. New York; Wiley, 1970. Vol. 1, pp. 157–283.

27 Ellis, J. D., A. V. Carron, and D. A. Bailey. Physical performance in boys from 10 through 16 years. *Human Biology,* 1975, *47,* 263–281.

28 Fernstrom, J. D., and R. J. Wurtman. Nutrition and the brain. *Scientific American,* 1974, 230(2), 84–91.

29 Forbes, G. B., and G. H. Amirhakimi. Skinfold thickness and body fat in children. *Human Biology,* 1970, *42,* 401–418.

30 Frisch, R. E. Fatness in girls from menarche to age 18 years, with a nomogram. *Human Biology,* 1976, *48,* 353–359.

31 Garai, J. E., and A. Scheinfeld. Sex differences in mental and behavioral traits. *Genetic Psychology Monographs,* 1968, 77, 169–299.

32 Goldstein, H. Factors influencing the height of seven-year old children—results from the National Child Development Study. *Human Biology,* 1971, *43,* 92–111.

33 Halverson, C. F., and J. B. Victor. Minor physical anomalies and problem behavior in elementary school children. *Child Development,* 1976, *47,* 281–285.

34 Hartnett, J. J., K. G. Bailey, and C. S. Hartley. Body height, position, and sex as determinants of personal scale. *Journal of Psychology,* 1974, *87,* 129–136.

35 Jacobziner, H. Accidents: A major child health problem. *Journal of Pediatrics,* 1955, *46,* 419–436.

36 Johnston, F. E., V. V. Hamill, and S. Lemeshaw. *Skinfold thickness of youths 12–17 years, United States.* Rockville, Md.: Health Resources Administration, National Center for Health Statistics, 1974.

37 Jones, M. C. Psychological correlates of somatic development. *Child Development,* 1965, *36,* 899–911.

38 Kaplan, B. J. Malnutrition and mental deficiency. *Psychological Bulletin,* 1972, *78,* 321–334.

39 Kelley, J. E., and C. R. Harvey. *Decayed, missing and filled teeth among youths 12–17 years.* Rockville, Md.: Health Resources Administration, National Center for Health Statistics, 1974.

40 Kelley, J. E., M. J. Sanchez, and L. E. Van Kirk. *An assessment of the occlusion of the teeth of children.* Rockville, Md.: Health Resources Administration, National Center for Health Statistics, 1973.

41 Kleck, R. E., S. A. Richardson, and L. Ronald. Physical appearance cues and interpersonal attraction in children. *Child Development,* 1974, *45,* 305–310.

42 Krebs, D., and A. A. Adinolfi. Physical

attractiveness, social relations, and personality style. *Journal of Personality and Social Psychology*, 1975, *31*, 245–253.

43 Kreze, A., M. Zeliner, J. Julås, and M. Garbara. Relationship between intelligence and relative prevalence of obesity. *Human Biology*, 1974, *46*, 109–113.

44 Krogman, W. M. Growth of head, face, trunk, and limbs in Philadelphia white and Negro children of elementary and high school age. *Monographs of the Society for Research in Child Development*, 1970, *35*, (3).

45 Landy, D., and H. Sigall. Beauty is talent: Task evaluation as a function of the performer's physical attractiveness. *Journal of Personality and Social Psychology*, 1974, *29*, 299–304.

46 Lerner, R. M. The development of personal space schemata toward body build. *Journal of Psychology*, 1973, *84*, 229–235.

47 Lerner, R. M., and E. Gellert. Body build identification, preference and aversion in children. *Developmental Psychology*, 1969, *1*, 456–462.

48 Lerner, R. M., S. A. Karabenick, and M. Meisels. Effect of age and sex on the development of personal space schemata towards body build. *Journal of Genetic Psychology*, 1975, *127*, 91–101.

49 Lewis, V. G., J. Money, and N. A. Bobrow. Psychologic study of boys with short stature, retarded osseous growth and normal age of pubertal onset. *Adolescence*, 1973, *8*, 445–454.

50 Litt, I. F., and M. I. Cohen. Age of menarche: A changing pattern and its relationship to ethnic origin and delinquency. *Journal of Pediatrics*, 1973, *82*, 288–289.

51 Lohman, T. G., R. A. Boileau, and B. H. Massey. Prediction of lean body mass in young boys from skinfold thickness and body weight. *Human Biology*, 1975, *47*, 245–262.

52 Mack, R. W., and J. Ipsen. The height-weight relationship in early childhood. Birth to 48 month correlations in an urban, low-income Negro population. *Human Biology*, 1974, *46*, 21–32.

53 MacMahon, B. *Age at menarche: United States*. Rockville, Md.: Health Resources Administration, National Center for Health Statistics, 1973.

54 Malina, R. M., P. V. V. Hamill, and S. Lemeshaw. *Body dimensions and proportions, white and Negro children 6–11 years*. Rockville, Md.: Health Resources Administration, National Center for Health Statistics, 1974.

55 Marshall, W. A. and A. V. Swan. Seasonal variation in growth rates of normal and blind children. *Human Biology*, 1971, *43*, 502–516.

56 Mathes, E. W., and A. Kahn. Physical attractiveness, happiness, neuroticism and self-esteem. *Journal of Psychology*, 1975, *90*, 27–29.

57 Mattsson, A. Long-term physical illness in childhood: A challenge to psychosocial adaptation. *Pediatrics*, 1972, *50*, 801–811.

58 Meredith, H. V. Somatic changes during human postnatal life. *Child Development*, 1975, *46*, 603–610.

59 Miklasheoskaya, N. N. Sex differences in growth of the head and face in children and adolescents. *Human Biology*, 1969, *41*, 250–262.

60 Mins, P. R., J. J. Hartnett, and W. R. Nay. Interpersonal attractiveness and help in volunteering as a function of physical attractiveness. *Journal of Psychology*, 1975, *89*, 131.

61 Moss, M. E., R. Miller, and R. A. Page. The effects of racial context on the perception of physical attractiveness. *Sociometry*, 1975, *38*, 525–535.

62 Mueller, W. H. Parent-child correlations for stature and weight among school aged children: A review of 24 studies. *Human Biology*, 1976, *48*, 379–397.

63 Nash, H. Ascription of maturity to human figure drawings by preschool children. *Journal of Genetic Psychology*, 1973, *122*, 319–328.

64 Nathan, S. Body image in chronically obese children as reflected in figure drawings. *Journal of Personality Assessment*, 1973, *37*, 456–463.

65 Onat, T. Prediction of adult height of girls based on the percentage of adult height at the onset of secondary sex characteristics at chronological age and at skeletal age. *Human Biology*, 1975, *47*, 117–130.

66 Peterson, R. A. The natural development of nocturnal bladder control. *Developmental Medicine and Child Neurology*, 1971, *13*, 730–734.

67 Rapier, J., R. Adelson, R. Carey, and K. Croke. Changes in children's attitudes toward the physically handicapped. *Exceptional Children*, 1972, *39*, 219–224.

68 Rich, J. Effects of children's physical attractiveness on teachers' evaluations. *Journal of Educational Psychology*, 1975, *67*, 599–609.

69 Robbins, P. R. Personality and psychiatric illness: A selective review of research. *Genetic Psychology Monographs*, 1969, *80*, 51–90.

70 Roberts, J. *Examination and health history findings among children and youths, 6–17 years: United States*. Rockville, Md.: Health Resources Administration, National Center for Health Statistics, 1973.

71 Roche, A. F., J. Roberts, and P. V. V. Hamill. *Skeletal maturity of children 6–11 years.: Racial, geographic area, and socioeconomic differentials*. Rockville, Md.: Health Resources Administration, National Center for Health Statistics, 1975.

72 Root, A. W. Endocrinology of puberty. I. Normal sexual maturation. II. Aberrations of sexual maturation. *Journal of Pediatrics*, 1973, *83*, 1–19, 187–200.

73 Sanchez, M. J. *Periodontal disease among youths 12–17 years*. Rockville, Md.: Health Resources Administration, National Center for Health Statistics, 1974.

74 Scheinfeld, A. *Heredity in humans*, rev. ed. Philadelphia, Lippincott, 1971.

75 Schrimshaw, N. S. Early malnutrition and central nervous system function. *Merrill-Palmer Quarterly*, 1969, *15*, 375–388.

76 Spock, B. *Raising children in a difficult time*. New York: Norton, 1974.

77 Staffieri, J. R. A study of social stereotypes of body image in children: In W. R. Looft (ed.), *Developmental psychology: A book of readings*. Hinsdale, Ill.: Dryden Press, 1972. Pp. 289–296.

78 Stern, E., A. H. Parmelle, Y. Akiyama, M. A. Schultz, and W. H. Y. Wenner. Sleep cycle characteristics in infants. *Pediatrics*, 1969, *43*, 65–70.

79 Stewart, M. A. Hyperactive children. *Scientific American*, 1970, *222*(4), 94–98.

80 Stone, L. J., and J. Church. *Childhood and adolescence: A psychology of the growing person*, 3d ed. New York: Random House, 1973.

81 Tanner, J. M. Physical growth. In P. H. Mussen (ed.), *Carmichael's man-*

ual of child psychology, 3d ed. New York: Wiley, 1970. Vol. 1, pp. 77–155.

82 Tanner, J. M. Growing up. *Scientific American*, 1973, *229*(3), 35–43.

83 Thomas, J. K. Adolescent endocrinology for counselors of adolescents. *Adolescence*, 1973, *8*, 394–406.

84 Thomas, W. D. Maturation age: Another dropout factor? *Canadian Counsellor*, 1972, *6*, 275–277.

85 *Time* Article: Medicine: Unvaccinated kids. *Time Magazine*, Sept. 8, 1975, p. 48.

86 Tizard, J. Early malnutrition, growth and mental development in man. *British Medical Bulletin*, 1974, *30*, 169–174.

87 Waber, D. P. Sex differences in cognition: A function of malnutrition rate? *Science*, 1976, *192*, 572–574.

88 Walánski, N. The stature of offspring and the assortive mating of parents. *Human Biology*, 1974, *46*, 613–619.

89 Weiss, N. S., P. V. V. Hamill, and T. Drizel. *Blood pressure levels of chil-dren 6–11 years: Relationship of age, sex, race and socioeconomic status.* Rockville, Md.: Health Resources Administration, National Center for Health Statistics, 1973.

90 Whiting, J. W. M., T. K. Landauer, and T. M. Jones. Infantile immunization and adult stature. *Child Development*, 1968, *39*, 59–67.

91 Woods, M. B. The unsupervised child of the working mother. *Developmental Psychology*, 1972, *6*, 14–25.

CHAPTER 6

MOTOR DEVELOPMENT

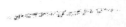

otor development means the development of control over bodily movements through the coordinated activity of the nerve centers, the nerves, and the muscles. This control comes from the development of the reflexes and mass activity present at birth. Until this development occurs, the child will remain helpless.

However, this condition of helplessness changes rapidly. During the first 4 or 5 years of postnatal life, the child gains control over *gross movements*. These movements involve the large areas of the body used in walking, running, jumping, swimming, and so on. After 5 years of age, major development takes place in the control of *finer coordinations,* which involve the smaller muscle groups used in grasping, throwing and catching balls, writing, and using tools.

Unless environmental obstacles or physical or mental handicaps interfere with normal motor development, the 6-year-old will be ready to adjust to the demands of school and to participate in the play activities of peers. Society expects this of children. Some of the most important developmental tasks of the preschool and early school years consist of the development of motor skills based on the coordinated use of different teams of muscles. (See Box 2–9 for a list of the developmental tasks of early childhood.)

Children who measure up to social expectations make good personal and social adjustments unless some personality obstacle stands in their way. On the other hand, children who fall below social expectations develop feelings of personal inadequacy which weaken their motivation to try to learn what their age-mates are already learning.

Being able to control their bodies as well as, if not better than, their peers is important to children for a number of reasons, some of which are given in Box 6–1. Figure 6–1 shows how motor development contributes to children's personal and social adjustments.

Principles of Motor Development

In numerous longitudinal studies, groups of babies and young children have been tested and observed over a period of time to see when certain forms of motor behavior appear and to discover whether these forms are similar for other children of the same age. Extensive studies show that various motor performances involving the arms, wrists, and fingers, such as reaching, grasping, and thumb opposition, develop in a predictable sequence (2, 5, 42, 53). Many other studies have concentrated on motor performances involving the feet, legs, and whole body, such as walking, jumping, running, and hopping. In addition, a few studies have been made of the age and sequence of development of specific skills, such as those involved in self-feeding and self-dressing, and throwing and catching balls (6, 30, 45, 55, 58). From these

---

BOX 6–1

CONTRIBUTIONS OF MOTOR DEVELOPMENT

GOOD HEALTH
Good health, which is vital to the child's development and happiness, is partially dependent on exercise. If motor coordination is so poor that the child performs below the standards of the peer group, the child will then derive little satisfaction from physical activities and will have little motivation to take part.

EMOTIONAL CATHARSIS
Through strenuous exercise, children get rid of pent-up energy and free their bodies from the tensions of anxiety and frustration. They are then able to relax both physically and psychologically.

INDEPENDENCE
The more children can do for themselves, the greater their self-confidence and happiness. Dependency leads to feelings of resentment and personal inadequacy.

SELF-ENTERTAINMENT
Motor control enables children to engage in activities which give them enjoyment even in the absence of playmates.

SOCIALIZATION
Good motor development contributes to the child's acceptance and provides opportunities to learn social skills. Superior motor development puts the child in line for a leadership role.

SELF-CONCEPT
Motor control leads to feelings of physical security, which are soon translated into psychological security. Psychological security, in turn, leads to a generalized self-confidence which affects all areas of behavior.

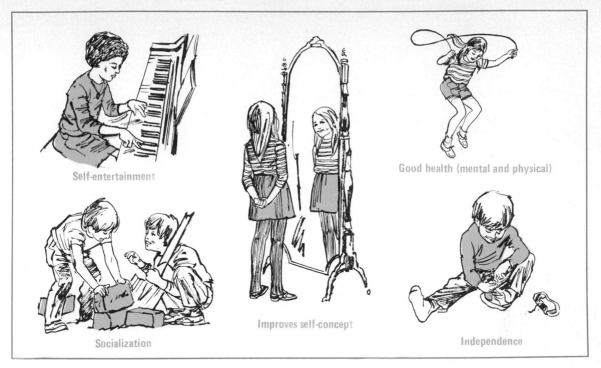

Figure 6–1. Motor development contributes to the child's development.

Motor Development Depends on Neural and Muscular Maturation

Development of the different forms of motor activity parallels the development of different areas of the nervous system. Because the lower nerve centers, located in the *spinal cord,* are better developed at birth than the higher nerve centers, located in the brain, reflexes are better developed at birth than voluntary activities. Within a short time after birth, the important reflexes needed for survival, such as sucking, swallowing, blinking, knee jerk, and patellar tendon reflex, strengthen and become better coordinated. Others that are less useful, such as the Babinski, the plantar or toe-grasp reflex, the palmar or hand-grasp reflex, the Moro, and the Babkin reflexes gradually wane and disappear before the end of the first year of life.

Mass activity, likewise present at birth, gradually develops into simple patterns of voluntary activity which form the basis for skills. The *cerebellum,* or lower brain, which controls balance, develops rapidly during the early years of life and practically reaches its mature size by the time the child is 5 years old. The upper brain, or *cerebrum,* especially the frontal lobes which control skilled movements, likewise develops in the early years.

Skilled movements cannot be mastered until the muscular mechanism of the child matures. The striped or *striated muscles,* which control voluntary movements, develop at a slow rate throughout the childhood years. Voluntary coordinated action is impossible before they are sufficiently mature.

Learning of Skills Cannot Occur until the Child Is Maturationally Ready

Trying to teach the child skilled movements before the nervous system and muscles are well developed will be wasted effort. This is equally true of practice the child may initiate. Such training may produce some

A
Four months
Sees but cannot contact

B
Five months
Palmar scoop

C
Eight months
A cube in each hand

D
Nine months
Pincer grasp perfected

temporary gain, but the long-term effects will be insignificant or nil.

Motor Development Follows a Predictable Pattern

Motor development follows the laws of developmental direction. See page 30 for a description of these laws and Figure 2–3 for a graphic representation of these laws. The cephalocaudal (head-to-foot) sequence of development is shown by the fact that, early in babyhood, there is greater movement in the head region than in the rest of the body. As the baby's neuromuscular mechanisms mature, there is more and better controlled movement in the trunk and later in the leg region. Motor development also proceeds in the proximodistal (from main axis to remote areas) direction. In reaching for an object, the baby uses shoulders and elbows before wrists and fingers.

The predictable pattern of motor development is evident in the change from *mass* to *specific* activities. With the maturation of the neuromuscular mechanisms, mass activity is replaced by specific activities, and gross random movements give way to refined movements which involve only the appropriate muscles and limbs.

Within different patterns of motor development, there are predictable stages. In the development of prehension, which forms the foundation for hand skills, there are predictable stages which occur at predictable ages. While each of these is distinct from the others, each is dependent on the stage preceding it and influences the stage following it (32, 45). Four stages of this sequence are shown in Figure 6–2.

That motor development is predictable is shown by evidence that the age at which babies start to walk is consistent with the rate of their total development. A baby who sits early, for example, walks earlier than babies who sit later. Because of this consistency in rate of development, it is possible to predict with a fair degree of accuracy when a baby will start to walk on the basis of evidence of the rate of development in other motor coordinations. Breckenridge and Vincent have pointed out that a fairly accurate way to predict

Figure 6–2. Pattern of development of hand skills. (*Adapted from E. L. Vincent and P. C. Martin: Human psychological development. Ronald; 1961. Used by permission.*)

the age at which babies will start to walk is to multiply the age at which they begin to creep by $1\frac{1}{2}$ or the age at which they sit alone by 2 (9).

It Is Possible to Establish Norms for Motor Development

Because early motor development follows a predictable pattern, it is possible to establish norms, based on mean ages, for different forms of motor activity. These norms can be used as guidelines to enable parents and others to know what to expect and at what ages to expect it of their children. They can also be used to assess the normalness of a child's development.

For example, the fact that certain reflexes wane at certain ages while others strengthen and become better coordinated is used by doctors to assess the baby's development both at birth and during the months following birth. Norms for different patterns of voluntary activity, such as sitting, standing, reaching, and grasping, are used to assess the intellectual development of babies before they are able to be tested by standard intelligence tests which rely heavily on the use of speech. The Bayley Scales of Infant Development, for example, serve this purpose (6).

There Are Individual Differences in the Rate of Motor Development

Even though motor development follows a pattern that is similar for all in its broader aspects, individual differences occur in the detail of the pattern. These affect the ages at which different individuals reach different stages. Some of these conditions speed up the rate of motor development while others retard it. The conditions that have been reported to have the greatest impact on the rate of motor development are given in Box 6–2.

Sequence of Motor Development

Experimental studies of motor development have revealed that there is a normal pattern of achieving muscle control and have indicated the ages at which the average child is able to control different parts of the body. Box 6–3 summarizes the findings of these studies (6, 7, 15, 36, 59, 65). Note how the development of motor control follows the laws of developmental

---

BOX 6–2

SOME CONDITIONS THAT INFLUENCE THE RATE OF MOTOR DEVELOPMENT

- Genetic constitution, including body build and intelligence, has a marked influence on rate of motor development.
- The more active the fetus, the more rapid is motor development in early postnatal life unless unfavorable environmental conditions interfere.
- Favorable prenatal conditions, especially maternal nutrition, encourage more rapid postnatal motor development than unfavorable prenatal conditions.
- A difficult birth, especially when there is temporary brain damage, delays motor development.
- Good health and nutrition during early postnatal life speed up motor development unless there are environmental obstacles.
- Children with high IQs show more rapid motor development than children with normal or below normal IQs.
- Stimulation, encouragement, and opportunities to move all parts of the body speed up motor development.
- Overprotectiveness stifles developmentally ready motor abilities.
- Firstborns tend to be ahead of later-borns in motor development because of parental encouragement and stimulation.
- Prematurity usually delays motor development because the level of development at birth is below that of full-term infants.
- Physical defects, such as blindness, delay motor development.
- Sex, racial, and socioeconomic differences in motor development are due more to differences in motivation and in child-training methods than to hereditary differences. These differences and the reasons for them will be explained later in this chapter.

---

direction. Studies have also shown predictable patterns in the way children achieve motor control in specific activities. In early *walking*, for example, there are predictable patterns in body posture and foot positions. The body is erect and motion comes from the use of the legs alone. As an aid to maintaining equilibrium, the baby's arms are held outright, much like those of a tightrope walker, or are pulled up to the body. The feet are turned outward, and the legs are stiff. There is a rhythmic alternation of the two legs. The head is held sightly forward, and the baby looks

BOX 6–3

SEQUENCE OF MOTOR DEVELOPMENT

HEAD REGION
- Ocular pursuit movements: 4 weeks
- "Social smiles" (in response to another's smile): 3 months
- Eye coordination: 4 months
- Holding the head up:
  In a prone position: 1 month
  In a sitting position: 4 months

TRUNK REGION
- Turning:
  From side to back: 2 months
  From back to side: 4 months
  Complete: 6 months
- Sitting:
  Pulls to sitting position: 4 months
  With support: 5 months
  Without support: 9 months
- Organs of elimination:
  Bowel control: 2 years
  Bladder control: 2 to 4 years

ARMS AND HANDS
- Defensive movements: 2 weeks
- Thumb-sucking: 1 month
- Reach and grasp: 4 months
- Grasp and hold: 5 months
- Picking up object with opposed thumb: 8 months

LEGS AND FEET
- Hitching (backward movement in sitting position—see Figure 6-3): 6 months
  Crawling (prone body pulled by arms and leg kicks): 7 months
- Creeping:
  On hands and knees: 9 months
  On all fours: 10 months
- Standing:
  With support: 8 months
  Without support 11 months
- Walking:
  With support: 11 months
  Without support: 12 to 14 months

Figure 6–3. Hitching. (*Adapted from L. H. Burnside: Coordination in the loco-motion of infants.* Genetic Psychology Monographs, *1927, no. 2. Used by permission.*)

straight ahead instead of at the floor. This is necessary if balance is to be maintained, though it usually results in many falls. Falls are caused also by poor general coordination and the fact that the baby raises the feet far from the floor and so loses balance. Figure 6–4 shows the characteristic body posture of the baby in the early stages of walking.

When the baby first starts to walk with support, the steps are short and erratic. They increase in length until the baby is about 15 months old, and thereafter they become quite regular. Noticeable changes are also apparent in the width of step. In early stepping, the toes of the two feet are approximately 5 centimeters apart, and the heels do not touch the floor. When the baby begins to walk without support, the width of the step increases sharply. It continues to increase until the end of the second year. Also, as the baby begins to walk, the whole sole of the foot is placed in contact with the floor. At first, the toes turn outward, but with improvement in walking the feet become parallel (11, 55, 65, 72).

Studies of the patterns of control over the organs of *elimination* have also shown predictable patterns, though there are individual differences in the ages at which control is achieved. Control of the bowels, for example, precedes control of the bladder and daytime bladder control precedes night control (7, 50, 60).

Figure 6–4. Body posture in early walking. (*Adapted from L. H. Burnside: Coordination in the locomotion of infants.* Genetic Psychology Monography, *1927, no. 2. Used by permission.*)

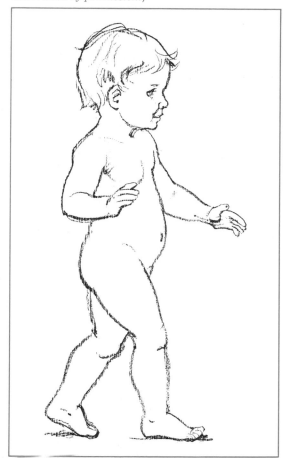

Motor Skills

Motor skills are fine coordinations in which the smaller muscles play a major role. In defining "skill," Cronbach (16) writes:

> A skill can be described in such words as automatic, rapid, accurate, and smooth. It is wrong, however, to think of a skill as some single, perfected action. Any skilled performance, even writing the letter **a**, is a series of hundreds of nerve-muscle coordinations. A skilled movement is a very complex process involving differentiation of cues and continual correction of errors.

A well-learned skill develops into a *habit*. As Hilgard et al. described it, a habit is "any sort of smooth-running repetitive activity, composed of recognizable movement patterns . . . A person commonly pays little attention to the details of his habitual performances. . . . Habits . . . are relatively automatic, repeated movement patterns, especially as they are revealed in skilled movements" (35).

After babies gain control over the gross body movements, they are ready to begin to learn skills. These skills are based on the foundations laid by maturation that has changed the random, meaningless activity, present at birth, into coordinated movements. When, for example, maturation of the arm and hand muscles has resulted in the ability to grasp and hold objects, the baby is ready to learn the skill of self-feeding with a spoon. Similarly, when maturation has resulted in the ability to walk, the baby is ready to learn to skip, hop, and jump.

Childhood—The Ideal Age for Learning Motor Skills

Childhood is often called the "ideal age" for learning motor skills. There are a number of reasons for this.

First, children's bodies are more pliable than those of adolescents and adults and, hence, all learning is easier.

Second, children have fewer previously learned skills that will conflict with the learning of a new skill and, by so doing, make the learning of the new skill more difficult than it otherwise would be.

Third, children are, on the whole, more adventuresome than they will be as they grow older. They are, as a result, eager to try something new. This provides the motivation necessary to put the effort into the learning.

Fourth, while adolescents and adults find repetition boring, children enjoy it. As a result, they are willing to repeat an act over and over again until the muscle patterns have been trained to perform effectively.

BOX 6–4

ESSENTIALS IN LEARNING MOTOR SKILLS

READINESS TO LEARN
When learning is correlated with readiness to learn, the skill is far superior to that learned with equal time and effort by those maturationally unready to learn.

OPPORTUNITY TO LEARN
Many children are deprived of opportunities to learn motor skills by parents who are afraid they will hurt themselves or by living in an environment which does not provide learning opportunities.

OPPORTUNITIES FOR PRACTICE
Children must be given as much time to practice as is needed to master a skill. However, the quality of the practice is far more important than the quantity. If children practice in a hit-or-miss fashion, poor habits of performance and inefficient movements will develop.

GOOD MODELS
Because imitating a model plays such an important role in learning motor skills, if good skills are to be learned, children must have good models to imitate.

GUIDANCE
Children need guidance if they are to imitate a model correctly. Guidance also helps them to correct errors before they are so well learned that it is difficult to correct them.

MOTIVATION
Motivation to learn is essential to keep interest from lagging. Common sources of motivation to learn motor skills are the personal satisfaction children derive from the activity, the independence and prestige in the peer group motor skills give them, and compensation for feelings of inadequacy in other areas, especially schoolwork.

EACH MOTOR SKILL MUST BE LEARNED INDIVIDUALLY
There is no such thing as a general hand skill or a general leg skill. Instead, each skill must be learned individually because it differs in some respect from every other skill. Holding a spoon for self-feeding, for example, differs from holding a crayon for coloring. (See Figure 6–5)

SKILLS SHOULD BE LEARNED ONE AT A TIME
Trying to learn several motor skills simultaneously, especially if they use the same muscle teams, is confusing to children and results in poor skills and wasted time and effort. After one skill has been mastered, another skill then can be learned without confusion.

Figure 6–5. Because every motor skill is slightly different from every other skill, it must be learned individually. (*Adapted from Bil Keane: "The Family Circus."* Register and Tribune Syndicate, *July 3, 1975. Used by permission.*)

7-3
1975, The Register and Tribune Syndicate

"That's all right for lollipops, but you have to hold pencils a different way."

Fifth, because children have fewer duties and responsibilities than they will have as they grow older, they have more time to devote to the mastery of skills than adolescents and adults have. Even if they do have sufficient time later, they are likely to become bored with the repetition that learning the skill requires and, as a result, they will not master it fully.

Essentials in Learning Motor Skills

Motor skills will not develop through maturation alone. Instead, they must be learned. Studies of how children learn motor skills have revealed that there are eight conditions essential to this learning. These eight essentials are explained in Box 6–4.

If any one of these essentials is lacking or deficient, development of the skill will fall below the child's capacity. When, for example, little or no guidance is given the child when learning the skill of self-feeding with a spoon, the skill will be learned more slowly and less efficiently than it would have been, had the child been shown how to use the spoon. The skill is likely, also, to fall far short of the socially approved way of holding a spoon.

Methods of Learning Motor Skills

The method the child uses to learn a motor skill is important to the quality of the skill eventually learned. While any method may, in time, enable the child to develop a skill, some methods are far more efficient and result in better quality skills than other methods.

Box 6–5 lists the three most common methods children use in learning motor skills. In each case, the advantages and disadvantages of each method are explained. This should point out why guidance is so essential to efficient learning. By contrast, an ineffectual learning method will cause the child to fall below the level of efficiency one might expect from the time and effort the child put into the learning.

Improvement in Motor Skills

In the early stages of learning a motor skill, body movements are clumsy and uncoordinated and many unnecessary movements are made. When children are learning to throw balls, for example, they throw with their whole bodies. With practice, ball-throwing skills improve and movements become coordinated,

---

BOX 6–5

COMMON METHODS OF LEARNING
MOTOR SKILLS

TRIAL-AND-ERROR LEARNING
Having no guidance and no model to imitate, the child tries out different acts at random. This usually results in a skill below the child's capacities.

IMITATION
Learning by imitating or observing a model (e.g., a parent or an older child) is faster than learning by trial and error, but is limited by faults in the model. A child will not learn to swim well, for example, if a poor swimmer is imitated. Even if the model is good, the child is not likely to be an efficient observer.

TRAINING
Learning under guidance and supervision in which the model demonstrates the skill and sees that the child imitates it correctly is especially important in the early phases of learning. Faulty movements and bad habits, once established, are hard to eliminate.

---

rhythmic, and more graceful. The individual movements of the arms, hands, head, legs, feet, and trunk become fused into a pattern (64).

As motor skills develop, speed, accuracy, strength, and economy of movements increase. *Speed,* for example, increases at a fairly uniform rate throughout childhood and up to the sixteenth or eighteenth year; the increase is greatest in the early childhood years and then slows down as the child approaches puberty. *Accuracy,* as measured by laboratory tests of tracing and aiming at a target, improves up to 13 or 14 years and then comes to a standstill. The greatest increase in accuracy comes early in childhood. For example, 6-year-olds, are nearly twice as accurate in their movements as 3-year-olds. *Steadiness,* as measured by how little movement occurs when the finger, hand, arm, or whole body is held as nearly motionless as possible, improves with age. The period of greatest improvement has not yet been determined. *Strength* increases with physical development, but not markedly until puberty, when there is rapid growth in the size of the muscles (3, 20, 43, 64, 65).

The motor skills most likely to show the greatest improvement are those learned in school, in supervised play groups, or in summer camps. These skills include writing, drawing, painting, clay modeling, dancing, and those related to games and sports. The latter range from such simple movements as throwing a ball to such complicated skills as diving or synchronized swimming.

The reason for the improvement in these skills is that teachers or play supervisors direct children's efforts into the right channels from the start. In addition, they are alert to possible errors and are ready to correct these errors before repeated practice makes them habitual. As a result, children show greater proficiency in skills in which they have received guidance than in skills learned at home where parents have too little time to give them guidance or in those learned when playing with peers. Often peers provide poor models and are too inexperienced to provide guidance in learning skills.

Some Common Motor Skills of Childhood

Some motor skills are commonly found among all children in a given culture because of similar learning experiences and similar adult expectations. In our culture, for example, all children are expected to learn to feed and dress themselves, to write, and to play the games approved by the social group. Furthermore, they are expected to learn these skills at approximately the same age as other children learn them. They are among the developmental tasks of childhood.

The skills that children in the American culture of today are expected to learn are mainly those involving the hands and arms and those involving the legs and feet. Because maturation of muscle coordination follows the laws of developmental direction, hand skills can be learned earlier than leg skills. Furthermore, because hand skills are, for the most part, more useful to children than leg skills, children spend more time and expend more effort in learning them. As a result, hand skills are not only more numerous than leg skills, but, for the most part, they are better learned and, consequently, of better quality than leg skills.

In the following pages, a description will be given of some of the common hand and leg skills that have been studied to date. Most of the skills are ones learned during the preschool years. There are two reasons for this: *first,* early childhood is the age when

many motor skills are learned and, *second,* it is far more difficult to make studies of how older children learn motor skills because of the difficulty of getting them to participate in the experiments and to allow observation over the length of time needed to master the skills.

Some of the motor skills that have received the most scientific attention and have been studied most extensively have yielded norms that are used in tests to measure the intelligence of children during infancy and the early babyhood years when use of tests involving language is impossible. In the Stanford Revision of the Binet Scale, for example, the ability to copy has been used to measure children's intellectual development at different ages. Children are expected to be able to copy a circle at 3 years of age, a square at 5 years, a diamond at 7 years and to reproduce a simple geometric figure from memory at 10 years (62).

Hand Skills

Control of the muscles of the arms, shoulders, and wrists improves rapidly during the childhood years and almost reaches the adult level of perfection by the time the child is 12 years old. Control of the fine muscles of the fingers, by contrast, develops at a slower rate. The control necessary for speedy writing or the playing of musical instruments is not normally attained until children are 12 or older (6, 20, 44).

Of the many skills of childhood, those that have been studied most extensively are self-feeding skills, self-dressing skills, self-grooming skills, writing, copying, ball throwing and catching, and block building. All of these studies have used large enough groups and have covered a long enough period of time to yield age norms at which different skills are mastered and to show whether the pattern of mastery is similar for most children. Two areas will be used as illustrations, self-feeding and ball throwing and catching.

SELF-FEEDING During the latter part of the first year of life, babies try to hold a bottle or cup and reach for the spoon with which they are being fed. By the age of 8 months, they can hold their bottles after they have been placed in their mouths; a month later, they can remove the bottle as well as put it back in their mouths. By the time they are 11 or 12 months old, babies can hold their cups temporarily and try to feed themselves with their spoons. At first, they hold the cup with both hands but, gradually, with practice, they can hold it with one hand. In first spoon-feeding, babies usually spill most of the food on their spoons but, with practice, they spill less and less.

By the end of the second year, young children can use forks as well as spoons. During the third year, they can spread butter or jam on their bread with a knife. A year later, most young children, if given opportunities for practice and guidance in how to do so, are able to cut tender meat with a knife. By the time they are ready for school, at 6 years, most children have mastered all the tasks used in self-feeding (9, 20).

BALL THROWING AND CATCHING   Some babies roll and may even attempt to throw balls before they are 2 years old. Even at 4, however, few can throw well. By 6 years, most children are proficient though there are marked variations at every age.

Because ball catching is even more difficult than ball throwing, it is later in developing. At 4 years, for example, few children are proficient at this skill, while at 6, approximately two-thirds are. At first, children use the whole body to grasp the ball when it is thrown to them. Then they use the arms, with less random movement. Shortly after they are 6 years old, they begin to perfect a coordinated movement of the hands to catch the ball between the palms (6, 20, 21, 27, 39).

Leg Skills

After babies reach 18 months of age, motor development in the legs consists primarily of the perfection of walking and the acquisition of related skills. Before babies are 2 years old, for example, they can walk sideways and backwards, they can stand on one foot with help and, a year later, without help. Before their second birthdays, babies can walk on tiptoe and, between the fifth and sixth years, they can walk well enough to balance on a narrow plank elevated on one end or to follow a chalk mark on the floor (6, 9, 68).

Fewer studies have been made of leg skills than of hand skills. Those that have been made have emphasized the patterns of development of these skills and the approximate ages at which children can be expected to acquire them. The leg skills that have received the most scientific attention are running, hopping, skipping, jumping, climbing, swimming, and tricycling and bicycling. Climbing and tricycling and bicycling will be used as illustrations of how these skills develop.

CLIMBING   Even before babies can walk, they climb steps by crawling and creeping. The pattern of stair climbing is almost identical to that of creeping. Babies who creep on their hands and knees, for example, climb stairs on their hands and knees; those who creep on hands, one knee, and one foot climb stairs in that fashion. In going down stairs, babies generally go down backwards.

Before babies are 2 years old, they can walk upstairs and downstairs with help, hold the railing of the stairs or the hand of a person. This they do in an upright position. At first, one foot is placed on the step and the other is drawn up to it. The same foot is used every time to make the advance. This ability is acquired as children approach their third birthdays.

A similar method is used for going downstairs. Gradually, with practice, children let go of the railing and use their legs alternately, as in walking. This adult method of step-climbing is attained by 4 years of age, provided children have ample opportunity to practice (6, 9, 20). Figure 6–6 shows the characteristic stages in acquiring the skill of step climbing.

TRICYCLING AND BICYCLING   By the age of two years, a few toddlers can ride tricycles. Most, however, push their tricycles around and ride on them only when held on the seat by someone. Between 3 and 4 years, however, all young children who have had an opportunity to learn to ride tricycles can do so.

After achieving enough skill in tricycle riding to feel self-confident, many young children use their tricycles for stunting, such as riding backwards, turning corners on two instead of three wheels, and riding while standing up. Because stunting is a hazard to good personal and social adjustments, this matter will be discussed in more detail in the section on hazards in motor development at the end of this chapter.

By the time children are 6, and sometimes before, they graduate to bicycles. Because riding bicycles is a more difficult and more complicated motor skill, involving balance as well as locomotion, it usually requires six months to a year of practice before the skill is so well mastered that children can ride without falls or trying to stunt.

Variations in Children's Skills

Just because certain skills are "common" among American children does not mean that they are universal. Some children, for example, may have no opportu-

Figure 6-6. Stages in step climbing.

nity to learn to swim and others may have little or no motivation to learn self-grooming skills because their parents assume this responsibility for them.

Studies of skills learned by children have identified some of the conditions responsible for variations in these skills. There are, for example, *sex* differences in skills. No significant sex differences in motor development have been found during the early years if boys and girls are given equal training, encouragement, equipment, and opportunities for practice (25). As a result of cultural pressures, sex differences in motor skills begin to appear around the kindergarten age, however, and become more and more marked as children grow older.

Cultural pressures influence sex differences in skills mainly by limiting learning opportunities. Among elementary school children, boys are generally superior to girls in skills requiring strength and endurance —skills which are considered more sex appropriate for boys. In ball throwing, for example, boys show greater gains than girls primarily because boys receive more encouragement to become proficient in this skill (21). On the other hand, while boys are superior to girls in motor skills requiring speed and coordination of gross bodily movements and in mechanical ability, girls are superior to boys in manual dexterity as shown in finer coordinations (25).

Children from the poorer *socioeconomic* groups, it has been reported, learn motor skills, especially self-help skills, earlier than those from better socioeconomic backgrounds. This is not because they are maturationally ready to learn them earlier but rather because their parents have less time to do things for them than have parents from a better socioeconomic status. This is true also for *family size*. Children from large families are expected to learn more skills at an earlier age than children from small families (9).

Body build plays an important role in determining the number and quality of the skills children learn. Children with mesomorphic builds, given opportunities to do so, learn more and better quality motor skills than those of ectomorphic or endomorphic builds. The mesomorph has greater strength and energy, thus making the learning of skills easy and pleasurable. By contrast, the ectomorph has less strength and endurance while the endomorph tends to be clumsy and awkward and to tire easily because of a flabby body and weak muscles (18, 23).

Knowing how important skills are to group belonging, children who are *popular* or who want to be accepted by their peers are more strongly motivated to learn skills than are children who are less popular or who prefer solitary activities (13, 44, 63). Skills also vary according to children's *personalities*. Children, for example, who suffer from feelings of inadequacy often bolster their self-concepts by learning motor skills that have prestige in the eyes of the peer group, as in the case of swimming (40).

Age is also an important factor in variations in motor skills. The older the child, the more skills, the greater the variety of skills, and the better their quality (3, 20, 23).

Functions of Motor Skills

Different motor skills play different roles in children's personal and social adjustments. Some skills, for example, help children to achieve the independence they crave while others help them to achieve social acceptance. Because it is impossible for children to learn a large number of motor skills simultaneously, they concentrate on learning the skills that will aid them in achieving the type of adjustment that is important to them at that time. When, for example, children are anxious to be independent, they concentrate on mastering the skills that will make independence possible. When, on the other hand, they crave peer acceptance, they concentrate on learning the skills needed for group belonging.

Motor skills can be divided, roughly, into four categories according to the functions they serve in the child's personal and social adjustments. These categories are explained in Box 6-6. Note that some of the skills involve the use of the legs but more involve the use of the arms and hands while others involve the use of the muscles of the entire body.

Of these categories, the self-help skills are usually learned first because often it is important to children to be independent before it is important to them to become members of a peer group. Until children are old enough to go to school, they have no real need for school skills. As a result, they have little motivation to learn them.

Handedness

Handedness means the predominant use of one hand. There are two criteria used to determine handedness; *first,* preference for one hand as compared with the other and, *second,* the proficiency or skill with which a person uses one hand as compared with use of the other hand.

People are said to be "right-handed" if they use the right hand *most* of the time and "left-handed" if they favor the left hand. Few people are so predominantly right- or left-handed that they *always* use the preferred hand. At all ages, not in childhood alone, shifts in hand usage are common though they tend to decrease as children approach adolescence.

People are referred to as "ambidextrous" or, as it is sometimes called, "mixed-handed," if they use both hands equally well and approximately an equal amount of the time. Left-handers tend to be more ambidextrous than right-handers. The reason for this is that when, as children, they showed a preference for their left hands, they were often taught to perform certain formal skills, such as writing or painting, with their right hands. In time, they built up a repertoire of skills they could carry out equally well with their right or left

---

BOX 6-6

FUNCTIONAL CATEGORIES OF CHILDREN'S SKILLS

SELF-HELP SKILLS
To achieve independence, children must learn motor skills that will enable them to do things for themselves. These skills include self-feeding, self-dressing, self-grooming, and self-bathing. By the time children reach school age, these skills should have reached the level of proficiency to enable children to take care of themselves with almost the speed and adeptness of adults.

SOCIAL-HELP SKILLS
To be an accepted member of a social group—either the family, the school, or the neighborhood group—the child must be a cooperative member. Skills such as helping with the work of the home, the school, or the peer group will go a long way to win the acceptance of the group.

PLAY SKILLS
To enjoy the activities of the peer group or to amuse themselves when away from peers, children must learn play skills such as ball play, roller skating, drawing, painting, and manipulating toys.

SCHOOL SKILLS
Much of the work of the early school years involves motor skills, such as writing, drawing, painting, clay modeling, dancing, or wood work. The more numerous and the better these skills are, the better the adjustments children will make to school and the greater their achievements in the academic as well as the nonacademic areas of schoolwork.

---

hands. By contrast, right-handers generally show less ambidexterity than left-handers (47).

A majority of hand skills require the use of one hand or of one hand aided by the other. The hand that does most of the work is known as the "dominant hand" and, if the act requires help, the other hand plays the role of helper and is known as the "auxiliary hand." In writing, for example, the dominant hand—whether the right or the left—holds the pencil or pen and does the writing while the other, the auxiliary hand, holds the paper in place.

In most cultures, for reasons as yet unexplained, more people are right-handed than left-handed. It has been reported, for example, that between 90 and 95 percent of all Americans today are right-handed and that more males than females are left-handed (17, 25, 35).

Development of Handedness

According to tradition, a child is born either right-handed or left-handed and any attempt to change this pattern will produce such ills as nervous tension, stuttering and stammering, or reading disorders. Whether handedness is hereditary or the result of training and social conditioning has been debated for many generations. Extensive research, however, indicates that training and social conditioning determine handedness and that there is no such thing as "natural handedness."

Studies of how handedness develops have shown that, in the early months of life, babies are ambidextrous, with no preference for either the right hand or the left. By the time they are 8 months old, most begin to show a slight preference for the right hand, though they shift from one hand to the other, depending largely on the position of the person or object they are reaching for. If the person or object is closer to their right, for example, they will use the right hand (2, 49, 56).

During the second year of life, shifting from right- to left-hand usage continues, but is not as frequent as during the first year. Then, between the ages of 2½ and 3½ years, there is a marked shift to bilatererality, with both hands being used with approximately equal frequency and proficiency. From the ages of 4 to 6 years, unilateral preference predominates and shifts from the use of one hand to the other are relatively infrequent (2, 10, 29). This means that when children enter school, they are predominantly either right- or left-handed, seldom ambidextrous. However, there is evidence that, when motivated to do so, children, adolescents, and even adults can acquire new skills with either hand without experiencing any emotional upset (10, 33, 34, 47).

Advantages of Hand Dominance

There is evidence that dominant handedness is advantageous. The reason for this is that, with the establishment of dominance come not only feelings of stability and security but also opportunities to develop levels of skill that would be impossible if attempts were made to use both hands with equal frequency. If a child learns to perform the majority of skills with one hand, the auxiliary hand is then trained to work with the dominant hand, and as a team the two can operate with great efficiency. Most children who lack hand dominance have less strength, speed, and accuracy in movement than those who are either right- or left-handed (3, 21, 34).

In the development of hand dominance, there is no evidence that the right hand is superior to the left hand and that a nation of right-handed people is superior to a nation of left-handers. It has, however, become traditional to regard the right hand as the preferred hand and much of the American culture has been built on this traditional preference. For example, machines, tools, home appliances, sporting equipment, and desk chairs are designed for right-handers. Only the typewriter, which has been called the only "left-handed machine in general use" because the most frequently used keys are on the left, is easier for left-handers to master. Methods of teaching, such as teaching handwriting in the elementary school, are also geared to right-handers (34, 48). Some of the many advantages of being right-handed are explained in Box 6-7.

The advantages of being right-handed do not end with childhood. When, for example, left-handed people apply for work that requires the manipulation of complicated machinery, they often find that even if they can adapt the training methods to their left-handed needs, they still find it difficult to come up to the speed of their right-handed coworkers. Many employers feel that left-handers are harder to train than right-handers, are slower workers, and tend to be accident-prone. This limits the employment opportunities of left-handers (48).

Hazards in Motor Development

Most people think of awkwardness as the only serious hazard in the child's development of motor coordinations and skills. While unquestionably awkwardness is a serious hazard to good personal and social adjustments, it is, by no means, the only hazard. Other hazards may and do have serious psychological repercussions. Some of these hazards are discussed below.

Delayed Motor Development

Delayed motor development means motor development below the norm for the child's age. As a result, the child does not learn the developmental tasks the social group expects children of that age to learn. A baby, for example, who falls below the norm in walking and self-feeding is regarded as "backward."

There are many *causes* of delayed motor development, some of which are controllable and some not. It may come from brain damage at birth or unfavorable conditions in the prenatal or early postnatal environment. More often, however, it comes from lack of opportunity to learn motor skills because of unfavorable environmental conditions, of parental overprotectiveness, or of lack of motivation on the child's part to learn them. It has been reported, for example, that restrictive mothers lower the child's level of competence in motor activities while stimulating mothers raise it (69).

The *effects* of delayed motor development are hazardous to good personal and social adjustments. There are two reasons for this. First, it has an unfavorable effect on children's self-concepts. As a result, it often leads to emotional and behavioral problems. When, for example, children try to do things to achieve the independence they crave and fail to do them successfully enough to be independent, they become frustrated when they must rely upon others for help. As they grow older and compare their achievements with those of their age-mates, they feel inferior when they discover how far short their achievements fall. Feelings of frustration and inferiority always lead to emotional and behavioral problems which are hazardous to good adjustments. Second, delayed motor development is hazardous because it does not provide the foundations on which motor skills can later be laid. When the learning of skills is delayed because of delay in laying the foundations on which the skills depend, children are at a disadvantage when they begin to play with other children. This is because early social contacts are mainly in the form of play. If children lack the motor skills necessary to play with their age-mates, they will be excluded from the play group, thus depriving them of the fun their age-mates have and of opportunities to learn social and play skills when their age-mates are learning them.

Unrealistic Expectations about Skills

Unrealistic expectations are expectations based more on hopes and desires than on the individual's potentials. In the area of motor development, children are expected to gain motor control and to learn skills before they are maturationally ready to do so.

Some unrealistic expectations come from parents,

BOX 6–7

IMPORTANT ADVANTAGES OF RIGHT-HANDEDNESS

LEARNING IS FACILITATED
Most equipment and systems of teaching motor skills favor the right-handed person. The left-hander has to try to adapt to them.

GUIDANCE AND DEMONSTRATIONS ARE MORE MEANINGFUL
Since most models are right-handed, the right-handed child finds demonstrations and explanations easier to follow than the left-hander.

SKILLS ARE SPEEDIER AND LESS FATIGUING
Since right-handers are favored in guidance and demonstrations, they usually develop superior motor skills and greater speed. Left-handers become fatigued from trying to keep up to the pace set by right-handers; they become frustrated because they are slower and have more difficulty achieving their levels of aspiration.

CONFORMITY TO SOCIAL EXPECTATIONS IS FACILITATED
Being right-handed in a right-handed culture enables children to conform to the pattern set by the majority. By contrast, being left-handed makes them feel different and conspicuous. Right-handedness also facilitates the social skills, such as following the accepted pattern of using eating utensils and shaking hands as a form of greeting.

PERSONALITY IS FAVORABLY AFFECTED
Conforming to the behavior of one's age-mates and to the expectations of the social group leads to favorable self-judgments. Many left-handed children feel inadequate and self-conscious because they are different.

some from teachers, and some from children themselves. Regardless of the source, they are hazardous to children's personal and social adjustments.

Unrealistic *parental* expectations may come from the parents' desire to have others think of their children as "precocious" and of themselves as "good parents." They may come from trying to have their children conform to the norms given in books on child rearing. Or, they may come from using older siblings as standards and expecting younger siblings to conform to these standards.

Another common unrealistic parental expectation is based on parental beliefs that children can learn several unrelated motor skills without adequate time to master each of these skills. In the case of self-dressing, for example, the skills needed to put on shirts are so different from the skills needed to put on socks and shoes that, until each has been mastered, children cannot be expected to do any part of the self-dressing process successfully. As a result, children will derive little satisfaction from the independence self-dressing normally gives and will feel inadequate when their achievements fall far short of parental expectations.

Within a family, the children most likely to be subjected to unrealistic parental expectations are first-borns and those who have been prematurely-born. In the case of the former, parental ignorance of what children are maturationally capable of or parental pride is likely to give rise to unrealistic expectations. In the case of children who were born permaturely, some parents, as was pointed out in Chapter 4, push them to catch up to children of the same age who were born at full term. However, no child in the family is likely to be spared from being subjected to unrealistic parental expectations about motor control and motor skills.

Some *teachers* have unrealistic expectations about children's motor abilities because they are "norm-conscious" and expect all children to conform to the norms they learned about in their teachers' training courses. Others use children in their classes or children in the same family whom they taught earlier as the basis for the norms they use to judge individual children. A younger sibling, for example, is expected to learn to write, to crayon, or to draw as well and at the same age as an older sibling taught several years earlier by the same teacher.

Children themselves may have unrealistic expectations about motor skills. Even the most complicated skill looks easy to children when they watch a competent person perform it quickly and accurately. They have no appreciation of how complicated the skill is or how long the person worked to perfect it. When children try to carry out the skill, they realize that it is far more difficult than it looked. After trying unsuccessfully to carry out the skill, they become discouraged and give up. This fosters a feeling of personal inadequacy.

Unrealistic expectations, whether they originate in parents or teachers or in children themselves are psychologically damaging to children. Not being able to live up to expectations makes children feel inferior and inadequate—feelings that undermine self-confidence and weaken motivation to learn other skills. If, in addition, children are criticized or scolded, they become resentful and feel martyred. This has an unfavorable effect on their social adjustments, not only with those responsible for the unrealistic expectations but also with others in no way involved in the situation.

Failure to Learn Important Motor Skills

If children fail to learn the motor skills that are important to them or to members of the peer group, it plays havoc with their personal and social adjustments. For example, because self-help skills are necessary to achieving independence, children who fail to learn these skills when a desire for independence becomes strong—during the second and third years—feel inferior and become rebellious when they must rely on others for help.

Similarly, when children want to be accepted members of a peer group, failure to learn the play and social-help skills that contribute heavily to social acceptance results in poor social adjustments as well as poor personal adjustments. Children will think of themselves as inferior because they cannot do what their peers do and martyred because they are not accepted as members of the peer group.

Poor Foundation Skills

According to tradition, "Practice makes perfect." This is true *only* if the foundation skills are good. Poor foundations, resulting from learning by trial-and-error or by imitating a poor model, will not result in good—and certainly not "perfect"—skills regardless of how much time and effort are devoted to practice.

The hazardous nature of accepting this traditional belief comes from adult pressure on children to continue practice regardless of the kind of motor skill they are learning. If the foundation skill is poor, proficiency in the new skill will not only fall short of the child's capacity but, even worse, this low level of proficiency will become so ingrained in the child that any improvement becomes difficult or almost impossible. When this happens, children feel frustrated that their time and effort have produced such poor results, and these results will be a constant source of feelings of inferiority when they compare their skills with those of age-mates who learned by better methods.

Stunting

Once children learn a skill well enough to gain satisfaction from it, they often begin to "stunt" or to carry out the skill in an unorthodox way to gain greater satisfaction, attention, and publicity. When young children, as was pointed out earlier, master the skills needed to ride their tricycles, they may try to ride them in some unorthodox way—riding backwards or not holding onto the handlebars. This gives them personal satisfaction from feelings of successful achievement and from the admiration or envy of their peers.

As children grow older and peer admiration becomes increasingly important to them, they add to the pleasure of achievement the satisfaction of the attention their stunting draws. In addition, successful accomplishment of a dare has great prestige value for children.

In spite of the satisfaction stunting gives, there is potential psychological damage from it. This comes from the effect on children's personal and social adjustments. Because stunting often leads to accidents, with the physical and psychological repercussions that accompany accidents (see page 128 for a discussion of this matter), stunting is hazardous to good personal adjustments even though it may, temporarily, give children feelings of personal satisfaction and superiority. It is hazardous to good social adjustments because members of the peer group regard children who stunt as "show-offs" and think they are "silly" to take such chances—even though they may, in fact, admire and envy them.

Left-Handedness

Left-handedness is a *potential* hazard to good personal and social adjustments. It becomes a *real* hazard under two conditions.

First, if children realize they are different because they are left-handed and if they interpret this to mean that they are inferior, it will affect their attitudes toward self and, in turn, their behavior. If, for example, they are the only left-handers in their classes, and if teachers make a point of demonstrating skills with the left hand for them, thus calling their classmates' attention to their differentness, or if they acquire the nickname, "Southpaw," the effect on their self-concepts is very likely to be unfavorable. This hazard tends to increase as childhood progresses and as children become more and more anxious to be like their peers. Feeling embarrassed and self-conscious about their differentness usually reaches a peak during the self-conscious years of puberty and early adolescence.

Second, left-handedness becomes a real hazard to good personal and social adjustments if it interferes with learning skills and results in learning skills which children believe are below their capacities. When, for example, children try to imitate a right-handed model or follow instructions given to right-handers, they are likely to become confused. This makes learning more difficult for them than it otherwise would be and results in a skill below their capacities. In play with peers and in schoolwork, this can be and often is a hazard to good personal adjustments because it increases their feelings of differentness. It is also a hazard to good social adjustments because it leads to unfavorable social attitudes, especially attitudes of peers when their play skills fall below those of their age-mates.

Because left-handedness is a potential personal and social hazard, two possible approaches to it can be taken. The *first* is to prevent left-handedness from becoming a habit. Learning to use one hand in preference to the other is always easier if directed and if learning occurs before a conflicting habit has been established. This does not mean that children should be *forced* to use their right hands if they definitely prefer doing things with their left hands. Instead, if objects are presented to the right hand and if the children are guided in learning skills with their right hands from the very beginning, the chances are good that right-handedness will be established (2, 34).

The *second* approach to the left-handedness problem is to change from left- to right-handedness when it becomes apparent that children are beginning to show a preference for their left hands. The longer the shift to the right hand is put off, the more difficult it will be. The reason is that changes in accustomed patterns of behavior always require adjustments and these always lead to nervous tension. If children are forced to change instead of being encouraged to do so, they will likely become resistant. This will increase their confusion and tension.

There is no evidence that changing handedness, per se, will cause serious psychological difficulties, as tradition holds, especially if the change is undertaken before left-handed habits have become strongly established. It is true, however, that the tension aroused when there is interference with partially established habits *may* lead to stuttering and other forms of nervous behavior, such as nail biting and thumb sucking. These are more likely to be *symptoms* of the tension resulting from the method used to break an old habit and establish a new one than of the change of handedness. Normally, the tension thus created will tend to subside when the change has been made. If the child's resistance is extreme and if there is too long a delay in making the change, the stuttering or other nervous mannerisms may become fixed habits that will persist throughout life.

The extent and duration of psychological damage resulting from attempts to change the child from a left- to a right-hander will vary according to four conditions.

First, the degree of motivation the child has to make the change. If children *want* to change to right-handedness, they will be far more anxious to put the time and effort needed into making the change than if they are satisfied to be left-handed.

Second, the age of the child when attempts are made to change to right-handedness. As was pointed out above, the longer the shift is delayed, the harder it will be for children to change and the more confusing it will be to do so.

Third, whether the child is encouraged or forced to make the change. If children can see any personal advantage to being right- rather than left-handed and if they are promised help in making the change, their motivation to do so will strengthen their desire to make the necessary effort.

Fourth, the personality make-up of the child. Personality influences the effect changing handedness will have. A high-strung, nervous child, for example, may suffer great and long-lasting damage while a child who is placid and easy-going may suffer none.

Hildreth has suggested conditions under which changes from left- to right-handedness can be carried out with minimum psychological damage to children (34). These conditions are as follows:

- The child is under 6 years of age.
- The child uses both hands interchangeably.
- The handedness index is bilateral.
- A trial period shows no permanent difficulty.
- The child is agreeable to the change.
- The child is above average in intelligence.

Awkwardness

Children should be regarded as awkward or clumsy *only* if control over the movements of their bodies falls below the accepted standards for their ages. Some children may seem to be awkward because they are judged by inappropriate standards. A 2-year-old, for example, who is large is likely to be judged awkward if standards of motor development for 3-year-olds are used. Similarly, children who are mentally precocious enough to be in grades above those of their age-mates are very likely to be judged by standards for their apparent ages, not their real ages.

Studies of awkwardness in children have revealed that there are many *causes*. These studies have revealed that some of the causes are controllable while others are not. They have also revealed that a child may be awkward for several reasons or for only one. Of the many causes of awkwardness, the following have been found to be most common: delay in maturation, a poor physical condition which weakens motivation to get the exercise needed to develop motor skills, extreme ectomorphic or endomorphic body builds which motivate children not to exercise enough to acquire skills, a very low IQ, which is accompanied by retardation in motor development, a very high IQ, which encourages interest in intellectual rather than motor activities, lack of opportunity and motivation to develop muscle control, and emotional tension that interferes with muscle coordinations (17, 38, 40, 58, 69).

There are also intraindividual differences in awkwardness for a number of reasons, three of which are common. *First,* children who are temporarily nervous, tense, and emotionally upset are more awkward than they normally are. Emotional disturbances make the muscles tense and even rigid, thus making control difficult. Normally well-coordinated children, under such conditions, become clumsy and awkward.

Second, during periods of rapid growth, such as the puberty growth spurt, established patterns of motor coordination are upset. Rapid maturers are more awkward at this time than slow maturers who have time to adjust to their newly enlarged hands and feet.

Third, children differ in the degree of motor control they have in different situations. As a result of differences in learning opportunities, in the time spent in acquiring skills, and in motivation, children are well coordinated in some activities and awkward in others. A child who has plenty of opportunity to practice ice skating but little opportunity to play ball or ride a bicycle, for example, will be a proficient skater but below the norm in ball playing and bicycling.

Studies of motor coordination in childhood have shown that the *psychological damage* of awkwardness is, in many respects, even greater than the physical. In

BOX 6-8

SOURCES OF PSYCHOLOGICAL DAMAGE FROM AWKWARDNESS

FEELINGS OF INFERIORITY

When children begin to associate with other children, they compare their activities and achievements with those of their age-mates. If their performances fall short, they feel inferior. If this happens frequently, they will begin to think of themselves as inferior, thus laying the foundations for inferiority complexes.

JEALOUSY OF OTHER CHILDREN

Jealousy develops when awkward children envy those who perform better than they do, especially if the good performers are commended by adults for their good performances and awkward children are criticized and scolded for their poor performances. Jealousy makes children unhappy; it also makes other children reject them as playmates.

RESENTMENT TOWARD ADULTS

Children rarely blame themselves for their awkwardness. Instead, they generally find a scapegoat to blame, usually a parent or teacher. This lays the foundation for a martyr complex. Feeling guiltless, children are not motivated to try to overcome their awkwardness.

SOCIAL REJECTION

Awkwardness is a handicap to children's social contacts with members of the peer group. If other children laugh at their clumsiness and do not want to play with them, awkward children's feelings of inadequacy and resentment are intensified.

DEPENDENCY

Children who lack self-confidence because of their awkwardness do not try to do their best. As a result, they become dependent on others and this increases their feelings of inadequacy.

TIMIDITY

Normally, physical timidity decreases as childhood progresses. Awkward children do not follow this pattern. Instead, they do not engage in motor activities because they are afraid they will not perform successfully. Physical timidity may become so generalized that they are afraid of *any* new situation. As a result, they work far below their capacities and often fail when they should succeed.

BOREDOM

Awkward children who are cut off from the activities of their age-mates become bored and restless. Instead of expending their energies in wholesome play, they often engage in troublesome activities, in retaliation for their rejection by the peer group or in the hope of winning the group's attention and approval. This pattern of social adjustment may become habitual.

Box 6-8 are listed the major sources of this psychological damage.

There is further evidence that the damage often leaves a scar on the child's personality—a scar that may never be completely eradicated even though the awkwardness itself is overcome. Many cases of inferiority complex in adolescence and adulthood have been traced in part to awkwardness during the childhood years (17, 24, 38, 40).

The psychological damage of awkwardness also manifests itself in the type of social adjustments children make. Studies of awkward children have revealed that they often become almost apologetic in posture and gait, in the way they shake hands, and in the manner in which they enter a room (9, 17). This kind of behavior, which is a direct reflection of lack of self-confidence and feelings of inadequacy, creates an unfavorable impression on others—peers as well as adults. As a result of unfavorable social judgements, awkward children tend to make poor social adjustments as well as poor personal adjustments.

Chapter Highlights

1 Motor development, which comes from the coordinated activities of nerve centers, nerves, and muscles, is partially responsible for overcoming the helplessness characteristic of newborn infants.

2 From longitudinal studies of babies and young children, five general principles of motor development have emerged: motor development depends on neural and muscular development; learning skills cannot occur until the child is maturationally ready; motor development follows a predictable pattern; it is possible to establish norms for motor development; and there are individual differences in rate of motor development.

3 Muscle control is achieved in a predictable way, following the laws of developmental direction.

4 Childhood is called the "ideal age" for learning skills because children's bodies are more pliable than those of adolescents and adults, children have fewer previously learned skills to conflict with new learning, they are more adventuresome and eager to learn, they enjoy repetition, and they have more time to devote to learning skills than they will have as they grow older.

5 In the learning of motor skills, readiness and opportunities to learn, motivation, a good model, and guidance are some of the most important essentials.

6 Motor skills are learned by trial-and-error, by imitation, and by teaching. Of these, teaching is the best and trial-and-error the poorest method.

7 Improvement in motor skills is judged by speed, accuracy, strength, and steadiness.

8 Motor skills of children are divided into two categories—hand and leg skills. Hand skills are more numerous and more useful to children and, hence, better learned.

9 Motor skills, whether of the hands or legs, may also be divided into four categories, according to their functions, and are called self-help skills, social-help skills, play skills, and school skills.

10 There are two criteria for determining handedness, preference and proficiency in use.

11 There is scientific evidence that handedness results from training and social conditioning and that right-handedness is an advantage in the American culture of today.

12 There are many hazards in motor development, the most common of which are delayed motor development, unrealistic expectations about skills, failure to learn skills important to the child's personal and social adjustments, poor foundation skills, stunting, left-handedness, and awkwardness.

13 There is no scientific evidence that the traditional belief that practice makes perfect is true if the skill that is being learned is of poor quality.

14 Left-handedness becomes a hazard to good personal and social adjustments if it makes children self-conscious and if it interferes with their mastery of skills.

15 Awkwardness is always a hazard to good personal and social adjustments because it makes children feel conspicuous and inadequate and because it leads to unfavorable social judgements.

Bibliography

1 Adelson, E., and S. Fraiberg. Gross motor development in infants blind from birth. *Child Development,* 1974, *45,* 114–126.

2 Ames, L. B., and F. L. Ilg. The developmental point of view with special reference to the principle of reciprocal neuromotor interweaving. *Journal of Genetic Psychology,* 1964, *105,* 195–209.

3 Annett, M. The growth of manual preference and speed. *British Journal of Psychology,* 1970, *61,* 545–559.

4 Bakwin, H., and R. M. Bakwin. *Behavior disorders in children,* 4th ed. Philadelphia: Saunders, 1972.

5 Bayley, N. Comparisons of mental and motor test scores for ages 1–15 months by sex, birth order, race, geographical location and education of parents. *Child Development,* 1965, *36,* 379–411.

6 Bayley, N. *Bayley's scales for infant development.* New York: Psychological Corporation, 1968.

7 Benjamin, L. S., W. Serdahely, and T. V. Geppert. Night training through parents' implicit use of operant conditioning. *Child Development,* 1971, *42,* 963–966.

8 Bernbaum, M., J. Goodnow, and E. Lehman. Relationships among perceptual-motor skills: Tracing and copying. *Journal of Educational Psychology,* 1974, *66,* 731–735.

9 Breckenridge, M. L., and E. L. Vincent. *Child development: Physical and psychological development through adolescence,* 5th ed. Philadelphia: Saunders, 1965.

10 Bruml, H. Age changes in preference and skill measures of handedness. *Perceptual and Motor Skills,* 1972, *34,* 3–14.

11 Burnett, C. N., and E. W. Johnson. Development of gait in childhood. *Developmental Medicine and Child*

Neurology, 1971, *13,* pt. I, 196–202, pt. II, 207–215.

12 Chalmers, D. K., and M. E. Rosenbaum. Learning by observing versus learning by doing. *Journal of Educational Psychology,* 1974, *66,* 216–224.

13 Chevrette, J. M. The effect of peer observation on selected tasks of physical performance. *Journal of Psychology,* 1968, *70,* 113–119.

14 Connolly, K., K. Brown, and E. Bassett. Developmental changes in some components of a motor skill. *British Journal of Psychology,* 1968, *59,* 305–314.

15 Coursin, D. B. Nutrition and brain development in infants. *Merrill-Palmer Quarterly,* 1972, *18,* 177–202.

16 Cronbach, L. J. *Educational psychology,* 2d ed. New York: Harcourt, Brace & World, 1963.

17 Dare, M. T., and N. Gordon. Clumsy children: A disorder of perception and motor organization. *Developmental Medicine and Child Neurology,* 1970, *12,* 178–185.

18 Davies, C. T. M., C. Barnes, and S. Godfrey. Body composition and maximal exercise performance in children. *Human Biology,* 1972, *44,* 195–214.

19 Dayhaw, L. T. Guiding handedness in the development of the child. *Education,* 1953, *74,* 196–199.

20 Denkla, M. B. Development of motor co-ordination in normal children. *Developmental Medicine and Child Neurology,* 1974, *16,* 729–741.

21 Dusenberry, L. A study of the effects of training in ball-throwing by children ages three to seven. *Research Quarterly of the American Association for Health, Physical Education and Recreation,* 1952, *23,* 9–14.

22 Eckert, H. M. Variability in skill acquisition. *Child Development* 1974, *45,* 487–489.

23 Ellis, J. D., A. V. Carron, and D. A. Bailey. Physical performance in boys from 10 through 16 years. *Human Biology,* 1975, *47,* 263–281.

24 Ely, K. P., A. Healey, and G. L. Smidt. Mothers' expectations of their child's accomplishment of certain gross motor skills, *Development Medicine and Child Neurology,* 1972, *14,* 621–625.

25 Garai, J. E., and A. Ocheinfeld. Sex differences in mental and behavioral traits. *Genetic Psychology Monographs,* 1968, *77,* 169–299.

26 Gesell, A. The ontogenesis of infant behavior. In L. Carmichael (ed.), *Manual of child psychology,* 2d ed. New York: Wiley, 1954. Pp. 335–373.

27 Govatos, L. A. Motor skill learning. *Review of Educational Research,* 1967, *37,* 583–598.

28 Grant, W. W., A. N. Boelsche, and D. Zin. Developmental patterns of two motor functions. *Developmental Medicine and Child Neurology,* 1973, *15,* 171–177.

29 Groden, G. Lateral preferences in normal children. *Perceptual and Motor Skills,* 1969, *28,* 213–214.

30 Gutteridge, M. V. A study of motor achievements of young children. *Archives of Psychology, New York,* 1939, no. 244.

31 Hallahan, D. P., J. M. Kauffman, and C. S. Mueller. Behavioral observation and teacher rating correlates of motor and vocal behavior in preschoolers. *Journal of Genetic Psychology,* 1975, *126,* 45–52.

32 Halverson, H. M. An experimental study of prehension in infants by means of systematic cinema records. *Genetic Psychology Monographs,* 1931, *10,* 107–286.

33 Hardyck, C., R. Goldman, and L. Petrinovich. Handedness and sex, race, and age. *Human Biology,* 1975, *47,* 369–375.

34 Hildreth, G. The development and training of hand dominance. *Journal of Genetic Psychology,* 1950, *75,* 197–220; *76,* 39–144.

35 Hilgard, E. R., R. C. Atkinson, and R. L. Atkinson. *Introduction to psychology,* 5th ed. New York: Harcourt, Brace & Jovanovich, 1971.

36 Hindley, C. B. Racial and sexual differences in age of walking: A reanalysis of the Smith et al. (1930) data. *Journal of Genetic Psychology,* 1967, *111,* 161–167.

37 Hindley, C. B., A. M. Filliozat, G. Klackenberg, D. Nicolet-Meister, and E. A. Sand. Differences in age of walking in five European longitudinal samples. *Human Biology,* 1966, *38,* 364–379.

38 Isaac, D. J., and B. M. O'Connor. Use of loss of skill under stress to test a theory of psychological development. *Human Relations,* 1973, *26,* 487–498.

39 Keogh, B. K., and J. F. Keogh. Pattern copying and pattern walking performance of normal, educationally subnormal boys. *American Journal of Mental Deficiency,* 1967, *71,* 1007–1013.

40 Koocher, G. P. Swimming competence and personality change. *Journal of Personality and Social Psychology,* 1971, *18,* 275–278.

41 Kopp, C. B. Fine motor abilities of Infants. *Developmental Medicine and Child Neurology,* 1974, *16,* 629–636.

42 Kravitz, H., and J. J. Boehm. Rhythmic habit patterns in infancy: Their sequence, age of onset and frequency. *Child Development,* 1971, *42,* 399–413.

43 Leithwood, K. A., and W. Fowler. Complex motor learning in four-year-olds. *Child Development,* 1971, *42,* 781–792.

44 Martens, R. Social reinforcement effects on preschool children's motor performance. *Perceptual and Motor Skills,* 1970, *31,* 787–792.

45 Martin, P. C., and E. L. Vincent. *Human biological development.* New York: Ronald, 1960.

46 McGraw, M. B. Neuromuscular development of the human infant as exemplified in the achievement of erect locomotion. *Journal of Pediatrics,* 1940, *17,* 744–771.

47 Miller, E. Handedness and the pattern of human ability. *British Journal of Psychology,* 1971, *62,* 111–112.

48 *New York Times* report: Left-handers buck right-handed life. *The New York Times,* Dec. 29, 1968.

49 Palmer, R. D. Development of a differential handedness. *Psychological Bulletin,* 1964, *62,* 257–272.

50 Peterson, R. A. The natural development of nocturnal bladder control. *Developmental Medicine and Child Neurology* 1971, *13,* 730–734.

51 Pikler, E. Some contributions to the study of the gross motor development of children. *Journal of Genetic Psychology,* 1968, *113,* 27–39.

52 Rand, C. W. Copying in drawing: The importance of adequate visual analysis versus the ability to utilize drawing rules. *Child Development,* 1973, *44,* 47–53.

53 Rheingold, H. L., W. C. Stanley, and J. A. Cooley. Method for studying exploratory behavior in infants. *Science,* 1962, *136,* 1054–1055.

54 Rosenbloom, L., and M. E. Horton. The maturation of fine prehension in young children. *Developmental Medicine and Child Neurology,* 1971, *13,* 3–8.

55 Scrutton, D. S., and P. Robson. The

gait of 500 normal children. *Physiotherapy*, 1968, *54*, 363–368.

56 Seth, G. Eye-hand coordination and "handedness": A developmental study of visuo-motor behavior in infancy. *British Journal of Educational Psychology*, 1973, *43*, 35–49.

57 Shirley, M. M. *The first two years of life*. Minneapolis, Minn: University of Minnesota Press, vol. 1, 1931, vol. 2, 1933.

58 Solomons, G., and H. S. Solomons. Factors affecting motor performance in four-month-old infants. *Child Development*, 1964, *35*, 1283–1296.

59 Sontag, L. W. Implications of fetal behavior and environment for adult personalities. *Annals of the New York Academy of Sciences*, 1966, *134*, 782–786.

60 Stein, Z., and M. Susser. Social factors in the development of sphincter control. *Developmental Medicine and Child Neurology*, 1967, *9*, 692–706.

61 Tautermannová, M. Smiling in infants. *Child Development*, 1973, *44*, 701–704.

62 Terman, L. M., and M. A. Merrill. *Stanford-Binet Intelligence Scale*, 3d ed. Boston: Houghton Mifflin, 1960.

63 Thomas, J. R., and B. S. Chissom. Differentiation between high and low sociometric status for sixth-grade boys using selected measures of motor skill. *Child Study Journal*, 1973, *3*, 125–130.

64 Todor, J. I. Age differences in integration of components of a motor task. *Perceptual and Motor Skills*, 1975, *41*, 211–215.

65 Touwen, B. C. L. A study on the development of some motor phenomena in infancy. *Developmental Medicine and Child Neurology*, 1971, *13*, 435–446.

66 Trieschmann, R. B. Undifferentiated handedness and perceptual development of children with reading problems. *Perceptual and Motor Skills*, 1968, *27*, 1125–1134.

67 Turnure, J. E., and J. E. Rynders. Effectiveness of manual guidance, modeling and trial and error procedures on the acquisition of new behaviors. *Merrill-Palmer Quarterly*, 1973, *19*, 49–65.

68 Vincent, E. L., and P. C. Martin. *Human psychological development*. New York: Ronald, 1961.

69 Wenar, C. Executive competence in toddlers: A perspective observational study. *Genetic Psychology Monographs*, 1976, *93*, 189–285.

70 Whitener, S. F., and K. W. James. The relationship among motor tasks for preschool children. *Journal of Motor Behavior*, 1973, *5*, 231–239.

71 Witryol, S. L., and J. E. Calkins. Marginal social values of rural school children. *Journal of Genetic Psychology*, 1958, *92*, 81–93.

72 Zelazo, P. R., N. A. Zelazo, and S. Kolb. "Walking" in the newborn. *Science*, 1972, *176*, 314–315.

CHAPTER 7

CHAPTER 7

SPEECH DEVELOPMENT

Much of the helplessness of newborn infants stems from their inability to communicate their needs and wants in forms others can understand and their inability to understand the words and gestures used by others. This helplessness is rapidly reduced in the early years of life as children gain control over the muscles needed for the various communication mechanisms.

The ability to speak also fills another important need in children's lives—the need to be a part of the social group. While they may be able to communicate with members of the social group by means other than speech, their position in the group will be marginal until they are able to talk to group members.

As is true of other areas of development, the early years of life are critical for speech development. During this time, the foundations for later speech development are laid. While early deficiencies can, to some extent, be compensated for later and while inefficient patterns can be corrected, the early foundations are likely to leave a permanent mark on children's patterns of speech. They may, for example, correct grammatical errors as they grow older; but, when they speak in excitement, these early grammatical errors are likely to creep in because they have become well-learned speech habits.

Meaning of "Speech"

Many people use the terms "speech" and "language" interchangeably. However, they are not synonymous. *Language* encompasses every means of communication in which thoughts and feelings are symbolized so as to convey meaning to others. It includes such widely differing forms of communication as writing, speaking, sign language, facial expression, gesture, pantomime, and art.

Speech is a form of language in which articulate sounds or words are used to convey meaning. Because it is the most effective form of communication, it is the most important and most widely used. As Jakobson has pointed out, "All sane human beings talk, but almost half of the world's people are totally illiterate, and the actual use of reading and writing is an asset of a scarce minority (40)."

Speech is a motor-mental skill. It not only involves the coordination of different teams of muscles of the vocal mechanism but it also has a mental aspect—the

association of meanings with the sounds produced. Not all sounds made by children, however, can be regarded as speech. Until children have gained enough control over the neuromuscular mechanism to produce clear, controlled, and distinct sounds, their vocal utterances are merely articulate sounds. Furthermore, until they learn to associate meanings with these controlled sounds, no matter how correctly they are produced, their speech will be mere "parrot talk"—imitative speech—because it lacks the mental element of meaning.

In judging whether children are speaking in the correct sense of the term or are merely using "parrot talk," two criteria must be used. *First,* children must know the meanings of the words they use and associate them with the objects they represent. The word "ball," for example, must refer to balls only not to toys in general. *Second,* children must pronounce their words so that they are readily understandable to others. Words that are comprehensible only to those who, because of constant contact with children, have learned to understand them or to guess at what they are trying to say do not meet this criterion.

It is often difficult to know when real speech begins. Many utterances of young children satisfy only one of these two criteria. Children may, for example, pronounce the word "milk" perfectly but they may use it to refer to anything they drink. Or, they may call milk "mil" and limit the use of this term to milk. In neither example can the utterance be considered real speech (48).

Undoubtedly, the marked variations reported in size of vocabulary of preschool children are due to the failure to apply *both criteria* of speech. When parents or other caretakers list the words children use, they tend to apply only the criterion of correct pronounciation. They assume that because children pronounce a word correctly, they automatically know its meaning.

Speech: A Tool for Communication

Communication means an interchange of thoughts and feelings. This interchange can be carried out with any form of language—gestures, emotional expressions, speech, or written language—but it is most commonly and most effectively done by speech (3).

During the early years of childhood, not all speech is used for communication. Young children often talk to themselves or to their toys while they are playing. However, as their interest in becoming a part of the social group develops, they reserve most of their speech for communicating with others and only infrequently talk to themselves or to their toys.

Essentials of Communication

If communication is to fulfill its function of interchange of thoughts and feelings, there are two essential elements. *First,* children must use a form of language that is meaningful to those with whom they are communicating. If, for example, they use a gesture, it must be in a form that can be understood, such as pointing to an object they want others to look at. When communication is by speech, it must be in words and grammatical structures the listener can understand (74). When, for example, children are accustomed to speaking in English, they will not understand what is said to them in German.

Second, children must understand the language used by others to communicate with them. They must, for example, know that when a person points to an object, it means that they are expected to look at that object. When communication is in the form of speech, they must understand what is said to them in that language.

Studies have shown that, at every age, the passive or "comprehension" vocabulary is larger than the active or "speech" vocabulary. Babies, for example, can comprehend the general meaning of what others say long before they can speak. This comes not from understanding the actual words but rather from understanding the speakers's voice intonations, gestures, or facial expressions. Until children are about 18 months old, speakers must reinforce their words with gestures if they want children to comprehend exact meanings. Even simple directions, such as "Put the cup on the table," must be supplemented by gestures of pointing to the cup and the table if children are to comprehend what they are being asked to do (16, 50).

Comprehension is more difficult in some areas of speech than in others. Commands, for example, are better understood by young children than statements of fact. This is partly because commands are usually accompanied by gestures, such as the lifting of the hand when one says "No-no," and partly because commands are given in a decisive tone of voice (36).

As children grow older, their comprehension improves, as does their ability to speak. However, their comprehension vocabularies continue to be greater than their speech vocabularies. This is true of adolescents and adults as well as of children.

Role of Speech in Communication

Even before they reach their first birthdays, babies discover how important the ability to communicate with others is. When they discover that their early attempts to communicate by crying or by using gestures are not always understood, they have a strong motivation to learn to speak. As soon as they are developmentally ready to do so, they try to learn to speak because they find that speech is a better tool for communication than crying, gestures, and other prespeech forms they had to use earlier.

Of the many ways in which speech plays an important role in a child's life, the most important are given and explained in Box 7–1. At different times throughout the childhood years, speech serves different functions, though at no time is there evidence that it is unimportant to children's personal and social adjustments.

Prespeech Forms of Communication

Learning to speak is a long and complicated process. Until the child is maturationally ready to learn, nature provides certain stopgap forms of communication. If this were not so, the period of helplessness would be greatly prolonged. Most children do not say even their first words until they are 12 to 15 months old. Their communication must be in forms preliminary to speech. They will continue to use these prespeech forms of communication until they have mastered sufficient linguistic skill to use meaningful words that can be understood both by the child and by others.

During the first year and a half to two years of postnatal life, until they have learned enough words to use as a form of communication, babies use four prespeech forms of communication: *crying;* explosive sounds which soon develop into *babbling; gestures;* and *emotional expressions.* Of these four, the second—babbling—is the most important in speech development because it becomes the basis for real speech.

HOW SPEECH CONTRIBUTES TO CHILDREN'S PERSONAL AND SOCIAL ADJUSTMENTS

SATISFACTION OF NEEDS AND WANTS
Being able to explain their needs and wants to others instead of having to wait for them to understand the meaning of their cries, gestures, or facial expressions eliminates much of the frustration babies experience when they cannot be understood.

ATTENTION FROM OTHERS
All children like to be in the limelight of attention. They soon discover that they can achieve this goal by asking questions, by using forbidden words, by expressing unconventional ideas, or merely by dominating the conversation.

SOCIAL RELATIONSHIPS
The ability to communicate with others in a way they can understand is essential to group belonging. Children who are able to communicate well are better accepted by members of the social group and have a better chance of playing leadership roles than those who lack the ability to communicate or who are afraid to use it.

SOCIAL EVALUATIONS
Children, like adults, are evaluated by members of the social group in terms of what they say and how they say it. Social background, racial origin, sex-appropriateness, and many other personal characteristics are signaled to others by speech.

SELF-EVALUATION
Children can tell from the comments of their listeners how they feel about what they have said and whether others are favorably or unfavorably impressed. This provides the basis for self-evaluation.

ACADEMIC ACHIEVEMENT
Children whose speech performance, in terms of pronunciation and grammatical structure, is below that of their classmates are usually judged to be intellectually inferior to them, and they tend to receive grades below their intellectual capacities. Size of vocabulary also influences children's abilities to express themselves in speech and writing, both of which are essential to school success.

INFLUENCE ON THOUGHTS AND FEELINGS OF OTHERS
Making derogatory comments or saying unpleasant things to and about others makes children unpopular with their age-mates as well as with adults. Saying pleasant things, by contrast, increases children's chances of social acceptance.

INFLUENCE ON BEHAVIOR OF OTHERS
Children who speak well and with confidence can influence their peers to behave as they want them to behave better than those who speak hesitatingly and with a limited vocabulary or poor grammatical forms. One of the characteristics of a child leader is the ability to speak better than the other group members.

As is true of all stopgap measures, prespeech forms of communication should be abandoned when their usefulness ends. If children continue to use them after they are developmentally ready to learn to speak, it will be damaging to their personal and social adjustments, as will be explained later in connection with the hazards of speech development.

Crying

In the early days of postnatal life, most vocalization consists of crying. As Ostwald and Peltzman have explained, "Crying is one of the first ways in which the infant is able to communicate with the world at large" (76). Through cries, babies make known their need for someone to relieve their hunger, pain, fatigue, and other unpleasant bodily states and to satisfy their desire for attention.

To make this communication easier for others to understand, nature provides for differentiation in the tonal quality of the cries as early as the third or fourth week of life. Pain, for example, is expressed by loud, shrill cries interrupted by groaning and whimpering while hunger cries are loud and interrupted by sucking movements.

Comprehension of the meaning of cries is aided by the intensity of the cries and by bodily movements that accompany crying. The louder and the more persistent the cry, the stronger the baby's need. A very hungry baby, for example, will have a louder and more persistent cry than a baby who is less hungry. The sucking movements that occur when the hunger cry is temporarily interrupted likewise aid in the interpretaition of the meaning of the cry.

In spite of these aids in interpretation of the meaning of a cry, the meaning is not always interpreted correctly. As a result, its communicative value is lessened. A person who is accustomed to taking care of babies, but especially of a particular baby, can generally understand the meaning of the cries better than an outsider can.

VARIATIONS IN CRYING Individual variations in the *amount of crying* are greater than variations in the tonal qualities of cries. Some babies cry very little, while others cry excessively—or more than normal for

their age and level of development. The amount of crying varies according to how promptly and how adequately their needs and wants are met. If they are met promptly, the baby will then cry only in pain and genuine distress.

Some babies continue to cry excessively after the first 2 weeks of life. In most cases, it has been reported that the parents of these babies wait a long time before heeding their cries or they are inconsistent about responding to them (63, 82).

Crying varies also according to *time of day*. These times coincide with times in the baby's schedule. Crying is, for example, most frequent before the scheduled time for feeding and before the time the baby is put to bed for the night. As babies become adapted to scheduled times for eating and sleeping, crying at

Figure 7-1. Amount of crying by hour of the day for a group of infants, 1 to 3 weeks of age, and a group of babies, 12 to 13 weeks of age. (*Adapted from F. Rebelsky and R. Black: Crying in infancy.* Journal of Genetic Psychology, *1972, 121, 49–57. Used by permission.*)

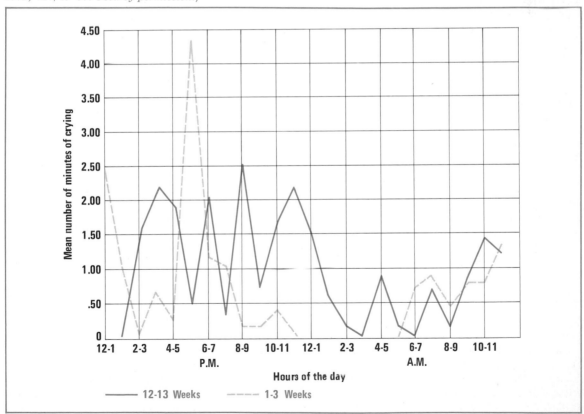

these times decreases (7, 8). Figure 7–1 shows the amount of crying babies do at different times during the day and night during the first 3 weeks of life and when they are 12 to 13 weeks old.

Social reactions to crying influence the amount of crying babies do. How parents and siblings, for example, react to a baby's cries depends partly on the baby's age and partly on their own beliefs regarding the function of crying. It is commonly believed that the only means of communication young babies have is crying. Parents, therefore, expect babies to cry. This expectation, in turn, affects babies' behavior; they learn that they must cry to get their needs and wants attended to. They are thus conditioned to cry because other methods have failed to bring them what they want. Babies then learn to cry instead of learning to use noncrying methods of communication.

DECREASE IN CRYING   During the first 2 weeks of life, crying occurs at irregular intervals. Often, for no apparent reason, the infant begins to cry intensely, sometimes even in sleep. Beginning with the third week, there is normally less crying and, by the third or fourth month, night waking and crying decrease,

Figure 7-2. Pattern of decline in crying during the first year of life. (*Adapted from M. D. S. Ainsworth, S. M. Bell, and D. J. Stayton: Individual differences in the development of some attachment behaviors.* Merrill-Palmer Quarterly, *1972,* 18, *123–143. Used by permission.*)

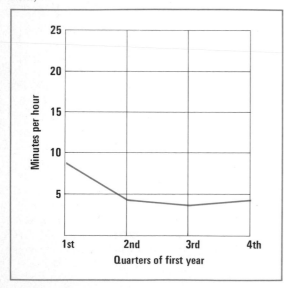

though daytime crying is still frequent. Normal, healthy babies, however, show a decrease in daytime crying by the time they are 6 months old, provided their wants and needs are met with reasonable speed (1). Figure 7–2 shows the pattern of decrease.

Even when babies can say a few words, their need for crying as a form of communication has not come to an end. Not until they have adequate vocabularies to express their needs, wants, thoughts, and feelings in a way that can be understood by others have they reached a point where crying is no longer necessary. When they reach this point will depend on learning opportunities, abilities, and motivation. Young children who have learned that crying is a tried and trusted method of coping with their needs and wants will not readily give it up without assurance that a substitute method will work equally effectively.

For all children, however, the *curve for crying should go down as the curve for speech rises*. If the speech curve rises slowly, the crying curve will have to descend slowly. But, if the speech curve rises rapidly, the crying curve should descend rapidly, though this is not always true. The reason for this is that, even after children have adequate vocabularies, they still will not automatically and immediately give up crying. They will do so more quickly, however, if they are *taught* how to get what they want by speaking instead of by crying and if the rewards of speech are as great or even greater than the rewards from crying. With guidance and encouragement, children should be almost ready to abandon crying as a form of communication by the time they reach the kindergarten age and certainly by the time they are ready to enter the first grade. Unless they do, they are likely to win the reputation of being "crybabies"—a reputation that can play havoc with both their personal and their social adjustments.

Cooing and Babbling

The second prespeech form of communication is called "cooing" or "babbling." In addition to cries, babies make may simple sounds during the early months of life, such as grunts of pain or disgust, squeals of delight, yawns, sneezes, sighs, belching, coughing, guttural barking sounds, growls, and cries that sound like the whine of a young pig or the bleat of a goat. These are known as cooing. As the baby's neuromuscular mechanisms develop, explosive sounds change into babbling (98).

COOING Early explosive sounds are caused by chance movements of the vocal mechanism. The sounds themselves depend largely on the shape of the oral cavity and the way it modifies the stream of air expelled from the lungs and passing over the vocal cords. They are unlearned and are universally found, even among the deaf. Because they have no significance for the baby and are not used as a form of communication, they may be regarded as a *playful activity* which gives the baby enjoyment. Many of these early cooing sounds will disappear, but some will develop into babbling and, still later, into words.

BABBLING Gradually, the number of sounds the baby can produce increases. There is, as well, an increasing definiteness of utterance of various sounds. At first, vowels are combined with consonants, for example, "da," "ma," "ugh," or "na." Later, with practice, vocal control makes it possible for the baby to repeat these sounds by stringing them together, as in "ma-ma-ma-ma" or "ugh-ugh-ugh." This is real babbling, or "lalling" (57).

Owing to the growing ability to control the flow of air over the vocal cords, the baby can pronounce sounds at will. Babbling is, therefore, a form of vocal gymnastics, voluntarily produced, but without a real meaning or association for the baby.

Some babies begin to babble as early as the second month of life. After that, there is a rapid increase, with a peak between the sixth and eighth months. Then babbling gradually gives way to the use of words. However, some babies continue to babble into the second year (5, 45).

How much babbling babies do and how soon they abandon babbling in favor of speech will be greatly influenced by how much they are encouraged to babble (20, 85, 95). When people babble to them and give them new babbling models to imitate, babies not only babble more than those who lack such stimulation but, even more important, they learn a larger repertoire of babbling sounds. This makes the pronounciation of words easier for them. As a result, they are likely to abandon babbling in favor of speech earlier than babies who lacked this preliminary training in vocalization. Figure 7–3 shows how parental attention to babbling increases its frequency and prepares babies for early speech.

In early scientific investigations of babbling, it was common to refer to babbling as "play speech." The justification for doing so was that because babies

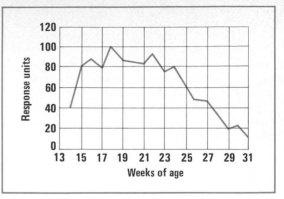

Figure 7-3. Parental attention to the baby's babbling increases its frequency and then it declines as the baby begins to use words. (*Adapted from R. G. Wahler: Infant social development; Some experimental analyses of an infant-mother interaction during the first year of life.* Journal of Experimental Child Psychology, *1969, 7, 101–113. Used by permission.*)

enjoy babbling, they use it as a form of amusement, especially when they are alone and they derive pleasure from listening to their own voices (52, 106).

Labeling babbling as "play speech" suggests that it has no value other than the immediate enjoyment it gives. This is not correct. It has great long-term value for three reasons. *First,* it is verbal practice that lays the foundations for developing the skilled movements required in speech. True, without babbling the baby would eventually learn to speak, but babbling hastens the learning process by providing the basic skills needed to control the vocal mechanism for the more highly complicated skills of speech (7, 20, 69).

Second, babbling encourages the desire to communicate with others. When with people who are talking to each other, babies often try to babble their way into a conversation. Furthermore, because babies babble more when people talk to them than when they are silent, this indicates a desire on the part of babies to communicate with them (62, 105).

Third, babbling helps babies to feel that they are a part of the social group. This feeling is intensified when members of the group talk to them or babble in response to their babbling. By feeling that they are a part of the social group, babies are spared the feeling of social isolation that inability to communicate always brings (7, 40).

Gestures

The third preliminary form of communication consists of gestures—movements of the limbs or the body which serve as *substitutes* for, or *supplements* to, speech. As a substitute for speech, gestures take the place of words; an idea is conveyed to others by meaningful movements of the limbs or some part of the body. As a supplement to speech, gestures emphasize the meaning of spoken words. Unlike babbling, which is fundamentally a form of play, gestures have the serious purpose of communication, just as crying has (24, 45, 65).

Most gestures made by babies are easy to understand. They, therefore, serve as a satisfactory substitute for speech until babies can communicate in words. Some commonly observed gestures of babyhood are identified in Box 7–2.

The need for gestures as a substitute for speech does not end when babies say their first words. Until children have time to build up a large enough vocabulary to express their wants, needs, thoughts, and feelings in words, they will continue to use gestures to make their incomplete sentences meaningful. The early sentences of young children are, therefore, a combination of words and gestures. As speech improves, the need for gestures decreases. Before children enter school, their vocabularies should be large enough to enable them to make themselves understood without the use of gestures (11, 63).

Emotional Expressions

The fourth prespeech form of communication is the expression of emotions through facial and bodily changes. The pleasant emotions are accompanied by pleasant vocalizations in the form of cooing, chuckling sounds, and laughs, while the unpleasant emotions are accompanied by whimpering and crying (13, 54).

When babies are happy, for example, they relax their bodies, wave their arms and legs, and smiles appear on their faces. This is accompanied by pleasant vocal sounds. By contrast, anger is expressed by tensing their bodies, by slashing movements of the arms and legs, by tense expressions on their faces, and by cries of anger.

Because babies have not yet learned to control the expressions of their emotions, it is easy for others to interpret them and to know how babies feel about people and situations. As children grow older, they learn to control emotional expressions and this decreases their communicative value. However, control over facial expressions is rarely so complete that it eliminates their communicative value. Even adults are not so well controlled that it is impossible to tell from their facial expressions whether fear, anger, disgust, happiness, or some other emotion is being experienced (24, 104).

Expressions of the emotions are a useful prespeech form of communication for a second reason—they are easy for babies to interpret when they are used by others. Babies quickly notice a changed expression on

---

BOX 7–2

SOME COMMON GESTURES OF BABYHOOD

GESTURE	MEANING
• Allows food to run out of mouth	• Satisfied or not hungry
• Pouts	• Displeased
• Pushes nipple from mouth with tongue	• Satisfied or not hungry
• Pushes object away	• Does not want it
• Reaches out for object	• Wants to have it
• Reaches out to person	• Wants to be picked up
• Smacks lips or ejects tongue	• Hungry
• Smiles and holds out arms	• Wants to be picked up
• Sneezes excessively	• Wet and cold
• Squirms and trembles	• Cold
• Squirms, wiggles, and cries during dressing or bathing	• Resents restriction on activities
• Turns head from nipple	• Satisfied or not hungry

the parent's face and a change in the tone of the parental voice. They may not, for example, understand the meaning of the words, "That was naughty," but they understand that they have done something to displease the person from the facial expression and tone of voice of that person (13).

Like gestures, emotional expressions continue to be a useful form of communication even after children have learned to speak. They reinforce words, as gestures do, and, as such, become supplements to speech rather than substitutes for speech as they were when babies had not yet learned to speak. Furthermore, they are likely to be more persistent than gestures because learning to control the overt expressions of the emotions is more difficult than learning to break the gesture habit.

How Children Learn to Speak

Speech is a skill and, like all skills, it must be learned. Speech consists of, first, the ability to produce certain sounds in combinations that are recognizable as words—the *motor* aspect of speech—and, second, the ability to associate meanings with these words—the *mental* aspect of speech. The muscle coordinations needed to produce sound combinations that are recognizable as words are certainly as complicated as the most intricate motor skills and require as much time and practice to learn. Furthermore, the necessity of associating meanings with words and of learning grammatical forms adds to the complexity of the speech skills.

Methods of Learning to Speak

Learning to speak is a skill and, like all skills, it can be learned by different methods, the most important of which were described in Box 6-5. However, as is true of all skills, training produces the best results. While children may learn to speak by trial-and-error or by imitating a model, the skill is likely to be less effective than when learned by training. In training, children are not only given a good model to imitate but they also receive guidance and help in following the model accurately. Equally important, they will be shown how to correct an incorrect imitation of the model before practice results in a habit that falls far short of the model (26, 42, 92).

Because speech is a motor-mental skill, children must, in addition to learning how to pronounce words, learn to associate meanings with these words. Only then will words become symbols for the people or objects they represent.

Learning to associate meanings may be done by trial-and-error, by imitation, or by training. When trial-and-error is used, children have just as good a chance of associating incorrect meanings with words as correct meanings. If, for example, the name of the family dog is "Spot," the child may associate the word "Spot" with all dogs and refer to them by that label—"I like spots."

When using imitation, once again children may associate the correct meaning and yet they may not. If, for example, a person says, "Here are some knives and forks" and then shows the child both knives and forks without designating the correct label for each, the child may call the knives "forks" and vice versa.

Figure 7–4 shows how learning to associate meanings with words through guidance and supervision—training—eliminates the possibility of making the errors so common in the other types of learning. Guidance and supervision of the child's association of a specific word with a specific object greatly minimizes the child's mistakes.

Figure 7-4. A baby learns to associate meaning with an object, and then a word becomes a symbol or label for the object. (*Adapted from M. E. Breckenridge & E. L. Vincent:* Child development: Physical and psychologic development through adolescence, *5th ed. Saunders, 1965. Used by permission.*)

Essentials in Learning to Speak

Just as there are certain essentials in learning motor skills, so there are certain essentials in learning to speak. While these essentials are similar to those in learning motor skills, because the elements of motor skills are somewhat different from the elements of speech skills the application of these essentials is of necessity somewhat different.

As is true of learning motor skills, learning to speak will be delayed and the quality of speech will be below the child's potential and below the level of speech of age-mates if any one of these essentials is missing (48, 69). The six essentials in learning to speak are explained in Box 7–3.

Pattern of Learning to Speak

The pattern of learning to speak is much the same for all children. The rate of development varies, however. Studies of the development of motor control and of speech have revealed that the pattern of speech development closely parallels the pattern of motor development. It also closely parallels the pattern of mental development. The reason for this is that speech is dependent on both motor and mental development (52, 68, 70).

In speech development, the pattern is one of spurts followed by resting periods, or *plateaus*—times when no apparent improvement occurs. Whenever a new motor act is being established, there will be a temporary plateau in the pattern of speech development. Between the ages of 9 and 18 months, for example, the urge to walk seems to be more powerful than the urge to talk. After walking becomes automatic, the baby's attention is directed to talking, and there are rapid gains in speech. From 18 months to 4 or 5 years of age, children master the ability to speak but they have much more to learn before they reach adult language competence.

When children enter school, their eagerness to learn—a characteristic of first graders—gives them a strong motivation to learn new words. The role played by school experiences in learning to speak will be discussed in detail in the following section, under the heading "Vocabulary Building."

In spite of the fact that children learn to speak in a predictable pattern, there are individual differences in the rate with which they follow this pattern, in the size and quality of their vocabularies, and in the correctness of pronounciation and grammatical structure of their speech (12, 39, 49). There are a number of conditions contributing to these variations, the most important of which are given in Box 7–4.

BOX 7–3

ESSENTIALS IN LEARNING TO SPEAK

PHYSICAL READINESS TO SPEAK
The ability to speak depends upon the maturation of the speech mechanism. At birth, the oral canal is small, the palate is flat, and the tongue is too large for the oral cavity. Until they take on a more mature shape, the nerves and muscles of the vocal mechanism cannot produce the sounds needed for words.

MENTAL READINESS TO SPEAK
Mental readiness to speak is dependent on the maturation of the brain, especially the association areas of the brain. This readiness usually develops between the age of 12 and 18 months and is regarded as the "teachable moment" in speech development.

A GOOD MODEL TO IMITATE
If children are to learn to pronounce words correctly, and later to combine them into correct sentences, they must have a model of good speech to imitate. This model may be people in their environment, speakers on radio or television, or actors in the movies. If they lack a good model, learning to speak will be difficult and the end result below their potentials.

OPPORTUNITIES FOR PRACTICE
If deprived of opportunities to practice speaking for whatever reason, children become angry and frustrated when they cannot make others understand them. This often weakens their motivation to learn to speak.

MOTIVATION
If young children discover that they can get what they want without asking for it, and if substitutes for speech such as crying and gestures serve their purpose, their incentive to learn to speak will be weakened.

GUIDANCE
The best ways to guide learning to speak are, *first,* to provide a good model, *second,* to say words slowly and distinctly enough that children can understand them and, *third,* to provide help in following this model by correcting any mistakes children may make in imitating the model.

BOX 7–4

CONDITIONS CONTRIBUTING TO VARIATIONS IN LEARNING TO SPEAK

HEALTH
Healthy children learn to talk sooner than those who are unhealthy because they have a stronger motivation to be members of a social group and to communicate with the members of the group.

INTELLIGENCE
Children with high IQs learn to talk sooner and show a marked linguistic superiority over those of lower intellectual levels.

SOCIOECONOMIC STATUS
Children from the higher socioeconomic groups learn to talk earlier, they express themselves better, and they talk more than those from the lower socioeconomic groups. This is mainly because those from the higher groups are given more encouragement to talk and more guidance in learning how to do so.

Figure 7–5. Comparison of the speech development of twins and singletons during the early years of life. (*Adapted from R. J. Dales: Motor and language development of twins during the first three years.* Journal of Genetic Psychology, *1969,* 114, *263–271. Used by permission.*)

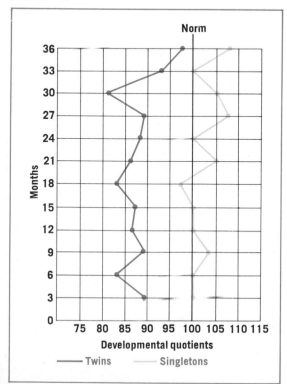

SEX
Boys, as a group, lag behind girls, as a group, in learning to talk. At every age, boys' sentences are shorter and less grammatically correct, their vocabularies are smaller, and their pronunciations are less accurate than girls'.

DESIRE TO COMMUNICATE
The stronger the desire to communicate with others, the stronger will be the child's motivation to learn to talk and the more willing the child will be to spend the time and effort needed for this learning.

STIMULATION
The more children are stimulated to talk, by being talked to and being encouraged to respond, the earlier they will learn to talk and the better the quality of their speech.

SIZE OF FAMILY
An only child or a child from a small family usually speaks earlier and better than children from large families because parents can give more time to teaching them to speak.

ORDINAL POSITION
Age for age, the speech of firstborns is superior to that of later-borns in the same family. This is because parents can spend more time teaching and encouraging them to talk than they can for later-born children.

CHILD-TRAINING METHODS
Authoritarian child training, which emphasizes that children should be "seen but not heard," is an obstacle to learning, while permissive and democratic child training encourages learning.

MULTIPLE BIRTHS
Children of multiple birth are generally delayed in their speech development because they associate mainly with one another and learn to understand their own jargons. This weakens their motivation to learn to speak so others can understand them. Figure 7–5 shows how twins lag behind the norm for their ages in early speech development.

CONTACTS WITH PEERS
The more contacts children have with peers and the more anxious they are to be accepted as members of the peer group, the stronger will be their motivation to learn to talk.

PERSONALITY
Well-adjusted children tend to speak better, both qualitatively and quantitatively, than those who are poorly adjusted. In fact, speech is often regarded as an indication of the child's mental health.

Major Tasks in Learning to Speak

Learning to speak involves three separate and yet interrelated processes—learning to pronounce words, building a vocabulary, and forming sentences. Because these processes are interrelated, failure to master one of them will jeopardize the whole speech pattern.

Each of these three major processes in learning to speak will be described below and information will be given about how and when they are learned. Because some of the processes are more difficult to master than others, their learning will be delayed.

Pronunciation

The first task in learning to speak is learning to pronounce words. Pronunciation is learned by imitation. Children literally "pick up" the pronunciation of words from the people with whom they associate. A young child's entire pattern of pronunciation will change rapidly if placed in a new environment where people pronounce words differently. Because of the child's flexibility in sound imitation—due to the plasticity of the vocal mechanism and the absence of well-developed habits of pronunciation—some parents and educators contend that early childhood is the proper time to begin learning a foreign language. If children learn the correct pronunciation then, they contend, they will "speak like natives." But, if they wait until junior or senior high school before learning, they will always speak the foreign language with an American accent.

Children differ markedly in the correctness of their pronunciation and in their accents. Variations in *correctness* of pronunciation depend partly upon the rate of development of the vocal mechanism but mostly upon the guidance young children receive in combining sounds into meaningful words. Variations in *accent* result from imitating models whose pronunciation differs from that in general use, as in the case of the bilingual child who imitates the accent of a foreign-born parent.

Vocabulary Building

The second task in learning to speak is vocabulary building. In vocabulary building, children must learn to associate meanings with sounds. Since many words have more than one meaning and since some words that sound alike—rain, reign, and rein—have different meanings, vocabulary building is far more difficult than pronunciation. Furthermore, there is a greater chance for error in the learning of correct sound-meaning associations than in pronouncing words.

Children first learn the meaning of those words for which they have the greatest need. However, until their vocabularies are adequate to meet their needs, they continue to use substitutes, such as gestures. As they grow older and abandon prespeech forms, they frequently use slang terms as substitutes.

Children learn two kinds of vocabularies: a general vocabulary and multiple special vocabularies. The *general* vocabulary consists of such words as 'man," "nice," and "go," which can be used in a variety of different situations. The *special* vocabularies, on the other hand, consist of words with specific meanings that can be used only in certain situations. Since words in the general vocabulary are the ones that are used most, they are learned first. At every age, the general vocabulary is larger than the special vocabularies (46, 53, 59, 91). Box 7–5 spells out the major characteristics of general and special vocabularies.

Increase in vocabulary comes not only from learning new words but also from learning new meanings for old words. For example, children may first use the word "orange" to refer to the fruit. Later, they discover that the word "orange" also refers to a color and, still later, that it is a complex color, made up of a combination of red and yellow.

It has been estimated that the mean number of different words used at 18 months is 10 and at 24 months, 29.1. The average vocabulary of a 2-year-old contains 200 to 300 words (17, 99). Figure 7–7 shows the increase in vocabulary size during the preschool years.

After children enter school, their vocabularies grow rapidly, owing to direct teaching, new experiences, leisure reading, and radio and television listening. It is estimated that the average first grader knows between 20,000 and 24,000 words, or 5 to 6 percent of the words in a standard dictionary. The sixth grader knows approximately 50,000 words, and the child entering high school about 80,000 words, or 22 percent of the words in a standard dictionary (26, 77, 91, 92).

Individual differences in vocabulary size at every age are due to differences in intelligence, environmental influences, learning opportunities, and motivation to learn. Girls on the average, it has been reported, have larger vocabularies at every age than do boys (5, 12, 43).

BOX 7–5

CHILDHOOD VOCABULARIES

GENERAL VOCABULARY

- *Nouns.* The first words used by children are nouns, generally monosyllables, taken from favorite babbling sounds.

- *Verbs.* After children have learned enough nouns to apply names to people and objects in the environment, they begin to learn verbs, especially those that designate action, such as "give," "take," or "hold."

- *Adjectives.* Adjectives appear in a baby's vocabulary from the age of 1½ years. The adjectives most commonly used at first are "good," "bad," "nice," "naughty," "hot," and "cold." These are applied principally to people, food, and toys.

- *Adverbs.* Adverbs are used at about the same age as adjectives. The earliest adverbs to appear in the child's vocabulary are generally "here" and "where."

- *Prepositions and pronouns.* These appear last because they are the most difficult to use. Young children become confused about when to use "I," "me," "my" or "mine," for example, and avoid their use as long as possible, substituting their own names for the pronoun.

SPECIAL VOCABULARIES

- *Color vocabulary.* Most children know the names of the primary colors by the age of 4. How soon they will learn other color names depends on their interest in colors and on opportunities to learn.

- *Number vocabulary.* In the Stanford-Binet Intelligence Scale, the 5-year-old is expected to count three objects; the 6-year-old is expected to understand the words "three," "nine," "five," "ten," and "seven" well enough to count out that number of blocks.

- *Time vocabulary.* By the age of 6 or 7, children usually know the meaning of morning, afternoon, night, summer, and winter.

- *Money vocabulary.* Four- or five-year-olds begin to label coins according to their size and color.

- *Slang vocabulary.* Between 4 and 8, most children, especially boys, "go tough," using slang to express emotions and to conform to the peer group.

- *Swearing vocabulary.* Swearing is used mainly by boys, starting at the school age, to identify themselves with the big boys, to compensate for feelings of inferiority, to assert their masculinity, and to attract attention. See Figure 7–6.

- *Secret language.* This is used mostly by girls after 6 years of age to communicate with their friends. It may be *verbal* (known as "pidgin English" because it is a distortion of English), *written* (symbols), or *kinetic* (gestures).

Figure 7–6. Swearing by children is often used as a way of attracting attention. (*Adapted from Hank Ketcham: "Dennis the Menace," Field Newspaper Syndicate, March 25, 1976. Used by permission.*)

"NOW HERE'S A WORD THAT'S *GUARANTEED* TO MAKE EVERYBODY STOP TALKIN' AND *LOOK* AT YOU."

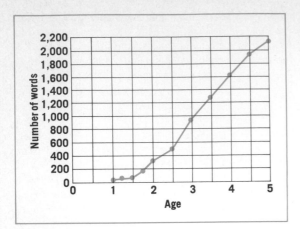

Figure 7–7. Increase in vocabulary with age. (*Adapted from L. P. Lipsitt: Learning processes of human newborns.* Merrill-Palmer Quarterly, *1966,* 12, *45–71. Used by permission.*)

Sentence Formation

The third task in learning to speak, combining words into sentences that are grammatically correct and can be understood by others, is by far the most difficult of the three. That is why this task is mastered later than the other two. That is why, also, it is more likely to be subject to error.

At first, children use one-word sentences—a noun or verb which, when combined with a gesture, expresses a complete thought. Saying "give" and pointing to a toy means, for example, "give me the toy." Children use single-word sentences from approximately 12 to 18 months of age. Two-year-olds combine words into short, often incomplete sentences containing one or two nouns, a verb, and occasionally an adjective or adverb. They simply omit prepositions, pronouns, and conjunctions. Typical sentences are "Hold doll," "Go bed," "Go bye-bye," and "Want drink." By the time children are 4, their sentences are nearly complete; a year later, they are complete in that all parts of speech are used (99).

An analysis of the sentences of children under the age of 8 reveals an early decline in the use of incomplete as well as structurally complete but functionally incomplete sentences. There is a slight but steady increase in the use of simple sentences, compound and complex sentences, and elaborated sentences (19).

One of the most common forms of sentences children use are questions. Meyer and Shane have made a study of the form and function of children's questions and have reported that this type of sentence follows Piaget's model of cognitive development. According to them (64):

Question-asking behavior reflects the logic of their thinking processes. At the preoperational stage, the child's questions concerning physical causality reflect largely undifferentiated cognitive structures in which the child's concerns with motivations and intentions are not separated from the causal explanation. When the child moves into the concrete operations stage, his questioning behavior reflects a higher level of differentiation: thus the questions separate physical causality from psychological causality. . . . The question-asking behaviors of children at the level of "concrete operations" are initially concerned with physical causality and then shift to a diverse number of categories.

At every age, children show marked individual differences in both the length and pattern of their sentences. Bright children and those from the higher socioeconomic groups usually use longer and more complex sentences than the average. When playing with their contemporaries, children are likely to converse in phrases rather than complete sentences. When with adults, they lengthen their sentences somewhat, but in a classroom situation, where there are both children and a teacher, they lengthen them even further.

Amount of Talking

After children have learned to speak, they talk almost incessantly. This is similar to the way they react to the ability to walk. Once they learn to walk, they walk just for the sake of walking. In both walking and speaking, these newly acquired skills give them feelings of importance.

While young children prefer to talk to people, they also talk when they are alone, playing with their toys. They even talk to people who pay little or no attention to what they are saying or who do not bother to answer their questions. It has been estimated that, on the average, 3- to 4-year-olds speak 15,000 words a day, or approximately 5 1/2 million words a year. Every year, as they grow older, they speak more and use more different words (2).

Ordinarily, children talk less and less as puberty approaches and progresses. This is largely because they are not feeling up to par physically, but it is also due to their concern about the many problems that puberty gives rise to. They not only talk less, but when they do talk they often tend to be sullen, disagreeable, and quarrelsome.

Individual Differences in Amount of Talking

The amount of talking children do is influenced by a number of factors, one of the most important of which is their *need for speech as a compensation* for other needs not met in their lives. Children, for example, who are deprived of affection, talk more when they are with adults and make more demands on them for attention than do children who feel secure in the affection of parents and peers.

In families where *authoritarian child training* is used and where there is an acceptance of the traditional belief that "children should be seen but not heard," children learn to talk less than in homes where either permissive or democratic discipline is used. In the former, children are permitted to talk when and as much as they please while in the latter, they are encouraged to express their opinions and to participate in family conversations as part of the democratic philosophy of the home.

Children from *large families* generally learn to talk less than those from small families partly because authoritarian training usually prevails in large families and partly because curbs on the amount of talking every family member does is essential to avoid bedlam. *Firstborns* are generally encouraged to talk more and are given more parental help in learning to talk than are their later-born siblings.

Intellectual ability is an important factor determining how much children talk. Children with high IQs usually are earlier, more interesting, and more fluent talkers than those who are less bright. Because of their speech ability, they are encouraged by adults and peers to talk more than their less bright age-mates who usually have less of interest to contribute to a conversation. *Popular* children learn that one of the ways to win peer acceptance is to contribute to conversations. As a result, they develop the habit of talking more than do those who are less well-accepted

or who are overlooked and neglected by the peer group.

Girls, as a group, talk more than boys, as a group, though there are marked individual differences within each sex group. Because family activities tend to be less well organized in members of the lower *socioeconomic* groups than in families of the middle or higher groups, children receive less encouragement to talk and less training in how to participate in conversations. Children from *one-parent* homes or homes where the mother works outside the home have less opportunity and encouragement to engage in family conversations. As a result, they do not develop the habit of talking at home as do children where these family conditions do not exist.

While children from *bilingual families* may talk as much at home as children from monolingual families, they talk less when with their peers. The reason for this will be discussed in detail in the section of this chapter related to hazards of speech development.

Significance of Amount of Talking

The earlier children begin to talk, the more practice they get and the greater their verbal facility. This increases their self-confidence. By contrast, children whose speech development is delayed get less practice, age for age, and this affects their verbal facility. A delay of 6 months to a year, for example, in starting to talk will mean, in many cases, that children are not ready linguistically to start school at the age of 6. Once they start to talk, they may catch up to the speech level of their age-mates, but lack of practice is likely to deprive them of the self-confidence essential to fluent speech. As a result, they hesitate to express themselves orally. This handicaps them in their academic and social adjustments.

As children grow older, they talk more and more with one another. This helps them to play together in a social way and adds enjoyment to their play. Quiet children find themselves left out of the play group. While they may not be rejected by their age-mates, they are often neglected because they have little of interest to contribute to the group. As a result, quiet children tend to develop feelings of inadequacy—feelings that may persist even after they catch up with their age-mates in verbal facility and are willing to talk more than they did when feelings of inadequacy developed because of their limited verbal facility. A close relationship has been reported between the amount of talking children do and their popularity. Children who talk most, other things equal, are the most popular (100). This matter will be discussed in more detail in Chapter 10.

Content of Speech

The content of children's speech has been clasified into two major categories: Egocentric speech and socialized speech (2, 30, 38). The characteristics of these two categories are given in Box 7–6.

Most of the young child's speech is egocentric. As the desire to be one of a social group increases, the child uses speech as a social tool. When this will occur is difficult to tell. Experimenters have reported ages ranging from 2 to 7 or 8 years. During these years, children talk more to peer group members than to adults if peer group members are available (60).

The shift from egocentric to socialized speech depends not so much upon chronological age as upon other factors. The child's personality is an important determinant. Egocentric children will continue to talk about themselves at every age and will show little interest in getting the other person's point of view. However, even egocentric children, as they grow older and as their desire to be accepted members of the peer group strengthens, tend to shift to more socialized speech. As the size of the peer group grows larger, their speech becomes less and less egocentric (2, 58).

When children are with their age-mates, socialized speech tends to predominate. When with adults, egocentric speech predominates. This is mainly because adults encourage children to talk about themselves by asking them questions about what they like to do, what they expect to do when they grow up, etc. This encouragement of egocentric speech is lacking when children are with age-mates. Consequently, children learn to steer their conversations into channels that will hold the attention and win the approval of their peers, thus strengthening their acceptance in the peer group (86).

Conversational Topics

What children talk about is influenced by their ages, the breadth of their experiences, and their personality patterns. Mainly, they talk about themselves and their activities, their families, and their relationships with different family members. Many topics that characterize adult conversations appear in a rudimentary form in the conversations of preschool children—topics such as clothes, likes and dislikes, where one lives, and matters of everyday routine.

Among older children, the variety of topics is wider, owing to the diversity of their experiences. Much of their conversation centers around school activities; their own experiences and accomplishments; their families and pets; sports; trips; clothes; movies, television programs, comics, and other forms of entertainment; and tabooed subjects, especially sex and sex organs. Children feel freer to discuss these topics with contemporaries than with adults (2, 16, 18, 23, 31, 93).

Methods of Presentation

Methods of presenting what they say often have more influence on people's reactions to children than the content of what they say. Young children tend to use matter-of-fact statements or questions; older children, as they shift from egocentric to socialized speech,

---

BOX 7–6

MAJOR CATEGORIES OF SPEECH CONTENT

EGOCENTRIC SPEECH
In egocentric speech, children talk either for their own enjoyment or for the pleasure of associating with anyone who happens to be present. They make no attempt to exchange ideas or to pay attention to the other person's point of view. Egocentric speech is, thus, pseudoconversation or monologue. There is no real communication present. Its major value in speech development is that it helps children to acquire facility in speaking and to discover how people react to what they have to say. This later proves to be an aid in socialized speech.

SOCIALIZED SPEECH
Socialized speech is speech that is adapted to the speech or behavior of the person to whom the individual is speaking. It occurs when children are able to shift their mental perspectives and are able to view a situation from other than their own viewpoints. They are then able to communicate and to engage in an exchange of ideas. Because questions command more attention than statements, much early socialized speech takes the form of asking questions.

BOX 7–7

COMMON FORMS OF UNSOCIAL PRESENTATION

EXAGGERATIONS

Between 5 and 7 years, when imagination outpaces reasoning, children tend to exaggerate what they say. When they discover that exaggerations bring them more attention than matter-of-fact remarks, they consciously or unconsciously exaggerate whenever they want attention and approval from others.

BOASTING

Boasting is a form of exaggeration in which children "embroider" statements of fact to make them more colorful and to increase their attention value. It is greatest between the ages of 8 and 12 years, when children are most anxious to impress their peers and to ensure their status in the peer group. What children boast about is determined largely by the values of the peer group—material possessions, skills, achievements, or family status.

NAME-CALLING

Name-calling is a form of boasting in which children who want attention or want to impress others with their superiority try to deflate the importance of other children by using derogatory names for them—"idiot," "dumbell," or "fatty." It is most common in the latter part of childhood.

CRITICISM

Critical comments about others serve to inflate the egos of children who feel inferior and to call attention to them-

selves. Criticism is used mainly to comment on the behavior, appearance, and personality of the person who is criticized—the person's lack of knowledge, clumsiness, clothing or stinginess, for example.

TATTLING

Tattling is a form of criticism in which children voice a complaint to a parent, teacher, or some other adult about the way another child or adult has treated them. Because this is one of the quickest and surest ways of winning social disapproval from adults as well as peers, most children abandon tattling when desire for social acceptance becomes strong.

DEROGATORY COMMENTS

Beginning around 3 years of age, many children use derogatory comments to inflate their egos, to relieve injured feelings, and to let others know how they feel about them. Older children do not reserve their derogatory comments for age-mates and siblings. Instead, they talk about adults in a derogatory manner when they discover that it is "the thing to do" among their age-mates. In this way, they are indirectly telling their age-mates that they are not "tied to parental apron strings" and that they are "good sports." Derogatory comments usually reach their peak in the early part of puberty and are often of an intensity that can be labeled "vitriolic."

tend to present their thoughts and feelings in more dramatic, attention-getting methods than they used for egocentric speech. As a result, what they say tends more often to be unsocial than social. Some of these unsocial forms of socialized speech are explained in Box 7–7. While some of these unsocial forms of presentation are learned by trial-and-error, many are learned by imitating the unsocial speech of peers, parents, or other adults.

Significance of Content of Speech

Studies of the content of children's speech at different ages gives much more than information about the size and correctness of their vocabularies and their ability to combine words into grammatically correct sentences. It gives information about their dominant inter-

ests, how they feel about other people and situations, and what concepts they have of themselves.

From what children say, one can tell what their aspirations are and how they feel about their achievements. It is also possible to get information about their emotional states—whether they are happy, frightened, angry, jealous, or envious of others. Speech content is, thus, a thermometer of children's emotional reactions.

Hazards in Speech Development

Because speech development is very complicated, owing to the fact that it involves both comprehension of what others say and the ability to speak in a way that others can understand, it is inevitable that there are many hazards in this area of development. Unless these hazards are recognized and either prevented or minimized, speech will fall below the child's capacities.

The impact of speech on children's personal and social adjustments is even greater than the impact of motor development. This is because speech has a greater influence on children's social adjustments than their skills have. And the kind of social adjustments children make affects their personal adjustments.

Some of the most common and most important hazards in speech development are discussed below. Most of them can be prevented or minimized. Consequently, it is important to be forewarned about them so as to make the difficult tasks involved in speech development easier for children.

Excessive Crying

Excessive crying means crying more than is normal for a child's age and level of development. If babies and young children cry no more than is normal for their ages, crying will have no damaging effects and may even be beneficial.

The reason for this is that normal crying provides babies with the exercise needed for muscle growth and coordination. It also stimulates their appetites and encourages sound sleep. In young children, normal crying is often an outlet for emotional tension. When thwarted in what they want to do, young children become angry and this leads to tension and nervousness. A good cry releases this pent-up energy and restores body homeostasis. It also releases antagonisms against the people who have thwarted them and, in so doing, helps to establish a more pleasant relationship with them.

Excessive crying, by contrast, is physically and psychologically damaging at any age. The longer the crying lasts and the more intense it is, the more harmful its effects. Some of the physical and psychological damages of excessive crying are given and explained in Box 7–8.

Excessive and prolonged crying may develop into a habit. Once formed, such a habit will not be outgrown

---

BOX 7–8

PHYSICAL AND PSYCHOLOGICAL DAMAGES OF EXCESSIVE CRYING

PHYSICAL DAMAGE
- *Depletion of energy.* Because babies literally "cry all over," excessive crying depletes their energy and exhausts them. This interferes with normal eating and sleeping and, in turn, with normal physical growth. If crying continues until they become somewhat hysterical, they cannot stop crying even when the cause of the crying has been removed. This further depletes their energy.

- *Upsets in body homeostasis.* Excessive crying, when prolonged, upsets the normal functioning of the entire body. This results in variability in gastrointestinal functions, regurgitations, vomiting, night waking, enuresis, and general nervous tension which is expressed in such mannerisms as thumb-sucking and nail-biting. When crying leads to a hysterical state, the upset in homeostasis is not only intensified but is also prolonged.

PSYCHOLOGICAL DAMAGE
- *Parental Attitudes.* When babies cry more than parents consider normal, they worry and become over-

concerned or they ignore the cries, hoping to teach their babies that they cannot get what they want by being ornery. In either case, babies are psychologically damaged—by parental overprotectiveness or by the build-up of feelings of helplessness and insecurity which they will later interpret as parental rejection.

- *Home climate.* Excessive crying annoys all members of the family and puts a strain on everyone. As a result, the home climate becomes frictional. Since the child is largely responsible, relationships with different family members deteriorate, and the child comes to feel unloved and unwanted.

- *Social reactions.* Unless adults and age-mates outside the home can see a real reason for the crying, they will be impatient and intolerant, regarding the child as a crybaby. This leads to social rejection, which is psychologically damaging. It deprives the child of opportunities to learn social skills and provides the basis for unfavorable self-evaluation.

---

nor will it disappear of its own accord. Instead, it will have to be unlearned and replaced with forms of communication that are more socially acceptable. The sooner this is done, the easier it will be for children and the less damage they will suffer.

Difficulties in Comprehension

Because the ability to communicate depends on the ability to understand what others say as well as on the ability to speak, children who cannot understand what others are trying to communicate to them will be handicapped socially. Feeling socially isolated will lead to feelings of inadequacy, inferiority, and martyrdom. Later, when children go to school, their academic achievements will fall below their intellectual capacities. If they are not sure of what the teacher's questions mean, they will hesitate to speak in class and this will lead to unfavorable evaluations of their knowledge.

There are a number of reasons for difficulties in comprehension, four of which are very common. *First,* the child's vocabulary may be so limited that the words others use are unfamiliar. In the case of slang and swear words, for example, the child may be at a loss to know what the speaker who refers to someone as a "kook" or a "nitwit" means (29, 34).

Second, when people speak rapidly, young children have difficulty in catching the words. As a result, their comprehension is blurred. After the age of 6, comprehension increases rapidly though more slowly for rapid presentation and for more difficult material (36, 74). This is illustrated in Figure 7–8.

Third, if children have grown up in a bilingual home where the family language is not English, their English vocabulary may be so limited that, when they talk to people outside the home, they will find that many of the words are unfamiliar. This interferes with their comprehension of what the speaker is saying (51).

Fourth, very often difficulties in comprehension stem from failures to listen attentively to what others are saying. This is especially true of young children who are so egocentric that they are more interested in what they want to say than in what others are saying to them (3).

Delayed Speech

When the level of speech development falls below the level of children of the same age in quality, as shown by word use and accuracy, children are handicapped

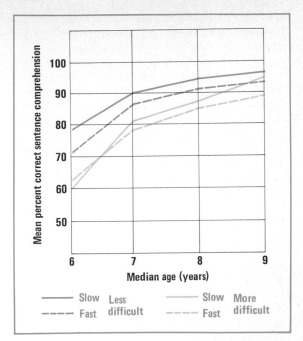

Figure 7–8. Improvement in comprehension of easy and difficult sentences, given slowly and rapidly, after school entrance. (*Adapted from N. W. Nelson: Comprehension of spoken language by normal children as a function of speaking rate, sentence difficulty and listener age and sex.* Child Development, *1976, 47, 299–303. Used by permission.*)

in their social relationships just as they are when their play skills fall below those of their age-mates. This affects the social adjustments children make. And, because members of the social group regard their speech as "babyish," it has a damaging effect on their self-concepts.

Should children continue to use babytalk and gestures when their age-mates are speaking in words, it will reinforce their belief that the children are too young to play with them. This will deprive children of opportunities to learn the play skills their age-mates are learning and further jeopardize their social acceptance.

Delayed speech not only affects children's personal and social adjustments but it also affects their academic adjustments. The most serious effect is on the ability to read—the basic subject of children's early school careers. Later, it may affect their ability to spell. Falling behind academically, combined with problems in social acceptance, will lead to a dislike for school

(12, 35, 77). This will further impede their academic achievements.

There are many causes of delayed speech, the most common of which are: *low-grade intelligence* which makes it impossible for children to learn to speak as well as their age-mates of normal or superior intelligence; *lack of motivation* because children discover that they can communicate adequately by prespeech forms; encouragement by parents to continue to use *"baby talk"* because they think it is "cute"; limited *opportunities to practice* speech because of strict limitations on how much talking they are permitted to do at home; constant association with *younger siblings* or *twins* who can understand their jargon; and the use of a *foreign language* in the home which delays the learning of English.

Unquestionably one of the most common and most serious causes of delayed speech is *failure to stimulate* children to speak, even when they are first starting to babble. When children are not encouraged to babble, it delays their use of words and they continue to lag behind their age-mates who are given more encouragement to talk (12, 43, 69, 96). That lack of stimulation is a serious cause of delayed speech is shown by the fact that when parents not only speak to their children but use a wide variety of words, their children's speech develops rapidly. Middle-class children, for example, whose parents are anxious to have them speak early and well, are far less likely to experience delayed speech than are lower-class children whose parents fail to give them this stimulation, either because of lack of time or because they do not realize how important it is to speech development (28, 43, 69, 96).

Defective Speech

Defective speech is inaccurate speech; it varies *qualitatively* from the norm for the child's age and contains more than the usual errors for that age. Defective speech differs from delayed speech, described above, which is quantitatively below the norm for the child's age due to a smaller vocabulary, poorer pronunciation, and less well formed sentences than is normal for children of that age.

The term "defective" is popularly applied only to defects in pronunciation. In its broader sense, however, it can be applied to *any* form of speech that is incorrect. Most speech defects can be categorized into three groups—defects in word meanings, defects in pronun-

ciation, and defects in sentence structure. These three categories are described below.

DEFECTS IN WORD MEANINGS The first common category of speech defects is association of the wrong meaning with a word. In every language, a number of meanings are associated with words that *sound alike,* even though their spelling may be different. For example, "rain," "rein," and "reign" sound alike but have very different meanings and different spelling. Under such conditions, it is not surprising that, while learning meanings, the child makes many wrong associations.

Such errors interfere with communication. They affect the child's comprehension of what others say as well as the ability of others to understand what the child says. In addition, such errors are responsible for some of the disciplinary problems of childhood. Many cases of what appears to be willful breaking of rules come from children's misinterpretation of the words used in the rules. This matter will be discussed further in the chapter on moral development.

DEFECTS IN PRONUNCIATION The second common category of speech defects is defects in pronunciation. Most defective pronunciation is due to faulty learning and can be corrected relatively easily. Some is due to malformation of parts of the speech mechanism, such as the teeth, palate, lips, or jaws. It may also be caused by imperfect hearing and muscular weakness or partial paralysis of the tongue and lips, as in some cases of cerebral palsy. Under such conditions, defective speech is more persistent and correction is far more difficult.

From 18 months to 3 or 4 years of age, most children make many mistakes in pronunciation. This is popularly referred to as "baby talk" and is regarded by many parents, grandparents, and other adults as "cute" or "appealing."

The errors that characterize baby talk generally come from faulty learning that has not been corrected. The faulty learning that gives rise to baby talk is more often the result of children's crude perceptions of words than of inability to pronounce the elemental sounds. Furthermore, in their zeal to talk to others, children often talk so quickly that they omit the harder parts of words. In saying "cream," for example, they are likely to omit the letter *r* because it takes considerable effort to pronounce two consecutive consonants.

The most common errors in pronunciation, made by young children, are given in Box 7–9.

As children grow older, errors in pronunciation do not automatically disappear, though they become less frequent. Children from homes where they have poor models of speech to imitate continue to make errors in pronunciation even when their errors in pronunciation are corrected in school (33, 77, 79).

Even mild defects in pronunciation, such as baby talk, are handicaps to children's personal and social adjustments. School children who mispronounce their words feel conspicuous and embarrassed. They dislike being called on to speak in class because they are afraid their classmates will laugh at them.

Many maladjustive forms of behavior stem from feelings of inadequacy caused in part by, or intensified by, defects in pronunciation. Defective speech thus becomes a part of the syndrome of maladjustment. Often a vicious circle is set into motion. Children with defective pronunciation, for example, may fail to take advantage of educational opportunities and thus become underachievers. Knowing that they are not living up to their potentials, they become anxious and this exaggerates their feelings of inadequacy. The more pronounced their feelings of inadequacy, the more likely it is to aggravate their mispronunciations.

DEFECTS IN SENTENCE STRUCTURE The third common category of speech defects is grammatical errors. Even the child with good speech models in the home makes many grammatical errors. The young child's major problems in sentence structure are in the use of pronouns and verb tenses. Few 2-year-olds use pronouns correctly; among 3-year-olds, about 75 percent do.

From the age of 3, children tighten their hold on grammar, though they continue to make grammatical mistakes throughout the elementary school years and into high school and college. Children from the lower socioeconomic groups who often hear patterns of incorrect speech in the home tend to make more grammatical errors at every age than do children from the more privileged homes. It has been reported that there is a high correlation between the grammatical errors made by children and those by their parents (19, 56, 61).

Often children's grammatical mistakes seem funny to adults, but they are psychologically damaging to children. That is why they should not be taken lightly

or ignored in the hopes that children will outgrow them or correct them when they study grammar in school. Some examples of the psychological damage of defective grammar are given in Box 7–10.

Speech Disorders

The term, "speech disorder," refers to a serious defect in pronunciation. It differs from a defect in pronunciation *first* because it is not caused by faulty learning but by some defect in the vocal mechanism or by persistent emotional tension and *second* because it cannot be corrected by learning correct pronunciations; rather, the cause of the trouble that has led to the disorder must be removed.

Speech disorders are especially common in families where one or both parents are neurotic, where parent-child relationships are poor, where there is a dominant mother and submissive father, or where the mother ignores the child, is exceptionally possessive or demanding, or sets excessively high levels of aspiration for the child. They are often correlated with dependency, soiling, destructiveness, restlessness in sleep, temper tantrums, negativism, timidity, and food finickiness. All this suggests that speech disorders are a part of the *syndrome of poor adjustment.* (9, 103).

Disorders of speech may develop at any time during the life-span. They are most likely to develop, however, during the preschool years when children are trying to master the task of learning to speak and when any emotional disturbance is likely to upset this learning. Many speech disorders, developed during the pre-

BOX 7–10

PSYCHOLOGICAL DAMAGE FROM
DEFECTIVE GRAMMAR

INCORRECT THINKING
Defects in sentence structure can give a totally unintended meaning to a sentence. They affect the child's understanding of what others say as well as their understanding of what the child is trying to communicate. Should the child say "I ate my lunch" instead of "I eat my lunch," it will create the impression that the child has already eaten when, in reality, it means that the child is now ready to eat.

UNFAVORABLE SOCIAL IMPRESSIONS
Judgments by others are often made on the basis of first impressions. The child whose grammar is defective will create a less favorable impression than one whose speech is correct. Furthermore, speech becomes a "status symbol" as the child grows older.

UNFAVORABLE SELF-EVALUATION
When children realize that they are unfavorably judged by others, even though they may not realize why, they will evaluate themselves unfavorably. This will have a damaging effect on their personalities. Grammatical mistakes lead to unfavorable self-concepts and feelings of inferiority long before childhood comes to an end.

HABITUAL PATTERNS OF SPEECH
With repetition, grammatical mistakes become habitual. If the child becomes accustomed to hearing words in certain combinations, any change in the combinations sounds incorrect. A child, for example, who has become accustomed to saying "He done," will claim that it sounds funny to say "He did," and will resist making the change.

school years, become habitual and are far more noticeable when their speech is compared with that of their age-mates. The most common speech disorders of childhood are outlined in Box 7–11 along with a brief explanation of their causes.

Bilingualism

Bilingualism is the ability to *use* two languages. It involves not only speaking and writing but also the ability to understand what others are attempting to communicate both orally and in writing. Truly bilingual children are as much at home in a foreign language as in the mother tongue. They are able to speak, read, and write both languages with equal facility.

Few children are truly bilingual. Most are more adept in the use of one language than the other. There are many combinations of binguality: Children may be able to understand and use both languages equally well; they may be able to speak both but write only one; or they may be able to understand both but speak only one.

When children are expected to learn two languages *simultaneously,* they must learn two different words for every object they name and for every thought they wish to express. They must learn two sets of grammatical forms—one often conflicting with the other. And, they must learn how to pronounce the same letters or same letter combinations differently. These learning tasks are very confusing for young children who have not yet learned one language well enough to feel at ease in using it.

When learning the second language is begun *after* the first has progressed to the point where it can be used automatically, the tasks involved in learning the second are still far from easy. The reason for this is that conflicts in pronunciation, in grammar, and in word associations will be confusing. In addition, the speech mechanism is not so easy to control as it was when children were younger. Consequently, learning to pronounce words in a different language is far more difficult than learning to pronounce new words in the language children are accustomed to use.

For some children, bilingualism is a serious obstacle to learning to speak correctly. However, it is important to realize that the effects on children's speech and on their personal and social adjustments depend not so much upon bilingualism, per se, but upon the conditions that it gives rise to. Of the many conditions that influence the effect of bilingualism on children's speech and on their personal and social adjustments, those explained in Box 7–12 are most common and most serious.

From a careful study of these conditions, it is logical to conclude that bilingualism is more of a handicap than an asset to a child, especially during the preschool years. This opinion is widely held by psychologists and educators (25, 33, 41, 51). It is also a handicap to older children, especially when their use of English falls below the level of their age-mates who are monolinguals.

Difficulties in Conversing

Most children encounter two difficulties in conversing with others. Both of these difficulties give rise to hazards in their social adjustments. And, because of unfavorable social reactions to them, they become hazards to their personal adjustments.

The first difficulty children encounter in conversations with others relates to the *amount of talking* they do. Some children talk too much and try to dominate the conversation while others talk too little and gain the reputation of being "Silent Sams." Very few strike a happy medium and give others an opportunity to talk while, at the same time, carrying their load in the conversation.

Talking too much often annoys others and creates the impression that the talkers are egocentric. Furthermore, children's endless chatter tends to bore others because "chatterbox" children rarely have enough of interest to say to hold the attention of their listeners. By contrast, children who contribute little or nothing to a conversation may create the impression that they are "stupid" or that they feel so superior to others that they do not want to waste their time talking to them. However their failure to talk is judged, it has an unfavorable effect on their social adjustments.

The second problem children who have difficulties in conversing with others encounter is *what to talk about*. If they talk about themselves, their possessions, their achievements, or their interests, they find that their listeners begin to be bored or annoyed by their egocentric talk. If they talk about tabooed subjects, such as sex or if they criticize parents or other family members, they may find that their talking arouses social disapproval (100).

Most children find it even more difficult to know what to say to adults than to their age-mates. If they have been permitted or even encouraged to talk about themselves at home, they do not know what to talk about to adults outside the home. The same is true when they are with age-mates. As a result, they either talk about themselves or remain silent, both of which create unfavorable impressions on their listeners.

Socially Unacceptable Speech

A child whose speech is socially unacceptable makes a poor impression and often acquires an unfavorable reputation. The effect on personal and social adjustments may be severe. Furthermore, if talking in a so-

---

BOX 7–11

COMMON SPEECH DISORDERS OF CHILDHOOD

LISPING

Lisping consists of letter-sound substitutions. The most common substitutions are *th* for *s* or *z,* as in "Thimple Thimon," and of *w* for *r,* as in "wed wose." Lisping is usually caused by deformation of the jaw, teeth, or lips and a tendency to cling to infantile speech. A missing front tooth may cause a temporary lisp. Lisping in adolescence is usually due to a space between the upper front teeth.

SLURRING

Slurring is indistinct speech due to inactivity of the lips, tongue, or jaw. It is sometimes caused by paralysis of the vocal organs or lack of development of the musculature of the tongue. When emotionally upset or excited, a child may rush through words without pronouncing each one distinctly. Slurring is most common during the preschool years before speech has become habitual.

STUTTERING

Stuttering is hesitant, repetitious speech accompanied by spasms of the muscles of the throat and diaphragm. It comes from a breathing disturbance due to partial or total incoordination of the speech muscles. It resembles stage fright in that the person seems at a loss to know what to say. It is usually accompanied by stammering, a deadlocking of speech in which the speaker is temporarily unable to produce any sound. Then, as muscular tension is released, a flood of words pours out, soon to be checked by another spasm. Stuttering begins when the child is between 2½ and 3½. Normally, it decreases as the child makes better social and home adjustments, only to flare up again when the child enters the broader environment of the school.

CLUTTERING

Cluttering is rapid and confused speech which is often mistaken for stuttering. It usually occurs in children whose motor control and speech development are delayed. It is an exaggeration of the errors of speech made by normal people. Unlike the stutterer, clutterers can improve their speech if they pay attention to what they want to say.

---

cially unacceptable manner becomes habitual, it will be an increasingly serious handicap each year. A survey of some of the far-reaching effects of socially unacceptable speech will highlight its significance.

BOX 7–12

CONDITIONS ASSOCIATED WITH BILINGUALISM THAT ARE HAZARDOUS TO GOOD ADJUSTMENTS

EFFECT ON SOCIAL ADJUSTMENTS

When the dominant language is different from the one used by the children with whom a child associates, the child finds it difficult to communicate with them. This leads to problems in social adjustment.

EFFECT ON SCHOOLWORK

Since bilingual children are not linguistically ready for school, they feel insecure and are handicapped educationally from the very start of their school careers.

EFFECT ON SPEECH DEVELOPMENT

Learning two languages simultaneously in the early years is likely to delay development in both languages and to lead to more speech errors than is normal for the child's age. Figure 7–9 shows a comparison of bilingual and monolingual children in different tests of linguistic achievement. Realization of their speech inferiority makes children nervous and emotionally excited—a condition that often leads to stuttering.

EFFECT ON THINKING

Bilingual children are often confused in their thinking and this makes them self-conscious about talking. If they are so self-conscious that they refuse to converse with peers, they will likely experience social neglect or rejection.

EFFECT ON SOCIAL DISCRIMINATION

About the time children reach school age, they discover that people associate different stereotypes with different accents. The child is then judged by peers as well as by adults in terms of the stereotype. If the stereotype is unfavorable, it is likely to lead to prejudice and discrimination.

EFFECT OF DIFFERENTNESS

If the dominant language is a foreign one, the child is likely to have a home environment in which the pattern of living, the child-training used, and the manner of dressing and eating will be different from those of age-mates. This syndrome of "differentness," constantly apparent in speech, especially if the child has a foreign accent, is likely to be a serious handicap to social adjustments.

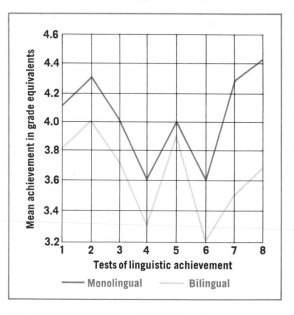

Figure 7-9. Comparison of bilingual with monolingual children in different tests of linguistic achievement. (*Adapted from Sister M. A. Carrow: Linguistic functioning of bilingual and monolingual children,* Journal of Speech and Hearing Disorders, *1957, 22, 371–380. Used by permission.*)

First, children who talk mostly about themselves think more about themselves than about others. Egocentric speech is thus not an isolated pattern of behavior; instead, it is part of the syndrome of egocentrism. Studies of social acceptance have revealed that children who are egocentric are less popular than those who think of others and consider their welfare. This will be discussed more fully in the chapters on social adjustments and personality.

On the other hand, just because children talk about other people and other things is no guarantee that they will talk about them in a manner that will lead to good social adjustments. For example, children who are constantly boasting make other children feel inferior. They also resent the implication that the boaster is superior. Boasters are likely to acquire the reputation of having "swelled heads" or of being "stuck up," —a reputation that will play havoc with their social adjustments.

Boasting also affects children's personal adjustments. While they may derive temporary ego-satisfaction from it, they build up an unrealistic concept of themselves and their abilities. As their capacity for reasoning increases, they will recognize the gap between what they say they are and what they really are—a gap that will lead to self-dissatisfaction and discontent. To close this gap, they often look for scapegoats upon whom they can project the blame for their not being, in reality, what they boasted they were.

Second, criticism in its many related forms—tattling, name-calling, and derogatory comments—may be ego-inflating for the child, but it is ego-deflating for the person who is criticized. It irritates people and breaks up friendships. Criticism within the family is one of the causes of deterioration in family relationships as children grow older. Parents and older relatives regard a child's critical comments as impertinence or lack of respect and reprove the child for them. Siblings, too, resent name-calling, tattling, and critical comments,

and they generally retaliate in kind. If parents try to stop the quarreling that ensues, they are accused of playing favorites, and parent-child relationships deteriorate still further.

Third, a cynical and belligerent attitude damages both children and those who are subjected to the expression of such attitudes. Not only are children building up habits of speech which will lead to social rejection with its accompanying psychological damage, but they are also building up distorted concepts of their superiority and their right to bully others. Those who bear the brunt of these comments cannot escape wondering whether they are as inadequate and inferior as those who bully them suggest.

Fourth, children can be permanently damaged by repeated criticism. The "female inferiority complex," for example, is largely the result of the critical and derogatory comments girls are subjected to by brothers and male classmates. The more important a critical person is to a child, the more the child will be influenced by what the person says. Thus there is little evidence of the truth of the old saying, "Sticks and stones will hurt my bones, but words will never harm me"; critical and derogatory words certainly *will harm* a child.

Chapter Highlights

1 Speech is only one of many forms of language, but it is the most useful and most widely used form. It is also the most difficult skill to master because of its mental aspect.

2 There are two criteria that must be applied to vocal utterances to determine if they are speech: (1) the speaker's knowledge of the meaning of the word used and (2) the ability to pronounce it in a way that it can be understood by others.

3 If speech is to be a useful form of communication, the speaker must use words that are meaningful to others and must be able to understand the meaning of words used by others.

4 Speech contributes to children's personal and social adjustments by satisfying their needs and wants, by giving them attention from others, by facilitating social relationships, by providing a basis for evaluation by members of the social group and for self-evaluation, by contributing to academic achievement,

and by enabling children to influence the behavior, thoughts, and feelings of others.

5 Before children are physically and mentally ready to learn to speak, nature provides four stopgap forms of communication for them—crying, gestures, babbling, and emotional expressions. From the long-term point of view, babbling is the most important because it provides the foundations for speech.

6 As is true of learning all skills, speech can be learned by trial-and-error, by imitation, or by training. Of these, training is the best because it involves guidance in learning to imitate a model.

7 There are six essentials in learning to speak—physical readiness, mental readiness, a good model to imitate, opportunities for practice, motivation, and guidance.

8 There are three major tasks in learning to speak: building a vocabulary—both general and special—by associating meanings with words, learning to pronounce words, and combining words into grammatically correct sentences.

9 The amount of talking children do varies according to their needs for speech as a compensation for unfulfilled needs, the child-training method used in the home, family size, ordinal position, intelligence, popularity, sex, presence of the mother in the home, and whether the family is bilingual or monolingual.

10 Children's speech may be egocentric—in which they talk about themselves—or socialized—in which they talk about other people and their activities and interests. As children grow older, socialized speech gradually replaces the egocentric speech of early childhood.

11 Even when socialized speech is used, children often present what they say in unsocial forms, such as exaggerations, boasting, criticism, name-calling, tattling, and derogatory comments. These unsocial forms of speech are damaging to children's personal and social adjustments.

12 The most common hazards in speech development are excessive crying, difficulties in comprehension, delayed speech, defective speech, speech disorders, bilingualism, difficulties in communication, and unsocial forms of speech.

13 Delayed speech means speech patterns below the norm for the child's age; defective speech means speech that varies qualitatively from the norm for the child's age because of faulty learning; and speech disorders are serious defects in pronunciation due not to faulty learning but to defects in the vocal mechanism or persistent emotional tension.

14 Bilingualism is a hazard to children's social adjustments because it makes communication with others difficult and to their personal adjustments because bilingualism makes them different from their peers and this leads to feelings of being inferior.

15 Difficulties in conversing often result in children's talking too much or too little, while difficulties in knowing how to present what they want to say often result in making socially unacceptable comments. Both of these difficulties are hazards to good personal and social adjustments of children.

Bibliography

1 Ainsworth, M. D. S., S. M. Bell, and D. J. Stayton. Individual differences in the development of some attachment behaviors. *Merrill-Palmer Quarterly,* 1972, *18,* 123–143.

2 Alvy, K. T. Relation of age to children's egocentric and cooperative communications. *Journal of Genetic Psychology,* 1968, *112,* 275–286.

3 Asher, S. R., and S. L. Oden. Children's failure to communicate: An assessment of comparison and egocentrism explanations. *Developmental Psychology,* 1976, *12,* 132–139.

4 Baldwin, T., P. T. McFarlane, and C. J. Garvey. Children's communication accuracy related to race and socioeconomic status. *Child Development,* 1971, *42,* 345–357.

5 Bar-Adon, A., and W. F. Leopold. (eds.), *Child language: A book of readings.* Englewood Cliffs, N. J.: Prentice-Hall, 1971.

6 Bates, E., L. Camaioni, and V. Volterra. The acquisition of performatives prior to speech. *Merrill-Palmer Quarterly,* 1975, *21,* 207–226.

7 Beckwith, L.: Relationships between infants' vocalizations and their mothers' behavior. *Merrill-Palmer Quarterly,* 1971, *17,* 211–226.

8 Bell, S. M., and M. D. S. Ainsworth. Infant crying and maternal responsiveness. *Child Development,* 1972, *43,* 1171–1190.

9 Berry, M. F. *Language disorders of children: Their bases and diagnosis.* New York: Appleton-Century-Crofts, 1969.

10 Blank, M. Cognitive functions of language in the preschool years. *Developmental Psychology,* 1974, *10,* 229–245.

11 Braine, M. D. S. Children's first word combinations. *Monographs of the Society for Research in Child Development,* 1976, No. 164.

12 Bruck, M., and G. R. Tucker. Social class differences in the acquisition of school language. *Merrill-Palmer Quarterly,* 1974, *20,* 205–220.

13 Buck, R. Nonverbal communication of affect in children. *Journal of Personality and Social Psychology,* 1975, *31,* 644–653.

14 Childers, P. R. Listening ability is a modifiable skill. *Journal of Experimental Education,* 1970, *38,* 1–3.

15 Condon, W. S., and L. W. Sander. Neonate movements as synchronized with adult speech: Interactional participation and language acquisition. *Science,* 1974, *183,* 99–101.

16 Davis, A. J., and G. Lange. Parent-child communication and development of categorization styles in preschool children. *Child Development.* 1973, *44,* 624–629.

17 deHirsch, K. A review of early language development. *Developmental Medicine and Child Neurology,* 1970, *12,* 87–97.

18 Deutsch, F. Observational and sociometric measures of peer popularity and their relationship to egocentric communication in female preschoolers. *Developmental Psychology,* 1974, *10,* 745–747.

19 deVilliers, J. G., and P. A. deVilliers. A cross-sectional study of the acquisition of grammatical morphemes in child speech. *Journal of*

Psycholinguistic Research, 1973, *2,* 267–278.

20 Dodd, B. J. Effects of social and vocal stimulation on infant babbling. *Developmental Psychology,* 1972, *7,* 80–83.

21 Donaldson, M., and G. Balfour. Less is more: A study of language comprehension in children. *British Journal of Psychology,* 1968, *59,* 461–471.

22 Doty, D. Infant speech perception. *Human Development,* 1974, *17,* 74–80.

23 Dreger, R. M. Spontaneous conversation and story-telling of children in a naturalistic setting. *Journal of Psychology,* 1955, *40,* 163–180.

24 Duncan, S. Nonverbal communication. *Psychological Bulletin,* 1969, *72,* 118–137.

25 Feldman, C., and M. Shen. Some language-related cognitive advantages of bilingual five-year-olds. *Journal of Genetic Psychology,* 1971, *118,* 235–244.

26 Ferguson, C. A. *Studies of child language development.* New York: Holt, Rinehart & Winston 1973.

27 Francis, H. Social background, speech and learning to read. *British Journal of Educational Psychology,* 1974, *44,* 290–299.

28 Fraser, C., and N. Roberts. Mothers' speech to children of four different ages. *Journal of Psycholinguistic Research,* 1975, *4,* 9–16.

29 Friedlander, B. Z. Receptive language development in infancy: Issues and problems. *Merrill-Palmer Quarterly,* 1970, *16,* 7–51.

30 Garvey, C., and R. Hogan. Social speech and social interaction: Egocentrism revisited. *Child Development,* 1973, *44,* 562–568.

31 Glucksberg, S., and R. M. Krauss. What do people say after they have learned to talk? Studies of the development of referential communication. *Merrill-Palmer Quarterly,* 1967, *13,* 309–316.

32 Groff, P. Children's speech errors and their spelling. *Elementary School Journal,* 1973, *74,* 88–96.

33 Hahn, J., and V. Dunston. Bilingualism and individualized parent education: An organic approach to early childhood education. *California Journal of Educational Research,* 1974, *35,* 253–260.

34 Hall, J. W. Word recognition by children of two age levels. *Journal of Educational Psychology,* 1968, *59,* 420–424.

35 Hallahan, D. P., J. M. Kauffman, and C. S. Mueller. Behavioral observation and teacher rating correlates of motor and vocal behavior in preschoolers. *Journal of Genetic Psychology,* 1975, *126,* 45–52.

36 Harris, R. J. Children's comprehension of complex sentences. *Journal of Experimental Child Psychology,* 1975, *19,* 420–433.

37 Holzman, M. The verbal environment provided by mothers for their very young children. *Merrill-Palmer Quarterly,* 1974, *20,* 31–42.

38 Hoy, E. A. Measurement of egocentrism in children's communication. *Developmental Psychology,* 1975, *11,* 392.

39 Hunt, J. McV., G. E. Kirk, and C. Lieberman. Social class and preschool language skill: IV. Semantic mastery of shapes. *Genetic Psychology Monographs,* 1975, *92,* 115–129.

40 Jakobson, R. Verbal communication. *Scientific American,* 1972, *227*(3), 73–80.

41 Janco-Worrall, A. D. Bilingualism and cognitive development. *Child Development,* 1972, *43,* 1390–1400.

42 Jessen, B. L., and D. W. Kaess. Effects of training on intersensory communication by five-year-olds. *Journal of Genetic Psychology,* 1973, *123,* 115–122.

43 Jones, P. A., and W. B. McMullan. Speech characteristics as a function of social class and situational factors. *Child Development,* 1973, *44,* 117–121.

44 Jones, S. J., and H. A. Moss. Age, state, and maternal behavior associated with infant vocalizations. *Child Development,* 1971, *42,* 1039–1051.

45 Kaplan, E., and G. Kaplan. The prelinguistic child. In J. Eliot (ed.), *Human development and cognitive processes.* New York: Holt, Rinehart & Winston, 1971. Pp. 358–381.

46 Karpf, R. J., A. E. Goss, and M. Y. Small. Naming, selection, and ordering of color ("hue") by young children. *Journal of General Psychology,* 1974, *90,* 297–314.

47 Katz, N., E. Baker, and J. Macnamara. What's in a name? A study of

how children learn common and proper names. *Child Development,* 1974, *45,* 469–473.

48 Kavanagh, J. F., and J. L. Cutting. (eds.) *The role of speech in language.* Cambridge, Mass.: M.I.T. Press, 1975.

49 Kirk, G. E., J. McV. Hunt, and F. Volkmar. Social class and preschool language skills. V. Cognitive and semantic mastery of number. *Genetic Psychology Monographs,* 1975, *92,* 131–153.

50 Krauss, R. M. Language as a symbolic process in communication; A psychological perspective. In W. R. Looft (ed.), *Developmental psychology: A book of readings.* Hinsdale, Ill.: Dryden Press, 1972. Pp. 387–401.

51 Laosa, L. M. Bilingualism in three United States Hispanic groups: Contextual use of language by children and adults in their families. *Journal of Educational Psychology,* 1975, *67,* 617–627.

52 Lenneberg, E. H., and E. Lenneberg (eds.): *Foundations of language development: A multidisciplinary approach.* New York: Academic Press, 1975. 2 vols.

53 Lerner, R. M., and C. Schroeder. Kindergarten children's active vocabulary about body build. *Developmental Psychology,* 1970, *5,* 179.

54 Lewis, W. C., R. N. Wolman, and M. King. The development of the language of emotions. *American Journal of Psychiatry,* 1971, *127,* 1491–1497.

55 Longhurst, T. M., and T. A. M. Schrandt. Linguistic analysis of children's speech: A comparison of four procedures. *Journal of Speech and Hearing Disorders,* 1973, *38,* 240–249.

56 Love, J. M., and C. Parker-Robinson. Children's imitation of grammatical and ungrammatical sentences. *Child Development,* 1972, *43,* 309–319.

57 Macnamara, J. Cognitive basis of language learning in infants. *Psychological Review,* 1972, *79,* 1–13.

58 Maratsos, M. P. Nonegocentric communication abilities in preschool children. *Child Development,* 1973, *44,* 697–700.

59 Maratsos, M. P. Preschool children's use of definite and indefinite

articles. *Child Development*, 1974, *45*, 446–455.

60 Marshall, H. R. Relations between home experiences and children's use of language in play interactions with peers. *Psychological Monographs: General and Applied*, 1961, *75* (5).

61 Marwit, S. J., and K. L. Marwit. Grammatical responses of Negro and Caucasian second graders as a function of standard and nonstandard English presentation. *Journal of Educational Psychology*, 1973, *65*, 187–191.

62 McCall, R. B. Smiling and vocalization in infants as indices of perceptual-cognitive processes. *Merrill-Palmer Quarterly*, 1972, *18*, 341–347.

63 McNeill, D. The development of language. In P. H. Mussen (ed), *Carmichael's manual of child psychology*, 3d ed. New York: Wiley, 1970. Vol. 1, pp. 1061–1161.

64 Meyer, W. J., and J. Shane. The form and function of children's questions. *Journal of Genetic Psychology*, 1973, *123*, 285–296.

65 Michael, G., and F. N. Willis. The development of gestures as a function of social class, education and sex. *Psychological Record*, 1968, *18*, 515–519.

66 Minke, K. A. Operant conditioning of a grammatical form class with second-grade children. *Journal of Genetic Psychology*, 1972, *121*, 21–30.

67 Mittler, P. Biological and social aspects of language development in twins. *Developmental Medicine and Child Neurology*, 1970, *12*, 741–757.

68 Moerk, E. L. Piaget's researches applied to the explanation of language development. *Merrill-Palmer Quarterly*, 1975, *21*, 151–169.

69 Moerk, E. L. Verbal interaction between children and their mothers during the preschool years. *Developmental Psychology*, 1975, *11*, 788–794.

70 Moore, T. E. (ed.) *Cognitive development and the acquisition of language*. New York: Academic Press, 1973.

71 Mueller, E. The maintenance of verbal exchanges between young children. *Child Development*, 1972, *43*, 930–938.

72 Mysak, E. D. Organismic development of oral language. *Journal of Speech and Hearing Disorders*, 1971, *26*, 377–384.

73 Neal W. R. The effect of environmental deprivation on speech and language development: Implications for child caseworkers, *Child Care Quarterly*, 1972, *1*, 157–172.

74 Nelson, N. W. Comprehension of spoken language by normal children as a function of speaking rate, sentence difficulty, and listener age and sex. *Child Development*, 1976, *47*, 299–303.

75 Osser, H., M. D. Wang, and F. Zaid. The young child's ability to imitate and comprehend speech: A comparison of two subcultural groups. *Child Development*, 1969, *40*, 1063–1075.

76 Ostwald, P. F., and P. Peltzman. The cry of the newborn. *Scientific American*, 1974, *230*(3), 84–90.

77 Palermo, D. S., and D. L. Molfese. Language acquisition from age five onward. *Psychological Bulletin*, 1972, *78*, 409–428.

78 Pozner, J., and E. Saltz. Social class, conditioned communication, and egocentric speech. *Developmental Psychology*, 1974, *10*, 764–771.

79 Quay, L. C. Language dialect, age and intelligence test performance in disadvantaged black children. *Child Development*, 1974, *45*, 463–468.

80 Rabin, K. H. Relationship between egocentric communication and popularity among peers. *Developmental Psychology*, 1972, *7*, 364.

81 Ramey, C. T., and L. L. Ourth. Delayed reinforcement and vocalization rates of infants. *Child Development*, 1971, *42*, 291–297.

82 Rebelsky, F., and R. Black. Crying in infancy. *Journal of Genetic Psychology*, 1972, *121*, 49–57.

83 Rebelsky, F., and C. Hanks. Fathers' verbal interaction with infants in the first 3 months of life. *Child Development*, 1971, *42*, 63–68.

84 Riegel, K. F. Development of language: Suggestions for a verbal fallout model. In D. C. Charles and and W. R. Looft (eds.), *Readings in psychological development through life*. New York: Holt, Rhinehart & Winston, 1973. Pp. 171–190.

85 Routh, D. K. Conditioning of vocal

response differentiation in infants. *Developmental Psychology*, 1969, *1*, 219–226.

86 Rubin, K. H. The relationship between spatial and communicative egocentrism in children and young and old adults. *Journal of Genetic Psychology*, 1974, *125*, 295–301.

87 Sachs, J. The status of developmental studies of language. In J. Eliot (ed.), *Human development and cognitive processes*, New York: Holt, Rhinehart & Winston, 1971. Pp. 381–394.

88 Shantz, C. U., and K. E. Wilson. Training communication skills in young children. *Child Development*, 1972, *43*, 693–698.

89 Shatz, M., and R. Gelman. The development of communication skills: Modifications in the speech of young children as a function of the listener. *Monographs of the Society for Research in Child Development*, 1973, *38*, 1–38.

90 Snow, C. E. Mothers' speech to children learning language. *Child Development*, 1972, *43*, 549–565.

91 Storck, P. A., and W. R. Looft. Qualitative analysis of vocabulary responses from persons aged six to sixty-six plus. *Journal of Educational Psychology*, 1973, *65*, 192–197.

92 Suppes, P. The semantics of children's language. *American Psychologist*, 1974, *29*, 103–114.

93 Thomas, V. Children's use of language in the nursery. *Educational Research*, 1973, *15*, 209–216.

94 Tizard, B., O. Cooperman, A. Joseph, and J. Tizard. Environmental effects on language development: A study of young children in long-stay residential nurseries. *Child Development*, 1972, *43*, 337–358.

95 Todd, G. A., and B. Palmer. Social reinforcement of infant babbling. *Child Development*, 1968, *39*, 591–596.

96 Tulkin, S. R., and J. Kagan. Mother-child interaction in the first year of life. *Child Development*, 1972, *43*, 31–41.

97 Vincent-Smith, L., D. Bricker, and W. Bricker. Acquisition of receptive vocabulary in the toddler-age child. *Child Development*, 1974, *45*, 189–193.

98 Watson, J. S. Smiling, cooing, and

"The Game." *Merrill-Palmer Quarterly*, 1972, *18*, 323–339.

99 Wehrabian, A. Measures of vocabulary and grammatical skills for children up to age six. *Developmental Psychology*, 1970, *2*, 439–446.

100 Welkowitz, J., G. Cariffe, and S. Feldstein. Conversational congruence as a criterion of socialization in children. *Child Development*, 1976, *47*, 269–272.

101 Whitehurst, G. J., G. Novak, and G. A. Zorn. Delayed speech studied in the home. *Developmental Psychology*, 1972, *7*, 169–177.

102 Wohman, R. N., W. C. Lewis, and M. King. The development of the language of emotions. IV. Bodily referents and the experience of affect. *Journal of Genetic Psychology*, 1972, *121*, 65–81.

103 Worster-Drought, C. Speech disorders in children. *Developmental Medicine and Child Neurology*, 1968, *10*, 427–440.

104 Young, R. D. Children's perception of emotion and empathic responses. *Perceptual and Motor Skills*, 1974, *38*, 971–976.

105 Zelazo, P. R. Smiling and vocalizing: A cognitive emphasis. *Merrill-Palmer Quarterly*, 1972, *18*, 349–365.

106 Zelazo, P. R., J. Kagan, and R. Hartmann. Excitement and boredom as determinants of vocalization in infants. *Journal of Genetic Psychology*, 1975, *126*, 107–117.

CHAPTER 8

EMOTIONAL DEVELOPMENT

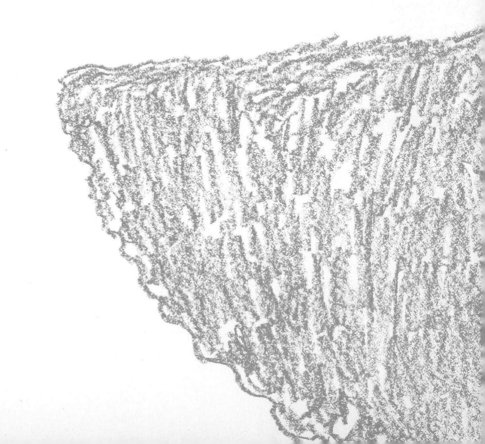

Because emotions play such an important role in life, it is essential to know how they develop and how they affect personal and social adjustments. Studying children's emotions is difficult because getting information about the subjective aspects of the emotions can come only from introspection—a technique which children cannot use successfully while they are still young.

Even studying their emotional reactions by observation of the overt expressions, especially facial expressions and actions associated with different emotions, is difficult as children become interested in conforming to social expectations. They learn, for example, to control the overt expressions of fear, anger, jealousy, or even grief when they discover that such emotional expressions serve as unfavorable social evaluations of them.

Because of these methodological difficulties, much of the scientific interest in children's emotions has been focused on the effects of emotions on children's personal and social adjustments. These studies have shown that *all* emotions, not just the pleasant ones, play an important role in the child's life and that each contributes to the kind of personal and social adjustments the child makes. The benefits or damages to children's personal and social adjustments may be physical or psychological or both. The most important effects of children's emotions on their adjustments are explained in Box 8–1.

In view of the important role the emotions play in the child's life, it is not surprising that some of the traditional beliefs about emotions that have grown up over the years to explain emotions have persisted in the absence of accurate information to substantiate or contradict them. And, until this scientific evidence is available, these traditional beliefs are not only likely to persist but, even more important, to influence the way in which parents and other adults who play caretaker roles will react to children's emotions.

For example, there is a widely accepted belief that some people are born more emotional than others. Consequently, it has been an accepted fact that there is nothing that can be done to change this characteristic. In ancient times, this difference in emotionality was explained as the result of differences in body humors. More recently, it was attributed to differences in the endocrine glands. In both cases, however, it was assumed that these differences were genetic and, hence, there was nothing that could be done to change them.

Differences in emotionality were also linked to hair color. People with red hair, for example, were said to be naturally "fiery" tempered while blonds were believed to have inherited weak emotionality and brunets were thought of as "naturally" warm and loving people.

Today, while it is conceded that there may be genetic differences in emotionality, evidence points to environmental conditions as largely responsible for differences in emotionality. Differences in emotionality of newborn infants have been attributed, in part, to differences in emotional stress experienced by their mothers during pregnancy—as was explained in Chapter 3. There is also evidence that children brought up in an exciting environment or subjected to constant pressures to live up to unrealistically high parental expectations may develop into tense, nervous, and highly emotional people.

Pattern of Emotional Development

The ability to respond emotionally is present in the newborn infant. The first sign of emotional behavior is general excitement due to strong stimulation. This diffuse excitement is reflected in the newborn's mass activity. At birth, however, the infant shows no clearcut responses that can be identified as specific emotional states (9, 64, 79).

Often before the period of the neonate is over, the general excitement of the newborn becomes differentiated into simple reactions that suggest pleasure and displeasure. *Unpleasant responses* can be elicited by abruptly changing the baby's position, making sudden loud noises, hampering the baby's movements, allowing the baby to wear wet diapers, and applying cold objects to the skin. Such stimuli cause crying and mass activity. *Pleasant responses,* on the other hand, are apparent when the baby sucks. They can also be elicited by rocking, patting, providing warmth, and holding the baby snugly. The baby shows pleasure by a general relaxation of the entire body, and by pleasant sounds in the form of coos and gurgles (64).

Even before babies are a year old, emotional expressions are recognizably similar to those of adults. Furthermore, babies display an increasing repertoire of emotional responses—joy, anger, fear, and happiness. These responses can be aroused by a wide range of stimuli, including people, objects, and situations which were ineffective when babies were younger.

HOW EMOTIONS AFFECT CHILDREN'S PERSONAL AND SOCIAL ADJUSTMENTS

**EMOTIONS ADD PLEASURE TO
EVERYDAY EXPERIENCES**
Even such emotions as anger and fear add pleasure to life by giving children some excitement. Mainly, their enjoyment comes from their pleasant aftereffects.

EMOTIONS PREPARE THE BODY FOR ACTION
The more intense the emotion, the more it upsets homeostasis to prepare the body for action. If this preparation is not needed, it will make children nervous and edgy.

**EMOTIONAL TENSION DISRUPTS
MOTOR SKILLS**
Bodily preparation for action plays havoc with motor skills, causing children to become awkward and clumsy and leading to such speech disorders as slurring and stuttering.

**EMOTIONS SERVE AS A FORM
OF COMMUNICATION**
Through the facial and bodily changes that accompany the emotions, children can communicate their feelings to others and determine what the feelings of others are.

**EMOTIONS INTERFERE WITH
MENTAL ACTIVITIES**
Because concentration, recall, reasoning, and other mental activities are severely affected by strong emotions, children perform below their intellectual potentials when emotionally disturbed.

**EMOTIONS ACT AS SOURCES OF SOCIAL
AND SELF-EVALUATION**
People evaluate children in terms both of how they express their emotions and of what their dominant emotions are. How they treat children, based on their evaluations, serves as the basis of children's self-evaluations.

**EMOTIONS COLOR CHILDREN'S OUTLOOKS
ON LIFE**
How children view their roles in life and their position in the social group is markedly influenced by whether they are shy, frightened, aggressive, curious, or happy.

EMOTIONS AFFECT SOCIAL INTERACTIONS
All emotions, pleasant and unpleasant, encourage social interaction. From them, children learn how to modify their behavior to conform to social expectations and standards.

**EMOTIONS LEAVE THEIR MARK
ON FACIAL EXPRESSIONS**
Pleasant emotions improve children's looks while unpleasant emotions distort the face and make children less attractive than they are. Because people are attracted or repelled by facial expressions, the emotions play an important role in social acceptance.

EMOTIONS AFFECT THE PSYCHOLOGICAL CLIMATE
In the home, the school, the neighborhood, or the play group, children's emotions affect the psychological climate and it, in turn, affects them. A childish temper tantrum annoys and embarrasses others, charging the emotional climate with anger and resentment. This makes children feel unloved and unwanted.

**EMOTIONAL RESPONSES WHEN REPEATED
DEVELOP INTO HABITS**
Any emotional expression that gives children satisfaction will be repeated and, in time, develop into a habit. As children grow older, if they find social reactions to their emotional expressions unfavorable, unrooting the habit will be difficult, if not impossible.

As children grow older, their emotional responses become less diffuse, random, and undifferentiated. Young babies, for example, show displeasure merely by screaming and crying. Later, their reactions include resisting, throwing things, stiffening the body, running away, hiding, and verbalizing. With increasing age, linguistic responses increase and motor responses decrease.

Not only does the general pattern of emotionality follow a predictable course but the patterns for different emotions are likewise predictable. Temper tantrums, for example, reach their peak between 2 and 4 years of age and are then replaced by more mature patterns of angry expressions, such as sullenness and orneriness. The predictable patterns of development for the different emotions will be discussed in the section of this chapter dealing with common emotional patterns.

Variations in Patterns of Emotional Development

Even though the pattern of emotional development is predictable, there are variations in frequency, intensity, and duration of the different emotions and in the ages at which they appear. These variations begin to appear before babyhood ends and become more frequent and more pronounced as childhood progresses.

All emotions are *less violently expressed* as children grow older due to the fact that children learn how people feel about violent emotional outbursts, even those of joy and the other pleasant emotions. And, because children curb some of their emotional expressions, emotions tend to persist longer than they did when they were expressed more violently.

Variations are also due in part to children's physical states at the time and their intellectual levels and in part to environmental conditions. *Healthy children* tend to be less emotional than those whose health is poor while *bright children,* as a group, respond emotionally to a wider range of stimuli than those who are less bright. They also tend to have more control over their emotional expressions (22, 53).

Variations are influenced by *social reactions* to emotional behavior. When these social reactions are unfavorable, as in the case of fear or jealousy, the emotions will appear less frequently and in a better controlled form than they would if social reactions were more favorable.

The success with which emotions meet *children's needs* influences variations in the different emotional patterns. If temper tantrums meet children's needs for attention and give them what they want, they will not only continue to use tantrums for these purposes but they will increase the intensity of the tantrums, thus hoping to increase their value to them as means to desired ends.

Boys, as a group, express emotions that are regarded as *sex-appropriate* such as anger, more frequently and more intensely than those considered more appropriate for girls, such as fear, anxiety, and affection (13, 27, 57). Jealousy and temper tantrums are more common in *large families* while envy is more common in *small families.* Jealousy and temper outbursts are also more common and more intense among *firstborns* than among later-born children of the same family (14).

Authoritarian *child training* encourages the development of anxiety and fear while permissive or democratic training encourages the development of curiosity and affection. Children of families with low *socioeconomic status* tend to have more fears and anxieties than those of higher socioeconomic status (22).

Conditions Responsible for Emotional Development

Studies of children's emotions have revealed that their development is due both to maturation and learning, and not to either alone. That a certain emotional reaction does not appear early in life is no proof that it is not innate. It may appear later, with the maturing of the brain or of the endocrine system.

Maturation and learning are so closely interwoven in the development of the emotions that at times it is difficult to determine their relative effects. What evidence there is about the roles played by maturation and learning in emotional development is presented below.

Role of Maturation

Intellectual development results in an ability to perceive meanings not previously perceived, to attend to one stimulus for a longer time, and to concentrate emotional tension on one object. The growth of imagination and understanding and the increase in ability to remember and anticipate likewise affect emotional reactions. Thus children become responsive to stimuli to which they were impervious at an earlier age (9, 40, 82).

Development of the endocrine glands is essential to mature emotional behavior. The baby is relatively lacking in the endocrine products that sustain some of the physiological response to stress. The adrenal glands, which play a dominant role in the emotions, show a sharp decrease in size soon after birth. Shortly later they begin to grow; they gain rapidly up to 5 years, slowly from 5 to 11, and more rapidly up to 16 years, by which time they have regained their birth size. Until their size has increased, little adrenin is produced and secreted. Their influence on the emotional states in childhood is marked (9, 57).

Role of Learning

Five kinds of learning contribute to the development of emotional patterns during childhood. What these methods are and how they contribute to children's emotional development are explained in Box 8–2.

Regardless of which method is used, children must be developmentally ready to learn before learning can take place. Newborn infants, for example, are incapable of expressing anger except by crying. With maturation of the nervous system and muscles, children develop the potential for many differentiated reactions. Their learning experiences will determine which of the potential reactions they will actually use to show their anger.

Relative Importance of Maturation and Learning

Both maturation and learning influence the development of the emotions, but learning is more important, primarily because it is controllable. Maturation is also somewhat controllable, but only by means that affect physical health and the maintenance of homeostasis, that is, through control of the glands whose secretions are triggered by the emotions.

In contrast, there are many ways to control what children learn to respond to emotionally. This can be done by direct teaching and guidance, by control of the environment to ensure that desirable emotional patterns will be established, and by professional help

---

BOX 8–2

LEARNING METHODS INVOLVED IN EMOTIONAL DEVELOPMENT

TRIAL-AND-ERROR LEARNING

Trial-and-error learning involves mainly the response aspect of the emotional pattern. Children learn in a trial-and-error way to express their emotions in forms of behavior that give them the greatest satisfaction and to abandon those that give little or no satisfaction. This form of learning is more commonly used in early childhood than later, but it is never completely abandoned.

LEARNING BY IMITATION

Learning by imitation affects both the stimulus and the response aspects of the emotional pattern. From observing the things that arouse certain emotions in others, children react with similar emotions and in methods of expression similar to those of the person or persons observed. A disruptive child, for example, may become angry at a teacher's rebuke. If the child is popular with age-mates, they are likely to become angry at the teacher also.

LEARNING BY IDENTIFICATION

Learning by identification is similar to learning by imitation in that children copy the emotional reactions of another person and are emotionally aroused by a stimulus similar to that which arouses the emotion in the person imitated. It differs from imitation in two ways: first, children imitate only those they admire and have strong emotional attachments for; second, the motivation to copy the admired person is stronger than the motivation to imitate just anyone.

CONDITIONING

Conditioning means learning by association. In conditioning, objects and situations which, at first, fail to call forth emotional reactions come to do so later as a result of association. Conditioning is related to the stimulus aspect of the emotional pattern, not to the reaction it calls forth. Figure 8–1 shows how fear of an animal, not formerly feared, can develop. Note the important role played by association. In time, emotions learned by conditioning may spread to objects and situations that are similar to the one the child was conditioned to respond to emotionally. This is shown in part 4 of Figure 8–1. Conditioning occurs easily and quickly during the early years of life because young children lack both the reasoning ability and the experience to assess a situation critically and to recognize how irrational many of their emotional responses are. After early childhood, conditioning is increasingly limited to the development of likes and dislikes.

TRAINING

Training, or learning under guidance and supervision, is limited to the response aspect of the emotional pattern. Children are taught the approved way of responding when a particular emotion is aroused. Through training children are stimulated to respond to stimuli that normally give rise to pleasant emotions and discouraged from responding emotionally to stimuli that give rise to the unpleasant emotions. This is done by control over the environment whenever possible.

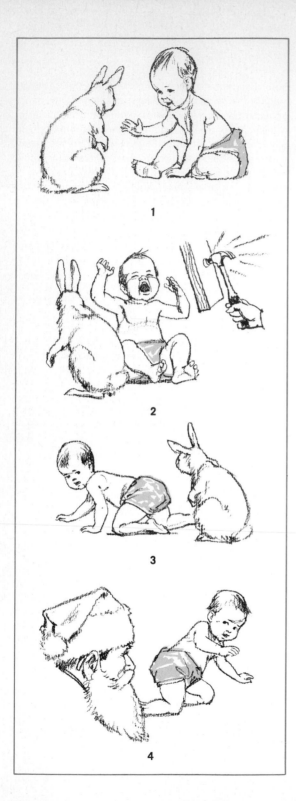

to eliminate undesirable patterns of response before they develop into well-established habits.

It has been found, for example, that environmental changes directly affect children's emotions. Children who have been accustomed to having the mother's undivided attention may bitterly resent her preoccupation with a new baby and may express anger and jealousy by frequent and intense emotional outbursts. These can be prevented by seeing to it that the children get their fair share of the mother's attention. Through teaching and guidance, they can be helped to understand why there are times when a baby requires the mother's time. And they—again by manipulation of the environment—can be given extra attention when the mother has free time.

Control over the learning pattern is both a positive and a preventive measure. Once an undesirable emotional response is learned and incorporated into a child's emotional pattern, it is not only likely to persist but to become increasingly difficult to change as the child grows older. It may even persist into adult life and require professional help to change it. That is why childhood may rightly be regarded as a "critical period" in emotional development (8, 22, 40).

Characteristics of Children's Emotions

Because of the influence of maturation and learning on emotional development, it is understandable that the emotions of young children often differ markedly from those of older children and adults. Unless this is recognized, adults will tend to regard the young child's emotional reactions as "immature." Furthermore, it is illogical to expect *all* children of a given age to have similar emotional patterns. Individual differences are inevitable because of differences in maturational level and learning opportunities.

Regardless of individual differences, however, cer-

Figure 8–1. How emotions can be conditioned. (1) Infant's response to a rabbit before conditioning; (2) the unconditioned stimulus which was presented simultaneously with the rabbit on several occasions; (3) the infant's response to the rabbit after conditioning; and (4) the generalization of conditioning to a Santa Claus beard. (*Adapted from G. G. Thompson: Child psychology, rev. ed. Houghton Mifflin, 1962. Used by permission.*)

tain characteristic features of children's emotions make them different from those of older persons. These features are described in Box 8–3.

Common Emotional Patterns

After the early months of babyhood, differentiated emotional patterns emerge. The most common patterns, the stimuli which arouse them, and the typical responses of each pattern are discussed in the following sections.

Fear

Certain fears are characteristically found at certain ages and may, therefore, be called the "typical fears" for those age levels. There is no sudden shift from one kind of fear to another, however, but rather a gradual shift from specific fears to general ones (18, 66, 75).

The most common fear-provoking stimuli in *babyhood* are loud noises, animals, dark rooms, high places, sudden displacement, being alone, pain, and strange persons, places, and objects. Figure 8–2 shows how rapidly fear of strangers develops during babyhood.

Young children are afraid of more things than either babies or older children. From 2 to 6 years of age is the

Figure 8–2. Fear of strangers develops rapidly during the latter part of babyhood. (*Adapted from S. Scarr and P. Salapatek: Patterns of fear development during infancy.* Merrill-Palmer Quarterly, *1970,* 16, *53–90. Used by permission.*)

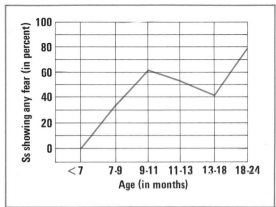

BOX 8–4

**FACTORS RESPONSIBLE FOR VARIATIONS
IN CHILDREN'S FEARS**

INTELLIGENCE

Precocious children have fears characteristic of those of an older age level and retarded children, those of a lower level. While most children of 3 years, for example, have fears that are situationally determined, precocious 3-year-olds usually have generalized and imaginary fears. Furthermore, precocious children tend to have more fears than their average age-mates because they are more aware of the possibility of danger.

SEX

At all ages, girls as a group show more fears than boys as a group. Also, it is more socially acceptable for girls to fear certain things, such as snakes and bugs.

SOCIOECONOMIC STATUS

Lower-class children at all ages have more fears than children from middle- and upper-class backgrounds. They are especially afraid of violence, which troubles middle- and upper-class children very little.

PHYSICAL CONDITION

If children are tired, hungry, or in poor health, they will respond with greater fear than normally and will be frightened in many situations which do not normally excite their fears.

SOCIAL CONTACTS

Being with others who are frightened predisposes children to be frightened also. As the number of individuals in the group increases, fears are shared and the total number of fears for each child increases.

ORDINAL POSITION

Firstborns tend to have more fears than later-borns because they are subjected to greater parental overprotectiveness. The more younger siblings associate with other siblings, the more fears they learn.

PERSONALITY

Insecure children tend to be frightened more easily than children who are emotionally secure. The extrovert learns more fears by imitating others than the introvert.

peak period of specific fears in the normal pattern of development. The reason for this is that young children are more capable of recognizing dangers than babies are, but their lack of experience makes them

less capable than older children of recognizing that they are not personal threats (8, 22, 38, 43).

Among older children, fears are concentrated on fanciful, supernatural, or remote dangers; on the dark and on imaginary creatures associated with the dark; on death or injury; on the elements, especially thunder and lightning; and on characters recalled from stories, movies, comics, and television. Older children have many fears related to self or status; they are afraid of failing, of being ridiculed, and of being "different" (4, 38, 43).

Regardless of the child's age, an important characteristic of all fear stimuli is that they occur *suddenly* and *unexpectedly;* the child has little opportunity to adjust to them. Fear of strangers in a baby is due in part to being accustomed to seeing a familiar face and being unable to adjust quickly to the sudden appearance of a stranger. As children grow older, and become more mature intellectually, they can adjust more quickly to sudden and unexpected circumstances. As a result, many conditions that aroused fear when they were younger no longer do so.

VARIATIONS IN FEARS Just because some fears are "typical" for a given age level does not mean that all children of this age level experience them. There are marked variations not only in the conditions that give rise to fear in childhood but also in the number and intensity of the fears different children experience. Some children, for example, have many more, and more intense, fears than others (62).

Variations in children's fears at different age levels reflect differences in mental and physical development as well as in individual experiences which determine what children learn to fear and how they learn to express their fears (22, 84). The chief causes of these variations are outlined in Box 8–4.

Individual differences in fear responses are even greater than the factors described in the box would seem to indicate. Fear does not depend simply on a given stimulus, but on the surrounding circumstances and the condition of the child at the time the stimulus occurs. To be able to predict whether a given child will show fear in a given situation, one must know the child's physiological and psychological condition at that time and the history of the child's fear reactions.

FEAR RESPONSES In babies, the fear response is typically one of helplessness. Cries are babies' calls for help. They hide their faces and get as far away from the feared object or person as possible. After they are able to creep or walk, they hide behind a person or piece of furniture and remain there until the fear subsides or until they feel it is safe to emerge.

As children grow older, overt fear responses are curbed by social pressure. The crying reactions cease, though the characteristic facial expressions remain, and the child withdraws from the feared object.

Not only do older children check the impulse to show fear, but they try to keep away from a situation that they think will be frightening. If confronted with a fear stimulus, they may express their fear indirectly in a general motor discharge that is more like a temper outburst than a fear reaction. Figure 8–3 shows some of the typical fear responses in the older child.

Fear-related Emotional Patterns

There are a number of emotional patterns that are fear-related in that the dominant aspect of these patterns is fear. The most important are shyness, embarrassment, worry, and anxiety. Each of these will be explained in this section.

SHYNESS Shyness is a form of fear characterized by shrinking from contact with others who are strange and unfamiliar. It is always *aroused* by people, never by objects, animals, or situations. Studies of babies have revealed that during the middle of the first year of life shyness is an almost universal reaction to strangers or to familiar people because of different clothes or hair styles. Refer to Figure 8–2. That it is fear of the unfamiliar that give rise to shyness is shown by the change that occurs in babies as soon as they become accustomed to a stranger or recognize the person whom they already know. Typically, then, babies stop crying and react in a friendly way. Shyness in the presence of strangers is so common at this age level that it is often labeled the ''strange age'' or the ''period of infantile fearfulness'' (18, 19, 66).

The reason for this period of fearfulness is that, at 6 months, babies are intellectually mature enough to recognize the difference between familiar and unfamiliar people, but they are not mature enough to recognize that their unfamiliarity poses no threat. As babies come in contact with more and more people,

Figure 8–3. Some typical ways of showing fear in childhood.

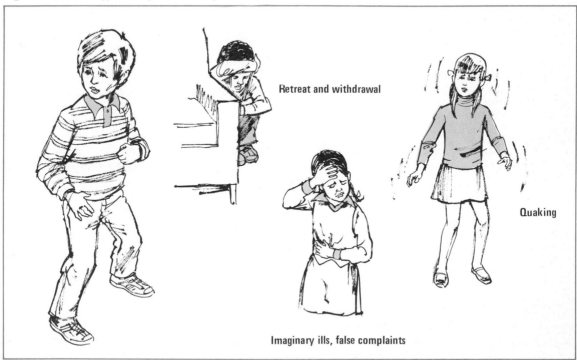

Retreat and withdrawal

Quaking

Imaginary ills, false complaints

they discover that strangers are often pleasant play-mates or companions. Consequently, their shyness becomes less intense and of briefer duration. If, however, shyness is extremely intense and frequent, it may lead to a generalized timidity that affects children's social relationships long after babyhood is over. They then become "shy children."

Few children, as they grow older, escape an occasional experience of shyness. Children may be shy in the presence of a guest in the home, a new baby-sitter, or a new teacher. Or they may experience shyness when their parents or peers are in the audience when they recite, sing, or participate in a Sunday school pageant or school play. Their shyness comes from uncertainty about how others will react to them, or fear that others will laugh at them.

In babies, the usual *response* in shyness is crying, turning the head away from the stranger, and clinging to a familiar person for protection. See Figure 8-4. Later, when babies are able to creep or walk, they run away and hide, as they do when they are frightened. Only after they are sure that there is no real danger are they willing to approach the stranger.

Older children show their shyness by blushing, by stuttering, by talking as little as possible, by nervous mannerisms, such as pulling at the ears or clothing, shifting from one foot to the other, and bending the head to one side and then raising it coyly to look at the

Figure 8-4. Crying when left alone with a stranger as compared with crying when alone with a familiar person. (*Adapted from E. Spelke, P. Zelazo, J. Kagan, and M. Kotelchuck: Father interaction and separation protest.* Developmental Psychology, *1973, 9, 83–90. Copyright 1973 by the American Psychological Association. Reprinted by permission.*)

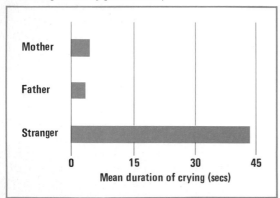

stranger. They try to make themselves as inconspicuous as possible by dressing like everyone else and by speaking only when spoken to.

EMBARRASSMENT Like shyness, embarrassment is a fear reaction to people, not to objects or situations. It differs from shyness in that it is not *aroused* by strangers or by familiar people in unfamiliar clothes or roles but rather by uncertainty about how people will judge one and one's behavior. It is, therefore, a state of self-conscious distress.

Because embarrassment depends on the ability to know what members of the social group expect and to assess whether or not one can live up to their expectations, it develops later than shyness. It is usually not present in a child less than 5 or 6 years of age.

As children grow older, embarrassment is heightened by memories of experiences in which their behavior fell below social expectations. This tends to exaggerate their fear of how others will judge them in the future. Since embarrassment predisposes children to be awkward and to speak haltingly, it often results in behavior that leads to unfavorable social judgments.

A number of studies have shown that memories of humiliating and ego-deflating experiences play an important role in heightening embarrassment. Both adolescents and adults report that such memories form the basis of unfavorable self-concepts. This becomes a circular situation: The more powerful the memories of past embarrassments, the poorer the self-concept and the more prone one is to interpret the reactions of others as unfavorable, thus giving rise to new embarrassments (35, 55, 73).

Most of the common *responses* in shyness—blushing, nervous mannerisms, stuttering, and avoidance of situations which formerly gave rise to the emotion—are also characteristic of embarrassment. Because of the similarity, it is not always easy to know whether the child's behavior is an indication of shyness or of embarrassment.

There is one major difference, however. Shy children speak as little as possible, even when asked a question. Embarrassed children, on the other hand, usually speak out; they are intent on explaining and justifying their behavior in the hopes of dispelling the unfavorable social judgments that caused their embarrassment. By contrast, shy children are taciturn.

WORRY Worry is usually described as "imaginary fear" or "borrowing trouble." Unlike real fear it is not *aroused* directly by a stimulus in the environment but is a product of the child's own mind. It comes from imagining dangerous situations which could arise. Worry is normal in childhood, even in the best-adjusted children.

Before children are capable of worrying, they must reach a stage of intellectual development in which it is possible for them to imagine things not immediately present. This does not happen until children are almost 3 years old. Worries become more frequent and more intense as childhood progresses. Ordinarily worrying reaches a peak just before the child becomes sexually mature, after which it declines. The decline is related to intellectual development. As the ability to reason improves, the child is able to see how illogical many worries are.

What children worry about is greatly influenced by what is significant in their lives at that time. Despite marked individual differences, certain worries are typical for American children at various age levels. The most common worries center around the home, family and peer relationships, and school problems, with the latter becoming more prominent as children progress in school. Typical family worries relate to the health and safety of family members and to being scolded or punished by the father or mother. School worries center around being late, failing tests, being scolded or punished by the teacher, doing reports, and being left behind. As acceptance in the peer group becomes increasingly important, worries center around social-adjustment problems, such as how to be more popular. As puberty changes begin, worries center around the body and sex-appropriate development. Refer to page 121 for a more complete discussion of sources of concern during puberty.

The way in which worry is *expressed* depends upon children's personality patterns. Children who feel inferior and inadequate tend to internalize their worries, thinking about them and exaggerating them out of all proportion. Better-adjusted children, by contrast, are more likely to discuss their worries with people they think will be sympathetic. Children who feel both insecure and rejected often verbalize their worries in the hopes of winning sympathy and, through it, improving their social acceptance. Extroverts at all ages verbalize their worries more than introverts.

However, almost all children express their worries by their facial expressions. They "look worried" and others then know that they are worried. Only as children grow older and realize that worry is not a particu-larly acceptable emotional pattern will they try to conceal their facial expressions. Some children, however, deliberately try to look worried in order to win attention and sympathy.

ANXIETY   Anxiety is an uneasy mental state concerning impending or anticipated ill. It is marked by apprehension, uneasiness, and foreboding from which the individual cannot escape; it is accompanied by a feeling of helplessness because the anxious person feels blocked, unable to find a solution for problems. The uneasy mental state characteristic of anxiety may in time become a generalized "free-floating" anxiety in which children experience a mild state of fear in any situation which is perceived as a potential threat.

Though anxiety develops from fear and worry, it is distinguished from them in several respects. It is more vague than fear. Unlike fear, it does not come from an existing situation, but from an *anticipated* one.

Like worry, anxiety is due to imaginary rather than real causes. Anxiety differs from worry, however, in two respects. *First,* worry is related to *specific* situations, such as parties, examinations, or money problems, whereas anxiety is a *generalized* emotional state. *Second,* worry comes from an *objective* problem, whereas anxiety comes from a *subjective* problem.

Anxiety depends upon the ability to imagine something not present, so it develops later than fear. It is often found during the early school years and tends to increase during childhood, especially from the fourth to the sixth grades. It does not wane during puberty but becomes more intense. Whether it will wane later depends largely upon the environment in which pubescents live, the pressures put on them to achieve beyond their capacities, and many other conditions.

Anxiety often develops after a period of frequent and intense worry that undermines children's self-confidence and predisposes them to generalized feelings of inadequacy. Contagion may also be responsible for the development of anxiety. If children are closely associated with anxious people—a mother or a sibling, for example—they may imitate anxiety. If they are already suffering from anxiety, association with anxious people will tend to increase it.

In its milder forms, anxiety may be *expressed* in readily recognizable behavior, such as depression, nervousness, irritability, mood swings, restless sleep, quick anger, and extraordinary sensitivity to what others say or do. Anxious children are unhappy children because they feel insecure. They may blame themselves because they feel guilty about not coming up to the expectations of parents, teachers, and peers, and they often feel lonely and misunderstood. Their self-dissatisfaction is generalized rather than being limited to a specific situation.

BOX 8–5

CLOAKS FOR CHILDHOOD ANXIETY

■ *Boisterous and show-off behavior.* By showing off, anxious children try to convince themselves and others of their competence.

■ *Boredom.* Anxiety makes children bored, restless, and disturbed, and they cannot concentrate on anything long enough to become interested in it.

■ *Ill-at-ease.* Whether alone or with others, anxious children feel insecure and show their anxiety by nervous mannerisms and speech problems.

■ *Avoidance of anxiety-threatening situations.* Children avoid threatening situations by going to sleep, even though not tired, by keeping themselves so busy that they have no time to think, or by withdrawing into a fantasy world.

■ *Characteristic reactions.* Anxious children over- or underreact. A slight criticism may send them into a fit of rage, or a vicious attack may be met with an apparently calm suppression of all anger.

■ *Out-of-character behavior.* A friendly child who is anxious may show a streak of cruelty or a usually kind child may commit a brutal act.

■ *Excessive eating.* Anxious children almost always become nibblers of sweets and, as a result, become overweight.

■ *Excessive use of mass media.* Anxious children tend to use television and other mass media more than their age-mates. In this way, they escape temporarily from anxiety-threatening situations.

■ *Excessive use of defense mechanisms.* While all children use defense mechanisms, especially projection of blame on others, anxious children use them excessively in the hope of freeing themselves from the vague uneasiness caused by feelings of guilt and inadequacy.

In its stronger forms, anxiety may not be so easily recognizable. Some of the common cloaks children may use to hide anxiety are given in Box 8–5. Most of these are used unconsciously and they keep the children themselves, as well as others, from recognizing their anxious states.

Anger

Anger is a more frequently expressed emotion in childhood than fear in its different forms. The reason for this is that anger-provoking stimuli are more numerous and children discover at an early age that anger is an effective way of getting attention or what they want. Each year, the number of anger-arousing situations increases and children tend to display more anger. By contrast, fear reactions decrease because children come to realize that, in most instances, there is no real need for fear.

The frequency and intensity with which children experience anger varies from child to child. Some children can withstand anger-provoking stimuli better than others. In a particular child, the ability to withstand such stimuli varies according to the need that is being blocked, the child's physical and emotional condition at the time, and the situation in which the stimuli occur. One child may react with petty annoyance, another may react with an angry outburst, and still another with withdrawal, showing intense disappointment and feelings of inadequacy.

STIMULI TO ANGER In general, the situations that give rise to anger involve restraint: interference with movements children wish to make, either by others or by their own inabilities; blocking of activities already in progress; thwarting of wishes, plans, and purposes children want to carry out; and a number of cumulative irritations. At different ages, some of these are more effective in arousing anger than at other ages.

Babies respond with angry outbursts to minor physical discomforts, interference with physical activities, and impositions of restraints connected with physical activities, and impositions of restraints connected with care, as in bathing and dressing. Their inability to make themselves understood through babbling or through their early attempts to speak likewise irritate them. Then, too, they become angry if people do not give them as much attention as they crave or if their possessions are taken away from them.

Preschool children are angered by many of the same

conditions that anger babies. They especially resent interference with their possessions, and they fight continually with other children who grab their toys or interfere with their play. They become angry when toys or other objects do not work as they want them to and when they make mistakes in what they are attempting to do. In addition, they become angry when ordered to do something they do not want to do at that moment.

In *older children*, thwarting of desires, interruption of activities in progress, constant faultfinding, teasing, "lecturing," or making unfavorable comparisons with other children will lead to anger. Older children frequently set goals beyond their reach. When they fail to reach these goals, they become angry at themselves or at the people they believe have stood in their way. They also become angry when they feel that they or their friends are unjustly reprimanded or punished or when they are slighted, neglected, or ridiculed by other children.

ANGER RESPONSES Responses to anger can be roughly divided into two major categories: impulsive and inhibited. *Impulsive responses* are usually called aggression. They are directed against persons, animals, or objects. They may be physical or verbal, and they may be mild or intense. Violent outbursts of anger, or temper tantrums, are typical in young children. Children do not hesitate to hurt others by any method at their disposal—hitting, biting, spitting, kicking, punching, poking, or pulling. Around the age of 4 years, language is added to the repertoire of angry responses. Figure 8–5 shows the ages at which temper tantrums reach their peak and then wane. Note the sex differences.

Impulsive expressions of anger are more common than inhibited expressions. They appear earlier, are more annoying to others, and are more socially unacceptable. Most impulsive expressions of anger are *extrapunitive*, in that they are directed against others. Some are *intrapunitive*, in the sense that children direct the anger at themselves.

Inhibited responses are kept under control or "bottled up." Children may withdraw into themselves, thus fleeing from the offending person or object. They may become apathetic, suggesting indifference or "lack of guts." Such behavior is labelled *impunitive*. Actually, apathetic children are not so indifferent to anger-provoking stimuli as they seem. They may simply feel that resistance is futile, that it is to their best interests to accept the frustrations, or that it is better for them to

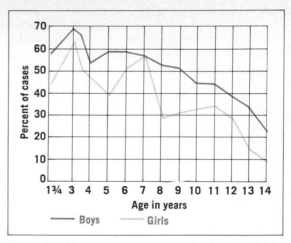

Figure 8–5. Temper tantrums normally decrease with age. (*Adapted from J. Macfarlane, L. Allen, and M. P. Honzik:* A developmental study of behavior problems of normal children between twenty-one months and fourteen years. *University of California Press, 1954. Used by permission.*)

conceal their anger than to express it and run the risk of punishment or social disapproval. They may, however, show that they are angry by acting hurt, being sullen, feeling sorry for themselves, or threatening to run away.

Jealousy

Jealousy is a normal response to actual, supposed, or threatened loss of affection. It is an outgrowth of anger, giving rise to an attitude of resentment directed toward people. Often some fear is combined with anger in the jealousy pattern. The jealous person feels insecure in relationship with a loved one and is afraid of losing status in that person's affection. The situation that calls forth jealousy is always a *social* one. There are three major situational sources of jealousy, the importance of each varying with the age of the child.

First, most childhood jealousies are homegrown: that is, they originate in conditions that exist in the home environment. Because the new baby takes much of the time and attention older children have become accustomed to receiving, they feel neglected. They then become resentful toward the new baby and the mother.

Parental favoritism results in a similar reaction. Without realizing it, many parents show a disproportionate interest in a child who happens to be especially attractive, affectionate, or gifted. Or the favored child may be sick or handicapped. Most often, parental favoritism is based on sex preferences. While fathers generally claim that they want sons, they are usually more lenient and affectionate toward daughters. Mothers generally prefer sons and are more lenient with them. The nonpreferred child quickly perceives this differential treatment and resents it. This matter will be discussed in more detail in the chapter on family relationships.

Second, social situations in the school are responsible for many of the jealousies of older children. Jealousy engendered in the home often carries over to the school and makes children regard everyone there—teachers as well as classmates—as threats to their security. To safeguard their security, children then develop a proprietary attitude toward the teacher and the classmates they select as friends, becoming angry if they show an interest in anyone else. While jealousy normally wanes when children make good adjustments to school, it may flare up if the teacher compares a child with classmates or an older sibling.

Third, situations in which children feel that they have been deprived of material possessions other children have may make them jealous of these children. This kind of jealousy comes from *envy*—an emotional state of anger or resentment directed toward another who has these envied material possessions. Envy is thus a form of covetousness. Among siblings, "two of everything" does not necessarily solve the jealousy problem. Older children feel that they should have more than their younger siblings because of their seniority.

JEALOUS RESPONSES The behavior of jealous children varies, depending on the situation. In one situation, a child may attack a person while, in another, the

---

BOX 8–6

COMMON CHILDHOOD REACTIONS TO JEALOUSY

DIRECT RESPONSES

Direct responses to jealousy may be aggressive attacks—biting, kicking, hitting, pushing, punching, and scratching—or socially approved attempts to outdo one's rival in competition for the attention and affection of the loved person. When jealousy springs from envy, children may be motivated to engage in socially disapproved acts, such as cheating or stealing. They may complain about what they have, make sour-grapes comments about the things they crave, or blame their parents for not providing them with the things their playmates have. It is also common for jealous children to make belittling comments about the person who has aroused their jealousy. See Figure 8–6.

INDIRECT RESPONSES

Indirect responses are more subtle than the direct ones and, therefore, harder to recognize. They include reversion to infantile forms of behavior, such as bed-wetting and thumb-sucking; bids for attention in the form of new fears or food idiosyncrasies; general naughtiness; destructiveness; verbal expressions, such as tattling and name-calling; unwonted displays of affection and helpfulness; venting of feelings on toys or animals; and subdued behavior, as in grieving.

Figure 8-6. Making belittling comments is a common way of showing jealousy in childhood. (*Adapted from Hank Ketcham: "Dennis the Menace."* Field Newspaper Syndicate, *Jan. 15, 1975. Used by permission.*)

"WHY ALL THE FUSS? THEY'RE NOT THAT SCARCE, ARE THEY?"

same child may try to win the person's favor. Most of the jealous behavior among children, however, shows an underlying feeling of insecurity and uncertainty. It suggests that children are trying to vindicate or prove themselves, even when they have no visible rivals. The large repertoire of jealous responses children use can be divided into two categories, indirect and direct. The common patterns of behavior in each are explained in Box 8-6.

Predictable *age differences* are noted in children's responses to jealousy. Among young children, the responses are mainly direct and aggressive. Among older children, they are more varied and indirect, although some aggressiveness does occur, usually at school and on the playground. Age differences are also apparent in the frequency with which children experience jealousy. Two peaks occur, the first at 3 years and the second just before puberty, at 11 years.

Grief

Grief is a psychic trauma, an emotional distress resulting from the loss of something loved. In its milder forms, it is known as *sorrow* or *sadness*. Regardless of its intensity or the age at which it occurs, grief is one of the most unpleasant emotions.

For most children, grief is not a very common emotion. There are three reasons for this. *First,* parents, teachers, and other adults try to insulate children from the painful aspects of grief on the grounds that it can play havoc with childhood happiness and lay the foundations for an unhappy adulthood. *Second,* because children, especially when they are young, have short memories, they can be helped to forget their grief if their attention is diverted to something pleasant. *Third,* the provision of a substitute for what children have lost—a loved toy or parent—can often turn their grief into happiness.

Each year, children normally experience more grief because they are not as thoroughly shielded from it as when they were younger. Their memories are better, and even diverting their attention or providing a substitute for their loss does not make them forget. In addition, they encounter more situations which give rise to grief.

GRIEF RESPONSES   Reactions to the loss of a cherished person or thing may be overt or inhibited. What they are and their characteristic forms of expression in childhood are explained in Box 8-7.

BOX 8-7

CHARACTERISTIC FORMS OF EXPRESSION OF GRIEF IN CHILDHOOD

OVERT EXPRESSIONS
The typical overt expression of grief in childhood is crying. The crying may be so anguished and prolonged that children will enter a state of near hysteria that will last until they are near exhaustion. If they interpret the loss as a punishment for their misbehavior, it will intensify their grief.

INHIBITED EXPRESSIONS
Inhibited expressions of grief consist of a generalized state of apathy marked by a loss of interest in things going on in the environment, loss of appetite, sleeplessness, a tendency to experience fearful dreams, refusal to play, lack of communication with others, and general listlessness. Prolonged grief leads to anxiety, with all its undesirable accompaniments.

Curiosity

Maw and Maw have described the curious child in the following way (52):

[The child] (a) reacts positively to new, strange, incongruous, or mysterious elements in his environment by moving toward them, exploring them or manipulating them; (b) exhibits a need or a desire to know more about himself and/or his environment; (c) scans his surroundings seeking new experiences; and/or (d) persists in examining and/or exploring stimuli in order to know more about them.

STIMULI TO CURIOSITY   The stimuli that give rise to curiosity in childhood are myriad. Children are interested in everything in their environments, including themselves. They are curious about their bodies, the different parts of their bodies, what they do, and why they have the forms they have. They want to know about the inside of their bodies also—where the stomach, heart, lungs, etc., are and what they do.

Children are also curious about people—why they dress, act, and speak as they do, why older people are different from younger, and why males are different from females. They are curious about familiar objects—a cake of soap or a kettle—and about those that are used occasionally or seasonally—a rug shampooer or a lawnmower. Long before children enter school, they are curious about mechanical devices such as light switches, television sets, or automobiles (42, 52, 74).

As the environment expands, so do children's curiosities. They are especially interested in sudden changes. When, for example, the mother changes her hair style or the father starts to wear glasses, or when new draperies appear in the living room, children notice the change at once and want to know what caused it. Changes in their own bodies likewise arouse their curiosity. A permanent tooth to replace a lost baby tooth will be examined in the mirror, as will the changes in their bodies that occur at the time of puberty (42, 53).

CURIOSITY RESPONSES   Babies express curiosity by tensing the face muscles, opening the mouth, stretching out the tongue, and wrinkling the forehead. This is a "state of wariness" akin to fear. When babies realize there is nothing to fear, they try to examine by looking at, grabbing, and *exploring* by handling and shaking everything within their reach.

Social pressures, in the form of warnings and punishment, check young children's use of exploration to satisfy their curiosity. Therefore, as soon as they are able to ask *questions*, they do so about the things that have aroused their curiosity. The "questioning age" begins around the age of 3 and reaches its peak just about the time children enter first grade in school. When they are old enough to read, most children start to substitute *reading* for questioning if they feel that their questions are not answered to their satisfaction (52, 53, 74).

Joy, Pleasure, Delight

Joy is a *pleasant* emotion. In its milder forms, it is known as pleasure, delight, or happiness. While all children experience varying intensities of joy, variations in the amount of joy they experience and the way they express it can to some extent be predicted. There are, for example, predictable age trends, with younger children experiencing joy in more pronounced forms than older children.

Among *babies,* the pleasant emotions of joy, happiness, and delight come from physical well-being. They are also associated with the baby's activities such as cooing, babbling, creeping, standing up, walking, and running.

Preschool children respond to more stimuli than babies. Their pleasure comes mainly from activities in which others are involved, primarily their age-mates, and is particularly strong when their achievements surpass those of their age-mates.

In *older children,* the stimuli that aroused pleasant emotions at the younger ages continue to bring pleasure. Physical well-being, incongruous situations, play on words, slight calamities, and sudden or unexpected noises never fail to call forth a smile or a laugh. Perhaps the most common cause of pleasure or even joy in older children is successful achievement of goals they have set for themselves. The harder they must strive to reach the goals, the greater their pleasure when they finally succeed.

At *puberty,* when bodily changes begin to occur, joy becomes less and less frequent. This is not because the environment contains fewer joy-provoking stimuli but because children's outlooks on life have changed. Pubescents are often overwhelmed with anxiety about themselves and the way their bodies are developing. They do not feel in top physical condition most of the time and they are often greatly dissatisfied with their performances in many areas of their lives.

JOY RESPONSES   Joyful expressions range from a quiet, calm, self-satisfied contentment to a bubbling-over exuberance. Laughter begins to appear around the fourth month of life and becomes increasingly frequent and intense with age. Some conditions that give rise to laughter in the first year of life are *auditory* stimuli (lip popping or saying "boom, boom"), *tactile* stimuli (blowing in the baby's hair), social stimuli (playing games such as peek-a-boo), and *visual* stimuli (pretending to suck the baby's bottle or crawling on the floor) (77). Figure 8–7 shows how laughter aroused by these stimuli increases during the first year of life.

Laughter is contagious. When with others, children laugh more than when alone. This is true of babies and becomes increasingly more true when children are older and want to do whatever their peers are doing.

As children grow older, they learn to express their joy in the socially approved pattern for the group with which they are identified. They learn that gloating over a person they have defeated is poor sportsmanship; they therefore learn not to show their joy, even though inwardly they may be glowing with pleasure.

The joyful emotions are always accompanied by smiling or laughing and a general relaxation of the entire body (69). This contrasts markedly with the tenseness that occurs in the unpleasant emotions. Little children also express their happiness in motor activities. They jump up and down; roll on the floor; crow with glee; clap their hands; hug the person, animal, or object that has given rise to their joy; and laugh uproariously.

Social pressures force older children to control their expressions of joy so that they will not be considered "immature." As a result, they are less noisy and rambunctious than younger children, although they may laugh in a loud, raucous manner and may even slap friends on the back or hug them when they are especially happy (77).

Affection

Affection is an emotional reaction directed toward a person, an animal, or a thing. It indicates warm regard, friendliness, sympathy, or helpfulness, and it may take a physical or verbal form. Learning plays an important role in determining the *particular* persons or objects to which affection is directed. Children tend to like most those who like them and are "friendly" in their relationships with them. Their affection is directed mainly to people. Animals and inanimate "love objects" are sometimes substitutes for human objects of affection.

To be a pleasant emotion and to contribute to good adjustment, affection must be reciprocal. There must be an emotional linkage between children and significant people in their lives. Bossard and Boll have labeled this reciprocal relationship the "empathic complex" (14). Garrison has emphasized the need for balance in the relationship (29):

Love seems to be a two-way affair and grows best when it is both given and received. A constant rejection in the home may leave the child's capacity for giving forth affection undeveloped, or may cause him to seek affection from individuals outside the home. Over-affection and indulgence may have as undesirable effects as lack of affection or rejection. . . . There is, therefore, the danger that overaffection for one or both parents will tend to exclude affection for children of the child's own age level.

Since the affection children have for others is conditioned by the kind of relationship that exists between them, it is understandable that children's affection for different family members will vary. In general, young children have greater affection for their mothers than for their fathers because their mothers are more constant companions to them and, as a rule, are less strict

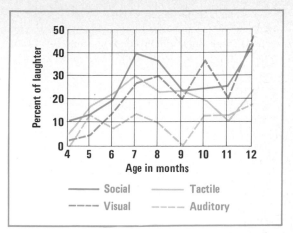

Figure 8–7. Some laughter-provoking stimuli during the first year of life. (*Adapted from L. A. Sroufe and J. P. Wunsch: The development of laughter in the first year of life.* Child Development, *1972, 43, 1326–1344. Used by permission.*)

disciplinarians than fathers. Children show greater affection for siblings who show affection for them and who do not criticize, tease, bully, or ignore them (33, 84).

Outside the home, the same principle holds. Children show the greatest affection for peers, teachers, and other adults who like them and give evidence of this in their speech and behavior. Teachers who show an interest in children and a willingness to help them will quickly win their affection. Within the peer group, children select as their friends those who like them and show affection for them.

AFFECTIONATE RESPONSES Affection is first shown in an outgoing, striving, approaching kind of behavior. Babies under 5 months of age fix their gaze on a person's face, kick, hold out and wave their arms, try to raise their bodies, smile, and turn their trunks. By the sixth month, babies have enough control over their arm movements to reach the loved one. They respond to cuddling by reaching for the loved one's face and by mouth fondling.

After the first year, young children show affection for others in much the same uncontrolled manner as they express other emotions; they tug, pat, stroke, and kiss the loved person or object. Kissing is a less frequent expression of affection in young children than hugging or patting, though they like to be kissed by others. Young children want to be constantly with the people

BOX 8–8

CONDITIONS CONTRIBUTING TO EMOTIONAL DOMINANCE

HEALTH CONDITIONS

Good health encourages the dominance of the pleasant emotions, while poor health encourages the dominance of unpleasant emotions.

HOME CLIMATE

If children grow up in a home environment where happiness prevails and where friction, jealousy, animosity, and other unpleasant emotions are kept to a minimum, the chances are that they will become happy children.

CHILD TRAINING

Authoritarian child training, where punitive methods are used to enforce strict obedience, encourages a dominance of unpleasant emotions, while democratic or permissive child training leads to a more relaxed home climate which promotes the expression of the pleasant emotions.

RELATIONSHIPS WITH FAMILY MEMBERS

A frictional relationship with parents or siblings will arouse so much anger and jealousy that these emotions will tend to dominate the child's home life.

RELATIONSHIPS WITH PEERS

The child who is well accepted by members of the peer group will experience a dominance of the pleasant emotions, while a child who is rejected or neglected by the peer group will experience a dominance of the unpleasant emotions.

OVERPROTECTIVENESS

Overprotective parents, who dwell on the potential danger in everything, encourage the dominance of fear in children.

PARENTAL ASPIRATIONS

If parents have unrealistically high aspirations for their children, children will become embarrassed and ashamed and feel guilty when they realize, from parental criticism, that they have fallen below these expectations. Repeated experiences of this kind will soon make the unpleasant emotions the dominant ones in their lives.

GUIDANCE

Guidance, with emphasis on understanding why some frustrations are necessary, can prevent anger and resentment from becoming dominant emotions. Without it, these emotions are likely to become dominant, especially when the frustrations seem unfair to a child.

Much the same pattern of behavior is shown in relation to pets or toys. Favorite toys are hugged and patted until they are literally loved to pieces. A pet animal is hugged and stroked until it is almost choked. Typically, young children take with them, wherever they go, the toys for which they have deep affection: they want to play constantly with a pet animal.

After children enter school, they tend to feel that physical demonstrations of affection are childish and they are embarrassed by them. They prefer, instead, verbal expressions. Boys, for example, will refer to their friends as "good guys," while girls refer to theirs as "my friends." Even their affection for family members is shown by calling them by pet names, by wanting to be with them, and by confiding in them as they do to peers whom they especially like.

Emotional Dominance

Emotional dominance means that, of all the emotions, one or a few come to have a predominant influence on the person's behavior. Children are not born with a dominance of pleasant or unpleasant emotions, or with a dominance of one specific emotion. Instead, the emotions that will become dominant forces in their lives depend mainly on the environments in which they grow up, the relationships they have with significant people, and the guidance they receive in controlling their emotions. The most important conditions that contribute to emotional dominance are described in Box 8–8.

Effects of Emotional Dominance

The emotions that become dominant affect children's personalities and, through them, their personal and social adjustments. The dominant emotions determine what each child's *temperament* or "prevailing mood" will be.

Temperament is persistent. It decides the child's characteristic adjustment to life. One who has a "cheerful disposition," or who is temperamentally cheerful, will take minor obstacles in stride and show little or no annoyance. One who has a "bad disposition" will express anger out of all proportion to the stimulus that produced it. A child who is temperamentally apprehensive will tend to experience more fear than other children.

At one time people believed that temperament was hereditary, that it was determined by "body humors," glands, and even body build. Today, there is evidence that it is largely a product of learning, although health and endocrine balance are important influences. The predominant emotional stimuli of the early, formative years and the way the child learns to respond to them will eventually determine the child's temperament (57, 83).

Temperament is reflected not only in characteristic methods of adjusting to life but also in children's facial expressions. Even in repose, the facial expression reveals whether a child's disposition is sad, happy, or irritable. The child's face often tells the story more eloquently than the child's actions.

A predominance of the pleasant emotions, such as affection, love, joy, and happiness, is essential to normal development. These emotions lead to feelings of security which help children approach their problems with self-confidence and assurance, react to minor obstacles with a minimum of emotional tension, and maintain their emotional balance even when major obstacles are encountered. Children whose emotions are predominantly pleasant are happy and well liked by others; they make a success in whatever they do. Because they are pleasant to be with, they not only are popular but also are often selected for leadership roles in the peer group.

Control of Emotional Dominance

There are three conditions that make control of emotional dominance possible. As a result, it is possible to see to it that the predominate emotions will be pleasant ones.

First, since certain emotions contribute more to successful adjustment than others, those emotions should be particularly encouraged. The good aspects of the less desirable emotions should also be developed. Curiosity is so important to the child's intellectual development that it should be especially encouraged. Similarly, the good effects of fear—a cautious approach to things new and different until it is apparent that they are not harmful—should be encouraged.

Second, to make sure that the emotions become a source of good in the child's life, parents and teachers *should provide guidance to help the child develop the most valuable forms of emotional expression.* For example, the child can be guided to use curiosity in creative and intellectual pursuits. Left to chance, curiosity

can lead the child into dangerous situations. The child can also be taught to direct anger into socially acceptable channels rather than restraining it and allowing it to become a source of pent-up hostility or destructive behavior.

Third, since the stimulus for most emotions comes from the environment, control of the environment can ensure that desirable emotions will be dominant. When discipline requires that the child be frustrated, for example, a habit of resenting authority or of feeling martyred can be prevented if the child knows why frustration is necessary at times and if the child has many other experiences that enhance happiness. Praise for good sportsmanship in accepting frustrations may take the sting out of some of them.

Emotional Balance

In emotional balance, the dominance of unpleasant emotions can be counteracted to some extent by pleasant emotions, and vice versa. In emotional balance, ideally, the scales should be tipped in favor of the pleasant so they can counteract, to some extent at least, the psychological damage from a dominance of the unpleasant emotions.

Throughout the first and sometimes into the second year of life, it is possible to control the environment so that the baby will experience a maximum of the pleasant emotions and only a minimum of the unpleasant. Once the child is able to move around freely, however, this is no longer possible. As motor skills improve and independence increases, a great many things in the environment call forth anger, fear, jealousy, and the other unpleasant emotions.

Emotional balance can be achieved in two ways. The first is *control of the environment* to see that unpleasant emotions are quickly outweighed by pleasant ones so that the balance will be in favor of the pleasant. This is rarely possible beyond the babyhood years.

The second and by far the more practical way is to help children *develop emotional tolerance*—the ability to withstand the effects of the unpleasant emotions. Since anger is the most common unpleasant emotional experience in childhood, frustration tolerance, or the ability to accept frustrations, is the most important form of emotional tolerance for children. How this can be achieved is explained in the section of this chapter dealing with emotional control.

In addition to developing tolerance of the unpleasant emotions children must learn to tolerate joy, affection, curiosity, and other pleasant emotional states so that they do not become so dependent on everything being rosy that they cannot withstand unpleasant emotions when they arise.

Why Emotional Balance Is Essential

If children experience too many of the unpleasant emotions and too few of the pleasant, their outlook on life will be distorted and they will develop "unpleasant dispositions." Their facial expressions will become sad, sullen, or generally disagreeable. This will make them less appealing to others and militate against good social adjustments. In turn, their self-dissatisfaction will increase and lead to minor or major personality maladjustments.

This, of course, does not mean that children should be overprotected. It does mean, however, that they should be protected from unreasonable and excessive fears, jealousies, angers, and other unpleasant emotions. In the case of anger, for example, if children gradually learn to tolerate frustrations when they are young, they will not develop the habit of aggressive attacks on all frustrating situations as they grow older.

Emotional Control

The *popular* concept of emotional control emphasizes suppression of overt responses to emotion-provoking stimuli. According to this concept, a person who has been aroused to anger stifles the reactions—facial, bodily, and verbal—that normally accompany anger and by so doing presents a picture of emotional calm. The more the person can suppress these overt responses, the better emotional control the person is judged to have.

The *scientific* concept of emotional control is very different from the popular concept. Using the word "control" as it is defined in any standard dictionary to mean "to exert restraining or directing influence over," the scientific concept of emotional control means to direct emotional energy into useful and socially approved channels of expression. True, the scientific concept does put emphasis on restraint, but that is not the same as suppression. When people are restraining the overt expression of their emotions, they are also attempting to turn the energy engendered by their bodies as a preparation for action into useful and socially acceptable patterns of behavior. This is very different from the popular concept, which requires that emotional energy be bottled up inside them.

To achieve emotional control in the scientific meaning of the term, the individual must give as much attention to the mental aspect of an emotion as to the physical. Simply expressing the emotion in a socially acceptable form is not enough. The mental aspect of the emotion needs guidance too, lest it keep the emotional state alive and predispose the person to react emotionally to later stimuli which, of their own accord, would be incapable of arousing emotional responses. Just finding a socially acceptable way to react to anger, for example, does not guarantee that people will stop being angry. In fact, the more they think about the cause of their anger, the angrier they are likely to become and the more convinced they will be that their anger was justified.

It is obvious, therefore, that children must learn how to handle the stimuli that give rise to emotions as well as the responses that normally accompany them. To do this, children must be capable of assessing the stimuli and deciding whether an emotional reaction is justified or not.

The achievement of emotional control is imperative if children are to develop normally. There are two major reasons why this is so. *First,* the social group expects all children to learn to control their emotions and it judges them in terms of their success in doing so. Although adults may be indulgent about emotional outbursts when children are very young, they disapprove of such reactions when children grow older. Children soon discover, then, that unbridled expressions of their emotions will not be tolerated. *Second,* once a pattern of emotional expression has been learned, it is difficult to control it and even more difficult to eliminate it. The sooner children learn to control their emotions, the easier it will be for them (29, 65, 83).

Effects of Emotional Control on Behavior

The physical and mental preparation for action generated whenever an emotion is aroused can be released in a number of ways. One's usual way of responding will depend largely on what provides the greatest satisfaction, wins social approval, or avoids the disapproval of significant people. Of the many ways children release pent-up energy, the most common are shown in Box 8–9.

Several of the ways children commonly react to anger-provoking stimuli are shown in Figure 8–8. Since no one way of expressing a controlled emotion is always best, children will choose the one that meets their needs and, if possible, at the same time gains social approval. Unless it uses up *all* the energy engendered by the emotion, however, there will be unfavorable aftereffects on children's physical and mental well-being. Even the most constructive indirect expression of anger will not be adequate, for example, unless it clears the system of the energy produced by the anger. An emotional explosion may clear the system, but it fails to win the approval of the group. As a result, it does not give satisfaction.

Emotional Catharsis

Clearing the system of pent-up energy, which occurs when the emotional expressions are controlled, is known as "emotional catharsis." Unless the *physical* energy built up in preparation for action is released, body homeostasis will be upset. In the same way, unless the *mental* states that accompany the emotions are handled properly, they can lead to such unfavorable attitudes that the child will make poor personal and social adjustments.

When the body is set for action, the stirred-up mental state—whether it takes the form of anxiety, jealously, or hostility—is likely to prolong the physical agitation. That will prolong the mental turbulence. As a result, there is a circular cause-and-effect relationship which is likely to continue until something is done to end it. The needs that have been thwarted must be met either directly or indirectly. If children cannot use up the energy in a direct expression of the emotion, they must get rid of it in an indirect way.

The need to clear the body of pent-up emotional energy was recognized as far back as the time of Hippocrates in ancient Greece, during the fourth century B.C. Not until around the turn of the present century, however, was it recognized that the need for emotional catharsis also applied to the mind.

Essentials of Emotional Catharsis

Just letting off emotional steam may relieve the system of excess physical energy temporarily, but it will not necessarily change the child's point of view or remove the source of emotional distress. The fundamental

---

BOX 8–9

COMMON WAYS OF RELEASING PENT-UP EMOTIONAL ENERGY

MOODINESS
Moodiness is a drawn-out state of the emotions caused by bottled up emotional energy and allowing it to smolder. The unpleasant emotions are most likely to be controlled, so children are sullen, morbid, reticent, or bad humored. They become listless and work below their capacities; their interest in people and things wanes, and they become preoccupied with themselves and their own feelings.

SUBSTITUTE RESPONSES
Emotional energy can be released by substituting a more socially acceptable response for the one normally associated with the emotion. When angry, children may substitute name-calling for hitting or kicking, or may do something useful or constructive.

DISPLACEMENT
In displacement, emotional responses are directed against a person, animal, or object unrelated to the stimulus. Instead of hitting or shouting at them, for example, angry children attack an innocent victim.

REGRESSION
One of the common ways of expressing thwarted emotions in childhood is regression—going back to earlier, perhaps infantile forms of behavior. Jealous children, for example, may wet their beds or claim that they need help in dressing.

EMOTIONAL EXPLOSIONS
In emotional explosions, children react violently to a seemingly trivial stimulus. When angry they have temper tantrums out of all proportion to what angered them. As older children know they are expected to develop frustration tolerance, their emotional explosions often lead to feelings of inadequacy, guilt, and shame.

---

principle of psychotherapy gives a clue to how one may go about effecting an emotional catharsis that will clear both the mind and the body. By bringing to the surface the repressed causes of emotional disturbance, by analyzing them, by subjecting them to reality testing to see how justified they are, and then by finding satisfactory ways to give expression to the drives

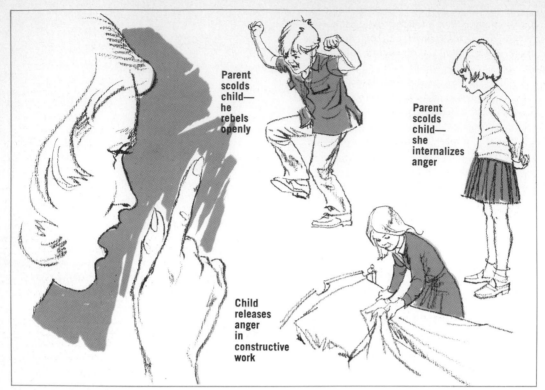

Parent scolds child— he rebels openly

Parent scolds child— she internalizes anger

Child releases anger in constructive work

Figure 8–8. Three common ways of reacting to anger. (*Adapted from M. E. Breckenridge and E. L. Vincent:* Child development; Physical and psychological development through adolescence. *5th ed. Saunders, 1960. Used by permission.*)

which have been thwarted, children will change their attitudes and develop a more wholesome point of view.

PHYSICAL CATHARSIS Any activity that uses up the energy generated by the bodily changes that accompany the emotions will serve as a catharsis for this energy and restore homeostasis. Among children, the three most common and most beneficial cathartic activities are strenuous exercise, laughing, and crying. These are not equally approved by the social group, however.

Strenuous activity, whether in play or work, is socially acceptable. Children can let off emotional steam by running, swimming, or playing ball as well as by cutting grass, shoveling snow, or using a hammer and saw. To achieve the desired cathartic effect, the activity must not only be socially acceptable but must also be satisfying to the individual. Children who are

forced to mow the grass, for example, will not get the cathartic value from this activity that they would get if they performed it voluntarily. Their resentments will keep their emotional states alive instead of reducing them.

A good *cry* will, likewise, go a long way toward clearing the body of excess tension. Children soon discover, however, that crying is not socially approved. Even if they cry in private, the telltale redness of their eyes may give them away. In addition, they feel guilty and ashamed of acting "like a baby" and know that they would be ridiculed and scorned if others knew about their crying.

Much the same problem arises with *laughter*. Only if children laugh when others laugh, at a joke or at a comic scene in a movie or on the television screen, can they laugh loudly enough to get the emotional catharsis they need without incurring social disapproval.

MENTAL CATHARSIS   To achieve mental catharsis, children must change their attitudes toward the situations that give rise to their emotions. This means that they must learn emotional tolerance and gain insight into the causes of their anger, grief, fear, jealousy and so on. They are too inexperienced, however, to handle this problem without help.

Guidance, therefore, is absolutely essential but children cannot benefit from it unless they are willing to communicate with others. No one can help them unless they are willing to do so. This they may do indirectly, through such techniques as doll-play therapy, or directly, through discussion and examination of their problems. Older children who are unwilling to communicate with others may help themselves to some extent by identification with characters in the mass media or by daydreaming. However, these outlets are far less valuable than direct discussions of their problems with people who can help them get a better perspective on them.

Aids to Emotional Catharsis

Even if the environment is such that children experience few demands to control their emotions, all children should learn how to discharge excess emotional energy so that they will suffer minimum physical and psychological damage when control is needed. Box 8–10 contains a list of aids to emotional catharsis.

These aids suggest how children can be encouraged to learn to use emotional catharsis at an early age—before they develop the habit of controlling their emotions in ways that will be damaging to good personal and social adjustments. If children learn how to use emotional catharsis, they will gain satisfaction both from their emotions and from the approval of the social group.

Hazards in Emotional Development

Because emotions play such an important role in determining what kinds of personal and social adjustments children will make, not only during childhood but also as they become adolescents and adults, their development must be of the kind that will make good adjustments possible. Anything that interferes with good emotional development will play havoc with children's adjustments.

BOX 8–10

AIDS TO EMOTIONAL CATHARSIS

- Some strenuous physical exercise daily in either play or work.
- An understanding of how strenuous exercise aids physical and emotional well-being.
- The development of a sense of humor so that one can laugh even at oneself.
- An understanding that crying is not always babyish. It can be good for children if they know when and where to use it.
- A close, affectional relationship with at least one family member. A parent can help children develop a more mature perspective on their problems.
- An intimate friend to whom one can confide troubles and verbalize complaints that the child would hesitate to discuss with an older person.
- A willingness to talk over problems with a sympathetic person. Most children, unless discouraged from doing so, will talk freely about *everything,* including their problems.
- A respect on the part of others for the underlying causes of one's emotional arousal. When children are afraid, for example, there is a reason for it. If parents, teachers, and others recognize this, children will then be willing to discuss their fears with them.

Furthermore, because the foundations for the different emotional patterns are laid early in life, the early years are critical in determining what forms these patterns will take. If, for example, children derive satisfaction from exploring anything and everything that arouses their curiosity, the habit may become deeply rooted before they discover that unbridled exploring is disapproved of by members of the social group and that, as a result of their exploratory behavior, they have acquired the reputation of being "snoopers."

To highlight the seriousness of potential hazards to good emotional development, the most common are discussed below. Some of these hazards develop early in a child's life while others do not appear until children are approaching puberty.

Emotional Deprivation

Emotional deprivation does not mean that children are deprived of *all* emotional experiences. Such total deprivation would be impossible. Instead, it means that children are deprived of a reasonable share of pleasant emotional experiences, especially curiosity, joy, happiness, and affection. Most children, unfortunately, grow up in environments that provide an abundance of unpleasant emotional experiences—anger, fear, jealousy, and envy—but a dearth of pleasant emotional experiences.

In its narrowest sense, emotional deprivation refers to deprivation of affection. This, in turn, denies children of opportunities to experience such pleasant emotions as joy, happiness, and affection from others. Children who grow up under such conditions are "emotionally starved." This results in serious physical as well as psychological damage. They are denied not only the ego-satisfying experience that being loved by others provides, but they are denied also the intimate social relations which affection and love encourage.

CAUSES OF DEPRIVATION OF AFFECTION   There are many conditions responsible for deprivation of affection. Babies or young children may be institutionalized or they may be deprived, through the death of one or both parents, of a steady source of affection. Even when children live with their parents, they may be deprived of affection because of parental rejection, neglect, or mistreatment of them, or because parents believe that showing affection "spoils" children (40, 65, 69).

Deprivation of affection may, on the other hand, result from children's rejections of their parents because they find that their parents do not meet their needs or because they are ashamed of their parents. This is especially likely to develop when children reach the peer-conscious age of middle childhood and discover that their parents are "different" from their peers' parents.

When children reject their parents, there is a strained parent-child relationship and parents cannot supply their children with affection. Children who are unpopular with their peers and those who have poor relationships with their parents and other family members are deprived of two of the most important sources of affection and the security affection brings.

EFFECTS OF DEPRIVATION OF AFFECTION   Numerous studies of human babies and young children and Harlow's famous study of infant monkeys have all shown that deprivation of affection during the earlier months and years of life can be hazardous to the individual's physical, mental, emotional, and social devel-

opment. Of the many areas of development that are likely to be damaged by deprivation of affection, the following are the most common (20, 32, 65, 71).

First, babies deprived of affection suffer a delay in normal growth and development. This is due to the fact that the baby's depressed state, resulting from lack of affectionate care, inhibits secretions of the pituitary hormones, including the growth hormone. As a result, their growth is stunted. Figure 8–9 shows the effect of emotional deprivation on a male twin who was rejected by the mother at the age of 4 months while the female twin received normal affection. At the age of 13 months, the female twin was near normal size while the male twin was the size of a 7-month old baby. This Gardner has labeled as a case of "deprivation dwarfism," the seriousness of which he explained thus: "Deprivation dwarfism is a concrete example . . . that demonstrates the delicacy, complexity and crucial importance of infant-parent interaction" (28).

In addition to stunting growth, emotional deprivation has been found to cause listlessness, emaciation, quietness, loss of appetite, general apathy, and psychosomatic illnesses. In extreme and prolonged cases of emotional deprivation, babies die (28, 65).

Second, motor development, as shown in sitting, standing, and walking, is usually delayed, and the young child is thus more clumsy and awkward than age-mates.

Third, speech development is delayed; the child often develops a speech disorder such as stuttering.

Fourth, intellectual development is delayed. The child is unable to concentrate and is easily distracted. This interferes with learning, recall, and reasoning (40, 71).

Fifth, children deprived of love are handicapped in learning how to get along with people. They respond negatively to the advances of others, tending to be uncooperative and hostile. They feel inadequate and show their resentment in aggressiveness, disobedience, and other forms of asocial behavior (44).

Sixth, the unfavorable emotional and social reactions resulting from deprivation of affection leave their mark on the child's developing personality. The emotionally starved child is self-bound, shows little interest in others, and is selfish and demanding (40, 71).

Many factors influence the way children are affected by emotional deprivation. For a summary of these factors, their effect on physical and psychological development, and whether their impact will be temporary or permanent, see Box 8–11 (20, 41, 65).

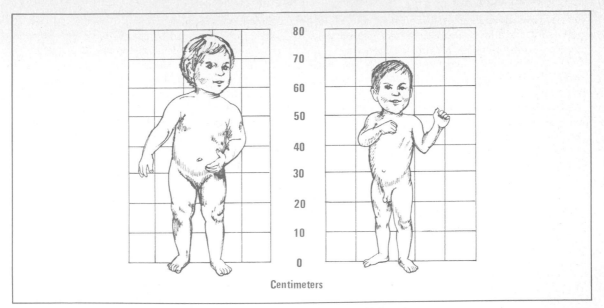

Figure 8–9. How emotional deprivation affects the growth of a baby. (*Adapted from L. I. Gardner: Deprivation dwarfism.* Scientific American, *1972, 227 (1), 76–82. Copyright 1972 by Scientific American, Inc. All rights reserved. Used by permission.*)

LONG-TERM EFFECTS OF EMOTIONAL DEPRIVATION
While it was formerly believed that deprivation of sources of emotional satisfaction during the early years of life would automatically lay the foundations for adult personality disorders, there is evidence today that this may not be so. Some evidence suggests that conditions other than emotional deprivation per se may be responsible (3, 16, 58). There is also evidence that the tendency to develop an "affectionless or psychopathic character" is often offset by favorable experiences later in childhood (16, 63).

While deprivation of affection is not the only cause of maladjustments in adolescence and adulthood, it is an important contributing factor. It has been reported that maladjustments resulting directly or indirectly from deprivation of affection range from general unhappiness to antisocial behavior, psychopathic personality, psychoneuroses, or even certain forms of psychosis, such as schizophrenia. Emotional deprivation is likely to increase the tendency toward maladjustment when it is accompanied by other unfavorable conditions (44, 65, 78).

Several examples will serve to illustrate how long-lasting the effects of deprivation of affection can be.

Rebellion against authority in adolescence is often increased if adolescents feel that they have never received the affection they crave. Teen-age marriages are often a means of satisfying a longing for affection and emotional security never completely satisfied by love from parents, siblings, or peers. Poor adjustment in marriage and at work and poor attitudes toward the law in adult life are likewise increased by feelings of insecurity engendered by deprivation of affection during the early years of childhood (3, 65).

Too Much Affection

Just because deprivation of affection is damaging to good personal and social adjustments does not mean that the more affection children receive, the better adjusted they will be. In fact, too much affection can be as hazardous to good adjustments as too little affection.

Parents who are oversolicitous and overdemonstrative do not encourage children to learn to express affection for others. Instead, they encourage children to focus affection on themselves and to demand and expect affection from others. As a result, such children

FACTORS THAT INFLUENCE THE EFFECTS OF DEPRIVATION OF AFFECTION

DEGREE OF DEPRIVATION

A slight frustration of desire for affection whets a child's desire for it. For example, a child competing with siblings for the mother's or father's attention becomes friendly and eager to please. Pronounced deprivation of affection leads to many of the serious effects reported in the text.

WHEN THE DEPRIVATION OCCURS

The critical period for deprivation of affection is from 6 months to 5 years of age. Deprivation after 5 years has minor effects because the child can find substitute satisfactions. Before that time, it has little effect because an emotional attachment was never firmly established.

PERSON FROM WHOM THE CHILD IS SEPARATED

After becoming accustomed to the care and love of the mother or mother surrogate, a baby or young child cannot comprehend the sudden withdrawal—even temporarily—of this source of emotional security. As a result, the child feels unwanted, unloved, and rejected.

EXTENT OF SEPARATION

When young children are separated from the mother or mother substitute for a long time, the effects are more serious than when the separation is temporary. If the deprivation lasts for less than 3 months, reestablishment of emotional interchange will lead to a resumption of normal physical and mental development.

PERSONALITY

Some children are dependent and crave more or less constant attention and affection while others can be happy with less. Self-bound children have less craving for affection than do those who are outer-bound.

ORDINAL POSITION

Firstborn children, accustomed to constant attention and affection from the mother, are more damaged by emotional deprivation than are their later-born siblings.

FAMILY SIZE

Children from large families are accustomed to fewer contacts with the mother and are less damaged by emotional deprivation than only children. Since children from large families are often cared for by mother substitutes, they do not become dependent on any one person for affection.

SATISFACTORY SUBSTITUTE SOURCE OF AFFECTION

Much of the psychological damage from emotional deprivation can be avoided if there is a satisfactory substitute for the child's original source of emotional satisfaction. In adoption, babies or young children soon adapt themselves to their substitute parents and make good adjustments.

---

are unable to establish the *empathic complex*—an emotional linkage with others. This creates the impression that children are disinterested in other people and have little affection for them, an impression that militates against their being accepted as members of the peer group (14).

Too much parental affection has another serious effect. It encourages children to concentrate their affection on one or two people exclusively. This is hazardous because it causes children to feel anxious and insecure when those on whom they have concentrated their affection are absent or when their behavior suggests that the relationship is threatened. Such children find it especially difficult to establish friendly relationships with peers. This leads to loneliness and feelings of martyrdom because they resent the fun their peers have (50, 88).

Dominance of Unpleasant Emotions

Dominance of the unpleasant emotions is hazardous to good personal and social adjustments because unpleasant emotions tend to color children's outlooks on life and their self-concepts. They also encourage the development of patterns of adjustment that are obstacles to good social relationships. Several examples of how unpleasant emotions that are frequent and severe can affect children's adjustments will suffice to show how hazardous they are.

So long as *shyness* is only a passing phase in early babyhood, it is not serious. Since it is an almost universal reaction at this age, babies are not unfavorably judged when they show shyness. If shyness becomes a persistent pattern of emotional behavior, however, it can have serious effects on children's personal and social adjustments and serve no useful purpose. Some of the effects of shyness are shown in Box 8–12.

Like shyness, *embarrassment* contributes to poor personal and social adjustments, leads to unfavorable self-concepts, and undermines self-confidence. It differs from shyness, however, in that it often serves as a motivation to learn to behave in a way that will conform to social expectations. A child who has been embarrassed for not saying "thank you" when this was expected will be motivated to remember to say the expected words in the future.

Frequent embarrassments can make childhood an unhappy period and can lay the foundations for personality maladjustments that come from feelings of inferiority and social rejection. There is little evidence, however, that embarrassment leads to a generalized feeling comparable to the timidity induced by an excess of shy experiences. Many children forget embarrassing experiences because they learn to behave in a way that keeps them from recurring or because they are able to rationalize them by projecting the blame on others (35, 55).

When children experience *grief* too frequently or too intensely, it can have a damaging effect on their personal and social adjustments. Grief is especially damaging to children because their intellectual immaturity and limited experience make it impossible for them to understand why the loss occurred. Their vivid imaginations encourage them to exaggerate the importance of what they have lost and to misinterpret the cause of the loss. To highlight the damages of childhood grief, its major consequences for personal and social adjustment are given in Box 8–13.

Heightened Emotionality

Heightened emotionality means a frequency and intensity of emotional experiences beyond what is normal. In judging heightened emotionality in a child, one must consider the normal pattern of emotionality for *that particular child.*

Any emotion may be experienced more frequently or more intensely at some times than at others. On some days, for example, everything seems to break right;

BOX 8–12

EFFECTS OF SHYNESS ON PERSONAL AND SOCIAL ADJUSTMENTS

- If persistent, shyness leads to a generalized timidity which causes children to be afraid to try anything new or different. This results in achievements below their potentials.
- Fear of strangeness can, unless checked, become a generalized fear of anything that differs from the accustomed. This militates against the child's trying to do anything new—a fear that stifles creativity.
- Shy children contribute little to the group, so they are not popular. Generally, they are not disliked, but are overlooked and neglected. This contributes to poor adjustment because of lack of social learning experiences.
- Shyness makes it difficult for children to play leadership roles because of their inability to communicate effectively and creatively with others.
- Shy children are afraid to talk to others so other people do not talk to them. This encourages children to become self-bound.
- Except in babyhood, when shyness is normal, shy children are likely to be unfavorably judged by others. They are also likely to be considered less bright than they are.
- Since self-evaluation reflects social evaluation, shy children judge themselves as others judge them. This may and often does contribute to the development of an inferiority complex.

---

consequently, the person experiences more happiness and more intense forms of happiness on those days. When the happy emotions predominate, the person is said to be in a state of *euphoria*—a sense of well-being and buoyancy. When the most frequent and intense emotions are unpleasant, whether they be anger, fear, jealousy, or envy, the person is said to be in a *state of disequilibrium,* feeling grumpy, disagreeable, and out of sorts. When there is no heightened emotionality—when the emotions are calm—the person is in a state of *equilibrium* (2).

All children experience euphoria, equilibrium, and disequilibrium. What proportion of their time will be characterized by each varies from child to child and, in the same child, from time to time. Many children, unfortunately, experience more disequilibrium than euphoria during periods of heightened emotionality.

EFFECTS OF GRIEF ON PERSONAL
AND SOCIAL ADJUSTMENTS

- Grief may lead to feelings of martyrdom if children interpret their loss as a punishment for their naughtiness.
- Grief-stricken children may become resentful if they feel that their parents or others could have prevented the loss.
- Grief may lead to feelings of guilt if children believe that they could have prevented the loss.
- Grief-stricken children may withdraw from people and become self-bound, thus eliminating opportunities for socialization.
- Grief may encourage children to escape from reality by daydreaming or by contemplating suicide.
- Grief will militate against achievement if children are so preoccupied with their loss that they cannot concentrate on what they are doing.
- Grief may be intensified by anxiety, with all its damaging effects.

(Refer to Chapter 2 for an earlier discussion of states of equilibrium and disequilibrium.)

CONDITIONS CONTRIBUTING TO HEIGHTENED EMOTIONALITY   Heightened emotionality may come from physical, psychological, or environmental conditions. Frequently, more than one condition is operative. Should children become upset because their schoolwork has fallen below their expectations, for example, they are likely to become nervous. Nervousness in turn, will interfere with eating and sleeping. The more hungry and tired children are, the more likely they are to react emotionally to any situation, even those which normally call forth little or no emotion. Thus a vicious circle is set in motion with both physical and psychological causes, often stemming from environmental causes, making their contributions. The common conditions contributing to heightened emotionality are described in Box 8–14.

MANIFESTATIONS OF HEIGHTENED EMOTIONALITY   Heightened emotionality is readily recognized by the behavior that accompanies it. If it stems from one of the unpleasant emotions, it is marked by moods and rages which come and go with greater or lesser violence, often outside the range of conscious control or even awareness. Which form it will take will depend not so much upon the intensity of the emotional state as upon what the child has learned is socially acceptable or will bring the least disapproval.

If heightened emotionality is expressed in moodiness, children are likely to be grouchy, glum, surly, or rude. Should pleasant emotions predominate, children will be happy and cheerful, singing, offering to help people, saying pleasant things to everyone, hugging friends or pets, and even skipping and dancing instead of walking. If curiosity is raised to a high pitch, children become nervous and edgy, asking innumerable questions, and prying into everything.

Some nervous tension always accompanies heightened emotionality. It may be expressed by thumb-sucking in young children, nail-biting in older children, scratching the head, giggling, or bursting into tears. When the emotion is strong, it is likely to lead to temporary stuttering or slurring. The extremely happy child, like the very angry or anxious child, will stumble over words, repeat syllables, choke in the middle of a word, or speak so rapidly that one word is run into another.

During euphoria or disequilibrium, children are predisposed to react emotionally more readily and more intensely than they normally do. If the emotions are unpleasant ones, they are ready to fly off the handle and go into temper tantrums at the slightest provocation. If the emotions are pleasant, children are predisposed to laugh uproariously at a joke which, under other circumstances, they might find "stupid." They will be overpleased by a gift or more demonstrative in their display of affection than usual. Whatever the stimulus, children will *over-react* to it because they are already in a state of readiness to react. Their reactions then, will tend to be less focused and directed than when they are calmer.

EFFECTS OF HEIGHTENED EMOTIONALITY   Heightened emotionality is far more often characterized by the unpleasant emotions than the pleasant, and therefore generally produces a state of disequilibrium. Most of the studies of the effects of heightened emotionality have concentrated on this state rather than on euphoria.

When euphoria is extremely intense, and this is relatively infrequent, there is reason to assume that its effects will be similar to those of disequilibrium. The basis for this assumption, in the absence of experimental proof, is that *any* intense emotion, whether pleasant or unpleasant, is accompanied by bodily preparation for action which affects the person's accustomed pattern of adjustment.

Many of the effects of heightened emotionality are closely related to the general effects of the emotions on adjustment, as explained in Box 8–1. When the emotions are heightened, however, the good effects referred to in Box 8–1 tend to become more damaging than beneficial (37, 56, 67). Box 8–15 lists the most common effects of heightened emotionality.

Failure to Learn Emotional Control

No one expects young children to control their emotions—pleasant or unpleasant. They know that it is normal for young children to have temper tantrums when they are frustrated in what they want to do, to run away, cry and hide when they are frightened, to explore anything that arouses their curiosity or to ask innumerable questions about it, and to laugh uproariously when they are amused or happy.

However, by the time children are ready to go to school, they are expected to have learned some control over their emotions. Each year, as they grow older, they are expected to have increasingly more control.

When children fail to live up to these social expectations, it leads to unfavorable social judgments of them. Realizing how unfavorably others are judging them makes children embarrassed and ashamed, feelings that are hazardous to good personal as well as social adjustments.

The major source of failure to learn emotional control is not learning to analyze a situation before responding to it emotionally. The old admonition of "counting ten before you speak" when angry is good training for children today because it encourages them to take time to analyze a situation before reacting to it emotionally. This is true for all emotions, not for anger alone.

Failure to learn emotional control is especially common among children brought up by authoritarian or permissive child-training methods. In the case of the former, children may exert control over their emotions while their parents are present to avoid punishment. But, when parents are absent, children have little motivation to control their emotions. In the case of permissive child training, because parents do not expect children to control their emotions, they have little motivation to learn to do so.

Children brought up in homes where democratic

> **BOX 8–14**
>
> ### CONDITIONS CONTRIBUTING TO HEIGHTENED EMOTIONALITY
>
> **PHYSICAL CONDITIONS**
> Whenever homeostasis is upset, owing to fatigue, poor health, or developmental changes, children experience heightened emotionality.
> - *Poor health,* due to malnutrition, digestive disturbances, or disease.
> - An *irritating condition,* such as hives or eczema.
> - Any *chronic disturbance,* such as asthma or diabetes.
> - *Glandular changes,* especially at puberty. Glandular upsets may also come from chronic emotional stress, as in free-floating anxiety.
>
> **PSYCHOLOGICAL CONDITIONS**
> Important psychological influences include level of intelligence, level of aspiration, and anxiety.
> - Poor *intellectual equipment.* Children of the lower intellectual levels, on the average, have less emotional control than bright children of the same ages.
> - Failure to attain one's *level of aspiration.* Repeated failures may lead to a more or less constant state of anxiety.
> - *Anxiety* after a particularly strong emotional experience. The aftereffects of a frightening experience, for example, will predispose children to be afraid in almost any situation where they feel threatened.
>
> **ENVIRONMENTAL CONDITIONS**
> Constant tension, an overcrowded schedule, and too many exciting experiences overstimulate the child.
> - *Tension* caused by constant bickering and quarreling.
> - An excessive number of *restraints,* as in authoritarian discipline.
> - *Parental attitudes* of overanxiety and overprotectiveness.
> - An authoritarian atmosphere at *school.* An overdemanding teacher or a class assignment ill-suited to their abilities will antagonize children and send them home in a bad humor.

child training is used get into the habit of analyzing a situation before reacting to it because their parents give them reasons for doing what they are supposed to do. This is in direct contrast to children brought up by authoritarian methods where "mother knows best" and no reasons are given to children for what they are told to do. Children brought up permissively get into the habit of reacting to all situations impulsively and this habit carries over to their emotional behavior.

Failure to Learn Emotional Tolerance

Failure to learn how to tolerate unpleasant emotions is hazardous to good personal and social adjustments because, sooner or later, all children must face situations that give rise to these emotions. If they go to pieces emotionally then, they will be unfavorably judged by members of the social group.

Not only is failure to learn emotional tolerance hazardous to good social adjustments because of the unfavorable judgments of such children as "immature," but also it is hazardous to good personal adjustments. Children who must face unpleasant experiences feel insecure, inferior, and inadequate. They often feel martyred because they have been subjected to these unpleasant experiences. Children's first experiences with grief, for example, may be overwhelming if they have been protected from all grief-provoking experiences during the early years of their lives.

As children grow older and their social horizons broaden, there will be no one to protect them against the experiences that will give rise to unpleasant emotions as their parents were able to do when they were young and when their environments were limited mainly to the home. If they have not learned to tolerate unpleasant emotions by gradually becoming accustomed to experiencing them when they are young, the task of learning emotional tolerance as they grow older will be extremely difficult for them.

The children most likely to be deprived of opportunities to learn emotional tolerance are first- and, in many cases, last-born children in a family, both of whom tend to be overprotected. Children brought up permissively are also likely not to learn emotional tolerance because they can avoid any situation not to their liking instead of having to face it as children do when authoritarian or democratic methods are used in their training.

Stumbling Blocks to Emotional Catharsis

Most children can find a source of *physical catharsis,* but some unfortunately cannot. Unpopular children, for example, may have no one to play with. Finding little enjoyment in solitary play, they spend their playtime reading, daydreaming, watching TV, or wondering what to do with their free time. Children with physical handicaps or overprotective parents will likewise be cut off from a ready source of physical catharsis. True, they could clear their systems of pent-up energy by laughing or crying, but children who lack playmates find little to laugh about. Although they may want to cry, they refrain because they know it will increase the lack of social acceptance they already have and jeopardize their chances for gaining social acceptance in the future.

Sources for *mental catharsis* may also be difficult for children to find. If children can talk over their difficulties with parents, teachers, or intimate friends, who will react sympathetically and help them solve their problems, they have a ready source of mental catharsis. Some children, however, do not have intimate friends in whom they can confide because they have never learned to establish close, warm, and friendly relationships with people—the empathic complex discussed earlier. Other children have such authoritarian home or school environments that they are afraid to communicate their problems to their parents or teachers.

When children fail to learn emotional catharsis, they are faced with two alternatives; they must bottle up their emotions or they may express them, regardless of how they do so. In either case, they will face consequences that are hazardous to good personal or social adjustments or to both. If they bottle up their emotions, it will be damaging to their physical and mental health. Furthermore, because it is unlikely that children will be able to bottle up their emotions indefi-nitely, they will eventually express them in reactions out of proportion to the stimuli that gave rise to them. This will result in social judgments of them as "immature." If, on the other hand, they express their emotions at the time they are aroused, even in a mild form, they are likewise likely to be judged as being "immature." These unfavorable social judgments will affect their self-evaluations and, thus, be hazards to good personal adjustments.

Chapter Highlights

1 All emotions play important roles in children's lives through the influence they have on children's personal and social adjustments.

2 Even though the pattern of emotional development is similar for all children, there are variations in this pattern. As a result, different stimuli are able to arouse similar emotions, and the responses made in each emotion will vary from child to child.

3 Emotional development is controlled by maturation and by learning, the five most important forms of which are learning by trial-and-error, by imitation, by identification, by conditioning, and by training.

4 To judge children's emotions fairly, it is essential to realize that they differ from adult emotions in intensity, in frequency of appearance, in permanency, in strength, in individually, and in their ability to be detected by behavioral symptoms.

5 The two most common emotions of childhood are fear and its related emotional patterns—shyness, embarrassment, worry, and anxiety—and anger.

6 Anger is commonly expressed by impulsive actions—usually called "aggression"—in young children, while in older children the responses tend to be inhibited. Fear reactions likewise become increasingly more inhibited as children grow older.

7 In addition to fear and anger, other common emotional patterns in childhood include jealousy, grief, curiosity, joy in its different degrees of intensity, and affection.

8 Emotional dominance—the tendency for the pleasant emotions to be predominant or vice versa—is responsible for temperament. Emotional dominance can be controlled in childhood through control over the environment.

9 Because control over the environment becomes increasingly difficult as children grow older, all children should learn emotional tolerance—the ability to accept and adjust to unpleasant emotional experiences—if emotional balance is to be achieved.

10 Emotional control consists of learning to assess emotion-provoking stimuli before responding to them and of learning to express the emotions in socially-approved patterns of behavior. This is essential if children are to make good personal and social adjustments.

11 To cope with pent-up emotional energy, emotional catharsis, if used effectively, enables children to gain insight into the situations that aroused their emotions. In addition, emotional catharsis clears their bodies of the energy bottled up to avoid the social disapproval that follows emotional outbursts.

12 Being deprived of affection is hazardous to good personal and social adjustments because of its damaging effects on children's physical, mental, social, and emotional developments. Too much affection, on the other hand, causes children to become self-bound and unable to establish emotional linkages with others—the empathic complex.

13 When unpleasant emotions become dominant, which is often due to failure to learn emotional tolerance, they color children's outlooks on life unfavorably and this makes good personal and social adjustments difficult, if not impossible.

14 Heightened emotionality—the tendency to experience more frequent and more intense emotions than is normal for the individual—militates against favorable social judgments and this results in unfavorable self-evaluations. This is true also of failure to achieve the emotional control the group expects of children of their ages and levels of development.

15 The two major stumbling blocks to emotional catharsis are lack of opportunity to express pent-up emotional energy in socially approved patterns of behavior and lack of opportunity to discuss the situa- tions that gave rise to unpleasant emotions, thus get- ting a healthier perspective on them and preventing their damaging effects on personal and social adjust- ments.

Bibliography

1 Acker, L. E., N. A. Acker, and D. Person. Generalized imitative affection: Relationship to prior kinds of imitation training. *Journal of Experimental Child Psychology*, 1973, *16*, 111–125.

2 Ames, L. B., and F. L. Ilg. The developmental point of view with special reference to the principle of reciprocal neuromotor interweaving. *Journal of Genetic Psychology*, 1964, *105*, 195–209.

3 Anderson, R. E. Where's Dad? Paternal deprivation and delinquency. *Archives of General Psychiatry*, 1968, *18*, 641–649.

4 Angelino, H., J. Dollins, and E. V. Mech. Trends in "fears and worries" of school children as related to socioeconomic status and age. *Journal of Genetic Psychology*, 1956, *89*, 263–276.

5 Archibald, H. C., D. Bell, C. Miller, and R. D. Tuddenham. Bereavement in childhood and adult psychiatric disturbance. *Psychosomatic Medicine*, 1962, *24*, 343–351.

6 Arthur, B., and M. L. Kemme. Bereavement in childhood. *Journal of Child Psychology and Psychiatry and Allied Disciplines*, 1964, *5*, 37–49.

7 Averill, J. R. Grief: Its nature and significance. *Psycological Bulletin*, 1968, *70*, 721–748.

8 Baider, L., and E. Rosenfeld. Effect of parental fears on children in wartime. *Social Casework*, 1974, *55*, 497–503.

9 Bakwin, H., and R. M. Bakwin. *Behavior disorders in children*, 4th ed. Philadelphia: Saunders, 1972.

10 Banham, K. M. Senescence and the emotions: A genetic theory. *Journal of Genetic Psychology*, 1951, *78*, 175–183.

11 Berecz, J. M. Phobias of childhood: Etiology and treatment. *Psychological Bulletin*, 1968, *70*, 694–720.

12 Berkowitz, L. Experimental investigations of hostility catharsis. *Journal of Consulting and Clinical Psychology*, 1970, *35*, 1–7.

13 Bledsoe, J. C. Sex and grade differences in children's manifest anxiety. *Psychological Reports*, 1973, *32*, 285–286.

14 Bossard, J. H. S., and E. S. Boll. *The sociology of child development*, 4th ed. New York: Harper & Row, 1966.

15 Bousfield, W. A., and W. D. Orbison. Ontogenesis of emotional behavior. *Psychological Review*, 1952, *59*, 1–7.

16 Bowlby, J., M. Ainsworth, M. Boston, and D. Rosenbluth. The effects of mother-child separation: A follow-up study. *British Journal of Medical Psychology*, 1956, *29*, 211–247.

17 Bronson, G. W. The development of fear in man and other animals. *Child Development*, 1968, *39*, 409–431.

18 Bronson, G. W. Fear of visual novelty: Developmental patterns in males and females. *Developmental Psychology*, 1970, *2*, 33–40.

19 Bronson, G. W. Infants' reactions to unfamiliar persons and novel objects. *Monographs of the Society for Research in Child Development*, 1972, *37* (3).

20 Caldwell, B. M. The effects of psychosocial deprivation on human development in infancy. *Merrill-Palmer Quarterly*, 1970, *16*, 260–277.

21 Chittick, E. V., and P. Himelstein. The manipulation of self-disclosure. *Journal of Psychology*, 1967, *65*, 117–121.

22 Croake, J. W. Fears of children. *Human Development*, 1969, *12*, 239–247.

23 Douglas, V. I. Children's responses to frustration: A developmental study. *Canadian Journal of Psychology*, 1965, *19*, 161–170.

24 Dunbar, F. Homeostasis during puberty. *American Journal of Psychiatry*, 1958, *114*, 673–682.

25 Elliott, F. Shy middle graders. *Elementary School Journal*, 1968, *69*, 296–300.

26 Frost, B. P. Anxiety and educational achievement. *British Journal of Educational Psychology*, 1968, *38*, 293–301.

27 Garai, J. E., and A. Scheinfeld. Sex differences in mental and behavioral traits. *Genetic Psychology Monographs*, 1968, *77*, 169–299.

28 Gardner, L. I. Deprivation dwarfism. *Scientific American*, 1972, *227* (1), 76–82.

29 Garrison, K. C. *Growth and development*, 2d ed. New York: Longmans, 1959.

30 Goode, W. J. The theoretical importance of love. *American Sociological Review*, 1959, *24*, 38–47.

31 Greenwood, E. The importance of play. *Menninger Quarterly*, 1968, *22*, 22–28.

32 Harlow, H. F. The nature of love. *American Psychologist*, 1958, *13*, 673–685.

33 Hollander, J. W., M. P. Duke, and S. Nowicki. Interpersonal distance: Sibling structure and parental affection antecedents. *Journal of Genetic Psychology*, 1973, *123*, 35–45.

34 Holt, R. R. On the interpersonal and intrapersonal consequences of expressing or not expressing anger. *Journal of Consulting and Clinical Psychology*, 1970, *35*, 8–12.

35 Horowitz, E. Reported embarrassment memories of elementary school, high school and college students. *Journal of Social Psychology*, 1962, *56*, 317–325.

36 Hutt, C. Curiosity in young children. *Science Journal*, 1970, *6*, 68–71.

37 Isaac, D. J., and B. M. O'Connor. Use of loss of skill under stress to test a theory of psychological development. *Human Relations*, 1973, *26*, 487–498.

38 Jersild, A. T., C. W. Telford, and J. M. Sawrey. *Child psychology*, 7th ed. Englewood Cliffs, N. J.: Prentice-Hall, 1975.

39 Kaplan, B. L. Anxiety—a classroom close-up. *Elementary School Journal*, 1970, *71*, 70–77.

40 Kohn, M., and J. Cohen. Emotional impairment and achievement deficit in disadvantaged children—fact or

myth? *Genetic Psychology Monographs*, 1975, *92*, 57–78.

41 Kotelchuck, M., R. R. Zelazo, J. Kagan, and E. Spelko. Infant reaction to parental separations when left with familiar and unfamiliar adults. *Journal of Genetic Psychology*, 1975, *126*, 255–262.

42 Kreitler, S., E. Zigler, and H. Kreitler. The nature of curiosity in children. *Journal of School Psychology*, 1975, *13*, 185–200.

43 Lazar, E. Children's perceptions of other children's fears. *Journal of Genetic Psychology*, 1969, *114*, 3–11.

44 Leifer, A. D., P. H. Leiderman, C. R. Bennett, and J. A. Williams. Effects of mother-infant separation on maternal attachment behavior. *Child Development*, 1972, *43*, 1023–1218.

45 Lewis, W. C., R. N. Wolman, and M. King. The development of the language of the emotions. *American Journal of Psychiatry*, 1971, *127*, 1491–1497.

46 Lewis, W. C., R. N. Wolman, and M. King. The development of the language of emotions: II. Intentionality in the experience of affect. *Journal of Genetic Psychology*, 1972, *120*, 303–316.

47 Lewis, W. C., R. N. Wolman, and M. King. The development of the language of emotions: III. Type of anxiety in the experience of affect. *Journal of Genetic Psychology*, 1972, *20*, 325–342.

48 Lintz, L. M., R. H. Starr, and G. R. Medinnus. Curiosity rewards in children. *Psychological Reports*, 1965, *16*, 1222.

49 Longstreth, L. E. Birth order and avoidance of dangerous activities. *Developmental Psychology*, 1970, *2*, 154.

50 Maas, H. S. Preadolescent peer relations and adult intimacy. *Psychiatry*, 1968, *31*, 161–172.

51 Maurer, A. What children fear. *Journal of Genetic Psychology*, 1965, *106*, 265–277.

52 Maw, W. H., and E. W. Maw. Self concepts of high- and low-curiosity boys. *Child Development*, 1970, *41*, 123–129.

53 Maw, W. H., and E. W. Maw. Social adjustment and curiosity of fifth grade children. *Journal of Psychology*, 1975, *90*, 137–145.

54 Messer, S. The effect of anxiety over intellectual performance on reflec-tion-impulsivity in children. *Child Development*, 1970, *41*, 723–735.

55 Modigliani, A. Embarrassment and embarrasability. *Sociometry*, 1968, *31*, 313–328.

56 Moore, T. Stress in normal childhood. *Human Relations*, 1969, *22*, 235–250.

57 Morgan, C. T. *Physiological psychology*, 3d ed. New York: McGraw-Hill, 1965.

58 Munro, A. Parent-child separation: Is it really a cause of psychiatric illness in adult life? *Archives of General Psychiatry*, 1969, *20*, 598–604.

59 Nighswander, J. K., and G. R. Mayer. Catharsis: A means of reducing elementary school students' aggressive behavior? *Personnel and Guidance Journal*, 1969, *47*, 461–466.

60 Parry, M. H. Infants' responses to novelty in familiar and unfamiliar settings. *Child Development*, 1972, *43*, 233–237.

61 Pielstick, N. L., and A. B. Woodruff. Exploratory behavior in children. *Psychological Reports*, 1968, *22*, 515–531.

62 Poznanski, E. O. Children with excessive fears. *American Journal of Orthopsychiatry*, 1973, *43*, 428–438.

63 Rathban, C., H. McLaughlin, C. Bennett, and J. A. Carland. Later adjustment of children following radical separation from family and culture. *American Journal of Orthopsychiatry*, 1965, *35*, 604–609.

64 Ricciuti, H. N. Social and emotional behavior in infancy: Some developmental issues and problems. *Merrill-Palmer Quarterly*, 1968, *14*, 82–100.

65 Roberts, A. R. (ed.) *Childhood deprivation*. Springfield, Ill.: Charles C Thomas, 1974.

66 Robson, K. S., F. A. Pedersen, and H. A. Moss. Developmental observations of diadic gazing in relation to the fear of strangers and social approach behavior. *Child Development*, 1969, *40*, 619–627.

67 Rollins, B. C., and C. Calder. Academic achievement, situational stress, and problem-solving flexibility. *Journal of Genetic Psychology*, 1975, *126*, 93–105.

68 Ross, H. S. The influence of novelty and complexity on exploratory behavior in 12-month-old infants. *Journal of Experimental Child Psychology*, 1974, *17*, 436–451.

69 Rothbart, M. K. Laughter in young children. *Psychological Bulletin*, 1973, *8*, 247–256.

70 Russell, G. W. Human fears: A factor analytic study of three age levels. *Genetic Psychology Monographs*, 1967, *76*, 141–162.

71 Rutter, M. Maternal deprivation reconsidered. *Journal of Psychosomatic Research*, 1972, *16*, 241–250.

72 Sadler, W. A. Creative existence: Play as a pathway to personal freedom and community. *Humanitas*, 1969, *5*, 57–79.

73 Sattler, J. M. A theoretical, developmental, and clinical study of embarrassment. *Genetic Psychology Monographs*, 1965, *71*, 19–59.

74 Saxe, R. M., and G. E. Stollak. Curiosity and the parent-child relationship. *Child Development*, 1971, *42*, 373–384.

75 Scarr, S., and P. Salapatek. Patterns of fear development during infancy. *Merrill-Palmer Quarterly*, 1970, *16*, 53–90.

76 Schaffer, H. R., A. Greenwood, and M. H. Parry. The onset of wariness. *Child Development*, 1972, *43*, 165–175.

77 Sherman, L. W. An ecological study of glee in small groups of preschool children. *Child Development*, 1975, *46*, 53–61.

78 Skard, A. G. Maternal deprivation: The research and its implications. *Journal of Marriage and the Family*, 1965, *27*, 333–343.

79 Sontag, L. W. Implications of fetal behavior and environment for adult personalities. *Annals of the New York Academy of Science*, 1966, *132*, 782–786.

80 Spelke, E. P. Zelazo, J. Kagan, and M. Kotelchuck. Father interaction and separation protest. *Developmental Psychology*, 1973, *9*, 83–90.

81 Spinelta, J. J., and S. Rigler. The child-abusing parent: A psychological review. *Psychological Bulletin*, 1972, *77*, 296–304.

82 Sroufe, L. A., and J. P. Munsch. The development of laughter in the first year of life. *Child Development*, 1972, *43*, 1326–1344.

83 Stagner, R. M. *Psychology of personality*, 4th ed. New York: McGraw-Hill, 1974.

84 Tulkin, S. R. Social class differences in attachment behaviors of ten-

month-old infants. *Child Development*, 1973, *44*, 171–174.

85 Tryon, A. F. Thumb sucking and manifest anxiety: A note. *Child Development*, 1968, *39*, 1159–1163.

86 Unger, H. E. The feeling of happiness. *Psychology,* 1970, *7*, 27–33.

87 Venn, J. R., and J. C. Short. Vicarious classical conditioning in nursery school children. *Journal of Personality and Social Psychology,* 1973, *28*, 249–255.

88 Wayne, D. The lonely school child. *American Journal of Nursing,* 1968, *68*, 774–777.

89 Wolman, R. N., W. C. Lewis, and M. King. The development of the language of emotions: IV. Bodily referents and the experience of affect. *Journal of Genetic Psychology,* 1972, *121*, 65–81.

90 Ziv, A., and H. Shauber. Contribution to a cross-cultural study of manifest anxiety in children. *Human Development,* 1969, *12*, 178–191.

CHAPTER 9

SOCIAL DEVELOPMENT

According to tradition, some people are born social and some unsocial. The people who turn inward and prefer their own company to that of others—the introverts—are "naturally" that way, and those who are social and turn outward—the extroverts—are that way because of their hereditary endowment. The person who is against society—the antisocial person—and who often becomes a criminal has, according to tradition, inherited "bad blood" from one or both parents.

There is little evidence that people are born social, unsocial, or antisocial, and much evidence that they are made that way by learning. However, learning to be a social person does not come overnight. Children learn in cycles, with periods of rapid improvement followed by plateaus in which there is little improvement or even by phases of regression to lower levels of social behavior. How soon children recover lost ground or rise from the plateaus depends largely on the strength of their motivation to become socialized.

When childhood comes to an end, most children are far from satisfied with the progress they have made in social development. This is true even when their development has been normal. Studies of the sources of unhappiness reported by adolescent boys and girls put great emphasis on social problems. Adolescents feel, for example, that they are far from the goal of learning how to get along with people, how to treat friends to avoid quarrels and the breakup of friendships, how to be at ease in social situations, and how to develop their leadership qualities (1, 48).

Meaning of Social Development

Social development means acquisition of the ability to behave in accordance with social expectations. Becoming socialized involves three processes which, although they are separate and distinct, are so closely interrelated that failure in any one of them will lower the individual's level of socialization (34, 38). These three processes are described in Box 9–1.

Relatively few people, either children or adults, totally succeed in all three of these processes. Most, however, wish to win social approval and, therefore, they conform to group expectations. They do so, for example, by learning to use fronts to cover up thoughts and feelings that might be considered unacceptable. They learn not to look bored, even though they may be bored; not to talk about tabooed subjects in the presence of those who disapprove; and not to look pleased when someone they dislike is hurt.

Social versus Nonsocial

The terms "social" and "nonsocial" are so loosely used in everyday language that it is often difficult to know exactly what is meant by them. To distinguish between these different categories, the accepted definitions, which are the ones used in this text, are given in Box 9–2.

In childhood, there is a strong drive to be with others and to be accepted by them. When this need is not met, children will be unhappy. When it is met, they will be satisfied and happy. Some children, for example, are satisfied with gregarious behavior, but most are happy only when they are accepted members of a social group. Some children derive satisfaction from violating social expectations, but when they discover that they are rejected by the members of the group for such behavior, their satisfaction is short-lived. Anything which interferes with socialization and acts as a barrier to acceptance by the group tends to lead to unhappiness.

BOX 9–1

PROCESSES IN SOCIALIZATION

LEARNING TO BEHAVE IN SOCIALLY APPROVED WAYS
Every social group has its standards of what is approved behavior for its members. To become socialized, children must not only know what this approved behavior is, but they must also model their own behavior along the approved lines.

PLAYING APPROVED SOCIAL ROLES
Every social group has its own patterns of customary behavior that are carefully defined and are expected by members of the group. There are approved roles, for example, for parents and children and for teachers and pupils.

DEVELOPMENT OF SOCIAL ATTITUDES
To become socialized, children must like people and social activities. If they do, they will make good social adjustments and be accepted as members of the social group with which they are identified.

Essentials of Socialization

What children's attitudes toward people and social experiences will be and how well they will get along with other people will depend largely on their learning experiences during the early, formative years of life. Whether they will learn to conform to social expectations and become socialized depends upon four factors, which are as follows:

First, ample opportunities for socializing are essential because children cannot learn to live socially with others if they spend most of their time alone. Each year, they need more opportunities to be not only with others of their own ages and levels of development but also with adults of different ages and backgrounds (22). Figure 9–1 shows how opportunities for social contacts results in improved social behavior.

Second, children must not only be able to communicate with others when they are with them in words that others can understand, but they must also be able to talk about topics that are understandable and interesting to others. Socialized speech, as was pointed out in the chapter on speech development, is an important aid to socialization, but egocentric speech militates against it.

Third, children will learn to be social only if they are motivated to do so. Motivation depends largely on how much satisfaction children derive from social activities. If they enjoy their contacts with other people, they will want to repeat these contacts. If, on the other hand, social contacts give them little enjoyment, they will shun them whenever possible.

Fourth, an effective method of learning under guidance is essential. By trial and error, children learn some of the behavior patterns necessary for good social adjustment. They also learn by role practice—by imitating the people they identify with. However, they will learn more quickly and the end results will be better if they are taught by a person who can guide and direct their learning and choose their associates so that they will have good models to imitate.

Influence of the Social Group on Social Development

At all ages people are influenced by the social group with which they have constant association and with which they want to be identified. This influence is greatest during childhood and the early part of adolescence, the time of greatest psychological plasticity.

BOX 9–2

SOCIAL AND NONSOCIAL PEOPLE

- *Social* people are those whose behavior reflects success in the three processes of socialization. As a result, they fit into the group with which they are identified and are accepted as group members.
- *Gregarious* people are social people who crave the presence of others and are lonely when by themselves. They are satisfied merely to be with others, regardless of the nature of the contact.
- *Nonsocial* people are those whose behavior does not reflect success in the three processes that characterize a social person.
- *Unsocial* people are nonsocial people who are ignorant of what the social group expects and, as a result, behave in a manner that falls short of social expectations. Because of this, they are not accepted by the group and are forced to spend much of their time in solitude.
- *Antisocial* people are nonsocial people who know what the group expects but, because of antagonistic attitudes toward people, they violate the group mores. As a result, they are neglected or rejected by the group.

The pattern of influence in childhood is predictable though it varies somewhat from child to child and even in the same child at different ages. This pattern is so universal that it is possible to predict which members of the social group will have the greatest influence on the child at a given age.

PATTERN OF INFLUENCE During the preschool years, the *family* is the most important socializing agency. From 7 years of age on, group pressures are more important than they were when children were younger or than they will be when children grow up.

When children enter school, *teachers* begin to exert an influence over their socialization, though *peer* influence is usually greater than either teacher influence or family influence. A study of the relative influence of peers and parents in children's decisions at different ages found that, when advice from the two differs, children are more likely to be influenced by peers than by parents as childhood progresses (99).

The strong influence of the peer group during the latter part of childhood comes partly from the child's desire to be acceptable to, and accepted by, the group

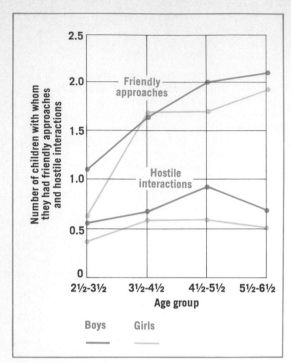

Figure 9–1. There is a decline in hostile interactions and an increase in friendly approaches to members of the peer group as children grow older and have more social experiences. (*Adapted from H. R. Marshall: Relations between home experiences and children's use of language in play interactions with peers.* Psychological Monographs, *1961,* 75, *no. 5. Used by permission.*)

and partly from the fact that the child spends more time with the peer group.

In spite of this predictable pattern, the influence of the social group varies. A number of factors contribute to the variations, and these, too, are largely predictable. The most important are described in Box 9–3.

AREAS OF INFLUENCE   The group's influence on the social development of children is especially strong in three areas, each of which is important to their personal and social adjustments. The *first* area of influence is on the desire to conform to social expectations. "Conformity" is behavior intended to fulfill group expectations. It reflects the willingness of individuals to model their behavior, attitudes, and values along lines that conform to group expectations. Some

people conform only in public and do what they please in private. Others conform both in public and in private.

Some children conform out of necessity rather than choice. They crave popularity and affection from their peers, especially when they feel they do not get the affection they want at home. To achieve these desired ends, they are willing to pay the price of conformity. Willingness to conform is especially strong during the latter part of childhood when the desire for social acceptance reaches a peak (21).

The *second* way in which the group influences children is by helping them to achieve independence from their parents and become individuals in their own right. Through their association with peers, children learn to think independently, to make their own decisions, to accept points of view and values not shared by their families, and to learn patterns of behavior approved by the group.

The *third* important influence of the group is on children's self-concepts. Even before children know why people accept or reject them, they sense what their opinions are and what their reactions mean. If the opinions of others are favorable, children will think favorably of themselves; if they are unfavorable, children will come to dislike and reject themselves.

Social Expectations

What the social group expects of children is defined in terms of developmental tasks or learning experiences that have been found to be appropriate for different age levels. See Box 2–9 for a list of developmental tasks. Before children enter school, for example, they are expected to relate emotionally by showing affection for and interest in their parents, siblings, and other people; they are expected to distinguish right from wrong in simple situations and act according to the socially approved pattern in these situations. During the elementary school years, children are expected to learn to get along with their age-mates, to play appropriate sex roles, and to conform to more complex standards of right and wrong (45).

Variations in Social Expectations

One of the major difficulties children encounter in learning approved social behavior is that each of the subcultures of society has its own definition of what is acceptable. Aggressiveness, for example, is approved by some subcultures and disapproved by others. Subcultures also differ in the standards they set for children of different ages and for members of the two sexes.

Within a subculture, accepted patterns vary from one age group to another. Girls, for example, may find that they can play roles similar to those of boys while they are still preschoolers but, as they grow older, they discover that there are socially approved female sex roles they are expected to play. This matter will be discussed in detail in the chapter on sex-role development.

Different racial and religious subcultural groups likewise have their standards of approved behavior which often differ markedly from those of other racial and religious groups. Similarly, approved behavior in urban areas may not conform to the standards of approved behavior for suburban and rural groups (6).

One of the problems children whose parents are mobile face is learning what the social expectations are of the new group with which they are identified. If, for example, their families move from the city to the suburbs, or from one area of the country to another, children are likely to discover very different social expectations in their new environments. Unless they conform to these new expectations, their social acceptance will be jeopardized.

Degree of Conformity to Social Expectations

How much conformity a particular social group demands of its members before it will accept them varies. In some cultures, a person may retain some individual qualities and still be acceptable. In others, no deviation is approved (17, 39).

In a tightly knit social group, greater conformity is expected of its members than in a group that is less tightly knit. In the former, by control of the environment and a uniform method of training in the home, school, and community, an attempt is made to mold every child into a prescribed pattern.

Children who grow up in a culture that tolerates some individuality will be accepted by the group, even though their behavior is not a photostat of other children's of the same age. In a regimented culture, on the other hand, a nonconformist of any degree will be punished by social rejection. The more clearly defined the cultural group's concept of the "ideal person"—the

---

BOX 9–3

FACTORS CONTRIBUTING TO VARIATIONS IN SOCIAL GROUP INFLUENCES

ACCEPTABILITY TO THE GROUP
Popular children, and those who see the possibility of gaining group acceptance, are influenced more by the group and less by their families than children who do not get along well with their peers. Children who see slight chance of being accepted by the group have little motivation to conform to its standards.

SECURITY OF STATUS
Children who feel secure in the group will feel free to express any disagreement they have with the judgments of other group members. Those who feel insecure, by contrast, will conform closely and will follow other group members.

TYPE OF GROUP
The influence of the group comes from the social distance—the degree of affective relationship—between group members. In the *primary* group (the family or peer group) bonds of intergroup relations are stronger than in the *secondary* (organized play groups or social clubs) or *tertiary* (people the child comes in contact with on buses, trains, and so on). As a result, the primary group has the greatest influence on children.

DIFFERENT MEMBERS OF THE GROUP
Within a group, the greatest influence usually comes from the leader and the least from those who are least popular.

PERSONALITY
Children who suffer from feelings of inadequacy or inferiority are more influenced by the group than those who have greater self-confidence and greater self-acceptance. Children with authoritarian personality patterns are most influenced by the group because they have a constant fear of not being liked by their peers.

AFFILIATION MOTIVE
The stronger the affiliation motive—the desire to be accepted—the greater the susceptibility to influence from group members, especially those with high status in the group. The more attractive the group seems to children, the more anxious they are to be accepted by it, and the more willing they are to allow themselves to be influenced by it.

person who will fit best into the pattern of life prescribed for the members of the group—the greater the conformity required for social acceptance.

Some specific examples of variations in demand for conformity will show how cultural groups differ. A cultural group that places high value on education as a stepping-stone to upward social mobility expects great conformity to school standards as a means to the desired end. Members of such a group develop this conformity in their children by using more authoritarian child-training methods than are used in families where less emphasis is placed on social mobility. Because of the high value middle-class American families place on social mobility, they expect greater conformity to socially approved standards of behavior on the part of their children than middle-class English families, who are less oriented toward upward mobility. In addition, the indifference to outside criticism by the English results in less pressure for conformity on the part of children than is found among American families, who, on the whole, are anxious to avoid criticism (23, 39).

Variations in standards of conformity are by no means the only source of difficulty children experience in trying to satisfy social expectations. There are many others, some of which are as great as the variations described above. The most important are given in Box 9–4.

Normally, conformity to group expectations is greater as children grow older. When they reach the peer-conscious age of late childhood, for example, they are more prone to conform to group expectations than they are during the more individualistic stage of the preschool years. This is illustrated in Figure 9–2. Note that at all ages, females tend to be more conforming than males.

However, at any age, children who feel insecure have a strong need for social approval and are more conforming than those who are more socially secure. Children who are self-bound and more concerned about their own interests and affairs than about those of others conform less than those who are more anxious for social approval (23, 70, 96).

Importance of Early Social Experiences

Since social or unsocial patterns of behavior are established during the formative childhood years, early social experiences largely determine what sort of adults children will become. Predominantly happy experiences encourage the child to seek more such experiences and to become a social person. Too many unhappy experiences are likely to lead to unwholesome attitudes toward *all* social experiences and toward people in general. They encourage the child to become unsocial or antisocial (27, 30).

Early social experiences may be with family members or with people outside the home. As a general rule, experiences in the home are more important during the preschool years while experiences with outsiders become more important after children enter school. Each year, as the desire for status in the group grows, attitudes and behavior are increasingly influenced by pressures from the members of the group (21, 99).

BOX 9–4

DIFFICULTIES IN CONFORMING TO SOCIAL EXPECTATIONS

- An inherent tendency may make conformity to social expectations difficult, if not impossible. A boy with a small build and weak musculature is incapable of conforming in a culture where the male ideal is a well-built athlete.
- A child who has been molded to fit the demands of one cultural group may have difficulty conforming if shifted to another group. A child from an immigrant or socially mobile family may encounter this problem.
- Conformity to social expectations is difficult if the child does not approve of the group's ideals.
- The child who has learned the proper behavior for one age level may find it difficult to adjust to the approved pattern for an older level.
- The child may be confused about what the approved pattern of behavior is. A girl, for example, may not know that she is regarded by the group as "too old" to be a tomboy.
- The child may be deprived of opportunities to learn socially approved patterns of behavior. A boy without a father may have no male model to imitate.
- The child to whom social acceptance is less important than being an individual will have little motivation to follow the approved pattern.

Family Influences

Relationships with family members, not parents alone, but siblings and grandparents, affect children's attitudes toward outsiders. If, for example, children have frictional relationships with grandparents, it will affect their attitudes toward outsiders who are elderly.

However, no one member of the family or one specific aspect of family life is responsible for socializing children. If the overall home environment favors the development of good social attitudes, the chances are that children will become social persons and vice versa.

Studies of social adjustment have revealed that personal relationships in the home are highly influential: *relationships* between parents, between children and their siblings, and between them and their parents. The *position* of the child in the family—whether the oldest, the middle, the youngest, or an only child—is also important. Older children, or those with siblings widely separated in age or of different sexes, tend to be more withdrawn when they are with other children. Children with siblings of the same sex as they are find it difficult to make associations with other children of the opposite sex but easy to make associations with children of the same sex (10, 53, 68).

The *size of the family* in which children grow up not only affects their early social experiences but also leaves its mark on their social attitudes and patterns of behavior. Only children, for example, often get more attention than is good for them. As a result, they come to expect similar treatment from outsiders and are resentful when they do not get it.

The social behavior and attitudes of children reflect the *treatment* they receive in the home. Children who feel that they are rejected by their parents or siblings may assume attitudes of martyrdom outside the home and carry these attitudes into adult life. Such children may turn within themselves and become introverts. By contrast, acceptant, loving parents encourage extroversion in their children (86).

Parental expectations motivate children to put forth effort to learn to behave in a socially acceptable way. As children grow older, for example, they learn that they must overcome aggressiveness and different patterns of unsocial behavior if they want to win parental approval (84).

In the early years of life, the most important influence on children's social behavior and attitudes is

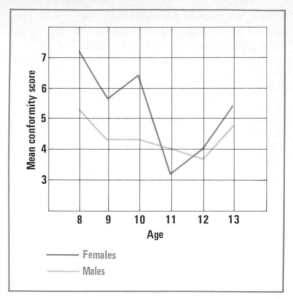

Figure 9–2. Degree of conformity at different ages in childhood. (*Adapted from D. S. Strassberg and E. Wiggen: Conformity as a function of age in preadolescents.* Journal of Social Psychology, *1973, 91, 61–66. Used by permission.*)

likely to be the *child-training method* used by their parents. Children who are brought up in democratic homes make the best social adjustments. They are socially active and outgoing. Those who are indulged, on the other hand, tend to become inactive and withdrawn. Children who are subjected to authoritarian child-training methods tend to be quiet and nonresistant, and their curiosity and creativity are restricted by parental pressures (35, 61).

In sum, the home is the "seat of learning" for social skills. Only when children have satisfactory social relationships with members of their family can they fully enjoy social relationships with people outside the home, develop healthy attitudes toward people, and learn to function successfully in the peer group.

Outside Influences

Early social experiences outside the home supplement home experiences and are important determinants of children's social attitudes and behavior patterns. If their relationships with peers and adults outside the home are pleasant, they will enjoy social contacts and want to repeat them. If, on the other hand, these contacts are unpleasant or frightening, children will shun them and fall back on family members for their social contacts.

BOX 9–5

EFFECTS OF EARLY SOCIAL EXPERIENCES

PERSISTENCE OF SOCIAL BEHAVIOR
Because patterns of behavior, learned early, tend to be persistent, they determine behavior in social situations as the child grows older. If these patterns lead to good social adjustments, they will be an asset; if not, they will prove to be a social liability.

CONSISTENCY OF SOCIAL ATTITUDES
Because attitudes, once formed, are less amenable to change than behavior patterns, the child who prefers interacting with people to interacting with objects develops more social know-how and, as a result, is more popular with peers than is the child whose attitudes toward social activities are less favorable.

EFFECT ON SOCIAL PARTICIPATION
Early social experiences determine the extent of the individual's social participation both in childhood and later. When social experiences are pleasant, the individual is likely to be more active than when the experiences are unpleasant.

EFFECT ON SOCIAL ACCEPTANCE
There is a close relationship between liking for social activities and social acceptance. The more favorable the child's attitude toward social activities, the more popular the child is likely to be.

EFFECT ON CHARACTERISTIC PATTERNS OF BEHAVIOR
Early social experiences determine whether the child will become predominantly social, unsocial, or antisocial and whether the child will become a leader or a follower.

EFFECT ON PERSONALITY
Early social experiences leave their mark on the child's personality—a mark that is likely to remain consistent throughout life. Positive attitudes toward self are most often found in a person whose early social experiences were favorable.

When children enjoy contact with outsiders, they will be motivated to behave in a manner that will win their approval. Since the desire for social approval and acceptance is especially strong during the latter years of childhood, the influence of the peer group is stronger then than during the preschool years when young children have less interest in peer play than older children have.

If children's playmates are older than they are, they try to keep up with them and, as a result, they develop more mature patterns of behavior than their age-mates usually have. However, if the older children are so bossy that the younger children do not enjoy playing with them, they are likely to choose younger children as playmates, bossing them as they were bossed by their older playmates. This leads to unsocial patterns of behavior. When children's playmates and siblings are all of their own sex, they often have difficulty in making good social adjustments with playmates of the opposite sex (29, 71).

Effects of Early Social Experiences

Studies of people of all ages have revealed the significance of early social experiences not only during childhood but also later in life (47, 67, 82, 84, 100). Some of the effects these early social experiences have on the individual's personal and social adjustments are explained in Box 9–5.

From studies of children over a period of time, Waldrop and Halverson have concluded that "sociability at 2½ years was predictive of sociability at 7½ years" (100). Because attitudes and behavior patterns tend to be persistent, the necessity of laying good foundations in the early years of life is apparent. If, on the other hand, the foundations are such that children get off to a bad start in their social lives, they are likely to acquire reputations of being unsocial. When this occurs, it has a seriously damaging effect on personal and social adjustments (49).

The Pattern of Social Development

Social development follows a pattern, an orderly sequence of social behavior which is similar for all children within a cultural group. There are also patterns in children's attitudes toward and interest in social activities and choice of companions. Because of this, it is possible to describe a timetable for socialization.

In this timetable, the true "socialization age" begins with formal entrance into school, either kindergarten or first grade. Children who have always acted upon their own impulses now try to use adult criteria to evaluate people and situations. By the time they are 10 years old, they can modify some of their impulses to conform to the demands of the social group (52).

Normally, all children pass through the several stages of socialization at approximately the same age. As in other kinds of development, bright children are accelerated, while dull children are retarded. Lack of opportunities for social contacts and for learning how to get along successfully with others will likewise delay normal development.

Reasons for the Pattern of Social Development

In spite of individual age-level variations in socialization, variations in the pattern itself are slight. There are two reasons. *First,* the pattern of physical and mental development is similar for all children, even though minor variations do occur, owing to differences in intelligence, health, and other factors. Consequently, children are ready to master the developmental tasks of socialization at much the same age.

Second, within a cultural group, social pressures and social expectations lead to similar learning experiences for all children. When a child's social behavior varies markedly from that of other children of the same age, it generally means that the child has made poor social adjustments or has developed unfavorable social attitudes. In either case, the trouble can generally be traced to lack of opportunities to learn to be social or lack of motivation to take advantage of the opportunities available.

Values of Knowing the Pattern

Knowing the pattern of development makes it possible to predict what normal social behavior will be at a given age. Consequently, parents, teachers, and other adults are less likely to regard a child as backward or precocious or antisocial.

Another value of understanding the pattern of social development is that it provides a schedule for training.

Children can be encouraged to develop those skills and attitudes which will be expected of them if they are to gain acceptance in the group. When children reach school age, for example, they are expected to be able to make social contacts with peers without adult interference.

The following pages present a survey of the normal pattern of social development from the earliest months of life until adolescence. The survey describes a timetable for socialization. Its aim is to show what is usual in social behavior at different ages and what, as a result, will be expected at those ages. At each major stage—babyhood, early childhood, later childhood, and puberty—only the behavior and attitudes most characteristic of that period will be discussed in detail. It should be assumed, however, that, once they have developed, they will continue to play a role in the child's social relationships unless environmental forces cause them to change. Resistant behavior in babyhood, for example, may lead to negativism if young children are not granted independence in keeping with their developmental status. Since prejudice and discrimination normally do not develop until children enter school, they will be discussed in the section about social development in late childhood, but emphasis will be placed on the foundations of prejudice laid earlier.

Beginnings of Social Behavior

At birth, babies are nongregarious. So long as their bodily needs are taken care of, they have no interest in people. During the first month or two of life, they merely respond to stimuli in their environment, regardless of whether these stimuli come from people or objects. They do not, for example, distinguish clearly between people's voices and other noises.

Socialization in the form of *gregarious* behavior begins around the third month, when babies can distinguish between people and objects in their environment and when they respond differently to them. By that time, their eye muscles are strong enough and sufficiently coordinated to enable them to look at people and objects and follow their movements, and to see them clearly. Their hearing is also sufficiently developed by then to enable them to distinguish sounds. As a result of this development, they are maturationally ready to learn to be social.

Reactions to Adults

Babies' first social responses are to adults because, normally, adults are babies' first social contacts. By the time babies are 3 months old, they turn their heads when they hear human voices and smile in response to a smile or clucking sound. They express pleasure in the presence of others by smiling, kicking, and waving their arms (15, 57, 93). *Social smiles,* or smiles in response to people as contrasted with reflex smiles elicited by touching the baby's cheek or lips, are regarded as the beginning of social development (93).

During the third month, babies cry when left alone but they stop crying when they are talked to or diverted by a rattle or some other mechanical device. They recognize their mothers and other familiar people and show fear of strangers by crying and turning their heads (76).

In the fourth month, babies make anticipatory adjustments to being lifted, they show selective attention to faces, they look in the direction of the person who leaves them, they smile at a person who speaks to them, they show delight in personal attention, and they laugh when being played with.

From the fifth to the sixth months, babies react differently to smiling and scolding, and they can distinguish between friendly and angry voices. They recognize familiar people with smiles and show definite expressions of fear in the presence of strangers. During the sixth month, social advances become more aggressive. Babies, for example, pull the hair of the person who is holding them, they grab the person's nose or eyeglasses, and they explore the person's facial features.

By 7 or 9 months of age, babies attempt to imitate speech sounds as well as simple acts and gestures. At 12 months, they can refrain from doing things in response to "no-no." They show their fear and dislike of strangers by drawing away and crying when a stranger approaches them. From the age of 15 months, babies show an increasing interest in adults and a strong desire to be with them and imitate them. At 2 years, they can cooperate with adults in a number of simple activities, such as helping with their baths or with their dressing.

Thus, it is apparent that in a relatively short period of time babies change from passive members of the family group who receive much attention and give little in return, to active members who initiate social contacts and participate in family activities. They have passed from nongregarious to gregarious and to social stages in the developmental pattern.

Reactions to Other Babies

The first real indication that babies notice another baby occurs between the ages of 4 and 5 months when they smile at another baby or show an interest in the baby's cries. Friendly contacts between babies begin usually between 6 and 8 months and consist of looking, reaching out, and touching another baby. Unfriendly contacts consist of attempting to grab something from another baby—attempts which often result in fights. Between 9 and 13 months, babies explore other babies by pulling their hair or clothes, imitate the behavior and vocalizations of other babies, and show for the first time cooperative use of toys. When a toy is taken away by another baby, it is usual for babies to become angry, fight, and cry.

Social reactions toward babies and children develop rapidly during the second year. From the thirteenth to the eighteenth months, babies smile and laugh in imitation of other babies or children. Their interest shifts from play materials to other babies or children, and there is less fighting and more cooperative play. During the last half of the second year, babies regard play materials as a means of establishing social relationships. They cooperate with their playmates, modify their behavior to adjust to the playmate's activity, and engage in simple games with young or older children.

Behavior in Social Situations

As a result of contacts with others, both adults and babies, certain social responses begin to be established (16, 27, 97). These early responses, outlined in Box 9–6, are the foundations upon which later social behavior develops.

The influence of early social behavior on later development has been emphasized by scientific studies. Babies, for example, who depend on their mothers to take care of their needs and wants, even when they are maturationally ready to learn to do these things for themselves, develop a generalized dependency on all adults and even on other children. This makes the achievement of independence difficult for them. Similarly, babies who are permitted to do as they please later find it very difficult to conform to the rules of the playground or school (16, 19, 30).

FOUNDATIONS OF SOCIAL BEHAVIOR LAID IN BABYHOOD

- *Imitation.* Babies become a part of the social group by imitating others. They first imitate facial expressions, then gestures and movements, then speech sounds, and, finally, total patterns of behavior.

- *Shyness.* By the third or fourth months, babies can distinguish between familiar people and strangers. Until late in the first year, they react to strangers by whimpering, crying, hiding their heads, and clinging to the person who is holding them.

- *Attachment behavior.* When babies are able to establish warm, loving relationships with their mothers or mother substitutes, the pleasure they derive from this association motivates them to try to establish friendly relationships with other people.

- *Dependency.* The more babies are cared for by one person, the more dependent they become on that person. They show their dependency by clinging to the person, crying when left with someone else, and expecting to be waited on even when they are capable of doing things for themselves.

- *Acceptance of authority.* Whether babies will learn to conform to the requests of those in authority will depend on how insistent those in authority are. Permissive attitudes encourage babies to reject authority.

- *Rivalry.* Rivalry develops in associations with other babies or children. It is shown by attempts to snatch toys or other objects from them, not because the babies want them but because it gives them pleasure to assert their superiority.

- *Attention seeking.* During the second year, babies try to get the attention of adults by vocalizations, especially crying, by grabbing at their clothes, by hitting them, and by doing forbidden things. If they are successful, they show their satisfaction by smiling or laughing.

- *Social cooperation.* Babies' cooperative play with adults is usually successful because adults are willing to do most of the sharing. With peers, social cooperation is usually unsuccessful because their peers are unwilling to share.

- *Resistant behavior.* During the middle of the second year of life, resistant behavior begins. It is expressed by tensing the body, crying, and refusal to obey. Unless babies are given opportunities to be independent, resistant behavior usually leads to negativism.

Although social attitudes and responses which lead to personal- and social-adjustment problems can be modified as children grow older, it is far easier to avoid the problems by laying good foundations in the first place. That is why babyhood is regarded as a critical age in socialization.

Social Development in Early Childhood

From 2 to 6 years, children learn how to make social contacts and how to get along with people outside the home, especially children of their own age. They learn to adapt themselves to others and how to cooperate in play activities. Follow-up studies of groups of children report that the social attitudes and behavior established during these early years usually persist with little change (3, 49).

Early childhood is often called the "pregang age." At this time, the number of contacts children have with other children increases and this determines, in part, how their social development will progress. Children who attend preschools—nursery schools, day-care centers, or kindergartens—usually have a decidedly larger number of social contacts with peers and make better social adjustments than children who have not had this preschool experience. The reason is that they are better prepared for active group participation than children whose social activities have been limited mainly to family members or children in the immediate neighborhood.

One of the many advantages of nursery schools, day-care centers, and kindergarten is that they provide social experiences under the guidance of trained teachers who promote enjoyable contacts and try to see that no children are subjected to treatment that might condition them to avoid social contacts. As a result, overall negative reactions to other children decrease. Negative reactions to teachers, however, sometimes increase slightly as children become more child- and less adult-oriented.

Relations with Adults

With each succeeding year, young children spend less time with adults and derive less enjoyment from being with them. At the same time, their interest in playmates of their own age increases and the enjoyment from being with them gets stronger. With their growing desire to be independent, children become resistant to adult authority.

In spite of their desire for independence, young children still try to gain attention and approval from adults. If they have derived satisfaction from attachment behavior in babyhood, they continue to try to establish warm, friendly relationships with other adults, especially family members (60).

However strong the desire for peer contacts, parents and teachers are still largely responsible for providing a model for developing social attitudes and for determining whether these will be attitudes of good will and friendly cooperation toward all or of intolerance and prejudice against those who are different.

Relations with Other Children

Before the age of 2 years, young children engage in solitary or parallel play. Even though two or three children play in the same room and with similar toys, little social interaction takes place. Their contacts consist primarily of imitating or watching one another or of attempting to take one another's toys.

From the age of 3 or 4, children begin to play together in groups, to talk to one another while they play, and to select from the children present those with whom they prefer to play. The most common behavior of these groups consists of watching each other, holding conversations, and making verbal suggestions.

A study of children at the preschool stage has revealed that as children advance in age, there is an increase in friendly approaches to other children and a decrease in hostile interactions (61). Age for age, boys made more friendly as well as more hostile approaches to other children. Refer to Figure 9–1.

Common Forms of Social Behavior

Some of the forms of social behavior developed in early childhood are based on foundations laid in babyhood. Some are new, based on new foundations. Many of these new foundations are laid from contacts with peers outside the home and from what children see on television, in movies, or in the comics they are permitted to look at.

Many of the patterns of behavior in social situations appear to be unsocial or even antisocial but, in reality, each is important in the socializing process. The foundations laid in early childhood will determine how children will adjust to people and to social situations when the environment becomes broader and when they do not have the protection and guidance of parents they had during the years of babyhood.

Box 9–7 gives a list of the different forms of behavior in social situations whose foundations are laid in early childhood. These are divided into two groups, social and unsocial behavior patterns. It is important to note, however, that even the unsocial patterns are often valuable learning experiences for young children. From them, children learn how others react to their behavior and they learn that, if they want to be accepted members of the social group, they must change their behavior.

While improvements in social behavior tend to predominate in early childhood as social experiences broaden and as children learn how people feel about their behavior and how it contributes to their acceptance or lack of acceptance by the peer group, some forms of behavior become unsocial or antisocial. How much improvement there will be depends on, *first,* how anxious children are to be socially accepted, *second,* their knowledge of how to improve their behavior and, *third,* their growing intellectual ability which enables them to see the relationship between their behavior and social acceptance.

Normally, the desire for social acceptance is great enough to provide the necessary motivation for improvement in social behavior. This is usually focused first on correcting unsocial patterns of behavior and, later, on strengthening social patterns. Children, for example, usually become less selfish and demanding and more cooperative and approving of social behavior as they grow older (20, 43). On the other

BOX 9–7

BEHAVIOR PATTERNS IN SOCIAL SITUATIONS DURING EARLY CHILDHOOD

SOCIAL BEHAVIOR PATTERNS

- *Cooperation.* Few children learn to play or work cooperatively with others until they are 4 years old. The more opportunities they have to do things together, the more quickly they will learn to do them in a cooperative way.

- *Rivalry.* When rivalry acts as a spur to children to do their best, it adds to their socialization. If, however, it is expressed in quarreling and boasting, it leads to poor socialization.

- *Generosity.* Generosity, as shown in a willingness to share with others, increases as selfishness decreases and as children learn that generosity leads to social acceptance.

- *Desire for social approval.* When the desire for approval is strong, it motivates children to conform to social expectations. Desire for adult approval usually comes earlier than desire for peer approval.

- *Sympathy.* Young children are incapable of sympathetic behavior until they have been in situations similar to those of a person in distress. They express their sympathy by trying to help or comfort a person in distress.

- *Empathy.* Empathy is the ability to put oneself in the position of another and to experience what that person experiences. This develops only when children can understand the facial expressions and speech of others.

- *Dependency.* Dependency on others for help, attention, and affection motivates children to behave in a socially approved way. Children who are independent lack this motivation.

- *Friendliness.* Young children show their friendliness by wanting to do things for and with others and by expressing their affection for them.

- *Unselfishness.* Children who have opportunities and encouragement to share what they have and who are not constantly in the limelight of family attention learn to think of others and to do things for them rather than concentrating on their own interests and possessions.

- *Imitation.* By imitating a person who is well accepted by the social group, children develop traits that add to their acceptance by the group.

- *Attachment behavior.* From foundations laid in babyhood, when the baby developed a warm and loving attachment to the mother or mother substitute, young children transfer this pattern of behavior to other people and learn to establish friendships with them.

UNSOCIAL BEHAVIOR PATTERNS

- *Negativism.* Negativism is resistance to pressures from others to behave in a certain way. It usually begins during the second year of life and reaches a peak between 3 and 6 years. Physical expressions, similar to temper tantrums, gradually give way to verbal refusals to do what children have been asked or told to do.

- *Aggression.* Aggression is an actual or threatened act of hostility, usually unprovoked by another person. Children may express their aggressiveness in physical or verbal attacks on another, usually a child smaller than they are.

- *Quarreling.* Quarrels are angry disputes that generally start when a person makes an unprovoked attack on another. Quarreling differs from aggression, *first,* because it involves two or more people while aggression is an individual act and, *second,* because one of the people involved in a quarrel plays a defensive role while, in aggression, the role is always aggressive.

- *Teasing and bullying.* Teasing is a verbal attack on another, but in bullying, the attack is physical. In both cases, the attacker gains satisfaction from watching the victim's discomfort and attempts to retaliate.

- *Ascendant behavior.* Ascendant behavior is the tendency to dominate others or to be "bossy." If properly directed, it can be a leadership trait, but it usually is not and, as a result, leads to rejection by the social group.

- *Egocentrism.* Almost all young children are egocentric in that their tendency is to think and talk about themselves. Whether this tendency will wane, remain constant, or grow stronger will depend partly on whether children realize that it makes them unpopular and partly on how anxious they are to be popular.

- *Prejudice.* The foundations of prejudice are laid in early childhood when children realize that some people are different in appearance and behavior from them and that these differences are regarded by the social group as signs of inferiority. It is unusual for young children to express prejudice by discriminating against those they recognize as different.

- *Sex antagonism.* An early childhood draws to a close, many boys are pressured by male relatives and peers to avoid associating with girls or playing "girls' games." They are also learning that the social group considers males superior to females. However, at this age, boys do not discriminate against girls, but they avoid them and shun activities regarded as girls' activities. See Figure 9–3.

"It was a pretty good party, 'cept there were GIRLS there."

Figure 9–3. During the latter part of the preschool years, boys develop a disdainful attitude toward girls and try to avoid girls and any activities in which girls are involved. (*Adapted from Bil Keane: "The Family Circus."* Register and Tribune Syndicate, *Sept. 27, 1975. Used by permission.*)

hand, prejudice and discrimination often increase and the cleavage between the sexes becomes greater (36, 37, 54).

Social Development in Late Childhood

After children enter school and come into contact with more children than during the preschool years, interest in family activities begins to wane. At the same time, individual play gives way to group games. Since group games require a large number of playmates, the older child's circle of friends gradually widens. With change in play interests comes an increasing desire to be with, and to be accepted by, children outside the home.

Upon beginning school, children enter the "gang age"—an age when social consciousness develops rapidly. Becoming socialized is one of the major developmental tasks of this period. Children become members of a peer group which will gradually replace the family in its influence over their attitudes and behavior. The peer group, as defined by Havighurst, is an "aggregation of people of approximately the same age who *feel* and *act* together" (45).

During the transition from the pregang age of early childhood to the gang age of late childhood, children shift from one group to another or from group to individual activities. The "shifting-group" stage bridges the gap between the pregang and the gang ages. The informal play group of the early school days consists of only two or three children. It is formed to carry out a specific play activity and is thus transitory. The activity itself, not friendship, is the basis for the organization of the group. Within the group, leadership swings from one child to another, depending on which child takes the initiative in a specific activity. There are many brief quarrels, but these have no permanent effect on the makeup of the group.

Childhood Gangs

The childhood gang is a spontaneous local group having no authorization from outside and no socially approved aim. Although adults may know that it is being organized, it is formed by the children themselves, without support from parents, teachers, or youth leaders. It is an attempt by children to create a society adequate to meet their needs. As such, it is a substitute for adult society and for what that society fails to give. It offers relief from adult supervision, though it may not be hostile to the adults in authority. The gang is not necessarily a product of substandard environments; it is also found in good environments.

GANG MAKEUP Gangs have a more definite structure than the informal groupings of younger children. Gang members are selected because they are able to do things the others enjoy doing, not because they live near each other or can do what one or two members want to do at the moment. The gang exists independently of activities and then selects the various activities it will engage in.

The typical gang is a *play group,* made up of children who have common play interests; its primary purpose is to have a good time, though, occasionally, having a good time may lead to mischief-making. From the ages of 6 or 7, boys and girls normally find increasing pleasure in being with groups of their own sex. As a result, gangs are usually unisexual in makeup. Some of the most important characteristics of gangs are shown in Box 9–8.

DIFFERENCES IN GANGS   Because different children have different social needs, the type of gang that meets the needs of one child will not necessarily meet the needs of another child. Children who have had opportunities for social contacts outside the home during the preschool years will be interested in becoming gang members earlier than children whose social contacts have been limited mainly to family members during this time. However, all children tend to lose interest in gang life at puberty.

Some gangs are large and some relatively small. The size of the gang is influenced partly by how many children are available for gang membership and partly by the type of activities they enjoy. Gangs, for example, that spend most of their time in games need more members than gangs that prefer more sedentary activities, such as constructing things or watching television together.

In some gangs, the leader is autocratic, while in others this would not be tolerated. Some are closely knit and surrounded with more secrecy than are others. In the former, there is less likelihood that new members will be welcomed than in the latter.

In most gangs, the children are of the same age and are in the same grade in school. In others, there are children of slightly different ages, though it is unusual for a gang to include children from different grades in school. When the gang is composed of children of different ages, the leader is almost always one of the oldest gang members.

The activities of gangs as well as their makeup reflect individual differences. The activities of some gangs border on rowdyism and in them there are constant attempts to test the barriers set by adults. In others, there is far less interest in any form of socially unacceptable behavior. Gangs in poorer neighborhoods are far more likely to engage in mischief-making and fighting with other gangs than are gangs in better neighborhoods.

INFLUENCE OF GANGS   As Havighurst has pointed out, there are four major ways in which the gang can help children become socialized (45). These four ways are explained in Box 9–9.

For the most part, gang life in childhood favors the development of good qualities. It teaches children to be democratic, to fit their desires and actions into

BOX 9–8

CHARACTERISTICS OF CHILDREN'S GANGS

- Gangs identify themselves by names, many of which are taken from the street or neighborhood where the members live or from popular books, comics, or movies.
- Gang members use secret signals, passwords, communication codes, or a private language to maintain their secrecy.
- Childhood gangs often use insignia—caps, armbands, or other decorations—to identify their members.
- Gangs sometimes have initiation ceremonies to test a new member's skill or physical endurance, to create loyalty within the group, and to make each member feel important because of being accepted.
- The preferred meeting place of the gang minimizes adult interference and maximizes opportunities for favored gang activities. Girls usually meet close to home, while boys meet as far from home as possible.
- Gang activities include all kinds of group play and entertainment, making things, annoying other people, exploring, and engaging in forbidden activities, such as gambling, smoking, drinking, and experimenting with drugs.

those of the group, to cooperate with group members, to develop skills which will enable them to do what their peers do, and to eliminate selfishness and antisocial individualism. In their competition for status, children try to improve themselves and to redirect their egocentric interests into channels that promote the group's interests. Figure 9–4 shows some of the most common ways in which gang belonging leads to improved socialization.

On the other hand, gang life favors the development of certain *undesirable* qualities. It sometimes encourages the use of slang and swearing, the telling of salacious stories and jokes, truancy, mischievousness, attitudes of contempt for rules and those in authority, the breaking of home ties and the shifting of loyalties from home to group activities, snobbishness, discrimination against members of minority groups or rival gangs, and the breaking down of ideals established in the home. Most of these undesirable effects of gang life are transitory. As children grow older, many of them can be eliminated.

One of the most valuable lessons children learn from

being members of a gang is to evaluate themselves realistically. In the home, where personal bias, stemming from parental affection, is strong, children learn to think of themselves as their parents think of them—as "superior" people. In the gang, this personal bias does not exist. If their contemporaries like them, children learn to think favorably of themselves and become self-acceptant people.

Patterns of Behavior Learned from Gang Membership

Gang life contributes to the development of a number of different kinds of social behavior. Some are outgrowths of attitudes and behavior patterns developed during the preschool years. Refer to Box 9–7 for a list of attitudes and behavior patterns learned at this time.

Figure 9–4. Some ways in which gang belonging leads to improved socialization in late childhood.

Others result from the broader social contacts of older children. Some interfere with social adjustments, although, on the whole, with modification and change as children grow older, they favor social adjustment. They are the foundations of social behavior normally found in adults. The most common of these new behavior patterns are discussed below.

SUSCEPTIBILITY TO SOCIAL APPROVAL AND DISAPPROVAL As soon as children begin to crave the companionship of other children, they also crave their approval of their dress, their speech, and their behavior. Should a conflict arise between the standards of the home and the school and those of the peer group, children will inevitably side with those of the peer group.

The craving for attention and social approval stems from feelings of insecurity and inadequacy. It is associated with such traits as timidity, jealousy, moodiness, and overdependency. Although all children want social approval and do all they can to avoid social disapproval, the more secure the children, the less likely they are to submerge their interests, needs, and desires and accept those of the group.

OVERSENSITIVENESS A common outgrowth of susceptibility to social approval and disapproval is oversensitiveness—the tendency to be easily hurt and to interpret what others say and do as hostile. To some extent, oversensitiveness is a measure of children's desire for social acceptance—a desire which makes them highly sensitive to the attitudes of adults as well as members of the peer group. It is also an effective method of coping with parents. When frustrated in what they want to do, older children soon discover that putting up a fight and being negativistic are poor weapons. Hurt feelings, however, baffle parents and often make them feel guilty. Oversensitiveness is seldom used outside the home because other children can see through it too easily.

SUGGESTIBILITY AND CONTRASUGGESTIBILITY A person who is *suggestible* is easily influenced by others. Like oversensitiveness, suggestibility is an outgrowth of a craving for attention and social approval. Suggestible children believe that their willingness to follow others in what they think and do will guarantee acceptance by them. Perhaps at no other age during the life span are people as suggestible as they are during late childhood.

Contrasuggestibility means thinking and acting contrary to suggestions from others. While accepting in a more or less unquestioning manner the suggestions of the peer group, older children begin to revolt against adults and to act in direct contradiction to them. Contrasuggestibility is similar to negativism in the younger child. Although negativism usually reaches its peak by the time children enter first grade, contrasuggestibility increases as childhood progresses and as children revolt more and more against what they regard as adult "bossiness."

COMPETITION During the gang age of late childhood, competition takes three forms: rivalry among group members for recognition within the group itself, conflicts between the gang and rival gangs, and conflicts between the gang and organized agencies of society. Each of these has a different effect on the socialization of children. The first is likely to lead to hostility and quarreling within the gang, thus serving to weaken the group and the loyalty of each member. The second serves to build up solidarity and feelings of loyalty, while the third, if it can be kept within constructive bounds, serves to develop independence.

Competition among older children is likely to lead to much quarreling. It may be expressed in aggressive fighting or in more subtle ways, such as criticism of others, ganging up on a single child who is disliked for annoying behavior or for belonging to a minority or rival group, teasing and bullying, ignoring a child or a group of children, or arguing without any real provocation and with the apparent desire to make the other person uncomfortable or annoyed.

GOOD SPORTSMANSHIP Good sportsmanship is the ability to cooperate with others to the extent of submerging individual personalities and promoting the spirit of the group. While it can be learned at home, it is far more likely to be a product of group life. From being members of a gang, children soon learn that they must play according to the rules of the game. Any infringement upon these, such as cheating, tattling, lying, or using underhanded methods, will not be tolerated. When working together for a common reward, children show positive interactions, such as helping each other and sharing materials. When competing, they have negative interactions, such as appropriating materials, making unfriendly remarks, and trying to obstruct or dominate others.

Good sportsmanship entails a willingness not only

to cooperate with others but also to share. As was pointed out in the earlier discussion of generosity among young children, generosity develops rapidly after the child enters school but especially rapidly during the fourth and fifth grades, when the desire to be an acceptable member of a gang reaches its peak. Children who want to be considered "good sports" must be generous with their material possessions, and they must also be generous in their attitudes toward losing to another, whether in school or in games. They discover that no matter how badly they want to win, if they should lose, they must share the pleasure of victory with the winner instead of pouting, complaining, or accusing the winner of being "unfair" (79, 80).

RESPONSIBILITY Closely related to good sportsmanship is responsibility—the willingness to assume one's share of the load. Studies of how responsibility is developed reveal that it, like many other kinds of social behavior, is "homegrown" in the sense that it has its roots in the child's early training (10). Children from large families, through necessity, must develop responsibility for their own affairs and for the care of younger siblings. Children who learn to assume responsibilities at home not only make better adjustments to the peer group but they also are likely to be selected for leadership roles. This gives them further opportunities to learn to assume responsibilities and the confidence that they can assume them successfully.

However, if too many responsibilities are placed on children too suddenly, it will undermine their self-confidence, especially if they meet with failure. For that reason, the development of responsibility must be gradual, starting with simple tasks and increasing as children gain confidence and experience in being responsible for their own affairs.

SOCIAL INSIGHT Social insight is the ability to perceive and to understand the meaning of social situations and of people in those situations. It is dependent upon *empathy*—the ability to put oneself in the psychological shoes of another and to perceive a situation from the other person's perspective. Stated differently, empathy is the ability to feel imaginatively and to think of oneself in the total mental-emotional attitude of another person.

Feshbach and Feshbach have explained the value of empathy to social insight in situations where aggression is involved. According to them (31):

The distress response of a child who is the object of an aggressive act may serve several adaptive functions. It "tells" the aggressor that the act has been effective as well as producing distress responses through empathy in the aggressor. Empathy, then, is a mechanism which may help terminate aggressive behavior before the object of aggression suffers serious injury.

Social insight normally increases with age, owing partly to mental maturation and partly to learning from social experiences. Only in very late childhood, however, is it sufficiently developed for children to be able to understand the behavior and feelings of other children to any great extent. Children whose social perception is superior to that of their peers usually make better social adjustments and receive greater social acceptance. The brighter the child, other things being equal, the more perceptive. This contributes to the popularity of bright children. And, the more popular children are, the more opportunities they have to develop social insight.

SOCIAL DISCRIMINATION Social discrimination means the tendency to make a distinction among people by certain tokens or cues. This distinction is usually accompanied by a tendency to treat them differently from others. This treatment may range from mere recognition of the difference to unfair or even cruel treatment.

Social discrimination appears early in childhood but is not well developed until the child becomes a member of a gang. Gang members assume the attitude that *any* member of their group is all right but that anyone who is not a member is inferior. This is a form of snobbishness, based on whether or not one belongs to the group. It soon becomes *generalized* to include anyone who is diffferent because of religion, race, socioeconomic status, age, or sex.

Children who discriminate against others treat them as inferiors because they are different, not because they are actually inferior. They regard them as belonging to an "outgroup" or a "minority group" because their status is considered inferior, not because their numbers are few. Children who belong to gangs, for example, feel that their status is superior to that of children who do not belong to gangs. They also feel that if the gang they are identified with is recognized as "superior," all other gangs are outgroups and, hence, inferior.

PREJUDICE   Back of discrimination is prejudice—a tendency to classify *all* who belong to other groups, whether they are social, religious, racial, or sex groups, as inferior and to treat them accordingly. It is based on a set of attitudes which cause, support, or justify discrimination. In prejudice, there is a tendency to *prejudge* as inferior all those who belong to a group against which there are unfavorable social attitudes, not because of what they are, but because of their identification with that group. Prejudice is made up of three elements, each of which influences behavior (3, 11). These three elements are explained in Box 9–10.

Very early, as was pointed out before, children become aware of differences between people. However, awareness of differences, per se, does not mean that they will be prejudiced. See Figure 9–5. Only when children become aware of social attitudes toward those who are different and only when pressure is placed on them to accept these attitudes does prejudice develop.

Awareness of differences comes during the preschool years. Racial awareness, for example, grows rapidly from the ages of 3 to 5 years. Prejudiced *attitudes* generally appear between 3 and 4 years, while prejudiced *behavior* comes slightly later. There are few indications of prejudiced behavior before children are 4 years old (50, 58, 88, 107).

What is sometimes interpreted as prejudice may not actually be such. Instead, it may indicate *bias*, not *prejudice*. Children may *prefer* to be with other children whose background is similar to theirs because they feel more at home with them. This does not mean that they dislike members of another group or feel superior to them. Prejudice involves hostility and discrimination. If the preference is for others of one's own kind, without any hostility toward members of another group, the cleavage between the child and members of another group may be due to a "comfort differential"—a feeling of greater "at homeness" with one group than with another—but *not* to prejudice (19, 33).

Prejudices are not a part of the child's hereditary endowment. Instead, they are a product of social *learning*. Some prejudices are learned through *unpleasant experiences* with a person of a certain group. This conditions children to dislike not only that person but all who are identified with that person because of their group affiliation. Some prejudices come from an uncritical acceptance of the *cultural values* of the home and of the social group. When certain groups are segregated in school or in the community,

for example, children assume that they are inferior because society treats them as if they were. Or, if cultural values emphasize the inferiority or superiority of certain accents, age levels, or nationalities, children learn to think of them as inferior or superior. Most prejudices come from *imitating* the attitudes and behavior

Figure 9–5. Some ways in which prejudice is expressed among children.

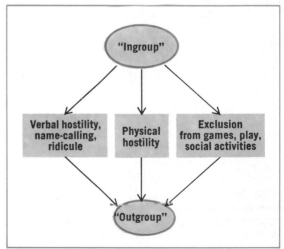

of parents, teachers, peers, neighbors, and characters in the mass media with whom children identify (50, 55, 63).

Few parents, teachers, or other adults actually *teach* children to be prejudiced. Their attitudes and behavior, however, their restrictions on playmate choice, and their tendency to stereotype—to attribute certain physical, behavioral, and mental characteristics to *all* individuals in a given racial or religious group—result in a pattern of prejudice which children imitate.

As children spend more and more time with the peer group, they "catch" some of their prejudices from the group members. In their desire to gain status in the group, older children accept the prejudices of the group because it is the "thing to do." In addition, prejudice gives the older child a *feeling of self-importance,*

Figure 9–6. A little boy may prefer to play with girls rather than with boys, provided he is not seen playing with them when other boys can tease him. (*Adapted from Hank Ketcham: "Dennis the Menace."* Field Newspaper Syndicate, *Nov. 20, 1970. Used by permission.*)

"I don't play with girls, Margaret . . ."

". . . Where people can see me!"

often serving as an outlet for frustration and thwarted aggression. Allport has said that prejudice may be a "psychological crutch" used by immature and psychologically crippled children, or it may come from a desire to conform to group expectations (3).

Almost anyone at any age may be the target of prejudice. In childhood, however, certain children are more likely to be the objects of prejudice than others. Traditionally, children from *minority groups,* whether the minority status be based on religion, race, nationality, socioeconomic level, or other conditions, are likely to be discriminated against.

Young children and *elderly adults* suffer more from childish prejudice than do older children and young adults. Children from *deprived areas* of cities are often the target of prejudice. Children with physical or mental *handicaps* face greater obstacles to social acceptance than members of minority groups. There is strong prejudice against a child who comes from a *deviant family* pattern, as in the case of illegitimacy or divorce (where divorice is relatively uncommon) or family stigmas arising from the socially disapproved behavior of some family member (10, 11, 50).

SEX ANTAGONISM Sex antagonism means an active, hostile opposition toward members of the opposite sex. It is popularly referred to as the "battle between the sexes."

In the early years of childhood, boys play with girls much as they did during babyhood; social harmony between the two is common. As late as the first, and sometimes the second, grade, boys *may* be willing to play with girls, provided the girls can keep up the pace the boys set. A boy may even prefer to play with some particular girl whom he especially likes. See Figure 9–6. Some boys at this time actually prefer girls' play activities, and some girls prefer boys' activities. These are exceptions, however. Most children during kindergarten and first grade begin to prefer persons—both children and adults—of their own sex. This tendency becomes more pronounced each year, reaching its peak just before and during puberty.

Because sex antagonism is a product of social pressures to play certain prescribed sex roles, how it develops and what effects it has on the personal and social adjustments of members of both sexes will be discussed in detail in the chapter on sex-role development. Although it is not exclusively a product of gang belonging in late childhood, there is ample evidence, as will be explained later, that children who belong to gangs normally develop more antagonism toward members of the opposite sex than do children who do not belong to a gang at this age.

Social Development at Puberty

With the beginning of puberty comes a change in social attitudes, a decline in interest in group activities, and a tendency to prefer solitude. As puberty progresses and the rate of puberty changes speeds up, social attitudes and behavior become increasingly antisocial.

Because of the antisocial behavior of this age, puberty is sometimes called the "negative phase" and a "period of disequilibrium." (Refer to Chapter 5 for an earlier discussion of the meaning of "negative phase.") These labels suggest that the child's attitude toward life is "anti"—that the child is negating some of the social characteristics developed so slowly and laboriously during the childhood years.

At this time, the pattern of social development is interrupted. Children are not, however, on a plateau in the continuum of social learning; instead they are skidding downward, often abruptly, from the point where they seemed close to the adult level. For most children, this interruption in the socialization process is only an interlude, unpleasant while it lasts but leaving few if any permanent scars.

Since the antisocial behavior of prepubescent or pubescent children is not the result of ignorance of social expectations, it cannot be called "unsocial." Typically, children know what society expects of them and have, in the latter part of childhood, conformed to those expectations. During puberty, children *intentionally* do the opposite of what is expected of them. They know, for example, that harassing younger children is regarded as poor sportsmanship, and yet they tease and bully younger siblings or neighborhood children.

Beginnings of Antisocial Behavior

It is impossible to predict exactly when antisocial behavior and attitudes will begin because there are such marked individual differences in the age of sexual maturing. On the average, however, puberty starts about a year earlier in girls than in boys. (See Chapter 5 for a more complete discussion of the age of sexual maturing.) The average age for the beginning of puberty changes in girls is 11 years, and in boys, 12 years. The first signs of antisocial behavior, therefore, can be expected at approximately these ages.

The worst aspects of antisocial behavior occur in the 6- to 12-month period preceding sexual maturity. This means, for girls, at some time between the twelfth and thirteenth birthdays, and for boys, between the thirteenth and fourteenth birthdays. After the peak has been reached, there is normally a rather rapid decline in antisocial behavior. Because girls, on the average, mature more rapidly than boys, the antisocial behavior characteristic of girls at this age is generally more pronounced than that of boys. Many boys, however, experience as pronounced reversals in their social development as girls.

After the worst of the negative phase has passed, with the advent of sexual maturity, young adolescents begin to climb upward again, slowly at first but then at increasing speed, motivated by a strong desire to be socially acceptable to the peer groups of both sexes. Whether the effects of the negative phase on future socialization will be left behind depends on many factors: when puberty occurs, how long it lasts, how closely it conforms to the norm of age-mates, and how parents, teachers, and peers treat children during this transitional period.

Causes of Antisocial Behavior

Without question, antisocial behavior at puberty is partly the result of rapid and far-reaching *physical* and *glandular changes*. A physical upheaval of the type that occurs during puberty could not occur without affecting behavior (25).

Antisocial behavior is also, perhaps to a very large degree, due to *environmental factors*. Since the child is beginning to look more like an adult—not only in size but also in body contour—parents and teachers decide that the time has come for the child to "put away childish things" and assume the responsibilities of maturity. The result is that new duties and responsibilities are assigned at a time when the child is not ready, physically, to assume them. Furthermore, after the carefree days of childhood, the child resents the sudden imposition of new duties and responsibilities and is likely to develop feelings of martyrdom. These feelings alone would be enough to lead to antisocial attitudes and behavior.

Feelings of martyrdom are most likely to occur when sexual maturing deviates markedly from that of age-mates, either in the time it occurs or in the time needed to complete it. Early-maturing children, for example, show characteristic negative-phase behavior sooner than their friends. Such behavior is met with intolerance because neither parents nor teachers expect or understand it.

Physical changes, accompanied by unfavorable physiological states, lead to self-concern and anxiety. Children who are excessively worried about themselves become excessively self-bound and thus unsocial.

Effects of Puberty Changes

Reversals in attitudes and behavior are almost inevitable at puberty. Sometimes the changes are so pronounced that children literally revert to behavior characteristic of the preschool years; sometimes they seem to be on the path to juvenile delinquency. In many respects, the changes seem worse than they actually are, partly because they follow so closely the socialized behavior characteristic of the gang age and partly because children who look almost like adults are judged by standards more in keeping with their size and general appearance than with their level of development. The most characteristic changes in social attitudes and behavior during the puberty period are given in Box 9–11.

CHANGES IN SELF-CONCEPT Studies of changes in self-concepts have revealed that children change their feelings about themselves as their bodies change and as the attitudes of significant people in their lives change. Studies of boys and girls from 9 to 13 years—when puberty changes are most rapid and their effects on behavior are most pronounced—show a downward trend in self-evaluation of intelligence, cooperativeness, generosity, sociability, popularity, and ability to be entertaining and amusing (1, 48).

CHANGES IN ATTITUDES AND BEHAVIOR The radical changes that occur at puberty, however devastating they may seem, are a normal part of the pattern of social development. Many kinds of antisocial behavior wane and disappear as sexual maturity is completed, and as the desire for social acceptance motivates young adolescents to conform to social expectations.

BOX 9–11

CHARACTERISTIC ATTITUDES AND BEHAVIOR AT PUBERTY

- Pubescent children sometimes have an antagonistic attitude toward everyone. They go around with chips on their shoulders and sneers on their faces.
- Pubescents are even more aggressive than preschoolers, instigating fights with peers and criticizing, arguing, and finding fault with almost everything adults do.
- Pubescents quarrel over the most trivial matters and pick fights with members of their gangs, criticizing whatever they do and delighting in hurting their feelings. As a result, many longstanding friendships are broken.
- According to pubescent children, social activities "bore" them, especially family gatherings and holiday celebrations.
- Pubescents spend much of their time in isolation, engaging in daydreams in which they play the role of martyrs or thinking about sex, exploring the genital organs, and masturbating.
- Pubescent children intentionally refuse to communicate with others except when necessary. When questioned, they shut out other people by answering, "I can't remember" or "I don't know."
- Pubescents are often shy in the presence of *all* people, not only strangers. Their shyness stems from anxiety over how others judge their changing bodies and their behavior. See Figure 9–7 for a graphic illustration of the puberty "shy age."

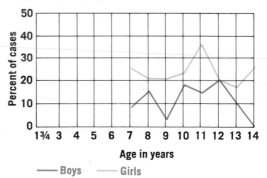

Figure 9-7. Shyness in childhood follows a different developmental pattern for boys and girls. (*Adapted from J. Macfarlane, L. Allen, and M. P. Honzik: A developmental study of the behavior problems of normal children between twenty-one months and fourteen years. University of California Press, 1954. Used by permission.*)

Even though they may have antagonized friends and alienated parents, teachers, and other adults while in the negative phase, their later behavior is so improved that ordinarily they are forgiven.

Deviant sexual development, however, often results in individual variations that are difficult to overcome. Early maturers show exaggerated forms of antisocial behavior earlier than average-maturing children for that age primarily because they cannot convince their parents and teachers that they want to be treated in accordance with their level of physical maturity, not in accordance with their chronological ages.

Children who lag behind their age-mates in sexual maturing—the late maturers—are usually treated by both age-mates and adults in accordance with their physical appearance rather than their chronological ages or academic status. People treat them like children because they look like children. In their fight to gain the status they feel they deserve, they often develop antisocial attitudes and patterns of behavior. The longer they lag behind in sexual maturing, the longer they reinforce their immature feelings and behavior through repetition (48).

Hazards in Social Development

In few areas are there more, and more serious, hazards to normal development than in the area of socialization. If social behavior falls below social expectations, it endangers children's acceptance by the group. When this happens, it deprives children of opportunities to learn to be social, with the result that their socialization falls further and further below that of their age-mates.

When their behavior falls below social expectations, children are judged unfavorably and this results in unfavorable self-judgments. The further children fall below the standards and expectations of the social group, the more damaging it is to their personal and social adjustments and the more unfavorable their self-concepts will be.

The most common hazards to socialization are discussed in the following pages. Each of these is controllable and, consequently, can be prevented.

Social Deprivation

Social deprivation means being deprived of opportunities to associate with people and, as a result, of oppor-

tunities to learn to be a social person. This deprivation may come from the fact that parents and other family members have too little time to devote to babies and, hence, babies lack the stimulation that provides the motivation to try to become parts of the family group. As they grow older, they may be deprived of opportunities to associate with children of their own ages because of geographic isolation or because their parents are afraid that contact with children outside the home will result in their children's "picking up germs." Or, children may have found their early social experiences, either in or outside the home, so unpleasant that they have little interest in contacts with people.

Regardless of what causes social deprivation, it encourages the prolongation of egocentrism, characteristic of all babies, and the tendency toward introversion. Once these unsocial tendencies develop, it is difficult to change them and to encourage the development of more social attitudes and behavior. That is why, as was stressed earlier, the babyhood years are the foundation years for socialization.

Social deprivation of *short* duration, especially as children grow older, tends to increase their motivation to win the attention and affection of others. If, for example, children are sent to their rooms for behaving in a socially unacceptable way, they will realize that it is to their personal advantage to behave in a more social way in the future if they want to avoid the social isolation of punishment and if they want to enjoy doing things with other family members.

On the other hand, *prolonged* social deprivation not only encourages introversion but it also makes children afraid to try to establish social contacts, should they be given the opportunity later. Because they feel inadequate to do things with others, they continue to isolate themselves from them.

Too Much Social Participation

Just because lack of opportunities for social contacts is hazardous to socialization does not mean that the more children participate in activities with others, the better socialized they will be. In fact, too much social participation is almost as hazardous to good socialization as too little participation.

Too much social participation may be harmful because it deprives children of opportunities to develop their inner resources, which will enable them to be happy when circumstances force them to be alone.

They will feel "lost" when they are not able to be with others and do things with them.

Under such conditions, they will tend to become indiscriminately sociable in the sense that they will want to be with others merely for the sake of social contacts regardless of congeniality of interests. This does not develop healthy social attitudes. Even worse, children who crave companionship of any kind just to avoid being alone become unstable in their interests and values. They change their interests and even their personalities to suit those of the adults or peers with whom they are associated in the hopes of winning their acceptance. They thus tend to be highly suggestible and easily influenced by anyone with whom they come in contact.

Because all children are different and have different social needs, there can be no set rule for too much social participation. On the other hand, it is possible to tell, from children's attitudes and behavior, if they are participating too much in social activities. If children are unhappy when alone, if they will play with anyone who is willing to play with them, and if they seem to be more conforming in their behavior than is usual for their ages and levels of development, that is fairly accurate evidence that their social participation is becoming a hazard to good socialization.

Overdependency

Babies and young children are, of necessity, dependent on others. Normally, children want to be independent as soon as they are developmentally ready to learn to be independent. Consequently, if they continue to be dependent on others—adults or age-mates—beyond the time when their age-mates are becoming independent, it will become a hazard to good personal and social adjustments. They will feel that they are inferior to their age-mates because they are unable to be as independent as they are, and in turn their age-mates will regard them as "babies" who are "tied to parental apron strings." This will jeopardize their acceptance as playmates by members of the peer group and thus further increase their feelings of inadequacy and inferiority.

In time, the tendency to depend on others leads to a generalized state in which children depend on anyone who is available, whether an adult or another child. They become highly suggestible and easily influenced by others. Even worse, they become afraid to be independent in their behavior and thinking because they

have never learned to be independent in similar situations when they were younger.

While any child may become overdependent, if brought up in a home environment where independence is discouraged, overdependency is especially common in children who suffer from some chronic disease, such as asthma or diabetes, and in firstborns who are far more likely to be encouraged to be dependent than their later-born siblings.

Overconformity

All children discover, sooner or later, that the social group judges and then accepts them on the basis of their willingness or ability to come up to its expectations. Older children, who are especially anxious to be accepted by the peer group, often overconform in the hopes that this will guarantee their acceptance.

However, this often defeats their purpose. Instead of judging them favorably, the group tends to regard them as "weak" or "spineless" because they lack even a reasonable amount of independence. In addition, overconformity results in a loss of individuality and this makes children seem so colorless and nondescript that they are neglected and overlooked by their peers because they seem to have nothing to offer to the group.

Overconformity is, thus, not only a hazard to good social adjustments but it is also a hazard to good personal adjustments. Children cannot have favorable opinions of themselves when they know that the group has an unfavorable opinion of them.

Nonconformity

Nonconformity, or failure to conform to group expectations, can be just as hazardous to good personal and social adjustments as overconformity. Children who do not conform to the accepted pattern of behavior of the group find themselves as social outcasts. As a result, they are not only deprived of the satisfaction of being members of a group but they are also deprived of the learning experiences which can come only from group belonging.

There are two common causes of nonconformity in childhood. *First,* children may not have the motivation to conform. Either they derive too little satisfaction from group activities or they find other activities than those of the group more satisfying. *Second,* they may lack the knowledge of what the group expects or how to fulfill these expectations. Children who have, for one reason or another, been deprived of pregang experience are ignorant of what their peers expect when they reach the gang age. By contrast, children whose home training stresses the values of the group, such as good sportsmanship and fair play, emphasizes the importance of reasonable conformity to group expectations, and provides good models to imitate—either parents or older siblings—will not find it difficult to learn to conform.

The only way nonconformists can improve their status in the group is to sacrifice some of their individualism and learn to conform, even if they do not wholeheartedly approve of the group expectations. If being individualists means more to them than social acceptance, they must be prepared to pay the price for individuality. If, on the other hand, being accepted by the group means more, they must be willing to pay the price demanded by the social group—conformity.

A slight deviation from accepted patterns of behavior, provided the group regards it as superior to the accepted pattern, not only is accepted but may even be imitated. Leaders, as will be pointed out in the next chapter, are neither extreme conformists nor extreme nonconformists. They do, it is true, deviate slightly from the accepted patterns of the group and, by so doing, they offer the group something new and interesting, which puts them in the limelight of attention.

Even more hazardous to good personal and social adjustments is *anticonformity*—choosing behavior patterns that are diametrically opposite to those approved by the group. Anticonformity almost always guarantees social rejection and social scorn. At no age is a rugged individualist accepted. If a person does not want to conform to group standards, the group does not want to accept that person as a member.

Prejudice

Prejudice is hazardous to children who are prejudiced, just as it is to their victims, though in a different way. Children who are prejudiced often become cruel, intolerant, rigid, and vindictive—traits which may become habitual and affect their relationships with people against whom they have no prejudice. Children who are the victims of prejudice come to believe that the social environment is hostile and that no one likes them. They are often subjected to teasing, bullying, and physical aggression and are either rejected or neglected. Some children who are victims of prejudice

withdraw from the group, or they may become excessively aggressive in their defensive reactions. Others turn their hostility against society in general and often develop into troublemakers or even juvenile delinquents. In time, prejudice distorts their personality patterns just as it distorts the personality patterns of children who are prejudiced (3).

The more aware children are of the prejudice people direct against them, the more damaged they will be psychologically. Being referred to as "niggers" or "kikes" leaves no question in children's minds about the group's attitudes toward them. Similarly, being discriminated against in an integrated school communicates to children that they are regarded as inferior.

Because prejudice is hazardous to good personal and social adjustments at all ages, many attempts have been made to prevent prejudice from developing in childhood or to modify it if it has already started to develop. This has been done by bringing children together so that they can get to know one another better. If prejudice is based on stereotyped beliefs, personal contact might correct the stereotype and thus reduce the prejudice. If it is based on unfavorable personal experiences, however, or if the contact is involuntary, as in many desegregated schools, personal contacts will not necessarily reduce the prejudice. They may even intensify it, especially in the short run (12, 36, 89, 105).

Helping children to develop better social insight about people against whom they are prejudiced by explaining why they are different may help to reduce prejudice (5). This has been done with some success through the use of multiethnic or "integrated" readers for elementary school children—readers which contain characters from different racial or ethnic groups—which show children of different backgrounds living, playing, and working together harmoniously in the same community setting. Similar attempts have also been made by showing minority children in important roles in comics and on television (40, 58, 107, 111).

Even in the absence of direct contact with children of other racial or ethnic groups, children who are prejudiced have been reported to develop greater insight and to develop more favorable attitudes after exposure to such stories and programs. However, there is no evidence, to date, that this exposure will necessarily replace prejudiced attitudes with a liking for members of minority groups (8, 103).

Since most prejudice in children comes not from personal contacts but from "social contagion," the most effective way of combating it is to make prejudice unfashionable. Children cannot be expected to have tolerant attitudes as long as members of the peer group approve intolerance. Children will not modify their prejudice until the rest of the group leads the way.

Peer-group prejudice is learned by social contagion from adult groups—mainly from parents—and children cannot be expected to modify their attitudes as long as they have a constant pattern of prejudice to imitate in their homes. Thus far, efforts to reduce prejudice have made little headway; the hopes of eliminating it completely are still very dim.

Pubescent Antisocial Behavior

Not only do children lose ground in their social development during puberty, but they also injure their social adjustments, their self-concepts, and their reputations among peers, family members, and teachers by their behavior.

Most children are able to counteract the harm they have done and resume the upward trend in the curve of socialization with no permanent damage. As with any setback, however, more effort and time are necessary than would be required had the setback not occurred. There are three important reasons for this in the case of antisocial pubescent behavior.

First, the most difficult aspect of the upward climb is the rebuilding of broken friendships. Most pubescent quarrels with peers are verbal. A psychological hurt conditions a child to have an unfavorable attitude toward the person who inflicted the pain, even though the child may forget the circumstances under which it was inflicted.

Second, negative phase behavior gives children a bad reputation. If their social milieu could be changed after the negative phase ended and if they could bury their unfavorable reputations and establish new friendships, the matter would not be so serious. But most children continue to live in the same neighborhood, attend the same school, and associate with the same people as they did during the negative phase. The job of building a new reputation is especially difficult because pubescent children have behaved antisocially in so many groups that their bad reputations are widely known.

Third, the upward climb is steepest for deviant maturers because they have a longer time to establish antisocial habits and acquire unfavorable reputations. In addition, deviant maturers are subjected to greater criticism and disapproval from every social group than their age-mates are. Social criticism and disapproval at any age lead to poor self-acceptance. Thus, deviant maturers must add to the other tasks of improving their social adjustments that of improving their self-concepts. The task is never easy, especially when a poor reputation makes social acceptance difficult.

Antisocial behavior at times other than at puberty, however, is serious. This is partly because it comes from causes other than physical, as does the antisocial behavior that accompanies the physical upheaval of puberty, and partly because it is likely to develop into a habit and be intensified at the time of puberty. Children who engage in antisocial behavior often develop into juvenile delinquents as they grow older. This is rarely true of the antisocial behavior that starts at puberty.

Chapter Highlights

1 Whether children develop into social, nonsocial, or antisocial people depends mainly on learning, not on heredity as tradition claims.

2 The three processes of socialization consist of learning to behave in a socially approved way, playing approved sex roles, and developing social attitudes.

3 The social group influences children's social development by encouraging them to conform to social expectations, by helping them to achieve independence, and by influencing their self-concepts.

4 What the social group expects in social behavior varies somewhat from one group to another, but all groups expect children to master the developmental tasks appropriate for their age levels.

5 Early social experiences, both inside and outside the home, are important in determining whether children want to be social, unsocial, or antisocial.

6 It is important to know that the pattern of social development is similar for all children because it makes it possible to predict what behavior to expect at different ages and it provides a schedule for training social skills and attitudes.

7 Social development begins early in childhood with the appearance of social smiling. The first social responses of babies are to adults and later, to other babies and children. The patterns of social behavior laid at this time form the foundations for later social development.

8 Early childhood is known as the "pregang age" because, at this time, children are learning to adjust to peers and to develop patterns of behavior that conform to social expectations.

9 There are a number of patterns of behavior in social situations during early childhood which, according to adult standards, are unsocial. However, they are valuable learning experiences because they show children what members of the social group will tolerate and what will lead to social approval and disapproval.

10 Social development during the gang age of late childhood helps children who are gang members to learn socially approved patterns of behavior, and this is an asset to the development of favorable self-concepts. Children who are not gang members are deprived of this socializing influence and are likely to develop unfavorable self-concepts.

11 Many of the patterns of behavior developed during the pregang period serve as foundations for the patterns developed during the gang age. However,

some of them, both social—such as good sportsmanship, responsibility, and cooperation—and unsocial—such as prejudice, discrimination, and sex antagonism—are intensified as a result of peer pressures.

12 Unsocial and antisocial behavior patterns develop during puberty. Most of these tend to be temporary and are replaced by more socially approved patterns after the radical physical changes of puberty are completed.

13 There are many hazards to social development, most of which are controllable if they are recognized in time and if remedial steps are taken to change them before they become habitual and lead to unfavorable reputations.

14 Among the less serious hazards in social development are social deprivation, too much social participation, overdependency, overconformity and nonconformity. These are likely to be corrected when children become gang members.

15 The most serious hazards in social development are prejudice and antisocial pubescent behavior, because they lead to unfavorable self-concepts and reputations. Deviant sexual maturing is especially hazardous to good socialization because its effects on personal and social adjustments tend to be persistent.

Bibliography

1 Adams, J. F. (ed.) *Understanding adolescence: Current developments in adolescent psychology,* 2d ed. Boston: Allyn & Bacon, 1973.

2 Ainsworth, M. D. S., S. M. Bell, and D. J. Stayton. Individual differences in the development of some attachment behaviors. *Merrill-Palmer Quarterly,* 1972, *18,* 123–143.

3 Allport, G. W. *The nature of prejudice.* Reading, Mass.: Addison-Wesley, 1954.

4 Anderson, S., and S. Messick. Social competency in young children. *Developmental Psychology,* 1974, *10,* 282–293.

5 Ayres, M. Counteracting racial stereotypes in preschool children. *Graduate Research in Education and Related Disciplines,* 1973, *6,* 55–74.

6 Baldwin, A. L., C. P. Baldwin, I. R. Hilton, and N. W. Lambert. The measurement of social expectations and their development in children. *Monographs of the Society for Research in Child Development,* 1969, *34*(4).

7 Baldwin, C. P., and A. L. Baldwin Children's judgments of kindness. *Child Development,* 1970, *41,* 29–47.

8 Best, D. L., S. C. Smith, D. J. Graves, and J. E. Williams. The modification of racial bias in preschool children. *Journal of Experimental Child Psychology,* 1975, *20,* 193–205.

9 Borke, H. The development of empathy in Chinese and American children between three and six years of age: A cross-cultural study. *Developmental Psychology,* 1973, *9,* 102–108.

10 Bossard, J. H. S., and E. S. Boll. *The sociology of child development,*

4th ed. New York: Harper & Row, 1966.

11 Brown, A. R. (ed.) *Prejudice in children.* Springfield, Ill.: Charles C Thomas, 1972.

12 Brown, G. A. An exploratory study of interaction among British and immigrant children. *British Journal of Social and Clinical Psychology,* 1973, *12,* 159–162.

13 Bryan, J. H., and N. H. Walbek. The impact of words and deeds concerning altruism upon children. *Child Development,* 1970, *41,* 747–757.

14 Cantor, G. N., and C. E. Paternite. A follow-up study of race awareness using a conflict paradigm. *Child Development,* 1973, *44,* 859–861.

15 Carpenter, J. C., J. J. Tecce, G. Stechler, and S. Friedman. Differential behavior to human and humanoid faces in early infancy.

Merrill-Palmer Quarterly, 1970, *16,* 91–108.

16 Coates, B., E. P. Anderson, and W. W. Hartup. The stability of attachment behaviors in the human infant. *Developmental Psychology,* 1972, *6,* 231–237.

17 Cohen, R., R. Bornstenin, and R. C. Sherman. Conformity behavior of children as a function of group makeup and task ambiguity. *Developmental Psychology,* 1973, *9,* 124–131.

18 Cohen, S. Peers as modeling and normative influences in the development of aggression. *Psychological Reports,* 1971, *28,* 995–998.

19 Cook, H., and D. W. Smothergill. Racial and sex determinants of imitative performance and knowledge in young children. *Journal of Educational Psychology,* 1973, *65,* 211–215.

20 Cook, H., and S. Stingle. Cooperative behavior in children. *Psychological Bulletin,* 1974, *81,* 918–933.

21 Coudry, J., and M. L. Siman. Characteristics of peer- and adult-oriented children. *Journal of Marriage and the Family,* 1974, *36,* 543–554.

22 Denzin, N. K. Play, games and interaction: The contexts of childhood socialization. *Sociological Quarterly,* 1975, *16,* 458–478.

23 Dodge, N., and G. A. Muench. Relationship of conformity and the need for approval in children. *Developmental Psychology,* 1969, *1,* 67–68.

24 Dorman, L. Assertive behavior and cognitive performance in preschool children. *Journal of Genetic Psychology,* 1973, *123,* 155–162.

25 Dunbar, F. Homeostasis during puberty. *American Journal of Psychiatry,* 1958, *114,* 673–683.

26 Emmerich, W. Continuity and stability in early social development. II. Teachers' ratings. *Child Development,* 1966, *37,* 17–27.

27 Escalona, S. K. Basic modes of social interaction: Their emergence and patterning during the first two years of life. *Merrill-Palmer Quarterly,* 1973, *19,* 205–232.

28 Feigenbaum, K. D., D. Geiger and S. Crevoshay. An exploratory study of 3-, 5-, and 7-year old females' comprehension of cooperative and uncooperative social interaction.

Journal of Genetic Psychology, 1970, *116,* 141–148.

29 Fein, G. G. The effect of chronological age and model reward on imitative behavior. *Developmental Psychology,* 1973, *9,* 283–289.

30 Ferguson, L. R. Origins of social development in infancy. *Merrill-Palmer Quarterly,* 1971, *17,* 119–137.

31 Feshbach, N. D., and S. Feshbach. The relationship between empathy and aggression in two age groups. *Developmental Psychology,* 1969, *1,* 102–107.

32 Fouts, G., and P. Liikanen. The effects of age and developmental level on imitation in children. *Child Development,* 1975, *46,* 555–558.

33 Fox, D. J., and V. B. Jordan. Racial preference and identification in black, American Chinese and white children. *Genetic Psychology Monographs,* 1973, *88,* 229–286.

34 Friedland, S. J. The development of role concepts. *Journal of Genetic Psychology,* 1973, *122,* 81–88.

35 Friedman, S. T. Relation of parental attitudes toward child rearing and patterns of social behavior in middle childhood. *Psychological Reports,* 1969, *24,* 575–579.

36 Fulcher, D., and D. G. Perry. Cooperation and competition in interethnic evaluation in preschool children. *Psychological Reports,* 1973, *33,* 795–800.

37 Galejs, I. Social interaction of preschool children. *Home Economics Research Journal,* 1974, *2,* 153–159.

38 Garvey, C., and R. Hogan. Social speech and social interaction: Egocentrism revisited. *Child Development,* 1973, *44,* 562–568.

39 Gingrich, D. H. Sex, grade level and religious-educational environment as factors in peer conformity. *Journal of Genetic Psychology,* 1973, *123,* 321–328.

40 Gorn, G. J., M. E. Goldberg, and R. N. Kanugo. The role of educational television in changing the intergroup attitudes of children. *Child Development,* 1976, *47,* 227–280.

41 Green, F. P., and F. W. Schneider. Age differences in the behavior of boys on three measures of altruism. *Child Development,* 1974, *45,* 248–251.

42 Greenberg, D. J., D. Hillman, and

D. Grice. Infant and stranger variables related to stranger anxiety in the first year of life. *Developmental Psychology,* 1973, *9,* 207–212.

43 Guilford, J. S. Maturation of values in young children. *Journal of Genetic Psychology,* 1974, *124,* 241–248.

44 Hartup, W. W. Aggression in childhood: Developmental perspectives. *American Psychologist,* 1974, *29,* 336–341.

45 Havinghurst, R. J. *Developmental tasks and education,* 3d ed. New York: McKay, 1972.

46 Isen, A. M., N. Horn, and D. L. Rosenham. Effects of success and failure on children's generosity. *Journal of Personality and Social Psychology,* 1973, *27,* 239–247.

47 Jennings, K. D. People versus object orientation, social behavior and intellectual abilities in preschool children. *Developmental Psychology,* 1975, *11,* 511–519.

48 Jones, M. C. Psychological correlates of somatic development. *Child Development,* 1965, *36,* 899–911.

49 Kagan, J., and H. A. Moss. *Birth to maturity: A study in psychological development.* New York: Wiley, 1962.

50 Katz, P. A., I. Katz, and S. Cohen. White children's attitudes toward Blacks and the physically handicapped: A developmental study. *Journal of Educational Psychology,* 1976, *68,* 20–24.

51 Katz, P. A., and S. R. Zalk. Doll preferences: An index of racial attitudes. *Journal of Educational Psychology,* 1974, *66,* 663–668.

52 Knox, W. E., and H. J. Kapferer. A discontinuity in the socialization of males in the United States. *Merrill-Palmer Quarterly,* 1971, *17,* 251–261.

53 Koch, H. L. The relation of certain formal attributes of siblings to attitudes held toward each other and toward their parents. *Monographs of the Society for Research in Child Development,* 1960, *25*(4).

54 Langlois, J. H., N. W. Gottfried, and B. Seay. The influence of sex of peer on the social behavior of preschool children. *Developmental Psychology,* 1973, *8,* 93–98.

55 Lerner, R. M., and C. J. Buehrig. The development of racial attitudes

in young black and white children. *Journal of Genetic Psychology*, 1975, *127*, 45–54.

56 Levine, L. E., and M. L. Hoffman. Empathy and cooperation in 4-year-olds. *Developmental Psychology*, 1975, *11*, 533–534.

57 Lewis, M. Infants' responses to facial stimuli during the first year of life. *Developmental Psychology*, 1969, *1*, 75–86.

58 Lichter, J., and D. W. Johnson. Changes in attitudes toward Negroes of white elementary school students after use of multiethnic readers. *Journal of Educational Psychology*, 1969, *60*, 148–152.

59 Loeb, R. C. Empathy and cooperation in 4-year-olds. *Developmental Psychology*, 1975, *11*, 533–534.

60 Maccoby, E. E., and S. S. Feldman. Mother-attachment and stranger reactions in the third year of life. *Monographs of the Society for Research in Child Development*, 1972, *37* (1).

61 Marshall, H. R. Relations between home experiences and children's use of language in play interactions with peers. *Psychological Monographs*, 1961, *75* (5).

62 Masters, J. C. Effects of social companion upon the imitation of neutral and altruistic behaviors by young children. *Child Development*, 1972, *43*, 131–142.

63 Maykovich, M. K. Correlates of racial prejudice. *Journal of Personality and Social Psychology*, 1975, *32*, 1014–1020.

64 McRae, K. N., and S. G. Lowe. Aggressive behavior in the preschool child. *Journal of Pediatrics*, 1968, *72*, 821–828.

65 Mithaug, D. E. The development of procedures for identifying competitive behavior in children. *Journal of Experimental Child Psychology*, 1973, *16*, 76–90.

66 Nias, D. K. The structuring of social attitudes in children. *Child Development*, 1972, *43*, 211–219.

67 Olpin, M., and K. L. Kogan. Child meets child: Social interaction between school-age boys. *Perceptual and Motor Skills*, 1969, *28*, 151–154.

68 Paluszny, N., and R. Gibson. Twin interactions in a normal nursery school. *American Journal of Psychiatry*, 1974, *131*, 293–296.

69 Parachse, E., and F. Curcio. Relationship of cognitive and affective behaviors to fear of strangers in male infants. *Developmental Psychology*, 1974, *10*, 476–483.

70 Pasternack, T. L. Qualitative differences in development of yielding behavior by elementary school children. *Psychological Reports*, 1975, *32*, 883–896.

71 Reuter, J., and G. Yunik. Social interaction in nursery school. *Developmental Psychology*, 1973, *9*, 319–325.

72 Rheingold, H. L., and C. O. Eckerman. The infant separates himself from his mother. In W. R. Looft (ed.), *Developmental psychology: A book of readings.* Hinsdale, Ill.; Dryden Press, 1972. Pp. 271–288.

73 Richardson, S. A., and A. Green. When is black beautiful? Colored and white children's reactions to skin color. *British Journal of Educational Psychology*, 1971, *41*, 62–69.

74 Richmond, B. O., and G. P. Weiner. Cooperation and competition among young children as a function of ethnic grouping, grade, sex and reward condition. *Journal of Educational Psychology*, 1973, *64*, 329–334.

75 Rosenfeld, H. M., and P. Gunnell. Effects of peer characteristics on preschool performance of low-income children. *Merrill-Palmer Quarterly*, 1973, *19*, 81–94.

76 Ross, S. H. The effects of increasing familiarity on infants' reactions to adult strangers. *Journal of Experimental Child Psychology*, 1975, *20*, 226–239.

77 Rubin, K. H. Egocentrism in childhood: A unitary construct? *Child Development*, 1973, *44*, 102–110.

78 Rubin, K. H., and F. W. Schneider. The relationship between moral judgment, egocentrism, and altruistic behavior. *Child Development*, 1973, *44*, 661–665.

79 Rushton, J. P. Generosity in children: Immediate and long-term effects of modeling, preaching and moral judgment. *Journal of Personality and Social Psychology*, 1975, *31*, 459–466.

80 Rushton, J. P., and J. Wiener. Altruism and congitive development in children. *British Journal of Social and Clinical Psychology*, 1975, *14*, 341–349.

81 Scarr, S. Social introversion-extroversion as a heritable response. *Child Development*, 1969, *40*, 823–832.

82 Schroeer, R. S., and D. Flapan. Assessing aggressive and friendly behavior in young children. *Journal of Psychology*, 1971, *77*, 193–202.

83 Schwarz, A. C., R. G. Strickland. and G. Kowlick. Infant day care: Behavior effects at preschool age. *Developmental Psychology*, 1974, *10*, 502–506.

84 Sears, R. R. Relation of early socialization experiences to self-concepts and gender role in middle childhood. *Child Development*, 1970, *41*, 267–289.

85 Shantz, D. W., and T. Pentz. Situational effects on justifiableness of aggression at three age levels. *Child Development*, 1972, *43*, 274–281.

86 Siegelman, M. "Origins" of extraversion-introversion. *Journal of Psychology*, 1968, *69*, 85–91.

87 Simner, M. L. Newborns' response to the cry of another infant. *Developmental Psychology*, 1971, *5*, 136–150.

88 Singh, J. M., and A. V. Yancey. Racial attitudes in white first grade children. *Journal of Educational Research*, 1974, *67*, 370–372.

89 Spencer, M. D., and F. D. Horowitz. Effects of systematic social and token reinforcement on the modification of racial and color concept attitudes in black and white preschool children. *Developmental Psychology*, 1973, *9*, 246–254.

90 Stabler, J. R., and E. E. Johnson. The meaning of black and white to children. *International Journal of Symbology*, 1972, *3*, 11–21.

91 Staub, E., and L. Sherk. Need for approval, children's sharing behavior, and reciprocity in sharing. *Child Development*, 1970, *41*, 243–252.

92 Strassberg, D. S. and E. Wiggen. Conformity as a function of age in preadolescents. *Journal of Social Psychology*, 1973, *91*, 61–66.

93 Tantermannová, M. Smiling in infants. *Child Development*, 1973, *44*, 701–704.

94 Taylor, S. P., and R. Pisano. Physi-

cal aggression as a function of frustration and physical attack. *Journal of Social Psychology,* 1971, *84,* 261–267.

95 Thompson, W. R., and J. E. Grusec. Studies of early experience. In P. H. Mussen (ed.), *Carmichael's manual of child psychology,* 3d ed. New York: Wiley, 1970. Vol. 1, pp. 465–654.

96 Tierney, M. C., and K. H. Rubin. Egocentrism and conformity in childhood. *Journal of Genetic Psychology,* 1975, *126,* 209–218.

97 Tulkin, S. R. Social class differences in attachment behaviors of ten-month-old infants. *Child Development,* 1973, *44,* 171–174.

98 Turnure, C. Response to voice of mother and stranger by babies in the first year. *Developmental Psychology,* 1971, *4,* 182–190.

99 Uttech, D. A., and K. L. Hoving. Parents and peers as competing influences in the decisions of children of different ages. *Journal of Social Psychology,* 1969, *78,* 267–274.

100 Waldrop, M. F., and C. F. Halverson. Intensive and extensive peer behavior: Longitudinal and cross-sectional analyses. *Child Development,* 1974, *45,* 19–26.

101 Ward, S. H., and J. Braun. Self-esteem and racial preference in black children. *American Journal of Orthopsychiatry,* 1972, *42,* 664–647.

102 Warner, L. G., and R. M. Dennis. Prejudice versus discrimination: An empirical example and theoretical extension. *Social Forces,* 1970, *48,* 473–484.

103 Williams, J. E., D. L. Best, and D. A. Boswell. The measurement of children's racial attitudes in the early school years. *Child Development,* 1975, *46,* 494–500.

104 Williams, K. H., J. F. Williams, and R. C. Beck. Assessing children's racial attitudes via a signal detection model. *Perceptual and Motor Skills,* 1973, *36,* 587–598.

105 Williams, R. L., W. H. Cormier, G. L. Sapp, and H. B. Andrews. The utility of behavior management techniques in changing interracial behaviors. *Journal of Psychology,* 1971, *77,* 127–138.

106 Yarrow, M. R., P. M. Scott, and C. Z. Waxler. Learning concern for others. *Developmental Psychology,* 1973, *8,* 240–260.

107 Yawkey, T. D., and J. Blackwell. Attitudes of 4-year-old black children toward themselves and whites based upon multi-ethnic social studies materials and experiences. *Journal of Educational Research,* 1974, *67,* 373–377.

108 Young, R. D. Children's perception of emotion and empathic responses. *Perceptual and Motor Skills,* 1974, *38,* 971–976.

109 Zahner, D. Suggestibility in relation to school grades, sex, and source of influence. *Journal of Genetic Psychology,* 1970, *116,* 203–209.

110 Zelazo, P. R. Smiling to social stimuli: Eliciting and conditioning effects. *Developmental Psychology,* 1971, *4,* 32–42.

111 Zimmerman, B. J., and G. H. Brody. Race and modeling influences on the interpersonal play patterns of boys. *Journal of Educational Psychology,* 1975, *67,* 591–598.

CHAPTER 10

CHAPTER 10

SOCIAL ADJUSTMENTS

In American culture today, parents and teachers are concerned about the kind of social adjustments children make. To them, the child's popularity or lack of it is so important that they do everything within their power to help the child to be a socially acceptable member of the peer group.

Most parents realize that there is a close relationship between a child's social adjustments and success and happiness in childhood as well as in later life. To ensure that their children will make good social adjustments, they provide them with opportunities to have social contacts with other children, and they try to motivate them to be socially active, hoping that this will lead to good social adjustments. See Figure 10–1.

Furthermore, they believe that a child who makes good social adjustments will be laying the foundations for success in adult life. If the child is well accepted by peers, they believe, it will result in behavior patterns and attitudes that will lead to a successful marriage and will be a stepping-stone to success in the vocational world, which will lead to upward social mobility.

Teachers are concerned about the social adjustments of their students because they know that well-accepted children are far more likely to do work in keeping with their capacities than are those who are rejected or ignored by their classmates. Furthermore, they are less disruptive in the classroom and far less likely to become truants and dropouts than those who make poor social adjustments.

Concern about the child's social adjustments on the part of parents and teachers is justified for two reasons. *First,* patterns of behavior and attitudes, formed early, tend to persist. Children who make good social adjustments in the first grade, for example, are far more likely to make good social adjustments when they reach high school and college than are children who make poor social adjustments during the first year of school. This, of course, does not mean that children who make a poor start will not improve their social adjustments as they grow older. But doing so will be a long and difficult task and the chances of success are far less than if better foundations had been laid during the preschool years.

Second, the kind of social adjustments children make leaves its mark on their self-concepts. This, likewise, contributes to the persistence of the pattern of social adjustments. Children, for example, who make poor social adjustments are unhappy and learn to dislike themselves. As a result, they often develop into self-centered, introverted, unsocial, or even antisocial individuals whose adult happiness and success are seriously jeopardized.

Figure 10–1. Because they believe that participation in social activities will guarantee good social adjustments, many parents urge their children to be socially active. (*Adapted from George Lichty and Fred Wagner: "Grin and Bear It."* Field Newspaper Syndicate, *Feb. 12, 1975. Used by permission.*)

"What are you doing in here studying? . . . You should be outside playing ball!"

Meaning of Social Adjustment

Social adjustment means the success with which people adjust to other people in general and to the group with which they are identified in particular. Well-adjusted people have learned such social skills as the ability to deal diplomatically with others—both friends and strangers—so that others' attitudes toward them will be favorable. People who make good social adjustments usually develop favorable social attitudes, such as a willingness to help others, even if they are personally inconvenienced. They are not self-bound.

Children are *expected* to become better adjusted to social life with each passing year and to conform to social expectations for their ages. No one expects babies to be well-adjusted people; they are too self-bound to consider others and too ignorant of social expectations to know how to conform to socially approved patterns of behavior. As children grow older, however, they are judged more critically.

Criteria of Social Adjustment

To determine how well adjusted children are socially, four criteria can be applied; any one alone is inadequate. Those four criteria are given in Box 10–1.

The first two criteria—overt performance and the ability to adjust to various groups—can be applied fairly successfully. Objective techniques of assessing attitudes and satisfactions, however, are more difficult to apply successfully. Children, for example, can be *asked* what their attitudes toward people are and how much they like social activities or their attitudes and satisfactions can be *inferred* from what they say about themselves, about other people, and about social activities. But one can never be sure that what they say is a true reflection of their attitudes. Children may say that they do not want to go out to play with other children because their play is boring or that they would rather stay at home and read or watch television. The obvious inference is that they derive less satisfaction from social then from solitary activities.

However, to be sure that their behavior or their statements reflect their real attitudes, one must observe children over a long enough period of time to see if there is a consistent pattern of behavior. When children claim, day after day, that they do not want to go out to play with other children but prefer to do things at home, there is little question about the fact that they have developed unfavorable social attitudes.

Difficulties in Making Good Social Adjustments

Making good social adjustments is far from easy. As a result, many children are poorly adjusted both socially and personally. Their childhood is unhappy, and unless they learn how to overcome their difficulties, they will grow up to be unhappy, maladjusted adults.

Many conditions contribute to the difficulties children experience in making good social adjustments, but four are paramount.

First, if poor patterns of social behavior are developed in the home, children will find it difficult to make

BOX 10–1

CRITERIA OF SOCIAL ADJUSTMENT

- *Overt performance.* When children's social behavior, as judged by the standards of the group with which they are identified, comes up to group expectations, they will be accepted members of the group.

- *Adjustment to different groups.* Children who can adjust reasonably well to the different groups with which they come in contact—adult as well as peer groups—are regarded as socially well adjusted.

- *Social attitudes.* Children must exhibit favorable attitudes toward people, toward social participation, and toward their roles in the social group if they are to be judged as socially well adjusted.

- *Personal satisfaction.* To be socially well adjusted, children must be reasonably satisfied with their social contacts and with the roles they play in social situations, whether that of leader or follower.

good social adjustments outside the home, even though they may be strongly motivated to do so. Children brought up by authoritarian methods, for example, frequently develop attitudes of resentment toward all in authority. With too permissive training in the home, children come to disregard the wishes of others, feeling that they can be laws unto themselves.

Second, if the home provides poor models for children to imitate, they will be seriously handicapped in their social adjustments outside the home. Children who are rejected by parents or who imitate deviant parental behavior may develop unstable, aggressive personalities which may push them into revengeful acts or even criminality as they grow older.

Third, lack of motivation to learn to be social is often a result of unfavorable early social experiences in the home or outside the home. Children, for example, who have been teased or bullied by older siblings, or have been made to seem unwanted in their play, will have little motivation to try to make good social adjustments outside the home.

Fourth, even when children have a strong motivation to learn to make good social adjustments, they may have little guidance and help in this learning. If parents believe, for example, that children will "outgrow" their aggressiveness as they become older and have more experience in social contacts, children may not associate their aggressiveness with their lack of peer acceptance and, as a result, they will make no effort to be less aggressive.

Role of Companions in Social Adjustments

The need for companionship is shown early in life when babies stop crying when someone comes to be with them. As babies grow older, the need for companionship increases. Children need companions not only for personal satisfaction but also for learning experience. From being with others, children learn what the group regards as acceptable behavior and what is regarded as unacceptable behavior.

Kinds of Companions

Different companions play different roles in the socialization process. If children's companions are appropriate for their ages and levels of development, they will contribute heavily to good social adjustments. If, on the other hand, they are developmentally inappropriate, they will not only interfere with children's social adjustments but they will also contribute to poor personal adjustments and add to children's unhappiness.

Having only older siblings for companions, for example, is developmentally inappropriate for children

because they are usually forced into the follower role. As a result, they soon begin to question their ability to play any other role, regardless of how bitterly they resent playing the follower role.

Children's companions may be divided into three major classifications; each influences socialization at different periods. These three kinds of companions and their characteristics are explained in Box 10-2.

Pattern of Companionship Needs

The kind of people who meet children's companionship needs is determined by the stage of their social development. Because the pattern of social development changes as children grow older, so do their companionship needs.

IN BABYHOOD In the gregarious stage of early babyhood, babies are satisfied to associate with anyone who is available for them to watch and listen to. What little social interaction occurs is initiated more often by others than by the baby.

Before babies are a year old, they want playmates as well as associates. Adults and older children are preferred companions during the last half of the first year and the second year. These people satisfy babies' desires for playmates because they will play with them when they want to be played with and in a way they want. Babies of their own age will not cater to their egocentric needs nor will young children. One- to two-year-olds are definitely family-oriented in their choice of companions.

IN EARLY CHILDHOOD During the preschool years, young children's companions are usually adults in the family, siblings, and, later, children from the neighborhood or the nursery school, kindergarten, day-care center, or Sunday school group with which children are identified. Adults in the family and siblings often serve as playmates. Between the ages of 2 and 4 years, children may find that family members are unable or unwilling to devote enough time to playing with them to meet their companionship needs. As a result, they crave the companionship of their peers. Not having had an opportunity to learn to play with their peers in a cooperative way, however, many young children at first merely watch them or join them in parallel play—playing independently beside them but not with them. Their peers are, thus, associates, not playmates.

BOX 10–2

COMPANIONS IN CHILDHOOD

- *Associates* are people who satisfy children's companionship needs by being in their environment. Children can watch and listen to them but they have no direct interaction with them. They may be of any age or either sex.
- *Playmates* are people with whom children engage in pleasurable activities. They may be of any age or either sex, but children ordinarily derive greater satisfaction from those of their own age and sex whose play interests are similar to theirs.
- *Friends* are people with whom children can not only play but also communicate by exchanging ideas and confidences, asking advice, and criticizing. Children of their own age, sex, and level of development are preferred as friends.

Gradually, with more opportunity to be with peers, children learn how to play with them. They then enter what is known as the "associative play stage" of social development—a stage in which children play with other children in similar if not identical activities. Much of the time young children are with their peers, however, is still spent in onlooker roles. Consequently, their companions are more often associates than playmates.

Before children are 4 years old, they normally want their companions to be playmates, and they try to engage in play activities with them. Children, at this age, select one or two children from those who are available and prefer to play with them. At first their playmates may be of either sex, but, even before children are ready to enter school, they show a preference for playmates of their own sex. They have more interests in common with children of their own sex because they also will have learned, through social pressures, to play in a sex-appropriate way. At this time, also, children begin to show a preference for playmates of their own racial and religious groups because, as is true of playmates of their own sex, they have more play interests in common. Furthermore, because young children are relatively unaware of social-class differences, they are willing to play with children from any socioeconomic background, provided they find them congenial playmates (2, 9, 38, 48).

In the strictest sense, young children cannot call their companions "friends" even though they often use this label. They are not friends because there is little communication between them. In the discussion of speech development in Chapter 7, it was explained that the talk young children engage in when they are playing with their peers is mainly egocentric, not social. They may engage in name-calling, boasting, and criticism, but there is seldom an exchange of ideas and rarely an exchange of confidences.

IN LATE CHILDHOOD When children enter school and begin to be interested in group play, they set new criteria, in addition to old ones, for the selection of playmates. While most school-age children must select their companions from their immediate neighborhoods, within the neighborhood group they prefer children of the same sex, size, chronological age, mental age, social maturity, and interests as theirs. As they grow older, personality traits become important, especially such traits as cheerfulness, generosity, friendliness, cooperativeness, honesty, even-temp-

eredness, sense of humor, and good sportsmanship (8, 22, 34, 37, 51).

Older children show a definite preference for playmates of their own racial groups. By the fifth grade, they also take socioeconomic status into consideration. Regardless of social class, almost all children like to have playmates who are successful in games and who, as a result, have prestige in the eyes of the group. From associating with them, children feel that their own prestige is increased (37, 48, 51). During late childhood, boys and girls select from their playmates those who are most congenial to them and with whom they can communicate as well as play. These children then become their friends. Each year, as they grow older, the need for friends becomes stronger, reaching a peak when the puberty changes begin (2, 9, 14, 57, 66).

IN PUBERTY In puberty, as interest in play decreases, owing to the physical changes which sap their energy, and as anxiety about these changes increases, children want confidantes rather than playmates. Since family members rarely meet their companionship needs at this age, pubescent children select as their friends members of their former gangs or adults who "understand" them and welcome their confidences.

Qualities Needed for Successful Companionship

Whether companions play the role of associates, playmates, or friends, they must have certain qualities if they are to satisfy the child's needs. Some of these qualities are important in all three companionship roles; others, in only one or two of the roles.

Of these qualities, four stand out. They are listed in Box 10-3 together with an explanation of the way they help meet the child's companionship needs.

Number of Companions

How many companions children should have to satisfy their companionship needs will vary with their age and developmental level. As a general rule, the number increases as children grow older. The preschool child is happy with one or two playmates, either family members or peers. The gang-age child needs three or four, and the number increases as gang play becomes more highly organized. But, by puberty, one com-

BOX 10–3

QUALITIES ESSENTIAL TO THE SATISFACTION OF COMPANIONSHIP NEEDS

INTEREST IN AND AFFECTION FOR THE CHILD

In all three kinds of companions, children must feel that they are the recipients of interest and affection. The interest and affection, however, must be appropriate for their developmental levels or they will frustrate the children's companionship needs.

SIMILARITY OF INTERESTS

Interests in common lead to comfortable feelings of being at home with others, and this facilitates communication and expressions of affection. This is true of all companions, but especially of friends.

SIMILARITY OF VALUES

Children have more respect for and greater congeniality with those who see things from the same frame of reference as they do and, as a result, "speak the same language." This is true of playmates as well as friends because similar values contribute to enjoyable play just as they contribute to successful communication.

GEOGRAPHIC PROXIMITY

If companions are to satisfy children's companionship needs, they must be readily available when children want them. Because children are not able to go from one part of the community to another without using public transportation or being transported by family members or adult neighbors, their companions must live in an area which children can easily reach by walking or bicycling.

How Companions Socialize Children

All three kinds of companions contribute to the socialization of children, though the roles they play differ. From imitating their *associates,* children learn patterns of behavior that lead to good or poor adjustment. If, for example, they imitate aggressive associates, either peers or adults, it will militate against good adjustments with their playmates.

From *playmates,* children learn patterns of behavior that they use in adjusting to social situations. They learn, for example, to be good or poor sports, to cheat or to play fairly, to be kind to those who are different or to discriminate against them, and to play the role of leader or follower successfully or unsuccessfully.

Above all other kinds of companions, *friends* exert the greatest influence on the socialization of children. Several friends can generally contribute more to socialization than one because each can contribute something different. One child, for example, may help children to see why they should act in a sex-appropriate way, another may show them the value of being cooperative instead of aggressive, while still another may help them to develop social insight and learn to be sympathetic. A single child, because of inexperience, is usually unable to do the entire socialization job successfully. By contrast, a group, made up of children of different interests, abilities, and backgrounds, can usually do the job better.

panion who can play the role of a trusted friend—or, at the most, two—will usually be adequate.

Within an age group, children differ in the number of companions required to satisfy their companionship needs. Children who are extroverted and prefer the companionship of others to being alone, need more companions than do children who are more introverted and, as a result, less social in their interests and activities (35).

How many companions children will need likewise is influenced by their play interests. Playing games of a strenuous type, for example, will require more playmates than playing sedentary games. Bright children tend to be satisfied with fewer companions than their age-mates who are less bright. This, however, may be

Shifts in Childhood Companions

Children's companions come and go. This is true of associates, playmates, and friends. This is due not to one cause alone but to many, the most common of which are given in Box 10–4.

While children change companions frequently at all ages, shifts are more frequent and more noticeable at some ages than others. Around the age of 5 years, there is a marked shift as children begin to prefer playmates of their own sex. Boys drop their girl playmates, and when girls must then choose new playmates, they generally select members of their own sex.

During the gang age of late childhood, shifts in playmates and friends are common. Today's playmate is

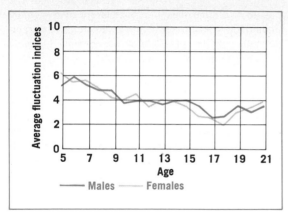

Figure 10–2. Friendship fluctuations through-out childhood and adolescence. (*Adapted from C. A. Skorepa, J. E. Horrocks, and G. G. Thompson: A study of friendship fluctuations of college students.* Journal of Genetic Psychology, *1963, 102, 151–157. Used by permission.*)

replaced by a different one tomorrow, a best friend be-comes an enemy, or a casual acquaintance becomes a best friend—quickly and often for little reason. Figure 10–2 shows the pattern of fluctuations in children's playmates and friends from 5 years until the end of adolescence. Note that, for both boys and girls, the shifts gradually decrease as childhood progresses and then remain relatively constant throughout adoles-ence (15, 34, 63, 83).

Learning Experiences in Shifts of Companions

Shifts in companions are valuable learning experi-ences for children and, as such, they play an important role in socialization. From these shifts, children learn four important things.

First, because shifts in companions almost always mean a period of unhappiness and loneliness, children learn how important companions are to them. This provides them with the necessary motivation to learn to behave in a way that will prevent shifts from occur-ring in the future, or at least decrease their number.

Second, children learn what types of companions do not meet their companionship needs, thus helping them to focus on those who do meet these needs. If, for example, they find that they get little enjoyment from playing with bossy children, they will avoid such

children in the future and select as playmates and friends those who are less prone to being bossy.

Third, as children discover what kinds of children do not meet their companionship needs, they will be-come more selective, trying out potential playmates and friends before establishing a close relationship with them.

Fourth, children learn that their playmates and friends will break off the relationship if they treat them in an antisocial way or if their behavior falls short of

---

BOX 10–4

WHY CHILDHOOD COMPANIONS
COME AND GO

CHANGES IN INTERESTS
As interests in play activities, academic work, or conver-sational topics change, children shift to companions whose interests are similar to theirs.

CHANGES IN VALUES
With changed interests and with greater maturity of behavior, children attach importance to different play activities or ways of behaving in social situations. They then choose companions whose values match their own.

ANTISOCIAL BEHAVIOR
Children whose behavior is antisocial beyond the time when their age-mates begin to behave in a more socially approved way find their former playmates and friends shifting to companions whose behavior is more social-ized then theirs.

LACK OF SOCIAL INSIGHT
Children whose social insight is less developed than that of their age-mates are regarded as tactless and heart-less. When they fail to show sympathy for their com-panions, they are likely to be rejected.

PRESSURES FROM OTHERS
Parental or peer pressures to select other playmates or friends, because of their sex, religion, race, socioeco-nomic status, or characteristic patterns of behavior, often cause children to give up an old companion in favor of one approved by parents or peers.

SOCIAL AND GEOGRAPHIC MOBILITY
When children's families move up or down the social scale or go into a new neighborhood or new community, children are forced to find new companions.

group values. This provides them with a strong motivation to conform to social expectations. It also encourages them to put group interests and activities first and, thus, to become social rather than egocentric.

Social Acceptance

In everyday speech, it is usual to refer to a child who achieves social acceptance as "popular." To the sociologist and psychologist, there is a subtle distinction between social acceptance and popularity. *Social acceptance* means being chosen as a companion for an activity in a group of which one is a member. It is an index of the success with which children take their place in the social group and the extent to which other group members like to work or play with them.

Popularity, on the other hand, means the general admiration in which people are held even by those who do not associate with them. Popular children, for example, may have few playmates or friends but many admirers. They are liked because they exhibit qualities other children admire even though they may not envy them for these qualities. Furthermore, because many of their peers admire them, such children are in line for leadership roles, especially if their popularity is based on respect from the group.

Active members of a group are not necessarily popular or accepted. Sometimes children who participate in many school activities and push themselves into many different groups are thoroughly disliked by their classmates. There is no direct relationship between children's desire for social contacts and their social acceptance. Furthermore, there is no indication that there are any children who are completely lacking in the desire to relate to their peers. Some children, however, prefer close, personal contacts with others; they are socially companionable, and "chummy." Others, by contrast, prefer to keep their distance and are regarded as "aloof."

Categories of Social Acceptance

If social acceptance is viewed as a straight line, along which different degrees of acceptance are pinpointed, the category of star will lie at one end of the line and that of social isolate will lie at the other. Few children fall in either of these extreme categories. Instead, most fall between the two extremes, enjoying varying degrees of social acceptance (9, 30, 51, 66, 88).

BOX 10–5

CATEGORIES OF SOCIAL ACCEPTANCE

STAR

Almost everyone in the group claims the star as an intimate friend, even though the star does not reciprocate many of these friendship choices. Everyone admires stars because of some outstanding quality or qualities. Very few children fall into this category.

ACCEPTED

Accepted children are liked by many members of the group. Their status is less secure than that of the star, and they can lose it if they persistently do or say things to antagonize members of the group.

ISOLATE

Isolates have no friends among their peers. Very few children fall in this category. There are two kinds of isolates: *voluntary isolates* withdraw from the group because of lack of interest in group members or their activities; *involuntary isolates* are rejected by the group even though they would like to be identified with it. "Subjective" involuntary isolates may think they are unwanted and isolate themselves from the group. "Objective" involuntary isolates, on the other hand, are actually rejected by the group.

FRINGER

Fringers are those who are on the borderline of acceptance. Like climbers, they are in a precarious position because they may lose what acceptance they have by doing or saying something that would turn the group against them.

CLIMBER

Climbers have gained acceptance in one group but want to gain acceptance in a socially more favored group. Their position is precarious because they can easily lose their acceptance in the original group and fail to gain acceptance in the new one if they do or say things that antagonize members of either group.

NEGLECTEE

Neglectees are neither liked nor disliked. They are neglected because they are shy, withdrawn, and nondescript. They have so little to offer that members of the group overlook them.

The categories of social acceptance are defined and explained in Box 10–5 and illustrated in Figure 10–3.

While categories of social acceptance are recognized by children, they do not use the technical names applied to them by psychologists and sociologists. Instead, they have their own names to designate these categories. These may change from generation to generation and from one group to another. Some commonly used names for different categories are "wheels" (the top crowd or those who run everything—the "stars"), "mice" (the quiet ones who are ineffectual and inoffensive—the "neglectees"), and the "drips" or "dopes" (those who are disliked and rejected by the group—the "involuntary isolates").

Within a group, not all children agree either upon those whom they will accept or reject or upon the degree to which they will accept or reject them. There is generally more agreement on those they dislike than on those they like. This means that *unpopular* children are more or less universally disliked by their age-mates, though they are disliked for different reasons and in different degrees. Furthermore, children tend to dislike many of their age-mates and to like only a few.

Awareness of Social Acceptance

The ability to perceive one's status in the group—*socioempathic ability*—is essential to good social adjustments because it determines how one will behave in social situations. Children, for example, who do not perceive their lack of social acceptance tend to behave as if they were liked. This is likely to increase their lack of acceptance because it will make other children think they are "pushy." On the other hand, children who perceive correctly that they are well accepted will make good social adjustments. The more accurately children can determine what their status is, the better they will know how to behave.

Figure 10–3. Varying degrees of a child's social acceptance.

Up to the age of 4 or 5 years, most children are unaware of how others feel about them. Gradually, their awareness grows as their social horizons broaden. Even before they enter school, they are able to verbalize this awareness in such comments as "He doesn't like me" or "No one wants to play with me." Gradually, children recognize levels of preference; they perceive that some children are better liked than others and that some people like them, some dislike them, and some ignore them.

Children's awareness of how well they are accepted by members of the social group comes from many sources, the six most common of which are given in Box 10–6. Although not all children use all these sources, most of them, especially as they grow older, use the majority of them. By so doing, there can be little doubt in their minds as to how the members of the social group feel about them and what status they have in the group.

While socioempathic ability normally increases with age, marked variations exist at every age level. Also, the ability to perceive one's own status in the group generally develops more slowly than the ability to perceive the status of others. This is to be expected because one can be more objective about matters which affect others than about those which affect oneself.

The correlation between *intelligence* and socioempathic ability is very close. *Sex differences* are also apparent in early childhood, with girls being superior to boys in this ability. Among older children, the gap between boys and girls narrows.

The more *anxious* children are to be accepted, the more aware they are of how others feel about them and the more accurate they are in judging their acceptance. Children who are *psychologically immature,* owing to parental overprotectiveness or authoritarian child training, tend to be less accurate than their peers.

Finally, accuracy in socioempathic ability varies according to how *popular* children are. Popular children have close contacts with their peers and, as a result, are quite aware of how others feel about them. Very unpopular children tend to underestimate their unpopularity, mainly because their lack of popularity has deprived them of opportunities to gain social insight. The ability to recognize *indifferent attitudes* is usually poorer than the ability to recognize acceptance or rejection. In spite of these variations, most children are well aware of how others feel about them by the time they reach the fifth grade. (27, 33, 34, 89, 91).

Traits Leading to Social Acceptance and Rejection

There is no such thing as a "popular" or "unpopular" personality pattern—a pattern that invariably leads to social acceptance or rejection. Even the most highly accepted child has some traits that are disliked. The child who is not accepted, on the other hand, may have some traits that are liked. In the accepted child, the disliked traits are compensated for by socially approved traits; in the rejected or neglected child, the desirable traits are overshadowed by the undesirable ones. No child needs to be a paragon of perfection to be accepted.

Social acceptance comes from others' reactions to the child's *total personality* rather than to specific traits. If the traits lead to acceptance by others, they are known as an "acceptance syndrome" or a constellation of traits that win acceptance from others. A constellation of traits that leads to rejection or neglect is known as an "alienation syndrome."

In the *acceptance syndrome* there are certain traits that are almost universally found. Almost all well-accepted children are friendly and cooperative. They adjust without making a disturbance, comply with requests, accept gracefully what happens, and have

---

BOX 10–6

COMMON SOURCES OF AWARENESS OF DEGREE OF SOCIAL ACCEPTANCE

- From the facial expression or tone of a person's voice, children get a clue as to how that person feels about them.
- The treatment children receive from others—peers or adults—tells them fairly accurately if they are liked or disliked.
- If others are willing to do what children want them to do or if they voluntarily imitate their speech, behavior, or clothes, children can be sure that they are liked.
- Children who have a number of playmates or friends know that they are better accepted than children who have only a few.
- From what others say to or about them, children can easily tell how others feel about them.
- What others call them is one of the most accurate clues to their level of acceptance. If people call children by derogatory nicknames, such as "Stink-pot," they know that they are less well accepted than if they are called by a more favorable nickname, such as "Pal."

good relationships with adults as well as children. They are kind to others, share what they have, are willing to take turns in any game the group plays, and show impartiality toward other members of the group. They assume responsibilities, participate in and enjoy social activities, feel secure in their status, and compare themselves favorably with their peers.

Well-accepted children are primarily group-centered rather than ego-centered; they think first of others, building up their egos instead of tearing them down to inflate their own. They also flatter others by focusing their comments on their good qualities instead of criticizing their undesirable ones. Children who are successful in games and in schoolwork tend to be highly accepted because being associated with them inflates the egos of those who are less successful.

Instead of being overconforming, well-accepted children are original, but they conform to the broad pattern of the group, observing its rules, regulations, and mores. They are flexible in the sense that they readily adapt their way of doing things to conform to social expectations. They are mature socially, emotionally, and intellectually. They, for example, show their social maturity by accepting people as they are—not criticizing them or trying to change them to fit into their own concepts of what they should be. Their social maturity is also shown in their social insight which enables them to size up and adjust quickly to different people in different social situations. Their emotional maturity is apparent in well-controlled, even-tempered behavior, free from anxiety, temper outbursts or displays of jealousy. They are intelligent and alert but not so intelligent that they are misfits in the group. They are usually good students not so much because they are more intelligent than their classmates but rather because they are conscientious students. (9, 33, 56, 57, 60, 65, 66).

It is important to realize that, while the traits given above contribute to social acceptance, this does not mean that the more developed they are, the greater the social acceptance children will enjoy. Having any trait in excess is likely to lead to poor acceptance, even when the trait per se is a highly admired one. Children, for example, have a better chance of social acceptance if they are generous rather than stingy. But, if they are overgenerous, handing out gifts right and left, they are likely to give the impression that they are trying to "buy" acceptance.

Just as there are certain traits almost universally found in the acceptance syndrome, so there are other traits almost universally found in the *alienation syn-*

drome. Children who lack social acceptance have ingrown, self-bound, and self-centered personality patterns. During the preschool years, children who are not fully accepted by their peers attack vigorously, strike others, push and pull. They try to escape responsibility by depending on adults or by running away. They dawdle over tasks assigned to them, refuse to comply with requests of others, and fail to conform to the routine of the home, the preschool, or the playground group.

As they grow older, children who are rejected or neglected not only antagonize their peers by their behavior but they also try to spoil their fun. They suffer from feelings of inferiority and lack any sense of belonging. They are more likely to have more personality disturbances than accepted children. Frequently, they feel so frustrated that they become aggressively antagonistic to adults in authority or to other children who play leadership roles. No matter how hard they try, they inevitably feel that they have failed. Such unfavorable self-concepts lead to poor adjustments and unsatisfactory social relationships. In addition, they undermine children's self-confidence and self-respect. (19, 32, 46, 47, 73, 92).

Effects of Social Acceptance

The kind of personal and social adjustments children make is greatly influenced by the extent to which their peers find them acceptable. Therefore, the impact of social acceptance is great, though it is more important in some areas of development than in others (59, 78, 88). Box 10–7 lists the chief effects of social acceptance on children's personal and social adjustments.

In a culture where high value is placed on social acceptance, and where parents, teachers, peers, and others use acceptance as an index of social success, children come to evaluate themselves in these terms. They measure their success or failure by the number of friends they have and by the security of their status in the group. This has a great impact on their self-concepts.

As was pointed out earlier, each year, as children grow older, their ability to perceive how others feel about them improves. They then have a better yardstick by which to evaluate themselves. This is back of much of the deterioration in the self-concept that occurs as children grow older (50).

Because children who are well accepted have more opportunities for participation in peer-group activities, and more motivation to do so, than have children who

EFFECTS OF SOCIAL ACCEPTANCE
DURING CHILDHOOD

CHILDREN WHO ARE WELL ACCEPTED

- Are happy and secure.
- Develop favorable self-concepts because others approve of them.
- Have opportunities to learn socially acceptable patterns of behavior and social skills which facilitate their poise in social situations.
- Are mentally free to turn their attention outward and to become interested in people and things outside themselves.
- Conform to group expectations and do not flout social traditions.

are less well accepted, they have opportunities to learn social skills. As a result, they become socially more competent than those who are less active. As Gottman et al. have stressed, "Popular children are more knowledgeable about how to make friends" (33). This adds to their social acceptance and, in turn, has a favorable effect on their self-concepts. Figure 10–4 shows the chain of events that leads to good personal and social adjustments.

Persistence of Social Acceptance

In general, persistence in sociometric status—the level of acceptance a person enjoys as assessed by objective measures—begins at the preschool level. This is shown by the fact that children at that age consistently choose the same playmates day after day. From then on, less and less shifting from one group to another occurs, though social acceptance varies somewhat with the activity engaged in. This means that chil-

dren who are well accepted in the preschool years have a greater likelihood of being well accepted throughout the elementary school years than have poorly accepted preschoolers.

Busk et al. have reported that sociometric status becomes constant by the time children reach the sixth grade (15). McGuire has stressed the fact that children who make poor social adjustments, owing to poor personal and social adjustments when they are young, tend to continue to make poor social adjustments as they grow older. Aggressive children, for example, continue to be aggressive even though they may modify their aggressiveness somewhat as they grow older. This, however, is not enough to have great impact on their sociometric status (62).

Even when there is a large turnover in the class—as the population changes or as children go from elementary to junior high school—social status within the group tends to remain constant. Social-acceptance scores are almost as constant as intelligence- and achievement-test scores. The child's acceptance score in one group, therefore, is a reliably accurate index of what the acceptance score in any similar group will be (20, 30, 56).

Most changes in social acceptance occur in the middle of the group of socially accepted children—those who are already partially accepted. It is highly unusual for those who are stars to fall from grace or for those who are quiet, withdrawn, and neglected to gain wholehearted acceptance. Those who are rejected because they are disliked tend to be more disliked the more often they come in contact with others.

The persistence of social acceptance standing can be explained in a number of ways, six of which are especially worth noting.

First, the personality characteristics which lead to acceptance, rejection, or neglect tend to remain stable or to intensity as children grow older. Only when their values of what they like or dislike in companions

Figure 10–4. The chain of events that leads to good personal and social adjustments.

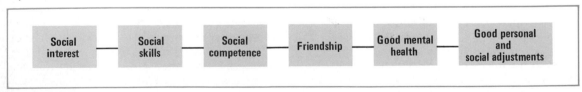

Social interest — Social skills — Social competence — Friendship — Good mental health — Good personal and social adjustments

change will children be likely to change their acceptance standing.

Second, the fundamental values, such as honesty, good sportsmanship, courage, and generosity, by which people judge children remain stable. If children's behavior does not conform to these values at one age, they are unlikely to gain acceptance at a later age unless they acquire characteristics that conform more closely to socially accepted values.

Third, within a group, children acquire reputations. Even if they change, their reputations generally do not. Each year, as they grow older, children discover that their peers give more attention to reputations in selecting playmates and friends than they did when they were younger.

Fourth, the more contacts children have with group members, and the closer these contacts are, the more likely they are to retain a stable status in the group.

Fifth, a favorable background in terms of family socioeconomic status contributes to stability of social acceptance because it helps children to acquire patterns of behavior and values that will continue to win social approval and acceptance as they grow older.

Sixth, children who have developed enough social and self-insight to evaluate themselves realistically will make better adjustments as they grow older than will children whose social adjustments are so poor that they have only limited opportunities to develop these abilities. (11, 15, 56, 62).

It must be recognized that persistence of social acceptance does not guarantee that children are well adjusted or that their social development is progressing in a manner that will ensure wholesome adjustments in adult life. If children are accepted by peers who admire and respect them, that is good. If, on the other hand, they are accepted because they are willing to play a role imposed on them by the group, even if that role is contrary to their standards and values, then the price of acceptance is too high. The temporary satisfaction they derive from this acceptance will be outweighed by the permanent damage it may do to their personalities and moral values.

Leaders and Followers

Because of the prestige associated with leadership, all children at some time or other want to be leaders. They are encouraged in this desire by their parents. Not only do many parents believe that being a leader is a sure

sign that their children have made superior social adjustments but they also derive vicarious satisfaction from their children's status in the group. Few children, however, achieve the status of leaders; most are followers.

Whether children will play the role of leader or follower does not depend so much upon the qualities they have as upon the relationship of their attributes to those of the group. As a result, children may be leaders in one group and followers in another group. So long as they are able to meet the needs of the group, they will be accepted as their leaders. When they are no longer able or willing to do so, they will be forced to relinquish their leadership roles and become followers.

Meaning of "Leader"

Leaders are accepted members of groups who more nearly represent the group's ideals than other group members. The other members are willing to follow them because they have demonstrated their mastery of social relationships, are able to elicit positive reactions toward themselves from the group members, and can contribute more than the other members to satisfy the needs of the group as a whole. Leaders are not just people in authority; instead they are the ones who can arouse emotional reactions from the group members. Because of this, they have the ability to get others to act in a certain way (36, 77).

Leaders in childhood can be divided, roughly, into two categories. The first is the *authoritarian* leader—one who is a bully and despot and who can lead by power alone. The authoritarian leader may win the respect of the group, but rarely wins its affection. The second is the *democratic* leader—one who shows great concern for the feelings and interests of the group members. Such a leader leads by making suggestions rather than by giving orders. In contrast to the authoritarian leader, the democratic leader wins both the respect and the affection of the group members.

Meaning of "Follower"

Followers, in childhood, like leaders, are accepted members of the social group with which they are identified; they retain this status as long as they are willing to do what the majority of the group members want to do and as long as they are willing to follow the leader.

Just as there are different kinds of leaders, so are there different kinds of followers. Some follow because following is easier than leading; others lack the qualities to be leaders. Some followers contribute little to the group and are content to go along with the crowd; others carry a heavy load for the leaders and will do the work while the leaders get the credit.

Some followers are constructive members of the group; others are destructive—the "tear-downers," who constantly criticize leaders and their policies. These are usually the children who wanted to be leaders but were not chosen; as a result, they are bitter and vindictive toward those who were chosen.

Characteristics of Leaders and Followers

The qualities that distinguish leaders from followers differ in *degree* rather than in kind. That is why children who are leaders in one group may not be leaders in another group. If, for example, children have athletic skills superior to those of other group members, they will have a good chance of being chosen as their leaders if the group interests are centered around games and sports. In other groups, their skills may be inferior to those of one or more group members: consequently, they will have little chance of being selected as leaders.

Certain differences between leaders and followers in childhood are predictable. While the traits that distinguish leaders also appear in followers, they are, as a rule, less developed in followers. Studies reveal that members of the peer group rate their leaders as having the best ideas, being best at getting others to do things, knowing best how others feel, and being the best looking (17, 41, 70). In commenting on the characteristics of leaders as compared with followers, Harrison et al. have said (36):

> Children chosen frequently as leaders are physically and mentally healthier, higher achievers in school, more socially adept than those children who were infrequently chosen as leaders. In short, leaders as a group displayed greater potential to excel physically, mentally, and socially.

Box 10–8 lists the characteristics that most clearly distinguish leaders.

Development of Leadership

Tradition holds that some people are born leaders, while others are born followers. As has just been pointed out, however, many children who are followers have the same traits as the leaders, perhaps even in a more highly developed form. The *use* children make of their abilities determines whether they will be leaders or followers. This, in turn, is determined largely by the training they had during the early years of life.

Two conditions have been found to play important roles in the development of leadership among children. The first is the influence of early experiences and the second, the type of child-training method used in the home.

The roots of leadership are found in *early childhood experiences*. Within a family, some children seem more predisposed to play leadership roles than others. This is not so much due to a difference in inherent abilities as to the treatment they receive from their parents and what the parents expect of them. Only children and oldest children are more likely to develop leadership abilities than younger children. The oldest children in a family are given many responsibilities, while only children become mature for their age because of their constant association with their parents (68).

Democratic *child training* during the early, formative years is far more likely to provide an environment conducive to the development of leadership qualities than strict authoritarian training. Under democratic child training, family relationships are generally good and children develop effective patterns of social adjustment in the home. They then carry these outside the home and are thus able to make satisfying peer adjustments. Children who make good peer adjustments have, in turn, many opportunities to learn to be leaders.

Pattern of Leadership Development

The pattern of development of leadership is predictable and similar for all leaders. During *babyhood,* when babies are put together, those who are dominant take the toys that appeal to them, even grabbing them away from other babies. They push, pull, kick, and do everything within their power to get the toy away from the other baby who is holding it.

Leaders in the *preschool years* are usually superior to other members of the group in size, in intelligence, and usually in age. Because of their superior size and intelligence, preschool leaders have more suggestions to offer for play, and thus the other children are willing to follow their lead. At this age, sex is an unimportant factor in leadership. Girls often assume the role of leadership over the boys as well as over the girls. Likewise, social status, nationality, and physical attractiveness are not so important now as they will be later. Fairness and responsibility to the group, on the other hand, are important characteristics of leaders at this age. Because of their ability to lead, young children who assume leadership roles develop marked self-confidence.

During the preschool years, leaders tend to be tyrannical bosses. They expect others to follow their wishes and become sullen or angry if they rebel. Should their techniques become too tyrannical, they will find themselves displaced and another child will be recognized as the group leader. In contrast to the bully, who tries to lead by brute force, the diplomat leads by artful and indirect suggestions, bargains, or even bribes and threats. The diplomat is usually able to hold the leadership role longer than the bully.

In *late childhood,* leaders represent the group's ideal. Should they fall short of group expectations, and should they display traits the group members dislike, they soon lose prestige and are replaced by another who, at the moment, more closely approximates the group's standards.

As childhood progresses, leaders are needed for different activities—school and class offices, sports, gangs, and community groups, like the Boy Scouts and Girl Scouts. The same child will not necessarily have the leadership qualifications needed for all such groups. Thus there is a tendency among older children to select leaders for *specific group activities*. Without doubt, however, the prestige and experience gained from leading one group activity carry over to other activities and give the child who has been a leader an advantage over another who may be equally suited for leadership but lacks experience.

The technique of leadership in older children differs from that which proves to be successful in younger children. Leaders can be authoritarian and despotic only when the group is very large and is unanimous in its admiration and respect for them. For the most part, however, leaders must give the rest of the group some

CONDITIONS AFFECTING PERSISTENCE OF LEADERSHIP

CONDITIONS ENCOURAGING PERSISTENCE

Stability of the Group
It is much easier for a child to continue to be a leader in a stable group than in one whose members come and go and in which, because of these shifts in membership, new interests and values appear.

Adaptability of the Leader
As children grow older, their social interests and needs change. Children who can and will change their methods of meeting their needs will have a far better chance of being retained as a leader than children who lack this flexibility.

Motivation to Be a Leader
Because the leadership role requires hard work and sacrifices of time, personal interests, and preferences, the child who does not get enough satisfaction from being a leader to be willing to make these sacrifices will lack the motivation to play this role.

CONDITIONS MILITATING AGAINST PERSISTENCE

Undemocratic Method of Selecting Leader
When a leader is selected by a teacher, camp counselor, or some other adult, the group members usually resent what they consider their own rights. Under such conditions, the chances are slim that the child will be able to retain the leadership position when the group is allowed to make its own choice unless the child demonstrates an ability to fill their needs.

Stopgap Leader
A leader selected to fill a gap caused by the withdrawal of a chosen leader will not be chosen again unless there is evidence of ability to meet the group's needs.

Failure to Meet Group's Needs
As the group's needs change, leaders must change their methods of meeting these needs. While a bossy leader may meet the needs of young children, the older child who continues to use bossy techniques will not meet the needs for independence and self-expression of older children.

choice; group members, in turn, must agree to the leader's suggestions and be willing to follow them.

Persistence of Leadership

According to tradition, "Once a leader, always a leader." This is not necessarily true, especially during early childhood. Young children who become leaders of their nursery school, kindergarten, or playground groups will not necessarily be the top executives in an important corporation when they are adults, nor will they necessarily be leaders in their high school or college days. While leaders come and go at all ages, leadership tends to become more persistent as childhood progresses.

There are certain conditions that encourage persistence of leadership during childhood and others that militate against it. The most common of these are explained in Box 10-9.

Effects of Being a Leader or a Follower

How playing a leadership or followership role will affect personal and social adjustments will be greatly influenced by how much children want to play these roles and what satisfaction they derive from doing so.

For some children, the satisfactions associated with the roles of leader and of follower outweigh the dissatisfactions. For others, the reverse is true. A brief critical analysis will help to show why some children prefer to be followers while others are unhappy unless they are leaders.

LEADERSHIP Judged by *objective* criteria, leadership is regarded as a certain index of good social adjustment. The larger the group and the more often a child is selected for leadership roles, the better adjusted the child is thought to be.

To judge a child's social adjustments fairly, however, one must also take into consideration the *subjective* criteria—how the child feels about being a leader. Most children enjoy the prestige of leadership and are willing to pay the price in terms of extra work and sacrifice of personal desires. They are even willing to give up close, personal friendships in order to be friendly with all who want to be their friends.

As a result of the favorable attitudes of the social group—peers and adults—the child leader develops a characteristic leader personality, often labeled a "dynamic" personality. This personality pattern is characterized by self-confidence, assertiveness, and an aloofness toward others that is manifested in lack of slavish conventionality and lack of close, warm friendships with a few selected members of the peer group.

FOLLOWERSHIP In the eyes of others, a follower is one who has made poor social adjustments. Every child, sooner or later, becomes aware of this *objective* judgment. The more emphasis parents and teachers place on "trying to be a leader," the more inadequate and the more resentful the child who is a follower becomes. In time, this results in a personality pattern that will militate against being *able* to be a leader, even though selected for such a role.

Some children do not want to be leaders and prefer the follower role. *Subjectively,* therefore, there is evidence that followers are making good adjustments because they are satisfied with the roles they are playing.

Children have different reasons for not wanting to be leaders and for preferring to be followers. It may be because they feel inadequate for the leader role, but more often it is because they have interests of their own which they find more absorbing than activities with a group. Or they may not like to dictate to, direct, or "boss" others: they resent being treated in that way; they do not want to give the time or put their energies into the work that leadership requires; they are afraid of criticism or failure which they feel may lower the acceptance they now enjoy; or they dislike the back-knifing of those who want to be leaders and who try, by such means, to take the leadership role from the present leader (41, 77).

When children are satisfied to be followers, they are content to allow others to do the work and assume responsibilities while they reap the benefits. This will not lead to feelings of inadequacy, especially if they are well accepted by the group and gain satisfaction from group activities.

Mobility

Mobility means the process of moving. There are two kinds of mobility that affect children's socialization: social and geographic mobility. *Social mobility* is the process of changing one's status in the social structure. With change in status there is inevitably a change

---

BOX 10–10

SOCIAL MOBILITY

HORIZONTAL MOBILITY
In horizontal mobility, there is a transition from one social group to another on the same level. The move is generally made for personal reasons. Children, for example, move to groups they find more congenial just as their parents move to neighborhoods they believe will be more congenial.

VERTICAL MOBILITY
In vertical mobility, there is a transition from one social stratum to another. The move may be ascending (upward mobility) or descending (downward). In *upward mobility,* people try to improve their status by identifying with a higher-level social group. They are motivated by a desire for advancement. In *downward mobility,* people become identified with a lower-level social group. The move is usually involuntary. Family misfortunes, for example, may force people to give up their associations with their former groups because they are no longer able to afford the clothes and other status symbols approved by the group. As a result, they lose their status in it.

---

in social relationships, and this involves problems of adjustment. Two kinds of social mobility and some of the characteristics of each are described in Box 10–10.

The person in the process of changing status in the social structure has been given a specific label by sociologists and psychologists—a label which indicates not only the direction of mobility but also the person's success in adjusting to the new group. People who try to climb up the social ladder are known as "climbers"; if they climb down or fall down the ladder, they are known as "sliders" or "decliners" or "skidders," depending on how rapid the descent is.

Between the climber and the slider are those who are trying to move upward. They are usually called "strainers" or "clingers." *Strainers* are people who are only tentatively accepted. As a result, their status gives them little satisfaction and security, and their social adjustments are poor. *Clingers* are peripheral to the group because they have not completely adopted its approved patterns. While they are not rejected, their status is precarious, and, at any time, should they say or do something the group disapproves of, they may forfeit what status they have.

Geographic mobility means moving to another place of residence. This move may be to a new house in the same neighborhood, to another part of the same community, from a rural to an urban or suburban community or vice versa, or even to another state, another region of the country, or to another country.

Many people think of social and geographic mobility as synonymous. They are not, though more often than not they go hand in hand. Only if the geographic move is so slight—as in the case of moving from one house to another in the same neighborhood—that it is possible to retain old social ties, will there not be social mobility when there is geographic mobility.

Even among adults who can go from one part of the community to another when they want to retain social ties after they move, these ties tend to weaken as new social ties are formed in the new area to which they have moved. Because children are less able to go from one part of the community to another than are adults and because they will be expected to attend a school in the new neighborhood to which they have moved, social mobility will be inevitable for them.

Reasons for Mobility

Whether children will be static or mobile will depend largely on their families. Some families are content to remain, year after year, in the same neighborhood, in the same community, or even in the same house. They retain, year after year, social ties with neighbors, friends, and relatives. Under such conditions, children are not forced to meet the problems mobility gives rise to unless they themselves want to move up the social ladder and become identified with a different group in the same neighborhood.

Many families in America today are not content to be static. Since World War II, mobility has become an increasingly serious problem for children as well as for their families. Many parents are anxious to have their children "better themselves," and so they move to neighborhoods or communities where their children will have greater advantages. Children themselves may have a strong drive to identify with a group that is regarded as superior to their present one.

Downward mobility is, likewise, a growing problem for children today. There are two major reasons: *First,* divorce and the breaking up of the home is far more common than in the past, and *second,* with the growth of big business, men are far more likely to lose their jobs than was true when business was on an individual or a smaller-group scale. If the financial stability of the

family is threatened, downward mobility is often inevitable.

Difficulties Encountered in Mobility

Mobility brings with it adjustment problems for all family members. Some of these are *practical* problems that require adjustments to accustomed patterns of doing things, such as using new shops, going to new doctors, dentists, schools, and churches, or making adjustments to new climates (55,71).

For all family members, however, *social* adjustments are far more difficult than adjustments to practical problems. For children, the two most difficult problems in social adjustment—regardless of what kind of mobility is involved—are achieving acceptance in the new group and accepting as their own the values and behavior patterns of the new group.

To gain *acceptance in the new group,* regardless of a child's age, there are two essentials: making a favorable impression on the group and showing enough aggressiveness to attract the attention of the group members without, at the same time, antagonizing them. Each year, these essentials become more important as children become more choosy about the choice of playmates and friends and as the gangs become more tightly knit units.

The importance of making a favorable first impression is well illustrated by a study of assimilation of newcomers into groups. The study reported a high correlation between acceptance on the first day in the classroom and 11 weeks later (93).

Well-controlled and well-camouflaged aggressiveness on the part of newcomers is likewise essential to gain entree into groups. Rarely do established groups take the initiative in making contacts with newcomers unless they make extraordinarily favorable first impressions. Instead, under most circumstances, newcomers must make the contacts by trying to talk to group members or by offering to make some contribution to the group (9). Since aggressiveness is often interpreted as pushiness, few children have enough social sophistication to know how aggressive they can be before creating such an unfavorable impression that it will lead to rejection by the group.

Learning to *conform to new standards* of approved attitudes and behavior is the second major difficulty in social mobility. This is true of all types of social mobility, but especially so for upward mobility where children in an established group are more choosy about accepting newcomers than in horizontal or downward social mobility. Unless children have some way of knowing what the approved patterns of behavior, values, attitudes, and beliefs of the group are, it is almost impossible for them to know what to conform to. Once children gain some acceptance, they can observe the approved patterns and model their behavior, values, attitudes, and beliefs along these approved lines in the hopes that, in time, the group will accept them fully.

Because downward social mobility has no appeal for children, they have little motivation to identify the approved standards of the new group or to conform to them. Consequently, children who are downwardly mobile have little chance of gaining acceptance by the group. Even if they do gain some acceptance, they gain little satisfaction from the companionship of children whom they and their parents regard as "inferior."

The difficulties children encounter in gaining acceptance in new social groups when they are mobile far outweigh the difficulties of adjustment to new living conditions and new patterns of life—the practical problems of mobility. For most mobile children, the problem of loneliness caused by lack of social ties is paramount. Parents often try to cope with this but, unfortunately, meet with only limited success. Once children reach the gang age of late childhood— the time when lack of companions is especially serious—children want to run their social lives as they wish and bitterly resent adult interference, a resentment that may and often does strengthen their resistance to accepting newcomers.

Hazards in Social Adjustments

Learning to adjust to different kinds of people and different kinds of social situations is an extremely difficult area of development during the childhood years. Because of this, there are many possibilities of developing unfavorable attitudes and behavior patterns.

Most of these unfavorable attitudes and behavior patterns could be prevented or quickly corrected if they were spotted in time and if efforts were made to correct them before they became deeply rooted habits. Unfortunately, many parents and teachers, while recognizing that these attitudes and behavior patterns lead to poor social as well as personal adjustments on the child's part, believe that the child will outgrow them and, as a result, they do nothing to correct them.

In few areas of the child's development is guidance and supervision more necessary than in making social adjustments. This is not only because of the many potential hazards every child faces in this area of development but also because of the important role social adjustment plays in the child's life, especially in the developing concept of self.

The following description of the common hazards to good social adjustments during the childhood years will show how many potential hazards there are in this area of development. It also will serve to alert those whose responsibility it is to guide the child's development to what these hazards are and to the long-term effects they can and often do have on personal and social adjustments.

Social Rejection and Neglect

What effect rejection and neglect by the social group will have on children will depend, to some extent, upon how important social approval and acceptance are to them. Voluntary and involuntary isolates, for example, have different social needs, with those of the former less than those of the latter (71, 89).

Although all children, to some extent, treat their age-mates in ways which, to adults, seem unsocial if not actually cruel, the most common victims of rejection or neglect are newcomers in a neighborhood who do not belong to any gang, those who are physically handicapped and cannot keep up with the pace set by their age-mates, or those who are so egocentric in their interests that they have little to offer the group (9, 14, 19, 66, 74).

Children who are constantly confronted with the high cultural value placed on social acceptance cannot fail to be psychologically damaged when they realize that their level of acceptance is interpreted as failure. Some of the forms this psychological damage takes are given in Box 10–11.

Substitute Companions

When children have strong needs for companionship that have not been satisfied, they usually find some substitute to meet their needs. The substitutes they choose will depend partly upon their ages and partly upon what is available. Young children generally find imaginary playmates a satisfactory substitute for real playmates. Older children, who have outgrown, mentally, the ability to endow imaginary companions with the life qualities of real friends, are more likely to turn to a pet. Many children also fall back on family members to meet their companionship needs when they are deprived, for whatever the reason, of peer-group companionship.

All these substitutes have some socializing influence on children. Children, for example, can practice language skills by talking to their imaginary companions and by playing simple games with them. In addition, playing with an imaginary companion stimulates creativity which can be transferred to play activities with real playmates.

In spite of any advantages that might come from having substitute companions, the hazards far outweigh the advantages. This is because they prevent children from learning behavior patterns and play skills which are essential if children are to be accepted by real companions. The hazards and advantages of each of the most common forms of substitute companions—family members, imaginary companions, and pets—are discussed below.

FAMILY MEMBERS Lonely children often turn to family members for the companionship their age-mates enjoy with peers. The family member may be a parent, a grandparent or other relative, or siblings, either younger or older than they are.

If the family member has the time and desire to do things with children, whether it be playing games with them or reading to them, children will derive satisfac-

tion and this will compensate, to some extent at least, for the loneliness they would otherwise experience.

However, these activities will not necessarily help them to learn the play skills their age-mates are learning at that time. A grandmother, for example, cannot roller skate with children or play the strenuous ball games their age-mates are learning to play at that time.

Furthermore, when the companion is a parent or grandparent, they offer children little competition and usually let them win in any play activity where competition is involved. This does not teach children to be competitive or good sports.

Should the companion be an older sibling, children can learn play skills from that sibling, but they will likely be forced into the follower role—a role that will either make them resentful or cause them to question their abilities to be leaders.

When children have younger siblings as companions, they are likely to assume the role of leader and learn to be bossy—a trait that will militate against playing the leadership role later with age-mates. Equally hazardous, they will be forced to play on a lower level than they are developmentally capable of when they play with younger siblings. This will make them unprepared to play with their age-mates, should an opportunity come later for them to do so.

IMAGINARY COMPANIONS To young children, imaginary companions are lifelike, possessing names, physical characteristics, and the ability to do things one normally associates with real children. Young children derive keen pleasure from playing with their imaginary playmates because they fill gaps in their social lives.

The usual age for imaginary companions is between 3 and 4 years, with 3½ years the high point. By the time children enter school and have real children available for playmates, they normally abandon their imaginary playmates, though they may play with them occasionally when they are lonely (7, 58, 82). The common characteristics of imaginary companions, the kind of child who usually has them, and many related matters will be discussed in Chapter 12.

In spite of the fact that imaginary companions meet the companionship needs of lonely children, they are hazardous for three reasons. *First,* they cannot teach children play skills or give them opportunities to learn them from cooperative play with other children. *Second,* children can and do assume leadership roles with their imaginary companions and dominate the play situation. This encourages children to be bossy—a habit which will militate against their playing leadership roles with age-mates or even being acceptable as followers in the peer group. *Third,* children have no opportunity to learn such patterns of behavior as social insight, cooperativeness, and good sportsmanship when they play with imaginary companions. This will handicap their acceptance by age-mates when they discover that imaginary companions no longer meet their companionship needs.

PETS   All children enjoy the companionship of pets and regard them as playmates with whom they can romp and play when they have no human companionship. While young children like pets of all kinds —birds, fish, hampsters, mice, turtles, rabbits, dogs, cats, etc.—older children get limited satisfaction from pets that do little to show their affection or even to hold their interest, or that are difficult to play with or show affection for. See Figure 10–5. Children want *playmates,* not just something to look at. For that reason, dogs and cats are usually the most satisfactory substitutes for human playmates for children of all ages.

Even though pets meet children's companionship needs, they, like imaginary companions, are hazard-

Figure 10–5. If pets are to serve as substitute companions, children must be able to play with them and show affection for them. (*Adapted from Bil Keane: "The Family Circus."* Register and Tribune Syndicate, *Oct. 17, 1973. Used by permission.*)

"Fish aren't very good pets. They're too hard to hug."

ous to children's acceptance by the peer group. They do not give children an opportunity to learn the play skills real companions regard as essential to group belonging, they cannot teach children social skills, such as cooperativeness and social insight, and, most serious of all, they encourage children to learn to be bossy.

Although pets as substitute companions do not have a direct socializing influence on children, they are often effective social aids. The companionship of a pet, for example, helps many timid children to make social contacts with other children and adults they would hesitate to make if they were alone. Even more important, children who learn to show affection for their pets are learning a pattern of behavior that enables them to establish an empathic complex with people instead of becoming self-bound. Consequently, pets can be regarded as less hazardous to good social adjustments than imaginary companions (53).

Attempts to "Buy" Social Acceptance

When children's social needs are not met by the acceptance they have, they may try to "buy" acceptance. This they do in many ways, the most common of which are using their allowances to "treat" their age-mates to candy, cones, or other sweets, by giving parties or by taking their age-mates to places of entertainment, such as movies or the circus, by offering to give them some of their material possessions they admire, or by saying flattering things to them.

Many parents, anxious that their children be well accepted, encourage them in their attempts to win social acceptance. This they do by providing them with the money necessary to buy this acceptance, by encouraging them to bring their age-mates to their homes for play, for meals, or for parties, or by "playing up" to the parents of the children whose acceptance their children are trying to win.

The usual targets of this "buying" of acceptance are the leaders of the gang or its best-accepted members. If children can win their acceptance, they feel that they can be assured of the acceptance of the other gang members.

While any child may try this technique of winning acceptance, the most likely to do so are children of higher socioeconomic-status families and newcomers to the community. In the case of the former, the children may find themselves discriminated against because they have acquired the reputation of being "stuck up" as a result of earlier boasting about their material possessions or because they have been cocky about expecting other children to do what they want to do. In the case of the latter, this technique is used in the hopes that members of an already-established gang will open the doors to them and accept them as members. This is more often done by trying to sell themselves by impressing others with their play skills than by monetary bribes.

Even though "buying" one's way into a group is not an uncommon practice among adults, it tends to be hazardous when used by children. They do not have the sophistication or the social know-how to do it in as subtle a way as adults do. It may win the desired result at first, but it rarely leads to permanent acceptance.

There are two reasons why this method of winning acceptance is hazardous when used by children. *First,* children are likely to get the reputation of being "pushy"—a reputation that will not contribute to their acceptance then or as they grow older. *Second,* and far more serious, it will not lead to good personal and social adjustments. If it works, it will weaken any motivation children otherwise might have to learn to behave in a more socially acceptable way. If it fails to work, children will become resentful toward those who accepted their generosity and then failed to reciprocate with their acceptance. Children will then think of themselves as martyrs and of other children as "mean," "selfish," and "grabby"—attitudes that cannot fail to lead to poor personal and social adjustments.

Shifts in Companions

Even though shifts in companions may be valuable learning experiences, as was explained earlier, they are potential hazards to children's personal and social adjustments. Whether they will become real hazards and, if so, how great these hazards will be, will depend on five conditions.

First, the age of the child when the shift occurs. In early childhood, when children's companions are mainly playmates, shifts are not as hazardous as they are when children are older and want their companions to be their friends as well as their playmates. Finding a companion to play with is easier than finding someone in whom they can confide and who shares similar interests and values.

Second, the number of children available for companions. When there are plenty of children available

for playmates and friends, as is true after children enter school, the seriousness of breaking off relationships is far less than during the preschool years when there may be other children available in the neighborhood but of different ages and levels of development, thus making them uncongenial companions.

Third, the reason for the shift. When companions move away, when children and their companions develop different interests and values, or when children are pressured to drop companions because of their racial, religious, or socioeconomic backgrounds, there is no evidence that the shift comes from unsocial behavior. However, if the shifts come because of quarrels that lead to hurt feelings, it is an indication that children are not learning to make good social adjustments. This is a danger signal, especially if children experience numerous shifts in their companions.

Fourth, the difficulty children experience in establishing new social relationships. In early childhood, establishing new social ties is relatively easy because most children will play with anyone who will play with them. However, during the gang age of late childhood, children become more choosy and the tightly knit group that makes up the gang is reluctant to accept new members unless they need extra players or unless they have reason to believe that those who want to become gang members will be congenial to the group as a whole.

Fifth, the reputation children acquire among their age-mates. This affects the ease or difficulty they have in making new social contacts. When children, for example, get the reputation of being "pushy," "poor sports," or "stuck up," their unfavorable reputations can be serious stumbling blocks to establishing new social relationships.

Regardless of what is responsible for shifts in companions, it is hazardous. When relationships are broken, even temporarily, children experience a period of loneliness. Because of their strong desire for companions, most children, under such circumstances, are willing to fall back on anyone who will accept them. If their new companions have interests and values different from theirs, for example, it may be a step backward in the socialization process, especially if, in their desire to have companions, lonely children are willing to conform to any interests and values to guarantee their acceptance in a group, regardless of what the group stands for.

An equally serious source of hazard is the feeling of

insecurity shifts in companions bring. Children who had, formerly, felt secure in the relationships with their playmates and friends may develop feelings of insecurity when they see their companions shifting away from them, regardless of who is to blame for these shifts. To prevent further shifts many children become overcomforming, hoping in this way to guarantee the security that comes with stable companions.

Dissatisfaction with Role in the Social Group

Whether children play the role of leader or follower, it can be hazardous to good personal and social adjustments. This hazard comes not from the role per se but from the dissatisfaction children have with the role the social group expects them to play. In fact, being a leader can be as hazardous to good personal and social adjustments as being a follower.

There are four common hazards associated with the *leader* role. The *first* comes from the effect being a leader has on children's self-concepts. Frequently children develop feelings of personal superiority when they are chosen as leaders, though they soon discover that these feelings must be well guarded or they will acquire the reputation of having a "swelled head"—a reputation that could quickly lead to loss of leadership status. However, these feelings of superiority are likely to come to the fore whenever they have to play the role of follower. Instead of being cooperative followers, they are likely to tell the leader how to do things, thus giving the impression that they are bossy or poor sports.

Second, since all child leaders have seen leaders come and go, they are aware of the possibility that this can happen to them too. If, for example, they hear grumblings of discontent, if their suggestions are challenged or if there is outright criticism of them and of the way they are playing the leadership role, much of their satisfaction from being leaders is counteracted by feelings of anxiety and resentment.

Third, should they be replaced by other leaders, their resentment against the group will be greatly increased and, in time, they will come to doubt their own leadership abilities. Psychological damage is especially likely to occur among children of low socioeconomic backgrounds who find that the leadership roles they once played are later taken over by children of better socioeconomic backgrounds, even though they may not be more competent leaders.

Fourth, when children do not want to be leaders because they feel inadequate for the role or because they are forced into this role by a teacher who wants to give all children some leadership experience or by peers who cannot find anyone else to fill this role, they are likely to be resentful or even martyred if they feel that "all the dirty work" is being thrust on them. These feelings militate against good personal and social adjustments on the part of children who do not want to be leaders but are forced into this role.

Children who rarely play leadership roles, and then only when appointed by a teacher or camp counselor, soon develop *follower complexes*—firmly established beliefs that they are incapable of being leaders. This often affects their attitudes toward accepting leadership roles later, should such roles be offered them. Studies of adolescent and adult women, for example, reveal that many of them shy away from semiexecutive or executive roles in business and industry, not because they lack the ability or training, but rather because they developed "follower complexes" during the years when the leadership roles in their classes in school and college were held mainly by boys, and when they learned that leadership was not considered sex-appropriate for girls. This matter will be discussed in detail in the chapter on sex-role development.

Even satisfied followers can be psychologically damaged if they are bossed by leaders or if their contributions are criticized by the leaders. The resentment this gives rise to colors their attitudes toward group belonging and their motivation to be contributors to group activities. As a result, this becomes a hazard to good personal and social adjustments.

Children who make the poorest personal and social adjustments are those who are forced to be followers when they want to be leaders. Even if they do not show their resentment openly, it will color their attitudes toward the group and toward their participation in the activities group members enjoy. If, on the other hand, they show their resentment by being "tear-downers" who try to persuade other group members to join their rebellion against the leaders, and who undermine the morale of the group by their hypercritical, negativistic attitudes, they will soon discover that the important members of the group resent them. In time, this is likely to result in their rejection by the group. Thus, judged objectively and subjectively, their social adjustments are most unsatisfactory, as are their personal adjustments.

Social Mobility

Whether social adjustment is judged by objective or subjective standards, the overall effects of social mobility are usually unfavorable. A family may improve its standard of living by upward mobility but the effects on the child's personal and social adjustments can be and often are damaging.

Downward mobility is even more hazardous to good personal and social adjustments. No one—adult or child—likes to skid down the social ladder. It is an ego-deflating experience because it implies failure. Furthermore, many people resent having to associate with those they regard as their inferiors. They consider their values, interests, and patterns of behavior inferior to those they have been accustomed to. Because downward mobility usually means living in a less desirable neighborhood, and having fewer material possessions, children are bound to be unhappy about their new status. All this, added to the belief that the new group is "inferior," weakens their motivation to try to identify with it. To make the situation worse, children are likely to find that their old social group—should they live near enough to make social contacts possible—will not accept them since they have changed their status and, with it, the neighbor-

---

BOX 10-12

SOME COMMON EFFECTS OF MOBILITY ON CHILDREN

LACK OF SOCIAL ACCEPTANCE
Lack of acceptance is especially difficult for children who have enjoyed acceptance in the group with which they were formerly identified. The better accepted they were in the old group, the less satisfied they will be to have to form friendships with fringers and social isolates if members of the established groups will not accept them.

EFFECTS ON FAMILY RELATIONSHIPS
Children of upwardly mobile families are constantly driven by their parents to form friendships with the "right" children and are criticized when they behave in a way that might jeopardize acceptance by the "right" children. Children of downwardly mobile families develop resentments against their parents for forcing them into downward mobility.

WEAKENING OF INTERGENERATIONAL TIES
Families that have risen above their kin, or skidded below them, tend to break off the close ties with relatives that give children feelings of security and identity. Even in horizontal mobility, kinship ties weaken when families move to new neighborhoods or new communities.

EFFECTS ON SCHOOLWORK
Since social mobility is usually accompanied by geographic mobility, children must shift to new schools. They often find that there are gaps in their schoolwork or that they are not as well prepared as their new classmates. Consequently, they may have to repeat a grade or they may find that their school marks in the new grade fall below those in their former grades. This is an ego-deflating experience for any child, but especially for one who has always been a good student.

CONFUSION ABOUT SOCIAL EXPECTATIONS
Because every social group has its own values and expectations, children may be confused when they discover that the values and expectations they learned in their former groups are judged as unacceptable by the new group. Until they learn and accept the values and expectations of the new group, their chances for acceptance will be slim.

LACK OF SENSE OF IDENTITY
Socially mobile children feel that they no longer belong to the group with which they were formerly identified or with the new group which has not yet accepted them. As a result, they feel socially isolated, insecure, and unsure of how to become a member of the new group.

OVERCONFORMITY
In hopes of winning a place in the new group, many socially mobile children overconform in dress, speech, beliefs, values, and patterns of behavior to those of members of the new group. As a result, they lose their sense of individuality.

EMBARRASSMENT
The insecurity of socially mobile children makes them self-conscious and embarrassed in social situations. For those who are downwardly mobile, this is intensified by shame—reactions that play havoc with their personal and social adjustments.

hood, school, and the ability to have the status symbols the group considers important.

Regardless of the form mobility takes—vertical, upward, or downward—and regardless of whether it is social alone or social and geographic, there are certain almost universal effects that lead to unhappiness and insecurity on the part of the mobile child (28, 42, 55, 71, 72, 86). How hazardous mobility is to children's personal and social adjustments will become apparent from the listing of important effects of mobility on children as given in Box 10–12.

From a careful study of these effects it should be apparent that the effects of mobility, so far as children are concerned, far outweigh any advantages there might be. Bossard and Boll have summed up the situation correctly when they said that "mobility has its advantages but we wouldn't wish them on anyone" (12).

Chapter Highlights

1   Social adjustment—the success with which people adjust to other people and to social situations—is judged by four criteria: overt performance, ability to adjust to any group, social attitudes, and personal satisfaction.

2   Companions, whether they play the role of associate, playmate, or friend, all contribute to the socialization of children, though in different ways at different ages.

3   Regardless of the role companions play in a child's life, to play it successfully they must have interest in and affection for the child, they must have interests and values similar to those of the child, and they must live close enough to the child to make frequent contacts possible.

4   How many companions children should have to meet their companionship needs will vary according to the age and the personality of each child, though, as a general rule, older children need more companions than do younger children.

5   Shifts in companions are less common among older children than among younger children, though shifts occur throughout the childhood years.

6   From shifts in companions, children learn how important companions are to them, the types of companions that meet their needs best, how to be more selective in the choice of their companions, and what patterns of behavior will and will not be tolerated.

7   Popularity and social acceptance—terms which are commonly used interchangeably differ in that admiration and respect play more important roles in popularity than in social acceptance.

8   There are different categories of social acceptance, ranging from stars to isolates, either voluntary or involuntary, with neglectees, fringers, and climbers falling between these two extremes.

9   Most children become increasingly aware of the degree of social acceptance they are able to achieve as they grow older, though perception of their acceptance varies greatly in every age group.

10   Acceptance does not come from one characteristic alone but from a constellation of characteristics, known as the "acceptance syndrome," all of which contribute to good social adjustments. By contrast, the "alienation syndrome" is made up of characteristics that contribute to rejection or neglect.

11   Leaders and followers have many characteristics in common but those of leaders differ from those of followers more in degree than in kind. However, the characteristics of leaders vary not only according to the group with which the child is identified but also according to the ages and interests of the group members.

12   Social mobility, which may be horizontal (moving from one social group to another on the same level) or vertical (moving up or down the social ladder), is usually accompanied by geographic mobility. This intensifies the adjustment problems that mobility gives rise to.

13   Because learning to adjust to different people and different social groups is extremely difficult for children, there are many potential hazards, the most common of which are social rejection and neglect, substitutes for peer companions, attempts to "buy" companionship, shifts in companions, dissatisfaction with one's role in the group, whether the leader or the follower role, and social mobility.

14 Substitute companions, whether family members, imaginary companions, or pets, are unable to socialize children as peer companions do and, as a result, are hazardous to good personal and social adjustments.

15 Children who are dissatisfied with the roles they play in the social group or who experience loneliness because of shifts in companions or mobility, suffer great psychological damage which adversely affects their self-concepts.

Bibliography

1 Adams, B. N. Occupational position, mobility, and the kin of orientation. *American Sociological Review*, 1967, *32*, 364–377.

2 Adams, G. R., and J. C. LaVoie, The effect of student's sex, conduct and facial attractiveness on teacher expectancy. *Education*, 1974, *95*, 76–83.

3 Ames, G. R., and A. F. Sakuma. Criteria for evaluating others: A reexamination of the Bogardus Social Distance Scale. *Sociology and Social Research*, 1969, *54*, 5–24.

4 Armentrout, J. A. Sociometric classroom popularity and children's reports of parental child-rearing behaviors. *Psychological Reports*, 1972, *30*, 261–262.

5 Bailey, R. C., P. Finney, and B. Helm. Sex-concept support and friendship duration. *Journal of Social Psychology*, 1975, *96*, 237–243.

6 Barrett, C. L., and H. Noble, Mothers' anxieties versus the effects of long distance move on children. *Journal of Marriage and the Family*, 1973, *35*, 181–188.

7 Benson, R. M., and D. B. Pryor. "When friends fall out": Developmental interference with the function of some imaginary companions. *Journal of American Psychonalytic Association*, 1973, *21*, 457–473.

8 Berkowitz, W. R. Perceived height, personality, and friendship choice. *Psychological Reports*, 1969, *24*, 373–374.

9 Bigelow, B. J., and J. J. LaGaipa. Children's written descriptions of friendship: A multidimensional analysis. *Developmental Psychology*, 1975, *11*, 857–858.

10 Blau, B., and J. Rafferty. Changes in friendship status as a function of reinforcement. *Child Development*, 1970, *41*, 113–121.

11 Bonney, M. E. Assessment of efforts to aid socially isolated elementary school pupils. *Journal of Educational Research*, 1971, *64*, 359–364.

12 Bossard, J. H. S., and E. S. Boll. *The sociology of child development*, 4th ed. New York: Harper & Row, 1966.

13 Brown, G. A. An exploratory study of interaction among British and immigrant children. *British Journal of Social and Clinical Psychology*, 1973, *12*, 159–162.

14 Bryan, T. H. Peer popularity of learning disabled children. *Journal of Learning Disabilities*, 1974, *7*, 621–626.

15 Busk, P. L., R. C. Ford, and J. L. Schulman. Stability of sociometric responses in classrooms. *Journal of Genetic Psychology*, 1973, *123*, 69–84.

16 Byrne, D., O. London, and K. Reeves. The effect of physical attractiveness, sex, and attitude similarity on interpersonal attraction. *Journal of Personality*, 1968, *36*, 259–271.

17 Clifford, C., and T. S. Cohn. The relationship between leadership and personality attributes of second grade children. *Journal of Social Psychology*, 1964, *64*, 57–64.

18 Cross, J. F., and J. Cross. Age, sex, race and the perception of facial beauty. *Developmental Psychology*, 1971, *3*, 433–439.

19 Deutsch, F. Observational and sociometric measures of peer popularity and their relationship to egocentric communication in female preschoolers. *Developmental Psychology*, 1974, *10*, 745–747.

20 Diab, L. N. A study of intragroup and intergroup relations among experimentally produced small groups. *Genetic Psychology Monographs*, 1970, *82*, 49–82.

21 Dion, K. K. Children's physical attractiveness and sex as determinants of adult punitiveness. *Developmental Psychology*, 1974, *10*, 772–778.

22 Dion, K. K., and E. Berscheid. Physical attractiveness and peer perception among children. *Sociometry*, 1974, *37*, 1–12.

23 Duck, S. W. Personality similarity and friendship choice: Similarity of what, when? *Journal of Personality*, 1973, *41*, 543–558.

24 Durogaiye, M. O. A. Behavior differences of sociometric status groups in a nursery school. *Child Development*, 1957, *28*, 103–111.

25 Early, C. J. Attitude learning in children. *Journal of Educational Psychology*, 1968, *59*, 176–180.

26 Elkins, D. Some factors related to the choice-status of ninety eighth-grade children in a school society. *Genetic Psychology Monographs*, 1958, *58*, 207–272.

27 Elliott, F. Shy middle graders. *Elementary School Journal*, 1968, *69*, 296–300.

28 Ellis, R. A., and W. C. Lane. Social mobility and social isolation: A test of Sorokin's dissociative hypothesis, *American Sociological Review*, 1967, *32*, 237–253.

29 Estvan, F. J. The social perception of nursery-school children. *Elementary School Journal*, 1966, *66*, 377–385.

30 Feldman, R. A. Group integration and intense interpersonal disliking. *Human Relations*, 1969, *22*, 405–413.

31 Feshbach, N. D. Sex differences in children's modes of aggressive responses toward outsiders. *Merrill-Palmer Quarterly*, 1969, *15*, 249–258.

32 Geller, D. M., E. Goodstein, M. Silver, and W. C. Steinberg. On being ignored: The effects of the violation of implicit rules of social interaction. *Sociometry*, 1974, *37*, 551–556.

33 Gottman, J., J. Gonso, and B. Rasmussen. Social interaction, social competence, and friendship in children. *Child Development*, 1975, *46*, 709–718.

34 Griffitt, W. B. Personality similarities and self-concept as determinants of interpersonal attraction. *Journal of Social Psychology*, 1969, *78*, 137–146.

35 Guilford, J. S. Maturation of values in young children. *Journal of Genetic Psychology*, 1974, *124*, 241–248.

36 Harrison, C. W., J. R. Rawls, and D. J. Rawls. Differences between leaders and nonleaders in six- to eleven-year-old children. *Journal of Social Psychology,* 1971, *84,* 269–272.

37 Hartup, W. W. Peer interaction and social organization. In P. H. Mussen (ed.), *Carmichael's manual of child psychology,* 3d ed. New York: Wiley, 1970. Vol. 2, pp. 361–456.

38 Haskett, G. J. Modification of peer preferences of first-grade children. *Developmental Psychology,* 1971, *4,* 429–433.

39 Hjelle, L. A. Accuracy of personality and social judgments as functions of familiarity. *Psychological Reports,* 1968, *22,* 311–319.

40 Hollander, E. P., and J. E. Marcia. Parental determinants of peer-orientation and self-orientation among preadolescents. *Developmental Psychology,* 1970, *2,* 292–302.

41 Isaacs, A. F. Giftedness and leadership. *Gifted Child Quarterly,* 1973, *17,* 103–112.

42 Jacobs, R. A. Mobility pains: A family in transition. *Family Life Coordinator,* 1969, *18,* 129–134.

43 Jersild, A. T., C. W. Telford, and J. M. Sawrey. *Child psychology,* 7th ed. Englewood Cliffs, N.J.: Prentice-Hall, 1975.

44 Jones, S. B. Geographic mobility as seen by the wife and mother. *Journal of Marriage and the Family,* 1973, *35,* 210–218.

45 Kingsley, R. F. Prevailing attitudes toward exceptional children. *Education,* 1967, *87,* 426–430.

46 Kleck, R. E., S. A. Richardson, and L. Roland. Physical appearance cues and interpersonal attraction in children. *Child Development,* 1974, *45,* 305–310.

47 Kohn, M., and B. Parnes. Social interaction in the classroom: A comparison of apathetic-withdrawn and angry-defiant children. *Journal of Genetic Psychology,* 1974, *125,* 165–175.

48 Krieger, L. H., and W. D. Wells. The criteria for friendship. *Journal of Social Psychology,* 1969, *78,* 109–112.

49 Landy, D., and H. Sigall. Beauty is talent: Task evaluation as a function of the performer's physical attractiveness. *Journal of Personality and Social Psychology,* 1974, *29,* 299–304.

50 Lazar, E. Children's perception of other children's fears. *Journal of Genetic Psychology,* 1969, *114,* 3–11.

51 Leinhardt, S. Developmental change in the sentiment structure of children's groups. *American Sociological Review,* 1972, *37,* 202–212.

52 Lerner, R. M., and E. Gellert. Body build, identification, preference, and aversion in children. *Developmental Psychology,* 1969, *1,* 456–462.

53 Levinson, B. M. *Pets and human development.* Springfield, Ill.; Charles C Thomas, 1972.

54 Loewenthal, K. How are "first impressions" formed? *Psychological Reports,* 1967, *21,* 834–836.

55 Long, L. H. Does migration interfere with children's progress in school? *Sociology of Education,* 1975, *48,* 369–381.

56 Lorber, N. M. Concomitants of social acceptance: A review of research, *Psychology,* 1969, *6,* 53–59.

57 Lott, A. J., B. E. Lott, and G. M. Matthews. Interpersonal attraction among children as a function of vicarious reward. *Journal of Educational Psychology,* 1969, *60,* 274–283.

58 Manosevitz, M., N. M. Prentice, and F. Wilson. Individual and family correlates of imaginary companions in preschool children. *Developmental Psychology,* 1973, *8,* 72–79.

59 Margolin, E. What do group values mean to young children? *Elementary School Journal,* 1969, *69,* 250–258.

60 Maw, W. H., and E. W. Maw. Social adjustment and curiosity of fifth-grade children. *Journal of Psychology,* 1975, *90,* 137–145.

61 McDavid, J. W., and H. Harari. Stereotyping of names and popularity in grade-school children. *Child Development,* 1966, *37,* 453–459.

62 McGuire, J. M. Aggression and sociometric status with preschool children. *Sociometry,* 1973, *36,* 542–549.

63 McKinney, J. P. The development of choice stability in children and adolescents. *Journal of Genetic Psychology,* 1968, *113,* 79–83.

64 Mims, P. R., J. J. Hartneff, and W. R. Nay. Interpersonal attraction and help volunteering as a function of physical attractiveness. *Journal of Psychology,* 1975, *89,* 125–131.

65 Minturn, L., and M. Lewis. Age differences in peer ratings of socially desirable and socially undesirable behavior. *Psychological Reports,* 1968, *23,* 783–791.

66 Mobe, P. A., and J. E. Williams. Relation of social attitudes to sociometric choices among second grade children. *Psychological Reports,* 1975, *37,* 541–554.

67 Morin, S. F., and R. L. Jones. Social comparison of abilities in blind children and adolescents. *Journal of Psychology,* 1974, *87,* 237–243.

68 Neetz, J. M. Birth order and leadership in the elementary school: A cross-cultural study. *Journal of Social Psychology,* 1974, *92,* 143–144.

69 Nelson, D. O. Leadership in sports. *Research Quarterly of the American Association for Health, Physical Education and Recreation,* 1966, *37,* 268–275.

70 Nelson, P. D. Similarities and differences among leaders and followers. *Journal of Social Psychology,* 1964, *63,* 161–167.

71 Orive, R., and H. B. Gerard. Social contact of minority parents and their children's acceptance by classmates. *Sociometry,* 1975, *38,* 518–524.

72 Packard, V. *The pyramid climbers.* New York: McGraw-Hill, 1962.

73 Patton, W. F., and E. Edwards. School readiness skills, personality characteristics and popularity of kindergarten children. *Perceptual and Motor Skills,* 1970, *31,* 689–690.

74 Rapier, J., R. Adelson, R. Carey, and K. Croke. Changes in children's attitudes toward the physically handicapped. *Exceptional Children,* 1972, *39,* 219–223.

75 Reese, H. W. Attitudes toward opposite sex in late childhood. *Merrill-Palmer Quarterly,* 1966, *12,* 157–163.

76 Richardson, S. A., and J. Royce. Race and physical handicap in children's preference for other children. *Child Development,* 1968, *39,* 467–480.

77 Riedesel, P. L. Bales reconsidered: A critical analysis of popularity and leadership differentiation. *Sociometry,* 1974, *37,* 557–564.

78 Roff, M., S. B. Sells, and M. M. Golden. *Social adjustment and personality development in children.* Minneapolis, Minn.: University of Minnesota Press, 1972.

79 Rubin, K. H. Relationship between egocentric communication and popularity among peers. *Developmental Psychology,* 1972, *7,* 364.

80 Scarlett, H. H., A. N. Press, and W. H.

Crockett. Children's descriptions of peers: A Wernerian developmental analysis. *Child Development*, 1971, *42*, 439–453.

81 Schachter, S. Birth order and sociometric choice. *Journal of Abnormal and Social Psychology*, 1964, *68*, 453–456.

82 Schaefer, C. E. Imaginary companions and creative adolescents. *Developmental Psychology*, 1969, *1*, 747–749.

83 Skorepa, C. A., J. E. Horrocks, and G. G. Thompson. A study of friendship fluctuations of college students. *Journal of Genetic Psychology*, 1963, *102*, 151–157.

84 Smith, C. R., L. Williams, and R. H. Willis. Race, sex and belief as determinants of friendship acceptance. *Journal of Personality and Social Psychology*, 1967, *5*, 127–137.

85 Spielberg, L., and R. Rutkin. The effects of peer vs. adult frustration on boys of middle childhood. *Journal of Psychology*, 1974, *87*, 231–235.

86 Sticht, T. G., and W. Fox. Geographical mobility and dogmatism, anxiety and age. *Journal of Social Psychology*, 1966, *68*, 171–178.

87 Sutton-Smith, B., and B. G. Rosenberg. Peer perceptions of impulsive behavior. *Merrill-Palmer Quarterly*, 1961, *7*, 233–238.

88 Thomas, J. R., and B. S. Chissom. Differentiation between high and low sociometric status for sixth-grade boys using selected measures of motor skill. *Child Study Journal*, 1973, *3*, 125–130.

89 Tulkin, S. R., J. P. Muller, and L. K. Conn. Need for approval and popularity: Sex differences in elementary school students. *Journal of Consulting and Clinical Psychology*, 1969, *33*, 35–39.

90 Vroegh, K. Masculinity and femininity in the elementary and junior high school years. *Developmental Psychology*, 1971, *4*, 254–261.

91 Wayne, D. The lonely school child. *American Journal of Nursing*, 1968, *68*, 774–777.

92 Ziller, R. C. The alienation syndrome: A triadic pattern of self-other orientation. *Sociometry*, 1969, *32*, 287–300.

93 Ziller, R. C., and R. D. Behringer. A longitudinal study of the assimilation of the new child in the group. *Human Relations*, 1961, *14*, 121–133.

94 Yasuda, S. A methodological inquiry into social mobility. *American Sociological Review*, 1964, *29*, 16–23.

CHAPTER 11

CHAPTER 11

PLAY
DEVELOPMENT

In few areas of development has there been a more radical change in attitude toward its importance to children's personal and social adjustments than in play. This is true not only of the scientist but also of the layman.

For generations it was believed that while play is fun, it is also a waste of time that could be spent more profitably on doing something useful. Since young children were incapable of doing anything useful, it was regarded as appropriate that they devote their time to play. However, when they were old enough to go to school, they were expected to learn to do things that would prepare them for life. Play activities were kept strictly for the end of the day or for holidays.

Since the turn of the present century, there has been a radical shift in attitudes toward play as a result of scientific studies of what play can do for the child's development. Instead of regarding play as a waste of time, scientists have pointed out that it is a valuable learning experience.

In no area, they have stressed, is this truer than in learning to be a social person. Because learning to be social is dependent upon opportunities to have contacts with members of the peer group and because these contacts are mainly in play activities, play is now regarded as an important tool for socialization.

Scientists have not been alone in stressing the importance of play to children's personal and social adjustments. Many parents, in keeping with the belief that children must be happy and carefree if they are to grow up to be well-adjusted adults, want their children to live in the world of play as long as possible. They provide them with all kinds of play equipment and free them from home duties and responsibilities. With the present-day emphasis on making good social adjustments, parents encourage their children to play with other children, and they choose homes in areas where playmates will be readily available.

Schools have acknowledged the educational value of play by introducing into the curriculum organized games and sports, dramatics, singing, and art.

Today more than ever before, manufacturers of toys and play equipment emphasize the educational value of their products. Many parents feel that if expensive toys have an educational as well as an amusing value, they must be worth the personal sacrifice needed to purchase them. Similarly, to counteract some of the criticism leveled against them, TV producers currently emphasize the educational value of children's television programs.

Meaning of Play

"Play" is a term so loosely used that its real significance is apt to be lost. In its strictest sense it means *any* activity engaged in for the enjoyment it gives, without consideration of the end result. It is entered into voluntarily and is lacking in external force or compulsion (101). Piaget has explained that play "consists of responses repeated purely for functional pleasure" (68). According to Bettelheim, play activities are those "having no rules other than those the player himself imposes and no intended end result in external reality" (5).

Play may be divided roughly into two categories, active and passive ("amusements"). What these two categories are and their important characteristics are explained in Box 11–1.

At all ages, children engage in both active and passive play. The proportion of time developed to each depends not on age, however, but upon health and the enjoyment children derive from each. While, typically, active play predominates in early childhood and amusements as children approach puberty, this is not always true. Some young children, for example, may

---

BOX 11–1

CATEGORIES OF PLAY

ACTIVE PLAY

In active play, the enjoyment comes from what the individual does, whether it is running just for the fun of running or constructing something with paints or clay. Children engage in active play less as they approach adolescence and have more home and school responsibilities and a lower energy level, owing to rapid growth and body changes.

AMUSEMENTS

In passive play or "amusements," the enjoyment is derived from the activities of others. The player expends a minimum of energy. The child who enjoys watching other children play, watching people or animals on television, looking at the comics, or reading books is playing with a minimum expenditure of energy, but the enjoyment may be equal to that of the child who expends great amounts of energy in the gym or on the playground.

prefer watching television to active play because they have not yet learned to play the games their age-mates enjoy and, as a result, are not accepted members of the peer group (63).

Play versus Work

"Work" differs from "play" in that it is an activity toward an end while, in play, the end result of the activity is of little or no importance. By contrast, in work, the activity is carried out not necessarily because it gives the individual enjoyment but rather because the individual wants the end result.

Work may be *voluntary,* in the sense that the individual elects to carry it out in the hopes of being rewarded for the effort by the end result. It may also be *involuntary* in that it is imposed on the individual by others. Involuntary work is usually called "drudgery." It has no element in common with play; it is not engaged in voluntarily, as play is, nor is the activity enjoyable to the individual as it is in play.

Although many people try to make a distinction between work and play activities, no activities may be classed exclusively as either. Whether an activity belongs in one category or the other depends not upon the activity itself but upon the individual's *attitude* toward it. Collecting, for example, is a form of play for a child or an adult who makes it a hobby, but it

is work for the person who collects articles to sell for a profit. Figure 11–1 shows that the same activity may be play, work, or drudgery.

Any activity that is directed toward an end other than enjoyment cannot rightly be called play. Games and sports are play to young children because winning or competing does not enter in; the only aim is to have fun. As children grow older, however, rivalry between gangs becomes important, and games or sports then become highly competitive. As a result, these activities become more like work than play. The end result is to beat the rival gang rather to enjoy the activity itself.

Relative Time Spent in Work and Play

How much time should be devoted to play and how much to work will depend on the age and the personal interests of the child. Some children derive their greatest satisfaction from work achievements, and others, from play. As children grow older, personal satisfaction from work often becomes increasingly important and satisfaction from play less important.

To date, there is not sufficient scientific evidence to indicate the relative amounts of time that should be devoted to work and to play to achieve the best personal and social adjustments. However, it is safe to conclude from the evidence now available, that

Figure 11-1. The same activity can be "work," "play," or "drudgery" for the child.

"Work"   **"Play"**   **"Drudgery"**

291

neither extreme—all work and no play or all play and no work—is as satisfactory as a combination of the two. Which should be given greater weight or whether they should be equal will depend on the age and personal needs of the individual child.

To determine whether children have the right combination of work and play for *them,* one can apply a relatively simple criterion. When children begin to be bored with play and ask, "What can I do now?" the scale has been too heavily tipped on the play side. If they are bored with their studies and home duties, or if they show signs of working below their capacities, it suggests that the work side of the scale has been overloaded. Consequently, it is safe to conclude that they need more time and opportunity for play (30, 56).

Contributions of Play

Play is such an accepted part of child life today that few people stop to consider the role it plays in the child's development. How important its contribution is Sutton-Smith has explained in this way: "The child's play consists of the four basic modes by which we know the world—imitation, exploration, testing and construction" (91).

Throughout the childhood years, play makes many contributions to children's personal and social adjustments. These contributions may differ somewhat from one level of development to another. When, for example, children put high value on sex appropriateness, as is true during the gang age of late child-

---

BOX 11–2

CONTRIBUTIONS OF PLAY TO CHILDREN'S DEVELOPMENT

PHYSICAL DEVELOPMENT
Active play is essential if children are to develop their muscles and exercise all parts of their bodies. It also acts as an outlet for surplus energy which, if pent-up, makes children tense, nervous, and irritable.

ENCOURAGEMENT OF COMMUNICATION
To play successfully with others, children must learn to communicate with them in terms they can understand, and they, in turn, must learn to understand what others are trying to communicate to them.

OUTLET FOR PENT-UP EMOTIONAL ENERGY
Play provides children with an outlet for the release of tensions due to the restrictions the environment places on their behavior.

OUTLET FOR NEEDS AND DESIRES
Needs and desires that cannot be satisfactorily met in other ways can often be met in play. A child who is unable to achieve a leadership role in real life may gain satisfaction for this desire by being a leader of toy soldiers.

SOURCE OF LEARNING
Play offers opportunities to learn many things—through books, television, or exploring the environment—that children would not have an opportunity to learn at home or in school.

STIMULANT TO CREATIVITY
Through experimentation in play, children discover that creating something new and different can be satisfying.

They then transfer their creative interests to situations outside the play world.

DEVELOPMENT OF SELF-INSIGHT
In play, children learn what their abilities are and how they compare with those of their playmates. This enables them to develop more definite and realistic concepts of themselves.

LEARNING TO BE SOCIAL
By playing with other children, children learn how to establish social relationships and how to meet and solve the problems these relationships give rise to.

MORAL STANDARDS
Although children learn in the home and school what the group considers right and wrong, the enforcement of moral standards is nowhere as rigid as in the play group.

LEARNING TO PLAY APPROPRIATE SEX ROLES
Children learn, at home and in school, what the approved sex roles are. However, they soon discover that they must also accept them if they want to become members of the play group.

DEVELOPMENT OF DESIRABLE PERSONALITY TRAITS
From contacts with members of the peer group in play, children learn to be cooperative, generous, truthful, good sports, and pleasant people to be with.

hood, play may prove to be a great help in creating the impression that they are sex appropriate. At an earlier age, when sex appropriateness is less important to them, play may makes its greatest contribution by helping them to learn social skills—something they value highly at that age.

In spite of the present-day emphasis on the socializing value of play, there is evidence that play makes other contributions to children's personal and social adjustments that are too important to be overlooked. Studies of children's play have revealed what these contributions are, the most important of which are explained in Box 11–2 (19, 63).

Characteristics of Children's Play

Studies of how children play have revealed that play during the childhood years has certain characteristics that differentiate it from the play of adolescents and adults. Although these characteristics may vary somewhat from child to child, they are so similar in their major aspects that they may be regarded as practically universal in American culture today. These characteristics are described below and their variations, when marked, are noted.

Play Is Influenced by Tradition

Young children imitate the play of older children, who have imitated the play of the generation of children preceding them. Thus, in every culture, one generation passes down to the next the forms of play it finds most satisfactory (81).

The influence of tradition is apparent in the seasonal patterns of children's play. Roller skates, jumping ropes, jacks, and bicycles come out on the first warm days of spring. With the approach of winter, children look forward to snow for sledding, snowball fighting, ice skating, and—in rural districts—sleigh riding (19).

Play Follows a Predictable Pattern of Development

From early babyhood to maturity, certain play activities are popular at one age and not at another, regardless of the environment, nationality, socioeconomic status, and sex of the child. These play activities are so universally popular and predictable that it is customary to divide the childhood years into specific play stages, each with its own name. These stages are described in Box 11–3.

Different kinds of play also follow predictable patterns. Block play, for example, has been reported to pass through four distinct stages. In the first, children merely handle, explore, carry blocks, and pile them in irregular masses; in the second, they construct rows and towers; in the third, they develop techniques for

---

BOX 11–3

STAGES IN PLAY DEVELOPMENT

EXPLORATORY STAGE
Until babies are about 3 months old, their play consists mainly of looking at people and objects and in making random attempts to grab objects held in front of them. From then on, their hands and arms come under enough voluntary control to enable them to grasp, hold, and examine small objects. After they can creep, crawl, or walk, they examine everything within their reach.

TOY STAGE
Toy play begins in the first year and reaches a peak between 5 and 6 years. At first, children merely explore their toys. Between 2 and 3 years, they imagine that their toys have life qualities—that they are capable of acting, talking, and feeling. As children develop intellectually, they are no longer able to endow inanimate objects with life qualities, and this dampens their interest in toys. Another factor that contributes to a decline in toy play is that it is mainly solitary and children want companionship. After entering school, most children regard toy play as "baby play."

PLAY STAGE
After children enter school, their play repertoires greatly increase, giving this stage its label. At first, they continue to play with toys, mainly when alone, and, in addition, they become interested in games, sports, hobbies, and other more mature forms of play.

DAYDREAM STAGE
As children approach puberty, they begin to lose interest in the play activities they formerly enjoyed and spend much of their play time in daydreaming. The characteristic daydreams of pubescents are of the martyr type, in which they see themselves as mistreated and misunderstood by everyone.

building more complicated designs; and in the fourth, they dramatize and reproduce actual structures (20, 28, 96).

Definite patterns have also been reported in children's drawings, in their interest in reading, in watching television or looking at comics, and in the types of games and sports they engage in. These patterns will be described later in connection with the different kinds of play of childhood.

The Number of Play Activities Decreases with Age

The number of different play activities engaged in gradually decreases as children grow older. Comparative studies have reported that among 8-year-olds, an average of 40.11 different play activities are engaged in during 1 week, while among persons 12 years old and older, the average is 17.71. Activities involving play with other children likewise decrease with age. At $7^1/_2$ years, the average is 27, as compared with 21 at $11^1/_2$ years and 13 at $16^1/_2$ years (21, 87).

The decrease is due to a number of reasons. Older children have less *time* available for play, and they want to spent it in ways that give them greatest enjoyment. As their *attention span* increases, they can concentrate on a play activity longer instead of flitting from one to another as they did when they were younger. Children abandon some activities because they have become *boring* or are regarded as babyish. For example, kindergarten children show a decreasing interest in blocks as other materials—paints, clay, crayons, and chalk—offer a greater variety of interesting activities.

The narrowing of the number of play activities may be the result of *lack of playmates*. Children who are not accepted in the peer group find themselves limited to activities they can enjoy alone. This is especially true for older children because most of the play at this age centers in gang activities.

Play Becomes Increasingly Social with Age

Because babies are egocentric, it is understandable that their play would be more solitary than social. Stone has explained that, even when the baby plays with the mother, the baby is "often a plaything, while the mothering one is the player. In time, both the child and the mothering one are mutually players and playthings" (86).

When young children first begin to play with agemates, there is little interaction or cooperation in their play. Instead, they engage in "onlooker play"—play in which children watch what other children are doing—or in "parallel play"—play in which children play in their own way, side by side with other children. When there is any interaction, there is little give and take. Instead, the interaction consists mostly of grabbing toys from another child and fighting when the child refuses to give up a toy.

As the number of social contacts increases, the quality of their play becomes more social. By the time children reach the school age, most of their play is social, as shown in cooperative play activities, provided they have achieved acceptance in a gang and, with it, an opportunity to learn to play in a social way (21, 36, 66, 75).

The Number of Playmates Decreases with Age

Young children will play with anyone who is available and willing to play with them. When they find children who are playing in a more interesting way, they shift from the children they are playing with to new ones. In a neighborhood or preschool group, children regard all group members as potential playmates.

After children become members of a gang, all this changes. They want to play with a small, select group—"my" gang—whose members have common interests and whose play gives them particular satisfaction. Older children limit the number of their playmates and spend most of their playtime with them (21, 75). Figure 11–2 shows the decline in number of playmates of children of high and low socioeconomic status.

Play Becomes Increasingly Sex Appropriate

Babies and very young children make little distinction between boys' toys and girls' toys, and children of both sexes play in much the same way. By the time they enter school, however, boys are clearly aware that boys do *not* play with certain toys unless they want to gain the reputation of being sissies (53, 59).

Boys not only drop their girl playmates when they enter school but they also shy away from all play activities which are not regarded as appropriate for them. Even when girls prefer play activities which the social group regards as "masculine," they, like boys, are influenced by social pressures to play in a sex-appropriate manner. As a result, the sex appropriateness of *all* children's play increases each year (4, 31).

Childhood Play Changes from Informal to Formal

The play of young children is spontaneous and informal. They play when, and with what toys, they wish, regardless of time and place. They do not need special play equipment or special play clothes. Gradually, play becomes more and more formal. During the gang age, for example, children feel that special clothing, special equipment, and a special place for play are essential. Appointments are made to meet and play at a definite time and place.

Play Is Less Physically Active As Children Grow Older

During the first three grades in school, children care little about sedentary play until late in the day, when they are tired. Then they like to watch television or be read to. From grade four on, however, there is a gradual increase in the amount of time spent in reading, going to the movies, watching television, listening to the radio, listening to music, and watching sports events.

Interest in active play reaches its lowest point during early puberty. At that time, children not only withdraw from active play but also spend little time reading, playing indoor games, or even watching television. Most of their playtime is devoted to daydreaming—a form of play that requires a minimum expenditure of energy.

Play Is Predictive of Children's Adjustments

The kind of play children engage in, the variety of their play activities, and the amount of time they spend in

play are all indications of their personal and social adjustments. Children, for example, who engage mainly in solitary play at ages when their peers are playing with other children are usually poorly adjusted, as shown by their lack of acceptance by members of the peer group (10, 40, 63, 75).

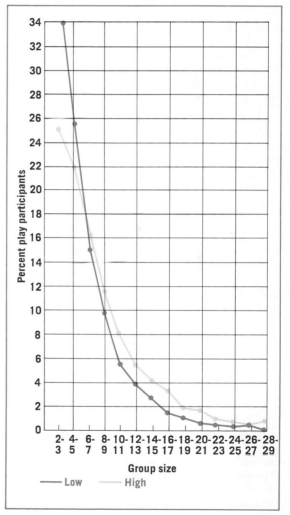

Figure 11–2. Percentages of play participants in different group sizes in schools of high and low socio-economic status. (*Adapted from R. R. Eifermann: Level of children's play as expressed in group size.* British Journal of Educational Psychology, *1970,* 40, *161–170. Used by permission.*)

There Are Marked Variations in Children's Play

Although all children pass through similar and predictable stages of play, not all children play the same way at the same age. Variations in children's play may be traced to a number of factors, the most important of which are given in Box 11–4 (16, 19, 63, 75).

Common Play Activities of Childhood

A survey of the different kinds of play children engage in will show how large the play repertoire of the typical child is. It is important to note, however, that not all children engage in all the play activities discussed below, though most children engage in a majority of them at some time or other.

Because there are so many play activities, they will be subdivided into two major categories, active play and passive play, generally called "amusements." These two categories will be discussed in detail below. In general, active play predominates in the early years of childhood and amusements in the closing years of childhood. However, at all ages throughout the childhood years, both types of play are represented in children's repertoire of play activities.

Both active play and amusements give children enjoyment and meet their play needs. Each type makes its contribution to their personal and social adjustments. However, at certain ages, one type gives more enjoyment and, as a result, meets children's play needs better than the other type. What these contributions are will be briefly discussed in connection with the different types of play activity that fall within each of the two major categories.

Active Play

Active play is play in which the enjoyment comes from what the children themselves do. While most children engage in different forms of active play, how much time they will spend on each and how much enjoyment they will derive from each vary greatly. These variations are due to a number of factors, six of which are especially important.

First, health affects active play. Healthy children spend more time in active play and derive more satisfaction from it than do children whose health is so poor that active play quickly tires them.

Second, because active play requires playmates, as children pass from the solitary play of babyhood to the social play of childhood, the degree of social acceptance children enjoy will determine how much time they will spend in active play and how much enjoyment they will derive from it.

The *third* factor responsible for variations in active play is the level of the child's intelligence. Very bright and very dull children, as a rule, spend less time in active play than do those whose intellectual level is closer to the average. This is mainly because their interests are out of step with those of more average intelligence and, as a result, they find such play less interesting to them than to the child whose play interests are geared to an average intellectual level.

Fourth, girls as a group engage in active play less often than boys not because they are less healthy or get less enjoyment from such play, but rather because they are discouraged from doing so by adults who regard very active play as sex-inappropriate for girls. This matter will be discussed in more detail in the chapter on sex roles.

Fifth, most active play requires some equipment to stimulate it. Babies who have few toys or young children who have little equipment for construction, for make-believe play, or for games are likely to turn to amusements where equipment in the form of a television set, books and magazines to look at, or a radio to listen to are more readily available.

Sixth, the environment in which children grow up influences the kind and amount of active play they engage in. In a cold climate, for example, winter games and sports are popular, but, for children who grow up in a warm climate, they would be impossible to engage in.

In the following pages, the different forms of active play popular among American children are discussed and a brief evaluation of each is given.

Free, Spontaneous Play

Free, spontaneous play is an active form of play in which children do what they want, when they want, and how they want. There are no rules and regulations. Children continue to play as long as the activity gives them enjoyment and then stop when their interest lags and, with it, their enjoyment.

The stimulus that gives rise to free, spontaneous play is anything new and different in the environment or toys that are especially designed for exploration. The more complex the object, the longer the time spent in exploring it.

As early as 3 months of age, babies begin to explore their toys or anything within their reach. This they do by sucking, banging, pulling at them or even by merely looking at them if they are beyond reach. By the end of the second year of life, interest in free, spontaneous play begins to wane. Because of this waning interest, free, spontaneous play may be regarded as "baby play."

There are three reasons for this early waning of interest in free, spontaneous play. *First,* as most of this play is solitary, children lose interest in it when they want to have playmates. *Second,* because enjoyment from this type of play comes mainly from exploring, when their curiosity has been satisfied with what is available to explore or what they are permitted to explore, they lose interest. *Third,* because of their rapidly growing intellectual abilities, children derive more enjoyment from more complicated play activities.

EVALUATION Even though exploratory play is annoying to parents, destructive of cherished possessions, and sometimes dangerous to children, it helps children to gain knowledge about things in their environment. It encourages children to be resourceful and to take the initiative in amusing themselves and to be self-sufficient when there is no one available to play with.

Children who, as babies, were permitted to explore and who were given toys that offered opportunities for exploration, learn what enjoyment they can get from exploring. As a result, they continue to engage in this form of play, to a limited extent and in a more controlled and sophisticated way, throughout childhood and even into adolescence and adulthood (28, 73, 89, 104). This matter will be discussed later in the section on active play.

Dramatic Play

Dramatic play—often called "make-believe play"—is a form of active play in which children, through overt behavior and language, deal with materials or situations as if they had attributes other than those they actually have. This type of play may be reproductive or productive—often called "creative"—in form.

In *reproductive* dramatic play, children try to reproduce in their play a situation they have observed in real life or in the mass media. By contrast, in *productive* dramatic play children use situations, actions, and speech from real-life situations in new and different forms. Reproductive dramatic play usually precedes productive.

In both reproductive and productive dramatic play, the children themselves play important roles, impersonating characters they admire in real life or in the mass media, or would like to be. The other actors are, at first, their toys—dolls, stuffed animals, soldiers, etc.—and later, their age-mates. The scenes at first are reproductions of real-life situations—a house, a store, or a doctor's office. Later, the scenes are more likely to be reproductions of those they have seen in the mass media—a battle scene or an operation in the hospital.

At first, dramatic play is solitary play. Later, as children become interested in playing with their age-mates, it becomes social with cooperation between children as they play different roles in the dramatizations. Whether solitary or social, dramatic play requires equipment. Children, for example, do not enjoy playing house unless they can transform the place where they are playing into the scene of the event they are playing.

As their intellectual abilities develop, especially their abilities to imagine, children transfer their interest from reproductive to productive dramatic play. Because productive dramatic play is a form of creativity, it will be discussed in the following chapter.

Dramatic play usually begins around the second year of life when children play with their toys as if they were real people or animals. They react to them in ways they have observed adults or older children react to the people or animals they represent. Gradually, as

their intellectual abilities increase, their dramatizations become more elaborate and complex. Instead, for example, of merely rocking a doll as if it were a baby, children duplicate the routine of caring for a baby—feeding or bathing it, or wheeling it in a carriage.

By the time children are ready to enter school, they begin to lose interest in dramatic play. However, their interest may continue for several years if their age-mates find it an enjoyable gang activity. Waning of interest in dramatic play comes mainly from an increase in realism and a decrease in ability to endow inanimate objects with living qualities. Dramatic play is, thus, typically early childhood play, just as free, spontaneous play is typically "baby play."

EVALUATION In spite of its relatively short duration as a play interest, dramatic play contributes much to children's personal and social adjustments. From practice in role-taking, children learn what the group considers appropriate for a role—whether as a parent, a pupil, or a soldier. They learn to view a situation from the frame of reference of the person they impersonate in their play. This helps them to develop social as well as self-insight.

Equally important, from dramatic play children learn to gain satisfaction from their own efforts instead of waiting to be amused by someone else. And, they learn to be cooperative members of a play group, playing the roles assigned to them by the group instead of demanding that they play only roles of their own choosing. This encourages them to be good followers which, as was stressed in the preceding chapter, is essential to good social adjustments (16, 63, 75).

Daydreaming

Daydreaming is a form of active play in which the activity is mental, rather than physical. Like dramatic play, the roles children adopt in their daydreams are dramatic, heroic, fanciful, and remote from daily life.

Like dramatic play, daydreams may be reproductive or productive. At first, they are largely r*eproductive*. In daydreams, children reproduce experiences in daily life in much the same way as they occurred in their everyday experiences. When, for example, the daydream is about going to a circus, children reproduce in their daydreams what happened on that occasion.

Soon, however, mundane experiences give way to more fanciful ones. Instead of merely going to a circus, for example, children see themselves as lion tamers or clowns, doing the things they saw the lion tamer or clown do in the circus. With this change, their daydreams become *productive* or creative. Since most daydreams are of this type, they will be discussed in more detail in the chapter on creativity.

. About the time children enter school, daydreaming begins to replace make-believe play. It normally reaches a peak during puberty or early adolescence. It is a popular form of play among older children when they are bored or restricted in their activities, as when they must sit through a long drawn-out family meal. Well-adjusted children usually daydream only when they cannot engage in other forms of play. Poorly adjusted children, by contrast, substitute daydreaming for play with other children.

EVALUATION Most people condemn daydreaming as a "waste of time" or as making children maladjusted to everyday life, which is usually far less exciting and glamorous than the daydream world. They also claim that it encourages mind-wandering and, as a result, children work below their capacities in school. By condemning it, they overlook some of the benefits children can and do derive from daydreaming.

Daydreaming, unquestionably, is a pleasurable form of activity that children can engage in when conditions make it impossible for them to engage in other forms of play. More important, it stimulates their imaginations and encourages creativity. In addition, it may serve as a source of motivation for children to do in real life what they have enjoyed doing in their daydreams.

If, however, daydreams are too unrealistic, children will be unable to match in real life their accomplishments in the daydream world. As a result, they will feel that they are failures. Under such conditions, the benefits they otherwise would derive from daydreaming are counteracted by feelings of inadequacy and inferiority (6).

Constructive Play

Constructive play is play in which children use materials to make things not for utilitarian purposes but rather for the enjoyment they derive from making them. At first, most constructive play is *reproductive*. Children reproduce in their constructions objects they coo in everyday life or in the mass media, such as mud pies to represent the pies they see baked at home or an Indian wigwam like those they see in books or on the television screen.

Up to the age of 4 or 5 years, children put together objects without a preconceived plan or pattern. If, by chance, they resemble a familiar object, such as a house or a bridge, they are delighted. By the time they are 5 or 6 years old, children use materials specifically and appropriately for making things according to a preconceived plan.

About this time, they begin to introduce originality in their constructions. Construction, thus, becomes a form of *productive play*. This form will be discussed in detail in the chapter on creativity.

Young children are pleased with whatever they make and proudly display it to others. Even before they enter school, however, they begin to be critical of their workmanship, especially in drawing and painting. They then not only stop boasting about their constructions but they often cover them up or destroy them if others come to look at them.

EVALUATION Constructive play contributes to self-sufficiency and to socialization. Because children derive enjoyment from making things when alone, they learn to amuse themselves when playmates are not available. They also learn to behave in a social way when they construct things with playmates by being cooperative and appreciative of their achievements. Constructive play also stimulates creativity.

If, on the other hand, children develop unrealistically high aspirations for their constructions, as often happens when they follow a model made by an adult or shown in a book of instructions, they are disappointed when their constructions fall below the standards they had hoped to achieve.

Also, if their constructions are ridiculed by peers or criticized by adults, it dampens their enthusiasm for this type of play because it kills the enjoyment they otherwise would derive from it. As a result, one of the important play activities of childhood and one that might be carried over to the adult years as a hobby is likely to be abandoned in favor of other play activities that contribute less to their personal and social adjustments then as well as in adult life.

Music

Music may be active or passive play, depending on how it is used. If children produce music by singing or by playing an instrument, just for the fun of it, or if they use music as a supplement to some other form of active play, such as dancing, it is active play. When, on the other hand, enjoyment comes from listening to the music produced by others, either by instruments or by singing, it is a form of amusement.

Music may also be reproductive or productive in form. If children reproduce the words and tunes produced by others, or if they dance to music in the way they have been taught to dance, it is *reproductive*. On the other hand, if they make up their own words for songs or produce their own tunes for words written by others, or if they make up original dance steps to accompany music, it becomes *productive* and, as such, is a form of creativity.

Singing is the most frequent form of musical expression because it requires no technical training. Children's favorite songs vary according to their major current interests. During the first four grades of school, children's songs are the most popular. As children grow older, there is an increased interest in classical, folk, and patriotic songs and less interest in religious and holiday songs. Interest in popular and dance music increases with age (35, 67, 72).

EVALUATION   Like constructive play, music can be a contributor to self-sufficiency and socialization. Children who derive enjoyment from singing, from playing musical instruments or from dancing to music can develop the ability to amuse themselves while, at the same time, learning to be creative. Music can also help to socialize them by encouraging cooperation with age-mates in producing music by singing, by playing instruments, or by dancing with them.

Unfortunately, many children for whom music could and should be a source of enjoyment, not only during childhood but also through life, are discouraged from engaging in this form of play by the critical attitudes of adults or prohibitions on their music because it "annoys" their parents and neighbors. In addition, their enjoyment is dampened by critical comments about the quality of the music they produce.

Collecting

Collecting is a common play activity of children from all racial, religious, and socioeconomic backgrounds. It begins during the preschool years, usually by the time children are 3 years old. At first, children collect anything and everything that attracts their attention, regardless of its usefulness. It gives them pleasure to pick up things and carry them home, where they usually put them with their toys or other possessions. Once collected, they are often forgotten. After children

start to play with other children, however, they often trade what they have collected for things their playmates have collected.

From the time children enter school until they reach puberty, collecting things that interest them at the moment or are similar to what their playmates collect is one of the most popular forms of play for both boys and girls. It gives them a sense of pride to have larger collections than their playmates, and they often engage in long trading or bartering sessions.

Collecting is not motivated by a desire to make use of what is accumulated. Thus, collecting is play in the strictest sense because the enjoyment comes more from the activity itself than from any practical value it might have. Older children usually keep their collections in some systematic arrangement, as in carefully labeled envelopes or jars. Systematizing their collections is fun for older children, but it also enables them to display their collections better and thus win the admiration and envy of peers as well as adults.

Although young children are random collectors, older children collect those things which have prestige in the peer group. If peers are interested in foreign stamps or pictures of athletes, for example, they will be interested too, hoping to collect a larger number of these prestigious items than their peers do.

EVALUATION   Whether engaged in as a solitary or social form of play, collecting contributes to children's personal and social adjustments. It makes them self-sufficient in their play and it encourages the development of such social skills as fair play, sharing, cooperation, and competition. It also helps children to learn new meanings and to become orderly.

If, on the other hand, children become too absorbed in making collections and classifying them, they are likely to spend a disproportionate amount of time in solitary play and shun play that will socialize them. In addition, absorption in their collections may result in feelings of superiority which will be reflected in their attitudes toward the collections of their age-mates and in what they say to them about their collections. This can and often does lead to social neglect or rejection.

Exploring

Just as babies derive keen enjoyment from exploring anything new or different, so do older children. The exploratory play of older children, however, differs from the exploratory activities of the free, spontaneous play of babies in four ways. These are described in Box 11–5.

There are sex differences in exploring, with boys engaging in it more often than girls. When girls do explore, they are likely to be less adventuresome than boys, to stay closer to home, and to have more adult supervision. This, it is important to realize, is not because girls are less curious or less adventuresome by nature than boys but rather because stricter restrictions are placed on their play activities than on boys'.

EVALUATION Exploring makes many contributions to children's personal and social adjustments, three of which are especially important. *First,* it increases children's knowledge and encourages them to seek information to supplement the knowledge they gain from their own explorations. *Second,* it encourages the development of such desirable personality traits as initiative, self-reliance, good sportsmanship, and calmness in the face of emergencies. And, *third,* it is an aid to socialization. When away from the protection and guidance of parents and teachers, children are forced to adjust to the wishes of the group, a learning experience that will be invaluable wherever they are.

On the minus side, exploring can and sometimes does encourage foolhardiness, thus often leading to accidents with their psychological damage. (See pages 127–128 for a discussion of this matter.) One or more accidents or narrow escapes may be so intimidating that children will abandon exploring as a form of play and thus be deprived of the benefits it gives.

Games and Sports

Games and sports are contests with set rules, undertaken for amusement or a stake. As Bettelheim has explained, they are "activities characterized by agreed-upon and often externally imposed rules and requirements to use the activity in an intended manner, not as fancy dictates" (5).

Sports are always physical contests, while *games* may be either physical or mental. Sports usually, though not always, involve either greater physical exertion or more rigid rules than games. The term "sport" is usually reserved for contests of highly organized teams, such as baseball, football, or basketball, though it can apply to individual outdoor contests, such as track, tennis, or hunting. Children's contests fall largely in the category of games, though sports begin to be popular as children approach adolescence

---

BOX 11–5

CHARACTERISTICS OF EXPLORING IN CHILDHOOD

PLANNING AND ORGANIZATION
Unlike babies and young children who spontaneously explore anything new and different, older children plan their explorations and organize some of their friends into a group to accompany them. Before they start out, they know where they want to go and what they want to do.

REMOTE ENVIRONMENTS
Having explored their immediate environments when they were younger, older children want to go to places remote from the familiar. Urban children, for example, may want to explore rural areas while rural children want to see the "big city" they have heard about.

GROUP VERSUS SOLITARY BEHAVIOR
Much of the enjoyment children derive from exploring comes from sharing their adventures with their age-mates. Unlike babies or younger children, older children get less enjoyment from exploring alone than from exploring with others. Exploring is one of the favorite activities of children's gangs.

GUIDANCE AND DIRECTION
The exploratory behavior of babies and young children is infrequently guided and directed but that of the gang-age child often is. Schools, scout groups, and camps plan tours to new, different, and interesting places too remote for children to go alone or which they would not be permitted to explore without adult supervision. Supplementary information given by the leaders or guides adds to the enjoyment children derive from these explorations.

(16, 63, 75, 81, 95). Box 11–6 lists the common kinds of childhood games with a brief description of each.

As children develop an interest in sports, they want to acquire the play skills needed for successful participation. At first, play is largely individual, and children concentrate on playing a better game than any of the other players. Because of this egocentric interest, young children are not good team players. Gradually, however, as they learn to cooperate with other players, children derive more satisfaction from sports. By the time they approach adolescence, most children are good team players (93, 95).

BABY GAMES

Simple games, played with family members or older children, appeal to babies before they are a year old. These traditional games, passed down from generation to generation, include pat-a-cake, peek-a-boo, and pigs-to-market.

INDIVIDUAL GAMES

By the time children are 4 or 5 years old, they play games to test their skills rather than just for fun. Play is individual and competition is with their own past achievements. The rules are few and are often modified or even violated. These games include walking on street curbs, jumping down steps, hopping on one foot, bouncing balls, and playing jacks.

NEIGHBORHOOD GAMES

While children are becoming interested in individual games, they are also developing an interest in neighborhood games of the undefined-group type in which any number can play. They may be organized by an older person or invented by the children themselves. Traditional games of this type include tag, hide-and-seek, statues, and cops-and-robbers.

TEAM GAMES

Team games begin to be popular with children between the ages of 8 and 10 years. They are highly organized and have rules and strong competition. At first, only a few children play but the number of players increases as skills improve and competition becomes stronger. Typical games of this type are modifications of baseball, football, basketball, and track.

INDOOR GAMES

Indoor games are less strenuous than outdoor games and are played mainly when children must stay indoors because of fatigue, illness, or bad weather. At first, they are played with parents or siblings and, later, with peers. Rules become stricter and competition keener as children grow older. Traditional games in this category include jacks, cards, guessing games, and puzzles.

EVALUATION Games and sports are not only pleasant forms of play but they also have great value as socializing agents. From them, children learn how to get along with other children, to cooperate in different activities, to play the role of leader as well as follower, and to evaluate themselves and their abilities realistically by comparing themselves and their achievements with those of their age-mates.

Children who lack social acceptance in the peer group must play games alone or with family members if they want to engage in this kind of play. While adults can teach children how to play games and are often willing to play with them, they usually fail to teach them how to be good sports. This is because adults are inclined to allow children advantages, as was explained earlier, while their age-mates will not. Having been accustomed to winning when playing with adults, many children are poor sports if they are losers when playing with age-mates.

Amusements

Amusements are forms of passive play in which children derive enjoyment with minimum effort from the activities of others. When, for example, children find reading difficult, they ask someone to read to them or they amuse themselves by looking at the pictures accompanying the text.

For some children, amusements are more enjoyable than active play, but for others, the reverse is true. For all children as they approach puberty, amusements begin to replace active play in popularity.

While some amusements can be enjoyed with members of the peer group, such as going to the movies or watching television, most amusements are carried out in solitude. Lack of social contacts does not diminish the enjoyment children derive from amusements as it does in active play.

Many adults regard the time children spend on amusements as a "waste of time" and claim that they would derive more benefit from active play. They imply, by these attitudes, that amusements make no contributions to children's personal and social adjustments. Such is not the case. Amusements not only make important contributions, but they also supplement the values derived from active play. However, some of the values of active play, such as its contribution to health and to the development of motor coordinations, are missing in amusements. Box 11–7 lists the most important contributions to children's personal and social adjustments made by amusements. Note how many of them relate to the important contributions of play listed in Box 11–2.

The most common forms of amusements among American children today are described in the following pages. As is true of active play, each will be evaluated to show its contributions to children's personal and social adjustments.

Reading

Long before children are able to read and even before they are able to comprehend the meaning of any but the simplest words, they like to be read to. Until they can read with minimum effort—and for many children, this is not before the third or fourth grades—reading for enjoyment is not a popular form of amusement. However, children continue to enjoy being read to, as they did when they were younger.

Once children have learned to read easily and well, they turn to reading as a form of amusement when they are tired, when they lack playmates because of geographic isolation, lack of social acceptance, or illness, or when they lack interest in the active play of their age-mates. Reading is most common in the late afternoons or evenings, when children are tired, when bad weather prevents them from playing outdoors, or on Sundays and holidays when playmates are not readily available.

Children from the more favored socioeconomic groups spend more time reading than those from the less favored groups. This difference is not necessarily due to a difference in intellectual level. Children from the better socioeconomic groups have more reading material readily available in the home and they receive more encouragement to read for pleasure than do children from less favored homes (24).

PREFERRED THEMES OF CHILDREN'S READING In spite of the popular belief that *young children* like highly imaginative stories, there is evidence that they prefer stories about things that "could happen." Stated in another way, they prefer stories that are sprinkled with a *bit* of unreality to those about what actually happened or those which are so far removed from their experiences that they cannot understand them (6, 24, 41).

Most young children prefer stories about familiar people and animals. They like these characters for their personal qualities or their humor. Since they are able to identify with animals, they derive great enjoyment from hearing about what they do (2, 41).

Because young children tend to be egocentric, they like stories that center around themselves. A story that tells how they digest their food, or what makes them hot or cold, has great fascination for them. If adults substitute storytelling for reading to young children, this egocentric interest is strong.

Cultural pressures influence the reading interests of *older children*. They read what is considered appropriate for members of their sex. Children from the middle and upper socioeconomic groups read what parents and teachers think appropriate, while children from the lower groups read what they wish, with a minimum of adult supervision (24).

With intellectual growth and school experience, older children become more realistic. They regard fantasy as "babyish" or "phony" and lose interest in stories where fantasy is involved, such as animals

---

BOX 11–7

IMPORTANT CONTRIBUTIONS OF AMUSEMENTS TO CHILDREN'S ADJUSTMENTS

- Amusements are an important source of knowledge.
- From amusements, children learn words and how to use them to communicate with others.
- By identification with characters in the mass media, children develop social insight which will help them to adjust to social life.
- Understanding themselves better comes from identification with characters in the mass media who have problems similar to theirs.
- Observing how characters in the mass media meet and solve their emotional problems helps children to handle the mental aspect of their own emotional problems successfully.
- Amusements provide outlets for children's needs and wants which are not provided by real-life situations.
- From observing how people in the mass media react to those who fail to conform to social expectations in the form of rules or laws, children develop a strong motivation to learn to conform.
- To be able to enjoy different kinds of amusements, children must learn to concentrate, to remember, and to reason. This aids their intellectual development.
- Many forms of amusement provide the materials for creativity and the motivation for children to use them to do something original.
- From the mass media, children learn what different roles in life embody and how people react to those who fail to play those roles satisfactorily.
- Many forms of mass media provide models of socially approved personality traits which children can use as models for their own personality development.

behaving like humans or fairy tales where characters do things children know do not happen in real life.

Children then turn their reading interests into three popular channels, adventure and violence, glamor and love, and educational topics. Which of these three major areas they will prefer will depend partly on their ages and reading abilities, partly on what their friends read, and partly on their own interests and personality patterns.

Regardless of children's backgrounds, they prefer pleasant settings for their stories and positive group interactions, characteristic of middle-class people, to the stark settings and negative group interactions of inner-city people. As the main characters of their readings, they prefer the "hero-type" to the "villain-type" (6, 45). In a study of children's books with high and low library circulation it was reported that the most popular books were those with heroes children could identify with because they had qualities they ad-mired and would like to possess. Books with villains as the main characters were far less popular because of their undesirable traits. Figure 11–3 shows the greater popularity of books with heroes as the main characters and the traits commonly associated with both heroes and villains in these books (9).

Another common characteristic of the preferred themes of children's readings is the strong preference they have for happy endings. Typically, children dislike anxiety-producing elements and want their stories to end happily. As Babbitt has explained (2):

> It does not work for every child's story, but perhaps it does apply to all that we remember longest and love best and will keep reading to our children and our children's children as a last remaining kind of oral history, a history of the essence of our own childhood. I am referring, of course, to The Happy Ending. Not, please, to a simple "happily ever after," or to the kind of contrived final sugar coating that seems tacked on primarily to spare the child any glimpse of what really would have happened had the author not been vigilant; not these, but to something which goes much deeper, something which turns a story ultimately toward hope rather than resignation.

POPULAR READING MEDIA IN CHILDHOOD   Three media provide reading material for children: books, newspapers, and magazines. Of these, books are the most popular and newspapers the least popular, though there are marked age as well as individual differences.

Young children like small *books* that they can handle and carry around easily; they like large, brightly colored pictures of people, animals, and familiar objects, and they like a minimum of reading matter, preferably in large letters which they can see easily without eyestrain. What reading matter there is must be in simple, understandable words and short sentences.

As children grow older and can read some of the words in their books, they continue to like the illustrations, just as they did when they were younger. Too much emphasis on description, whimsy, and scenes or customs that are unfamiliar to them tend to be boring.

As Schramm et al. have pointed out, "The newspaper is the last of the great media to which the child is introduced" (79). This seldom happens until children are 7 years old. After the introduction, children devote more

Figure 11–3. Children's preferences for heroes rather than villains and the traits admired in these characters. (*Adapted from R. H. Bloomer: Characteristics of portrayal and conflict and children's attraction to books. Psychological Reports, 1968, 23, 99–106. Used by permission.*)

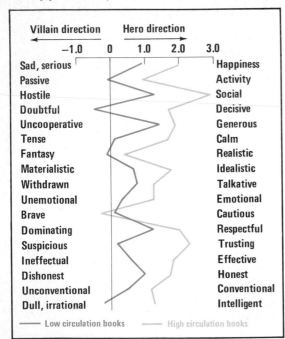

time to *newspaper* reading every year. As they approach puberty, they often spend more time reading newspapers than books.

When children first begin to read newspapers, their main interest is the comic strips. Gradually, as a result of their studies and their discussions of current events in school, they begin to read the news of the day, foreign news, political news, and even editorials.

Interest in *magazine* reading parallels interest in newspaper reading. At first, children merely look at the pictures. Later, they read some of the shorter stories, and last, the editorials and letters to the editor. At all ages, they prefer magazines with brightly colored ads and with stories and articles that are short, easy to read, and sex appropriate (24, 79).

EVALUATION Psychologically, reading is one of the healthiest forms of play. There are many reasons for this. It encourages children to become *self-sufficient* and to develop resources within themselves so that they can enjoy their leisure time when playmates are not available. Such resources will be valuable throughout life. When children enjoy reading for fun, they not only form *healthy attitudes* toward reading that will carry over to their schoolwork, but they acquire reading *proficiency* which will be an asset in all their studies.

Reading, regardless of the media used, encourages *creativity*. This is true of all reading themes, not of fantasy alone. Children who broaden their interests and acquire new knowledge through reading are laying the foundations for their own creative activities. This will be discussed in more detail in the following chapter.

Reading provides children with *insight* into their own problems and offers clues to how best to solve them. Equally important, as many children lack people they like and admire enough to want to identify with, in their reading they often find sources of *identification* which fit their needs and provide motivation in the molding of their own personalities (6).

In spite of the benefits derived from reading, it should not be assumed that the more reading children do, the greater the benefits. Too much play time devoted to reading indicates that children, for one reason or another, gain too little satisfaction from active and other forms of passive play to want to engage in them. Too much reading, therefore, can be regarded as a danger signal of poor personal and social adjustments.

Looking at Comics

Comics are cartoon stories in which the story element is less important than the pictures. They may be in book form, in comic strips in newspapers or magazines, or in cartoons. For the most part, children can understand the stories told by comics with a minimum amount of reading. That is why they have such a strong appeal to children who are still struggling to learn to read and who, as a result, must give more attention to the mechanics of reading than to the meaning of what is being read.

Most of the comics published today relate to adventure rather than comedy, and their appeal is principally emotional. Comics are "skewed toward reality." When the situation is real, the people are unreal; when the situation is unreal, the people are real.

The characters are occasionally humorous, but for the most part they are serious and are intent on dangerous adventure and noble deeds. To accomplish these ends, they use methods ranging from magic to violence. Good usually triumphs over evil in comics. Many of the comics today have animal characters and many of them are humorous (12).

The subject matter of the comics includes adventure, humor, romance and sex, animal antics, and detective stories. Some are based on literary classics or stories from the Bible. Approximately equal space is devoted to humor, sex, and crime.

Because children growing up in America today are literally surrounded by comics, it is not surprising that looking at the comics is one of their favorite forms of amusement. Box 11–8 explains some of the reasons children have for liking comics.

PREFERRED COMICS The appeal of various kinds of comics follows a predictable pattern. Among *preschoolers*, the favorites are those in which animals, such as Bugs Bunny and Mickey Mouse, dress and talk like human beings. In fact, however, preschool children like all comics, provided they contain no element of terror.

In *late childhood*, at the beginning of the hero-worship age, children like comics with heroes or heroines they can identify with. They like adventure, mystery, and thrills and, as they approach puberty, romance and love. Sex and crime also have a great appeal for children during the gang age, as does humor. As these new themes become popular, interest in

BOX 11–8

WHY CHILDREN LIKE COMICS

- Through identification with characters in the comics, children have an excellent opportunity to gain insight into their own personal and social problems. This may help them to solve their own problems.
- Comics appeal to children's imagination and to their curiosity about the supernatural.
- Comics offer children a temporary escape from the humdrum reality of daily life.
- Comics are easy to read. Even poor readers can get the gist of their meaning from the pictures.
- Since comics are inexpensive, even children from poor families can have some of their own.
- Because many comics are exciting, mysterious, and humorous, they provide children with the motivation to learn to read, which many children's books do not.
- If in serial form, comics give children something to look forward to.
- In comics, the characters often do or say things children themselves do not dare to do, even though they would like to. This provides a vicarious pleasure for them.
- The characters in comics are often strong, brave, and good looking, thus giving boys and girls heroes and heroines to identify with.
- The art in comics is colorful and simple enough for children to understand.

animal comics and those centering on family life lose their appeal (12, 79).

EVALUATION   Many educators and parents oppose the child's preoccupation with comics. Others approve of their looking at comics or at least condone it. Both sides present arguments to substantiate their points of view (12, 23, 105). Box 11–9 gives some of the most common arguments.

The pro and con arguments presented in the box indicate the lack of agreement on the effects of the comics. They have both good and bad features so far as mental health, academic work, and personality development are concerned. As long as reading the comics is a favorite form of play among American children, any child who is not permitted to read them will be regarded as "different," and this can be very damaging psychologically.

By contrast, devoting an *unreasonable* portion of playtime to comics is not only unwise but the source

of potential psychological harm. If children *want* to devote more time to the comics than their age-mates do, this may be regarded as a danger signal of poor personal and social adjustments.

Going to Movies

Going to the movies is far less popular with children today than it was a decade or two ago. There are two major reasons: *First,* children get much the same sort of pleasure from watching television as from going to the movies, especially since many of the popular movies are shown on TV; and *second,* movies have become so expensive that many children cannot afford to attend even the "kiddie shows" without making great inroads upon their allowances.

This does not mean that going to the movies is no longer a form of amusement for American children. They do go to the movies—though less frequently than in the past—and they see movies on the television screen in their homes or in the homes of friends. Movies have the same appeal today as they did in the days when TV was not a part of every American home and children had to go to the theater to see them. In fact, watching movies, whether in a movie theater or on television is one of children's favorite amusements.

Interest in movies as a form of recreation develops later than many other play interests. Most preschoolers cannot understand enough of what is shown on the movie screen to be able to concentrate on it for an entire show, and thus they become bored and restless. This, of course, is not true of movies made especially for their age level.

Furthermore, as many movies have a "thrill" element involving shooting and noise, many preschoolers become frightened. Not realizing that it is only make-believe, they often shut their eyes and cry in fear. This lowers their interest in going to the kiddie shows at the neighborhood movie theaters and even in watching movies on television.

By the time children are 6 or 7 years old, they can concentrate for a longer time, especially when what they see or hear is amusing to them. They have a better understanding of what they are hearing and seeing and thus find it more interesting. In addition, older children know that a movie is only make-believe and are, therefore, less frightened by violent or aggressive scenes.

MOVIE PREFERENCES   What children see on the screen, whether on the television screen or in a theater, depends on what is available at the times they can watch. If, however, there is a choice, young children prefer comics and animated films, especially those with animals as the main characters. They can understand these and they usually lack terror elements.

For older children, by contrast, the thrill element of a film is its major appeal. Regardless of how the thrill is produced, they want to see something that excites them and has an element of terror, violence, or suspense. Anything that offers excitement, adventure, or mystery appeals to them because it is in sharp contrast to their daily lives. It is for this reason that older children often prefer movies to books, games, and sports (1).

EVALUATION Any form of play that has a strong appeal to children will, inevitably, affect their attitudes and behavior. Some of the ways movies influence children are given in Box 11–10. How much influence movies have is determined by many factors, four of which are especially common.

First, what children get from movies depends on their needs and background. Children with low aggression, for example, are usually more aggressive after seeing a film with an aggressive theme. Seeing aggression on the screen gives it a stamp of approval and encourages them to release the aggressiveness they have inhibited.

Second, the more closely a picture relates to experiences children have had, the greater the likelihood that they will understand and remember it. A very exciting film, on the other hand, tends to stifle critical attitudes and, as a result, children are apt to remember it in an uncritical way and this increases the influence it has on them.

Third, because children with low IQs tend to be less critical than those with higher IQs, they tend to be more influenced by what they see on the screen than do children with higher IQs.

Fourth, when children identify closely with one of the characters on the screen, they share, vicariously, the experiences of the character. This influences their behavior later. If the character is aggressive, for example, this tends to increase children's aggressiveness.

Radio Listening

Before the advent of television, listening to the radio was an even more popular amusement than going to the movies. Now listening to the radio has lost much of its appeal for young children, though many older children find radio listening meets their play needs better than television watching.

Interest in listening to the radio begins earlier than interest in movies. Babies enjoy hearing music and listening to others speak, even though they cannot understand what they are saying. Few children, however, show much interest in the radio until they are 3 years old. From then on, interest in radio listening increases.

The time spent in listening to the radio varies

BOX 11–9

EVALUATION OF COMICS

ARGUMENTS IN FAVOR OF COMICS

- The comics supply the child of limited reading ability with an enjoyable reading experience.
- Comics may be used to motivate the child to develop reading skills.
- The educational attainment of the child who reads comics frequently is almost identical with that of one who reads them infrequently.
- The child is introduced to a wide vocabulary, many words of which are encountered in other reading.
- The comic book provides an excellent technique for disseminating propaganda, especially antiprejudice propaganda.
- The comics provide the child with a source of emotional catharsis for pent-up emotions.
- The child may identify with comic book characters who embody admired qualities.

ARGUMENTS AGAINST COMICS

- The comics distract the child from more worthwhile literature.
- Since the pictures tell the story, the poor reader may make no effort to read the text.
- There is little or no progression of reading experience within the comics.
- The art, stories, and language of most comic strips are inferior.
- Material relating to sex, violence, and fear overstimulates and often frightens the child.
- The comics keep the child from engaging in other forms of play.
- By portraying antisocial behavior, comics encourage aggressiveness and juvenile delinquency.
- The comics make real life seem dull and uninteresting.
- The comics stereotype people, and this encourages prejudice.

BOX 11-10

HOW MOVIES INFLUENCE CHILDREN

- Movies give children pleasure by taking them into a new world of people and animals doing things that they cannot do.
- In the movies, children find an excitement not found in their everyday lives, an excitement more vivid than they can get from their reading, even from the comics.
- Ideas that can be used in other play activities are derived from movies about cowboys, spacemen, Indians, etc.
- Movies provide information about how to behave in social situations, and children use this to increase their social acceptance.
- Information is remembered longer when seen on the screen with sound than when presented in print with only an occasional illustration, as in books, newspapers, and magazines.
- Movies provide information about many different kinds of people—people with whom children have little or no personal contact. Whether this will foster tolerance, prejudice, or liking will depend largely on how the people are presented on the screen.
- Moving pictures have a pronounced emotional effect on children. In young children, this may be expressed in nightmares, daydreams, eating and sleeping problems, or nervous mannerisms. In older children, the effects are much milder and less frequent because they realize that what they see on the screen is merely make-believe.
- Watching movies for too long at one time may cause eyestrain and general fatigue. Horror movies are especially fatiguing both physically and emotionally.

dren like plays dealing with adventure, mystery, crime, and comedy, and they like popular dance music.

Quiz shows appeal to older children, as do plays about domestic life, slapstick comedies, sports reports, and, occasionally, the news of the day. For the most part, older children dislike programs of a serious nature, such as classical music and educational, religious, or historical talks (34).

EVALUATION There is a tendency to overestimate the unfavorable effects of radio listening and to underemphasize the educational and other advantages. Without question, however, the amount of time spent in radio listening and the kind of program habitually listened to are important determinants of its effects.

The *favorable* effects of radio listening have been listed as follows: it offers children a form of entertainment within the home and thus keeps them with the family; it increases children's knowledge about history, geography, current events, literature, and other subjects and it supplements what they learn in school; it improves their speech by increasing their vocabularies, improving their grammar, and giving them a good model of diction; it encourages them to read to supplement their knowledge of subjects they have heard over the air; and it offers them models with whom they can identify, thus acting as an incentive to self-improvement.

Critics of radio listening emphasize the *harmful* effects. These are most pronounced when children concentrate on programs of violence, crime, and mystery. Terrifying programs may affect the general physical condition of children by producing nightmares, nervous tension, loss of sleep, and poor appetite.

Children who spend much of their time listening to the radio get too little exercise for normal development and a healthy physical condition. Their schoolwork may suffer because they do not give enough time to their studies and do not concentrate when they are studying. As with any other form of amusement, too much time spent in listening to the radio may be regarded as a danger signal of poor personal and social adjustment.

Listening to Music

Popularity of listening to music as an amusement begins early. Babies enjoy being sung to and listening to music on records, radio, or television. This enjoyment increases as children grow older, reaching a

greatly. Some children spend several hours a day—more than is spent in playing with other children or reading. Other children spend almost no time on this amusement, especially if television watching is readily available for them (1, 34).

PROGRAM PREFERENCES In general, preferences for radio programs at different ages follow preferences in reading and movies. Preschool children like to listen to programs which deal mainly with animals and familiar people doing familiar things. They also like simple music, whether vocal or instrumental.

By the age of 6 years, children begin to lose interest in children's programs. They now want programs that are more exciting and entertaining. Young school chil-

high point at puberty when interest in active play sharply decreases.

Just as babies and young children like simple stories, so they like simple music. They can comprehend anything simple, but anything complex fails to hold their attention because they cannot understand it. In the case of music, they like plenty of rhythm and simple renditions.

Some children prefer singing to orchestral and single-instrument music, although, for others, the reverse is true. However, most like any music, provided it is not too complex for them to understand.

Children will listen to music from any source, but they prefer music on records, if given a choice. The reason for this preference is that it enables them to listen to the music of their choice and enables them to repeat favorite music over and over again. When listening to music on radio or television, they are limited to what is available at times when they can listen and they are unable to hear, time after time, their favorite music.

An added advantage to listening to music on records is that they can play records while studying. Many older children, claiming that they can study better while listening to music, turn on their phonographs or radios when they study. In many homes where there is only one radio or television set, this very likely would not be permitted.

EVALUATION Listening to music makes important contributions to children's personal and social adjustment. It gives them a form of enjoyment when they are alone, it relaxes them when they are tired, it often serves as a form of catharsis for pent-up emotional energy, and it serves as a foundation for a hobby that will give them lifelong enjoyment. Because listening to music is a popular form of amusement among children, being able to listen to music with their age-mates and to talk about their favorite songs acts as a bond that encourages social acceptance.

On the negative side, listening to music is detrimental to good adjustments only when it becomes so time-consuming as to use time that should be spent in active play or when it encourages excessive daydreaming or poor concentration. Children who habitually listen to music while studying, for example, may readily develop a habit of mind-wandering that will play havoc with their schoolwork and, as they grow older, with any work they may do except routine work in a factory or office.

Television Watching

Television combines the appealing features of the movies and radio and is one of the most popular amusements during the childhood years. In fact, it has been called the "electronic Pied Piper"—a label suggesting that it literally lures children away from other forms of play.

Many babies are introduced to television while they are still in their cribs. For them, television is a built-in

---

BOX 11–11

FACTORS INFLUENCING CHILDREN'S INTEREST IN TV

- *Age.* Preschoolers show a greater interest in television than school-age children, who have broader play interests and more playmates, and are more critical of what they see on TV.

- *Sex.* Age for age, boys spend more time watching television than girls. Boys find reading more difficult than girls; also, television shows often concentrate on the thrills that boys like.

- *Intelligence.* At all ages, bright children derive less satisfaction from television than their less bright age-mates, and they begin to lose interest in it sooner.

- *Socioeconomic status.* TV is more popular with children of the lower socioeconomic groups than with those of the higher. This becomes more true as childhood progresses, in part because children in the lower groups have fewer opportunities for other forms of play.

- *Academic achievements.* Age for age, good students are less interested in television than poor students. They often regard it as a waste of time to watch the programs that are available.

- *Social acceptance.* There is a close relationship between the amount of social acceptance children enjoy and their interest in TV. The more accepted they are, the less interest they have in television and vice versa.

- *Personality.* Television appeals more to children who are poorly adjusted, both personally and socially, than to those who are well adjusted. Self-bound children watch TV more than those who are outer-bound.

---

baby sitter because it keeps them amused when no one is available to act in this role. For some preschool children and even older children, television watching is an *added* play activity, not merely a substitute for active play and other forms of passive play. But for many children it is more popular and more consuming of their play time than all other play activities.

The appeal of television varies markedly from child to child and from age to age in the same child. Some of the factors responsible for these variations are listed and discussed briefly in Box 11–11.

TIME SPENT ON TELEVISION For far too many children, the time spent on television watching is out of all proportion to the amount of time devoted to other forms of play. In commenting on how much time *preschoolers* spend watching television, Murray has said: "On the average, preschoolers spend approximately half of an adult's work week sitting in front of the television screen" (62). From the time children are 3 years old until they enter school at 6, there is a sharp increase in the amount of time spent in television watching (62). This is shown in Figure 11–4.

Figure 11–4. Time spend daily watching television by children of different ages. (*Adapted from H. R. Marshall: Relations between home experiences and children's use of language in play interactions with peers.* Psychological Monographs, *1961,* 75, *no. 5. Used by permission.*)

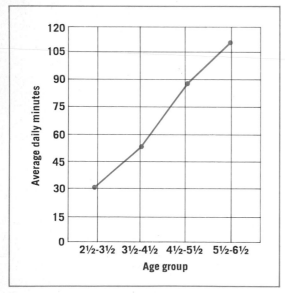

Studies show that the average *schoolchild* spends from 20 to 21 hours a week before the television screen, with a decrease of approximately 3 hours during the summer months (62).

The amount of time children spend in watching television is not, however, foolproof evidence of their interest or lack of interest in it. The time may be regulated by family rules, by the demands of schoolwork or home duties, by whether the family owns one television set or more, or none at all, by how many family members there are to share the watching time, and many other conditions.

PROGRAM PREFERENCES When children first start watching television, they watch any program available at the time. Soon, however, they begin to show definite program preferences. Preschool children like dramatizations involving animals and familiar people, music, cartoons, and simple comedy. First- and second-grade children like puppet shows, cowboy movies, harmless mysteries, humor, family-life situations, and prize-presenting programs. By the third and fourth grades, children are interested in imaginative programs, such as those about rockets and spaceships, and in variety shows, mystery and detective stories, dramatic plays, and music. Fifth- and sixth-grade children continue to like these programs, but they also like presentations dealing with science and feats of skill. Stories, comedy, cartoons, and music are popular at every age, while educational programs tend to be unpopular, especially among children with lower intellectual levels. Only if the educational program is presented in an entertaining way, like Sesame Street, will it have as strong appeal to children of all intellectual levels as programs that concentrate on entertainment (47, 62, 88).

Program preferences of young children are greatly influenced by guidance and encouragement from parents. Later, teachers help them to choose the programs they consider most interesting as well as most wholesome and informative. Among older children, program preferences are influenced more by peers than by parents or teachers.

EVALUATION In view of the amount of time children spend in television watching, it is logical to assume that it has a profound influence on them. Because of this influence, popular concern about television is understandable. Ever since its arrival, parents, educators, law-enforcing officers, and the clergy have shown a great concern about its effects on the child. Concern has ranged from the inroads television makes on reading and other leisure-time activities to its effect on moral behavior and its relationship to the increase in juvenile delinquency. The blame has not been placed on television per se as much as on the kind of programs available to children.

All studies of the effects of television watching have indicated that how much influence it has on children depends upon many conditions, three of which are especially important.

First, how much influence television has and whether this influence is good or bad is determined by the amount of guidance and supervision children have in their watching (76). If parents take time to interpret what children see on the screen, as they do when they read to them or provide them with books to read, children will understand and interpret correctly what they see. Furthermore, with guidance and supervision of programs children see, they can learn healthy patterns of behavior and values that will lead to good socialization rather than to unhealthy values and unsocial patterns of behavior. As Leifer et al. have pointed out, "Television is not only entertainment for children, but it is also an important socializer for them" (48).

Second, how much children remember of what they see on the screen and how correctly they understand it will have a marked influence on the effect it has on them. If they interpret violence on television, for example, to mean that this is the socially approved pattern of behavior and the correct model for them to imitate, its effect will be vastly different than if they interpret it to mean a socially disapproved pattern of behavior.

Third, how television affects children depends on what kind of children they are as a result of other experiences. Schramm et al., from their study of the influence of television on over 6,000 children, have stressed this factor as an important determinant of the effect of television in this way (80):

> More important than what television brings to the child is what the child brings to television. And this is our responsibility. What kind of child are we sending to television? . . . If we use television as a baby sitter, at the cost of other human contacts, we are obviously remiss. If we do not introduce our children to books, simply because television is so easily available, then we are being foolish. If we do not help our children to build up healthy contacts with other humans their own

age, simply because television "keeps them at home," then we are truly doing them an unkindness.

Concern about the effects of television watching on children has given rise to research studies to discover just how great its influence on children's attitudes and behavior is and whether this influence is immediate, long-term, or both. Some of the studies have concluded that television watching is a good influence; others that it is damaging. There is almost unanimous agreement, however, on one point: The well-adjusted child is less likely to be adversely affected, either temporarily or permanently, than the poorly adjusted child, and the healthy child less than the unhealthy.

Of the many effects of television watching that have been reported, the ones listed and briefly explained in Box 11–12 have received the most attention (29, 48, 61, 74, 76, 97).

However, if the psychological damage of television watching is to be reduced and if the psychological benefits are to be increased, it should be evident that there must be more guidance and control over what programs children see than is given in most homes. It should also be evident that in this area of play children need more guidance and control than in any other, even in the reading of comics (54, 76).

Unfortunately, this guidance and control are often lacking. If the themes and pictures in comics are harmful, parents and teachers try to keep them out of the child's reach. Social pressure in many communities has forced merchants to remove harmful comics from their shelves. Unfortunately, far too many parents show little concern about the quality of television their children watch. They *encourage* their children to watch when they are tired or fretful, regardless of what is on. Since many parents believe that television has an educational value, they permit children of all ages to spend more time watching than is good for them. Parents in the lower socioeconomic groups are more permissive about television watching than those in the middle and upper groups.

Play Hazards

Because of the widespread interest in the effects of television watching on children and the concern about its damaging effects, it would be logical to assume that this is the only serious hazard in children's play. This is far from the truth.

BOX 11–12

REPORTED EFFECTS OF TELEVISION ON CHILDREN

PHYSICAL EFFECTS
Watching television often interferes with schedules of eating and sleeping. Digestion may then be upset, and children will get less sleep than they need.

EFFECTS ON OTHER FORMS OF PLAY
Television watching cuts into the time available for other play activities, especially outdoor play with other children. It also leaves little time for creative play or different forms of amusement.

EFFECTS ON SCHOOLWORK
Television presents material in such an exciting and vivid way that schoolbooks can hardly compete with it for children's interest and attention. As a result, they often find schoolbooks and schoolwork boring.

EFFECTS ON FAMILY RELATIONSHIPS
Television watching often restricts social interactions among family members and limits conversation.

MOTIVATION TO ACQUIRE KNOWLEDGE
Some children are motivated to follow up what they see on the television screen by reading to fill in the gaps in their knowledge of the subjects.

EFFECTS ON ATTITUDES
Characters in television are usually presented as stereotypes. Children then come to think of all people in a given group as having the same qualities as the people on the screen. This influences children's attitudes toward them.

EFFECTS ON VALUES
A constant diet of programs showing crime, torture, and cruelty may, in time, blunt children's sensitivities and encourage the development of values that are not in keeping with those held by the majority of the social group. If children become habituated and desensitized to violence, they will accept such behavior as a normal pattern of life.

EFFECTS ON BEHAVIOR
Since children are imitators, they feel that what has the stamp of approval of a television program must be an accepted way for them to behave. Because law-abiding heroes or heroines are less glamorous than those who win attention by violence and other unsocial acts, children tend to use the latter to identify with and imitate.

EFFECTS ON SPEECH
Children's speech is greatly influenced by what they hear the people on television say and how they say it. This may lead to improved pronunciation and grammatical forms but it will not necessarily give children good patterns of presentation of what they say. See Figure 11–5.

MODELS FOR LIFE ROLES
Television characters present models for different life roles, for sex-appropriate behavior, and for careers. This gives children insight into what the social group expects of them.

EFFECTS ON BELIEFS
Many children believe that anything said on television is true and that the television announcers know more about everything than parents, teachers, and doctors. This is likely to lead to a general gullibility.

Figure 11–5. What children say and how they say it is often influenced by what they hear on television. (*Adapted from "Nancy" by Ernie Bushmiller, United Features Syndicate, July 18, 1974. Used by permission.*)

There are many other hazards which, though not necessarily as damaging as television watching is claimed to be, are nonetheless too damaging to children's personal and social adjustments to be overlooked. A brief summary of some of these hazards will show why this is correct.

Too Much Play Time

Some parents, influenced by the old saying that "All work and no play makes Jack a dull boy," conclude that the more playtime their children have, the brighter and better adjusted they will be. As a result, they free their children from many of the activities that might be regarded as work, and they encourage them to spend the major part of their waking hours in play. Even after their children reach school age, such parents insist that the schools give little or no homework, and they free their children from household chores to enable them to have as much time for play as possible. (17)

Depriving children of an opportunity to balance play with work activities is hazardous to good personal and social adjustments. This is true of toddlers, just as it is of preschool and school-age children. There are three important reasons for this.

First, a steady diet of play becomes boring to children because it is monotonous. Even with a large variety of equipment to stimulate many different kinds of play, there will be so much repetition that the excitement and enjoyment of play will wear off and children will become bored. Boredom, in turn, makes children lethargic and prone to expend far less energy in doing everything than they are capable of. This can and often does lead to the habit of underachievement. As a result, too much play can make "Jack" just as "dull" a boy as too much work.

Second, children are deprived of the pleasure of social recognition they could get if they achieved success in some work activity, whether in the home, the school, or the community. The reason is that far less social recognition is given for play achievements than for work achievements. Even among high school or college athletes, only the outstanding players on their teams are likely to receive social recognition for their achievements.

Third, depriving children of the opportunity to engage in activities that are regarded as "work" encourages children to think of work as something that should be avoided as long as possible because it is an unpleasant activity. In time, this may lead to an antiwork attitude which will be hazardous to good personal and social adjustments as well as to successful achievements throughout life.

Imbalance between Active Play and Amusements

Active play and amusements both make important contributions to good personal and social adjustments. When there is an imbalance between them, whether in favor of active play or amusements, children are deprived of the benefits they should be getting from the type of play that is occupying too little of their playtime.

Imbalance in favor of either active play or amusements has many causes. It may be due to too much *equipment* for one type of play and too little for the other. The child may have, for example, plenty of equipment for all kinds of outdoor play but very little for indoor play, especially dramatic, creative, and constructive play.

The *environment* in which the child grows up may be responsible for the imbalance. Urban children, whose parents live in crowded sections of a city, are likely to be deprived of play space and, because of danger from traffic, unable to use equipment for active play, such as skates, bicycles, or sleds.

A child with a *special ability,* such as mechanical or artistic talent, often favors play in which the special ability can be used. Recognizing the talent, parents are likely to encourage the use of that ability in play and to provide play equipment needed to make the play enjoyable.

When parents believe that certain kinds of play are beneficial to the child and others are likely to be harmful, *parental encouragement* to engage in the types of play they regard as beneficial and discouragement or prohibition of engaging in the types they regard as harmful may result in an imbalance in the child's play activities.

Peer pressures are likewise an important cause of play imbalance. If gang-mates want to spend their play time almost exclusively in games and sports, the child will follow their lead and ignore preferred play activities, such as constructions. Peer influence on the child's preoccupation with television watching and looking at comics is especially strong.

Imbalance between active play and amusements not only affects children's personal and social adjustments, but it also deprives them of opportunities to explore a wide variety of play activities to discover which meet their play needs best. Children, for example, who spend most of their playtime on games and sports may never discover the enjoyment they might have had from constructions or dramatizations.

Narrowing the field of play activities is damaging also to the development of play interests that can serve as hobbies as children grow older. Concentration on active play in childhood provides little opportunity to develop interests in less active play, which, as the person grows older, must of necessity replace the strenuous play activities of children.

Imbalance between Social and Solitary Play

Whether play is predominantly social or solitary will be influenced by the degree of social acceptance children enjoy and pressures put on them by parents, teachers, and peers to play with age-mates rather than alone. The more emphasis parents and others put on the importance of doing things with others rather than alone, the greater the imbalance between social and solitary play.

Unquestionably both types are important and both contribute to children's personal and social adjustments. Children who prefer solitary to social play, regardless of the reason for this preference, will come to think of themselves as "different," "queer," or "inferior" because that is the way members of the social group are likely to think of them.

Should they, on the other hand, prefer social to solitary play to the extent that solitary play gives them little enjoyment, they will be ill-equipped to engage in solitary play, should conditions, such as illness or moving to a new community where they do not belong to gangs, necessitate their playing alone. Furthermore, if they have learned to think of solitary play as characteristic only of those who are rejected or neglected, they will have little motivation to try to learn to enjoy solitary play. This is unfortunate because solitary play can contribute to personal and social adjustments just as social play can. As Moore et al. have explained, "Solitary play is a normal and probably functionally beneficial activity rather than an indication of poor social adjustment" (60).

Emphasis on Sex-appropriate Play Activities

Before babies are a year old, pressures are put on them to play with toys regarded as appropriate for their sex. This pressure takes two forms: first, babies are given toys considered appropriate for members of their sex and are encouraged to play with them; second, they are denied opportunities to play with toys regarded as appropriate for members of the other sex.

Later, as toddlers, preschoolers, or school-age children, these pressures become stronger. They come from peers as well as from parents. Generally these pressures are stronger on boys than on girls until girls approach puberty when pressure to play in a sex-appropriate way are equally as strong as on boys.

Expecting children to play as the social group defines as sex appropriate is hazardous to good personal and social adjustments. Children resent not being able to play as they wish to play and being forced to play in a way that does not meet their play needs. Furthermore, if they do not have either the interest in playing, or the ability to play, in a sex-appropriate way, they will develop feelings of inadequacy and inferiority when their play skills fall below those of their peers (14, 33). This matter will be discussed in more detail in the chapter on sex roles.

Inappropriate Play Equipment

Almost all play, with the exception of daydreaming, requires some equipment. However, this equipment does not have to be designed especially for play. Few children, even those from the poor socioeconomic groups, lack toys and play equipment. On the other hand, far too often the equipment children have for play is inappropriate for them. Consequently it does not meet their play needs and, as a result, they lack the enjoyment and stimulation play normally gives a child. That is why it becomes a hazard to good personal adjustments. If children do not learn to play as their age-mates play, due to inappropriate equipment, it then becomes a hazard to their social as well as their personal adjustments.

There are a number of reasons why children's play equipment is inappropriate for them. Of these, the most common and most serious are explained in Box 11–13. In each case, an attempt will be made to show why it is inappropriate and, thus, hazardous to personal and social adjustments.

Too Much or Too Little Guidance in Play

Many adults assume that children will "instinctively" know how to use play equipment. As a result, they provide children with equipment but fail to show them

COMMON REASONS WHY PLAY EQUIPMENT IS INAPPROPRIATE FOR CHILDREN

DANGER

Most commercially made play equipment is so carefully controlled by law that it is only infrequently dangerous. Homemade equipment, on the other hand, can be and often is dangerous, whether it is a swing tied to a bough on a tree or button eyes on a homemade doll. If this equipment leads to an accident, it can condition children to dislike play related to the area in which the accident occurred or make them afraid to engage in any play that is new or different.

ADULT PREFERENCES

Because most play equipment for children is selected by parents, relatives, or friends of the family, their preferences dominate the choice. Parents who have nostalgic memories of the types of books they enjoyed when they were children often give their children books of the same type. If these books do not interest the children, it will color their attitudes toward reading so unfavorably that they will shun reading as a form of amusement.

TOO LITTLE VARIETY

If children show an interest in a particular type of play, parents are likely to provide equipment for that type of play and skimp on equipment for other types. This limits the range of children's play activities and deprives them of opportunities to try out different types of play.

**SELECTION ACCORDING TO
CHRONOLOGICAL AGE**

Almost all manufactured play equipment is marked for "ages 2–3 years," "ages 4–6 years," etc. The underlying assumption is that *all* children of those ages will find the equipment suited to their play needs. This is rarely true. The more children deviate, physically and mentally, from the norms for their ages, the less appropriate this equipment will be for them. This will dampen their interest in play with that equipment and may dampen their interest in play in general.

EQUIPMENT TOO COMPLEX FOR THE CHILD

When play equipment is bought for children to "grow into" or is handed down from an older sibling who has outgrown it, it may be too complicated for the child to use without help from others. Having to rely on others to help them to use their play equipment not only stifles children's interest in using it, but, even more seriously, it makes them feel inadequate and inferior.

EQUIPMENT TOO SIMPLE FOR THE CHILD

When equipment is too simple for children's physical and mental development, it provides no stimulation and bores them. This makes children dislike the type of play for which the equipment was meant and may condition them unfavorably toward all related play activities. Books that are too simple for children's level of intelligence, for example, can condition them unfavorably toward reading just for fun.

EQUIPMENT THAT IS TOO FRAGILE

At every age, play involves some exploration. Equipment that is too fragile for this loses its stimulating value if children are not permitted to explore it. It leads to feelings of guilt if children are reproved for damaging it during their explorations. In either case, it is harmful to their attitudes toward play and deprives them of the benefits play could give them.

how to use it. Other adults assume that, if children are to get the enjoyment they should from play, they must be "taught" how to play. Both of these assumptions are hazardous because they influence the amount of enjoyment children derive from their play and this, in turn, affects the benefits they get from it.

When children are given toys and other play equipment but are not shown how to use them, their interest in and enjoyment from playing with them quickly wanes. After they have explored the toys or other play equipment, there is nothing left for them to do. Just being given a ball, for example, does not mean that children will automatically know how to throw or catch it or to play different kinds of ball games. Similarly, they must be given guidance in using materials for construction—pencils, paints, clay, sand, or blocks, for example—if they are to enjoy making things.

Too much guidance, on the other hand, makes play seem like work to children. They get the impression, from the way they are being shown how to use their equipment, that they are being "taught." Play then resembles a school lesson, with the end result far more important than the enjoyment of the activity itself.

Furthermore, they often develop feelings of resentment against the person who seems to be forcing them to play in a way that is not necessarily to their liking.

Drawing the line between too little and too much guidance must, of necessity, be done for each individual child. What is too much guidance for one child may be too little for another and vice versa. However, a good rule to follow in determining the right amount of guidance for children is how children react to it. If they accept guidance readily and comply graciously with suggestions given them, it suggests that they are getting the right amount of guidance.

If, on the other hand, children quickly lose interest in a play activity and show signs of being bored, it suggests that they have not had enough guidance to stimulate their interest in the play activity or that they are not aware of the number of potentialities in the equipment they have. Too much guidance becomes readily apparent in children's attitudes. If they rebel against being told how to play or if they become resentful and defensive when their play achievements are criticized, it suggests that play is being treated as work and, as a result, it is losing the benefits it would otherwise give.

"Happy Endings"

In its narrow sense, the term "happy endings" refers to mass media—stories in books, on television or radio, or in the movies. In its broader sense, it can be applied to the outcome of any play activity. Winning a game, for example, can be called a "happy ending" for the player just as a drawing or a block construction that is praised by a parent or peer can be called a "happy ending" for that play activity. One of the hazards of playing games with adults or older children, as was pointed out earlier, is that they tend to let children win regardless of how poorly they play. When children play with younger children, they almost always win. This encourages them to believe that all play will end happily for them.

Happy endings of *active play* can be and often are hazardous to good personal and social adjustments. When children become accustomed to winning in games, to being praised for any construction they make, or to being conquering heroes in their daydream worlds, they come to think of themselves as having more ability than they actually have and to believe that they will always come out on top. If, for example, children are permitted to win games played with adults, it will be hard for them to take a defeat when playing with their peers. Refer to the discussion of potential hazards of parents as substitute companions on page 278. Not having an opportunity to experience failure, they do not develop failure tolerance. As a result, they are not learning to be good sports when they lose in games or when they do not receive the praise they have been accustomed to receive for their play achievements. Similarly, if they are accustomed to being heroes in their daydream worlds, they will have difficulty in adjusting to not being heroes in real life.

Happy endings in *amusements* are psychologically damaging not because they foster unrealistic concepts of the individual but rather because they foster unrealistic concepts of life and its experiences. As Zimet has pointed out, even textbooks for children present people as living in a "falsely glamourized fantasy world" (103). As a result, he contends, it is logical that children's concepts of life would become distorted.

If everything turns out successfully in the mass media, it is not surprising that children expect everything in their lives to turn out successfully also. When this does not happen, they are likely to feel that they are martyrs who are being discriminated against by members of the social group. This leads to poor social adjustments just as unrealistic self-concepts lead to poor personal adjustments.

Chapter Highlights

1   Play differs from work and drudgery not because of the activity but because of the individual's attitude toward the activity.

2   Play makes many contributions to children's personal and social adjustments and, as such, it is an important learning experience, not just a "waste of time" as was formerly believed.

3   There are many characteristics of children's play, the most important of which are that it is influenced by tradition, it follows a predictable pattern of development, the number of its activities decreases with age, it becomes increasingly social with age, the number of

playmates decreases with age, it becomes increasingly sex appropriate and changes from informal to formal, it is less physically active as children grow older, and it is predictive of children's adjustments.

4   Marked variations in children's play are due to health, motor development, intelligence, sex, environment, socioeconomic status, amount of leisure time, and play equipment.

5   Play activities are usually divided into two categories—active play in which the enjoyment comes from what the child does and passive play or amusements in which the enjoyment comes from the activity of others. Normally, active play predominates in early childhood and passive play in the latter part of childhood though, at all ages, both types of play are represented in the child's play repertoire.

6   There are variations in the amount of active play children engage in because of such conditions as health, the child's social acceptance, level of intelligence, sex, play equipment, and the environment in which the child lives.

7   The most common forms of active play in childhood include free, spontaneous play, dramatizations, daydreaming, constructive play, music, collecting, exploring, games, and sports.

8   All forms of active play contribute to children's personal and social adjustments provided too much of the child's time is not devoted to any one form.

9   Amusements make many contributions to children's personal and social adjustments that cannot be made by active play and, as a result, they are important supplements to active play.

10   The most common forms of amusements for American children today include being read to or reading for pleasure, looking at comics, going to movies, listening to music or the radio, and television watching.

11   Of all types of amusements in childhood, television watching is commonly regarded as most hazardous to personal and social adjustments because, first, more time is spent on it than other forms of play and, second, it is less often supervised by parents and other adults than other forms of play.

12   In spite of the popular belief that TV watching is the major play hazard of childhood, there are others that are too serious to be overlooked: devoting too much time to play, an imbalance between active play and amusements or between social and solitary play, too much emphasis on sex-appropriate play activities, inappropriate play equipment, too much or too little guidance in play, and happy endings.

13   Because equipment is needed for most play, equipment that does not meet children's play needs because it is too complex or too simple for their level of development, too concentrated in one area of play, or dangerous is hazardous to good personal and social adjustments.

14   Too much guidance in play can be as hazardous to good adjustments as too little. In the case of the former, it dampens children's interest in play by making it seem like schoolwork and, in the latter, it deprives children of knowing how to use the play equipment available and, thus, getting the enjoyment they should from their play.

15   Happy endings in active play in the form of having these activities come out to their liking encourages the development of unrealistic self-concepts in children. Too many happy endings in amusements are hazardous because they encourage children to develop unrealistic concepts of life and what they can expect of different life situations.

Bibliography

1   Anast, P. Personality determinants of mass media preferences. *Journalism Quarterly*, 1966, *43*, 729–732.

2   Babbitt, N. Happy endings? Of course, and also joy. *The New York Times*, Nov. 8, 1970.

3   Barnes, K. E. Preschool play norms: A replication. *Developmental Psychology*, 1971, *5*, 99–103.

4   Bates, J. E., and P. M. Bentler. Play activities of normal and effeminate boys. *Developmental Psychology*, 1973, *9*, 20–27.

5   Bettelheim, B. Play and education. *School Review*, 1972, *81*, 1–13.

6   Bettelheim, B. *The uses of enchantment: The meaning and importance of fairy tales.* New York: Knopf, 1976.

7   Birnie, L., and J. H. Whiteley. The effects of acquired meaning on children's play behavior. *Child Development*, 1973, *44*, 355–358.

8   Bishop, D. W., and C. A. Chace. Parental conceptual systems, home environment, and potential creativ-

ity in children. *Journal of Experimental Child Psychology*, 1971, *12*, 318–338.

9 Bloomer, R. H. Characteristics of portrayal and conflict and children's attraction to books. *Psychological Reports*, 1968, *23*, 99–106.

10 Brooks, J. B., and D. M. Elliott. Prediction of psychological adjustment at age thirty for leisure time activities and satisfactions in childhood. *Human Development*, 1971, *14*, 51–61.

11 Bruner, J. S. Play is serious business. *Psychology Today*, 1975, *8* (8), 81–83.

12 Butterworth, R. F., and G. G. Thompson. Factors related to age-grade trends and sex differences in children's preferences for comic books. *Journal of Genetic Psychology*, 1951, *78*, 71–96.

13 Cline, V. B., R. G. Croft, and S. Courrier. Desensitization of children to television violence. *Journal of Personality and Social Psychology*, 1973, *27*, 360–365.

14 Cramer, P., and K. A. Hogan. Sex differences in verbal and play fantasy. *Developmental Psychology*, 1975, *11*, 145–154.

15 Dansky, J. L., and C. W. Silverman. Effects of play on assortive fluency in preschool-aged children. *Developmental Psychology*, 1973, *9*, 38–43.

16 Denzin, N. K. Play, games, and interaction: The contexts of childhood socialization, *Sociological Quarterly*, 1975, *16*, 458–478.

17 D'Heurle, A., and J. M. Fiemer. On play. *Elementary School Journal*, 1971, *72*, 118–124.

18 Drabman, R. S., and M. H. Thomas. Does media violence increase children's toleration of real-life aggressions? *Developmental Psychology*, 1974, *10*, 418–421.

19 Durrell, D. E., and P. Weisberg. Imitative play behavior of children: The importance of model distinctiveness and prior imitative training. *Journal of Experimental Child Psychology*, 1973, *16*, 23–31.

20 Eckerman, C. O., and H. L. Rheingold. Infants' exploratory responses to toys and people. *Developmental Psychology*, 1974, *10*, 255–259.

21 Eifermann, R. R. Level of children's play as expressed in group size.

British Journal of Educational Psychology, 1970, *40*, 161–170.

22 Eifermann, R. R. Social play in childhood. In R. E. Herron and B. Sutton-Smith (eds.), *Child's play*. New York: Wiley, 1971. Pp. 270–297.

23 Ellis, G. T., and F. Sekyra. The effect of aggressive cartoons on the behavior of first grade children. *Journal of Psychology*, 1972, *81*, 37–43.

24 Emans, R. What do children in the inner city like to read? *Elementary School Journal*, 1968, *69*, 118–122.

25 Erikson, E. H. Sex differences in the play configurations of American pre-adolescents. In R. E. Herron and B. Sutton-Smith (eds.), *Child's play*. New York: Wiley, 1971. Pp. 126–144.

26 Eron, L. D., L. R. Huesmann, M. M. Lefkowitz, and L. D. Walder. Does television violence cause aggression? *American Psychologist*, 1972, *27*, 253–266.

27 Fagot, B. I., and I. Littman. Stability of sex-role and play interests from preschool to elementary school. *Journal of Psychology*, 1975, *89*, 285–290.

28 Fenson, L., J. Kagan, R. B. Kearsley, and P. R. Zelazo. The developmental progression of manipulative play in the first two years. *Child Development*, 1976, *47*, 232–236.

29 Feshbach, N. D. The effects of violence in childhood. *Journal of Clinical Child Psychology*, 1973, *2*, 28–31.

30 Fingarette, H. All work and no play. *Humanitas*, 1969, *5*, 5–19.

31 Fling, S., and M. Manosevitz. Sex typing in nursery school children's play interests. *Developmental Psychology*, 1972, *7*, 146–152.

32 Freeman, N. H., and R. Janikoun. Intellectual realism in children's drawings of a familiar object with distinctive features. *Child Development*, 1972, *43*, 1116–1121.

33 Friedlander, B. Z., H. S. Wetstone, and C. S. Scott. Surburban preschool children's comprehension of an age-appropriate informational television program. *Child Development*, 1974, *45*, 561–565.

34 Garai, J. E., and A. Scheinfeld. Sex differences in mental and behavioral traits. *Genetic Psychology Monographs*, 1968, *77*, 169–299.

35 Gardner, H. Children's sensitivity to musical styles. *Merrill-Palmer Quarterly*, 1973, *19*, 67–77.

36 Garvey, C. Some properties of social play. *Merrill-Palmer Quarterly*, 1974, *20*, 163–180.

37 Goldberg, S., and M. Lewis. Play behavior in the year-old infant: Early sex differences. *Child Development*, 1969, *40*, 21–31.

38 Goodnow, J. J., and S. Friedman. Orientation in children's human figure drawings: An aspect of graphic language. *Developmental Psychology*, 1972, *7*, 10–16.

39 Granza, A. F., and P. A. Witt. Choices of colored blocks in the play of preschool children. *Perceptual and Motor Skills*, 1969, *29*, 783–787.

40 Halverson, C. F., and M. F. Waldrop. The relations of mechanically recorded activity level to varieties of preschool play behavior. *Child Development*, 1973, *44*, 678–681.

41 Helson, R. Through the pages of children's books. *Psychology Today*, 1973, *7* (6), 107–117.

42 Herron, R. E., and B. Sutton-Smith. (eds.) *Child's play*. New York: Wiley, 1971.

43 Hicks, D. J. Girls' attitudes toward modeled behaviors and the content of imitative private play. *Child Development*, 1971, *42*, 139–147.

44 Hutt, C. Exploration and play in children. In R. E. Herron and B. Sutton-Smith (eds.), *Child's play*. New York: Wiley, 1971. Pp. 231–251.

45 Johns, J. L. Reading preferences of intermediate-grade students in urban settings. *Reading World*, 1974, *14*, 51–63.

46 Laurence, R., and B. Sutton-Smith. Novel responses to toys: A replication. *Merrill-Palmer Quarterly*, 1968, *14*, 159–160.

47 Lefkowitz, M. M., and L. O. Walder, L. D. Eron, and L. R. Huesmann. Preference for televised contact sports as related to sex differences in aggressiveness. *Developmental Psychology*, 1973, *9*, 417–420.

48 Leifer, A. D., N. G. Gordon, and S. B. Graves. Children's television: More than mere entertainment. *Harvard Educational Review*, 1974, *44*, 213–245.

49 Lesser, G. S. *Children and televi-*

sion: *Lessons from Sesame Street.* New York: Random House, 1974.

50 Levinsohn, F. H. Happy endings: TV's kindly offering. *School Review,* 1975, *84,* 109–115.

51 Liebert, R. M. Television and children's aggressive behavior: Another look. *American Journal of Psychoanalysis,* 1974, *34,* 99–107.

52 Liebert, R. M., and R. A. Baron. Some immediate effects of televised violence on children's behavior. *Developmental Psychology,* 1972, *6,* 469–475.

53 Liebert, R. M., R. B. McCall and M. A. Hanratty. Effects of sex-typed information on children's toy preferences. *Journal of Genetic Psychology,* 1971, *119,* 133–136.

54 Liebert, R. M., J. M. Neale, and E. S. Davidson. *The early window: Effects of television on children and youth.* New York: Pergamon Press, 1975.

55 Lurcat, L., and I. Kostin. Study of graphical abilities in children. *Perceptual and Motor Skills,* 1970, *30,* 615–630.

56 Margolin, E. Work and play: Are they really opposites? *Elementary School Journal,* 1967, *67,* 343–353.

57 Messer, S. B., and M. Lewis. Social class and sex differences in the attachment behavior and play behavior of the year-old infant. *Merrill-Palmer Quarterly,* 1972, *18,* 295–306.

58 Millar S. *The psychology of play.* New York: Jason Aronson, 1974.

59 Montemayer, R. Children's performance in a game and their attraction to it as a function of sex-typed labels. *Child Development,* 1974, *45,* 152–156.

60 Moore, N. V., C. M. Evertson, and J. E. Brophy. Solitary play: Some functional reconsiderations. *Developmental Psychology,* 1974, *10,* 830–834.

61 Mukerji, R. TV's impact on children: A checker-board scene. *Phi Delta Kappan,* 1976, *67,* 316–321.

62 Murray, J. P. Television and violence: Implications of the Surgeon General's Research Program. *American Psychologist,* 1973, *28,* 472–478.

63 Neumann, E. A. *The elements of play.* New York: MSS Information Corp., 1971.

64 Noble, G. Film-mediated aggressive and creative play. *British Journal of Social and Clinical Psychology,* 1970, *9,* 1–7.

65 Osborn, D. K., and R. C. Endsley. Emotional reactions of young children to TV violence. *Child Development,* 1971, *42,* 321–331.

66 Parten, M. B. Social play among preschool children. In R. F. Herron and B. Sutton-Smith (eds.), *Child's play.* New York: Wiley, 1971. Pp. 83–95.

67 Payne, E. Musical taste and personality. *British Journal of Psychology,* 1967, *58,* 133–138.

68 Piaget, J. *Play, dreams, and imitation in childhood.* London: Hienemann, 1951.

69 Piaget, J. *The grasp of consciousness: Action and concept in the young child.* Cambridge, Mass.: Harvard University Press, 1976.

70 Pulaski, M. A. S. Play as a function of toy structure and fantasy predisposition. *Child Development,* 1970, *41,* 531–537.

71 Rabinowitz, F. M., B. E. Moely, N. Finkel, and S. McClinton. The effects of toy novelty and social interaction on the exploratory behavior of preschool children. *Child Development,* 1975, *46,* 286–289.

72 Reiber, M. The effect of music on the activity level of children. *Psychonomic Science,* 1965, *3,* 325–326.

73 Roberts, G. C., and K. N. Black. The effect of naming and object permanence on toy preferences. *Child Development,* 1972, *43,* 858–868.

74 Rossiter, J. R., and T. S. Robertson. Children's television viewing: An examination of parent-child consensus. *Sociometry,* 1975, *38,* 308–326.

75 Rubin, K. H., T. L. Maioni, and M. Harnung. Free play behaviors in middle- and lower-class preschoolers: Parten and Piaget revisited. *Child Development,* 1976, *47,* 414–419.

76 Rue, V. M. Television and the family: The question of control. *Family Coordinator,* 1974, *27,* 73–81.

77 Sadler, W. A. Creative existence: Play as a pathway to personal freedom and community. *Humanitas,* 1969, *5,* 57–79.

78 Scheffler, R. G. The child from five to six: A longitudinal study of fantasy change. *Genetic Psychology Monographs,* 1975, *92,* 19–56.

79 Schramm, W., J. Lyle, and E. B. Parker. Patterns in children's reading of newspapers. *Journalism Quarterly,* 1960, *37,* 35–40.

80 Schramm, W., J. Lyle, and E. B. Parker. *Television in the lives of our children.* Stanford, Calif.: Stanford University Press, 1961.

81 Seagoe, M. V. Children's play in three American subcultures. *Journal of School Psychology,* 1971, *9,* 167–172.

82 Singer, J. L. *The child's world of make-believe: Experimental studies of imaginative play.* New York: Academic Press, 1973.

83 Singer, J. L. *The inner world of daydreaming.* New York: Harper & Row, 1975.

84 Smart, R. C., and M. S. Smart. Group values shown in preadolescents' drawings in five English-speaking countries. *Journal of Social Psychology,* 1975, *97,* 23–37.

85 Steuer, F. B., G. M. Applefield, and R. Smith. Televised aggression and the interpersonal aggression of preschool children. *Journal of Experimental Child Psychology,* 1971, *11,* 442–447.

86 Stone, G. P. The play of little children. In R. E. Herron and B. Sutton-Smith (eds.), *Child's play.* New York: Wiley, 1971. Pp. 4–14.

87 Stone, L. J., and J. Church. *Childhood and adolescence: A psychology of the growing person,* 3d ed. New York: Random House, 1972.

88 Streicher, L. H., and N. L. Bonney. Children talk about television. *Journal of Communication,* 1974, *24* (2), 54–61.

89 Strom, R. D. Toy talk: The new conversation between generations. *Elementary School Journal,* 1970, *70,* 418–428.

90 Sutton-Smith, B. Novel responses to toys. *Merrill-Palmer Quarterly,* 1968, *14,* 151–158.

91 Sutton-Smith, B. Child's play: Very serious business. *Psychology Today,* 1971, *5* (7), 66–69, 87.

92 Sutton-Smith, B. Piaget on play: A critique. In R. E. Herron and B. Sutton-Smith (eds.), *Child's play.* New York: Wiley, 1971. Pp 326–336.

93 Sutton-Smith, B. Play preference and play behavior: A validity study. In R. E. Herron and B. Sutton-Smith

(eds.), *Child's play*. New York: Wiley, 1971. Pp. 73–75.

94 Sutton-Smith, B. The useless made useful: Play as variability training. *School Review*, 1975, *83*, 197–214.

95 Sutton-Smith, B., and B. G. Rosenberg. Sixty years of historical change in the game preferences of American children. In R. E. Herron and B. Sutton-Smith (eds.), *Child's play*. New York: Wiley, 1971. Pp. 18–50.

96 Switzky, H. N., H. C. Haywood, and R. Isott. Exploration, curiosity, and play in young children: Effects of stimulus complexity. *Developmental Psychology*, 1974, *10*, 321–329.

97 Thomas, M. H., and R. S. Drabman. Toleration of real life aggression as a function of exposure to televised violence and age of subject. *Merrill-Palmer Quarterly*, 1975, *21*, 227–232.

98 *U. S. News & World Report:* How TV violence affects children—Official report. *U. S. News & World Report*, April 17, 1972, pp. 92–95.

99 Walk, R. D., K. Karusaitis, C. Lebowitz, and T. Falbo. Artistic style as concept formation for children and adults. *Merrill-Palmer Quarterly*, 1971, *17*, 347–356.

100 Walls, R. T., R. A. Moxley, and S. P. Gulkus. Collection preferences of children. *Child Development*, 1975, *46*, 783–785.

101 Weisler, A., and R. B. McCall. Exploration and play: Résumé and redirection. *American Psychologist*, 1976, *31*, 492–508.

102 Wolf, T. M. Response consequences to televised modeled sex-inappropriate play behavior. *Journal of Genetic Psychology*, 1975, *127*, 35–44.

103 Zimet, S. F. American elementary reading textbooks: A sociological review. *Teachers College Record*, 1969, *70*, 331–340.

104 Zunmernal, L. D., and G. Calovini. Toys as learning materials for preschool children. *Exceptional Children*, 1971, *36*, 642–654.

105 Zusne, L. Measuring violence in children's cartoons. *Perceptual and Motor Skills*, 1968, *27*, 901–902.

CHAPTER 12

DEVELOPMENT OF CREATIVITY

psychologists, sociologists, and other scientists have long recognized the importance of creativity to the individual and to society. In spite of this recognition, creativity is still one of the most neglected subjects in scientific research. There are many reasons for this neglect, five of which are especially important.

First, there was the traditional belief that creativity—commonly called "genius"—was hereditary and that nothing could be done to make people creative. It was believed that they were either born with the "divine spark" of genius or they were not.

Second, because it was believed that only a few people have the ability to create, it was thought that scientific research should concentrate on matters that affect the majority of the population, not the relatively few who are creative.

Third, it has been argued that the competent plodders—those with high intelligence and achievement drive—are more likely to be successful in life than those who are creative. The latter, it was argued, often live and die in poverty and their achievements are not recognized until after their deaths, if then. Consequently, with the rewards of creativity so uncertain, there was little incentive to encourage children in this direction.

Fourth, the traditional belief that creative people are sex inappropriate—that creative men are sissies and creative women more masculine than feminine—has discouraged parents from praising their children's creative urges. Many fathers, for example, oppose their sons' interest in music, art, writing, or even inventing, but praise their achievements in sports. A vocation in the business world, they argue, is more "practical" and more "masculine" than one in the arts. This negative attitude toward creativity has tended to discourage the development of scientific interest in it.

Fifth, creativity is difficult to study and even more difficult to measure. With present-day emphasis on the measurement of different human qualities—intelligence, personality, or mechanical ability—it is not surprising that scientists have shied away from research in an area that presents such methodological difficulties.

Meaning of Creativity

"Creativity" is one of the most loosely used and, hence, most ambiguous terms in psychological research today. It is even more ambiguous and more loosely used by laymen.

To appreciate the meaning of the term "creativity" as used by psychologists, an examination of common forms of popular usage of the term will help to show what is incorrect or only partially correct in these different forms and why psychologists have defined the term as it is now defined (2, 21, 91).

Popular Meanings of Creativity

There are many popular meanings of creativity, eight of which are commonly used.

First, one of the most popular meanings of creativity emphasizes making something that is new and different. Most people believe that creativity can be judged by the *product* or by what the person creates. But creativity does not always lead to products that can be observed and judged. In daydreaming, for example, a person creates something new and different, but the daydreamer alone knows what it is.

Consequently, creativity must be regarded as a *process*—a process by which something new, either an idea or an object in a new form or arrangement, is produced. The emphasis on the act of producing rather than on the end result of the act is accepted today as central to the concept of creativity.

A *second* popular meaning of creativity regards it as the haphazard creation of something new and original by chance, as when a child, playing with blocks, constructs a pile that resembles a house and then labels it a house. Similarly, when an artist is mixing colors and by chance produces a shade of red or green different from colors already commonly in use, the artist is credited with being "original."

There is little evidence that this popular concept of creativity is valid. Today, it is recognized that all creativity is goal-directed even though the goal may be no more than the immediate pleasure the person derives from the activities (34).

A *third* popular concept of creativity holds that what is created is always new and different from what already existed and, therefore, is unique. There is ample evidence that this concept is not correct or is only partially correct. Granted that all creativity involves the *combination of old ideas or products* into new forms, but the old are the basis for the new. The painter who produces a new red makes use of old colors just as the child, in creating a daydream world, makes use of scenes and actions experienced in daily life, or observed in the mass media. Furthermore, *uniqueness is a personal achievement,* not necessarily a universal achievement. People can, for example, be creative when they produce something *they* have never produced before, although it may have been produced in almost the same, or in even an identical, form by someone else.

A *fourth* popular notion of creativity is that it is a unique mental process—a process needed for no other purpose than to produce something new, different, and original. Instead, creativity involves a specific kind of thinking, labeled by Guilford as "divergent thinking." According to Guilford, *divergent thinking* makes excursions from the beaten track and seeks variety. It goes beyond the obvious and apparent, considering several possible answers to a problem, not one single correct solution. This contrasts with "convergent thinking," which follows the conventional path with the thinker using information at hand to arrive at a conclusion that leads to one right answer, an answer similar to that which others would reach (38).

Creative people like to explore things mentally and to try out lots of possibilities, even if they are wrong. This kind of thinking is often employed in day-to-day activities not usually considered creative. Creative people, however, are more flexible and fluent than convergent thinkers and do not confine themselves to the information at hand. This permits a richer flow of ideas and, as a result, it opens up a way toward solutions that are novel and, hence, creative (10).

Another characteristic of divergent thinking—the kind that is used in creativity—is that it makes leaps. It does not proceed in easily observable and definable phases as is true of convergent thinking. Convergent thinking is sequential; it proceeds one step at a time. It is guided by a purpose; thus, it examines alternatives and sets controls to check the veracity of the propositions being considered (38).

Fifth, creativity is often considered synonymous with high intelligence. This belief has been reinforced by the fact that people with very high IQs are labeled "genius"—a term which the layman equates with creativity. There is little evidence that high intelligence and high creativity always go hand in hand. Instead, creativity is just *one* aspect of intelligence, as is memory or reasoning.

Sixth, the common concept of creativity as a spark of genius which is inherent in a person and has no relationship to learning or environment suggests that creative people are vehicles. It suggests that they play no role in their creative behavior except to express in overt actions an inherent trait that their own experiences and decisions have little or nothing to do with. By contrast, there is evidence that, if people are to be creative, they must *acquire accepted knowledge* before they can use it in a new and original way (29).

Seventh, creativity is commonly regarded as synonymous with imagination and fantasy and, as such, is a form of mental play. Rather, as Goldner has said, creativity is an "organized, comprehensive, imaginative activity of the brain toward an original outcome." It is, thus, *innovative* rather than reproductive (36).

An *eighth* popular concept of creativity is that all people fall roughly into two major groups, the "conformers" and the "creators." Conformers do what is expected of them without disturbing or causing trouble for others. By contrast, creators contribute original ideas, different points of view, or new ways of looking at problems and attacking them. They do not follow the beaten path and are sometimes disturbing elements in the social group. The degree of the disturbance and of their acceptance depends on how far they deviate from the beaten path traveled by the majority.

This concept suggests that a child is either a creative person or a noncreative person, a conformer or a creator. It admits no variation in the degree of creativity one may possess. While the measurement of creativity is still in its infancy, owing mainly to the difficulty of devising ways to measure it accurately, there is enough evidence from observation and from the simple measurements now available to show that this notion is not true. Children can no more validly be divided into two major groups in terms of creativity than they can in terms of intelligence or any other characteristic. Instead, children possess *varying degrees of creativity* just as they possess varying degrees of intelligence. This means that, while children may be predominantly conformers, they also have some creative ability and vice versa.

Psychological Meaning of Creativity

Many definitions of creativity that might be acceptable to the psychologist are so brief that they do not cover all the important elements required in a workable definition. The one given by Drevdahl (29) has therefore been selected as a good, workable definition:

Creativity is the capacity of persons to produce compositions, products or ideas of any sort which are essentially new or novel, and previously unknown to the producer. It can be imaginative activity, or thought synthesis, where the product is not a mere summation. It may involve the forming of new patterns and combinations of information derived from past experiences, and the transplanting of old relationships to new situations and may involve the generation of new correlates. It must be purposeful or goal directed, not idle fantasy—although it need not have immediate practical application or be a perfect and complete product. It may take the form of an artistic, literary, or scientific production or may be of a procedural or methodological nature.

Since creativity is so complex and so often misunderstood, its important elements are brought together and presented in a concise form in Box 12–1 (2, 44, 91). A careful study of these elements will reveal two facts: *First,* creativity as viewed by the psychologist is very different from the popular concept of it, and *second,* creativity is a far more complex activity than most people recognize.

BOX 12–1

CHARACTERISTIC ELEMENTS
OF CREATIVITY

- Creativity is a process, not a product.
- The process is goal-directed, either for personal benefit or for the benefit of the social group.
- It leads to the production of something new, different, and, therefore, unique for the person whether it be verbal or nonverbal, concrete or abstract.
- Creativity comes from divergent thinking, while conformity and everyday problem solving comes from convergent thinking.
- It is a way of thinking; it is not synonymous with intelligence, which includes mental abilities other than thinking.
- The ability to create depends on the acquisition of accepted knowledge.
- Creativity is a form of controlled imagination that leads to some kind of achievement, whether in painting, block building, or daydreaming.

Relation of Creativity to Intelligence

Occasionally there are reports of people with highly creative talents whose intellectual levels are low, and it is well known that not all people with high intelligence are creators. Many bright children, for example, achieve academic success, but few exhibit a creative way of thinking that goes beyond "giving what the teacher wants."

Whether high intelligence and high creativity will go hand in hand depends largely on factors extraneous to both creativity and intelligence. Factors in the environment or within the person often interfere with the development of creativity. Strict authoritarian child-training methods in the home or school during the early, formative years may, for example, stifle creativity but not affect a high native intelligence. Under such conditions the correlation between intelligence and creativity will be low.

There is, however, a positive correlation between intelligence and creativity. This may at first sound contradictory. But remember that creativity, which leads to the production of something new, is dependent upon the ability to acquire accepted knowledge. That knowledge is then organized and manipulated into new and original forms. Creativity cannot function in a vacuum. It makes use of knowledge previously acquired, and this depends upon the intellectual abilities of the person.

In the absence of obstacles that interfere with the development of creativity, it is reasonably safe to say that the more intelligent the child the more creative the child *could* be. On the other hand, it is questionable whether a child with very low intelligence could ever be more than moderately creative even in the most favorable of environments.

The Creativity Syndrome

A number of studies have been made of the personality patterns of highly creative children, adolescents, and adults. These studies report that no single trait is characteristically found among those who are creative but rather a cluster of related traits, referred to as the "creativity syndrome."

Among the traits in the creativity syndrome are flexibility, nonconformity, need for autonomy, need for independence, high aspirations, self-discipline, playfulness, liking for manipulation of ideas (toying with ideas), assertiveness, reserve, self-assurance, sense of humor, open-mindedness, intellectual persistence, self-confidence, curiosity, enjoyment of calculated risk when success depends on own ability, sex-inappropriate interests, timidity in social situations, preference for fantasy to real adventure, venture-someness, and pursuit of self-chosen interests (1, 7, 72, 78).

From extensive studies of people who are regarded as "creative," Dellas and Gaier have concluded (26):

A particular constellation of psychological traits emerges consistently in the creative individual and forms a recognizable schema of the creative personality. This schema indicates that creative persons are distinguished more by interests, attitudes, and drives than by intellectual abilities . . . . The cognitive capacities that appear to be most frequently associated with the creative are an above-average intelligence and the effective use of this intelligence, the ability to produce unusual and appropriate ideas, an exceptional retention and more readily availability of life experiences, ideational fluency and the ability to synthesize remote or disparate ideas, discriminative observation, and a general cognitive flexibility. . . . The creative individual is possessed of superior ego strength and a positive, constructive way of reacting to problems. Intuitiveness also comes through as a hallmark of the creative person . . . . Independence in attitudes and social behavior emerge with striking consistency as relevant to creativity.

For the most part, there is little evidence that children who are creative are either maladjusted or lonely, as tradition holds. If they are, it is mainly because unfavorable social attitudes toward them have led to maladjustment and social isolation. The situation is very much the same with children who have very high IQs.

When the personality syndrome characteristic of creativity is combined with a high level of intelligence, it is likely to lead to successful achievement and to good personal and social adjustment. When combined with low intelligence—and this is not common—it is likely to lead to trouble both for the individual and for the social group. Children fitting the latter description often become rebellious, antagonistic, and troublesome nonconformists.

Values of Creativity

Popular belief about the value of creativity centers on what the creative person produces for the benefit and enjoyment of the social group and for social progress. The value of creativity to the person who is creative has often been almost completely overlooked. These values are much too important to be overlooked, as the following facts will attest to.

Creativity gives children tremendous personal *pleasure* and *satisfaction*—rewards that have a marked influence on their developing personalities. Nothing, for example, gives young children more satisfaction than to create something all by themselves, whether it be a house made out of a turned-over chair covered by a blanket or a drawing of a pet dog. And nothing is more ego-deflating than to have the creation criticized or ridiculed or to be asked what it is supposed to be (42).

Being creative is also valuable to young children because it adds *spice to their play*—the activities around which their life centers. If creativity can make play pleasurable, children will be happy and contented. This, in turn, will lead to good personal and social adjustments.

As children grow older, *achievement* is of major importance in their adjustment to life. Creativity that helps them to achieve success in areas that matter to them and are favorably viewed by people who are significant to them will be a source of great ego satisfaction (63).

One very important value of creativity that is often overlooked is its contribution to *leadership*. At any age, the leader must contribute something to the group that is important to the group members. The child leader's contribution may be in the form of suggestions for a new and different kind of play activity, or it may be suggestions about how to organize the gang into committees, each with special roles and special responsibilities to the group.

How important the leadership role is to the child's personal and social adjustments was discussed in detail in Chapter 10. If, in addition to the personal satisfaction children derive from creativity, they add to it the satisfaction of playing a leadership role, it will guarantee good social as well as personal adjustments.

The value of creativity is highlighted in the case of children who lack creativity. As Spock has commented, "The person who is strictly literal-minded has a limited usefulness to the world and a limited capacity for joy" (79).

Just because creativity is valuable does not mean that the more creative people are the greater will be their contributions to the social group and the happier and better adjusted they will be. Too much creativity is very likely to make people into "impractical dreamers"—those who create mentally but never seem to be able to put their dreams into practical forms that will benefit them or the social group. As a result, they will not achieve what they are potentially capable of. This will result in feelings of failure which are damaging to personal as well as social adjustments.

Discovery of Creativity

In the past, creative people were discovered only after they had produced something original, such as a picture, a musical composition, or an invention. With our present knowledge of how the ability to be creative—commonly known as "talent"—can be fostered or stifled by environmental influences, it has become apparent that waiting until the creative person has produced something worthy of attention may, for most children, mean waiting until it is too late.

Consequently, interest today is centered on ways of discovering *potential* creativity so that it can be given an opportunity to develop. Discovering potential creativity has proved to be a very difficult task. In the search, effort has been directed toward the construction of tests that will measure creativity or some aspect of it.

Some of the tests of creativity are verbal and some are visual. In the *verbal tests*, creativity is assessed in terms of the number of words children can associate with a given word, such as "bolt" or "rain." Or children may be asked to name all the round things they can think of or to tell how a carrot and a potato are alike (6, 26, 57, 64).

In the *visual tests* of creativity, patterned or line drawings are presented to children and their imagination is judged in terms of what they say the drawings mean to them.

One reason such tests have met with little success is that creativity is a rather nebulous concept. Are the things that are being tested creativity or are they some other ability? Furthermore, critics of the tests claim that they do not always meet the requirements of rigorous experimental design.

Teachers try to identify creativity by determining how original children are in solving problems or how much of a "personal touch" they give to storytelling, artwork, or compositions. These judgments are, of necessity, subjective and, consequently, of little scientific value. For the teacher, however, they serve as guidelines in discovering and encouraging creativity. For parents and others whose work is related to guiding the child's development, similar approaches must be used. Until reliable objective tests can be developed, creativity must, of necessity, be discovered by the way it is expressed in the child's activities.

Development of Creativity

Studies of creativity have shown that its development follows a predictable pattern. It appears early in life and is shown first in the child's play. Gradually, it spreads to other areas of life—schoolwork, recreational activities, and vocations (47, 70, 82).

Creative productions normally reach their peak during the thirties and forties. After that, they either remain on a plateau or gradually decline (27, 48). Erikson has called middle age a "crisis age" in which "generativity" (the tendency to create or to bring into existence) or "stagnation" will dominate (31).

Lehman has explained the early peak in creativity as due to environmental factors, such as poor health, family circumstances, financial pressures, and lack of free time. There is no evidence that the early peak or the subsequent decline is due to hereditary limitations (48).

Whether this pattern will be followed or not will depend largely upon environmental influences that facilitate or hinder the expression of creativity. Spock has emphasized how important early parental attitudes are toward the child's expressions of creativity when he said (79):

The parent who is introducing babies to the world of inanimate things—or failing to do so—shows them what fun can be gained by putting a batch of spoons in a saucepan, looking at pictures in a book, dancing to the music of the phonograph. When the parent teaches them in this positive spirit, it gives them a sense not only that things are to be enjoyed but also that they will be able to manipulate them successfully. Or if the parent has the opposite attitude, it may teach them that objects are to be suspiciously avoided because playing with them involves some kind of danger or parental wrath.

Arasteh has reported that the development of creativity may be obstructed at several "critical periods" during childhood and adolescence (7). Box 12-2 lists these periods and explains why they are regarded as critical. Some children are subjected to environmental factors that result in a stifling of their creativity at these periods while other children of the same age are not. A child who goes to kindergarten, for example, is likely to show greater creativity at that age than is the child who does not attend kindergarten. This is partly because the kindergarten environment promotes creativity and is less structured and evaluative than the typical home or neighborhood environment (22).

Variations in Creativity

In spite of the fact that creativity follows a predictable pattern, there are variations in this pattern. There are a number of factors responsible for these variations, five of which have been found to be important.

SEX Boys show greater creativity than girls, especially as childhood advances. In large part, this is due to the different treatment boys and girls receive. Boys are given more opportunities to be independent, they are prodded by peers to take more risks, and they are encouraged by parents and teachers to show more initiative and originality (7, 13, 25, 88). As Torrance has explained, "There is little doubt that the attitudes and treatment accorded girls and women by a society influence their creative development and behavior" (89).

SOCIOECONOMIC STATUS Children of the higher socioeconomic groups tend to be more creative than those of the lower groups. The former, for the most part, are brought up under democratic child-training methods, while the latter are far more likely to experience authoritarian training. Democratic control fosters creativity by giving children more opportunities to express their individuality and pursue interests and activities of their own choosing. Even more important, the environment of children of the higher socioeconomic groups provides more opportunities for gaining the knowledge and experience necessary for creativity. For example, young children from deprived homes

have very few creative materials to play with and little encouragement to experiment with clay, paints, and puppets as compared with those from more favorable socioeconomic environments.

ORDINAL POSITION Studies of order of birth and its effects on the child's development (refer to pages 60 to 62 for a discussion of these studies) have reported that children of different ordinal positions show different degrees of creativity. The explanation for these differences stresses environment rather than heredity. Middle, later-born, and only children are likely to be more creative than the first-born. Typically, the first-born is subjected to greater pressures to conform to parental expectations than those born later—pressures that encourage the child to be a conformer rather than a creator. An only child is spared

---

BOX 12–2

CRITICAL PERIODS IN
DEVELOPMENT OF CREATIVITY

5 TO 6 YEARS
Before children are ready to enter school, they learn that they must accept authority and conform to the rules and regulations of adults in the home and, later, in school. The stricter the authority, the more it will stifle creativity.

8 TO 10 YEARS
The desire to be accepted as a member of a gang reaches its peak at this time. Most children feel that, to be accepted, they must conform as closely as possible to the pattern set by the gang and that any deviation is a threat to acceptance.

13 TO 15 YEARS
Striving for peer approval, especially from members of the opposite sex, controls the young adolescent's pattern of behavior. Like the gang-age child, the young adolescent conforms in the hope of winning approval and acceptance.

17 TO 19 YEARS
At this age, striving for approval and acceptance as well as training for a chosen vocation may curb creativity. If the vocation necessitates conforming to a standard pattern and following specific orders and rules, as in most routine jobs, it will stifle creativity.

many of the parental pressures common in homes where there are siblings and is also given opportunities to develop individuality.

FAMILY SIZE Children from small families, other conditions being equal, tend to be more creative than children from large families. In large families, authoritarian child-training controls and less favorable socioeconomic conditions are more likely to prevail and militate against the development of creativity.

URBAN VERSUS RURAL ENVIRONMENTS Children from urban environments tend to be more creative than children from rural environments. Authoritarian training is more common in rural homes, and the rural environment offers less stimulation to creativity than the larger environments of cities and their suburbs (49, 88). Figure 12–1 shows a comparison of urban and rural groups—the latter based on studies of Amish children—in tests of creativity, originality, and flexibility.

INTELLIGENCE Age for age, bright children show more creativity than those who are less bright. They have more new ideas in handling social conflict situations and are able to formulate more solutions to these conflicts. That is one of the reasons they are more often selected as leaders than their less bright agemates (3).

Conditions Fostering Creativity

When it was believed that creativity was an inherited trait possessed by only a few children, it was believed that creativity would develop automatically and that there was no need for environmental stimulation or environmental conditions favorable for its development. By contrast, it is now known that *all* children have the potentials for creativity, though they differ in the degree of creativity they possess. Consequently, it is an accepted fact that, like any potential, the environment must provide opportunities for creativity to develop and the stimulation to do so.

This new point of view about creativity has led to research to determine which environmental conditions favor the development of creativity and which stifle it. This research has shown two important conditions.

First, the prevailing unfavorable social attitudes toward creativity must be overcome. The reason for this is that such attitudes influence peers, parents, and teachers and their treatment of potentially creative children. If conditions favorable to the development of creativity are to be established, this negative factor must be eliminated. This many parents try to do by stressing the normality of their creative children and by encouraging them to act like their peers and be interested in what their peers are interested in.

Second, the conditions that are favorable to **the** development of creativity must be present early in life when creativity starts to develop and must be continued until it is well developed. As Torda has explained (86):

Creativity depends not only on special inborn potentials but also on differences in the mental mechanisms by which the inborn qualities are expressed. These

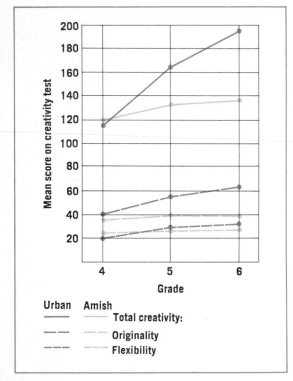

Figure 12–1. In tests of creativity, rural children score lower than those from urban areas. (*Adapted from M. L., Lembright and K. Yamamoto: Subcultures and creative thinking: An exploratory comparison between Amish and urban school children.* Merrill-Palmer Quarterly, *1965,* 11, *49–64. Used by permission.*)

mental mechanisms result from a special type of early adaptation. . . . Seemingly creative and noncreative persons make use of similar and different mental mechanisms. . . . Creative and noncreative persons differ in attitude (philosophy of life), what they hold important and what is anxiety-producing, and show differences in problem-solving skills. These differences originate partially in inborn qualities and partially in early adaptational processes rooted in parental attitudes.

A number of things can be done to foster creativity; the most important of these conditions and the roles they play in fostering creativity are given and briefly explained in Box 12–3.

Persistence of Creativity

The best way to study persistence is to trace the development of a group of children from early childhood into adulthood or even middle age. This approach has not, to date, been used to study creativity. The obstacle is not lack of scientific interest, but rather the lack of adequate measuring devices—standardized tests that can discover creativity in children and measure changes that take place as children grow older. The few tests that are available today, as was explained earlier, are regarded as experimental and far too unreliable to use for a genetic study.

Several studies of creativity over a short period of time have suggested that creativity remains persistent in the early years of life (66, 73). Scheffler, studying children from ages 5 to 6 years, reported that fantasies change somewhat during that time but tend to be more persistent than changeable (70). Kogan and Pankove traced creativity over a 5-year span and found that there was consistency during this period of time (46).

In *Genetic Studies of Genius,* Terman and Oden indirectly studied creativity from childhood into adulthood in connection with their study of the interests and activities of very bright children. They reported a persistence of creative interests through the years (85). Both Dennis and Lehman, who studied creativity mainly in the areas of science, have reported that those who achieved creative distinction in their field had shown interest from childhood days in the areas in which they achieved success (27, 48). These studies, however, were retrospective and, like all retrospection,

---

BOX 12–3

CONDITIONS THAT FOSTER CREATIVITY

TIME
To be creative, children must not be so regimented that they have little free time to toy with ideas and concepts and try them out in new and original forms.

SOLITUDE
Only when away from the pressures imposed on them by the social group can children be creative. As Singer has explained, "It takes time and solitude to develop a rich imaginative life" (73).

ENCOURAGEMENT
Regardless of how far short of adult standards their achievements fall, children must be encouraged to be creative and free from the ridicule and criticism that far too often are heaped on creative children.

MATERIALS
Play materials and, later, other materials must be supplied to stimulate experimentation and exploration, essential elements of all creativity.

STIMULATING ENVIRONMENT
Both the home and school environments must stimulate creativity by providing guidance and encouragement to use the materials that will encourage creativity. This should be done as early as babyhood and continued through the school years by making creativity an enjoyable and socially recognized experience.

UNPOSSESSIVE PARENT-CHILD RELATIONSHIP
Parents who are neither overprotective nor overpossessive encourage their children to be independent and self-reliant, two qualities that contribute heavily to creativity.

CHILD-TRAINING METHODS
Democratic and permissive child training in the home and school foster creativity while authoritarian training stifles it.

OPPORTUNITIES TO ACQUIRE KNOWLEDGE
Creativity cannot take place in a vacuum. The more knowledge children can acquire, the better the foundations on which to build creative productions. As Pulaski has said, "Children must have content in order to fantasize" (63).

they are subject to inaccuracies caused by the subjects' forgetfulness and tendency to exaggerate favorable qualities or experiences.

Helson has reported the results of a study of the childhood interest clusters related to creativity in women. Although this, too, was a retrospective study, Helson concentrated on the interests of the women, not on their achievements. Since childhood interests are less likely to be forgotten or exaggerated than childhood achievements, this study is of particular significance as evidence of persistence.

According to Helson's findings, creative women, as children, showed both interest in and experiences related to such creative activities as imaginative play, painting, writing stories, or putting on plays. This contrasted with noncreative women, who as children enjoyed tomboy activities involving aggression and competition, or those who enjoyed conventional games and play activities where creativity played only a very minor role (40).

Expression of Creativity in Childhood

In the following pages, some of the most common ways in which children at different ages express their creativity will be discussed. Each means of expression will be critically evaluated to determine whether it leads to good personal and social adjustment and brings satisfaction to the child.

Animism

Animism is the tendency to ascribe consciousness to inanimate objects. Young children have too little knowledge and experience to be able to distinguish between things which have life qualities and those which do not. They *assume* that, since they feel and act in certain ways in different situations, everything else does likewise.

It is difficult to tell just when animistic thinking begins because very young children cannot verbalize their thoughts. Thus, their thoughts must be judged in terms of their actions. This approach has led to the conclusion that animistic thinking begins around the time the child is 2 years old, reaches a peak between 4 and 5 years, and then declines rapidly, disappearing shortly after the child enters school (12, 50, 74).

The tendency of children to endow everything with the same life qualities they have is very often encouraged by parents. They read children stories or encourage them to look at comics, television programs, or movies in which trees, toys, animals, and objects of all sorts behave like human beings. They try to keep children from hurting themselves or objects during temper outbursts by saying, "Don't kick the poor chair or you will hurt his legs" or "How would you feel if I threw you around the way you are throwing poor dolly?" Under such conditions, it is understandable that children would endow inanimate objects with lifelike qualities. This is illustrated in Figure 12-2.

In trying to explain natural phenomena, such as clouds, stars, lightning, or snow, adults often encourage children to think of them as having living qualities. Only as children gain more experience and as they begin to understand explanations of the difference between animate and inanimate objects does their animistic thinking wane. Animism can, consequently, be regarded as a creative activity of early childhood, but it rarely continues after the child begins school.

EVALUATION That animism gives young children pleasure cannot be questioned. It adds enjoyment to their toy play during the years when they are too immature to spend much of their playtime with other people. When children become mature enough to understand that toys and toy animals do not have the qualities of people and real animals, they begin to lose interest in toy play and turn their attention to play in which toys are not needed.

There is no evidence that endowing inanimate objects with life qualities interferes in any way with children's personal and social adjustments. On the contrary, it helps children to imagine themselves in the place of others and, thus, to develop sympathy and empathy. Children, for example, who feel sorry for a toy that has been hit by another child in a fit of temper learn to feel sorry for people in similar situations. As a result, this helps children to learn to curb aggressive attacks on others. Equally important, identifying with a toy gives children a feeling of security that many young children lack. Taking a stuffed dog to bed, for example, has been found to help many young children to overcome their fear of the dark. They feel that the toy will protect them just as the family dog protects the family.

Dramatic Play

Dramatic play which, as was pointed out in the preceding chapter is often called "make-believe play," parallels animistic thinking. It loses its appeal just about the time children enter school. When reasoning ability and experience enable children to distinguish between reality and fantasy, they lose interest in make-believe play and turn their creative drives into other activities, usually constructive play.

At first, as was likewise pointed out in the preceding chapter, dramatic play is reproductive. In it, children reproduce with astonishing fidelity the behavior of people they are imitating and the situations of life or of the mass media they are using as themes for their dramatic play.

Very quickly, reproductive dramatic play is replaced by productive play in which children create the characters and themes of their play based on people and situations from life or from the mass media. Sometimes these creative productions closely approximate real people and real situations; sometimes they are mainly a product of imagination and bear little resemblance to real-life people or situations (19, 25, 74).

While the themes of dramatic play vary greatly, the way in which children act out the themes follows a definite and predictable pattern. Sonte and Church (81) have described the typical pattern of children's dramatizations:

"Naughty door! You hurt PJ's fingers! You naughty door!"

Figure 12–2. When children endow inanimate objects with life qualities, they react to these objects as they would to people or animals. (*Adapted from Bil Keane: "The Family Circus."* Register and Tribune Syndicate, *Dec. 6, 1973. Used by permission.*)

For a three-year-old, a block can be a doll, a train, a building, a cow. For the five-year-old, a block is a building material, and he wants some approximation of a real train to run in and out of the railroad station he makes with his blocks. The three-year-old can people a universe with sticks and stones and paper and rags—which, however, he does not try to shape in representational images. The four-year-old, to be a successful cowboy, wants some outstanding prop—a broad-brimmed hat, a cap pistol, or a neckerchief. For him, one element can stand for the whole configuration "cowboy." The five-year-old, though, is likely to feel dissatisfied in his role-playing unless he can wear the full regalia of his part.

EVALUATION   Only if dramatic play persists long beyond the time when children usually engage in this form of creative activity is there any likelihood that children will be damaged in their personal and social adjustments by it. Like animism, dramatic play is usually discarded by most children shortly after they enter school. By that time, they can no longer attribute living qualities to their toys and they are too realistic to want to pretend that their dramatizations are anything but make-believe. Furthermore, as the interest in peer activities increases and the desire for social acceptance becomes stronger, children want to do what their peers are doing. This means that, no matter how much enjoyment they might derive from dramatic play, they abandon it if their peers regard it as babyish and if they have substituted balls, bats, skates, and more grown-up play equipment for their toys. Only if dramatic play is a popular gang activity in late childhood does it persist after children become gang-oriented in their play interests.

Box 12–4 describes some of the ways in which dramatic play contributes to young children's personal *and* social adjustments. Though teachers in nursery schools and kindergartens recognize the value of dramatic play to *social* adjustment, parents often overlook

EVALUATION OF DRAMATIC PLAY

CONTRIBUTIONS TO PERSONAL ADJUSTMENT

- Dramatic play gives children pleasure and eliminates the boredom they might experience when no playmates are available.
- In dramatic play, children can go beyond the restrictions imposed by reality and thus learn the pleasures and benefits of creativity.
- Dramatic play enables children to realize their wishes vicariously, thus eliminating feelings of frustration when their wishes are blocked in daily life.
- Dramatizations serve as a source of emotional catharsis by enabling children to express frustrations in aggressive make-believe play.
- In dramatic play, children can increase their feelings of self-importance by playing roles associated with power and prestige (such as parental roles).
- By dressing up for roles in make-believe play, children begin to recognize the value of clothes.

CONTRIBUTIONS TO SOCIAL ADJUSTMENT

- Dramatic play shows children the pleasures of social contacts and encourages them to become outer-oriented.
- In make-believe play, children learn to be cooperative by playing roles that fit into the pattern of the roles played by others.
- Dramatic play helps children to learn, through imitation of real or mass-media models, approved social and sex roles.
- In dramatic play, children are motivated to speak, either in making suggestions about the dramatization or in playing their roles. Thus, they not only increase their vocabularies but they also gain confidence in their abilities to communicate with peers—a skill needed for social acceptance.

it, giving more attention to personal adjustment contributions (63).

Constructive Play

As children reach school age and are better able to distinguish between fantasy and reality, they lose interest in dramatic play and turn their attention to constructive play. This does not mean that construc-

tive play begins when dramatic play ends. Constructive play begins early, often sooner than dramatic play, but it is overshadowed by the more exciting play of make-believe. Then, when make-believe loses much of its thrill for children, they turn their attention to a type of creative play they found enjoyable earlier and devote much of their time to it.

Early constructive play is reproductive. Children copy what they have seen in everyday life. Later, as they grow older, they create constructions by using everyday objects and situations and changing them to suit their fancy.

The two most common and popular kinds of constructive play are making things and drawing. As in other creative play, there are marked variations in the frequency with which children engage in these activities and there are differences in the kinds of things they construct. Boys enjoy constructive play as much as girls, for example, but boys and girls of the same age usually follow quite different constructive play patterns.

In early constructive play, children *make things* from mud, sand, blocks, clay, paint, and paper and paste. In kindergarten, most children turn from block building to painting, modeling, puzzles, and collages. In late childhood, children build tents, playhouses, huts, snowmen, and dams.

Early *drawings* are usually copies of pictures in children's drawing books. They are, thus, reproductive. If given crayons or pencils and paper to draw as they please, drawings become constructive. Children create pictures of people or places, not so much as they remember them but as they would like them to be. They are uninterested in perspective and proportions. Instead, they put in details that interest them, such as buttons on a coat, while omitting essentials, such as a man's legs. By the time children enter school, their drawings show regard for perspective, relative size, and correctness of detail. Unless truly gifted, children, as a result of formal instruction they receive in drawing in school, show less originality in their drawings with each passing year (9, 18). Figure 12–3 shows, from a longitudinal study of one child's drawings, the decrease in originality that tends to occur after children enter school.

The drawings of young children usually represent familiar objects, rarely designs. The human form is most popular, with the adult form slightly more popular than the child's. Animals are less frequently drawn than houses and trees.

Among older children, more emphasis is placed on the drawing of machines, designs, animals, houses, flowers, and trees, and less on the human form. Older children frequently draw cartoons similar to comic strips; subject matter is varied, but favorite characters are teachers and peers whom they dislike (33, 37, 51, 77).

EVALUATION Constructive play contributes to good personal adjustment but does little toward improving social adjustment. Constructive play is usually carried out as a solitary rather than a group activity, and so it offers no help in making social adjustments. Only when children make things with another child or several children can it contribute to social adjustments in the same way as dramatic play.

Constructive play aids personal adjustment both directly and indirectly. *Directly,* its contribution comes from the ego satisfaction children receive from being able to construct something by themselves and from the social recognition they receive for their constructions. Unfortunately their constructive efforts are often criticized or ridiculed by peers, parents, or teachers. Such experiences are ego-deflating.

Indirectly, constructive play contributes to personal adjustments by eliminating boredom and any feeling of martyrdom children might have if they have no one to play with. Children who are bored often feel sorry for themselves. Even worse, they try to compensate for their boredom by engaging in daydreaming—a type of play that gives temporary satisfaction but, in the long run, can play havoc with good personal and social adjustments. This subject will be taken up in a later section of this chapter.

The contribution of constructive play to good personal adjustment does not end with childhood, as is true of dramatic play. Instead, constructive play often develops into a lifetime hobby. Thus, its contribution to personal adjustment persists.

Imaginary Companions

An imaginary companion is a person, an animal, or a thing which the child creates in fantasy to play the role of a companion. Because much play requires playmates to be enjoyable, the child who lacks a playmate often creates an imaginary one. A child who is timid or has had unpleasant early social experiences may prefer an imaginary playmate to a real one.

When the child wants a friend, the imaginary companion will serve as a real friend. Thus, imaginary companions, like real ones, may be either playmates or friends (as explained in the chapter on social adjustments). Regardless of the role the imaginary companion plays, the child derives satisfaction from feeling that someone is always present. A. A. Milne explains how a young child feels about an imaginary companion (58):

> Binker—what I call him—is a secret of my own,
> And Binker is the reason why I never feel alone.
> Playing in the nursery, sitting on the stair,
> Whatever I am busy at, Binker will be there.

Most imaginary companions are people—mainly children of the child's own sex and age. They have

Figure 12–3. (a) "Wolf, crouching," age 3–4, pen; (b) "My family," age 7–10, pencil. Creativity in drawings tends to decrease after the child receives formal instruction in drawing. (*Adapted from J. L. Brown: Precursors of intelligence and creativity: A longitudinal study of one child's development.* Merrill-Palmer Quarterly, *1970,* 16, *117–137. Used by permission.*)

names chosen by the child and physical and personality characteristics the child likes—often those the child would like to have. Imaginary companions can and will do anything the child wants them to do. This, of course, adds to the pleasure the child derives from them.

PREVALENCE OF IMAGINARY COMPANIONS Because the imaginary companion is a "secret of my own," children do not always tell others about their imaginary companions. Observing children and listening to what they say when they are playing alone, however, will often reveal that they have imaginary companions. This secrecy on the part of young children explains the methodological difficulty of finding out how common a creative activity having an imaginary companion is, what kind of children are most likely to have imaginary companions, and at what ages imaginary companions are likely to be most important in a child's life.

Studies of imaginary companions, more often based on retrospective reports than on direct observations of young children, suggest that imaginary companions are more prevalent among children of superior *intelligence* than among those of average intelligence (8, 39, 69). In a study of creative adolescents, Schaefer, for example, concluded that, as children, having an imaginary companion was more common in those who were bright, especially those with leanings toward literary creativity, than among those who were less bright or less interested in writing (69).

No one *personality* type predisposes children to have imaginary companions. Children who are happy and well adjusted have them during the preschool years just as other children do. It has been reported that they are most common among children who have such personality difficulties as timidity in the presence of other children, a domineering manner with other children, fear of physical activities, sensitivity, an undemonstrative manner, evasiveness, irresponsibility, eagerness to be in the limelight, and fear of being outdone by others (36, 39, 52, 69).

All children who lack the companionship they crave may compensate by developing imaginary companions to meet their needs. Imaginary companions are so common during the early childhood years that having one may be regarded as normal. However, if children *prefer* imaginary companions beyond the age when children normally have them, that may be regarded as a danger signal of poor personal and social adjustments.

EVALUATION Imaginary companions are, by no means, a satisfactory solution to the lonely child problem. Although it may help children to relieve their loneliness, it does not help them to make good personal and social adjustments. This matter was discussed in detail in the chapter on social adjustments, in the section on hazards in social adjustments.

Several studies have been made of college students who, as young children, had imaginary companions. The studies show little evidence of permanent damage from imaginary-companion experiences in early childhood. Comparatively, the students tend to be more introverted, to be less social in their interests, and to have less achievement motivation, but unless these tendencies are strong, they do not seriously impair social adjustment. The findings suggest, however, that children who have imaginary companions need guidance and help to guarantee that these tendencies be overcome before they become habitual patterns of personal and social adjustment (39).

Daydreaming

Like all play, daydreaming is an activity which is engaged in for the pleasure it provides. It is a form of mental play, and is usually called "fantasy" to distinguish it from more controlled expressions of imagination. Blazer has written: "Fantasy is an escape or defensive mechanism offering either solace or an illusionary release from unsatisfying reality or an imaginary satisfaction of wishes any actual gratification of which has been forbidden by repression" (15).

Daydreaming differs from make-believe play in that the roles children play in their daydreams are more fanciful, more heroic, and more remote from daily life. In a daydream, for example, a child may be a princess, an orphaned prince, a popular sports hero, or the President of the United States. The stuff of which daydreams are made often comes from the mass media—movies, television, books, or comics (73, 75, 91).

Regardless of the setting or the action of the daydream, the central character is always the dreamer. All other characters are subordinate, though their roles are related to and affect the actions of the dreamer. When, for example, a daydream centers around a circus, the dreamer is the lion tamer or the trapeze artist; others play subordinate and admiring roles.

Although daydreaming may begin early—and it does in bright children—it reaches a peak during puberty. It is a favorite form of entertainment among older children when they are bored or restricted in other play.

THEMES OF DAYDREAMS Although daydreams may have any imaginable setting and may relate to any activity, three major categories are most common and most popular in childhood. These are explained briefly in Box 12–5.

Normally, in well-adjusted children, conquering-hero daydreams predominate, though almost all well-adjusted children, at some time or other, engage in both suffering-hero and imaginary-invalid daydreams. In poorly adjusted children, on the other hand, suffering-hero and imaginary-invalid daydreams predominate.

As children approach puberty and begin to develop antisocial attitudes and to feel below par physically, suffering-hero and imaginary-invalid daydreams become increasingly frequent and vivid. In fact, they are almost universal during puberty though, of course, every pubescent child also engages in conquering-hero daydreams. Figure 12–4, showing different physical causes for absence from school among children at different ages, emphasizes how common imaginary invalidism (referred to as "illegal cause") is as children approach puberty.

EVALUATION Daydreaming is so widespread and so satisfying in childhood that an evaluation of its effects on personal and social adjustments is in order. In this evaluation, given in Box 12–6, it should become apparent that the obstacles daydreaming poses to good adjustment far outweigh its aids. This is especially true when daydreaming becomes habitual (73, 75).

White Lies

A very common expression of creativity among young children is the telling of "white lies"—often referred to as "tall tales." The white lie of childhood is very different from lying as adults think of it. A white lie is a falsehood told by a person who actually believes it is true. There is no intention of deceiving others and no motivation to do so. Children who tell white lies believe what they say because it is so vivid and seems so realistic to them that they assume it is true.

A "lie," by contrast, is a falsehood told with the deliberate intent to deceive. Children who resort to lies often do so to avoid punishment or criticism for something they know is forbidden or disapproved. Occasionally, children use lies to impress others and, as such, lying is a form of self-aggrandizement rather than self-protection. Whatever the motivation, children are fully aware that what they say is untrue.

Fundamentally, the difference between the two is that white lies are used for self-aggrandizement and lies for self-protection, though some lies, as was pointed out above, may also be for self-aggrandizement. Children who tell white lies exaggerate and embroider reality because they have discovered that this focuses attention on themselves and increases their prestige. A young child, for example, who tells family members at the dinner table about seeing a lion on the street discovers this has greater attention value than telling them about seeing a dog. And the

---

BOX 12–5

CATEGORIES OF DAYDREAMS

CONQUERING-HERO DAYDREAMS
Children see themselves as they would like to be in real life—cowboys, ballet dancers, beauty queens, or athletic heroes. The dreamers are always the central characters and all other characters pay homage to them.

SUFFERING-HERO DAYDREAMS
Children see themselves as martyrs who are misunderstood and mistreated by parents, teachers, siblings, peers, or society in general. In the end, the dreamers turn out to be heroes and those who mistreated them are penitent and try to do all within their power to compensate for the physical or mental pain they inflicted on them.

IMAGINARY-INVALID DAYDREAMS
Children see themselves as suffering from a physical ailment which prevents them from doing what other children of their age do. Imaginary-invalid daydreams are, thus, a form of suffering-hero daydream. When these daydreams are vivid, children actually believe that they are sick or suffering from a physical handicap, such as inability to run or to do things with one or both of their hands.

DEVELOPMENT OF CREATIVITY

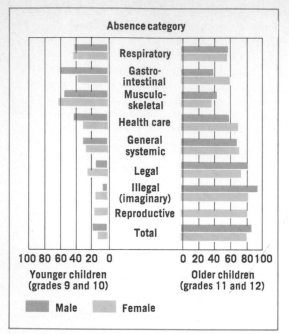

Absence category

	Respiratory
	Gastro-intestinal
	Musculo-skeletal
	Health care
	General systemic
	Legal
	Illegal (imaginary)
	Reproductive
	Total

100 80 60 40 20 0   0 20 40 60 80 100

Younger children   Older children
(grades 9 and 10)   (grades 11 and 12)

■ Male   ■ Female

Figure 12–4. Absence from school for imaginary illness (Illegal) increases markedly during early adolescence among both boys and girls. (*Adapted from K. D. Rogers and G. Reese: Health studies— presumably normal high school students. II. Absence from school.* American Journal of Diseases of Children, 1965, 109, *9–27. Used by permission.*)

child may actually believe it was seen on the street rather than on the television screen or in a book.

Many white lies originate in daydreaming. When children in the daydream world see themselves doing things they would like to do in real life, the ego satisfaction they receive from the daydream helps to reinforce their belief that they actually did these things.

If, in addition to their daydreams, children are encouraged to endow inanimate objects with life qualities and are told stories or see pictures of objects or animals doing and saying things that people in real life do, they are likely to believe that they actually were or could be real. This makes them more white-lie prone.

There is some evidence that white lies reach their peak of frequency and intensity between the ages of 4 and 5 years and then wane rapidly as children's reasoning improves and their knowledge increases. It is also likely that the environment in which children live

and how the significant people in their lives react will influence their tendency to tell white lies. Normally, white lies are infrequent after children are 6 years old and spend much of their play time with age-mates who tend to be less tolerant of white lies than parents are.

EVALUATION   There is no evidence that white lies contribute to good personal or social adjustments. Whether they will be detrimental and how detrimental they will be will depend largely on how adults or others who are significant in the child's life react.

Adults often regard a child's white lies with amused tolerance. They may even encourage children to tell tall tales because they are "cute" or amusing. The danger in this kind of adult reaction is that children interpret it to mean that people approve of telling white lies. They are not, therefore, motivated to examine critically what they have said to determine whether they imagined it or whether it actually happened. This adult reaction also encourages children to exaggerate whatever they say because this raises its attention value. Later, boasting and exaggerating—both of which are done with the intention of impressing others and, as such, are a form of lying—may become habitual. As was noted in the chapter on speech development, neither of these contributes to social acceptance.

A second common adult reaction to white lies is to *regard them as real lies* and to assume that the child is trying to deceive. This reaction stems from the adults' failure to realize that young children are mentally too immature to be able to distinguish between what they imagine and what actually happens. Since adults feel that a child who lies will make poor adjustments to life, they take punitive steps to prevent the behavior from becoming habitual. Whatever punitive action is taken, the child who is made to feel guilty and ashamed may develop a generalized feeling of guilt about *any* form of imaginative thinking. Adult disapproval may be reinforced by the reactions of older children who also fail to realize that the young child is often incapable of distinguishing imaginary from real experiences. Such unfavorable reactions may make the child feel that imagination itself is wrong. This will curb any natural ability to be creative.

The third and most wholesome adult reaction to white lies is to recognize them as *natural in early childhood but a potential source of social rejection.* This reaction, if accompanied by guidance to help children analyze what they said to determine whether they actually experienced it or just imagined it, will help children to become self-critical without being stifled by feelings of guilt.

Humor Production

Humor has two aspects: the ability to perceive the comic and the ability to produce it. Both aspects can add to social acceptance, because they help to create the impression that one is fun to be with and is a good sport.

Some forms of humor can be produced only by persons with a high level of intelligence, but most of the forms that have great appeal to children can be created by anyone of normal or even slightly below normal intelligence. They require divergent thinking, which enables the producer to perceive new ways to combine previously learned material into patterns that others will regard as humorous. They do not require the production of completely new material.

The creation of humor also requires a knowledge of the kind of situation that others perceive as comic and a motivation to turn one's creative energies into channels that will result in humorous patterns. As McGhee and Grodzitsky have pointed out, when the "child acquires a high level of conceptual mastery over some content area, he may perceive any inaccurate depiction of it as being funny." When, for example, he knows the socially approved roles for members of the two sexes, he regards any deviation from these roles as "funny" (56).

Knowledge of what others regard as comic comes partly from observation of what people laugh at in real-life stiuations and partly from observation of people's reactions to the comic in the mass media. Young children, for example, observe that almost everyone laughs when a person slips and falls on a banana peel and that they laugh even harder when the person in the predicament is someone who is regarded as superior because of age or position. Children also discover what makes people laugh from reading the comics, from stories their parents or teachers read to them, and from what they see on movie or television screens.

Children who want to be socially acceptable, especially if their acceptance is marginal, have a strong *motivation* to learn to produce humor as an aid to achieving this goal. They are willing to spend time and energy discovering what makes people laugh and creating humor that will win their approval.

Humor takes many forms, ranging from the simple to the complex and from the crude to the subtle. In Box 12–7 are given some of the most common outlets for humor creativity among American children today. The list shows that children's humor is largely dependent upon their observation of what makes others laugh. The creative element comes from the ability to take this information from past experiences and apply it to new situations. Children who see a clown getting a laugh when he trips over his oversized shoes, for example, may paddle around in their fathers' shoes, trip over their feet, and get a laugh from their age-mates (55).

BOX 12–6

EVALUATION OF DAYDREAMING

AIDS TO ADJUSTMENT

- Daydreaming is a source of enjoyment to all children, especially those who are unhappy with their real selves and their real-life roles.
- Daydreaming is an important wish-fulfillment experience for all children.
- In the secret world of daydreams, children can get the excitement they rarely find in real life, even greater excitement than from identification with characters in the mass media.
- Daydreaming provides a source of emotional catharsis for children. This comes from imagining that they are doing the things they would like to do in real life but are afraid to do.

OBSTACLES TO ADJUSTMENT

- Instead of motivating children to do what they are capable of, daydreaming far too often acts as a substitute for achievement.
- Daydreaming prevents children from engaging in active play, which is essential to a good physical condition and normal growth.
- Daydreaming may and often does give rise to strong emotions which upset body homeostasis.
- In the daydream world, children tend to develop romanticized self-concepts which are far removed from reality.
- When children indulge in suffering-hero daydreams, it builds up unsocial attitudes that intensify poor social adjustments.
- Imaginary-invalid daydreams encourage children to feel sorry for themselves and to become self-bound.
- Excessive daydreamers rarely have good self- or social insight. This intensifies poor personal and social adjustments.

BOX 12–7

COMMON FORMS OF HUMOR PRODUCTION

- Punning, or play on words by twisting their meanings or pronunciations
- Caricature drawings of people or animals doing humorous things
- Mimicry of the speech, singing, mannerisms, or actions of people or animals
- Jokes and smutty stories mainly about tabooed subjects, such as sex, or about people in authority
- Slips of the tongue, often intentional
- Stunting or doing "silly" things
- Dressing up to produce an incongruous appearance
- Clowning or "cutting up"
- Horseplay or "roughhousing" with peers
- Practical jokes to put others in a predicament
- Sarcasm or verbal caricatures of others

touch of originality will lead others to think that the humorist is not very original or funny after all.

A personal example will illustrate this point. When the writer was talking to a class of third graders, one of the youngsters held up his hand to ask a question. He began by saying, "Dr. Hislock," and then added, with apparent though, to the writer, studied embarrassment, "I mean Dr. Hurlock," to cover up what he wanted his classmates to think was a slip of the tongue. Understandably, this was greeted with a roar of laughter.

Twice more during the same class period, the youngster made the same slip of the tongue and twice more he tried to pretend that it was accidental and that he was embarrassed. On the first repetition, the laughter from his classmates was halfhearted. On the second, it was barely a ripple, and one of his classmates commented sarcastically, "Aw, turn off the record. We've heard it before."

Storytelling

Some children entertain their peers or younger siblings by telling them stories. If listeners react to their stories favorably, children are encouraged to continue to tell stories and, later, to write them down either as assigned work for English classes or as a hobby.

At first, storytelling is reproductive. Children tell stories that have been told to them or that they have read or heard over the radio or television. Later, their stories become creative. Children make up stories based on material from different sources, mainly from the mass media, and add original details to them.

It has been reported that the children most likely to engage in this form of creativity are those who, when they were younger, had imaginary companions and learned to talk to these companions as if they were real companions or friends (69). Storytelling has also been reported to be more common among bright children than among those who are less bright (30). This is true also of having imaginary companions, as was pointed out earlier.

EVALUATION Children who are able to make others laugh or who are able to put others in an inferior position will develop self-confidence and self-assurance. On the surface, one might conclude that humor production is an aid to personal adjustment.

One must look below the surface, however, to see if this form of creativity often leads to unfavorable social reactions that will counteract the aid it might be to personal adjustment. Although almost all humorous patterns are at first greeted with laughter and the humor producer receives initially favorable social reactions, later reactions may be quite the reverse.

Children who can make their classmates laugh by clowning or "cutting up," for example, may soon discover that they are regarded as "pests." Similarly, the first reaction to an off-color joke may appear to be favorable, but if it causes embarrassment to those who hear it, they will not have a high regard for the person who told the joke.

Three conditions often lead to unfavorable social reactions toward humorous productions. *First,* any humor that causes annoyance or interference with what others want to do will lead to social judgments that the creator of the humor is a pest. *Second,* humor that embarrasses or humiliates another person, especially when the person is unable to retaliate, is regarded as poor sportsmanship. And *third,* humor that is repeated without enough variation to give it a

EVALUATION There is little evidence that storytelling is harmful to personal and social adjustments and much evidence that it contributes to them. Children who can entertain their age-mates or younger children are bound to be well accepted by them and may even be selected for leadership roles. In addition, children acquire social insight by observing how listeners react to their stories. If, for example, listeners react more favorably to stories depicting kindness than to those centered around violence, children will discover how others feel about aggressiveness in its different forms of expression.

Not only does storytelling help children to make good social adjustments, it also helps them to make good personal adjustments. Knowing that they can hold the limelight of attention gives children self-confidence and self-assurance. In addition, it helps them to gain self-insight by discovering how others react to them and to the way they tell their stories. They learn how to talk to others and to acquire conversational skills, which are essential to social acceptance and to leadership roles.

In school, children who can write stories are likely to gain greater teacher approval than those who lack this capacity. Because of the emphasis put on language usage in the school curriculum, children who can write or read well gain an academic halo which spreads to others areas of the curriculum in which the child may be less able.

Storytelling is one of the few areas of creativity in which children are unlikely to encounter social criticism or ridicule. No matter how fantastic their stories may be, there is far less likelihood that listeners will criticize or ridicule them than there is in such creative productions as drawings, constructions, or humor. This absence of criticism and ridicule adds to the enjoyment children derive from this form of creativity. It encourages them to spend time and thought on improving skills in this area.

On the negative side, the only unfavorable effect of storytelling comes if children become so accustomed to embroidering their stories to increase their attention value that they develop the habit of exaggerating *everything,* including what they say about themselves. As was pointed out earlier, children who tend to exaggerate, especially when talking about themselves, encounter serious obstacles to good social adjustments because of the unfavorable social attitudes toward their exaggerations.

Aspirations for Achievement

Left to their own devices, most children would live in the present and let the future take care of itself. But they are not left to their own devices. Even before they enter school, parents, relatives, and family friends ask children what they are planning to do when they are grown up. Most adults regard a child who says, "I want to be President of the United States" or "I am going to be a doctor," as ambitious, and as courageous if the ambition is to be the first person to walk on the planet Mars.

In a culture which provides vast opportunities for its members to be and to achieve what they want, it is understandable that children at an early age would be subjected to pressures to create aspirations for the future. Aspirations, it is believed, motivate children to take advantage of the opportunities parents and society provide.

Social pressures to plan for the future are reinforced by competition with members of the peer group in play and schoolwork. As children compare what they can do with what their peers can do, it adds new meanings to their aspirations and puts new emphasis on the creation of aspirations that are both ego satisfying and admired by members of the social group. Thus, forming aspirations becomes an important area of creativity in childhood.

MEANING OF ASPIRATION   To the layman, "aspiration" is synonymous with "ambition." It suggests that the person is not only planning personal betterment but is carrying out this plan in real life. In the strictest sense, as used by the psychologist and defined in standard dictionaries, ambition means a desire for honor, power, or attainment. By contrast, aspiration means a longing for what is above one, with advancement as its goal. The subtle distinction between the two terms is that aspiration emphasizes the desire to improve or to rise above one's present status, while ambition stresses the end result—the attainment of power, honor, or some achievement.

If aspiration and ambition were synonymous, and meant honorable attainment, people would be satisfied if their achievements were recognized and applauded by others. Children, for example, would be satisfied if their parents praised them for the block houses they built or for the drawings they made. If, on the other hand, the desire to improve or to have what is above one is taken into consideration, children would not necessarily be satisfied with their block houses or their drawings just because their parents praised them. Instead, they would be satisfied *only* if their block houses or drawings met with the standards they set for themselves. This distinction is important because it helps to explain much of the dissatisfaction children—as well as adolescents and adults—experience in connection with their achievements and why, as a result, aspirations play such a large role in personal and social adjustments.

VARIETIES OF ASPIRATIONS   Aspirations vary not only in strength but, even more important, in kind. They may be *positive* or *negative*. In the former, the emphasis is on winning success or doing better than one has done before, while in the latter, the emphasis

is on avoiding failure. *Immediate* aspirations are goals the person sets for the immediate future—today, tomorrow, next week, or next month—while *remote* aspirations are goals set for the future, such as "when I grow up."

Childhood aspirations are likely to be *unrealistic* because knowledge and experiences at this age are limited. As a result, children are unable to assess their abilities accurately enough to know what they can and cannot do, or what environmental obstacles might prevent them from doing what they want to do. This prevents them from checking their divergent thinking with facts and gives their imaginations free rein.

Some aspirations relate to what children *want to be* and some to what they *want to accomplish*. The former are usually called "ideal self-concepts"—to be discussed in the following section—and the latter are called "aspirations for achievement"—to be discussed below.

Some aspirations are *verbalized* and some are not. Aspirations for achievement are more likely to be verbalized than ideal self-concepts. Verbalizing aspirations for achievement, children discover, leads to favorable social reactions; such children are regarded as "ambitious." Verbalizing ideal self-concepts, by contrast, often leads to unfavorable social reactions; children are regarded as conceited or, as their peers describe them, "they have swelled heads."

DEVELOPMENT OF ASPIRATIONS FOR ACHIEVEMENT
Aspirations for achievement are influenced more by environmental factors than by personal factors. Some environmental influences encourage the development of immediate aspirations and some encourage remote aspirations; some foster positive aspirations while others foster negative aspirations; some motivate the child to be realistic, and others, unrealistic.

Box 12–8 lists the environmental and personal factors that most affect the creation of aspirations for achievement. In early childhood, before children are old enough to know what their abilities, interests, and values are, their aspirations are largely shaped by their environments. As children grow older and are more aware of their abilities and interests, personal factors have a greater influence, but many of their aspirations are still environmental in origin.

EVALUATION   On the *positive* side, aspirations for achievement are important aids to personal and social adjustment. Personally, it is ego-inflating to children to think that they will achieve goals that are

---

BOX 12–8

FACTORS INFLUENCING ASPIRATIONS
FOR ACHIEVEMENT

PERSONAL FACTORS
- Children's wishes for what they want to achieve
- Personal interests, which influence the areas of children's aspirations
- Past experiences, with successes strengthening aspirations and failures weakening them
- The personality pattern, which influences both the kind and strength of children's aspirations
- Personal values, which determine what aspirations are important
- Sex, with boys aspiring higher than girls
- Socioeconomic status, with those of the middle and upper groups aspiring higher than those of the lower groups
- Racial background, with those of minority-group status often aspiring unrealistically high as a form of compensation

ENVIRONMENTAL FACTORS
- Parental ambitions, which are higher for first-born than later-born children
- Social expectations which emphasize that those who are successful in one area can be successful in *all* areas if they wish
- Peer pressures to set aspirations in areas important to the peer group
- Group emphasis on sex appropriateness of aspirations
- Cultural traditions which hold that *all* people can achieve anything they wish if they try hard enough
- Social values, which vary with area of achievement
- Mass media, which encourages achievement aspirations
- Social rewards for high achievement and social neglect or rejection for low achievement
- Competition with siblings and peers in the hope of showing one's superiority over them

highly valued by the social group. Their aspirations also motivate them to do all they can to achieve the goals they set for themselves. In addition, they act as guidelines to direct their energies into channels that will make attainment of their goals possible.

Aspirations for achievement aid social adjustments by giving others the impression that the child is a serious, conscientious person, not an impractical dreamer. Even when children's achievements fall below the group's expectations, most people give such children credit for trying and judge them more favorably than they would if they gave the impression that they lacked goal orientation.

On the *negative* side, aspirations for achievement can lead to poor personal and social adjustments if they are unrealistically high or low. Children who aspire beyond their capacities will, inevitably, fall below their own expectations as well as those of others. As a result, they will think of themselves as failures and this will encourage others to judge them as failures.

Children with unrealistically low aspirations are rarely satisfied with their achievements, especially if they feel that they might have done better. Nor is the social group likely to judge them favorably if there is reason to believe that they are not trying to make the most of their abilities. The effects of unrealistic aspirations on personality will be discussed in more detail in Chapter 18.

Concepts of Ideal Self

The concept of the ideal self is an aspiration children create of what they would like to be rather than what they would like to achieve. The latter has to do with aspirations for achievement, discussed above. The ideal self-concept includes what children would like to look like—their *physical self-concepts*—and what they would like their capacities to be—their *psychological self-concepts*.

Like aspirations for achievement, the ideal self-concept may be for the present or for the future. If the self ideal is for the future, it is most likely to be unrealistic, because very few children are satisfied with themselves as they are. As their social horizons broaden to include people outside the home, both peers and adults, and as their interest in the mass media increases, they are constantly comparing themselves with ideal models and seeing their shortcomings. Thus their self-dissatisfaction grows.

Children who are not completely satisfied with what they are will, at some time or other, create aspirations

of what they would like to be. Very bright children, owing to their better social and self-insight, are more likely to recognize their weaknesses than the less bright. As a result, their aspirations for what they would like to be are usually developed earlier and are likely to be more realistic.

DEVELOPMENT OF IDEAL SELF-CONCEPTS The material from which children create their ideal self-concepts comes mainly from contacts, either directly or indirectly, with real people they admire or from the characters they observe and admire in the mass media. Some of the most common sources of ideal self-concepts are given in Box 12–9.

At first, children identify with people in their immediate environments. Later, they choose models from more remote sources, such as the school, neighborhood, community, the nation, or even foreign nations. Fewer models come from literature than from movies, television, and newspapers because the characters in literature seem less real than those on the screen or in a newspaper photograph. As older children have more associations, both directly and indirectly, with people in positions of prestige, it is understandable that their influence becomes increasingly more important.

CHANGES IN IDEAL SELF-CONCEPTS Throughout childhood, ideal self-concepts change from time to time. There are two explanations for this. *First,* children identify with many different models. As they shift models, they revise their ideal self-concepts. This shifting of models comes as they make new social contacts and as they gain more understanding of what is socially approved and admired. The preschooler, for example, who wanted to be just like the policeman on the block learns, in time, that bankers have more prestige in the eyes of the social group than policemen. The child then begins to admire a friend of the family who is a banker and wants to be like the banker.

Second, as children grow older, ideal self-concepts become less specific and more composite. The young child wants to be a carbon copy of some admired person. Later, the ideal is a composite of traits, both physical and mental, which the child has admired in different people at different times. As children have more experiences with people, as they become aware of social values, and as they become more skilled in evaluating people, they find it difficult to regard anyone as the paragon that they ideally want to be. Consequently, they select characteristics from different models and combine them into models of their own.

When a girl, for example, finds that red hair has attention value and is highly admired by her peers, she wants to have red hair just like Mary Smith. Having heard people criticize Mary Smith's freckles, however, she wants to have a complexion like Mary Brown. Mary Brown has a beautiful complexion, and, as Mother says, "You could have one, too, if you didn't eat so much candy." She would choose the large, flashing eyes of her favorite actress as the model for her eyes and the tall, slender figure of her Sunday school teacher as the model for her figure.

EVALUATION On the *positive* side, having an ideal self-concept gives hope to children who are dissatisfied with themselves. It shows them that they can improve and be better satisfied with themselves. It also acts as a guideline, showing them what they should do to achieve the result they want. Having a model to imitate, children know what they must change in their looks or behavior to make themselves more like what they want to be.

If the model is a real person whose abilities and background are similar to their own, it can motivate children in a realistic way. Unfortunately, such a model often lacks glamor and loses its appeal at an early age.

On the *negative* side, ideal self-concepts can be detrimental to good personal and social adjustments. If the concept is too unrealistic—which is especially likely when it is a composite of different models—it will discourage children. Inevitably, they will discover that they are unable to achieve their ideal. This will, in time, weaken their motivation to try to improve themselves. At the same time, it will tend to encourage daydreaming where, with a minimum of effort, they can be whatever they would like to be. It will also encourage them to project the blame for their failure to come up to their ideals on parents or others. Regardless of how they cope with their failure to achieve their ideal selves, it will lead to poor personal and social adjustments.

If the child clings to a model which is inappropriate or which is disapproved of by the group, that, too, can lead to poor personal and social adjustments. The girl who clings to an ideal self modeled after a parent or teacher, for example, may find that peers consider her immature if they have shifted to more glamorous models, such as society leaders or actresses.

Hazards to Creativity

Creativity is so important to good personal and social adjustments that anything that prevents its development is hazardous. When environmental conditions foster the development of mental rigidity or convergent thinking, it will prevent the development of mental flexibility or divergent thinking (1, 10, 22).

Equally serious is anything that encourages spending too much time on certain forms of creativity that if engaged in occasionally, may bring favorable results but not if engaged in excessively. Occasional daydreaming, for example, may lead to good personal and social adjustments, but excessive daydreaming not only counteracts the good effects of daydreaming but it also proves to be harmful to these adjustments.

There are a number of hazards to good adjustments in the different areas of creativity. A survey of these hazards will highlight potential hazards in this area of the child's development and explain why and under what conditions they are hazardous.

Failure to Stimulate Creativity

Even though the foundations for creativity are innate, like all innate potentials, its development must be stimulated. Any condition that obstructs this stimulation will prevent its development.

Evidence, as was pointed out earlier, indicates that creativity appears early and is first shown in the way a baby plays with toys. At this time, any condition that obstructs its development may stifle it. One of the most common obstacles is lack of stimulation.

Lack of stimulation may come from ignorance of its importance on the part of parents and other people in the baby's environment, or it may come from the assumption that, because creativity is in an inborn characteristic, nature will provide for its development and stimulation is, therefore, unnecessary.

When children are old enough to go to school —whether nursery school, kindergarten, or first grade —they will be given stimulation but, by then, it may be too late. By that time, they may have become so accustomed to following a pattern set by others or to thinking in the way others think that acting or thinking in a creative way will be difficult or impossible. No amount of stimulation, then, will be adequate to break completely the habits already formed.

Inability to Detect Creativity in Time

Until young children have knowledge and skills on which to build creative thinking and activities, there will be no sure way for people in their environments to know what their potentials for creativity are. And, until there are tests to detect potential creativity, they will have no way to spot these potentials.

Under such conditions, it is not surprising that stimulation to the development of creativity is neglected. By the time there is some evidence that the child has the potentials for creativity, it may be too late for stimulation to result in the full development of these potentials.

Until tests or other methods can be devised to spot creativity at an early age, the only way to overcome this hazard is to go on the assumption that *every* child has the potentials for creativity, though in varying degrees, and to provide the necessary stimulation at an early age. If this is done, many potentially creative children will be given an opportunity to develop their creativity (26, 64, 65).

Unfavorable Social Attitudes toward Creativity

Social factors often militate against the development of creativity. These obstructive factors take two common forms: *first,* unfavorable attitudes toward children who are creative (see Figure 12–5.) and, *sec-*

Figure 12–5. Unfavorable social attitudes, especially when expressed by peers, tend to dampen young children's attempts to be creative. (*Adapted from Hank Ketcham: "Dennis the Menace."* Field Newspaper Syndicate, *October 14, 1976. Used by permission.*)

ond, lack of social rewards for creativity. In discussing unfavorable social attitudes, Torrance has said (87):

> In spite of the fact that these children have many excellent ideas, they readily achieve a reputation for having silly, wild, or naughty ideas. It is difficult to determine what effect this derogation of their ideas has on their personality development, as well as upon the future development of their creative talents. . . . Although their humor and playfulness may win some friends for them, it does not always make them "easier to live with." In fact, it may make their behavior even more unpredictable than otherwise and this probably makes their presence in a group upsetting.

Children soon discover that creativity is less of an asset than a high IQ in meeting the demands of the school. They also discover that the school encourages and rewards convergent or conventional thinking more than potentially creative divergent thinking.

Thus, the chances are that the "promise of youth" (which Terman and Oden reported as fulfilled by a high-IQ group) would not similarly be fulfilled by a highly creative group (85).

Not only do obstructive social attitudes and the lack of rewards discourage creativity but even worse, they often foster maladjustive behavior by developing in the child an unfavorable self-concept. While some creative children may withdraw from a social group that has a poor opinion of them, others are likely to retaliate by being troublesome and vindictive.

Unfavorable Home Conditions

Within the home there are many conditions that affect the development of creativity. Because the home is the child's first environment, any condition that stifles the development of creativity when it is maturationally ready to develop can be most damaging. Furthermore, conditions that stifle the development of creativity when the child is young are likely to persist and stifle the development of creativity as the child grows older.

Of the many possible home conditions that are unfavorable to the development of creativity, the most common are given in Box 12–10. The times when these unfavorable conditions present the greatest hazard are during the "critical ages" of creativity development, as given in Box 12–2.

Unfavorable School Conditions

School conditions also affect the development of creativity. If unfavorable, they can counteract much of the stimulation of creativity provided by a favorable home environment. That is one of the reasons why the age of school entry is a "critical period" in the development of creativity. (Refer to Box 12–2.)

Among the many school conditions that discourage the development of creativity are very large classes where regimentation is essential; strong emphasis on memorizing; discouragement of anything that does not fall within the prescribed pattern, whether it be original painting or original storytelling; a highly organized schedule of class activities; strict, authoritarian discipline; and the belief of teachers that creative children are hard to manage and their work harder to grade than that of the conformers. If teachers regard academic achievement as the only path to success in life, the obstacles to creative expression may be overwhelming (59, 65, 67).

Excessive Daydreaming

Daydreaming is one of the most potentially dangerous forms of creativity because it can so readily become an habitual method of escaping from unpleasant realities.

BOX 12–10

SOME HOME CONDITIONS
UNFAVORABLE TO CREATIVITY

DISCOURAGEMENT OF EXPLORATION
When parents discourage children from exploring or from asking questions, they are also discouraging the development of creativity.

REGIMENTATION OF TIME
If children are so regimented that they have little free time to do as they please, they will be deprived of one of the essentials in developing creativity.

ENCOURAGEMENT OF FAMILY TOGETHERNESS
Expecting all family members to do things together, regardless of personal interests and preferences, interferes with the development of creativity.

DISCOURAGEMENT OF FANTASY
Parents who believe that all fantasy is a waste of time and a source of unrealistic ideas do all they can to make their children realists.

PROVISION OF HIGHLY STRUCTURED PLAY EQUIPMENT
Children who are provided with highly structured play equipment, such as fully dressed dolls or coloring books with figures to be colored, are deprived of play opportunities that will encourage the development of creativity.

CONSERVATIVE PARENTS
Parents who are conservative to the point where they are afraid to deviate from the approved social pattern often insist that their children follow in their footsteps.

OVERPROTECTIVE PARENTS
When parents overprotect their children, they deprive them of opportunities to explore new or different ways of doing things.

AUTHORITARIAN DISCIPLINE
Authoritarian discipline makes any deviation from parent-approved behavior difficult or impossible.

The habitual use of daydreaming to escape unpleasant reality and to bolster the ego is extremely damaging to personal and social adjustments. But this does not justify saying that *all* daydreaming is dangerous. In fact, it can be said that too little daydreaming is almost as hazardous to good adjustments as too much.

If children—or adolescents or adults—never daydream, they are deprived of the pleasures daydreaming can bring to a life that is not entirely satisfying. Equally important, all people need some morale booster when they are discouraged and when their attempts to achieve success have failed or gone unnoticed. Seeing themselves as conquering heroes can motivate them to continue trying until they finally reach their goals. Without such a morale builder, they might let their anxieties and frustrations get so strong a hold on them that they would dominate their lives.

As a rule of thumb, there are two criteria that can be used to determine if children are daydreaming excessively. The *first* is by observing children's behavior and attitudes. If, when by themselves, they usually spend their time in a solitary play activity, such as doing something constructive, this is not indicative of an unhealthy attachment to daydreaming. On the other hand, if children normally spend hours at a stretch in isolation, doing nothing but looking into space, and if they show a strong preference for this kind of occupation, there can be no doubt that daydreaming has reached an unhealthy stage.

In addition to the amount of time involved, there is a *second* criterion of how healthy or unhealthy daydreaming is—the kind of daydream that predominates. Even though all children, at some time or other, engage in every kind of daydream, those who are extraordinarily attached to the suffering-hero or the imaginary-invalid categories will be most damaged psychologically. Children will be better adjusted, both socially and personally, if their daydreaming helps them gain self-confidence and self-assurance than if it fosters the belief that they are inferior and inadequate, as happens when their daydreams are predominantly of the suffering-hero or imaginary-invalid categories.

Chapter Highlights

1   In spite of scientific recognition of the importance of creativity, it has been subjected to little research partly because of the methodological difficulties involved, partly because it was believed to be characteristic of too few individuals to justify taking time from research related to more universal characteristics to study it, and partly because it was believed to be hereditary and, therefore, little could be done to control it.

2   Popular concepts of creativity put major emphasis on the products of creative people and on the originality of these products in the social group as a whole. The scientific concept emphasizes that creativity is a process or a way of thinking that leads to something new and different for the person involved.

3   Although creativity is not synonymous with a high level of intelligence, there is evidence that there is a positive correlation between the two. There is also evidence that there is a personality syndrome characteristic of creative people.

4   Because of the methodological problems involved in studying creativity, it is difficult to discover creativity until there are overt indications in the form of behavior or achievements.

5   While creativity develops according to a predictable pattern, there are critical periods when its development can be altered or stifled by unfavorable environmental influences.

6   If creativity is to develop normally, the prevailing unfavorable attitudes toward creative people must be overcome and conditions favorable to the development of creativity must prevail early in life when its most rapid development occurs.

7   In spite of the relatively few longitudinal studies of creative people, there is some evidence that it is a persistent characteristic.

8   There are many ways in which creativity is expressed during the childhood years, the most common of which are animism, dramatic and constructive play, imaginary companions, daydreaming, white lies, production of humor, storytelling, aspirations for achievement, and ideal self-concepts.

9   Animism and dramatic play can be aids to good personal and social adjustments, provided they do not persist beyond the time when they are normally engaged in by children and provided they do not become the preferred forms of play to the point where they occupy too much of the child's playtime.

10   White lies, which are used for self-aggran-

dizement rather than for the intent of deceiving others, as is true of lies, are the result of uneven development of imagination and reasoning. By the time children enter school, reasoning combined with peer pressures normally puts an end to white lies.

11 The ability to produce humor and to tell stories aids children's personal and social adjustments, provided they are not used excessively or in greatly exaggerated forms.

12 Aspirations for achievement, the products of personal and social factors, contribute to good personal and social adjustments, as long as they are not unrealistic for the child's abilities.

13 Ideal self-concepts, based first on people children admire and later on composites of different traits they

admire in different people, become hazards to good personal and social adjustments if they are so unrealistic that they result in feelings of failure and inadequacy on the child's part.

14 The most common hazards to creativity include failure to detect creativity in time to stimulate it when it is developing, unfavorable social attitudes toward creativity, conditions in the home and school that are unfavorable to the development of creativity, and excessive daydreaming.

15 Because of the hazards to good personal and social adjustment that come from excessive daydreaming, two criteria can be used to determine if it is excessive; first, the child's preference for this kind of play activity and second, the type of daydream that predominates.

Bibliography

1 Adcock, C. J., and W. A. Martin. Flexibility and creativity. *Journal of General Psychology*, 1971, *85*, 71–76.

2 Agnew, U. Originality: The art of being oneself. *Humanitas*, 1976, *12*, 49–58.

3 Albert, R. S., and R. C. Elliott. Creative ability and the handling of personal and social conflict among bright sixth graders. *Social Behavior and Personality*, 1973, *1*, 169–181.

4 Aldous, J. Family background factors and originality in children. *Gifted Child Quarterly*, 1973, *17*, 183–192.

5 Amato, A., R. Emans, and E. Ziegler. The effectiveness of creative dramatics and story telling in a library setting. *Journal of Educational Research*, 1973, *67*, 162–181.

6 Anastasi, A. *Psychological testing*, 4th ed. New York: Macmillan, 1976.

7 Arasteh, J. D. Creativity and related processes in the young child: A review of the literature. *Journal of Genetic Psychology*, 1968, *112*, 77–108.

8 Bach, S. Notes on some imaginary companions. *Psychoanalytic Study of the Child*, 1971, *26*, 159–171.

9 Baker, C. D. Children's art: An interdisciplinary approach. *Journal of Home Economics*, 1975, *67*, 11–14.

10 Bennett, S. N. Divergent thinking abilities—a validation study. *British*

Journal of Educational Psychology, 1973, *43*, 1–7.

11 Benson, R. M., and D. B. Pryon, "When friends fall out": Developmental interference with the function of some imaginary companions. *Journal of the American Psychoanalytic Association*, 1973, *21*, 457–473.

12 Bergonsky, M. D. A further note on the animism controversy. *Journal of Genetic Psychology*, 1975, *126*, 307–308.

13 Bhavnani, R., and C. Hurr. Divergent thinking in boys and girls. *Journal of Child Psychology and Psychiatry*, 1972, *13*, 121–127.

14 Bishop, D. W., and C. A. Chace. Parental conceptual systems, home play environment, and potential creativity in children. *Journal of Experimental Child Psychology*, 1971, *12*, 318–338.

15 Blazer, J. A. Fantasy and daydreams. *Child and Family*, 1966, *5* (3), 22–28.

16 Bloomberg, M. (ed.) *Creativity*. New York: College and University Press, 1973.

17 Boshier, R., and E. Thom. Do conservative parents nurture conservative children? *School Behavior and Personality*, 1973, *1*, 108–110.

18 Brown, J. L. Precursors of intelligence and creativity: A longitudinal study of one child's development. *Merrill-Palmer Quarterly, 1970, 16*, 117–137.

19 Bruner, J. S. Play is serious business. *Psychology Today*, 1975, *8* (8), 81–83.

20 Busse, T. V. Child-rearing antecedants of flexible thinking. *Developmental Psychology*, 1969, *1*, 584–591.

21 Carroll, J. L., and L. R. Laming. Giftedness and creativity: Recent attempts at definition: A literature review. *Gifted Child Quarterly*, 1974, *13*, 85–96.

22 Cohen, S., and S. Oden. An examination of creativity and locus of control in children. *Journal of Genetic Psychology*, 1974, *124*, 179–185.

23 Cottle, T. J. A simple change in creativity. *Journal of Creative Behavior*, 1973, *7*, 161–164.

24 Cowan, J. C. How parents can foster creativity in their children. In W. B. Michael (ed.), *Teaching for creative behavior*. Bloomington, Ind.: Indiana University Press, 1968. Pp. 330–341.

25 Cramer, P., and K. A. Hogan. Sex differences in verbal and play fantasy. *Developmental Psychology*, 1975, *11*, 145–154.

26 Dellas, M., and E. L. Gaier. Identification of creativity: The individual. *Psychological Bulletin*, 1970, *73*, 55–73.

27 Dennis, W. Creative productivity between the ages of 20 and 80 years. In B. L. Neugarten (ed.), *Middle age and aging: A reader in social psychology*. Chicago: University of Chicago Press, 1968. Pp. 106–114.

28 Dewing, K. Family influences on cre-

ativity: A review and discussion. *Journal of Special Education,* 1970, *4,* 399–404.

29 Drevdahl, J. E. Factors of importance for creativity. *Journal of Clinical Psychology,* 1956, *12,* 21–26.

30 Engle, G. D. Giftedness and writing: Creativity in the classroom. *Gifted Child Quarterly,* 1970, *14,* 220–229.

31 Erikson, E. H. Identity and the life cycle. Selected papers. *Psychological Issues Monographs,* vol. 1, New York: International Universities Press, 1967.

32 Foster, J. Creativity. *Educational Research,* 1973, *15,* 217–220.

33 Freeman, N. H., and R. Janikoun. Intellectual realism in children's drawings of a familiar object with distinctive feature. *Child Development,* 1972, *43,* 1116–1121.

34 Freud, S. *The standard edition of the complete psychological works of Sigmund Freud.* London: Hogarth Press, 1953–1962. 21 Vols.

35 Garfield, S. J., H. A. Cohen, R. M. Roth, and H. L. Berenbaum. Effects of group counseling on creativity. *Journal of Educational Research,* 1971, *64,* 235–237.

36 Goldner, B. B. *The strategy of creative thinking.* Englewood Cliffs, N.J.: Prentice-Hall, 1962.

37 Goodnow, J. J., and S. Friedman. Orientation in children's human figure drawings: An aspect of graphic language. *Developmental Psychology,* 1972, *7,* 10–16.

38 Guilford, J. P. *Intelligence, creativity and their educational implications.* San Diego, Calif.: R. R. Knapp, 1968.

39 Haynes, E. D. *Imaginary companions and personality.* Unpublished Master of Home Economics thesis, Colorado State University, Fort Collins, Colorado, 1970.

40 Helson, R. Childhood interest clusters related to creativity in women. *Journal of Consulting Psychology,* 1965, *29,* 352–361.

41 Isaacs, A. F. Being gifted is a bed of roses, with the thorns included. *Gifted Child Quarterly,* 1970, *15,* 54–56.

42 Jersild, A. T., C. W. Telford, and J. M. Sawrey, *Child psychology,* 7th ed. Englewood Cliffs, N.J.: Prentice-Hall, 1975.

43 Johnson, R. A. Differential effects of reward versus no-reward instructions on the creative thinking of two

economic levels of elementary school children. *Journal of Educational Psychology,* 1974, *66,* 530–533.

44 Khatena, J. Creative imagination, imagery and analogy. *Gifted Child Quarterly,* 1975, *19,* 149–160.

45 Khatena, J., and E. C. Dickerson. Training sixth grade children to think creatively with words. *Psychological Reports,* 1973, *32,* 841–842.

46 Kogan, N., and E. Pankove. Creative ability over a five-year span. *Child Development,* 1972, *43,* 427–442.

47 Laurence, R., and B. Sutton-Smith. Novel responses to toys: A replication. *Merrill-Palmer Quarterly,* 1968, *14,* 159–160.

48 Lehman, H. C. The creative production rates of present versus past generations of scientists. In B. L. Neugarten (ed.), *Middle age and aging: A reader in social psychology.* Chicago: University of Chicago Press, 1968. Pp. 99–105.

49 Lembright, M. L., and K. Yamamoto. Subcultures and creative thinking: An exploratory comparison between Amish and urban American school children. *Merrill-Palmer Quarterly,* 1965, *11,* 49–64.

50 Looft, W. R. Animistic thought in children: Understanding of "living" across its associated attributes. *Journal of Genetic Psychology,* 1974, *124,* 235–240.

51 Lurcat, L., and I. Kostin. Study of graphical abilities in children. *Perceptual and Motor Skills,* 1970, *30,* 615–630.

52 Manosevitz, M., N. M. Prentice, and F. Wilson. Individual and family correlates of imaginary companions In preschool children. *Developmental Psychology,* 1973, *8,* 72–79.

53 Marshall, H. R. Relations between home experiences and children's use of language in play interactions with peers. *Psychological Monographs: General and Applied,* 1961, *75* (5).

54 Maynard, F. *Guiding your child to a more creative life.* Garden City, N.Y.: Doubleday, 1973.

55 McGhee, P. E. Development of children's ability to create the joking relationship. *Child Development,* 1974, *45,* 552–556.

56 McGhee, P. E., and P. Grodzitsky. Sex-role identification and humor among preschool children. *Journal of Psychology,* 1973, *84,* 189–193.

57 Milgram, R. A., and N. A. Milgram. Group versus individual administration in the measurement of creative thinking in gifted and nongifted children. *Child Development,* 1976, *47,* 563–565.

58 Milne, A. A. *Now we are six.* New York: Dutton, 1927.

59 Ogilvie, E. Creativity and curriculum structure. *Educational Research,* 1974, *16,* 126–132.

60 Piers, E. V. Adolescent creativity. In J. F. Adams (ed.), *Understanding adolescence: Current developments in adolescent psychology* 2d ed. Boston: Allyn & Bacon, 1973. Pp. 191–220.

61 Pressey, S. L. Concerning the nature and nurture of genius. *Scientific Monthly,* 1955, *81,* 123–129.

62 Pulaski, M. A. S. Play as a function of toy structure and fantasy predisposition. *Child Development,* 1970, *41,* 531–537.

63 Pulaski, M. A. S. The rich rewards of make believe. *Psychology Today,* 1974, *7* (8), 68–74.

64 Quattrocki, C. G. Recognizing creative potential in preschool children. *Gifted Child Quarterly,* 1974, *18,* 74–80.

65 Ramey, C. T., and V. Piper. Creativity in open and traditional classrooms. *Child Development,* 1974, *45,* 557–560.

66 Renzulli, J. S., and C. M. Callahan. Developing creativity training activities. *Gifted Child Quarterly,* 1975, *19,* 38–45.

67 Rosenthal, R., S. S. Baratz, and C. M. Hall. Teacher behavior, teacher expectations, and genius in pupils' rated creativity. *Journal of Genetic Psychology,* 1974, *124,* 115–121.

68 Sadler, W. A. Creative existence: Play as a pathway to personal freedom and community. *Humanitas,* 1969. *5,* 57–79.

69 Schaefer, C. E. Imaginary companions and creative adolescents. *Developmental Psychology,* 1969, *1,* 747–749.

70 Scheffler, R. Z. The child from five to six: A longitudinal study of fantasy change. *Genetic Psychology Monographs,* 1975, *92,* 19–56.

71 Siegelman, M. Parent behavior correlates of personality traits related to creativity in sons and daughters. *Journal of Consulting and Clinical Psychology,* 1973, 40, 43–47.

72 Singer, D. L., and J. Rummo. Ideational creativity and behavioral style in kindergarten-age children. *Developmental Psychology*, 1973, *8*, 154–161.

73 Singer, J. L. The importance of daydreaming. *Psychology Today*, 1968, *1* (11), 19–26.

74 Singer, J. L. *The child's world of make-believe*. New York: Academic Press, 1973.

75 Singer, J. L. *The inner world of daydreams*. New York: Harper & Row, 1975.

76 Singer, J. L. Fantasy: The foundation of serenity. *Psychology Today*, 1976, *10* (2), 32–34, 37.

77 Smart, R. C., and M. S. Smart. Group values shown in pre-adolescents' drawings in five English-speaking countries. *Journal of Social Psychology*, 1975, *97*, 23–37.

78 Smith, R. L. The special theory of creativity. *Journal of Creative Behavior*, 1973, *7*, 165–173.

79 Spock, B. *Raising children in a difficult time*. New York: Norton, 1974.

80 Staffieri, J. R.: Birth order and creativity. *Journal of Clinical Psychology*, 1970, *26*, 65–66.

81 Stone, J. L., and J. Church. *Childhood and adolescence: A psychology of the growing person*, 3d ed. New York: Random House, 1972.

82 Sutton-Smith, B. Novel responses to toys. *Merrill-Palmer Quarterly*, 1968, *14*, 151–158.

83 Taylor, B. J., and R. J. Howell. The ability of three-, four-, and five-year-old children to distinguish fantasy from reality, *Journal of Genetic Psychology*, 1973, *122*, 315–318.

84 Taylor, I. A. Developing creativity in gifted young adults. *Education*, 1974, *94*, 266–268.

85 Terman, L. M., and M. H. Oden. *Genetic studies of genius: V. The gifted group at mid-life*. Stanford, Calif.: Stanford University Press, 1959.

86 Torda, C. Some observations on the creative process. *Perceptual and Motor Skills*, 1970, *31*, 107–126.

87 Torrance, E. P. *Guiding creative talent*. Englewood Cliffs, N.J.: Prentice-Hall, 1962.

88 Torrance, E. P. Peer influences on preschool children's willingness to try difficult tasks. *Journal of Psychology*, 1969, *72*, 189–194.

89 Torrance, E. P. Creative young women in today's world. *Exceptional Children*, 1972, *38*, 597–603.

90 Treadwell, Y. Humor and creativity. *Psychological Reports*, 1970, *26*, 55–58.

91 Ungesma, A. J. Fantasy, creativity, conformity. *Humanitas*, 1976, *12*, 49–58.

92 Varley, W. B., J. R. Levin, R. A. Severson, and P. Wolff. Training imagery production in young children through motor involvement. *Journal of Educational Psychology*, 1974, *66*, 262–266.

93 Wallach, M. A. Creativity. In P. H. Mussen (ed.), *Carmichael's manual of child psychology*, 3d ed. New York: Wiley, 1970. Vol. 1, pp. 1211–1272.

94 Ward, W. C., N. Kogan, and E. Pankove. Incentive effects in children's creativity. *Child Development*, 1972, *43*, 669–676.

CHAPTER 13

DEVELOPMENT OF UNDERSTANDING

Early interest in studying how children acquire an understanding of the world in which they live was aroused by G. Stanley Hall's report of children's misconceptions. This report, based on his study of what certain common words meant to children, appeared in the first issue of *Pedagogical Seminary* (later called *The Journal of Genetic Psychology*) in 1891 under the title, "Contents of Children's Minds on Entering School" (36).

In this study, using the questionnaire method which was in common use at that time, Hall and his coworkers reported that young children, when asked what certain common words meant to them, more often had incorrect than correct meanings associated with these words. One of the classic illustrations of their misconceptions was the reply that some city children made to the question, "What is a butterfly?": It was a fly made of butter.

Following Hall's study came many studies of concept development in childhood, covering almost every common area of child life. These studies were designed to find out how and when different categories of concepts develop and what is responsible for their accuracy or inaccuracy.

A second important stimulant to the study of how understanding develops came from Piaget's theory of cognitive development with its predictable ages and predictable changes in cognitive ability.

This theory has had a tremendous impact on interest in studying the development of understanding by psychologists, an interest that was aroused at the turn of the present century by Hall's earlier study of misconceptions. It has led to many studies to substantiate or refute the stages through which the child's cognitive development passes and the predictable ages at which these stages occur (75). The material derived from these studies has added valuable information to our knowledge of how understanding in general develops during the childhood years as well as in different areas of development.

Importance of Understanding

"Understanding" is the ability to achieve a grasp of the nature, significance, or explanation of something and to have a clear or complete idea of it. In short, it means the ability to comprehend. Understanding is achieved by applying previously acquired knowledge to new experiences and situations.

The kind of adjustment children make to life is greatly influenced by their understanding of their environments, of people, and of themselves. The child who understands the danger of automobiles, high places, and animals, for example, will be cautious; the child who lacks this understanding will not take proper precautions in a potentially dangerous situation and may be handicapped for life by some resulting physical disability.

When children do not understand their limitations, whether they are physical or mental, they will not understand why people treat them as they do, and they may misinterpret their actions. Children who do not recognize their physical limitations may feel that their lack of acceptance in a play group is due to discrimination whereas it is actually due to their lack of play skills. If these children do not come to understand the reason for their rejection, they will have little motivation to cultivate qualities that might increase their chances of acceptance.

Attitudes toward other people, toward things, and toward what is important in life are likewise dependent upon understanding. The child who does not understand that much of what is shown in movies or on television is merely make-believe is likely to develop unrealistic or false attitudes toward life.

One of the greatest values of understanding is that it enables children to adapt to changes, both personal and environmental. Changes in body form at puberty, with their accompanying changes in behavior and interests, provide a good illustration. The child who understands that these changes occur in a predictable pattern and who knows *why* they are taking place will react with less fear, anxiety, or resentment than the child who does not understand.

How Understanding Develops

Understanding comes from the maturation of the intellectual capacities of the child and from knowledge acquired by learning over a long period of time. When babies are born, they have no understanding of their environment. As William James pointed out, many years ago, they experience the world as a "big, blooming, buzzing confusion" (42). They do not know, for example, the source of the discomfort that motivates them to cry. All they know is that they are uncomfortable and that crying will bring help. As a result of maturation and learning, children gradually begin to understand what they see, hear, smell, taste, and feel. The environment then begins to be meaningful to them, and they begin to understand why they feel as they do.

Pattern of Development of Understanding

The ability to understand develops in a predictable way. According to Piaget, cognitive ability, which makes understanding possible, develops in two major periods involving four stages—the sensorimotor stage, the preoperational stage, the stage of concrete operations, and the stage of formal operations. These stages are not separate and distinct but rather are subdivisions of a continuous pattern of cognitive development.

The first major period of cognitive development is known as the "Period of Sensorimotor Intelligence," covering the first stage of the cognitive developmental continuum, and the second is known as the "Period of Conceptual Intelligence," including the other three stages. The first period is largely dominated by sensorimotor processes and the second by more abstract processes of reasoning and problem solving, in which the child is capable of using language and symbols.

During the *sensorimotor stage* of cognitive development, children begin to develop an understanding of themselves as separate and distinct from the environment, causality, time, and space. This understanding comes from sensorimotor exploration. The sensorimotor stage extends from birth to the time when children are 2 years of age.

The *preoperational stage* of cognitive development, which extends from 2 to 6 years of age, is the time when children are capable of using language and symbolic thinking. This is apparent in their imaginative play. It is a time of egocentric thinking in which children are unable to take the views of others and are unable to solve problems involving number concepts or classes of objects.

The third stage in cognitive development—the *stage of concrete operations*—extends from the time children are 6 years of age until they are 11 or 12 years old. At this time, the vague and nebulous concepts of the preschool years become concrete and specific. This enables children to begin to think deductively, to form concepts of space and time, and to categorize objects. They are able to take the role of others and this leads to a greater understanding of reality.

In the fourth and final stage of cognitive development—the *stage of formal operations*—which begins around the age of 11 or 12 years and extends onward, children are capable of considering all possible ways of solving problems and are able to reason on the basis of hypotheses and propositions. As a result, they can look at problems from different points of view and can take many factors into consideration when solving problems. Children's thinking then becomes more flexible and concrete, and they are able to combine information from a number of different sources (74, 75).

Role of Maturation in the Development of Understanding

Maturation provides a state of readiness to understand. Before understanding can progress, the child's brain and nervous system must develop, and the sense organs—used for perceiving—must become functionally mature. Understanding parallels mental growth. When mental growth is rapid, as in a very bright child, understanding is above the norm for the child's age level; in a dull child, understanding lags behind the norm. Similarly, a hierarchy of information-processing abilities, essential to understanding complex situations and behavior patterns, parallels the development of reasoning ability.

Studies of intellectual growth, based on the results of standardized tests of general intelligence, have revealed that there is an increase in general intelligence during the early years of life. The rate of increase slows down as children approach the adolescent years and then comes to a standstill or a near standstill in the latter part of adolescence or in the early adult years (2, 57, 88).

In spite of this predictable pattern, there are marked variations in the ages at which people reach their top level of intellectual functioning. The higher the level of innate intellectual ability, the longer general intelligence will continue to grow. Throughout the growth years, there are also variations in the rate of growth of general intelligence. Among some children, the growth rate fluctuates greatly and, among others, it is relatively stable. Variations tend to become less marked as children approach adolescence (2, 43). Variations in the pattern of growth of general intelligence are shown in Figure 13–1.

Not only is there a predictable pattern of growth in general intelligence but there are predictable patterns of development of specific intellectual capacities.

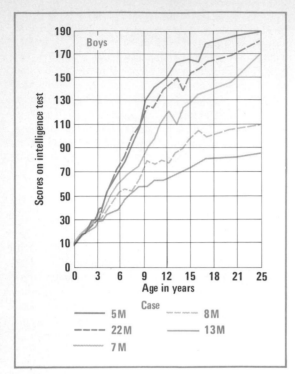

Figure 13–1. Individual growth curves of intelligence as measured by tests given to five males at intervals up to 25 years of age. (*Adapted from N. Bayley: Research in child development: A longitudinal perspective. Merrill-Palmer Quarterly, 1965, 11, 183–208. Used by permission.*)

Even though similar in their major aspects, these patterns are distinct and reach their mature levels at different ages. As Bayley has explained (2):

> Intelligence is a dynamic succession of developing functions, with the more advanced and complex functions in the hierarchy depending on the prior maturing of the earlier, simpler ones. . . . Intelligence is a complex of separately timed, developing functions.

In the pattern of intellectual development, for example, memory precedes reasoning and concrete reasoning precedes abstract reasoning. Memory for concrete material develops earlier and reaches its peak earlier than reasoning. These variations are important because of the effect they have on the child's ability to understand and the accuracy of understanding (2, 43, 93).

Role of Learning in the Development of Understanding

Learning is just as essential to understanding as maturation. Children must learn how to perceive differences in the things they see, hear, smell, taste, and feel. Understanding begins when children develop the ability to discriminate. At 2 weeks of age or earlier, for example, babies give momentary heed to a dangling ring, indicating that they notice something different in the environment. Later, their behavior indicates that they can discriminate differences in people. They will smile at the sight of people who are familiar and will cry when they are unfamiliar (34).

Understanding increases as the child's ability to perceive relationships between new and old situations increases. Handling objects, for example, increases the ability to perceive relationships because it causes the child's attention to be fixed, and this provides an opportunity to discover meanings (95). The more readily a child can associate new meanings with old experiences, the more meaningful the old experiences become and the more integrated they are in a system of interrelated ideas. The important role learning plays in understanding will be explained further in connection with the development of concepts.

Role of Concepts in Understanding

Understanding is based on concepts. *Concepts* are not direct sensory data; instead, they result from the elaboration and combination—the tying together, or linking—of discrete sensory experiences. The common elements in diverse objects or situations serve to unite objects or situations into a single concept.

Concepts are *symbolic* in that they depend upon the properties of both absent and present situations and objects. Frequently concepts have an *affective* quality—an "emotional weighting"—which becomes a part of the concept and which determines how the individual feels about the person, object, or situation of which the concept is a symbol. This emotional weighting determines, to a large extent, the kind of *response* the person will make. Concepts are thus *complex* relationships which are continuously changing with experience and with the accumulation of new knowledge. Their complexity may be illustrated by a simple drawing that shows their composite nature (see Figure 13–2).

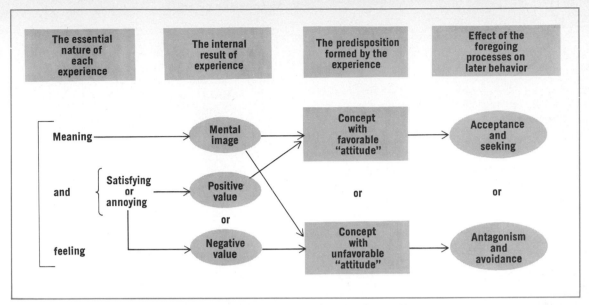

Figure 13–2. The composite nature of a concept. (*Adapted from A. D. Woodruff: Basic concepts of teaching. Chandler, 1961. Used by permission.*)

Concepts may relate to *objects;* to *people;* to *qualities,* such as "good" and "dishonest"; or to *relationships,* such as "above" and "when." They may be *definite* ("one-half teaspoon of salt") or *indefinite* (a "generous helping of salt"). Concepts are not always verbalized. A child may, for example, have a clear and accurate concept of what "generosity" means but not know the word that describes this quality.

Box 13-1 summarizes some of the outstanding characteristics of children's concepts. It tells briefly how children view their world and perceive their relationship to it.

Importance of Concepts

Concepts are important because they determine what one knows and believes and, to a large extent, what one does. If the concept includes a favorable attitude—or if it is emotionally weighted with a pleasant emotion—it will lead to positive actions in the form of acceptance and seeking. Concepts that are weighted with unpleasant emotions, on the other hand, lead to negative actions in the form of antagonism and avoidance. A child who has a favorable concept of "school," for example, will do better academic work and will have more favorable attitudes toward the teacher,

lessons, and everything connected with school than the child whose concept of "school" is unfavorable. The former will make better personal, social, and academic adjustments.

Equally important, the accuracy or inaccuracy of a child's concepts affects understanding. The more concepts a child has, the better developed they are, and the more accurate they are, the greater the understanding. Simple reading material, for example, employing meaningful words and illustrated with relevant pictures, can be better understood by a young child than material containing many different words on a page, many different ideas, involved sentences, and abstract or unfamiliar words. Even the mechanical devices of capitalization and punctuation may give the child a hint of the relationship a strange word has to the words surrounding it.

How Concepts Develop

For the most part, early concepts relate to common experiences in daily life. Most of these early concepts are partially or totally inaccurate. By the time children reach adolescence, they have built up a large store of concepts. In addition, they have added new meanings

CHARACTERISTICS OF CHILDREN'S CONCEPTS

CONCEPTS ARE INDIVIDUALIZED
Since no two children have precisely the same intellectual abilities or the same learning experiences, no two will have identical concepts. Similar training and similar values, however, will leda to similar concepts.

CONCEPT DEVELOPMENT FOLLOWS A PATTERN
As new meanings are associated with old, concepts change from simple to complex and from concrete to abstract. The time needed for these developmental changes depends on the children's intelligence and learning opportunities.

CONCEPTS ARE HIERARCHICAL
As concepts become more complex, the child attaches names to objects and to classes of objects, indicating a realization that they have elements in common as well as differences. The hierarchical structure of concepts is illustrated in Figure 13–3 (see page 359).

CONCEPTS DEVELOP FROM UNDEFINED TO SPECIFIC
The child first responds to the total situation rather than to any one part of it. Gradually, vague and undefined concepts develop into specific and differentiated concepts.

CONCEPTS DEVELOP FROM SPECIFIC TO GENERAL
With experience, the child is able to distinguish partial elements of objects and to group together those which have common features. Figure 13–4 (see page 360) shows how this is done.

CONCEPTS ARE EMOTIONALLY WEIGHTED
All concepts have some emotional weighting—the "affective aspect" of the concept. This weighting is added as new and old meanings are combined. In general, concepts that are subjective—concerned with self or with objects, people, and situations related to self—are more heavily weighted with feelings than are concepts that are more objective.

CONCEPTS ARE FREQUENTLY RESISTANT TO CHANGE
The more emotionally weighted a concept is, the more resistant to change it is. The reason is that emotionally weighted concepts are satisfying to children and, as a result, children cling to them until they develop others that give them equal or greater satisfaction.

CONCEPTS INFLUENCE BEHAVIOR
All concepts influence personal and social adjustments by influencing the quality of behavior. Favorable concepts lead to positive behavior; unfavorable concepts, to negative behavior.

---

to old concepts and corrected many inaccuracies in previously learned concepts.

Some concepts help the child to develop other concepts. For example, a child learns to perceive an older person's slipping and falling on a banana peel as funny because this act violates an already learned social concept about the dignity and respect accompanying adulthood. Similarly, the child who develops concepts of appropriate behavior and appearance for members of the two sexes can apply knowledge to the development of concepts of masculine or feminine beauty; the child thus learns to think of beauty not as an abstract concept but in relation to the concept of what is sex appropriate.

Concept development is a long and difficult process because of the limited knowledge and experience children have. They cannot perceive an object or situation in the same way that an adult can, even though their sense organs are equally mature. If concepts are to be accurate and if children are to develop concepts adequate to meet their needs for understanding the world in which they live, three essentials must be fulfilled (29). These are listed and explained in Box 13–2.

Sources of Meaning

As children acquire new meanings from new sources, they add them to old meanings previously learned. The ability to acquire meanings from new sources depends on maturational readiness. Since maturation is pre-

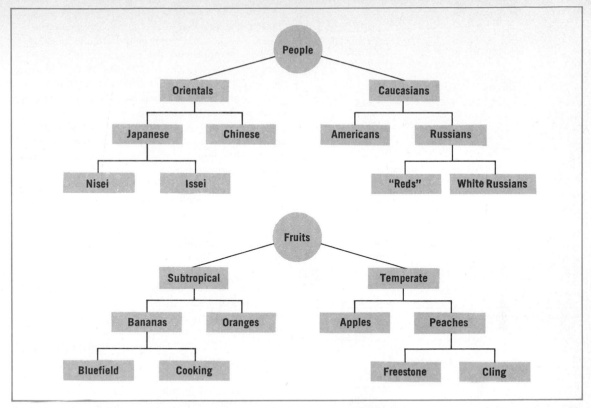

Figure 13–3. The hierarchical structure of concepts. (*Adapted from W. E. Vinacke: Stereotypes as social concepts.* Journal of Social Psychology, *1957, 46, 229–243. Used by permission.*)

dictable, even though there are individual differences, it is possible to know at approximately what age a new source of meaning will come into use. This pattern is explained below.

SENSORY EXPLORATION As Eckerman and Rheingold have explained, "It is through exploration that the infant learns about the world of people as well as of things" (22). Shortly after birth, babies begin to look and listen. Later, they smell, taste, and touch everything within their grasp. By so doing, they perceive meanings which fuse with meanings previously observed. This causes strange and unfamiliar objects to become familiar.

MOTOR MANIPULATION When motor coordination is sufficiently developed that the baby can handle things at will, beginning in the second half of the first year, motor manipulation supplements the information gained through sensory exploration. The baby discovers qualities such as smoothness, softness, and warmth. Too often, the "hands-off" policy, which many adults enforce, deprives the young child of one of the most valuable sources of information (35, 80).

QUESTIONING As soon as children are old enough to put words together, they begin to ask questions about the things that have aroused their curiosity. The "questioning age" begins around the third year and reaches its peak around the sixth year. However, children continue to use this method of gaining information throughout the rest of their lives. Its usefulness will depend upon the satisfaction children derive from it during the early years of childhood, before they are capable of using more difficult methods of getting the information they are seeking (24).

THE CONCEPTUAL LEARNING	THE SYMBOLIC LEARNING

"That's rain, Billy"

A specific concept of RAIN

"It's snowing, son"

+ A specific concept of SNOW

"Now the sun is shining, Buster"

+ A specific concept of SUNSHINE and HEAT

"It's cold and icy, now"

+ A specific concept of ICE and COLD

"All this is weather, my boy"

= A general concept of WEATHER

PICTORIAL MASS MEDIA What is seen in pictorial mass media, especially comics, movies, and television, forms the basis for many of the child's concepts. If teachers or policemen are constantly depicted in a particular way, the child will come to think that *all* teachers or *all* policemen have the characteristics observed in the pictures. This is one of the common ways in which stereotypes develop.

Most pictorial mass media contain elements of unreality, even though they may be skewed toward reality. Therefore, the child is likely to develop concepts that are unrealistic.

Educational films and educational television serve to develop more realistic concepts. A child whose concept of "elephant" is based only on a distant view of an elephant in a zoo enclosure, for example, will derive a more accurate concept from a film about the elephant in its natural habitat.

READING Before children learn to read, they build up a store of meanings by looking at pictures, being read to, or having stories told to them. Even the simplest story books introduce new meanings into children's lives. Careful observation of pictures enables children to gain information about people, objects, and situations they formerly had not understood. When reading is supplemented by discussions with adults or by educational films at school, children's understanding is greatly increased.

It is important to realize that acquiring new methods of gaining knowledge does *not* necessarily entail abandoning previously used methods. Instead, it means *adding* a new method to the old methods. Even when adults rely heavily on reading for acquisition of knowledge, they continue to use motor manipulation, sensory exploration, and questioning to supplement the knowledge they acquire through reading.

Factors Influencing Concept Development

Because children are subjected to different experiences inside and outside the home, it is to be expected that children of the same age and level of development will have different concepts. There are many factors

Figure 13–4. How specific concepts accumulate and make general concepts. (*Adapted from A. D. Woodruff: Basic concepts of teaching. Chandler, 1961. Used by permission.*)

responsible for concept development, the most important of which are explained briefly in Box 13–3.

Some Common Concepts of Children

In spite of the fact that concepts are a reflection of children's personal and unique development, some are so common among children in a given culture that they may be regarded as "typical." These include concepts of life and death, of causality, of space and weight, of numbers and time, of money, of beauty, of the comic, of the self, and of social relationships.

What these common concepts among American children today are, how they develop, and what effects they have on the child's personal and social adjustments will be described below. When concepts in a given category differ markedly from those held by other children, an attempt will be made to explain why this is so. Why, for example, do some children regard something as "pretty" or beautiful while other children, living in the same neighborhood, regard it as "ugly"? Or, why do some children develop favorable self- or social concepts while others develop unfavorable concepts?

Concepts of Life

Because of their limited experience and knowledge, most young children fail to distinguish between living and inanimate objects. Instead, they believe that all objects have the same life qualities as human beings and, therefore, are animate. The tendency to ascribe living qualities to inert objects—"animism"—was explained in detail in the chapter on creativity.

A number of studies have tried to discover when animism begins and how long it persists. In one of the most comprehensive and best-known studies, Piaget concluded that there are four successive stages in the animistic concepts of young children (73). These four stages and the ages Piaget has given for them are shown in Box 13–4.

Other studies have concluded that there are no clearly demarcated animistic stages through which children pass, but rather a gradual transition from one phase to another. Furthermore, children of the same age differ markedly. These studies also show that children distinguish between "living" and "having life." Living is more often applied to inanimate objects than

having life. When children say an object is "alive," they usually do not attribute sensory or functional characteristics to it. Thus their definition of alive differs from that of adults. To children, alive means "active." This is not animism in the true sense of the word (9, 59).

After children enter kindergarten or become members of a peer play group, they discover that fewer and fewer of their age-mates attribute life to inanimate objects. This influences their own thinking. By the time they are ready to enter school, most children have adequate criteria to enable them to distinguish between animate and inanimate and to realize that movement is not the sole criterion of life. They then use such criteria as thinking, feeling, and voluntary activities —qualities that are impossible for all but humans and animals (60, 84).

Concepts of Death

Concepts of death are slower in developing than are concepts of life. This is partly because young children have few contacts with death and partly because understanding the finality of death is more difficult for them than the activity associated with living.

About the time when children are able to understand the difference between inanimate and animate, they begin to be interested in death. Their first interest is impersonal unless a member of the family, a pet, or a peer dies. They regard it as inevitable, but they do not try to understand why it occurs or what happens to the person after death. Few children, unless they have experienced a long or severe illness, think of death in relation to themselves. To most children, death is associated with old age, not with themselves.

Gradually, however, as their contacts with people outside the home increase and as mass media play an increasingly important role in their lives, children begin to become interested in death and try to understand it. Between the ages of 5 and 9 years, concepts of death are usually first developed. While these may and often do change radically as children grow older, the foundations of these concepts, laid earlier, have a lasting influence on what their concepts of death will be (1, 48, 85, 98).

FACTORS INFLUENCING CONCEPTS OF DEATH
What concepts of death a child will develop will depend upon many different conditions in the child's life, four of which are especially common and influential.

First, mass media lay the foundations for many childish concepts of death. In spite of parental desire to spare children *firsthand* contact with death—even when a family member or pet animal dies—children sooner or later have *secondhand* experiences with it through the mass media. In newspapers or on the television or movie screens, they see pictures of people dying and being buried and the grief shown by those close to the person who has died.

The more the home, school, and neighborhood surround death with mystery, the more children are forced to base their concepts of death on information from mass media. What these concepts will be will depend largely on what kinds of mass media they enjoy. Children, for example, who are encouraged to read newspapers, news magazines, or to look at the news programs on television, will often be limited in information about death to pictures of murder or accidents. If, on the other hand, they enjoy fairy tales or religious stories, their concepts of death will be of a very different kind.

Second, the child's concept of death is greatly influenced by adults' reactions to death. In their attempt to shield the child from grief or in their absorption in their own grief when a member of the family or a close friend dies, parents may overprotect or ignore the child. Such circumstances not only affect the child emotionally, but even more important, they color the concept of death the child develops. As Barclay has explained, the child who is "surrounded by gaunt-eyed adults who do not see you or hear a word that you say can magnify the idea of death's enormity almost beyond belief" (1).

Third, the religious training children receive at home, in Sunday school, or church has a marked influence on their concepts of death. If, for example, children are told that "good children" go to Heaven where they will be eternally happy and where every wish will be granted, they will have far different concepts of death than will children who are constantly threatened with what will happen to them after death if they are "bad"—the eternal punishment of Hell. Children who come from religiously oriented homes tend to have more specific concepts of death than those who come from homes where religion plays a minor role.

Fourth, all children, sooner or later, have some first-hand experiences with death. Losing a family member, a pet, or a playmate introduces children to the finality of death and sometimes to the physical distortions that death brings.

When death occurs in the immediate family, even though children have been spared firsthand experiences with the dead person or the funeral and burial, they discover that the permanent absence of the family member means a revision in the pattern of family life. If, in time, the family member is replaced by a stepparent, an adopted sibling, or a new baby, children's concepts of death will be colored by their reactions to the replacements and by the changes in the patterns of their lives that death and the replacement have brought about (98).

CONCEPTS OF LIFE AFTER DEATH Children are not very much concerned about what happens after death. Unless religious instruction emphasizes Hell as a place of eternal punishment, children learn to think of life after death as pleasant. The concept formed in early childhood is likely to persist with few modifications until adolescence.

Children who receive little or no religious instruction about life after death seldom wonder about it or build up any concept of it. Religious instruction is likely to foster such unrealistic concepts that children have to

revise them radically when they reach adolescence and become aware of how unrealistic the concepts are (68, 98).

Concepts of Causality

The ability to see cause-and-effect relationships is more closely related to children's personal and learning experiences than to either their chronological or mental ages. If, for example, children have learned a number of religious and superstitious beliefs to explain natural phenomena or accidental happenings, they will have many more faulty concepts of causality than if their learning experiences had been more realistic.

Similarly, a child who reads books and comics or who sees movies and television programs with a fairy-tale slant will come to think that *magic* causes anything whose cause is not immediately apparent. A child often learns in religious instruction that *God* is responsible for everything. See Figure 13–5.

BOX 13–4

PIAGET'S STAGES IN ANIMISTIC THINKING

STAGE 1 (4 TO 6 YEARS)

Everything that moves in any way is regarded as conscious, even though it is stationary.

STAGE 2 (6 TO 7 YEARS)
Consciousness is attributed only to things that can move. The sun and a bicycle are regarded as conscious, while a table and a stone are not.

STAGE 3 (8 TO 10 YEARS)
The child makes an essential distinction between movement that is due to the object itself and movement that is introduced by an outside agent. Bodies that can move of their own accord, such as the sun or the wind, are looked upon as conscious, while objects that receive their movement from without, such as bicycles, are regarded as devoid of consciousness.

STAGE 4 (11 YEARS ON)
Consciousness is restricted to plants and animals, or to animals alone.

"God turns the sun off at night 'cause it's too expensive to keep it runnin' when everybody's asleep."

Figure 13–5. Concepts of causality are sometimes influenced by children's religious teaching. (*Adapted from Hank Ketcham: "Dennis the Menace." Field Newspaper Syndicate, May 23, 1970. Used by permission.*)

Figure 13–6. Many young children believe that a stork brings the new baby. (*Adapted from Art Gates,* The Atlanta Journal and Constitution Magazine, *Jan. 18, 1976. Used by permission.*)

In the pattern of development of concepts of causality, concepts of physical causality are usually developed earlier than concepts of psychological causality. For example, the child can understand what makes clouds move before being able to understand what makes people angry or frightened. This difference is due not so much to differences in personal experience as to differences in guidance. The child is told about physical causality at home and in school. Psychological causality, however, remains unexplained, and children must depend upon their own observations and interpretations (6, 8, 96).

A number of studies have been made of the pattern of development of concepts of causality. The three that have received the greatest amount of attention—concepts of birth, of bodily functions, and of germs—will serve to illustrate the pattern of development of concepts in the general category of causality.

CONCEPTS OF BIRTH Many young children think that babies are brought by a stork or that they come from God, from a store, or from the doctor's satchel. See Figure 13–6. Having had no opportunity to see the birth process, even in a pet animal, children base their concepts on what parents, other adults, siblings, or playmates tell them.

By the time children go to school, they generally observe a relationship between the arrival of a baby and the changes that take place in the mother's body. They realize that the mother's abdomen is enlarged before the baby arrives and that it assumes its normal shape after the baby's birth. However, children do not include in their concept how the baby got into the mother's body, the role of the father, or how the baby got out of the mother's body. Some children believe that the baby originates from the food the mother eats, while others believe that it was put in the mother's body by magic. Most children believe that the baby emerges into the world through the "belly button" (5, 69). Children's interest in birth and how their concepts of birth affect their attitudes and behavior will be discussed in detail in Chapter 15 on children's interests.

CONCEPTS OF BODILY FUNCTIONS Most young children think of the functioning of the body in terms of specific organs. Up to the age of 7 years, for example, they believe that the *brain* is in the head, that it is round and composed of bone, blood, and skin. Only after the fifth or sixth grade does their concept of the brain include flesh and cells.

To older children, *lungs* are represented as round bags, made of bone, skin, blood, and flesh. Some children locate the lungs in the head or neck; few locate them in the chest. Figure 13–7 shows two examples of children's placement of the important organs of the body. Even at the sixth-grade level, many children fail to include the sex organs in their placement of the body organs.

In the child's concept of the *digestive process*, digestion takes place in the mouth and stomach. The stomach, which is meant for storing or eating food, is usually located in the upper part of the trunk and is believed to be composed of skin, bone, flesh, and blood.

Children have little understanding of the relationship between eating, digestion, and elimination. Young children often believe that food goes from the mouth to the stomach and then to the arms and legs. Older children are more likely to include the intestines in the route that food takes through the body, though they may be confused about the roles played by the kidneys and the intestines. Even older children have poor concepts of the cause-and-effect relationship between eating and living (26, 31, 77).

CONCEPTS OF GERMS While many young children think that illness is caused by their disobedience or naughtiness, most school-age children believe that illness is caused by germs. To a young child, a germ is like a dot or an abstract figure. Children 8 years of age and older think of germs as abstract figures or animals—a fly or worm. They believe that germs enter the body through the mouth, nose, or skin and that they make the person ill, damage the body, or live in the body. Germs can leave the body, they believe, through the mouth, nose, skin, or anus and can be ejected by coughing, sneezing, or anal evacuation. When the doctor gives medicine, that pushes the germs out of the body (13, 47).

Concepts of Space

To judge space accurately, children must learn to compare it with familiar objects whose size or distance they know. They must learn to regard the degree of clearness of outline and color and the amount of visible detail as cues, and they must learn that different sensations in the eyes, resulting from convergence or strain, help them to interpret what they observe.

The distance of an object from the child affects the

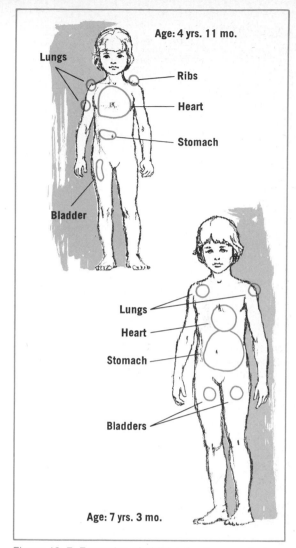

Figure 13–7. Examples of children's placement of some bodily organs at different ages. (*Adapted from E. Gellert: Children's conceptions of the content and function of the human body.* Genetic Psychology Monographs, *1962, 65, 293–405. Used by permission.*)

accuracy of judgment of its size. The child's own size also affects the judgment. The child tends to judge a close object as larger than it actually is and a distant object as smaller. By handling blocks, carts, tricycles, and other play equipment, the child soon learns to perceive short distances accurately. Longer distances,

COMMON SPACE CONCEPTS OF CHILDHOOD

GEOMETRIC FORM

A 6-month-old baby can distinguish between simple geometric forms, such as circles, squares, and triangles. By 2 years, children's concepts of form are well enough developed to enable them to insert geometric figures in holes on a form board. A year later, they can match objects on the basis of form.

DIFFERENT-SHAPED OBJECTS

Concepts of the size of different-shaped objects, such as a star and a square, are not well developed until after the child enters school and receives guidance in combating illusions.

RELATIVE SIZE

Concepts of relative size appear first between 3 and 4 years of age when the child can select the biggest and smallest from a number of objects. By 9, the child can judge middleness as accurately as bigness and smallness.

RIGHT AND LEFT

Up to 7 or 8 years, children have a nondifferentiated concept of right and left; they can apply the concept to their hands, arms, and legs but not to objects. See Figure 13–8. From then until 10 or 11 years, they develop a concrete differentiation of right and left and can apply it to objects outside themselves.

DIRECTION

Even elementary school children have difficulty identifying all but the cardinal directions and in describing locations. Concepts of direction gradually improve as children approach adolescence.

"This is my WRITE hand 'cause I write with it."

Figure 13–8. Young children use as cues to right and left what they do with their hands. (*Adapted from Bil Keane: "The Family Circus."* Register and Tribune Syndicate, *Feb. 12, 1975. Used by permission.*)

DISTANCE

The ability to judge distance develops slowly because the child must learn to use such cues as the relative size of familiar objects, e.g., houses in the distance and the clearness of detail.

DEPTH

Perception of depth is slow in developing. Even by school-entrance age, most children cannot see three dimensions in objects.

because they are unrelated to the child's own body—for example, the distance between two trees or the length of a street block—are extremely difficult for the young child to judge. Not until adolescence can a child perceive long distances accurately, and even then the judgments are often erroneous.

In school, the child learns the meaning of inches, feet, yards, pounds, and the standard measures of space and weight, though the concepts may be so formalized that the child has difficulty applying them to daily experiences. Box 13–5 shows some common space concepts a child develops and the usual ages at which they are developed.

Concepts of Weight

Judgments of weight depend upon judgments of size and upon knowledge of the weight of different materials. Young children judge mainly by size. That is why, when they pick up objects, they do not make the necessary muscular adjustments to handle them without breakage. A small toy or object, for instance, may slip through the fingers and break because the child did not expect it to be as heavy as it is.

Gradually, children learn from experience that certain things are "heavy" while others are "light." Of even greater importance, they learn that they must take into consideration what the object is made of as well as its size. In time, children learn that if they want to discover just what the weight of an object is they must pick it up, hold it with their fingers, or place it in the palm of the hand and then move the hand up and down. In this manner, a 5-year-old child can tell the difference between a 3- and a 15-gram weight when they are the same size. With practice, a child can tell the differences when weights vary only 3 or 4 grams (89).

In an experiment in which children were asked to estimate the weight of a milk bottle when filled and when empty, young children tended to underestimate both. With age, they gradually improved their estimates. In estimating the weight of two lumps of Plasticine, equal in size and in weight but different in shape, children showed a gradual increase in accuracy with age (47).

Number Concepts

Words relating to numbers are used soon after the child starts to speak. This early use of number words, however, is merely a form of "parrot speech." What a number really means to a child and when the child can use it in a meaningful way are difficult to determine. The development of number concepts appears to be a function of age and of educational development. Terman and Merrill found that the average child of 4 can count two out of a number of objects; the average child of 5 can count four; and the average child of 6 can count twelve (89).

Young children who go to nursery school or kindergarten generally learn the meaning of numbers sooner than those who do not go. Young children's concepts of numbers above 10 are generally vague and confused. For example, they often think of 100 and 1000 as similar.

After children begin school and have formal instruction in arithmetic, their number concepts develop rapidly. From grades 2 to 11, there is a gradual increase in understanding of indeterminate number concepts, such as "few," "several," "more" or "less," and "some." School textbooks place so much emphasis on *quantitative* concepts—number concepts relating to increase or decrease in amount—that children

gradually develop more definite and more accurate concepts of what numbers mean. References to "$15 a ton," a "500-mile trip," or a "trip of 20 days" may be relatively meaningless until the child has had instruction in their use and opportunities for comparison (12, 32, 82).

Many children, through hearing family members, teachers, or peers refer to certain numbers as lucky and others as unlucky, add these new meanings to their developing concepts of numbers. They learn to think of 7 and 11 as lucky numbers, as tradition holds they are, just as they learn to associate bad luck with 13 (56).

Time Concepts

Time concepts come into use in a relatively uniform sequence in the life of every child. The ability to tell at what time a thing happens in terms of another activity appears before the ability to give an actual clock time. Children know morning or afternoon at 4 years; what day it is, at 5 years; the names of the days of the week, at 5; and what time it is, at 7. At 7, they also know what month it is and what season. At 8, they know what year and what day of the month it is, and can name the month correctly.

By the time they are 5 years old, children can tell what time they go bed; by 6, when they have supper, when they get up, when they go to school, and when afternoon begins. Most children can tell their ages when they are 3 years old; when their next birthday will be, at 4; and how old they will be on the next birthday, by the time they are 5. While this pattern is similar for all children, just when a particular child will reach each stage in the pattern will depend largely upon intelligence and learning opportunities (23, 89).

In learning to tell time by the clock, most children follow a similar genetic sequence. They can first tell time and set the clock by the hour, then by the half hour, and later by the quarter hour. They must learn the meaning of the difference in the lengths of the hands, however, before they can do either. Most children learn to tell time during their sixth or seventh year (23, 37, 89).

CONCEPTS OF DURATION OF TIME   The ability to estimate time intervals develops only after the child has learned to relate time to different activities. Longer intervals are usually underestimated, while shorter ones are exaggerated; the best evaluation has been found in intervals from 30 seconds to 1 minute in duration. Up to the age of 8 years, children have difficulty judging the length of a second. When they use cues, such as counting aloud, they are able to increase their accuracy.

Unlike the younger child, the older child discovers that judgments of time are not influenced by the activity alone but by one's attitude toward it. When the activity is pleasant, time seems much shorter than it actually is (23, 41, 47).

CONCEPTS OF HISTORICAL TIME   The ability to think of the past as different from the present passes through two stages. In the first, or "negative," stage, the child learns that the past differs from the present because in the past, for example, people wore skins or worshiped idols. In the second stage, the child not only distinguishes historical periods but also forms a picture of successive epochs not unlike that formed by the adult. It is easier to understand periods of time in the past if the periods are pivoted around events rather than around people, dates, or places (23).

Because of the new methods of teaching history and the influence of different forms of mass media, children today learn about historical time earlier than their grandparents or parents did. When children see movies or TV programs or read "historical" comic books about King Arthur and the knights of the Round Table, for example, medieval Britain, with its life and customs, becomes far more meaningful than if they merely read stories about King Arthur. Similarly, if children see Biblical movies or movies based on events in ancient Rome or Egypt, the past becomes very meaningful to them.

Money Concepts

Money becomes meaningful to children only when they have an opportunity to use it. True, they may be able to identify different coins, but the names of the coins are relatively meaningless until children learn their value or know what different coins can buy. Because few children have much opportunity to spend money until they reach school age, the development of money concepts during the preschool years lags behind that of many other concepts.

At 5 years of age, the average child can name pennies only. A year later, most children can name pennies, nickels, and dimes, and some children know how many pennies there are in a nickel or dime. The 7-year-old knows what a quarter is, and many children can tell how many pennies there are in a quarter and ask for correct change in a store. At 8½ years, the child can match equivalent amounts with different coins, even when the money combinations are complex (62, 89).

MEANINGS RELATED TO MONEY   The child's concepts of money often contain meanings that have little direct relationship to the use of money for spending or saving or to how much the various denominations of money can buy. In learning these extraneous meanings and practices, the child uses parental attitudes as a model. As children come in contact with other adults, with mass media, and with members of the peer group, they not only associate new meanings with money but also add an emotional weighting to their developing money concept. The important new meanings related to money by the older child are shown in Box 13–6.

VARIATIONS IN MONEY CONCEPTS   Variations in children's concepts of money stem from differences in learning experiences. The child who *earns money* learns more about what money means in terms of time and effort than the child who receives money as an allowance or dole from parents. In general, experience with money decreases with a rise in number of *siblings in the family;* the more siblings there are, the less money each child has to spend.

Children have more experience in handling money if their *mothers work outside the home* because they have more home responsibilities involving the use of money. Children who *save* their money have a better understanding of its meaning than those who *spend* it. Children who *spend foolishly* learn more about the value of money than children who *spend wisely* or children whose spending is closely supervised.

As children grow older, they begin to *moralize* about the rightness or wrongness of the use of money. Children whose parents keep a close tab on the way they spend their allowances and point out the "foolishness" of certain expenditures and the "wisdom" of others begin to add new meanings to their developing concepts of money. By contrast, children who are allowed to spend as they choose do not develop these new meanings—or they may develop them much later.

Parental training in money matters plays an important role in children's concepts of money. Parents who handle money matters without consulting their children deprive them of opportunities to learn the meaning of money. This is true also of parents who feel that children should not be concerned about financial problems and, consequently, do not discuss such matters with them or in their presence. As a result, children have little motivation to learn about money. Consequently, when they reach adolescence, their money concepts are on a low level and are mainly egocentric.

Concepts of Beauty

To a child, as to an adult, nothing is beautiful or ugly in and of itself. What is perceived as beautiful or ugly depends upon the person's associations with it. If these associations are pleasant, the individual perceives the object as beautiful, regardless of how others perceive it. If associations are unpleasant, the child perceives it as ugly. Emotional weighting thus plays an important role in the development of this type of concept.

Young children regard people they like as beautiful, no matter how they may be judged by objective standards. When children go out into the neighborhood and school, they discover that other people have different standards of beauty. No longer, then, are things beautiful or ugly simply because they like or dislike them. Instead, their concepts of the beauty or ugliness of colors, of objects, and of the human face and form are then conditioned by group standards rather than by their personal reactions to them (30).

In addition to group standards, older children are influenced by mass communications. Even before they start school, older children have begun to think of beauty and ugliness in terms of what they see in pictures, books, magazines, and comics, and on the moving-picture or television screen. Heroes and heroines, their homes, and all their material possessions are regarded as beautiful while villains or "underdogs" and their possessions are regarded as ugly.

Each year, as children grow older, the influence of mass media on concepts of beauty increases. And, because older children and most of their friends see the same movies and television programs, read the same books, and look at the same comics, the influence of mass media is augmented by peer influences. The more the child identifies with characters in books or on the screen, the greater their influence on the child's concepts of beauty.

In spite of individual experiences that determine whether a person, an object, or a situation will be regarded as beautiful or ugly, many common concepts of beauty are a product of cultural standards. The influence of such standards on the individual child's

---

BOX 13–6

EXTRANEOUS MEANINGS ASSOCIATED WITH MONEY

LOVE
When parents shower children with toys and gifts, and say that this is because they "love them so much," children learn to think of money as a means of buying love from others.

FRIENDSHIP AND SOCIAL ACCEPTANCE
Many children who use their allowances to "treat" their friends find that this increases their social acceptance, and they associate this meaning with money throughout life.

CONTROL OF BEHAVIOR
Children who are bribed to study or to be on their good behavior learn to think of money as a way to control the behavior of others.

PAYMENT FOR SERVICES
When children are paid for household chores, they come to regard everything as having a "price tag." This colors their attitudes toward work in school and, later, in their jobs.

PRESTIGE
When children discover that social acceptance is greatly influenced by the socioeconomic status of the family and that the more material possessions they have, the greater their chances for acceptance, they learn to think of money as a source of prestige.

INDEPENDENCE
Children who earn money by doing household chores or after-school jobs discover that they can spend it as they wish. Their craving for independence colors their attitude toward schooling and plays an important role in their vocational selections.

DETERMINANT OF VALUE
Children learn to think that the more a thing costs the better it is and that the more money a person earns, the more successful that person is. Human and material worth are thus judged by a monetary yardstick.

PERSONAL SECURITY
From personal experiences of having savings in a piggy bank for making emergency purchases and from observations of elderly people who are economically secure after retirement, the child learns the value of saving as an essential to security at all ages.

concepts has been reported in a number of studies. The most important of these common concepts are discussed below.

CONCEPTS OF FACIAL BEAUTY   In studies of facial features, it has been found that there are developmental trends in aesthetic preferences for thickness of lips, width of mouth, distance between eyes, and length of nose. As children grow older, their preferences are increasingly similar to those of adults. Owing to social learning, children regard members of their own racial group and sex as most beautiful. Boys show a preference for pictures of boys, while girls think that girls are most beautiful. In addition, attractive people are perceived as having more desirable personalities and to be more competent than those who are unattractive (16, 20).

CONCEPTS OF BODILY BEAUTY   Cultural pressures largely determine concepts of bodily beauty. As early as kindergarten age, children dislike chubby builds and regard slender body builds as beautiful. Each year, as children grow older, their concepts of bodily beauty conform more closely to the cultural stereotype. Children whose body builds deviate from this stereotype—in weight, height, or sex appropriateness of appearance—are likely to be subjected to ridicule and to acquire nicknames that tell how members of the peer group feel about their bodies (15, 16, 55, 87).

CONCEPTS OF BEAUTY IN PICTURES   While children may be attracted by the new and unfamiliar in pictures, studies of what they consider beautiful have revealed that they like pictures of familiar people and animals doing familiar things. They like commonplace objects, such as houses, boats, trees, and airplanes, and action themes dealing with exciting events. Landscapes have little appeal for the young child, though the older child likes them if they contain familiar objects.

Realistic pictures appeal to children much more than those which are highly stylized. Colored pictures are preferred only when the colors are realistic. Children also like *simplicity* in pictures; the popularity of the comics is due partly to this factor. As children mature, they begin to like more complexity in drawings (10, 14).

CONCEPTS OF BEAUTY IN COLOR   At all ages, children like color. Which colors they perceive as beautiful, however, depends upon their personal likes and dislikes and upon the approved cultural attitudes toward different colors. Young children like colors that are bright and gaudy and perceive pastel shades and subdued hues as ugly. With increasing age, their attitudes change. By the time they reach adolescence, both boys and girls show a marked preference for duller shades and less saturated hues; they regard the saturated colors as "loud" or "hideous." Most children like blue, red, and green best, and black, white, yellow, and orange least.

Concepts of beauty in colors or pictures are influenced more by color than by form. Children like clothes of their favorite colors better than clothes that are more becoming or more fashionable but are in colors they dislike. In the case of pictures, they also like those with bright colors. That is one of the many reasons children have for liking comics.

In their concepts of color beauty, children incorporate meanings of color which come from their own experiences or are culturally determined. They learn to think of yellow as bright and cheerful—the color of the sun—and regard it as the color of happiness. By contrast, they associate brown and black with sadness; the emotional weighting of their concepts of these colors makes them regard them as "ugly."

Preferences for certain *color combinations* are very indefinite in young children. Red-blue and red-green are the favorite combinations of older children, while orange-green is the least favored combination. At every age, there are more pronounced individual differences for preferred color combinations than for preferred single colors. This is largely due to the different associations individuals make with various color combinations (11, 14, 46).

Concepts of the Comic

Whether children will perceive something as comic or not depends to a large extent upon the meaning they associate with it. This meaning may be derived from their own personal experiences or from their knowledge of what is culturally accepted as a source of the comic.

Comic perception may be either objective or subjective. In *objective* comic perception, people see humor in a situation in which others are involved; in the *subjective* type, they see humor in a situation involving themselves and their own acts. More intelligent people can see themselves in better perspective and can be amused by their own behavior. By contrast, those who are less intelligent or less personally and socially secure lack the insight to appraise themselves realistically or to perceive the incongruities of their behavior. As a result, subjective humor is more likely to be found in those of higher intellectual levels (63).

Perception of the comic does not always elicit laughter, especially among older children. They may have learned that social reactions will be unfavorable or that they will hurt the feelings of the person who is the target of their laughter. Young children, unaware of these possibilities, usually laugh at any situation they regard as comic (51, 63). Figure 8–7 shows some of the different types of stimuli that makes babies laugh.

Concepts of the comic follow a developmental pattern that is influenced, to some extent, by age, intelligence, and interests. This pattern is described below.

COMIC CONCEPTS IN YOUNG CHILDREN Although vocal play is one of the earliest forms of humor, babies also perceive comedy in annoying people, dropping things, and blowing bubbles in water. After the first year, children enjoy making faces, doing stunts, and hiding from people and then laughing. Among preschool children, humor is called forth mainly by slapstick situations involving physical incongruities, by noises and grimaces made by the child himself or by others, by word play, by the funny antics of animals, by comic drawings, and by simple jokes. Surprise and suspense are fundamental elements in the perception of the comic at this age (63, 86).

COMIC CONCEPTS IN OLDER CHILDREN Older children will join with others in laughing at anything, whether they think it is funny or not. Like younger children, they see humor mainly in incongruities or in the unusual: in the abasement of dignity; in people who defy authority—as they would like to do but fear doing because of punishment; and in the predicaments and misfortunes of others, especially those whom they look up to and respect. They will, for example, laugh heartily if a parent or teacher stumbles and falls. Clown acts in the circus or comedy situations in the movies or on the television screen also appeal to older children because they contain one or more of these elements of humor.

Because of their greater understanding of words, older children enjoy puns, riddles, and jokes. Practical jokes and jokes relating to forbidden subjects, such as sex, have a strong appeal. Practical jokes are usually aimed at people in authority or those against whom children are prejudiced. Children enjoy such jokes because they feel that they are getting even by making such figures appear ridiculous or by embarrassing them (66, 67, 78, 81, 83).

VARIATIONS IN PERCEPTION OF THE COMIC Although the ability to perceive the comic follows a

---

BOX 13–7

FACTORS RESPONSIBLE FOR VARIATIONS IN PERCEPTION OF THE COMIC

PAST EXPERIENCES
Past experiences and memories of these experiences determine whether or not new experiences are perceived as comic.

EMOTIONAL STATE
Perceptions of comic situations are greatly influenced by children's moods and emotional states. During a temper tantrum, children can see nothing humorous in situations that, under normal conditions, they would regard as very funny.

PHYSICAL STATE
When tired, children deem things less funny than they do when they are rested.

ATTITUDES OF OTHER PEOPLE
A joke that is amusing in one situation may seem meaningless or even repugnant in another if the attitudes of the group members toward it are unfavorable.

INTELLIGENCE
The more intelligent children are, the more meaning they can perceive and, as a result, the more humorous the situation becomes.

PERSONALITY
Children who feel insecure can rarely see the humor in situations in which they are involved. Instead, they prefer humor which bolsters their egos—objective humor in which they can laugh at others.

ABILITY TO EMPHASIZE
The ability to emphasize or to imagine oneself in the place of a person in a predicament influences one's reactions to a comic situation.

SOCIAL PRESSURES
When children discover that certain types of humor are approved and others are not, they try to avoid those that lead to social disapproval.

predictable pattern of development, the pattern varies from child to child. The factors chiefly responsible for the variations are explained in Box 13–7 (66, 83).

Self-concepts

Self-concepts are images people have of themselves. They are composites of the beliefs they have about themselves—their physical, psychological, social, and emotional characteristics, their aspirations, and their achievements. All self-concepts include physical and psychological self-images. The *physical* self-image is usually formed first and is related to the child's physical appearance—its attractiveness and its sex appropriateness or inappropriateness—and the importance of the different parts of the body to behavior and to the prestige they give the child in the eyes of others.

Psychological self-images are based on thoughts, feelings, and emotions; they consist of the qualities and abilities that affect adjustment to life, qualities such as courage, honesty, independence, and self-confidence, and aspirations and abilities of various kinds.

Coordinating physical and psychological self-images is often difficult for children. Consequently, they are apt to think of themselves as having dual personalities with a specific appearance and a specific personality make-up. As children grow older, the physical and psychological self-concepts gradually fuse and they perceive themselves as unified individuals.

ORIGIN OF SELF-CONCEPTS Self-concepts are based on what children *believe* the significant people in their lives—parents, teachers, and peers—think of them. They are thus "mirror images." If children believe these significant people think favorably of them, they

Figure 13–9. Self-concepts are mirror images of what children believe significant people in their lives think of them.

think favorably of themselves, and vice versa. Figure 13–9 shows how these mirror images are formed.

PATTERN OF DEVELOPMENT OF SELF-CONCEPTS
Concepts of self are hierarchical in nature; the most basic—the *primary* self-concept—is acquired first. It is founded on the experiences the child has in the home and is made up of many individual concepts, each resulting from experiences with different members of the family group.

The primary self-concept includes both physical and psychological self-images, though the former usually develop earlier than the latter. The *first* psychological self-images are based on children's contacts with siblings and comparison of themselves with their siblings. Similarly, early concepts of their roles in life, their aspirations, and their responsibilities to others are based on parental teachings and pressures.

As contacts outside the home increase, children acquire other concepts of themselves. These make up the *secondary* self-concepts. They relate to how children see themselves through the eyes of others. The primary self-concept frequently determines the selection of situations in which the secondary self-concepts will be formed. Children who have developed self-concepts characterized by beliefs of their own importance, for example, will select playmates who regard them much as their parents do.

The secondary self-concept, like the primary, includes physical as well as psychological self-images. Children think of their physical structures as people outside the home do, and they evaluate their psychological self-images, formed at home, by comparing them with what they believe teachers, peers, and others think of them.

Generally, though not always, the primary self-concept is more favorable than the secondary. When a discrepancy exists, children must close the gap between the two if they are to be happy and well adjusted. They may do this by trying to force others to change their unfavorable concepts so that these concepts will correspond to the favorable concepts children have of themselves. Because this rarely works, children must revise their unrealistic self-concepts so that they will more closely approach reality.

IMPORTANT ELEMENTS IN PATTERN OF DEVELOPMENT
All children add to their self-concepts meanings that their cultural group regards as important. These elements are added at predictable times

and are similar for all children, though variations in subsocieties affect them somewhat. The new meanings that are almost universally associated with self-concepts during the childhood years are shown in Box 13–8.

BOX 13–8

COMMON ELEMENTS OF SELF CONCEPTS

SEX DIFFERENCES
By the age of 3 or 4 years, children are aware of their sex and use such cues as hair styles and clothing to distinguish members of the two sexes. Awareness of differences in interests, achievements, and aptitudes develops after children enter school and reaches a peak during puberty. Gradually, an emotional weighting is added, based on an awareness of social attitudes toward "male" and "female."

SEX ROLES
Children learn the appropriate behavior for their sex by identifying with their parents and by parental training and pressures. Later they learn by identifying with adults or older children outside the home and with cultural stereotypes in the mass media. By the time children enter school, these meanings are added to their self-concepts, and emotional weighting, based on social attitudes toward the roles of the two sexes, becomes an important part of the self-concept.

RACIAL DIFFERENCES
Most children can distinguish their racial identification by the time they are 4 years old. They gradually learn the social attitudes toward members of their race and the prestige or lack of prestige associated with their racial group. How children are treated by peers as well as by other members of the social group contributes to the emotional weighting of their self-concepts.

SOCIAL-CLASS DIFFERENCES
Preschool children discover that there are differences in what people have and in the way they live. They learn that these are related to the father's occupation and that some people are labeled "rich" while others are labeled "poor." They add these meanings to their self-concepts. Figure 13–10 shows the cues children use to identify social-class belonging. The more important social acceptance is to children, the more emotional weighting they give to social-class membership.

DEVELOPMENT OF UNDERSTANDING

Working-class cues

Middle-class cues

Figure 13–10. Some cues used by children to identify social-class differences.
(*Adapted from G. Jahoda: Development of the perception of social differences in children from 6 to 10.* British Journal of Psychology, *1959, 50, 159–175. Used by permission.*)

Social Concepts

Social concepts, or concepts relating to people and social situations, usually develop slightly later than self-concepts. The baby and young child are egocentric, and their interests center more on themselves than on others. Also, the young child has limited social horizons, and so has few opportunities to develop social concepts.

PATTERN OF DEVELOPMENT OF SOCIAL CONCEPTS
By the time babies are a month old, they can differentiate the human voice from other sounds. A month or two later, they show an interest in people and are able to differentiate between those who are familiar and those who are strangers. Not until they are about 8 months old, however, do babies respond to the emotional behavior of others in a way that signifies they understand facial expressions (72).

Young children include in their developing social concepts not only an understanding of the feelings and emotions of others, as expressed in their overt behavior, but also an understanding of the underlying meaning of these emotions and feelings. Thus, the young child's social perceptions are colored by past experiences, by social pressures, by what they observe, and by what they have heard others say.

Older children size up both adults and their contempories fairly accurately and develop specific concepts of them in terms of socially approved behavior. Even within the family, children develop specific concepts of the approved social role for the mother, the father, the child, and the other family members. This topic will be discussed in detail in Chapter 17, Family Relationships.

In addition to general elements in social concepts, older children associate specific meanings based on their experiences with people of different races, socioeconomic groups, and of the two sexes. While some of these associated meanings may appear in the social concepts of young children, most are added to the social concepts as children's social horizons broaden to include the neighborhood, the school, and the community.

ASSOCIATION OF RACIAL MEANINGS Prejudice influences the child's developing concepts of members of different racial groups. Prejudice against a member of a minority group is usually not based on personal experience, but is a reflection of cultural patterns and stereotypes. Preschool children can distinguish people of different races on the basis of skin and hair color and other physical features, but the degree of difference between their own appearance and that of people of other racial groups determines the age at which they become aware of the difference (45).

Since children of minority groups are usually sensitized to racial differences earlier than those of majority groups, social concepts of minority-group children contain meanings of racial differences earlier. The child's concepts of race include not only the appearance of people of different racial groups but also their occupations, clothing, living quarters, personalities, and abilities. These associations become stronger as children grow older.

ASSOCIATION OF SEX-ROLE MEANINGS In the development of social concepts, children add meanings related to sex differences and approved sex roles.

While learning how they differ from members of the opposite sex, and what the approved sex role for members of their own sex is, children learn to judge others—parents, siblings, peers, and adults outside the home—in terms of these meanings. Children are well aware of what the social group expects of members of both sexes before childhood comes to an end (40). This matter will be discussed in detail in the chapter on development of sex roles.

ASSOCIATION OF SOCIAL-CLASS MEANINGS Social concepts also include meanings related to social-class identification. Even in the preschool years, some children make vague social distinctions on the basis of crude and concrete cues which enable them to compare their social milieu with that of others (92).

For most children, perception of social-class differences develops rapidly during the childhood years, reaching the adult level during early adolescence. Estvan and Estvan found that among elementary school children, the ability to understand and appreciate high socioeconomic status, as represented by a picture of a mansion, was more closely related to development of social maturity than to differences in children's social backgrounds. At the age of 6 years, for example, only 30 percent of the children studied were able to discriminate between the mansion and any other home situation; by 12, the percentage had risen to 68. With this increasing sensitivity to social-class differences came a higher regard for what the mansion symbolizes in our culture (25).

ASSOCIATION OF AGE MEANINGS Young children perceive age in relation to the person's size. A large child is judged to be older than a small child. In the case of adults, who vary less in size than children do, age is perceived in relation to certain cues, such as hair color, skin wrinkles, type of clothing or occupation. An elderly person who has dyed hair and who wears clothing designed for teenagers, for example, will be perceived by a child as younger than a person of the same age who has gray hair and wears clothing designed for the middle-aged or elderly.

By the time children are 9 years old, they begin to judge age more correctly. This is especially true of age judgments of children. Because of their interest in age and their tendency to select playmates and friends from those of their own chronological age level, older children have far more accurate concepts of age than they had when they were younger (49).

This accuracy, however, is limited to children's ages rather than adolescents' or adults' ages. Throughout childhood and even into adolescence, inaccuracies in judgments of age of older age groups continue to be common. As a result, their social concepts of older people tend to be less accurate than their social concepts of children.

Hazards in Development
Of Understanding

Failure to understand and misunderstanding are hazardous to personal and social adjustments. The seriousness of misunderstanding, as was pointed out earlier, was first highlighted by G. Stanley Hall's study, published in 1891. Since then, many studies of how lack of understanding or misunderstanding resulting from faulty concepts have appeared. All have substantiated Hall's conclusions that these are hazardous to children's adjustments.

Some of the most common causes of understanding below the norm for the child's age and of misunderstandings are discussed below. How they affect the child's personal and social adjustments will be explained to justify regarding them as "hazardous."

Developmental Lag in
Understanding

Developmental lag in understanding means the ability to understand at a level below that of the norm for the child's age. In school, for example, children of a given age are expected to have a level of understanding that will enable them to do the schoolwork that other children of the same age are capable of doing. Similarly, in the play group, age-mates expect each child to have an understanding of situations similar to that of the other group members. Failure to come up to these expectations means that the child will make poor adjustments to these situations.

Lag in understanding may be due to many causes, the two most common of which are intellectual development below the norm for the child's age and lack of opportunities to have experiences on which understanding is based. Regardless of the cause, the child's comprehension will fall below that of other children of the same age.

Studies of growth of general intelligence and of different intellectual abilities, especially the ability to learn, have revealed that their lag may be due to a poor hereditary endowment or, more likely, to environmental conditions that interfere with normal brain development during the critical months of late prenatal life and early postnatal life when the brain is developing most rapidly. Of the many conditions that interfere with normal brain development, as was pointed out earlier, are poor nutrition—of the mother before the child's birth and of the child after birth—and brain damage due either to unfavorable conditions in the prenatal environment or to unfavorable conditions during the birth process—anoxia or pressure on the fetal brain during a difficult birth or excessive maternal medication to ease birth pains.

A second common cause of lag in understanding is due to lack of opportunities to have experiences on which understanding is based. This may result from a culturally sterile environment, but more often it results from lack of stimulation to make use of environmental opportunities. Children who grow up in homes where the socioeconomic condition of the family is so low that few opportunities are available to them to have experiences outside their immediate environments and where parents are too peroccupied with the essentials of survival to provide their children with any more than the bare essentials lack stimulation of their innate abilities. As a result, these abilities do not develop as they would, had environmental conditions been more favorable.

That this plays an important role in lag in understanding has been demonstrated by children from such environments who have been placed in day-care nurseries while their mothers worked or in Head Start programs in school. As a result of good physical care, especially good nutrition, and opportunities to learn many things which they had no opportunity to learn in their homes, these children show an increase in their intellectual abilities and in their understanding.

Lack of experiences may also come from parental overprotectiveness. For fear that their children will hurt themselves if they explore the environment or that they will get "bad ideas" from mass media, overprotective parents deprive their children of learning experiences. They then seem "backward" or "stupid" in comparison with other children whose parents have not only given them opportunities to learn but who have also encouraged them to learn and have guided their learning.

Lag in understanding affects every area of life and of the adjustments children make. In school, for example, children whose understanding is below that of their age-mates cannot do the work the school expects the child to do at that age. First graders, for example, cannot read or do arithmetic as well as their classmates and, as a result, are forced to repeat first grade. That is why nursery school, kindergarten, and child-care center programs have proved to be so beneficial in filling in the gaps in development of understanding caused by earlier lack of opportunities to learn.

In social situations, lag in understanding is one of the important causes of poor social adjustments and poor social acceptance. Children whose social insight is below that of the members of the peer group do things that annoy their peers. This results in peer rejection or neglect. Children whose understanding of the comic is below that of the members of the peer group are judged as "stupid" or "poor sports" because they cannot understand jokes or cartoons which their age-mates regard as "funny."

Children whose understanding of their strengths and weaknesses is poor in comparison with that of their age-mates develop unrealistic self-concepts. When their age-mates do not treat them in accordance with how they believe they should be treated, children with poor self-understanding develop a resentment against their age-mates that increases their poor social adjustments. Poor social adjustments, in turn, contribute to poor personal adjustments.

Misconceptions

Misconceptions are faulty interpretations of different sensory experiences. Children frequently misinterpret what they see, hear, smell, feel, or taste. They may experience these sensations correctly, but they associate wrong meanings with them. Sometimes, for example, they believe that a stuffed animal has the qualities of a living animal because it closely resembles a real animal. Or, they may believe that an object at a distance is small because it looks small in comparison with near objects.

Misunderstanding, resulting from faulty concepts due to the association of wrong meanings with sensory experiences, may be traced to a number of causes, the most common of which are given and explained in Box 13-9.

Misconceptions, which lead to misunderstanding, have a serious effect on the child's adjustments. If they were only temporary, this would not be serious, but because they tend to be long lasting, their effects

can and often do have a persistent effect on the types of adjustment the child makes to life.

In their *schoolwork*, children are handicapped by misconceptions of the words used by teachers and in their textbooks. If concepts are limited or faulty, children may not be able to understand the teacher's explanations or understand what the teacher is trying to teach them.

Lack of understanding affects children's *play*. If they do not understand the rules of games and sports, their playmates will not want to play with them. When *reading* for pleasure or when watching *movies* or *television*, children will misinterpret what they see or hear if their concepts of certain words are faulty or if they habitually view life in an unrealistic way.

Partial or total misconceptions affect children's *attitudes* and, in turn, their behavior. If children develop the concept that certain people, actions, or situations are "bad," without adequate reason for doing so, they will react to them in a negative way. If their concepts were more accurate and if they evaluated the people or situations as "good," as many others do, their reactions would be more favorable.

Social relationships are greatly influenced by misconceptions. Children who misinterpret what other people say or do or who do not perceive their own and others' status in the group accurately will be greatly handicapped in their relationships with members of the group. As a result, they will not enjoy the social acceptance they would have had, had their understanding of others and of themselves been more accurate.

A common source of misconceptions that affect social relationships is the tendency to stereotype people. As was explained earlier, stereotyping is fostered by mass media, especially comics, movies, and television. Children who group people together because they have common physical or personal characteristics will react to them as if they were alike in every way. They are thus likely to behave in a manner that will lead to poor social relationships.

Misconceptions about *themselves*, due to faulty or unrealistic self-concepts, can and often do play havoc with children's personal adjustments. Seeing themselves as they would like to be or through the eyes of people who have unrealistic concepts of them, as often happens in the case of parents, children expect others to react to them in accordance with the concept they have of themselves. When they do not receive the treatment they expect, they become resentful of those

BOX 13-9

CAUSES OF MISCONCEPTIONS

INCORRECT INFORMATION

Incorrect information comes from three common sources during childhood. Children may (1) receive faulty information from parents in answer to their questions either because of parental ignorance or parental preoccupation with something that prevents their hearing the child's question correctly; they may (2) receive faulty information from siblings or peers whose knowledge is incorrect; or they may (3) receive it from unauthoritative or out-of-date mass media.

LIMITED EXPERIENCE

Limited experience makes it impossible for children to judge things accurately. Lack of critical attitude, resulting from limited experience, combined with undeveloped reasoning ability, may cause children to associate wrong meanings with what they observe without realizing how incongruous the association is.

GULLIBILITY

Children who have been brought up in authoritarian homes learn to believe that "mother knows best." This quickly spreads to the belief that anyone older or anyone in authority knows more than they do. As a result, they accept what is said or written without question.

FAULTY REASONING

Although reasoning ability normally increases with age, lack of training or opportunity to use reasoning ability because of authoritarian training in the home or school often causes children to reason inaccurately.

VIVID IMAGINATION

Because imagination outstrips reasoning in the development of different intellectual abilities, children do not have the check on their imagination that they will have later. As a result, they believe that what they imagine has actually happened, and they incorporate this faulty belief in their developing concepts.

UNREALISTIC THINKING

When children are encouraged to think unrealistically about things—including themselves—through constant exposure to the mass media, they are likely to develop the habit of thinking unrealistically. This plays havoc with understanding.

MISUNDERSTANDING OF WORDS

Because all concepts sooner or later acquire verbal labels, many children have limited or incorrect understanding of the words that serve as labels. This is especially true when the labels are verbal instead of written. How this can affect their understanding is illustrated in Figure 13-11.

CONFUSION

Misconceptions may be due to what, to children, seems to be conflicting information. When, for example, parents explain birth first in terms of the "birds and bees" and then later in terms of humans, it is not surprising that young children's concepts of birth become distorted by apparently conflicting facts.

Figure 13-11. Verbal labels, first learned in relation to specific objects, people, or situations, can lead to misconceptions if these verbal labels have different meanings when spelled differently. (*Adapted from Ernie Bushmiller:"Nancy."* United Features Syndicate, *Feb. 19, 1975. Used by permission.*)

who do not treat them as they expect to be treated. This leads to poor social relationships. Poor social relationships, in turn, affect children's self-concepts unfavorably and this leads to poor personal adjustments.

Difficulty in Correcting Misconceptions

Serious as misconceptions are to understanding, the difficulty in changing them, once they have developed, is an even greater hazard to children's personal and social adjustments. This is because, unless they are corrected, they will have a persistently unfavorable effect on children's behavior.

Although the *cognitive* aspect of a concept can be changed relatively easily as the child gathers more and more accurate information, the *affective* aspect—the emotional weighting—of the concept is likely to be persistent. If the child, for example, develops an unfavorable attitude toward school, parents and teachers can explain why an education is important. The child may understand and agree with all they say, but unless something can be done to improve the unfavorable attitude that plays such an important role in the child's concept of school, the concept of school will remain unfavorable.

The two categories of concepts that are most difficult to change are social and self concepts. This is serious because both contribute heavily to personal and social adjustments. In both cases, the emotional weighting of the concepts is especially heavy. This is primarily responsible for the difficulty in changing them.

When, for example, social concepts are based on stereotypes fostered by different forms of mass media, they have the halo of infallibility that comes from these sources. Persuading children that not all people in a specific racial, religious, or age group are the same is difficult because children have accepted their beliefs from the mass media which they have learned are infallible sources of information, just as they have learned to accept as infallible what their textbooks in school teach them.

Changing self-concepts is even more difficult than changing social concepts. This is because the emotional weighting of the former is greater than the emotional weighting of the latter. Furthermore, children are usually incapable of seeing below the surface of the speech and behavior of others. As a result, they fail to grasp the true motivation of the treatment they receive from others. Should, for example, a teacher give more time and attention to a slow learner than to one who learns more rapidly, children who learn rapidly may readily interpret this to mean that the teacher likes the slow learner better. This leads them to interpret this as "favoritism"—a common cause of children's dislike of a teacher and of school. It also makes children feel that they are inferior to the child who appears to be the object of the teacher's attention and interest.

Few adults are aware that children build up unfavorable self-concepts through misinterpreting the speech and behavior of others. Consequently, such concepts get a strong hold on children before they are detected and corrected. Even more important, few adults, whether parents or teachers, try to control the development of children's self-concepts to ensure that they will be both realistic and favorable. The result is that many self-concepts develop haphazardly and contain many misconceptions. Even though children develop better social and self-insight as they grow older, and, as a result, are able to make better appraisals of their appearance, abilities, achievements, and roles, their self-concepts are likely to be colored by the mirror images they formed earlier. And, because of the heavy emotional weighting of these early mirror images, changing them into more favorable self-concepts is an almost impossible task.

Chapter Highlights

1 Psychological interest in children's understanding was motivated by G. Stanley Hall's study of children's misconceptions at the turn of the present century and, more recently, by Piaget's theory of cognitive development.

2 The ability to understand is important because it determines the kind of personal and social adjustments children make.

3 Understanding develops according to a predictable pattern in which maturation and learning play important roles.

4 Because understanding is based on concepts,

how they develop and how accurate they are determine the quality of the child's understanding.

5 If concepts are to be accurate and adequate to meet a child's needs, three essentials must be fulfilled: the ability to see relationships, the ability to comprehend underlying meanings, and the ability to reason.

6 The meanings that make up concepts come from sensory exploration, motor manipulation, questioning, pictorial mass media, and reading.

7 The quality of the concepts children develop is influenced by many factors, the most important of which are the condition of the sense organs, intelligence, the opportunity to learn, the type of experiences the child has, sex, and personality.

8 Concepts of life are greatly influenced by animism and concepts of death by religious instruction and experiences with death itself, both direct and indirect.

9 Concepts of physical causality usually develop earlier than concepts of psychological causality because the former are easier for children to comprehend than the latter. Concepts of space, weight, numbers, time, and money are slow to develop partly because of their abstract nature and partly because children have limited experiences in these areas until they go to school.

10 Perception of beauty, whether in the area of personal attractiveness, pictures, or color, is influenced partly by a child's likes and dislikes and partly by peer and cultural pressures.

11 Whether objective or subjective, perception of the comic follows a predictable pattern that is influenced by the child's age, intelligence, and interests.

12 Self-concepts, or images children have of themselves, are mirror images of what they believe significant people in their lives—parents, teachers, and peers—think of them. They contain such common elements as meanings related to sex differences, sex roles, social class, and racial differences.

13 Social concepts—concepts related to people and social situations—are built up from children's experiences, both direct and indirect, with people in different social situations.

14 The major hazards in the development of understanding are developmental lag in understanding, misconceptions, and difficulties in changing misconceptions, once they have developed.

15 Misconceptions are hazardous to good personal and social adjustments partly because they lead to unfavorable behavior and partly because, as a result of their emotional weighting, they are difficult to correct and thus continue to affect adjustments unfavorably.

Bibliography

1 Barclay, D. Questions of life and death. *The New York Times*, July 15, 1962.

2 Bayley, N. The development of mental abilities. In P. H. Mussen (ed.), *Carmichael's manual of child psychology*, 3d ed. New York: Wiley, 1970. Vol. 1, pp. 1163–1209.

3 Berlyne, D. E. Children's reasoning and thinking. In P. H. Mussen (ed.), *Carmichael's manual of child psychology*, 3d ed. New York: Wiley, 1970. Vol. 1, pp. 939–981.

4 Bernstein, A. C. How children learn about birth and sex. *Psychology Today*, 1976, *9* (8), 31–35, 66.

5 Bernstein, A. C., and P. A. Cowan. Children's concepts of how people get babies. *Child Development*, 1975, *46*, 77–91.

6 Berzonsky, M. D. The role of familiarity in children's explanations of physical causality. *Child Development*, 1971, *42*, 705–715.

7 Berzonsky, M. D. A factor-analytic investigation of child animism. *Journal of Genetic Psychology*, 1973, *122*, 287–295.

8 Berzonsky, M. D. Some relationships between children's conceptions of psychological and physical causality. *Journal of Social Psychology*, 1973, *90*, 299–309.

9 Berzonsky, M. D. A further note on the animism controversy. *Journal of Genetic Psychology*, 1975, *126*, 307–308.

10 Black, K. N., T. M. Williams, and D. R. Brown. A developmental study of preschool children's preference for random forms. *Child Development*, 1971, *42*, 57–61.

11 Borich, C. D. Preferences for color, form, borders, lines, and dots by preschool children and adults. *Perceptual and Motor Skills*, 1970, *31*, 811–817.

12 Brainerd, C. J. The origin of number concepts. *Scientific American*, 1973, *228* (3), 101–109.

13 Campbell, J. D. Illness is a point of view: The development of children's concept of illness. *Child Development*, 1975, *46*, 92–100.

14 Cantor, G. N. Children's "like-dislike" ratings of familiarized and nonfamiliarized visual stimuli. *Journal of Experimental Child Psychology*, 1968, *6*, 651–657.

15 Caskey, S. R., and D. W. Felker. Social stereotyping of female body image by elementary school age girls. *Research Quarterly of the American Association for Health,*

Physical Education and Recreation, 1971, *42*, 251–255.

16 Cavior, N., and D. A. Lombardi. Developmental aspects of judgment of physical attractiveness in children. *Developmental Psychology*, 1973, *8*, 67–71.

17 Chapman, A. J. Humorous laughter in children. *Journal of Personality and Social Psychology*, 1975, *31*, 42–49.

18 Chapman, A. J., and W. A. Chapman. Responsiveness in humor: Its dependency upon a companion's humorous smiling and laughter. *Journal of Psychology*, 1974, *88*, 245–272.

19 Chapman, R. H. The development of children's understanding of proportions. *Child Development*, 1975, *46*, 141–148.

20 Clifford, M. M. Physical attractiveness and academic performance. *Child Study Journal*, 1975, *5*, 201–209.

21 Dion, K. K. Young children's stereotyping of facial attractiveness. *Developmental Psychology*, 1973, *9*, 183–188.

22 Eckerman, C. O., and H. L. Rheingold. Infants' exploratory responses to toys and people. *Developmental Psychology*, 1974, *10*, 255–259.

23 Elkind, D. Of time and the child. *The New York Times*, Dec. 11, 1970.

24 Endsley, R. C., and S. A. Clarey. Answering young children's questions as a determinant of the subsequent question-asking behavior. *Developmental Psychology*, 1975, *11*, 863.

25 Estvan, F. J., and E. W. Estvan. *The child's world: His social perception*. New York: Putnam, 1959.

26 Faterson, H. F., and H. A. Witkin. Longitudinal study of development of the body concept. *Developmental Psychology*, 1970, *2*, 429–438.

27 Fernstrom, J. D., and R. J. Wurtman. Nutrition and the brain. *Scientific American*, 1974, *230* (2), 84–91.

28 Fishbein, H. D., S. Lewis, and K. Keiffer. Children's understanding of spatial relations: Coordination of perspective. *Developmental Psychology*, 1972, *7*, 21–33.

29 Flavell, J. H. Concept development. In P. H. Mussen (ed.), *Carmichael's manual of child psychology*, 3d ed. New York: Wiley, 1970. Vol. 1, pp. 983–1059.

30 Gardner, H. Children's sensitivity to musical styles. *Merrill-Palmer Quarterly*, 1973, *19*, 67–77.

31 Gellert, E. Children's conceptions of the content and function of the human body. *Genetic Psychology Monographs*, 1962, *65*, 293–405.

32 Gelman, R., and M. F. Tucker. Further investigations of the young child's conception of number. *Child Development*, 1975, *46*, 167–175.

33 Gergen, K. J. *The concept of self*. New York: Holt, Rinehart & Winston, 1971.

34 Golden, M., and B. Birns. Social class and cognitive development in infancy. *Merrill-Palmer Quarterly*, 1968, *14*, 139–149.

35 Goodnow, J. J. Effects of activity handling, illustrated by uses for objects. *Child Development*, 1969, *40*, 201–212.

36 Hall, G. S. The contents of children's minds on entering school. *Pedagogical Seminary*, 1891, *1*, 139–173.

37 Harner, L. Yesterday and tomorrow: Development of early understanding of the terms. *Developmental Psychology*, 1975, *11*, 864–865.

38 Harris, L. J. Discrimination of left and right, and development of the logic of relations. *Merrill-Palmer Quarterly*, 1972, *18*, 307–322.

39 Harris, L. J., and E. A. Strommen. The role of front-back features in children's "front," "back" and "beside" placement of objects. *Merrill-Palmer Quarterly*, 1972, *18*, 259–271.

40 Hartley, R. E. Sex role pressures and the socialization of the male child. *Psychological Reports*, 1959, *5*, 457–468.

41 Hermelin, B. M., and N. O'Connor. Children's judgements of duration. *British Journal of Psychology*, 1971, *62*, 13–20.

42 James, W. *The principles of psychology*. New York: Holt, 1890.

43 Kagan, J., and N. Kogan. Individual variation in cognitive processes. In P. H. Mussen (ed.), *Carmichael's manual of child psychology*, 3d. ed. New York: Wiley, 1970. Vol. 1, pp. 1273–1365.

44 Kaplan, B. J. Malnutrition and mental deficiency. *Psychological Bulletin*, 1972, *78*, 321–334.

45 Katz, P. A. Perception of racial cues in preschool children: A new look. *Developmental Psychology*, 1973, *8*, 295–299.

46 Kimball, M. M., and P. S. Dale. The relationship between color naming and color recognition abilities of preschoolers. *Child Development*, 1972, *43*, 972–980.

47 King, W. H. The development of scientific concepts in children. *British Journal of Educational Psychology*, 1961, *31*, 1–20.

48 Koocher, G. P. Childhood, death and cognitive development. *Developmental Psychology*, 1973, *9*, 369–376.

49 Kratochwill, T. R., and J. A. Goldman. Developmental changes in children's judgements of age. *Developmental Psychology*, 1973, *9*, 358–362.

50 Kreitler, H., and S. Kreitler. Children's concepts of sexuality and birth. *Child Development*, 1966, *37*, 363–378.

51 Kreitler, H., and S. Kreitler. Dependence of laughter on cognitive strategies. *Merrill-Palmer Quarterly*, 1970, *16*, 163–177.

52 Kucǧaj, S. A., and M. P. Maratsos. On the acquisition of front, back, and side. *Child Development*, 1975, *46*, 202–210.

53 Lacoursiere-Paige, F. Development of right-left concept in children. *Perceptual and Motor Skills*, 1974, *38*, 111–117.

54 Lerner, R. M., and E. Gellert. Body build identification, preference, and aversion in children. *Developmental Psychology*, 1969, *1*, 456–462.

55 Lerner, R. M., and C. Schroeder. Physique-identification, preference, and aversion in kindergarten children. *Developmental Psychology*, 1971, *5*, 538.

56 Lindauer, M. S. Historical and contemporary attitudes toward numbers. *Journal of Psychology*, 1969, *71*, 41–43.

57 Little, A. A longitudinal study of cognitive development in young children. *Child Development*, 1972, *43*, 1024–1034.

58 Looft, W. R. Animistic thought in children: Understanding of "living" across its associated attributes. *Journal of Genetic Psychology*, 1974, *124*, 235–240.

59 Looft, W. R., and W. H. Bartz. Animism revived. In W. R. Looft (ed.), *Developmental psychology: A book of readings*. Hinsdale, Ill.: Dryden Press, 1972. Pp. 309–336.

60 Looft, W. R., and D. C. Charles. Modification of the life concept in chil-

dren. *Developmental Psychology,* 1969, *1*, 445.

61 Maratsos, M. P. Decrease in the understanding of the word "big" in preschool children. *Child Development,* 1973, *44*, 747–752.

62 Marshall, H. R. The relation of giving children an allowance to children's money knowledge and responsibility, and to other practices of parents. *Journal of Genetic Psychology,* 1964, *104*, 35–57.

63 McGhee, P. E. Development of the humor responses: A review of the literature. *Psychological Bulletin,* 1971, *76*, 328–348.

64 McGhee, P. E. Development of children's ability to create the joking relationship. *Child Development,* 1974, *45*, 552–556.

65 McGhee, P. E. Moral development and children's appreciation of humor. *Developmental Psychology,* 1974, *10*, 514–533.

66 McGhee, P. E. Children's appreciation of humor: A test of the cognitive congruency principle. *Child Development,* 1976, *47*, 420–426.

67 McGhee, P. E., and S. F. Johnson. The role of fantasy and reality cues in children's appreciation of incongruity humor. *Merrill-Palmer Quarterly,* 1975, *21*, 19–30.

68 Melear, J. D. Children's conceptions of death. *Journal of Genetic Psychology,* 1973, *123*, 359–360.

69 Moore, J. E., and D. G. Kendall. Children's concepts of reproduction. *Journal of Sex Research,* 1971, *7*, 42–61.

70 Nash, H. The judgment of body landmark heights. *Genetic Psychology Monographs,* 1967, *79*, 251–296.

71 Neisser, E. G. Emotional and social values attached to money. *Marriage and Family Living,* 1960, *22*, 132–139.

72 Odom, R. D., and C. M. Lemond. Developmental differences in the perception and production of facial expressions. *Child Development,* 1972, *43*, 359–369.

73 Piaget, J. *Six psychological studies.* New York: Random House, 1968.

74 Piaget, J. Piaget's theory. In P. H. Mussen (ed.), *Carmichael's manual of child psychology,* 3d ed. New York: Wiley, 1970. Vol. 1, pp. 703–732.

75 Piaget, J. *Science of education and psychology of the child.* New York: Orion Press, 1970.

76 Pick, H. L., and A. D. Pick. Sensory and perceptual development. In P. H. Mussen (ed.), *Carmichael's manual of child psychology,* 3d ed. New York: Wiley, 1970. Vol. 1, pp. 773–847.

77 Porter, C. S. Grade school children's perceptions of their internal body parts. *Nursing Research,* 1974, *23*, 384–391.

78 Prentice, N. M., and R. E. Fathman. Joking riddles: A developmental index of children's humor. *Developmental Psychology,* 1975, *11*, 210–216.

79 Rabinowitz, F. M., B. E. Moely, N. Finkel, and S. McClinton. The effects of toy novelty and social interaction on the exploratory behavior of preschool children. *Child Development,* 1975, *46*, 286–289.

80 Schaffer, H. R., and M. H. Parry. Perceptual-motor behavior in infancy as a function of age and stimulus familiarity. *British Journal of Psychology,* 1969, *60*, 1–9.

81 Shultz, T. R. Development of the appreciation of riddles. *Child Development,* 1974, *45*, 100–105.

82 Siegel, L. S. The sequence of development of certain number concepts in preschool children. *Developmental Psychology,* 1971, *5*, 357–361.

83 Sinnott, J. D., and B. M. Ross. Comparison of aggression and incongruity as factors in children's judgments of humor. *Journal of Genetic Psychology,* 1976, *128*, 241–249.

84 Smeets, P. M. The animism controversy revisited: A probability analysis. *Journal of Genetic Psychology,* 1973, *123*, 219–225.

85 Somerville, R. M. Death education as part of family life education: Using imaginative literature for insights into family crises. *Family Coordinator,* 1971, *20*, 209–224.

86 Sroufe, L. A., and J. P. Wunsch. The development of laughter in the first year of life. *Child Development,* 1972, *43*, 1326–1344.

87 Staffieri, J. R. A study of social stereotypes of body images in children. In W. R. Looft (ed.), *Developmental psychology: A book of readings.* Hinsdale, Ill.: Dryden Press, 1972. Pp. 289–296.

88 Starr, R. H. Cognitive development in infancy: Assessment, acceleration, and actualization. *Merrill-Palmer Quarterly,* 1971, *17*, 153–188.

89 Terman, L. M., and M. A. Merrill. *Stanford-Binet Intelligence Scale.* Boston: Houghton Mifflin, 1960.

90 Tizard, J. Early malnutrition, growth and mental development in man. *British Medical Bulletin,* 1974, *30*, 169–174.

91 Treadwell, Y. Humor and creativity. *Psychological Reports,* 1970, *26*, 55–58.

92 Tudor, J. F. The development of class awareness in children. *Social Forces,* 1971, *49*, 470–476.

93 Uzgiris, I. C. Patterns of cognitive development in infancy. *Merrill-Palmer Quarterly,* 1973, *19*, 181–204.

94 Walson, J. S. Cognitive-perceptual development in infancy: Setting for the seventies. *Merrill-Palmer Quarterly,* 1971, *17*, 139–152.

95 Weiner, B., and J. J. Goodnow. Motor activity: Effects on memory. *Developmental Psychology,* 1970, *2*, 448.

96 Whiteman, M. Children's conceptions of psychological causality as related to subjective responsibility, conservation and language. *Journal of Genetic Psychology,* 1976, *128*, 215–226.

97 Wilcox, R. M. Visual preferences of human infants for representations of the human face. *Journal of Experimental Child Psychology,* 1969, *7*, 10–20.

98 Zeligs, R. *Children's experiences with death.* Springfield, Ill.: Charles C Thomas, 1974.

CHAPTER 14

MORAL DEVELOPMENT

Early psychological interest in moral development was centered on discipline—the best type to use to ensure that children would learn to be law-abiding citizens and the effect of such discipline on their personal and social adjustments. Gradually psychological interest shifted to moral development—the normal pattern for this area of development and the ages at which children can be expected to behave in a socially approved way.

With the serious increase in juvenile delinquency, interest in studying the causes, cures, and prevention of juvenile delinquency became a psychological as well as a sociological concern. At first, this interest was limited to studies of the adolescent years because, correctly speaking, children are not regarded as "juvenile delinquents" regardless of how far their behavior deviates from socially approved standards.

In the past two decades, psychological studies of moral development have been spurred on by theories, based on research findings, of the predictable patterns of moral development during the childhood years. The best known and most influential of these theories are those of Piaget and Kohlberg.

Also the work of the Gluecks at Harvard University to determine what is responsible for juvenile delinquency has contributed two important findings which have stimulated psychological interest in other aspects of moral development. The first of the Gluecks' findings was that juvenile delinquency is not a new phenomenon in the adolescent years but rather a continuation of a pattern of unsocial behavior that had its origin in childhood. The Gluecks claimed that as early as 2 or 3 years of age it is possible to spot those children who will later become juvenile delinquents.

The second finding of the Gluecks was that there is a close relationship between juvenile delinquency and the environment, especially the home environment (28). This finding has spurred psychological interest in investigating the reasons for the discrepancy between moral knowledge and moral behavior even during the childhood years.

Today, studies of moral development have become one of the focal points of psychological research. As a result, present-day knowledge of this area of development provides a fairly complete picture of the pattern of moral development and the causes of deviation from this pattern.

Meaning of Moral Behavior

The terms "moral" and "immoral" are so loosely used that their true significance is often overlooked or ignored. Therefore, before any attempt is made to discuss moral development, it is necessary to understand the meaning of these labels. The definitions given in Box 14–1 are the ones which will be used in this discussion.

Children cannot be expected to know all the mores of the group nor can they be expected to behave in a truly moral way. By the time children reach adolescence, however, the members of the social group expect them to behave in accordance with the mores of the group. When they fail to do so it is generally because they do not want to rather than because of ignorance of group expectations (77, 78).

Behavior which may be called "true morality" not only conforms to social standards but also is carried out voluntarily. It comes with the transition from *external* to *internal authority* and consists of conduct regulated from within. It is accompanied by a feeling of personal responsibility for one's acts. It involves giv-

---

BOX 14–1

MEANING OF MORAL BEHAVIOR

MORAL BEHAVIOR
Moral behavior means behavior in conformity with the moral code of the social group. "Moral" comes from the Latin word *mores,* meaning manners, customs, and folkways. Moral behavior is controlled by moral concepts—the rules of behavior to which the members of a culture have become accustomed and which determine the expected behavior patterns of all group members.

IMMORAL BEHAVIOR
Immoral behavior is behavior that fails to conform to social expectations. Such behavior is not due to ignorance of social expectations but to disapproval of social standards or to lack of feeling of obligation to conform.

UNMORAL BEHAVIOR
Unmoral or nonmoral behavior is due to ignorance of what the social group expects rather than intentional violation of the group's standards. Some of the misbehavior of young children is unmoral rather than immoral.

ing primary consideration to the welfare of the group while relegating personal desires or gains to a position of secondary importance. True morality is rarely found in children, but it should appear during the adolescent years.

Moral development has both an *intellectual* and an *impulsive* aspect. Children must learn what is right and what is wrong. Then, as soon as they are old enough, they must be given explanations of why this is right and that is wrong. They must also have opportunities to take part in group activities so that they can learn what the group expects. Even more important, they must develop a desire to do what is right, to act for the common good, and to avoid wrong. This can be accomplished most successfully by associating pleasant reactions with what is right and unpleasant reactions with what is wrong. To ensure willingness to act in a socially desirable way, children must receive the approval of the group.

How Morality Is Learned

At birth, no child has a conscience or a scale of values. Consequently, every newborn infant may be regarded as unmoral or nonmoral. And, no child can be expected to develop a moral code alone. Instead, every child must be taught the group's standards of right and wrong.

Learning to behave in a socially approved manner is a long, slow process which extends into adolescence. It is one of the important developmental tasks of childhood. Before children enter school, they are expected to be able to distinguish right from wrong in simple situations and to lay the foundations for the development of a conscience. Before childhood is over, children are expected to develop a scale of values and a conscience to guide them when they must make a moral decision (35).

Sooner or later, most children learn that it is to their personal advantage to conform to group mores, even though they may not always agree with them. Some children, by contrast, are what has been called "socially stupid" because they violate the mores of the group either because they disapprove of them or because they feel they have the right to do as they please—that they are "above the law." But society does not condone violations of its mores. Such children pay the penalty in the form of social rejection—a

penalty that is far more harmful to their egos than the temporary pleasure they receive from disregarding the social mores.

In learning to be moral, there are four essential elements: learning what the social group expects of its members as spelled out in laws, customs, and rules; developing a conscience; learning to experience guilt and shame when the individual's behavior fails to conform to the expectations of the group; and having opportunities for social interactions to learn what members of the group expect. The role played by each of these essentials is described below (19, 25, 97).

Roles of Laws, Customs, and Rules in Moral Development

The first essential in learning to be a moral person is learning what the social group expects of its members. These expectations are spelled out for all group members in the form of laws, customs, and rules. In every social group, certain acts are considered either "right" or "wrong" because they further or are believed to further or hinder the welfare of the group members. The most important mores are incorporated into *laws,* with specific penalties for breaking them. Others, which are just as binding as the laws themselves, persist as *customs,* without specific penalties for breaking them.

Taking the material possessions of others, for example, is considered serious enough to hinder the welfare of the group. It is therefore a legal offense and has prescribed penalties attached to it. It is also customary not to handle the possessions of another without the owner's knowledge and consent. While violation of this custom will incur no legal action, social disapproval will be the penalty should there be any damage.

Lawmakers set the pattern of the moral behavior for the members of the social group. Parents, teachers, and others who are responsible for the guidance of children must help them learn to conform to the approved pattern. This they do by setting up *rules*—prescribed patterns for conduct—as guidelines.

Rules differ from laws in certain important ways. *First,* they are set by those who are responsible for the child's care; laws are set by the elected or appointed lawmakers of a state or country. *Second*, laws have set penalties for their infringement; breaking a rule is punished according to the wish or the whim of the person in charge of the child. *Third,* when people learn the laws, they also learn specific punishments for breaking each law. Few children are aware of the fact that they will be punished if they break a rule until they actually break it, nor do they know what, specifically, the punishment will be until they receive it. *Fourth,* the severity of the punishment for breaking a law varies with the seriousness of the act. When a rule is broken, the severity of the punishment varies according to how the person who inflicts the punishment feels at the time. The severity of the punishment is often totally unrelated to the seriousness of the act. *Fifth,* laws are more uniform and consistent than rules. A law is the same for all members of a state, a city, or a nation; rules often vary within a group. In the home, for example, there may be different rules for boys and girls and for younger and older children. In the school, one teacher may set quite different rules than another teacher. Even in the play group, rules for games and sports may differ, depending on the leaders and on the wishes of the members of the play group (23, 24, 64).

Young children are not expected to conform to laws and customs to the same extent that older children are. However, after they reach the school age, they are gradually taught the laws that apply to their lives—not taking things from stores, damaging the property of others, etc., and the customs of the social group with which they are identified—not taking things or even examining them without the knowledge and consent of the owners, showing politeness and deference toward older people, helping those who are handicapped, etc.

On the other hand, even young children are expected to learn and abide by rules set by parents and others in authority. When they reach school age, they are expected to learn and abide by the rules of the school and of the playground. As soon as they begin to play cooperatively with age-mates, they are expected to learn and to abide by the rules for different types of games, whether marbles, ball games, or running games.

Gradually, children learn the rules set by the different groups with which they are identified—in the home, the school, and the neighborhood. This forms the basis of their knowledge of what the different groups expect of them. They also learn that they are expected to conform to these rules and that failure to do so will result in punishment or lack of social acceptance. Thus, rules serve as guidelines for children's behavior and as sources of motivation to conform to social expectations just as laws and customs do for adolescents and adults.

Role of Conscience in Moral Development

The second essential in learning to be a moral person is the development of a conscience to act as an internal control over the individual's behavior. According to tradition, children are born with a "conscience," or the ability to *know* what is right or wrong. In keeping with this tradition is the belief that misbehavior is the result of some inherited weakness, the origin of which is ascribed to either the mother's or the father's side of the family. Those who hold to such beliefs maintain that children cannot be reformed; as a result, they see little need of devoting time and effort to moral training. The justification for corporal punishment was founded on the belief that such punishment would "drive out the devil" and thus make the "naturally bad" child into a good one.

Today it is widely accepted that no child is born with a conscience and that every child must not only learn what is right and wrong but must also use the conscience as a control over behavior. This is regarded as one of the important developmental tasks of the childhood years (37, 38, 48).

Conscience has been explained as a conditioned anxiety response to certain situations and actions that has been developed by associating aggressive acts with punishment. It has been called by such names as "inner light," "superego," and "internalized policeman" (18, 36). In the role of an internalized policeman, conscience ceaselessly keeps an eye on the individual's activities and "gives him a sharp tweak whenever he deviates from the straight and narrow path of duty" (18). The "voice of conscience" is not some kind of *deus ex machina* that has been implanted in some mysterious way in a human being; it is an internal standard which controls the individual's behavior (18).

Acquiring an internalized standard of conduct is too complex for young children. Consequently, their behavior must be controlled mainly by environmental restrictions. There is a gradual shift, however, from environmental to internalized controls. By the time children approach adolescence, the "internalized policeman" should have taken over much of the control of children's behavior. By the time children reach legal maturity, the transition should be complete, though this is by no means always true.

Roles of Guilt and Shame in Moral Development

The third essential in learning to be a moral person is the development of feelings of guilt and shame. After children develop a conscience, they carry it with them and use it as a guideline for their behavior. If their behavior does not come up to the standard set by their conscience, they feel guilty, ashamed, or both.

Guilt has been explained as a "special kind of negative self-evaluation which occurs when an individual acknowledges that his behavior is at variance with a given moral value to which he feels obligated to conform" (18). Children who feel guilty about what they have done have acknowledged to themselves that their behavior has fallen below the standards they have set for themselves.

Before guilt is experienced, however, four conditions must exist. *First,* children must accept certain standards of right and wrong or of "good" and "bad" as their own. *Second,* they must accept the obligation of regulating their behavior to conform to the standards they have adopted. *Third,* they must feel accountable for any lapses from these standards and acknowledge that they, not someone else, are to blame for these lapses. And, *fourth,* they must possess sufficient self-critical ability to recognize that a discrepancy has occurred between their behavior and their internalized standards of behavior (37, 70).

Shame has been defined as an "unpleasant emotional reaction of an individual to an actual or presumed negative judgment of himself by others resulting in self-depreciation vis-a-vis the group" (3). It can be nonmoral, as when a person commits a breach of propriety and is embarrassed, or moral, as when a person is unfavorably judged by others because of behavior that has fallen below their moral standards. *Shame relies on external sanctions alone, though it may be accompanied by guilt. Guilt relies on both internal and external sanctions.*

In true morality, guilt must be present. The person must conform to the mores of the group through inner-directed standards rather than outer-directed standards. As Ausubel has explained, "Guilt is one of the most important psychological mechanisms through which an individual becomes socialized in the ways of his culture. It is also an important instrument for cultural survival since it constitutes a most efficient watchdog within each individual, serving to keep his behavior compatible with the moral values of the society in which he lives" (3). If children felt no guilt, they would have little motivation to learn what the social group expected of them or to conform to these expectations.

Role of Social Interactions in Moral Development

The fourth essential in learning to be a moral person is having opportunities for interactions with members of the social group. Social interactions play an important role in moral development: *first,* by providing children with standards of socially approved behavior and, *second,* by providing them with a source of motivation, through social approval and disapproval, to conform to these standards. Without interaction with others, children would not know what socially approved behavior is nor would they have a source of motivation to behave in any way except as they wished.

Early social interactions occur within the family group. Children learn from parents, siblings, and other family members what this social group regards as right and wrong. From social disapproval or punishment for wrong behavior and from social approval or rewards for right behavior, children derive the necessary motivation to conform to standards of behavior prescribed by the family members.

As their social horizons broaden to include the neighborhood and school, children discover, in their play with peers and from communicating with them, that some of the standards of behavior they learned in the home are similar to those held by their peers and others are different. They may, for example, discover that tattling to parents about the behavior of siblings was not only acceptable but even approved by parents, but in the peer group it is strongly disapproved.

As social interactions with peers increase, so does peer influence. When there is a discrepancy between the moral standards of the home and those of the peer group, children often accept the standards of the peer group and reject those of the family group.

When children go to school, they discover that their conduct is controlled by school rules. Failure to conform to these rules brings punishment and teacher disapproval though it may, and sometimes does, bring peer approval. Cheating, for example, always brings teacher disapproval and some form of punishment. On the other hand, if it is "the thing to do," especially if it helps a classmate in a predicament, cheating is more likely to win peer approval than disapproval. Because peer approval is more important to most children than teacher approval, children meet the discrepancy between school rules and peer standards by conforming to the latter.

Through social interactions, children not only have an opportunity to learn moral codes, but they also have an opportunity to learn how others evaluate their behavior. If the evaluations are favorable, this will provide children with strong motivation to conform to the moral standards that have brought favorable social evaluations. If, on the other hand, the evaluations are unfavorable, children will change their moral standards and accept those which will guarantee the approval and acceptance they crave.

When children are well accepted by their peers, their chances for social interaction are greatly increased. This provides opportunities for learning moral codes and the motivation to conform to these codes. By contrast, children who are marginally accepted or rejected and neglected by the peer group are deprived of opportunities to learn the group's moral code and are frequently regarded as morally immature. Even though they may have a strong motivation to win social approval, they often fail to do so because, not knowing the moral code of the group, they continue to conform to the moral code approved in the home—a code that may conflict sharply with the group's code. They will be judged as "morally immature" and, like all immaturity of behavior, moral immaturity is a great handicap to social acceptance (50, 53, 73).

Because of the strong influence of the social group on children's moral development, it is important that the social group with which children are identified have moral standards that conform to those of the larger social group of the community. If, for example, the major play interests of a children's gang consist of "stirring up some excitement" by antisocial behavior, such as annoying neighbors or destroying their property in retaliation for their reporting the gang's activities to the parents of the gang members or to the police, the child who accepts the moral code of such a gang may readily develop into a juvenile delinquent.

By contrast, children whose social interactions are with other children whose moral codes conform to those of the home, the school, and the community at large will be laying foundations for moral behavior that will lead to good personal and social adjustments as they grow older. That is why, as was stressed earlier in the discussion of the influence of the peer group on the socialization of the child, the type of companions a child has is far more important than the number.

Pattern of Moral Development

Moral development is dependent upon intellectual development. It occurs in predictable stages related to stages in intellectual development. As children's abilities to perceive and understand change, children move on to a higher level of moral development. While the order in which these stages in moral development occur is constant, the ages at which children reach these stages differ according to the level of their intellectual development (19, 78).

By the time intellectual development reaches its mature level, moral development should also reach its mature level. When this does not happen, the individual is regarded as "morally immature"—a person who is intellectually capable of mature moral behavior but whose moral behavior is on the level of that of a child.

Of the many attempts to show how children's moral development is related to and dependent upon their intellectual development, the two most comprehensive studies are those of Piaget and Kohlberg. Both have shown, from studies of children of different ages, how moral development, in ability to make moral judgments and in behavior that conforms to approved social standards, follows a predictable pattern related to the sequence of stages in intellectual development.

Piaget's Stages in Moral Development

According to Piaget, moral development occurs in two clearcut stages. The first stage Piaget has called the "stage of moral realism" or "morality by constraint." The second stage he called the "stage of autonomous morality" or "morality by cooperation or reciprocity."

In the first stage, children's behavior is characterized by automatic obedience to rules without reasoning or judgment. They regard parents and all adults in authority as omnipotent and follow the rules laid down by them without questioning their justice. In this stage of moral development, children judge acts as "right" or "wrong" in terms of their consequences rather than in terms of the motivations behind them. They totally disregard the intentionality of the act. An act, for example, is regarded as "wrong" because it results in punishment either from other human beings or from natural or supernatural forces.

In the second stage of moral development, children judge behavior in terms of its underlying intent. This stage usually begins between 7 or 8 years of age and extends until children are 12 years old and older. Between the ages of 5 and 7 or 8 years, children's concepts of justice begin to change. The rigid and inflexible notions of right and wrong, learned from parents, are gradually modified. As a result, children begin to take into consideration the specific circumstances related to moral violations. To a 5-year-old, for example, lying is always "bad," but an older child recognizes that lying is justified in some situations and is not, therefore, necessarily "bad."

This second stage in moral development coincides with Piaget's "stage of formal operations" in cognitive development, when children are capable of considering all possible ways of solving a particular problem and can reason on the basis of hypotheses and propositions. This enables children to look at their problems from different points of view and to take many factors into consideration in solving them (72, 73, 74).

Kohlberg's Stages in Moral Development

Kohlberg has extended Piaget's research and has elaborated on Piaget's theory to include three levels of moral development instead of Piaget's two. Each of Kohlberg's three levels includes two stages.

In Level 1, "Preconventional Morality," the child's behavior is subject to external controls. In the first stage of this level, the child is obedience- and punishment-oriented and the morality of an act is judged in terms of its physical consequences. In the second stage of this level, children conform to social expectations to gain rewards. There is some evidence of reciprocity and sharing, but it is based on bartering rather than on a real sense of justice.

Level 2 is "Conventional Morality" or morality of conventional rules and conformity. In the first stage of this level, "Good Boy Morality," the child conforms to rules to win the approval of others and to maintain good relations with them. In the second stage of this level, children believe that if the social group accepts rules as appropriate for all group members, they should conform to them to avoid social disapproval and censure.

Level 3 Kohlberg has labeled "Postconventional morality," or morality of self-accepted principles. In the first stage of this level, the child believes that there should be a flexibility in moral beliefs that make it possible to modify and change moral standards if this will prove to be advantageous to group members as a whole. In the second stage of this level, people con-

form to both social standards and to internalized ideals to avoid self-condemnation rather than to avoid social censure. It is a morality based on respect for others rather than on personal desires (25, 52, 55).

Phases of Moral Development

If true morality is to be attained, moral development must take place in two distinct phases: *first,* the development of moral behavior, and *second,* the development of moral concepts. Moral knowledge does not guarantee moral conduct because behavior is motivated by factors other than knowledge. Social pressures, how children feel about themselves, how they are treated by family members and peers, desires at the moment, and many other factors influence how children will behave when a choice must be made. Studies of honesty, for example, have revealed correlations of approximately .25 between moral knowledge and moral conduct, suggesting that more often than not children do not conform to the standards they have accepted for their behavior (47).

DEVELOPMENT OF MORAL BEHAVIOR Children can learn to behave in a socially approved manner through trial and error, through direct teaching, or through identification. Of the three, direct teaching and identification are not only the best methods but also the most widely used (37, 63, 79). How each of these methods contributes to the development of moral behavior is explained in Box 14–2.

DEVELOPMENT OF MORAL CONCEPTS The second phase of moral development consists of the learning of moral concepts, or the principles of right and wrong, in an abstract, verbal form. This, of course, is too advanced for a young child. Training in moral principles must therefore wait until the child has the mental capacity to generalize and to transfer a principle of conduct from one situation to another.

Studies of concept development have revealed that moral concepts are at first specific and relate to the specific situations in which they were learned. As the child's capacity for comprehending relationships increases, concepts of right and wrong in different though related situations merge. As a result, general concepts are gradually learned as the child becomes able to recognize a common element in a variety of situations.

Because preschool children are incapable of abstract thinking, they define "good behavior" in terms

METHODS OF LEARNING MORAL BEHAVIOR

TRIAL-AND-ERROR LEARNING

When children learn to behave in a socially approved way by trial and error, they do so by trying out one pattern of behavior to see if it conforms to social standards and wins social approval for them. If it does not, they try out another method and still another until, eventually, more by chance than by plan, they hit upon a method that gives the desired results. This method is time- and energy-consuming and the end results are often far from satisfactory.

DIRECT TEACHING

In learning to behave in a socially approved manner, children must first learn to make correct specific responses in specific situations. This they do by conforming to the rules set down by parents and others in authority. If the objective aspects of different situations are similar, children transfer the patterns of behavior they have learned in one situation to other similar situations. When, on the other hand, these objective aspects are different, children will fail to see how what they learned in one situation applies to another situation.

IDENTIFICATION

When children identify with people they admire, they imitate the patterns of behavior they observe in these people, usually unconsciously and without pressure from them. Identification as a source of learning moral behavior becomes increasingly important as children grow older and rebel against discipline in the home and school. Having someone to identify with fills the gap and provides the anchorage necessary to the development of moral behavior.

by the time children reach adolescence, their moral codes are fairly well formed, though they are still subject to change if they are subjected to strong social pressures. When changes do occur, they usually involve a shift in emphasis. This shift is generally in the direction of conventional morality or the morality of the adult social group (4, 40, 78, 91, 97).

Meaning of Discipline

The popular concept of "discipline" is synonymous with "punishment." According to this concept, discipline is used only when the child violates the rules and regulations set down by parents, teachers, or adults in charge of the affairs of the community in which the child lives.

Discipline comes from the same word as "disciple"—one who learns from or voluntarily follows a leader. The parents and teachers are the leaders, and the child is the disciple who learns from them the ways of life that lead to usefulness and happiness. Discipline is thus society's way of teaching the child the moral behavior approved by the group (37).

The goal of all discipline is to mold behavior so that it will conform to the roles prescribed by the cultural group with which the individual is identified. As there is no single cultural pattern, there is no overall philosophy of child training to influence the disciplinary methods used. Thus the specific methods used within a cultural group vary widely, even though they all have the same objective—to teach children how to behave in a way that conforms to the standards of the social group with which they are identified.

of specific acts, such as "obeying mother" or "helping others" and "bad behavior" in terms of not doing these things. By the time children are 8 or 9 years old, their concepts become more generalized. They realize, for example, that "stealing is wrong" rather than that it is "wrong to steal a ball."

Generalized moral concepts which reflect social values are known as "moral values." The moral values of children are not static. Instead, they tend to change as children's social horizons broaden, and as they associate with more people and with people whose values differ from those they have learned at home. However,

Social Attitudes toward Discipline

Discipline has always been regarded as essential to the child's development, but ideas about what constitutes good discipline have undergone many changes. In the American culture, the strict, authoritarian discipline of earlier centuries, which was based on social customs and religious principles, has been replaced, in recent decades, by more lenient and, sometimes, even laissez-faire attitudes.

Bakwin and Bakwin have given the following reasons for changes in social attitudes toward discipline: the loss of influence of formal religion; the popularity of psychoanalysis with its emphasis on the dire effects of frustration and inhibition; the centering of attention on emotional development rather than spiritual development; the false doctrine that mistakes in child training register themselves permanently in the child's psyche; the consequent loss of parental self-confidence and, with it, authority; and a clearer but as yet incomplete understanding of the principles underlying child rearing. Furthermore, many parents are unwilling to make the effort necessary for proper discipline. They often fear that discipline will bring on resentments which will make their relationship with the older child difficult and unpleasant (4).

In recent years there has been a growing belief that wrong behavior is the result of the child's training rather than of innate sinfulness. This transition has led to the development of two conflicting views of discipline. As Spock has explained: "Some people believe that there are only two ways to raise children: with overpermissiveness, which produces brats, or with sternness and punishment, which makes good citizens. Neither of these extremes works well" (88).

These conflicting concepts of discipline are usually referred to as "negative" and "positive." According to the *negative* concept, discipline means control by external authority, usually arbitrarily applied. It is a form of restraint through distasteful or painful means. This is synonymous with punishment. Punishment does not, however, always weaken the individual's tendencies to act in a socially disapproved manner, nor does it guarantee that the abandoned activity will be replaced by more acceptable behavior.

The *positive* concept of discipline is synonymous with education and counseling in that it emphasizes *inner* growth—self-discipline and self-control. This, in turn, leads to motivation from within. Negative discipline forces immaturity on the individual, while positive discipline encourages maturity. Since the principal function of discipline is to teach the acceptance of needful restraint and to help direct the child's energies into useful and socially acceptable channels, positive discipline will achieve this end more successfully than negative discipline.

Need for Discipline

It has always been believed that children need discipline, but there have been changes in attitudes about why they need it. In the past, it was believed that discipline was necessary to ensure that children would adhere to the standards that society established and would tolerate no deviations from. Today it is recognized that children need discipline if they are to be happy, well-adjusted people. It is through discipline that they learn to behave in a socially approved way and, as a result, win the acceptance of members of the social group.

Discipline is essential to children's development because it fills certain of their needs. By so doing, it adds to their happiness and to their personal and social adjustments. Some of the many needs filled by discipline are explained in Box 14–3 (16, 30, 75).

In spite of the fact that all children need discipline, there are variations in their needs. There are many conditions that affect children's needs for discipline, six of which have been found to be especially important.

First, because there are variations in the rate of development for different children, all children of the same age could not be expected to have the same need for discipline nor could they be expected to need the same type of discipline. Discipline that is appropriate for one child may not be appropriate for another child of the same age. A few kind words, for example, may teach one child not to play with matches while another child of the same age may not understand the

---

BOX 14–3

SOME CHILDHOOD NEEDS FULFILLED BY DISCIPLINE

- Discipline gives children a feeling of security by telling them what they may and may not do.
- By helping children to avoid frequent feelings of guilt and shame for misbehavior—feelings that inevitably lead to unhappiness and poor adjustment—discipline enables children to live according to standards approved by the social group and, thus, to win social approval.
- Through discipline, children learn to behave in a way that leads to praise that they interpret as indications of love and acceptance—essentials to successful adjustment and happiness.
- Developmentally appropriate discipline serves as an ego-bolstering motivation which encourages children to accomplish what is required of them.
- Discipline helps children to develop a conscience—the "internalized voice" that guides them in making their own decisions and controlling their own behavior.

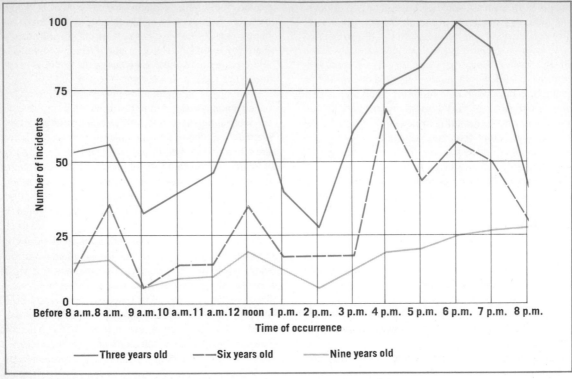

Figure 14–1 Frequency of discipline by the hour of occurrence and age of the child. (*Adapted from E. Clifford: Discipline in the home: A controlled observational study of parental practices.* Journal of Genetic Psychology, *1959, 95, 45–82. Used by permission.*)

words used in the prohibition and may need a tap on the fingers to make the prohibition meaningful.

Second, the need for discipline varies according to the time of day. Figure 14–1 shows when discipline is most often needed for children of different ages (11). Note that the peaks usually come at times when children are most likely to be tired.

Third, the activity in which children are engaged affects their need for discipline. Discipline is most likely to be needed in connection with routine activities, such as eating, going to bed, or preparing for school and is least likely to be needed when children are free to play as they choose. When, for example, children resist going to bed or dawdle over a meal, there is more need for discipline than there is when they are reading or playing with toys.

Fourth, the need for discipline varies with different

days of the week. Mondays and weekends are the times when discipline is most often needed.

Fifth, discipline is more often needed in large than in small families. The more children there are in the family, the less attention and supervision each can get from the parents, and the more likely there is to be sibling jealousy and animosity which leads to quarreling and other forms of troublesome behavior.

Sixth, the need for discipline varies with age. Older children need discipline less often than do younger children. As children grow older, they can communicate better and thus understand what is expected of them. Older children also need a different kind of discipline than do younger children. Instead of merely being told what to do and what not to do, older children need an explanation of why certain forms of behavior are acceptable and others are not. Explanations help to broaden their moral concepts and motivate them to do what is expected of them (4, 11, 37, 67).

Essentials in Discipline

If discipline is to fulfill its function of teaching children to conform to the standards of behavior set by the social group with which they are identified, it has four essential elements, whatever the disciplinary technique used. These are: rules as guidelines for behavior, consistency in those rules and in the techniques used to teach and enforce them, punishment for willful breaking of the rules, and rewards for attempts to model behavior along the approved lines (56).

Omission of any of these essentials will result in unfavorable attitudes on the part of the child and in behavior that will not conform to social standards and expectations. If, for example, children feel that they have been unfairly punished or if their efforts to conform to social expectations have not been appreciated by those in authority, it will weaken their motivation to try to live up to social expectations.

Because each of these four essentials plays an important role in moral development during the childhood years, they will be discussed separately. In each discussion, an attempt will be made to explain their roles in moral development and how they contribute to children's moral behavior.

Rules

The first essential of discipline is rules. Rules, as was explained earlier, are prescribed patterns for conduct. These prescribed patterns may be set by parents, teachers, or playmates. Their purpose is to supply children with guidelines for approved behavior in *that particular situation*. In the case of school rules, for example, they tell children what they must and must not do while in the schoolroom, the school corridors, the school lunchroom, the washrooms, or on the school playground. They do not, on the other hand, tell children what they must not do at home, in the neighborhood, or in a play group that is unsupervised by teachers.

Similarly, home rules tell children what they must and must not do in the home or in their relationships with family members—they must not take their siblings' possessions, must not "talk back" to their

parents, and must not fail to carry their load of family chores, such as helping with setting the table or cleaning their rooms. Playground rules are mainly concentrated on games and sports, though they also relate to group conduct, such as not tattling to parents or teachers about other group members.

FUNCTIONS OF RULES   Rules serve two very important functions in helping children to become moral people. *First,* they have an educational value. They acquaint children with what is regarded as acceptable behavior by members of that group. Children, for example, learn from rules about giving and getting help in their schoolwork—that submitting their own work is the only acceptable method the school has of judging their achievements.

Second, rules help to restrain undesirable behavior. If it is a family rule that no child may take the toys or other possessions of brothers and sisters without their knowledge and consent, children soon learn that this is regarded as unacceptable behavior because they are criticized or punished if they engage in this forbidden act.

If rules are to serve these two important functions, they must be understood, remembered, and accepted by the child. When rules are given in words that children do not *understand* or only partially understand, they are valueless as guidelines for behavior, and they fail to restrain undesirable behavior. When, for example, a child is told not to take "Mary's toys" without gaining Mary's permission, the child may not understand that this rule holds true for all children in the family or the school group, not for Mary alone. Or, the child may not understand that the rule about not playing on the street means any street, not just the street in front of the family house.

Even when children understand a rule, they may not remember it. When, for example, they are told the rule while busily engaged in some play activity, they may not pay enough attention to the rule to enable them to *remember* it several hours or days later.

Or, they may not *accept* the rule as a guide to their own behavior. They may feel that it relates only to another child, as when the teacher tells a child who turns in a perfect arithmetic assignment that in the future parents must not help the child. Or they feel that the rule is unfair and, consequently, they will not accept it. Why, they may argue, should they not get help from their parents when they have difficulty in understanding how to do some of their arithmetic problems, especially when the teacher is too busy to help them? (40, 83)

NUMBER OF RULES   How many rules there will be as guidelines for the child's behavior will vary according to the situation in which the rules are used, the age of the child, the attitude of the disciplinarian, the type of disciplinary technique used, and many other factors. In general, there are more rules in a school situation than in a home or play situation, but this is by no means always true.

Because a school group is larger than a family group, rules are essential to prevent the school situation from becoming chaotic. However, in a large family, more rules are needed than in a small one, just as is true of a large play group as compared with a small play group. It is the *size of the group,* rather than the situation per se, that determines how many rules will be needed to allow every member of the group to function successfully.

When the *disciplinary technique* is authoritarian, there will be more rules than when the technique is democratic. When the technique is permissive, the rules will be fewest. This holds true for school and home situations and for play situations when the leader is "bossy." If the *person in charge of the situation,* whether parent, teacher, or play leader, feels that rules are essential to curb unsocial behavior and to foster social behavior, more rules will be used than if the person in charge believed that control should come from the children themselves rather than from imposed rules.

The number of rules also varies according to the *activities* children are engaging in. In the home, for example, there are more rules for outdoor play than for television watching. In the school, there are more rules for schoolroom activities than for activities during the recess period. And, in a play group, there are more rules for games and sports than for creative or constructive play.

In general, more rules are needed for *young children* then for older children. As children approach adolescence, it is assumed that they have learned what the social group expects of them and that, consequently, rules as guidelines to behavior are no longer needed. However, since many children—as well as adolescents and adults—would be likely to slip quickly into undesirable behavior without rules, rules continue to serve as restraints on undesirable behavior—the second major function of rules (23, 67, 83).

EVALUATION OF RULES   Rules serve as the basis for moral concepts, and moral concepts, in turn, serve as the basis for a moral code. From rules, children learn what the social group regards as right and wrong. At first, this knowledge serves as the basis for specific moral concepts, related to specific behavior in the home, the school, or the play group.

Gradually, as children's intellectual abilities increase, they begin to see similar elements in the different specific concepts they have learned. And, as was pointed out earlier, these specific concepts are associated and become general moral concepts or moral values.

It is from the general moral concepts or moral values that children develop a moral code. They learn, for example, that taking things that belong to others is wrong in every situation—in the home, the school, or the play group. They learn that it is wrong to lie or intentionally deceive others no matter what the reason for their deceit. Stealing from others and lying thus become a part of the forbidden behavior in their moral codes.

The more similar the rules for different situations, the easier it will be for children to learn general moral concepts and, in turn, moral codes. When, on the other hand, school rules differ markedly from home or playground rules, or when there are few rules in one situation and many in another, it slows down the learning of moral concepts and this, in turn, slows down the development of moral codes.

Punishment

The second essential of discipline is punishment. Punishment comes from the Latin verb, *punire,* and means to impose a penalty on a person for a fault, offense, or violation in retribution or retaliation. Although not specifically said, it implies that this fault, offense, or violation was intentional in the sense that the person knew that the act was wrong but intentionally carried it out.

In the case of young children, one cannot assume that they wilfully carry out a forbidden act unless there is evidence that they had already understood and learned the rules the social group—whether parents or teachers—had taught them. However, as children grow older, it is assumed that they have been taught what is right and what is wrong. Consequently, it is assumed that *any* misbehavior is intentional.

These assumptions are, by no means, always correct. Even if children know a rule, this is not foolproof evidence, as was pointed out in the discussion of rules, that they understand the complete meaning of the rule. Under such conditions, punishment for wrongdoing is justified only if it has an educational value. And by the time children comprehend the meaning of words well enough to understand rules, verbal explanations should replace punishment.

FUNCTIONS OF PUNISHMENT Punishment plays three important roles in the moral development of children. The *first* function is restrictive. Punishment deters the repetition of socially undesirable acts. When children discover that certain acts will lead to punishment, they are usually deterred from carrying out these acts by memories of the punishments they have received in the past for these acts. Its restrictive value is also important in young children who have not yet learned what is right and wrong. Should they engage in an act that might be harmful to them, to other people, or to material possessions, a slap on the offending hand will usually put an end to the acts.

The *second* function of punishment is educational. Before children can understand rules, they can learn that certain acts are right and others wrong by being punished while carrying out wrong acts and by failure to receive punishment when they carry out acts that are permitted. As children grow older, they learn rules mainly by verbal teaching. However, they also learn, from experience, that failure to comply with rules will inevitably result in punishment. This, therefore, reinforces the verbal teaching. Another educational aspect of punishment is often overlooked is the teaching of the relative wrongness of different wrong acts. Children's criteria of the seriousness of their offenses are the frequency and severity of the punishments they receive. If punishment is consistent, they will always be punished for a wrong act. The seriousness of the wrong act is learned by the severity of the punishment they receive for it.

Motivation to avoid socially disapproved behavior is the *third* function of punishment. Recognition of the possible consequences of a wrong act is essential to motivation to avoid this act. When children are intellectually able to weigh alternative acts and the consequences associated with each, they must learn to decide for themselves whether a wrong act is worth its price. If they decide it is not, they will be motivated to avoid this act (59, 61, 66, 92).

KINDS OF PUNISHMENT In the past, most people thought of punishment in terms of corporal punishment—inflicting pain by slapping, spanking, whipping, and beating. This was regarded as the only really effective way of preventing children's misbehavior from recurring. This belief was reinforced by the old saying, "Spare the rod and spoil the child."

That many parents and even teachers felt that corporal punishment of children was a duty and responsibility was shown by the fact that, before administering the punishment, they frequently informed the child, "This hurts me more than it hurts you." However, they believed that any other form of punishment was worthless and an indication that those in authority were too "soft" and "weak" to carry out their duties and responsibilities (61, 92).

In the post-World War II era, the pendulum swung in the opposite direction, with the popularization of the works of Freud and his followers and the teachings of Spock. American parents and teachers entered what is often referred to as the "era of permissiveness" or "Spockism"—an era that reached its peak during the fifties and sixties. During this time, other forms of punishment gained widespread popularity. These included isolating children from the social group when they misbehaved, depriving them of some accustomed privilege, such as watching a favorite TV program, frightening them by telling them "the policeman will get you," shaming, ignoring or threatening them with loss of parental love, making unfavorable comparisons with siblings or other children, nagging, and harping on the children's misdemeanors. Most of these forms of punishment, as is true of corporal punishment, are aimed at restricting childish misbehavior. Many are used for older children as well as for preschoolers (29, 34, 56).

During the seventies, it has become increasingly evident, with the increase in juvenile delinquency, terrorism in the schools, and with the breakdown in respect for those in authority and for law, that the pendulum may have swung too far. As a result of the Supreme Court decision, permitting corporal punishment in the schools under certain restricted conditions, it has become evident that there must be a reassessment of the kinds of punishment used in both the homes and the schools. As a result, corporal punishment is returning to favor (see Figure 14–2) though in milder forms than were formerly used. However, there are still cases where corporal punishment is so severe that the child is permanently injured or even killed.

"It's a new way of disciplining children . . . I just read about it."

Figure 14–2 Spanking as a form of punishment is coming back into style. (*Adapted George Clark: "The Neighbors." Chicago Tribune–New York News Syndicate, Dec. 11, 1972. Used by permission.*)

EVALUATION OF PUNISHMENT In evaluating different forms of punishment, two criteria must be used. *First,* is the punishment developmentally appropriate? For example, does the child understand why the punishment is being given or is the child intellectually too immature to see the relationship between the punishment and the misbehavior for which the punishment is being given? As children grow older, they gradually make more mature judgments about punishment and, as a result, realize that they are to blame for the punishment they receive (43).

Second, does the punishment fulfill the three purposes of discipline given above: educational, restrictive, and motivational? Does it, for example, tell children why an act is wrong or does it tell them that they are "naughty" children? If it implies, as so often happens in the case of corporal punishment, that big people have the right to hit little people, it will not serve the educational function that all punishment is supposed to serve, namely, telling children why certain acts are wrong and that, therefore, they must not be repeated. Instead, it educates children to believe

that they have the right to hit smaller children—a belief that encourages the development of bullies.

Equally important, if the punishment used makes children resentful and rebellious, they will lack the motivation to try to behave in a socially more desirable way. Instead, they will try to retaliate, even if it is done by projecting their anger and resentment on some innocent victim instead of on the person who punished them. Or it may encourage them to become sneaky and try to outwit the person who punished them.

Contrary to popular opinion, corporal punishment is one of the least satisfactory forms of punishment because children seldom associate the punishment with the act for which they are being punished. Since the anger of the adult is a more dominant factor in the situation than the punishable act itself, children tend to associate the disciplinarian with pain rather than the wrong deed.

Because of the potentially harmful psychological effects of corporal punishment, it is now recognized that it should be used sparingly, preferably not much after children are able to understand the reasons for rules. There are, however, three conditions under which corporal punishment serves a useful purpose. *First,* if there is no other way to communicate a prohibition to children that might result in their hurting themselves or someone else. *Second,* if the punishment can be given during the forbidden act so that children will associate the two and understand why the act is forbidden. If given after the act, its educational value may be lost and it will then build up resentments and other unfavorable attitudes. *Third,* if the severity of the corporal punishment is regulated according to the severity of the misdeed, it will have an educational value. Unfortunately, the severity of corporal punishment is usually determined by the anger and annoyance of the punisher rather than by the severity of the misdeed. Consequently, much of the educational value of the punishment is lost and unfavorable attitudes are fostered.

The most effective form of punishment has a direct relationship to the act. For that reason, scolding, depriving children of an accustomed privilege, isolating them from family members or playmates when the wrong act had nothing to do with them, or sending children to bed without supper are not as effective as the adults who use them expect them to be. They are easy to use, it is true, and require little if any ingenuity, but they do not serve the purpose as well as individualized punishment. They have a number of advantages, however, as compared with corporal punishment. *First,* no physical pain is involved; *second,* the duration and severity of the punishment can be varied; *third,* no long period of time elapses between the act and the punishment during which the child feels abused or can plan revenge on the disciplinarian; *fourth,* when the punishment is over, a favorable relationship can be established with the punisher; and, *fifth,* the punisher's personal feelings are not revealed as overtly as in corporal punishment.

Studies of the effects of punishment have established a number of essential elements of *good* punishment—punishment that teaches the child why society will not tolerate certain patterns of behavior but does not arouse resentments that kill the child's motivation to put the learning into practice. The major essentials of good punishment are shown in Box 14–4.

Rewards

The third essential in discipline is the use of rewards. The term "reward" means any form of appreciation for an attainment. It does not have to be in the form of a material possession. Instead, it can be a word of approval, a smile, or a pat on the back.

As the term suggests, rewards *follow* attainments. Consequently, they differ from bribes, which are promises of rewards used to induce an act. Bribes are, consequently, given *before* the act, rather than after the act, as in the case of rewards.

Many parents and teachers feel that rewards are unnecessary because children should behave in a socially approved way without having to be "paid" for it. Others feel that rewards will weaken children's motivation to do what they should do. Consequently, they use rewards far less frequently than punishments. This is especially true as children grow older.

FUNCTIONS OF REWARDS Rewards play three important roles in teaching children to behave in a socially approved way. *First,* they have an educational value. If an act is approved, children know that it is good. Just as punishment tells children that their behavior is bad, so rewards tell them that it is good. And, like punishment, if rewards are varied in intensity to conform to the degree of effort children put into their behavior to ensure that it will conform to socially approved standards, the educational value of rewards is increased.

Second, rewards serve as motivations to repeat socially approved behavior. Because children react fa-

---

BOX 14–4

ESSENTIALS OF GOOD PUNISHMENT

- Punishment must be suited to the transgression, and it must follow the transgression as soon as possible so that the child will associate the two. If a child throws food on the floor in a fit of temper, the child must be made to clean it up immediately.
- The punishment used must be consistent so that the child will know that whenever a rule is broken, punishment is inevitable.
- Whatever form of punishment is used, it should be impersonal so that the child will not interpret it as "meanness" on the part of the punisher.
- Punishment must be constructive so as to motivate socially approved behavior in the future.
- An explanation of the reason for the punishment must accompany the punishment so that the child will see it as fair and just.
- Punishment must lead to conscience-building to guarantee future inner control of behavior.
- Punishment must not humiliate the child and arouse resentments.

---

vorably to approval as expressed in rewards, they try to behave in the future in a manner that will bring more rewards. And, *third,* rewards serve to reinforce socially approved behavior, and absence of rewards weakens the desire to repeat this behavior. If children are to learn to behave in socially approved ways, it must be worth their while to do so. Therefore, rewards must be used to build up pleasant associations with the desired behavior.

Just because rewards play an important role in discipline does not mean that they can replace the role played by punishment. Both are essential elements in learning to behave in a socially approved way. The role played by rewards is primarily positive—motivating children to do what is considered desirable—while the role of punishment is primarily negative—deterring children from engaging in socially disapproved behavior.

KINDS OF REWARDS Whatever reward is used must be developmentally appropriate for children. Otherwise, it will lose its effectiveness. Before children are able to understand words, for example, praise is of little value unless it is accompanied by a smile, a hug, or some other nonverbal form of communication. When, on the other hand, these nonverbal forms of communication are used for older children, they are far less effective than words of praise.

Perhaps the simplest and yet most effective reward is *social recognition*. A comment such as, "You cleaned up your room very well. I couldn't do a better job than you did," can always be tied in with the act. At the same time it always satisfies children's normal desires for praise. However, to be most effective, praise must be used judiciously, not just when the adult happens to be in a pleasant mood. If it is to have an educational value, it must reflect the degree of social approval for the act rather than the mood of the person who gives the praise.

Gifts are sometimes given as rewards for good behavior. A gift may be a token of affection, it may represent a respect for the child's abilities and achievements, it may serve as a form of encouragement, or it may be a token of confidence. In any instance, gifts add to the child's feeling of self-importance.

A *special treat,* such as being permitted to stay up beyond the usual bedtime to see a TV program or going to a movie, is especially useful as a reward for older children. They appreciate the feeling that their efforts to conform to social expectations have resulted in social recognition in forms that suggest that they are being treated as grown-ups rather than as children. To younger children, a more tangible reward, in the form of a gift, is usually better understood than a special treat. Hence, its value as a source of motivation to continued good behavior is greater (51, 86).

EVALUATION OF REWARDS It is commonly believed that praising or rewarding children for good behavior will make them conceited, but it has been found that when positive techniques, in the form of praise, encouragement, or balanced criticism, are used in school, desirable responses outweigh the undesirable in the ratio of 46 to 1. Even children who at first seem recalcitrant later show desirable responses (47).

As children grow older, rewards serve as a powerful source of motivation for them to continue to try to live up to expectations. If their efforts go unnoticed or unappreciated, they have little motivation, and what motivation they may have is often dampened by criticism and nagging about what they have done wrong.

Throughout the childhood years, rewards have an important educational value. They tell children that their behavior conforms to social expectations and

they motivate children to repeat this socially approved behavior. They are thus reinforcement agents for good behavior (5, 12, 21, 31, 57).

Consistency

The fourth essential of discipline is consistency. Consistency means a degree of uniformity or stability. It is not the same as constancy, which implies that there is no change. Instead, it means a tendency toward sameness.

If discipline were constant, there would be no change to meet changing developmental needs. In the case of rewards, discussed above, the same rewards would be used for children of all ages regardless of whether some other form might be more effective as children grow older. Consistency, by contrast, makes it possible to meet changed developmental needs while, at the same time, retaining enough uniformity so that children will not be confused about what is expected of them.

Consistency must be characteristic of all areas of discipline. There must be consistency in the rules used as guidelines for behavior, in the way these rules are taught and enforced, in punishment given for nonconformity, and in rewards for conformity. If, for example, children are punished one day for an act that the next day goes unnoticed, they will not know what is right and what is wrong. If an act is rewarded one day and is not rewarded the next day, the reinforcement value of rewards will be lost. In no area is consistency more important than in rules. If the mother sets one rule for a specific act, the father another, and the grandmother or baby-sitter still another, how can any child be expected to learn what is right and what is wrong?

FUNCTION OF CONSISTENCY Consistency in discipline plays three important roles. *First,* it has great educational value. When rules are consistent, it speeds up the learning process. This is because of its reinforcement value. It is, for example, far easier for children to learn the rule, "You must never take anything belonging to someone else without getting permission first," if it is always true, than it would be if children were allowed to take a sibling's toy without the sibling's consent and then punished because they took money from the mother's pocketbook without asking if they might have it.

Second, consistency has a strong motivational value. Children who discover that rewards always follow approved behavior but punishments always follow forbidden behavior will have a far stronger desire to avoid forbidden acts and to engage in approved acts than they would have if they were uncertain about how these acts would be treated. If, for example, there was at least a 50–50 chance of not being punished for a forbidden act, they might feel that the chance was worth taking.

Third, consistency fosters respect for rules and for people in authority. Even young children have less respect for those who can be "persuaded" not to punish them for misbehavior than they have for those who are uninfluenced by tears and pleadings. See Figure 14–3. Older children who develop a strong feeling of fair play from peer contacts build up resentments toward those whom they regard as "unfair." With this resentment comes a waning of respect.

EVALUATION OF CONSISTENCY The important role consistency plays in discipline has been highlighted by studies of the effects of inconsistency. This matter will be discussed in detail in the section of this chapter that deals with hazards in moral development.

On the positive side, however, there are certain important values of consistency. It speeds up the learning process and, by so doing, helps children to learn rules and to combine these rules into a moral code. As a result, children who have been subjected to consistent moral training tend, as a whole, to be more morally mature than age-mates whose moral training has been inconsistent.

Knowing that the discipline received at home and in school will be consistent fosters in children a respect for parents and teachers. As a result, they will have far less reason to be resentful toward them because they feel they have been unfairly treated than will children who have been subjected to inconsistent discipline.

Most important of all, children who have had consistent discipline have a stronger motivation to behave according to socially approved standards than have those whose discipline has been inconsistent. They feel that it is to their personal advantage to behave in the approved way because the rewards for good behavior outweigh any temporary pleasure misbehavior might give them. As a result, they are far less likely to develop into juvenile delinquents and adult criminals than are those whose discipline has been inconsistent (51, 81, 82).

To emphasize how important consistency is to chil-

"Mommy says 'no' and Daddy says 'yes', Grandma. Will you break the tie?"

Figure 14–3 Inconsistent discipline encourages children to try to get their way by persuading others to comply with their wishes. (*Adapted from Bil Keane: "The Family Circus."* Register and Tribune Syndicate, *Feb. 11, 1975. Used by permission.*)

dren's moral development, Spock has explained the role of parents in providing consistent discipline for their children. As he has pointed out: "For the system to work well, the parents must have ideals of one kind or another. They have to know what they expect of their children and communicate this to them clearly"(88).

Techniques of Discipline

In the past, there was only one approved technique of discipline. Today that is called "authoritarian discipline." As the name implies, training children to behave in a socially approved way was the responsibility of those in authority—parents, teachers, and others who acted as caretakers for children.

With the swing away from the beliefs that "Mother knows best" and that to "spare the rod will spoil the child" came the era of permissiveness in discipline. During this era, a new technique of discipline was widely accepted. This has been labeled "permissive discipline."

As it gradually became apparent that neither the authoritarian nor the permissive techniques served the goals of making morally mature people, a third disciplinary technique has evolved, known as "democratic discipline." This embodies the good features of the earlier forms and omits many of the weaknesses or bad features of them.

Kinds of Disciplinary Techniques

A brief description of each of the three kinds of disciplinary techniques will serve to show what the characteristics of each are and will emphasize their good and bad features.

AUTHORITARIAN DISCIPLINARY TECHNIQUES Strict rules and regulations to enforce the desired behavior characterize all kinds of authoritarian discipline. Techniques include severe punishment for failure to come up to expected standards and little or no recognition, praise, or other signs of approval when the child meets the expected standards.

Authoritarian discipline may range from reasonable restraints on the child's behavior to *rigid* restraints that permit no freedom of action except that which conforms to prescribed standards. Authoritarian discipline always means control through *external* force in the form of punishment, especially corporal punishment.

Even as children grow older, parents who use rigid authoritarian control rarely relax their control or abandon corporal punishment. Furthermore, they do not encourage children to make decisions regarding their acts. Instead, they tell them what to do, but they do not tell them why they should do it. Thus, children are deprived of opportunities to learn how to control their own behavior.

In families where authoritarian discipline is more reasonable, children are still restricted in what they may do and decisions for their acts are made for them. Their wishes are not completely disregarded, however, and there are fewer irrational restrictions, such as forbidding children to do what their peers do.

PERMISSIVE DISCIPLINARY TECHNIQUES Permissive discipline is really little or no discipline. It does not usually guide the child into socially approved patterns of behavior and does not employ punishment. Some parents and teachers, mistaking permissiveness for *laissez faire,* allow children to grope through situations too difficult for them to cope with alone with no guidance or control.

For many parents, permissive discipline is a protest against the rigid and harsh discipline under which they were brought up. In such cases, children often have no limits or boundaries set on what they may do; they are permitted to make their own decisions and act on them in practically any way they wish.

DEMOCRATIC DISCIPLINARY TECHNIQUES Democratic methods of discipline employ explanation, discussion, and reasoning to help children understand why they are expected to behave in a certain way. They emphasize the educational aspect of discipline rather than the punitive.

When children are young, they are given explanations of the rules they are expected to conform to in words they can understand. For example, if there is a rule that they must not touch the kitchen stove, they are told it will hurt them or they are shown, by having their hands held close to the stove, what "hurt" means and why they must not touch the stove. As they grow older, they are not only given explanations of the rules but they are given opportunities to express their opinions about the rules. If, for example, the rules differ from those of their friends, parents give them an opportunity to explain why they feel they should not be expected to conform to rules their friends do not have to conform to. If their reasons seem valid, parents who use democratic discipline are usually willing to modify or change the rules.

Democratic discipline uses punishments and rewards, with more emphasis on rewards than on punishment. Punishment is never harsh and it usually takes forms other than corporal punishment. It is used only when there is evidence that children have *wilfully* refused to do what was expected of them. When children's behavior comes up to expected standards, the democratic disciplinarian rewards them with praise or some other expression of approval.

The fundamental philosophy behind democratic discipline is that it will teach children to develop control over their behavior so that they will do what is right even when there is no one standing over them to threaten them with punishment if they do what they are not supposed to do. This *internal* control over behavior comes from educating children to behave in an approved manner and by showing them the rewards for doing so.

As is true of authoritarian and permissive discipline, there are variations in democratic methods of discipline that range from extreme leniency and little control to careful planning of children's activities so that their energies are directed into approved channels and diverted from activities disapproved by members of the social group. There are variations also in the amount of explanation given and in the willingness of disciplinarians to hear children's points of view about rules and punishments and to modify them if children's reasons seem valid.

Reasons for Choice of Disciplinary Techniques

Parents and teachers usually have *reasons* for using the disciplinary technique they choose; the choice is rarely based on whim. Box 14–5 shows some of the chief factors that influence the choice of disciplinary techniques.

Since the choice of disciplinary techniques is based on reasons which parents and teachers consider valid, the chances of convincing them that the technique they have chosen is not as good as another are slim. They tend to cling to the chosen technique, though

---

BOX 14–5

FACTORS INFLUENCING CHOICE OF DISCIPLINARY TECHNIQUES

SIMILARITY TO DISCIPLINE USED BY PARENTS
If parents and teachers feel that their parents did a good job in training them, they use a similar technique in training the children they are responsible for; if they feel the technique their parents used was wrong, they usually swing to an opposite technique.

CONFORMITY TO GROUP-APPROVED TECHNIQUES
All parents and teachers, but especially those who are young and inexperienced, are more influenced by what members of their group consider the "best" techniques than by their own convictions about what is best.

AGE OF PARENTS OR TEACHERS
Young parents and teachers tend to be more democratic and permissive than those who are older. They tend to exercise less and less control as children approach adolescence.

TRAINING FOR PARENTHOOD OR TEACHING
Adults who have had courses in child care and are more understanding of children and their needs use more democratic techniques than adults who lack such training.

SEX OF DISCIPLINARIAN
Women generally have a better understanding of children and their needs than men, and they tend to be less authoritarian. This is true of parents and teachers as well as of other caretakers.

SOCIOECONOMIC STATUS
Lower- and middle-class parents and teachers tend to be stricter, more coercive, and less tolerant than those of the upper class, but they are more consistent. The better educated they are, the more they favor democratic discipline.

CONCEPT OF ADULT ROLE
Parents who hold to the traditional concept of the parental role tend to be more authoritarian than parents who have accepted a more modern concept. Teachers who believe there should be a rigid routine in the classroom use more authoritarian discipline than those who have a democratic concept of teaching.

SEX OF CHILD
Parents are generally stricter with their daughters than with their sons. Teachers, likewise, tend to be stricter with girls.

AGE OF CHILD
Authoritarian discipline is far more commonly used for young children than for those who are older. Regardless of what technique they favor, most parents and teachers feel that young children cannot understand explanations, so they concentrate on authoritarian control.

DISCIPLINARY SITUATION
Fears and anxieties are usually handled nonpunitively, while defiance of authority, negativism, and aggression are more likely to encourage authoritarian control.

---

they may modify it to some extent as they discover, from their own experiences, that it does not work as well as anticipated.

Evaluation of Disciplinary Techniques

Since different disciplinary techniques will, of necessity, have different effects on the behavior and personality pattern of the child, each of the major categories of disciplinary techniques will be evaluated separately, with an attempt to show their good and bad features.

Even though *authoritarian discipline* in its strictest form is more damaging to a child at certain times during the developmental pattern than at others, there is *no* time when it does not leave an unfavorable mark on the child's behavior or personality. Overly strict parents who use harsh and punitive methods to achieve their ends may make the child conform to their standards and be a "good" child. But while there is surface goodness, there is apt to be smoldering resentment which will break out sooner or later, causing children to do many things they otherwise would not have done.

The overdisciplined child feels that the world is hostile, and acts accordingly. Too much rebellion against

too strict discipline may eventually lead to delinquency.

If the child's resentments against overly strict discipline and harsh punishment lead to even harsher punishment, they may be "driven underground" and then find new channels of expression. They may be expressed in aggressiveness toward other children—especially younger siblings and members of minority groups—and a hypercritical attitude toward all in authority.

Regardless of the child's manner of expressing resentment, it is likely to lead to maladjustive behavior. As Davitz has stated, "Punishment and rejection give rise to fear; fear promotes defensive reactions; and the defensive reactions elicit further punishment. This is the vicious circle of maladjustment. The child lives in an interpersonal world of constant threat. The consequence is unhappiness and fear" (13). The "vicious circle" of punishment, which leads to maladjustive behavior, is illustrated in Figure 14–4.

In spite of the undesirable effects of very strict authoritarian discipline on the child's behavior, there is evidence that, in its less severe form, authoritarian discipline leads to socialization of the child. This is because children, subjected to strict control by parents or teachers, learn to behave in a socially approved way. As a result, they are more acceptable to their peers and to adults than are children who have been allowed to behave much as they please.

The child's personality is also unfavorably affected by overly strict discipline. Children who are outwardly quiet, well-behaved, and nonresistant often harbor deep resentments which make them unhappy and suspicious toward everyone they come in contact with, especially people in authority. In addition, they often learn to be sly, secretive, and dishonest to avoid punishment when they defy authority (87).

When parents inhibit their desire to use corporal punishment, they usually substitute "psychological punishment," such as withdrawal of love. This kind of punishment is extremely harsh and, if repeated too often, can have a devastating influence on the child's personality. Studies of psychiatric patients, for example, have revealed that they experienced more psychological than physical punishment during their childhood (15, 32, 88).

When children are trained by *permissive* disciplinary techniques, they tend to become confused and insecure. Because of limited experience and mental immaturity which makes it impossible for them to make de-

Figure 14–4 The "vicious circle" of punishment. (*Adapted from M. E. Breckenridge and E. L. Vincent:* Child development: Physical and psychological development through adolescence, *5th ed. Saunders, 1965. Used by permission.*)

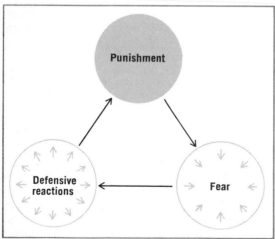

cisions about behavior which will conform to social expectations, they do not know what they should or should not do. As a result, they are likely to become fearful, anxious, and excessively aggressive. In addition, they are likely to become resentful because they feel that their parents care too little about them to take the trouble to guide them and thus help them to avoid mistakes. It is not unusual for such children to feel contempt for their parents' "softness."

The most serious effect of too lenient discipline comes from the reactions of people outside the home. In the school or neighborhood, the undisciplined child is soon labeled a "spoiled brat" or a "little monster"—neither label contributing to social acceptance.

Democratic discipline leads to good personal and social adjustments. It results in independence in thinking, initiative in action, and a healthy, positive, confident self-concept which is reflected in active, outgoing, and spontaneous behavior.

Greater freedom in the home, characteristic of democratic discipline, shows itself in better cooperation, greater persistence in the face of obstacles, better self-control, greater creativity, and a friendlier approach to people. In the school, teachers who have a warm, friendly, cooperative relationship with their pupils find that their pupils make better personal and social adjustments, are less troublesome, and do better schoolwork.

Unquestionably the most important contribution to children's personal and social adjustments made by democratic discipline is that it develops inner control. This gives children feelings of satisfaction to know that they are permitted to control their behavior and that they can do so in a way that will win social approval. Such children are far less likely to be plagued by feelings of guilt and shame than are those trained by authoritarian or permissive disciplinary techniques, and because their behavior usually conforms to social standards, they win social approval.

Evaluation of Discipline

Discipline should not be evaluated in terms of its immediate results. Nor should it be evaluated in terms of the child's moral behavior alone. Although a child can be forced into a pattern of adult-approved behavior and made into the "perfect child," the long-term effects on the child's attitudes toward discipline and

toward those in authority as well as on the child's personality may outweigh the temporary advantages.

Havighurst has warned that certain wholesome and unwholesome functions of discipline must be kept in mind when discipline is evaluated. Some of the major functions of discipline, both wholesome and unwholesome, as suggested by Havighurst, are given in Box 14–6 (35).

Criteria of Wholesome Discipline

There are three criteria that can be used in evaluating discipline. If the evaluation in each case is favorable, it suggests that the discipline used has fulfilled its functions and that the discipline may, as a result, be regarded as wholesome or "good."

The *first* criterion is the effect the discipline has on behavior. No one can expect a child, an adolescent, or an adult to behave in a socially approved manner at all times and in all situations. Discrepancies between moral knowledge and moral behavior are sometimes inevitable.

However, if children show a progressive improvement in their behavior as they grow older and if the discrepancies between moral knowledge and behavior become fewer and less serious with each passing year, there is justification for believing that children are gradually approaching the highest levels of moral behavior, as suggested by Piaget and Kohlberg, and that they are thus approaching moral maturity.

The *second* criterion that must be used in evaluating discipline is the effect the discipline has on children's attitudes toward those in authority and toward the discipline they have received. Children are sensitive to the fairness of parents, teachers, and others in authority. They become increasingly so as they grow older. If they consider the treatment they receive as "unfair," they become resentful and feel abused.

Whether the treatment is actually unfair or not is less important than the way children interpret it. Their grievances are important for two reasons: they affect children's attitudes toward people in authority and they affect children's willingness to try to conform to social expectations. Unfavorable repercussions from feelings of being unfairly treated are most likely to occur when children are kept from doing what members of the peer group are permitted to do.

On the other hand, children who feel that the discipline they receive is fair and that the restrictions placed on their behavior are for their own good have a far more favorable attitude toward the restrictions. They also have a more favorable attitude toward disciplinarians than children who feel that those in authority are "mean" or revengeful.

The *third* criterion in evaluating discipline is the effect of the discipline on the child's personality. If children feel that they have been unfairly restricted or unfairly punished, and if they feel that their efforts to conform to rules are unappreciated because they rarely receive any praise or other reward for their attempts to conform, it affects their self-concepts. When children believe that they have been the victims of unfair treatment, serious personality disturbances are likely to result.

Children, by contrast, who are disciplined fairly and consistently are well adjusted. They have a sense of freedom; their behavior is well integrated; and they have a realistic approach to life as well as a realistic concept of themselves. In addition, they develop feelings of adequacy and self-confidence (27, 30, 37, 80).

Hazards in Moral Development

With each passing year, reports from the Justice Department in Washington have indicated that the number of juvenile delinquents and adult criminals has been rising steadily. This information suggests that there is something seriously wrong with the moral development of children and adolescents.

Until the cause or causes of the rises in juvenile delinquency and adult criminality can be diagnosed, any attempt to reverse these trends will be futile. Consequently, attempts are being made by criminologists, sociologists, psychologists, and others to get to the root of the trouble in order to find ways to improve the moral development of children.

A number of suggestions about the causes have been made in the hopes of fixing the blame where it belongs. It has been suggested that the schools and colleges are to blame because they are too lenient and have been, until the recent Supreme Court decision, forbidden to use any form of corporal punishment on unruly pupils. Others have suggested that the lack of religious training in the home and in schools and the decline in church attendance are to blame. Still others have blamed the breakdown in family life and the increase in divorce, desertion, working mothers, and one-parent families for the trouble.

Perhaps the most unanimous suggestion about the cause of moral deterioration, as evidenced by the rise of different forms of delinquency and criminality, has centered on "permissiveness" or what is often referred to as "Spockism." Middle-aged and elderly people, when they compare the discipline they received as children with the discipline children today receive in the home and school, agree almost unanimously that this is where the real blame lies.

In the following pages, an attempt will be made to discuss the common hazards in the moral development of children today in the hopes of throwing some light on this serious social problem. It will become readily apparent that not one cause alone but many are responsible for the trouble, and that if improvements are to be made, they must be concentrated on improvements in disciplinary methods.

Belief That Discipline and Punishment Are Synonymous

As was pointed out earlier, many adults believe that discipline and punishment are synonymous. As a result, they believe that a good disciplinarian is one who uses punishment to deter misbehavior and to teach children what the social group will and will not tolerate.

Those who accept these beliefs logically believe the more unsocial the behavior, the harsher the punishment should be. They believe that the best way to teach children to behave in a socially approved way is to make socially disapproved behavior so unattractive that children will avoid it and turn their energies into socially approved behavior. They claim that only corporal punishment will achieve this goal.

There are two fallacies in these beliefs. *First,* studies of the effects of corporal punishment have shown, as was pointed out earlier, that instead of fostering the development of socially approved behavior, corporal punishment fosters the development of such unfavorable attitudes on the part of children that instead of improvements in their moral behavior it becomes increasingly immoral. There is little evidence that corporal punishment serves as a source of motivation to moral behavior.

The *second* fallacy is the belief that punishment can fulfill all the functions of discipline. This belief ignores the roles played by rules and rewards. It also ignores the fact that true morality comes from inner control of behavior rather than outer control. If children do not know what is right and wrong, if they are not rewarded for trying to conform to social expectations, and if they develop an unfavorable attitude toward those in authority because they regard them as punitive people, they will have little desire to try to conform to social expectations.

Difficulties in Learning Moral Concepts

Learning the moral values of the social group takes time, just as learning specific moral concepts does. This learning is made difficult for the child by a number of factors, the most important of which are given in Box 14–7.

In learning moral values, the child may be confused about what the social group expects. This will have adverse effects on the child's moral development for several reasons:

First, confusion slows the learning process. When there is a conflict between the code of the home and that of the peer group, children must decide which to follow. If their decision is in favor of the peer group, they will have to relearn at least part of what they learned at home. If, on the other hand, it is in favor of the home, they may try to reconcile the two codes by modifying each.

Second, confusion leads children to question the fairness of the concepts. When this happens, it weakens their motivation to accept the concepts they

regard as unfair. Rebellion against accepting moral concepts they regard as unfair usually reaches its peak during the gang age and extends into adolescence.

Third, and most seriously, confusion in moral concepts has an impact on moral decisions. When, for example, a conflict arises between one social group and another, children must decide which moral code to follow and then be prepared to accept the punishment and rejection of the other social group whose code they have violated. The more anxious children are for social acceptance, the more "group-linked" they will be in their moral decisions when they are with the group. To maintain their status in the group, many children do things with their gangs that they would not do if they were alone.

Inconsistency in Discipline

Unless discipline is consistent, children are at a loss to know what to do and whom to obey. Inconsistency may come in any area of discipline, but it is most common in rules, punishment, and in the disciplinary technique used.

The causes of inconsistency in disciplining children are numerous. Many parents and teachers are either unsure of what they want the child to do or unsure of what they should do to achieve the behavior they expect. Most parents—and many teachers as well—do not have a single pervasive philosophy about child training, nor are they consistent in the application of the method they generally use. They vary from leniency bordering on complete lack of control to such rigid standards that the child is given little freedom of action.

Not only do parents vacillate between lenient and strict discipline, but they often use a trial-and-error approach to see what method works best. Within one disciplinary incident, for example, parents often use many different methods of control; they try emotional appeals, humor, appeals to the child's self-esteem, bribes and coaxing, ignoring the child's behavior, punishing and diverting the child's attention. Furthermore, most parents have no one consistent method of punishment.

Fluctuation in the warmth of the parent-child relationship due to changes in the child's attitude toward parents and parents' attitudes toward the child is a common cause of inconsistency in discipline. When the relationship between parent and child is warm, for example, discipline tends to be lenient. On the other hand, when the relationship is strained, discipline usually becomes severe. If children try to live up to parental expectations, parents tend to be more lenient than if they make little effort to do so.

Perhaps the most common cause of inconsistency comes from the different concepts of discipline held by parents. When there is a disagreement, parents tend to settle on a stricter pattern of discipline than they would had a disagreement not arisen. Both parents seem to feel that they should be stricter than they usually are to convince the other parent that they are "good disciplinarians."

Severity or laxity of discipline, per se, is not as damaging to children as inconsistency. Studies of the causes of juvenile delinquency, for example, have revealed that children who later became delinquents and criminals usually had inconsistent discipline, and that children who were subjected to severe but consistent discipline rarely became delinquents or criminals (28).

Although it is not essential that parents agree entirely about discipline, it is essential that they support one another in specific instances, such as giving permission to do something or withholding permission. Otherwise, children will quickly learn to play one parent against the other and thus be able to do much as they please.

Criticism of one parent by the other regarding the method of discipline used is even more damaging than inconsistency. If the criticism is not made in front of children, it hurts them indirectly by making the criticized parent feel insecure in the disciplinary role. It also hurts children directly by weakening their respect for the disciplinarian. In time, this attitude may spread to all in authority.

Use of Bribes

Many adults disapprove of rewarding a child for socially approved behavior because they think of rewards as a form of bribery. The two are quite different, however. A *bribe,* as was explained earlier, is something used to induce or influence an act, and a *reward* is something given in return for an act. In bribery, children are *promised* a material object or a privilege if they will behave in the way a parent, a teacher, or some other adult in authority wants them to behave. In the case of rewards, children are given a material object, special privilege, or adult commendation *after* they have behaved in a socially approved way.

Although bribes can usually be counted on to bring about the desired behavior, they are bad for three reasons. *First,* they motivate children to behave in a socially approved way only when they are paid to do so. As a result, they do not lead to the development of inner control. *Second,* they lack the educational value of teaching children to assume responsibility for control over their own behavior. And *third,* they give children the choice of not behaving in a socially approved way if they feel they are not being paid enough to make it worth the effort.

If rewards are used too frequently, they begin to assume the characteristics of bribery. Children learn to expect a reward whenever they behave in a socially approved way. Then, if the reward is not forthcoming, it weakens their motivation to behave in a socially approved way in the future (31, 51, 86).

Discrepancies between Moral Concepts and Moral Behavior

Among adults as well as among children, there are many discrepancies between a person's moral code and the person's behavior. Abstract knowledge that it is wrong to cheat, for example, does not keep children from cheating when a situation arises in which they are tempted or when they find it to their personal advantage to do so. Similarly, children who say it is "wrong" to fight with their classmates are not always consistent in their behavior. Most people, however, are consistent in relating their moral beliefs to their behavior. It becomes a matter of honor to live up to their standards. If they do not, they feel guilty, and if caught, they feel ashamed.

Children whose behavior falls below social standards are rarely ignorant of the wrongs they do. In fact, even among juvenile delinquents, moral knowledge is very similar to that of nondelinquents. This is true even among young children; their misbehavior is sometimes due to causes other than ignorance of what is expected of them.

Studies of discrepancies between moral knowledge and moral behavior in childhood have revealed three common causes of these discrepancies (16, 28, 94). These three causes are explained in Box 14–8.

Discrepancies between moral knowledge and moral behavior are hazardous to good personal and social adjustments. They win social disapproval and this, in turns, jeopardizes children's chances of adult as well as of peer approval and acceptance. Equally serious, discrepancies between moral knowledge and moral behavior lead to feelings of guilt and shame—feelings that are hazardous to good personal adjustments.

When children are caught in cheating, for example, they may try to justify their act by claiming that "every-

---

BOX 14–8

CAUSES OF DISCREPANCIES BETWEEN
MORAL KNOWLEDGE AND MORAL BEHAVIOR

CONFUSION
Children are often confused about the rules they are expected to follow and what patterns of behavior are approved by the social group. There are five common causes of this confusion. Confusion often arises (1) when children must apply abstract moral concepts to situations that are new to them, (2) when there is a discrepancy between what parents or others in authority say is right and what they do, (3) when there is a discrepancy between behavior portrayed in the mass media and what they have been taught is right or wrong, (4) when their moral concepts differ from those of their peers, and (5) when moral concepts conflict with one another, as when concepts of honesty conflict with concepts of loyalty and cooperation, which gives rise to the dilemma of whether or not to cheat to help a friend.

EMOTIONAL FACTORS
In anger, for example, children may do things they know are wrong to "get even" with those who have angered them, or they may bully and tease younger children as a form of displacement of anger aroused by the way their age-mates ignore or reject them.

MOTIVATIONAL FACTORS
Children may find it expedient to behave in a way they know is not right. They may, for example, cheat in an examination because of parental pressures to get better grades than they are capable of or to avoid being left behind when their friends are promoted. They may steal from stores to have the material possessions they believe will increase their acceptance by their peers or they may "cut up" in school in the hopes of winning peer attention and increased peer acceptance.

---

one does it" or they may deny that they cheated in the hopes of warding off social disapproval and punishment. But they still know that their cheating was wrong and they feel guilty about it. In addition, they feel ashamed about having been caught in a socially disapproved act and about being accused of wrongdoing, even if they are successful enough in explaining why they cheated.

If children can convince themselves as well as

COMMON MISDEMEANORS OF CHILDHOOD

LYING

The lies of young children are not usually meant to deceive others, but are due primarily to fantasy. Some are due to exaggerations, inaccuracies, and imitation of dishonesty in others. Others are due to the child's attempt to avoid punishment or threat of punishment. Most lies of older children are due to fear of punishment, disapproval, or ridicule. Frequency of lying at different ages is shown in Figure 14–5 (next page).

CHEATING

Cheating in games is common among children of all ages because of the social esteem attached to winning. Cheating in school is common when emphasis is placed on grades. Bright children may cheat to help a less able classmate, to gain greater social acceptance, and to counteract the impression that they are "goody-goodies."

STEALING

While most children learn at an early age that it is wrong to take the possessions of others, they do so when they want something they feel they cannot get in other ways. Stealing is most common when children feel they will not be caught.

DESTRUCTIVENESS

In younger children, destructiveness is usually unintentional except as retaliation. Older children are less destructive than younger ones because of fear of punishment. Destructiveness usually occurs in group situations and is an expression of hostility toward the person whose property is destroyed. Figure 14–6 (next page) shows age differences.

TRUANCY

Among young children, truancy usually results from school phobias—a fear of school caused not by the school but by the home situation. Among older children, truancy usually results from dislike of school, caused by poor academic work, lack of peer acceptance, lack of promotion, or punishment for misbehavior.

others that there was no real discrepancy between their moral knowledge and their behavior, or that the discrepancy was not their fault, they can then free themselves of some of the feelings of guilt and shame. Only under such conditions can they escape the haz-

ards to personal and social adjustments that these discrepancies usually give rise to.

Misdemeanors

A misdemeanor is mischievousness, disobedience, or willful badness of a minor sort. Most little children learn, unfortunately, that they get more attention when they are naughty than when they are good. They therefore are often *intentionally* naughty when they feel that they are being ignored. Even though they are punished, the pleasure they derive from being in the spotlight far outweighs the temporary discomfort of the punishment.

The desire for attention does not lessen as children grow older. However, they are also motivated to do things they know are wrong by sheer boredom. It is a case of "idle hands get into mischief." In relatively few cases are misdemeanors in older children due to ignorance of the fact that they are doing something the social group regards as wrong.

Although children do countless things that adults regard as "naughty" or "bad," certain misdemeanors are almost universal. These may vary in frequency and seriousness from child to child and in the same child from one age to another. The most common childhood misdemeanors are described in Box 14–9 (41, 45, 60, 75).

Note that, of all these misdemeanors, dishonesty in one form or another is especially common. Sometimes dishonesty is unintentional though most often it is intentional. Children who have been subjected to strict discipline in which corporal punishment was freely applied try to escape punishment by using a form of dishonesty which they have discovered, from past experience, brings them immunity. Similarly, children who have been subjected to psychological punishment, especially threats of loss of parental love, scoldings, or unfavorable comparisons with siblings, are motivated to be dishonest to escape these ego-deflating and anxiety-producing punishments. By contrast, children who are subjected to more democratic discipline in the home and school have less motivation to be dishonest.

Dishonesty appears in the preschool years but is more pronounced in late childhood. Boys and girls learn, from their own experiences or from those of their friends, ways and means of deceiving others, especially parents and teachers. They may pretend to be ill to avoid an unpleasant task; they may hide broken objects or pretend that someone else did the damage, they may feign ignorance of a rule which they have broken; they may cheat in schoolwork or athletics; or they may steal.

VARIATIONS IN MISDEMEANORS The frequency, seriousness, and most common kinds of misdemeanors vary markedly at different ages, among different children at the same age, and under different conditions. Normally, misdemeanors increase with *age,* coming to a peak shortly before adolescence when children are making a transition from external to internal control and from parental to group authority.

The tendency to engage in misdemeanors shows a consistent *sex* difference from kindergarten age on. This is in favor of boys, with boys engaging in more and more serious misdemeanors at every age than girls. Refer to Figure 14–7. Misdemeanors of all kinds and of greater severity are more common in *large families* than in small families. *Only children* engage in fewer misdemeanors than children with siblings. In large families, *firstborns* commit fewer misdemeanors than their later-born siblings, but, in small families, the reverse is likely to be true.

Because rules for behavior differ according to the situation, *home misdemeanors* are different from *school misdemeanors.* Figure 14–7 shows common school misdemeanors. In both situations, they vary according to the type of *disciplinary technique* used. Misdemeanors are more common when authoritarian and permissive discipline are used than when the discipline is democratic.

Frequency of misdemeanors varies according to the *attention value* of the forbidden act. Because the use of slang and swearing has greater attention value than not doing assigned chores, children are far more likely to break rules relating to the use of forbidden words than those related to assigned chores. The greater the attractiveness of a forbidden act, the more misdemeanors there will be. Refer to Figure 7–6.

The *personality pattern* of the child has a great influence on the number and severity of misdemeanors. Quiet, shy, and retiring children tend to be far less prone to misdemeanors than are outgoing, adventuresome, and impulsive children (1, 2, 22, 37, 62, 75).

MISDEMEANORS AS DANGER SIGNALS Because all children misbehave at some time or other, only when the number and seriousness of their misdemeanors deviates either above or below the norm for their age

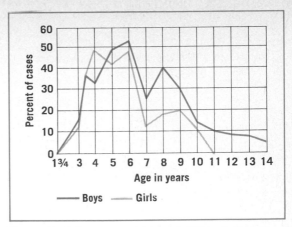

Figure 14–5 Frequency of lying at different ages in childhood. (*Adapted from J. Macfarlane, L. Allen, and M. P. Honzik:* A developmental study of the behavior problems of normal children between twenty-one months and fourteen years. *University of California Press, 1954. Used by permission.*)

and sex groups is there reason for serious concern. These deviations may be regarded as "danger signals" of potential future trouble. As Glueck has pointed out, potential juvenile delinquents can be spotted when children are 2 or 3 years old. The danger signal comes not so much from their behavior as from their attitudes toward their misbehavior. Being sly and trying to con-

Figure 14–6 Differences in destructiveness at different ages in childhood. (*Adapted from J. Macfarlane, L. Allen, and M. P. Honzik:* A developmental study of the behavior problems of normal children between twenty-one months and fourteen years. *University of California Press, 1954. Used by permission.*)

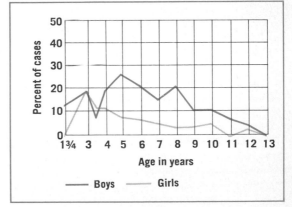

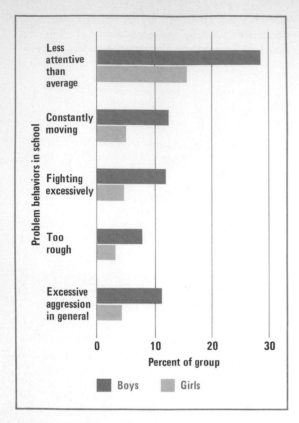

Figure 14–7 Percent of boys and girls, ages 6 to 11 years, who have been reported, in a nationwide survey, to have committed different kinds of school misdemeanors. (*Adapted from J. Roberts and J. T. Baird:* Behavior patterns of children in school: United States. *U. S. Department of Health, Education, and Welfare, 1972. Used by permission.*)

vince others that they did not misbehave or that someone else was responsible for their misbehavior is more of a danger signal than the misbehavior itself (28).

Children who are no trouble to their teachers or parents are showing danger signals of potential trouble in the future. They can be too good for their own good and for that of society. The reason for this is that they are usually hiding something behind a facade of model behavior—fear of punishment or social rejection, revenge, or some other unfavorable attitude. Sooner or later, these unfavorable attitudes will break loose and lead to unsocial behavior. All one has to do is read newspapers or watch television to find out how often "good" or "model" children pick up a shotgun

and blast away at their sleeping families or other innocent victims.

Children who are more troublesome for their age and sex than normal, *both* at home and in school, are sending out signals of potential trouble. If, on the other hand, children are more troublesome for their age and sex *either* in school or at home, it suggests that the trouble is not with the poor adjustment of the children, but with the environment in which they are more troublesome. Children whose teachers report them to be "good as gold," for example, may be the products of democratic training in the school and authoritarian or permissive training in the home. Under such conditions, if home misdemeanors are to be reduced, home discipline should duplicate school discipline. Obviously in the example above the school discipline works better than the home discipline (16, 30).

PSYCHOLOGICAL DAMAGE FROM MISDEMEANORS
Perhaps the most serious aspect of misdemeanors in childhood is that they tend to give children feelings of satisfaction which motivate them to repeat the behavior. However, to keep the level of satisfaction constant usually requires an increase in the strength of the stimulus. Children, for example, who derived satisfaction from taking a quarter from the mother's pocketbook when they were first graders, may have to steal a dollar when they are fifth graders. Like the alcoholic or drug addict, children who inflate their egos by misbehaving must have stronger and stronger doses to maintain a constant level of satisfaction.

Equally serious, misdemeanors deprive children of opportunities to learn to gain satisfaction from socially approved behavior. If they can gain satisfaction from misdemeanors, why would they want to be good, especially if they receive less attention and less admiration from the peer group when they are good?

If peer values remained constant, there would be less reason for concern. However, this is not so. One of the areas of greatest change with age is in moral values. Children who were admired for misbehaviors will find peer admiration rapidly fading unless they change the pattern of their behavior to conform to these changed values. If satisfaction from misdemeanors in childhood is great enough to weaken children's motivations to mend their ways as they grow older, they will continue to try to win peer approval by the tried and proven method of childhood by increasing the seriousness of the misdemeanors when they discover that misdemeanors in minor forms no longer work.

Because of changed moral values, children will discover, even before childhood is over, that many of their peers now disapprove of the misdemeanors they formerly envied and applauded in others. When this change in peer values reinforces the disapproval of the adult group, children begin to suffer the effects of shame and guilt. Gradually they begin to build up the belief that since their acts are considered unworthy of social approval, they, too, are unworthy. In time, this belief will develop into a generalized feeling of inadequacy and inferiority—an attitude that will warp mental health. That is why misdemeanors are such a serious hazard to personal and social adjustments.

Chapter Highlights

1 Psychological studies of moral development have been motivated by interest in discipline, the serious social problem of juvenile delinquency, theories of moral development, and evidence that the foundations for moral behavior are laid early in life.

2 Moral behavior is behavior that conforms to the standards of the group with which the individual is identified, but unmoral or immoral behavior fails to do so. This failure is due to disapproval of social standards or lack of feeling of obligation to conform to these standards—"immoral" behavior—or ignorance of social standards—"unmoral" behavior.

3 In the development of morality, there are four essentials; learning what the social group expects of its members as spelled out in laws, customs, or rules; development of a conscience; learning to feel guilt and shame when behavior falls below social standards; and opportunities for social interactions to learn what the social group expects of its members.

4 Moral development is related to and dependent upon intellectual development. It occurs in two clearcut stages, according to Piaget and in three stages, according to Kohlberg.

5 Moral development occurs in two distinct but interrelated phases—the development of moral behavior and the development of moral concepts.

6 Although the goal of all discipline is to mold the child's behavior into socially approved patterns, there is no universal agreement about the best disciplinary technique to use to achieve this goal.

7 Regardless of the disciplinary technique used, there are four essential elements: rules as guidelines for behavior; consistency in the rules used as guidelines and in the technique used to teach and enforce the rules; punishment for willful breaking of rules; and rewards for the child's attempts to model behavior along approved lines.

8 Rules serve as the basis for moral concepts and moral concepts, in turn, serve as the basis for the moral code that guides the child's behavior.

9 Punishment plays three important roles in moral development—it deters repetition of socially undesirable behavior, it tells children what the social group will and will not tolerate, and it motivates children to behave in a socially approved way.

10 Rewards are forms of appreciation for attainment, but bribes are promises of reward to induce good behavior. Rewards are good forms of motivation, but bribes lose their effectiveness unless their strength is constantly increased.

11 If discipline is to achieve its goal of inner control of behavior, there must be consistency in the rules used and in the punishments and rewards given.

12 Today, there are three commonly used techniques of discipline, called authoritarian, democratic, and permissive. There is evidence that the democratic technique produces better results than the authoritarian or permissive.

13 Three criteria can be used to evaluate discipline: the effect it has on the child's behavior; the effect it has on the child's attitude toward those in authority and the disciplinary techniques used; and the effect it has on the child's personality.

14 The common hazards in moral development include the belief that punishment and discipline are synonymous, difficulties in learning moral concepts, inconsistency in discipline, the use of bribes, discrepancies between moral concepts and moral behavior, and misdemeanors.

15 Common childish misdemeanors, which include lying, cheating, stealing, destructiveness, and truancy, are danger signals of poor personal and social adjustments in children.

Bibliography

1 Allen, V. L., and P. S. Allen. On the attractiveness of forbidden objects. *Developmental Psychology*, 1974, *10*, 871–873.

2 Armentrout, J. A. Parental child-rearing attitudes and preadolescents' problem behaviors. *Journal of Consulting and Clinical Psychology*, 1971, *37*, 278–285.

3 Ausubel, D. P. Relationship between shame and guilt in the socializing process. *Psychological Review*, 1955, *62*, 378–390.

4 Bakwin, H., and R. M. Bakwin. *Behavioral disorders in children*, 4th ed. Philadelphia: Saunders, 1972.

5 Baron, R. M., A. R. Bass, and P. M. Vietze. Type and frequency of praise as determinants of favorability of self-image: An experiment in a field setting. *Journal of Personality*, 1971, *39*, 493–511.

6 Biskin, D., and K. Hoskisson. Moral development through children's literature. *Elementary School Journal*, 1974, *75*, 153–157.

7 Blaker, K. E., and R. W. Bennett. Behavioral counseling for elementary-school children. *Elementary School Journal*, 1970, *70*, 411–417.

8 Breckenridge, M. E., and E. L. Vincent. *Child development: Physical and psychological development through adolescence,* 5th ed. Philadelphia: Saunders, 1965.

9 Carlsmith, J. M., M. R. Lepper, and T. K. Landauer. Children's obedience to adult request: Interactive effects of anxiety-arousal-apparent punitiveness of the adult. *Journal of Personality and Social Psychology*, 1974, *30*, 822–829.

10 Chandler, T. A. Transgression as a function of timing of punishment and age. *Genetic Psychology Monographs*, 1974, *89*, 3–23.

11 Clifford, E. Discipline in the home: A controlled observational study of parental practices. *Journal of Genetic Psychology*, 1958, *95*, 45–82.

12 Costantini, A. F., and K. L. Hoving. The effectiveness of reward and punishment contingencies on response inhibition. *Journal of Experimental Child Psychology*, 1973, *16*, 484–491.

13 Davitz, J. R. Contributions of research with children to a theory of maladjustment. *Child Development*, 1958, *29*, 3–7.

14 Denney, N. W., and D. M. Duffy. Possible environmental causes of stages in moral reasoning. *Journal of Genetic Psychology*, 1974, *125*, 277–283.

15 DePalma, D. J., and J. M. Foley (eds.) *Moral development: Current theory and research*. Hillsdale, N. J.: Laurence Erlbaum, 1975.

16 Dinkmeyer, D., and D. Dinkmeyer Jr. Logical consequences: A key to the reduction of disciplinary problems. *Phi Delta Kappan*, 1976, *57*, 664–666.

17 Drabman, R., and R. Spitalnik. Social isolation as a punishment procedure: A controlled study. *Journal of Experimental Child Psychology*, 1973, *16*, 236–249.

18 Eysenck, H. J. The development of moral values in children. VII. The contribution of learning theory. *British Journal of Educational Psychology*, 1960, *30*, 11–21.

19 Feldman, N. S., E. C. Klosson, J. C. Parsons, W. S. Rholes, and W. S. Ruble. Order of information presentation and children's moral judgments. *Child Development*, 1976, *47*, 556–559.

20 Ferdon, N. K. Chromosomal abnormalities and antisocial behavior. *Journal of Genetic Psychology*, 1971, *118*, 281–292.

21 Fish, M. C., and E. E. Loehfelm. Verbal approval: A neglected educational resource. *Teachers College Record*, 1975, *76*, 493–498.

22 Forbes, G. B., and D. Dykstra. Children's attribution of negative traits to authority figures as a function of family size and sex. *Psychological Reports*, 1971, *28*, 363–366.

23 Ford, F. R., and J. Herrick. Family rules: Family life styles. *American Journal of Orthopsychiatry*, 1974, *44*, 61–69.

24 Gagné, R. M., and V. K. Weigand. Some factors in children's learning and retention of concrete rules. *Journal of Educational Psychology*, 1968, *59*, 355–361.

25 Gash, H. Moral judgment: A comparison of two theoretical approaches. *Genetic Psychology Monographs*, 1976, *93*, 91–111.

26 Gecas, V., and F. I. Nye. Sex and class differences in parent-child interaction: A test of Kohn's hypothesis. *Journal of Marriage and the Family*, 1974, *36*, 742–749.

27 Glassco, J. N., N. A. Milgram, and J. Youniss. Stability of training effects on intentionality in moral judgment in children. *Journal of Personality and Social Psychology*, 1970, *14*, 360–365.

28 Glueck, E. T. A more discriminative instrument for the identification of potential delinquents at school entrance. *Journal of Criminal Law, Criminology, and Police Science*, 1966, *57*, 27–30.

29 Grusec, J. E., and S. A. Ezrin. Techniques of punishment and the development of self-criticism. *Child Development*, 1972, *43*, 1273–1288.

30 Gutkin, D. C. Maternal discipline and children's judgments of moral intentionality. *Journal of Genetic Psychology*, 1975, *127*, 55–61.

31 Haddad, N. F., J. C. McCullers, and J. D. Moran. Satiation and the detrimental effects of material rewards. *Child Development*, 1976, *47*, 547–550.

32 Hammer, M. The relationship between recalled type of discipline in childhood and adult interpersonal behavior. *Merrill-Palmer Quarterly*, 1964, *10*, 143–145.

33 Hardeman, M. Children's moral reasoning. *Journal of Genetic Psychology*, 1972, *120*, 49–59.

34 Hartlage, L. C., and J. Schlagel. Teacher characteristics associated with student classroom behaviors. *Journal of Psychology*, 1974, *86*, 191–195.

35 Havighurst, R. J. *Human development and education*. New York: Longmans, 1953.

36 Hoffman, M. L. Conscience, personality and socialization techniques. *Human Development*, 1970, *13*, 90–126.

37 Hoffman, M. L. Moral development. In P. H. Mussen (ed.), *Carmichael's manual of child psychology*, 3d ed. New York: Wiley, 1970. Vol. 2, pp. 261–359.

38 Hoffman, M. L. Father absence and conscience development. *Developmental Psychology*, 1971, *4*, 400–406.

39 Hoffman, M. L. Moral internalization, parental power, and the nature of parent-child interaction. *Developmental Psychology*, 1975, *11*, 228–239.

40 Irwin, M., and S. G. Moore. The young child's understanding of social justice. *Developmental Psychology*, 1971, *5*, 406–410.

41 Jonkins, R. L. Classification of behavior problems in children. *American Journal of Psychiatry*, 1969, *125*, 1032–1039.

42 Jensen, L. C., and G. E. Hafen. The effect of training children to consider intentions when making moral judgments. *Journal of Genetic Psychology* 1973, *122*, 223–233.

43 Jensen, L. C., and A. M. Rytting. Changing children's beliefs about punishment. *British Journal of Social and Clinical Psychology*, 1975, *14*, 91–92.

44 Jersild, A. T., C. W. Telford, and J. M. Sawrey. *Child psychology*, 6th ed. Englewood Cliffs, N.J.: Prentice-Hall, 1975.

45 Johnson, C. D., and J. Gormley. Academic cheating: The contribution of sex, personality and situation variables. *Developmental Psychology*, 1972, *6*, 320–325.

46 Jones, F. H., and W. H. Miller. The effective use of negative attention for reducing group disruption in special elementary school classrooms. *Psychological Record*, 1974, *24*, 435–448.

47 Jones, V. Character development in children: An objective approach. In L. Carmichael (ed.), *Manual of child psychology*, rev. ed. New York: Wiley, 1954. Pp. 781–832.

48 Kanfer, F. H., and J. Zich. Self-control training: The effects of external control on children's resistance to temptation. *Developmental Psychology*, 1974, *10*, 108–115.

49 Keasey, C. B. Sex differences in yielding to temptation: A function of the situation. *Journal of Genetic Psychology*, 1971, *118*, 25–28.

50 Keasey, C. B. Social participation as a factor in the moral development of preadolescents. *Developmental Psychology*, 1971, *5*, 216–220.

51 Keat, D. B. Survey schedule of rewards for children. *Psychological Reports*, 1974, *35*, 287–293.

52 Kohlberg, L. The development of children's orientation toward a moral order: Sequence in the development of moral thought. *Vita Humana, Basel*, 1963, *6*, 11–33.

53 Kohlberg, L. *Stages in the development of moral thought and action.* New York: Holt, 1969.

54 Kohlberg, L. Stages and aging in moral development: Some speculations. *Gerontologist*, 1973, *13*, 497–502.

55 Kuhn, D. Short-term longitudinal evidence for the sequentiality of Kohlberg's early stages of moral judgments. *Developmental Psychology*, 1976, *12*, 162–166.

56 Kurtines, W., and E. B. Greif. The development of moral thought: Review and evaluation of Kohlberg's approach. *Psychological Bulletin*, 1974, *81*, 453–470.

57 Lane, I. M., and R. C. Coon. Reward allocation in preschool children. *Child Development*, 1972, *43*, 1382–1389.

58 LaVoie, J. C. The effects of an aversive stimulus, a rationale, and sex of child on punishment effectiveness and generalization, *Child Development*, 1973, *44*, 505–510.

59 MacMillan, D. L., S. R. Forness, and B. M. Trumbull. The role of punishment in the classroom. *Exceptional Children*, 1973, *40*, 85–96.

60 Marshall, H. R. Behavior problems in normal children: A comparison between the lay literature and developmental research. In W. R. Looft (ed.), *Developmental psychology: A book of readings.* Hinsdale, Ill.: Dryden Press, 1972. Pp. 85–95.

61 Maurer, A. Corporal punishment. *American Psychologist*, 1974, *29*, 614–626.

62 McKinney, J. D. Teacher perceptions of the classroom behavior of reflective and impulsive children. *Psychology in the Schools*, 1975, *12*, 348–352.

63 McManis, D. L. Effects of peer-models vs. adult-models and social reinforcement on intentionality of children's moral judgments. *Journal of Psychology*, 1974, *87*, 159–170.

64 Merchant, R. L., and F. Rebelsky. Effects of participation in rule formation on the moral judgment of children. *Genetic Psychology Monographs* 1972, *85*, 287–304.

65 Moir, D. J. Egocentrism and the emergence of conventional morality in preadolescent girls. *Child Development*, 1974, *45*, 299–304.

66 Morris, W. N., H. M. Marshall, and R. S. Miller. The effect of vicarious punishment of prosocial behavior in children. *Journal of Experimental Child Psychology*, 1973, *15*, 222–236.

67 Nye, F. I., J. Carlson, and G. Garrett. Family size, interaction, affect and stress. *Journal of Marriage and the Family*, 1970, *32*, 216–226.

68 O'Leary, K. D., K. F. Kaufman, R. E. Kass, and R. S. Drabman. The effects of loud and soft reprimands on the behavior of disruptive students. *Exceptional Children*, 1970, *37*, 145–155.

69 Peck, R. F., and R. J. Havighurst. *The psychology of character development.* New York: Wiley, 1962.

70 Peretti, P. O. Guilt in moral development: A comparative study. *Psychological Reports*, 1969, *25*, 739–745.

71 Phillips, B. N. Problem behavior in the elementary school. *Child Development*, 1968, *39*, 895–903.

72 Piaget, J. *The moral judgment of the child.* New York: Free Press, 1965.

73 Piaget, J. *Science of education and psychology of the child.* New York: Orion Press, 1970.

74 Piaget, J. *Psychology and epistemology.* New York: Grossman, 1971.

75 Redl, F. Disruptive behavior in the classroom. *School Review*, 1975, *83*, 569–594.

76 Roberts, J., and J. T. Baird. *Behavior patterns of children in school: United States.* Rockville, Md.: U. S. Department of Health, Education, and Welfare, 1972.

77 Rothberg, C., and M. B. Harris. "Right," "wrong" and discrimination learning in children. *Journal of Genetic Psychology*, 1972, *120*, 275–286.

78 Rothman, G. R. The influence of moral reasoning on behavioral choices. *Child Development*, 1976, *47*, 397–406.

79 Rubin, K. H., and F. W. Schneider. The relationship between moral judgment, egocentrism, and altruistic behavior. *Child Development*, 1973, *44*, 661–665.

80 Rychlak, J. F., N. D. Tuan, and W. E. Schneider. Formal discipline revisited: Affective assessment and nonspecific transfer. *Journal of Educational Psychology*, 1974, *66*, 139–151.

81 Santrock, J. W. Father absence, perceived maternal behavior, and moral development in boys. *Child Development*, 1975, *46*, 753–757.

82 Schleifer, M., and V. I. Douglas. Effects of training on the moral judgment of young children. *Journal of Personality and Social Psychology*, 1973, *28*, 62–68.

83 Settlage, C. F. The value of limits in child rearing. *Children*, 1958, *5*, 175–178.

84 Shannon, W. V. What code of values

can we teach our children now? *The New York Times,* Jan. 16, 1972.

85 Shelton, J., and J. P. Hill. Effects on cheating of achievement anxiety and knowledge of peer performance. *Developmental Psychology,* 1969, *1,* 449–455.

86 Skidgell, A. C., S. L. Witryol, and P. J. Wirzbicki. The effect of novelty-familiarity levels on material reward preferences of first-grade children. *Journal of Genetic Psychology,* 1976, *128,* 291–297.

87 Sollenberger, R. T. Chinese-American child-rearing practices and juvenile delinquency. *Journal of Social Psychology,* 1968, *74,* 13–23.

88 Spock, B. *Raising children in a difficult time.* New York: Norton, 1974.

89 Stein, G. M., and J. H. Bryan. The ef-fect of a television model upon rule adoption behavior of children. *Child Development,* 1972, *43,* 268–273.

90 Stott, D. H. Classification of behavior disturbance among school-age children: Principles, epidemology and syndromes. *Psychology in the Schools,* 1971, *8,* 232–239.

91 Stouwie, R. J. An experimental study of adult dominance and warmth, conflicting verbal instructions, and children's moral behavior. *Child Development,* 1972, *43,* 959–971.

92 Straus, M. A. Some social antecedents of physical punishment: A linkage theory interpretation. *Journal of Marriage and the Family,* 1971, *33,* 658–663.

93 Swift, M., G. Spivack, O. DeLisser, A. Danset, J. Danset-Léger, and P. Win-nykamen. Children's disturbing classroom behavior: A cross-cultural investigation. *Exceptional Children,* 1972, *38,* 492–493.

94 Thornburg, H. D. Behavior and values: Consistency or inconsistency. *Adolescence,* 1973, *8,* 513–520.

95 Tuckman, J., and R. A. Regan. Size of family and behavioral problems in children. *Journal of Genetic Psychology,* 1967, *111,* 151–160.

96 Turiel, E., and G. R. Rothman. The influence of reasoning on behavior choices at different stages of moral development. *Child Development,* 1972, *43,* 741–756.

97 Yussen, S. R. Moral reasoning from the perspective of others. *Child Development,* 1976, *47,* 551–555.

CHAPTER 15

CHAPTER 15

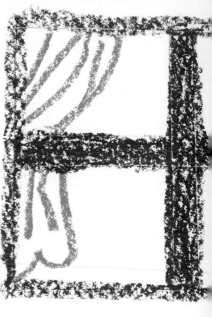

SOME COMMON CHILDHOOD INTERESTS

Many people fail to understand the true meaning of the term "interest." As a result, they often confuse it with what might correctly be called a "whim."

An *interest* has been explained as "something with which the child identifies his personal well-being" (72). Interests are sources of motivation which drive people to do what they want to do when they are free to choose. When they see that something will benefit them, they become interested in it. This, in turn, leads to satisfaction. When satisfaction wanes, so does interest.

By contrast, a *whim* is a temporary interest. It differs from interest not in quality but in persistence. While it lasts, it may be as intense and as highly motivating as an interest. But it soon begins to wane because the activity it has given rise to gives the individual only temporary satisfaction. Interests are more persistent because they satisfy important needs in the person's life.

Every interest satisfies some need in a child's life, even though this need may not be readily apparent to adults. The stronger the need, the stronger and more lasting the interest. Furthermore, the more often the interest is expressed in activities, the stronger it will become.

On the other hand, interests are subject to extinction through disuse. Should the environment in which children live limit opportunities to play with other children, for example, interest in playmates will begin to wane and a substitute interest will take its place. If children can find satisfactory substitutes for playmates, a time may come when they will have little interest in playmates. Children then may even claim that their peers "bore" them.

An activity that fails to satisfy, stimulate, or challenge the individual is called "boring.": the individual is unable to see how the activity can contribute personal benefit or satisfaction. *Boredom,* which consists of feelings of tedium and dissatisfaction, is thus the opposite of interest.

When children are bored, they are likely to get into mischief and cause trouble for others in the hope of stirring up some excitement, and thus turning a boring situation into an interesting one. For the most part, children experience boredom when they are forced to do things that do not fit their needs or give them satisfaction. Boredom is especially likely to occur in school, where the curriculum and method of teaching must be planned for the group rather than for the individual.

Failure to recognize the difference between interests and whims and to appreciate how whims can and often do lead to boredom, is important because of the effects interests and boredom have on children's personal and social adjustments. When children are forced to continue to do things after their interest has waned to the point where the activities are boring to them, it will result in attitudes and behavior that will play havoc with their adjustments to these situations and to their happiness. This matter will be explained more fully in the section dealing with hazards in the development of interests.

Importance of Interests

At all ages, interests play an important role in a person's life and have a great impact on the person's behavior and attitudes. At no time is this more true than during childhood. What kind of person the child will become is determined to a large extent by the interests developed during the childhood years.

Throughout the childhood years, interests provide a strong *motivation to learn.* Children who are interested in an activity, whether it is play or work, will put forth more effort to learn than will children who are less interested or bored. If learning experiences are to tap children's full resources, they must be timed to coincide with their interests. This is the "teachable moment"—the time when children are ready to learn because they are interested in what learning will bring them in personal advantages and satisfactions (34).

Interests influence the form and intensity of children's *aspirations.* When children begin to think about their future vocations, for example, they set goals for what they want to be and do when they are grown-up. The more convinced they are about what they want their future vocations to be, the greater will be their interests in activities, in the classroom or outside the classroom, that will lead to the achievement of their vocational aspirations.

Interests add *enjoyment* to any activity the individual engages in. If children are interested in an activity, the experience will be far more enjoyable to them than if they are bored. Furthermore, when children fail to derive enjoyment from activities, they do not put any more effort into the activities than is absolutely neces-

BOX 15–1
CHARACTERISTICS OF CHILDREN'S INTERESTS

**INTERESTS PARALLEL PHYSICAL
AND MENTAL DEVELOPMENT**

Interests in all areas change as long as physical and mental changes are taking place. Figure 15–1 shows changes in several interests with age. When growth slows down and a mature level of development is reached, interests become more stable. Children who develop more rapidly or more slowly than their age-mates will have interests that are different from those of their age-mates. Slow maturers, as was pointed out earlier, encounter social problems because their interests are those of a child, but their age-mates' interests are those of an adolescent.

**INTERESTS DEPEND UPON
READINESS TO LEARN**

Children cannot acquire interests before they are physically and mentally ready to do so. They cannot, for example, have a *real* interest in ball games until they have the strength and muscle coordination necessary for ball play.

**INTERESTS DEPEND UPON
OPPORTUNITIES TO LEARN**

Opportunities to learn depend upon the environment and the interests of the people—both children and adults—with whom children are associated. Because young children's environments are limited largely to the home, their interests are "homegrown." As their social horizons broaden, they acquire the interests of the people outside the home with whom they come in contact.

DEVELOPMENT OF INTERESTS MAY BE LIMITED

Physical and mental incapacities and restricted social experiences limit children's interests. A physically handicapped child, for example, cannot acquire the same interest in sports as children of the same age whose physical development is normal.

**INTERESTS ARE AFFECTED
BY CULTURAL INFLUENCES**

From parents, teachers, and other adults, children are given opportunities to learn what the cultural group considers appropriate interests, and they are deprived of opportunities to learn interests that the cultural group regards as inappropriate for them.

INTERESTS ARE EMOTIONALLY WEIGHTED

The emotional weighting—the affective aspect—of interests determines their strength. Unpleasant emotional weighting weakens interests, and pleasant emotional weightings strengthen them.

INTERESTS ARE EGOCENTRIC

Throughout childhood, interests are egocentric. Boys' interests in mathematics, for example, often stem from their belief that doing well in mathematics in school will be a stepping stone to a lucrative and prestigious job in the business world.

Figure 15–1. Some changes in interests as children grow up. Note that strong interests in childhood give way to weaker interests and vice versa. (*Adapted from J. E. Horrocks and M. C. Mussman: Developmental trends in wishes, confidence, and the sense of personal control from childhood to middle maturity.* Journal of Psychology, *1973,* 84, *241–252. Used by permission.*)

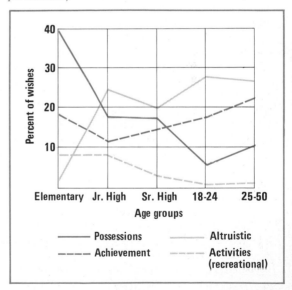

sary. As a result, their *achievements* fall far short of their capacities. This makes them feel guilty and ashamed—attitudes that further reduce their enjoyment in the activities.

To understand the important role interests play in children's lives, it is essential to know the characteristics of children's interests and also how they differ from adult interests. Box 15–1 gives the most important characteristics of children's interests.

Methods of Discovering Children's Interests

Because of the important roles interests play in the child's life, it is essential to discover and foster the interests that will aid the child's personal and social adjustments. How, one may ask, is it possible to know what a child's interests are and how is it possible to distinguish between interests and whims? Some of the ways of discovering children's interests are explained in Box 15–2.

Although one method alone might be sufficient to determine whether children are really interested in a specific activity or subject, it is safer to use several methods so that one can act as a check on the others. Unless this is done, what appears to be an interest may turn out to be a whim. By observing a child, for example, one might conclude that that child had a stronger interest in painting than is usual for that age because of the enthusiastic way the child goes about painting. Unless it is possible to observe that child over a long enough period of time to determine whether the enthusiasm persists, this observation should be supplemented with other methods—what the child talks about, reads, draws, or collects—to make sure that the interest is a true one, not just a whim.

Using several methods to substantiate an original assessment of an interest is also justified by the fact that children may engage in an activity because they may have nothing else to do. Many activities that occupy children's free time, such as listening to the radio or watching television, may not represent a strong interest but rather a lack of something more interesting to spend their time on.

Then, too, many children seem to be interested in activities which, in reality, have little interest for them. They engage in these activities because it is the "thing to do"—their friends engage in the activities and chil-

dren want to do what their friends are doing to avoid creating the impression that they are "different."

How Interests Develop

The child is not born with ready-made interests. Instead, interests are an outgrowth of learning experiences. The kind of learning from which an interest develops will determine how satisfying and how persistent the interest will be. To understand how interests develop, it is essential to know not only how they are learned but also how the different aspects of interests develop.

Aspects of Interests

All interests have two aspects, the cognitive and the affective. The *cognitive* aspect is based on concepts children develop about the areas related to the interests. The cognitive aspect of children's interest in school, for example, is based on their concepts of school. If they think of school as a place where they can learn about things that have aroused their curiosity and where they will have opportunities for contacts with peers that they have not had in their preschool years, their interest in school will be very different than if it were based on concepts of school which emphasize frustrations and restrictions on their activities by school rules and the hard work studying lessons requires.

Because childhood interests tend to be egocentric, the cognitive aspect of these interests centers around the question of what benefits and personal satisfaction they will give. Children, for example, want to satisfy themselves that the time and effort they expend in activities related to their interests will pay off in personal satisfaction and benefits. If there is evidence that they will benefit and gain satisfaction, their interests will not only persist but also grow stronger as the benefits and satisfactions become evident. The reverse will be true if there is little or no evidence of personal benefits or satisfaction.

Concepts that make up the cognitive aspect of interests are based on personal experiences and what is learned in the home, the school, and the community and from different forms of mass media. From these sources children learn what will satisfy their needs and what will not. The former will then develop into interests, and the latter will not. Children discover, for example, that their curiosity about what goes on inside their bodies can be satisfied by questions and by reading. So long as these activities give them satisfaction, their interest will persist. By contrast, interest in health does not satisfy personal needs so long as children are healthy or suffer from no troublesome ailments. Hence, they show little or no interest in health practices.

The *affective* aspect, or the emotional weighting, of the concepts that make up the cognitive aspect of interests is expressed in attitudes toward the activities interests give rise to. Like the cognitive aspect, the affective aspect is developed from personal experiences, from attitudes of significant people—parents, teachers, and peers—toward the activities related to these interests, and from attitudes expressed or implied in different forms of mass media toward the same activities.

Children, for example, who have pleasant relationships with teachers usually develop favorable attitudes toward school. Because their school experiences are pleasant, their interest in school is strengthened. By contrast, an unpleasant experience with a teacher can and often does lead to unfavorable attitudes that may, in time, weaken the child's interest in school. How this can happen is illustrated in Figure 15–2.

Although both aspects, the cognitive and the affective, play important roles in determining what children will and will not do, and what types of personal and social adjustments they will make, the affective aspect is more important than the cognitive for two reasons. *First,* the affective aspect plays a greater role in motivating action than the cognitive. A favorable emotional weighting of an interest strengthens the interest and increases the person's motivation to express the interest in action. An unpleasant emotional weighting has the opposite effect. It either produces boredom with its weakening effect on motivation or it leads to actions that jeopardize good personal and social adjustments.

Favorable attitudes toward school, for example, increase children's motivation to study and to become good "school citizens." Similarly, a vocation chosen because of favorable social attitudes toward it will motivate children to study to prepare themselves for their chosen vocation.

Second, the affective aspect of interests, once formed, tends to be more resistant to change than the cognitive aspect. Although, for example, inaccurate information about vocations—the cognitive aspect of vocational interests—can be corrected relatively easily

---

BOX 15–2

DISCOVERING CHILDREN'S INTERESTS

- *Observation of activities.* By observing what objects children play with, buy, collect, or use when there is an element of spontaneity in the activity, one can get a clue to their interests.

- *Questions.* When children ask questions persistently and frequently about something, they are more interested in that subject than in one they ask questions about only occasionally.

- *Topics of conversation.* What children talk about either with adults or with contemporaries gives a clue to what they are interested in and how strong the interest is.

- *Reading.* When free to select books to read or to have read to them, children select those which deal with topics that interest them.

- *Spontaneous drawing.* What children draw or paint spontaneously and how often they return to it will give a clue to their interest in a subject.

- *Wishes.* When asked what they would like to have if they could have anything they wanted, most children state very frankly wishes for things that interest them most.

- *Reports of what is of interest.* When asked to tell or to write down three or more things that interest them most, children indicate already-formed interests, which give a clue to where their satisfactions come from.

---

as children grow older and have more exposure to different jobs and more vocational guidance in school, changing the affective aspect of their interests is far from easy.

As in attitudes toward other people, as was stressed in the discussion of prejudice earlier, once attitudes toward vocations have been developed, they are likely to become persistent. Any change that is made is more likely to be quantitative than qualitative. An unfavorable attitude toward a vocation may, with increased knowledge and work experience, become less unfavorable than it originally was, but there is little likeli-

Figure 15–2. An unpleasant experience with a teacher may weaken a child's interest in school and dampen motivation to study. (*Adapted from Ernie Bushmiller: "Nancy."* United Features Syndicate, *Feb. 11, 1976. Used by permission.*)

hood that it will change from unfavorable to favorable. Consequently, because of the effect interests can have on behavior and on personal and social adjustments, in the development of interests, greater attention should be given to the development of favorable emotional weighting of these interests than to their cognitive aspects.

How Interests Are Learned

Most commonly, interests grow out of three kinds of learning experiences. *First,* in trial-and-error learning, children discover that something interests them. Interests acquired in this way may be long lasting or they may turn out to be whims, which quickly pass. When combined with guidance, trial-and-error learning is a valuable means of developing new interests because children have opportunities to try out what appeals to them to see whether or not it actually meets some needs in their lives.

Second, in learning through identification with people they love or admire, children take on other people's interests as well as their patterns of behavior. If, for ex-

ample, a boy's father is interested in shopwork as a hobby, the boy will be likely to develop an interest in shopwork also so that he can participate in the activity with his father.

Two important points about this method of learning interests should be noted. In the first place, if children do not have the skills or abilities to sustain these interests, the interests will give them little satisfaction and will soon subside. Second, and equally important, sources of identification shift as children grow older. When this happens, children then try to model themselves along the lines of the new people they identify with. This means a shift in interests that may cause a conflict between the new interests they are trying to develop and the old ones.

Third, interests may develop through the guidance and direction of a person qualified to assess children's abilities. Since this method of learning takes into consideration the child's abilities, it is much more likely to lead to the development of interests that will satisfy the child's needs more than either trial-and-error learning or identification.

Because of differences in abilities and in learning experiences, children's interests vary. This is more true of older than of younger children. However, while all children will develop certain interests that meet their individual needs, there are some interests that are almost universal in a culture because of the pressures put on all children in that culture to develop these interests. What these common interests of American children of today are will be discussed in the following pages.

Interest in the Human Body

Studies of children's interests in the body have shown that this interest follows a predictable pattern. This pattern is due in part to the development of intellectual abilities which enable children to perceive differences in their own bodies as they change and differences between their bodies and those of age-mates and adults. It is due more, however, to social pressures from peers and adults. Unless children were sick, for example, they would have little interest in health were it not for parental pressures to take measures to maintain good health, such as brushing their teeth, washing their hands before eating and after toileting to avoid germs, or taking vitamins to ensure good health.

In the pattern of development of interest in the body, interest is concentrated first on the *exterior* of the body and, later, on the interior of the body. One of the earliest exploratory behaviors of babies is concentrated on exploring the different parts of the exteriors of their bodies—their hair, their noses, their ears, and their navels.

When children begin to play with children outside the home, new interests are aroused in the exteriors of their bodies. They become interested in body build and how their body builds differ from those of age-mates. This interest is heightened when they discover that certain body builds are more socially approved than are others and that different body builds affect their energy level and ability to do things more than other body builds do. They discover, for example, that the mesomorphic build (heavy and muscular) is more socially approved than either the ectomorphic (tall and thin) or endomorphic (round and soft with flabby fat) builds and that children with mesomorphic builds can do more and tend to get less tired than those with either endomorphic or ectomorphic builds.

As children notice differences in other children's bodies and between children's and adults' bodies, their interest is concentrated on what causes these differences and why they exist. They want to know, for example, why women have "bumps" on their chests while men and children do not.

When their own bodies begin to change with the development of secondary sex characteristics, late in childhood, children become interested in the causes and reasons for these changes. They are also greatly interested in how these puberty changes make their bodies different from those of the opposite sex and from their own former childish bodies.

Because it is impossible for children to see the *interiors* of their bodies, interest in the different organs and their functions develops later than interest in the exterior of the body. However, even before children enter school, they are interested in knowing the names of the different organs and their functions. They want to know, for example, where the heart is, whether it is shaped like the Valentine Day's hearts, and what its function is. This interest is heightened when children take courses in hygiene in school or see pictures of different parts of the body in the mass media. This interest is illustrated in Figure 15–3.

Children are also interested in *body products,* such as saliva, blood, and sweat. So long as they are normal, everyday experiences, interest is unemotional.

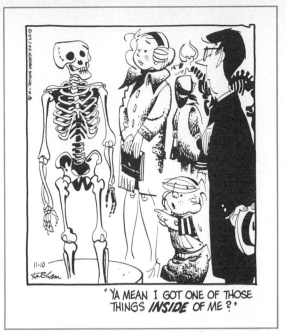

"YA MEAN I GOT ONE OF THOSE THINGS *INSIDE* OF ME?"

Figure 15–3. Interest in the interior of the body is heightened when children see pictures or other illustrations of what is inside their bodies. (*Adapted from Hank Ketcham: "Dennis the Menace."* Field Newspaper Syndicate, *Nov. 10, 1975. Used by permission.*)

The behavior of children during elimination, for example, is just as matter of fact as when brushing teeth. If, on the other hand, the body product is unusual, as in the flow of blood from a cut finger, the reaction is emotionally colored and the interest heightened. The child wants to know where the blood came from, how and why it clots, what causes the cut to heal, and why there is pain when there is a flow of blood from a cut (36).

Should a person *die,* older children are interested in what happens to the person's body after it has been put in a coffin and buried. They want to know how it can get out of the coffin after it has been buried and how it can get to Heaven. They also are interested in how a body that has been cremated can be changed into an angel's body.

Interest in Health

Interest in the body does not, as a rule, include interest in health. Most children take good health for granted and resent parental attempts to safeguard their good health by insisting that they use proper health precautions such as adequate sleep, regular meals, and protection against the elements. This is characteristic of well-adjusted children. They are not only not health-conscious but they also resent having adults, especially parents, attempt to make them interested in their health.

As children approach adolescence, this lack of interest in health gives way to an interest that is so strong that it often causes children to become health-conscious and health-preoccupied. This change from little or no interest to a strong interest is due to two things. *First,* children no longer enjoy the good health they did when they were younger. Although they are not ill, they often feel under par. Rapid physical growth saps their energy so that they fatigue easily. Rapid physical development, especially of the internal organs, causes minor discomforts such as digestive disturbances or occasional heart palpitations. These changes lead to an interest in their health.

Second, interest in health is aroused by children's realization of the role played by health in appearance. They discover, for example, that when they are not feeling up to par, their skin looks sallow and acne seems worse than usual. They also notice that when they are not feeling well everything, even those activities they most enjoy, seems to be too much effort to make it worth doing. As a result, interest in health often becomes an obsession. This is true of well-adjusted prepubescent children, not only of those who are poorly adjusted, as in the earlier years.

Closely related to interest in health is interest in germs. Children want to know what germs are, what they look like, how they get into the body, how they cause the body to become sick, how inoculations can prevent germs from making people sick, and how medicine can cure sickness.

Ways of Expressing Interest in the Body

The earliest form of expressing an interest in the body is through *exploration.* Even before babies are able to sit up, they investigate their bodies by looking at their hands and feet when they voluntarily move them; they investigate their hair, eyes, ears, and navels, and they put their fingers into any openings, such as their nostrils and ears. If they have an opportunity, they like to watch themselves in mirrors when they "make faces" or move different parts of the body.

When babies and young children are with other people, they explore them by pulling at their hair, feeling their hands or faces, and by wanting to feel a man's whiskers or a woman's breasts. A common peer play activity of preschoolers is exploring the bodies of playmates of their own and of the opposite sex.

By the time children have learned enough words to communicate with others, they ask endless *questions* about their bodies and bodies of other people. They also make *comments* about any aspect of the body of another person that differs from their own bodies. They comment, for example, on the difference in the genital organs of boys and girls, on the fact that adult bodies differ from children's bodies, and on any physical defect a child or adult may have.

The *mass media* provide children with ways to satisfy their interest in the human body. Pictures of different organs and how they function, of reproduction and childbirth, and of the different features on the exterior of the body are always fascinating to children. By the time they can read, they use *reading* to fill in the gaps of knowledge that they have been unable to get from other sources.

Of all mass media, comics prove to be one of the most common sources of information. Because the human body is usually exaggerated in the drawing of the comics, it has a greater attention value than other drawings. This is especially true of the secondary sex characteristics of males and females. These drawings serve as a basis for children's concepts of sex-appropriate appearance—one of their major interests in appearance.

Interest in Appearance

Throughout the early years of childhood, interest in appearance is relatively slight. So long as children are not conspicuously different from their age-mates or so homely or sloppy that people comment unfavorably about them, appearance is of little concern to young children. Missing teeth, for example, do not concern most 6-year-olds because most of their age-mates also have missing teeth. Even pressures to stand up straight and parental criticism of their sloppiness are not enough to arouse young children's interest in their appearance. In fact, the more parental concern and criticism children are subjected to, the stronger their resistance will be and the less their interest in their appearance.

About the time children enter school, there is a change in their attitudes toward appearance. Gradually their interest in appearance increases. By the time children reach adolescence, interest in appearance has become so strong that it is often an obsession. Some of the conditions responsible for increased interest in appearance as children grow older are explained in Box 15–3.

Areas of Interest in Appearance

Although interest in appearance increases as children grow older, different areas of interest develop at different ages. When they will develop will depend mainly on conditions that give rise to the realization of the role appearance plays in the individual child's personal and social adjustments. If, for example, a child's physical defect, such as a broken tooth, goes unnoticed by peers until the child reaches the self-conscious age of puberty, the child will have little interest in this blemish to appearance. On the other hand, a major physical defect, such as a facial birthmark, may be commented on by peers and adults while the child is still very young. As a result, interest in appearance will develop early.

Children who conform to stereotypes of *attractiveness* of different facial features discover that this is a personal asset. Consequently, it heightens their interest in their features. Similarly, if their body builds conform to the socially approved stereotypes of the "right" body build, their interest will be increased. Lack of conformity will lead to a negative interest in the form of concern, and a positive interest in how to improve or camouflage a body build that fails to conform to the approved stereotype (18).

As interest in sex-appropriate behavior begins to develop, even among preschoolers, so does an interest in a *sex-appropriate appearance.* Boys want to look "masculine" and girls, "feminine." Failure to create a sex-appropriate appearance is the source of major concern to them because they realize how it handicaps social acceptance (48).

Any *physical defect* that is noticeable and mars their appearance becomes a focal point of interest when children realize how it handicaps their relationships with others. Even if the reactions of others are colored

by sympathy and pity, children resent being treated differently from their age-mates. This heightens their interest in their defects.

Interest in *puberty changes,* as was stressed earlier (see pages 121–122), begins when the first sign of puberty changes appear and grows increasingly stronger as different secondary sex characteristics make their appearance. This interest, as was likewise explained earlier, is heightened by two sources of concern: being normal and being sex-appropriate. As puberty progresses, interest wanes in puberty changes provided the child's body is normal and sex appropriate in its appearance. Any deviation from these characteristics will keep the concerns alive and, by so doing, will prolong the child's interest into adolescence.

Interest in *grooming,* as an aid to an attractive appearance, does not develop until children become aware of the advantages of attractiveness. As this awareness develops, so does an interest in grooming. If, however, boys are associated with a gang whose members regard good grooming as a sign of a "sissy," their interest in grooming will be negative—they will want to be as sloppy and dirty as their parents will permit in the hopes of creating the impression of masculinity. (21, 29, 46, 47, 55).

Interest in Clothes

There are two conditions responsible for children's interest in clothes. *First,* at an early age, all children learn that the cultural group puts high value on clothes. This they learn first from parents and, later, from peers. When parents are constantly emphasizing the importance of the right clothes for the occasion or how certain garments help to improve one's looks, it makes children clothes-conscious. Later when it becomes apparent to them that clothes help to increase popularity among peers and facilitate playing leadership roles, this further reinforces children's realization of how much value the social group places on clothes.

Because clothes are important to the significant people in children's lives, they are important to them also.

Second, children discover at an early age that clothes satisfy some important needs in their lives. The more needs they can satisfy, the stronger will be the interest in clothes. Box 15–4 lists seven important needs that can be satisfied by clothes.

Gang-age children, for example, want to be accepted members of the peer group. They also want to be independent of adult domination and to create the impression that they are sex appropriate. All these needs can be satisfied by their clothes. This heightens their interest in them.

As children grow older, their needs change. When this happens, interest in clothes also changes. This is well illustrated in the need for attention. Preschoolers expect attention from adults when they have new clothes. If they do not get it, they will say, "See my new

---

BOX 15–4

SOME CHILDHOOD NEEDS SATISFIED BY CLOTHES

AUTONOMY

Babies satisfy their need for autonomy by removing their clothes and by trying to dress themselves. Preschoolers satisfy this need by selecting the clothes they want to wear and gang-age children by wearing clothes as they please, regardless of adult protests about the appropriateness of the clothes for the occasion or the sloppiness of the way they put them on.

IMPRESSION OF GROWING UP

Because children equate autonomy with age, they want clothes that create the impression that they are older than they are. One of the things they especially like about new clothes is that they are larger in size than old clothes—a condition that suggests to children that they are older because they are bigger.

ATTENTION

Children discover at an early age that clothes can have great attention value if they are brightly colored, ornamented, or new. Only when they realize that attention can be unfavorable are they willing to conform to adult standards of appropriateness and good taste.

INDIVIDUALITY

Children soon learn that clothes help to identify them as individuals. Even during the gang age they can retain

their identity by wearing clothes like the peer group but in their favorite colors.

IDENTIFICATION WITH THE PEER GROUP

Clothes are one of the quickest ways for children to show others that they are members of the peer groups they want to be identified with. How they wear their clothes is also a symbol of belonging.

SEX APPROPRIATENESS

When the peer group puts strong emphasis on sex appropriateness of appearance and behavior, children want clothes that proclaim their sex appropriateness. If this is unimportant to the peer group, children are unconcerned about having clothes that identify them with their sex group.

CAMOUFLAGE

All children become self-conscious about physical defects, physical features, or body builds that deviate markedly from those of their age-mates. They discover, often by trial and error, that clothes help to camouflage these characteristics. The more anxious they are to create a favorable impression as an aid to social acceptance, the more interested they are in clothes that serve as camouflages.

---

shoes," or "I am wearing a new sweater." Gang-age children are satisfied if members of the peer group show approval for their clothes because they are similar to theirs and are sex appropriate.

Areas of Interest in Clothes

Children's interest in clothes is different from that of adolescents and adults. As a result, different aspects of their clothes are important. Style and becomingness, for example, are very important to adolescents and adults but very unimportant to children. On the other hand, ornamentation and color with attention value are important to children but relatively unimportant to adults unless they conform to the prevailing styles.

While different aspects of clothes are the focal point of children's interests at different ages and among different children, there are several aspects of clothes that may be regarded as of universal interest to children, regardless of age, sex, and other factors. They are discussed below.

NEWNESS All children like new clothes and want to wear them in preference to their old clothes. Young children discover that newness has great attention value, and older children's interest is concentrated on the belief that newness implies that they are growing up because they have outgrown their old clothes.

One of the reasons children rebel against wearing hand-me-down clothes from older siblings is that they are "old clothes." Even the temporary pleasure of feeling that wearing clothes associated with an older sibling will make people think they are older is quickly overshadowed by their realization that the clothes are "old." Only if hand-me-downs are changed by dyeing or sewing on ornamentation to give them a new look will children be satisfied to wear them.

COLOR Children of all ages are especially interested in the color of their clothes. If a garment is of a favorite color, they will like it, whether it is becoming or not. Most young children like light and bright colors, primarily because they have great attention value. No red, for example, is too red or no green too green to appeal to young children. As children grow older, they show a preference for darker and less highly saturated hues of their favorite colors. They also learn to combine colors that are regarded as attractive combinations instead of combining their favorite colors, regardless of whether or not they harmonize or blend.

ORNAMENTATION Young children are far more interested in the ornamentation of their clothes than in their styles or fit. They discover that ornamentation has great attention value. Since girls' clothes can be ornamented more than boys', girls are interested in ornamentation of all kinds—ruffles, bows, braids, buttons, and costume jewelry. They regard such ornamentations not only as means of attracting attention but also as symbols of growing up. Many young girls put on every kind of ornament they own at one time in the hope of winning attention and arousing the envy of their peers, which adds to their feelings of self-importance.

Children soon learn that too much ornamentation wins social disapproval. They then become more selective, using not only less ornamentation but only that which is suitable for the occasion. As childhood draws to a close, much of the overdressing that young children enjoy is replaced by an interest in "correct" dressing.

MATERIALS Unlike the adult whose interest in materials is concentrated on their durability and appearance of expensiveness, the child's interest in materials is concentrated mainly on their feel. The child likes soft fabrics of all kinds and enjoys touching them. Furs are special favorites. It does not matter if the fur is real or expensive; if it has a soft feel, the child will like it.

Since soft materials, such as silks and velvets, are suitable only for dress-up clothing, liking for these materials adds greatly to the child's interest in dress-up clothes. By contrast, lack of interest in play clothes is due, in part, to the fact that they are made of sturdy, tough material (20, 31, 70).

Interest in Names

Young children are not interested in their names unless others comment favorably or unfavorably on them, thus calling attention to them. Instead, they accept their names in a matter-of-fact way, just as they accept their bodies. Their names have been a part of themselves ever since they were born, as have their bodies.

As their social horizons broaden and as they spend more and more time outside the home, children dis-

Figure 15-4. Names are symbols in the minds of others.

cover that people—peers as well as adults—regard names as labels or symbols of identity and that they, like everyone else, are judged by these labels. As Harari and McDavid have pointed out, "People, like inanimate objects, are often judged by their labels" (32). When this discovery is made, children begin to become interested in their names.

How people react to their names will determine how great an interest children will have in them. When the reactions are favorable, their interest will be weaker than when the reactions are unfavorable. When children sense or know that social reactions to their names are unfavorable, they develop an almost obsessive interest in them. If, for example, children feel that they are being discriminated against in the peer group because of a surname associated with an ethnic or religious group against which there is prejudice, they may beg their parents to change their names, or they may shun social situations whenever members of other ethnic or religious groups will be present.

Any name that is markedly different from the names of age-mates likewise arouses children's interest in their names. If social reactions toward the name are favorable, the child will like it. On the other hand, if children feel that different names make them conspicuous and different from their age-mates, they will dislike their names even if social reactions to them are neutral or even favorable. The stronger their dislike of their names, the stronger will be children's interest in them (10, 11, 12, 13, 43, 71).

There are many reasons why children dislike their names. Some of the most common causes for their dislikes are given in Box 4-10, which shows what names are potential hazards to children's personal and social adjustments. When, for example, children have pleasant associations with names, they will like them. Unpleasant associations, regardless of the cause, make children dislike their names. Figure 15-4 shows some common associations with names. John and Anne, for example, are associated with all-American boys and girls and, hence, are liked. By contrast, Percy is associated with a sissy and Jane with the cliché, "Plain Jane." As a result, both are disliked.

Interest in Different Names

Every child, in the American culture today, has at least two names, a given name and a family or surname. In addition, many children have other names, especially middle names, nicknames, and pet names which family members use when they speak to them. Box 15-5 lists the different names children may have.

How much interest children have in their different names will depend upon two conditions. *First,* the more often a name is used, the more interest children will have in it. Even a disliked name, if used only infrequently, will be of little interest to them. For example, few children use their middle names, at least until they reach adolescence. A boy will tell others that his name is "John Smith" instead of giving his full name, "John McHugh Smith," and a girl will inform others that she is "Mary Jones," not that she is "Mary Anne Jones."

Second, how much interest children have in each name they have will be greatly influenced by how

DIFFERENT KINDS OF NAMES

GIVEN NAMES
These names are often called "first names" or "Christian names." They are given to children at the time of birth and are legally registered with their birth certificates. Once registered, they cannot be changed except by legal actions. Usually given names are selected by parents, though occasionally other family members or friends may suggest the names to parents, who make the final decision about the matter.

FAMILY NAMES
Family names, often called "surnames" or "last names," are names borne by all members of the same family. Like given names, the family name is given to a child at birth and is registered on the birth certificate. Only with legal action, such as marriage or petition to the court for a change of name, can family names be changed. When children are legitimate, their family names are those of their fathers. Illegitimate children have the family name of the mother.

MIDDLE NAMES
Some children have one or more middle names—names between their given and their family names. Like given and family names, they are usually given to children at birth and are registered on their birth certificates. Should parents or children, for one reason or another, want to add a middle name later, this must be done with legal action to be valid. And, like given names or family names, middle names cannot be changed without legal action: Some people do not use their middle names except for legal documents.

NICKNAMES
Almost all children acquire nicknames when they begin to associate with peers. These often reflect the judgment of other children. They may be favorable or unfavorable, depending on how members of the social group judge the child. There are many ways in which nicknames are derived, the most common of which are: shortening of given names or family names, such as "Joe" for "Joseph" or "Beck" for "Beckman"; emphasis on some physical defect, such as "Fatso" or "Beanpole"; emphasis on personality defects as "Crybaby" or "Pipsqueak"; names based on nationality or place of origin, such as "Dago" or "Frenchie"; names coming from animals, such as "Pig" or "Ass"; names derived from initials, such as "Hel" from "Helen Elizabeth Leonard"; or names from family pet names, as "Junior" or "Sweetie."

PET NAMES
Pet names are bestowed upon children by family members. They are indications of endearment, as compared with ridicule, which is characteristic of nicknames. It is usually parents who give children their pet names though occasionally grandparents or older siblings have their own pet names for a child. It is not unusual for a child to have several pet names, each given by a different family member. A child, for example, may be called "Bunny" by the mother, "Junior" by the father, and "Kid" by an older brother.

KINSHIP NAMES
Within a family, every member has a kinship name—"mother," "father," "son," "daughter," "grandmother," etc. These kinship names are not usually used as a form of address for children, though parents sometimes use them as pet names, calling a boy "son" or a girl "daughter." Some children refer to their sisters as "sister" and their brothers as "brother." However, given names, nicknames, or pet names are more frequently used for children within the family.

---

much they dislike it. Their dislike, in turn, will be influenced by social reactions to their names. Nicknames and pet names, for example, are usually a focal point of interest in names among children because social reactions to these names are more often unfavorable than favorable.

During the childhood years, the names used for children are mainly given names, nicknames, and pet names. Consequently, their interest will be concentrated on these names. Unless there are several children in the same class in school with the same given names, family names will not be used in referring to children. Middle names are rarely used by children unless they dislike their given names so much that they beg family members to call them by their middle names.

Interest in family or surnames is slight except under three conditions: first, if they are different enough from the family names of peers to make them conspicuous; second, if they are associated with a minority group against which there is peer prejudice; and, third, if they are different from the parents' names. Children, for example, who have stepfathers may be embarrassed when their friends ask them why their names are different from their parents' names. Under such conditions, the family name becomes a source of concern and a focal point of interest.

Perhaps the strongest interest children have in their names is centered on their *nicknames* and on the pet names used by members of their families when addressing them. They learn, in their early contacts with peers, that these names are labels that call forth pronounced reactions, usually unfavorable. Children realize that both nicknames and pet names, as used by peers, are verbal caricatures, which emphasize some characteristic their peers are ridiculing.

For example, a girl whose nickname is "Kitty" (in short for her given name, "Katherine") will quickly realize that she is being ridiculed by peers when they call her "Kitty Kat." Similarly, a boy will not resent being called "Billy" because he realizes that social reactions to that nickname are favorable. But, if he is called "Billy Boy," he realizes that he is being ridiculed because his peers believe he is a "mother's boy" who is tied to parental apron strings.

So long as the environment is limited to the family circle, children's interests in *pet names* will be toned with favorable emotions. However, when they go out into the broader world, children soon discover that members of the peer group use pet names not as terms of endearment but as forms of ridicule. The little boy who was proud to be called "Junior" at home begins to hate that name when peers use it. Similarly, the little girl who derives great satisfaction from being called "darling" at home discovers that peers use that term in a derisive way. As in the case of nicknames, the more children dislike their pet names, the more they become focal points of interest.

Kinship names are accepted by young children in a matter-of-fact way. For the most part, they have heard these names applied to them by family members ever since they were old enough to understand their meanings. So long as kinship names remain in the family, and so long as they are not made into pet names, children will show little interest in them. When, on the other hand, family members begin to use the pet name "Sonny" for "son" and "Babe" for "baby," and when these pet names are picked up by their age-mates and used as nicknames, it is a different story. Their dislike for what they regard as a type of ridicule will make them keenly interested in these kinship names.

Interest in Status Symbols

A status symbol is a prestige symbol. It tells others that the person has a higher status than those with whom that person is identified. What is a status symbol at one age, however, will not necessarily be a status symbol at another. It depends on what is important and valued by the group with which the person is identified *at that time.* Going to a "name" school, for example, is a status symbol for an adolescent but not for a child, because the child does not realize how society rates different schools. Toys and playthings are status symbols for a child but not for an adolescent because they do not add to the adolescent's prestige in the eyes of the peer group.

Status symbols also vary according to the group with which the person is identified. Children in a school that places high value on sports regard athletic achievement as a prestige symbol. In another school, where emphasis is placed on scholarship and athletics are regarded merely as a way to get exercises, academic achievement is a far greater prestige symbol than athletic achievement.

Even before children spend much of their time with members of the peer group, they discover that attention from others can be facilitated by status symbols. This knowledge motivates an interest in status symbols. Each year, as children become increasingly aware of the role status symbols play in social acceptance, their interest in them increases.

Essentials of Status Symbols

For a status symbol to attract the child's interest, it must meet certain criteria. *First,* it must give the child satisfaction in the form of social attention, preferably from the peer group. Favorable attention, the child knows, is a stepping stone to group acceptance.

Second, a status symbol must be valued by others if it is to give the attention the child craves. A large number of toys is highly valued by young children, and so children who have more toys than their playmates will be envied. Satisfaction will come from the attention envy brings.

Third, with the child's growing realization of the role played by socioeconomic status, the status symbols that meet the child's needs best are those which proclaim to others, either directly or indirectly, a favorable socioeconomic status. An older child is more interested in the father's occupational standing than the younger child, for example, because the older child recognizes that socioeconomic status and occupation go hand in hand.

Fourth, to arouse a strong interest in the child, status symbols must be visible for all to see. Invisible status symbols, which are important to adolescents and adults, are too sophisticated for a child to understand. A child cannot, for example, understand the status-symbol value of club membership or family background. As a result, the child is not interested in them. Ryan (70) has described this criterion of status-symbol value thus:

> The child thinks in concrete rather than in abstract terms. It is much easier for him to attribute acceptance or rejection to something tangible such as possession of the uniform or symbol of the group than it is to attribute it to something intangible such as sportsmanship or friendliness.

Changes in Status Symbols

As social values change, so do the status symbols used to display the individual's possession of the objects or qualities valued. These changed values may come from age changes—with older children having values different from young children—or they may come from social mobility—moving from one group to another.

It is, for example, not a status symbol for children to be popular with members of the opposite sex when they are young. In fact, during the gang age, being popular with members of the opposite sex is likely to lead to the labels "tomboy" or "sissy." As puberty changes take place, this value changes. Being popular with members of the opposite sex is then a far more important status symbol than being popular with members of the same sex.

Moving from one group to another, with horizontal, upward, or downward social mobility, is likewise responsible for value changes. Upper- and lower-class children often have different values about aggressive behavior and about using slang and swear words. Profanity may be a status symbol for lower-class children, but it will not necessarily be for upper-class children.

The most marked change in values comes in the relative importance of quantity and quality. Young children are primarily interested in the *quantity* of status symbols they have. If they have more toys, more family television sets, and more cars than their peers, they feel superior. This increases their interest in status symbols.

As childhood draws to a close, children begin to appreciate *quality* in status symbols. Girls recognize that having more dresses than their peers is not necessarily synonymous with being superior to them unless their dresses are made of better material and come from more prestigious stores. Similarly, the older boy learns that a small foreign-made car of expensive design carries more prestige than a large car of inexpensive make. With this discovery, the child's interest shifts from quantity to quality.

As children begin to become cognizant of deviations from the average, they notice first those which are qualitatively inferior. They notice a dilapidated house sooner than one of equal size but in a better state of repair. In addition, they are far more attracted to upper-status patterns of living than to lower-status patterns and are more favorably impressed by things that are of better quality.

Some Common Childhood Status Symbols

There are certain status symbols that are universally used and understood in American culture today. What these are is explained in Box 15–6. (3, 23, 64, 70).

It is important to realize that these status symbols are not used by children of all ages. Some are more valuable at one age than at another. In the case of material possessions, toys are a status symbol for young children, but among older children athletic equipment and radios of their own are status symbols that are of little status-symbol value to preschoolers.

The prestige of the family in the community, as shown by leadership roles in different community organizations and club membership, is unimportant to young children because they do not understand the meaning of them. However, by the time children reach the fourth or fifth grades, they are able to understand the prestige value of these symbols.

Box 15–6

SOME COMMON STATUS SYMBOLS IN CHILDHOOD

MATERIAL POSSESSIONS
Among young children, toys and play equipment are important, but among older children, clothes, athletic equipment, collections of stamps, shells, etc., radio or television sets of their own, and comics serve as status symbols.

FAMILY POSSESSIONS
A large house with a big lawn, a game or recreation room, several cars, a boat, a private plane, and servants are vicarious prestige symbols for children at every age.

POPULARITY WITH PEERS
The larger the number of playmates and friends, especially those who are well liked by the peer group, the greater the prestige value of popularity.

ATHLETIC SUCCESS
At any age, skill in games and sports superior to that of peers is a status symbol.

ACADEMIC SUCCESS
Among young children, being a good reader is a status symbol, and among older children, good academic grades serve this purpose.

PARENTAL OCCUPATION
The parent's occupation, especially if it carries a title or is connected with a prestigious organization, becomes a status symbol for a child.

LEADERSHIP ROLES
Playing a leadership role, either by the child or by parents in business or community affairs, becomes a status symbol for the whole family.

CLUB MEMBERSHIP
When parents belong to community clubs, especially if they are private and exclusive clubs, children use this as a status symbol.

AUTONOMY
Having more freedom to do what they want, when they want, than their peers is always a status symbol for children at every age. Children brought up by permissive training more often have this status symbol than children from authoritarian or democratic families.

SPENDING MONEY
Having more spending money than peers, whether from an allowance or from earnings, has great prestige value during childhood.

EARNING MONEY
A child who earns money creates the impression of being older than peers, thus adding to the prestige status of an "earner."

TRAVEL
The more children travel, the further from home, and the more by prestigious carriers, such as boats or airplanes, the greater the status-symbol value of travel.

Ways of Showing Interest in Status Symbols

Children have many ways of showing their interest in status symbols. The ones they use depend partly on what they have found, from their own experiences, are most effective in giving them the attention they crave and partly on what they have found most effective when used by siblings or age-mates. However, at some time or other during the childhood years, almost every child uses most of the methods described below.

One of the earliest ways children show an interest in status symbols is *boasting* and *bragging* about what they have, what their families have, what they can do, and what their parents have done. In addition, children claim that their possessions and achievements are superior to those of their age-mates and that their parents' possessions and achievements are superior to those of their age-mates' parents.

When they visit in the homes of playmates, children compare what they see there with what they have in their own homes. If they feel that these are superior to what they have, they express *envy* and *dissatisfaction* with what they have. They tell their playmates that they wish they could have what their playmates have, and they complain to their parents about their not giving them what their playmates' parents give them. If they feel that their parents' status in the community is inferior to that of their playmates' parents, they often express their dissatisfaction and envy by asking their parents why they are not leaders in the community, and why their father does not have a better job. Or they make derogatory comments about their parents' lack of community achievements.

It is not uncommon, especially as children grow older, to express their interest in status symbols by *daydreams* in which they are surrounded by all the status symbols they crave. Some children take part-time after-school *jobs* to earn money to buy status symbols while, at the same time, being able to boast to their age-mates of their near-adult status as earners. Still others show how strong their interest in status symbols is by *appropriating* things from their play-mates or from stores which they believe will serve as important status symbols for them.

Many children discover that making derogatory comments about the possessions and achievements of others eliminates some of the envy and dissatisfaction they have. This *"sour-grapes" attitude* is easy for most adults to interpret. The more unfavorable comments children make about others, the stronger their interest in the possessions and achievements of those people.

Interest in Religion

Interest in religion is fostered by the training children receive in the home, Sunday school, synagogue, and by emphasis placed on religious observances in their daily lives. Children who are brought up to say grace before meals, who are expected to say prayers before going to bed, and whose parents read or tell them stories from the Bible, tend to have a greater interest in religion than those whose main contact with religion is a weekly visit to Sunday school.

As children grow older and spend increasingly more time with members of the peer group, playmates and friends will influence their interests. A child, for example, whose friends talk about religion and their religious observances will have a greater interest in religion than will a child whose friends show little or no interest in religion and have a negative attitude toward all religious observances.

Regardless of differences in religious instruction and social pressures to be interested in religion, all young children, at some time or other, become interested in those aspects of religion that are called to their attention by experiences in daily life. If they are told that rain, snow, and sunshine, for example, come from Heaven and that God lives in Heaven, it is natural that children will become interested in God and in

Heaven. If parental discipline is tied to religion and if children are threatened with "going to Hell" after they die if they constantly break family rules, it is logical that they will become interested in Hell—where it is, what happens there, who the Devil is, etc.

Areas of Religious Interest

Religion contains two elements: beliefs and practices. These are separate and distinct. Consequently, interest in one element does not necessarily guarantee interest in the other. Nor does it mean that interest in both elements will be equal. One person, for example, may be especially interested in religious observances and show slight interest in what is often regarded as "theology" or religious beliefs. The reverse may be true of another person. So it is with children. Some are primarily interested in religious observances and others are primarily interested in religious beliefs. Which interests them more is determined partly by the emphasis placed on these two elements in their early religious training and partly by which they find, from their own experiences, meets their needs better. Their interest in religion is, thus, primarily egocentric.

RELIGIOUS OBSERVANCES   Children who have a strong interest in religion devote considerable time to religious activities. Usually this interest persists as long as they enjoy the novelty of the activities and as long as they prove to be enjoyable and rewarding experiences for them.

Religious services, in churches and synagogues, appeal to young children because of their colorful pageantry. The ritual of the service intrigues them and they like to join in the singing. They also enjoy looking around at the people at worship, to see what they are doing. Interest is, thus, a mixture of reverence and curiosity. After a time, this interest wanes and children begin to rebel against going to these services.

Children enjoy going to *Sunday school* if the activities are forms of play—being read to, having an opportunity to sing, and participating in religious holiday celebrations. Children also enjoy being with their friends and playmates on days when, otherwise, they might not be permitted to go out to play with the neighborhood play groups.

As children grow older, the Sunday school activities often begin to resemble schoolwork. Children are expected to memorize parts from the Bible, to answer questions from assigned homework, and to recite what they were expected to learn. While there are some aspects of the Sunday school activities that still appeal to them, such as opportunities to sing, to be with their friends, and to participate in religious holiday celebrations, much of the activity of Sunday school becomes boring to them. Were it not for the fact that it gives them an opportunity to be with their friends, they would openly rebel against Sunday school attendance.

Older children like the *young people's organizations* of their churches and synagogues, such as gymnasiums for play and social gatherings in the cities, "socials" in the small communities, picnics, holiday celebrations, and outings. Their interest in these activities is primarily social rather than religious. As childhood draws to a close, participation in these activities begins to wane rapidly (22).

Interest in *prayer* follows much the same pattern as interest in other religious activities. Children under 8 years of age feel that prayer is a way of talking to God; they believe that God answers their prayers by telling them how to be good or what to do or not to do. They ask God for material things and for help in doing things they feel incapable of doing alone. Older children ask for help, seek forgiveness for misdeeds, and thank God for His help. On the whole, children's prayers are a "begging ritual" (50).

As children grow older, their interest in prayer usually wanes. They feel that most of their prayers, for material possessions, for help, or for guidance, are unanswered and, consequently, they receive no personal benefits from them. Figure 15–5 shows the typical transition in children's reactions to prayer as they grow older.

Family celebrations of religious holidays, on the other hand, retain their interest for children for a longer time. This is because they are more social than religious in nature. The celebration of Christmas, for example, becomes a festive day in the home with family gatherings, special food, decorations in which children take a part, and relaxation of rules and schedules. Interest in *family religious rituals,* such as grace before meals, Bible readings and prayers, wanes rapidly. These rituals are engaged in only because of parental pressures.

RELIGIOUS BELIEFS Children's religious beliefs reflect the teachings they have received at home, in Sunday school, in church, or in synagogue. If, for example, children are taught to think of God as a person who will become angry when they do something wrong and that He always punishes people for their sins, they will have very different beliefs about religion than will children to whom God has been presented in a different way (61). Since these beliefs are taught to

Figure 15–5. Typical transition in children's prayers.

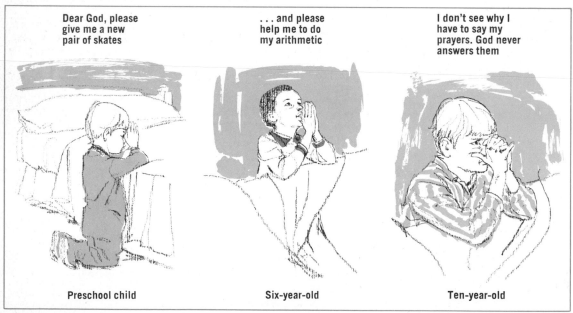

| Dear God, please give me a new pair of skates | . . . and please help me to do my arithmetic | I don't see why I have to say my prayers. God never answers them |

| Preschool child | Six-year-old | Ten-year-old |

children by parents and Sunday school teachers rather than by peers, children tend to accept them uncritically, just as they accept uncritically what parents and teachers tell them about other things.

To make it possible for young children to understand religion, religious concepts are taught in everyday language and by the use of everyday experiences. As a result, these concepts become concrete and realistic. Early religious beliefs are, thus, based on realistic concepts. Children learn to think of God, Heaven, Hell, angels, and the Devil in terms of the pictures they have seen of them or the stories they have been told about them.

Later, as children's comprehension increases and as their experiences become more varied, their concepts change. Their concept of God as a father, for example, will be influenced by their experiences with their own fathers and by the experiences their friends have with their fathers. Likewise, children's concepts of sin and forgiveness will reflect the way they have been treated when they misbehave.

As children grow older, their reasoning ability increases, their experiences broaden, and they learn, from teachings in school or from reading, facts that often conflict with what they had learned earlier at home and in Sunday school. They also discover that their friends may have concepts that differ from theirs. All this leads to confusion and doubt, which tends to weaken their religious beliefs.

At all times throughout childhood, children's beliefs about religion vary because they are built on concepts developed by different training and different experiences. However, certain religious beliefs are common among American children today (19, 50, 53, 62). These are given and briefly explained in Box 15–7.

Ways of Showing Interest in Religion

The earliest way in which children show an interest in religion is by *asking questions*. Between the ages of 3 and 4 years, most children begin to ask questions about religion, such as "Who is God?", "Where is Heaven?", "What is death?", "What are angels?", etc. (22, 26).

When children are able to comprehend the meaning of stories told or read to them (at about the same time they are able to ask questions), they like to hear *religious stories*. These stories appeal to them in much the same way as fairy tales do. Both relate to people,

---

BOX 15–7

SOME CHILDISH RELIGIOUS BELIEFS

- *God.* God is a very large person, dressed in white flowing garments, with a kind or stern face and white beard. He is a "watcher," and punishes those who misbehave, though He can be supplicated through prayer. He rewards those who are good and sends them to Heaven when they die.
- *Heaven.* Heaven is God's abode in the clouds where people have everything they want and where there is eternal peace and happiness.
- *Angels.* People who are good during life go to Heaven after death and become angels, dressed in flowing white garments.
- *Hell.* Hell is a place below the earth where there is eternal unhappiness and punishment for those who have been bad during their lives.
- *Devil.* Hell is ruled over by the Devil who is in the form of a man with horns and a tail. He carries a pitchfork and is red all over.
- *Miracles.* Miracles are acts which only God can do.
- *Bible.* The Bible is a book written by God. Every word of it is true and to doubt it is sinful.
- *Prayer.* Prayer is a way of asking God for something important.
- *Christmas.* Christmas is the time when Santa Claus comes down the chimney and fills stockings with gifts for children who have been good.
- *Easter.* Easter is the time when the Easter Bunny brings nests and baskets filled with candies and colored eggs.
- *Death.* When people die, they go to sleep and never wake up. Death may be caused by old age, by illness, or by disobeying God.
- *Life after Death.* After death, people go to Heaven or Hell, depending on whether they have been good or bad during life.

---

countries, and situations so different from the everyday environment that the child enjoys hearing them over and over. At different ages children show preferences for different parts of the Bible. Children under 8 years of age prefer stories relating to the birth and childhood of Jesus and the childhood of Samuel, Moses, Joseph, and David, while older children show a greater interest in the historical books of the Old Testament. Most children are interested primarily in persons and happenings rather than doctrines (60, 65).

Most religious storybooks for children are illustrated. Even young children are fascinated by these pictures and enjoy looking at them even when not being read to. *Looking at pictures* is usually accompanied by asking questions, especially about the differences in clothing, hair styles, and manner of living of people in Biblical times as compared with people today.

Older children often *talk to their friends* about religion. This is centered more on religious observances, such as form of worship in the church or in the home, than about religious beliefs. Although young children may talk to their friends about whether or not they believe in Santa Claus or the Easter Bunny, older children are far more likely to discuss such beliefs as the existence of Heaven or Hell or whether there are angels and a Devil.

As was pointed out earlier, at all ages in childhood, interest in religion is shown by *participating in religious observances* in the church, the synagogue, the Sunday school, or the home. As children grow older, interest in the social aspect of this participation becomes stronger in most children than interest in the religious aspect. Of all religious observances, the greatest interest is centered on *religious holidays,* which, as was pointed out earlier, appeal to children of all ages because of their pageantry and differentness from the usual religious observances.

The development of *religious doubt*—a tendency to question the value of religious observances, such as prayer, first, and later, religious beliefs, such as beliefs about Heaven and Hell—is a common expression of interest in religion in childhood. If children were not interested in religion, they would not spend the time and effort involved in questioning it. What forms doubting takes and the hazardous nature of doubting will be discussed in more detail later in the chapter, in the section related to hazards in the development of interests.

Interest in Sex

Although interest in sex is common among all children at all ages, it is greater after children enter school—nursery school, kindergarten, or first grade—because of more frequent and closer peer contacts than they had when their peer contacts were limited mainly to the neighborhood play group.

Throughout the school years, interest in sex increases, usually reaching a peak during the period of puberty changes. Because these changes occur mainly during the closing years of childhood, it can be stated with little question of its accuracy that at no period in life, with the possible exception of early marriage, is interest in sex so preoccupying as in the part of puberty that overlaps the closing years of childhood.

There are certain conditions in childhood that are responsible for this increase in interest in sex as children grow older. Unquestionably, one of the most important of these is *peer pressures.* It is the thing to do to talk about sex—as is true of any tabooed subject—when with gang members and away from listening adult ears. Being able to tell or to understand smutty jokes and to find humor in them makes a contribution to the child's reputation of being a "good sport."

As children of today are surrounded by sex in the *mass media,* all forms of mass media—comics, movies, television, and newspapers—contribute pictures and information about sex that increase children's interest in it. Rating of movies and television shows as "unsuitable for children" or "suitable only with parental guidance," further heightens children's interest in sex.

The *occurrences of everyday life*—the arrival of a new baby in the family or the neighborhood, a pet that has a litter of young, the marriage of a neighbor or family member, the enlargement of a woman's body during pregnancy followed by a flattening of the abdomen and an enlargement of the "bumps" on her chest after the arrival of a baby—all help to keep interest in sex alive during the childhood years.

Parental, peer, and school emphasis on *sex differences* and *sex appropriateness* adds to children's interest in sex. Unquestionably, one of the strongest contributors to children's interest in sex is *sex education.* When parents make a point of taking their children aside, away from siblings, and telling them behind closed doors the "facts of life," ending with the admonition not to talk about these matters to anyone, can children escape becoming greatly interested in this mysterious aspect of life? Sex education classes in school, set aside as special classes which can be attended only with written consent of parents, add their share to heightening children's interest in sex.

Pattern of Interest in Sex

In spite of the fact that interest in sex is greatly influenced by environmental conditions, there is a pattern of interest that is almost universal among children in the American culture today. During the first year of life, in the process of exploring their own bodies, *babies* sooner or later touch their sex organs and discover that this results in a pleasurable sensation. When they discover their navels, they find it fun to put their fingers into the "hole." Other than this exploratory play, there is little evidence of interest in sex until the child is between 2 and 3 years of age.

During the *preschool* years, interest in sex is concentrated mainly on where babies come from, why some animals have many babies at one time but humans have only one or possibly two, why the male and female bodies are different, why children's bodies differ from those of adults, and why members of the two sexes wear different clothes and do different things.

With association with peers, in preschool or in first grade, interest in sex is not only increased but it is greatly broadened. *Older children* now want to know not only where babies come from but also what the role of both parents is in producing babies and what the birth process is. In the same way, there is an extension of their interest in sex differences. Now they want to know what makes males and females different, what makes adult bodies different from children's bodies, why the social group expects members of the two sexes to dress and behave differently, and why members of one sex are not expected or permitted to do some of the things that members of the other sex are expected and permitted to do.

When *puberty* changes begin to appear, either on the surface of their own bodies or on the bodies of their friends and classmates, interest in sex shifts to

---

BOX 15-8

METHODS OF SATISFYING INTEREST IN SEX

ASKING QUESTIONS
Among preschool children, the most common questions relate to the origin of babies, the coming of another baby, the sex organs and their functions, and physical sex differences. Among older children, the emphasis is on the origin of babies, the process of birth, and the father's part in reproduction.

EXPLORATION OF THE SEX ORGANS
At first, children explore their own sex organs, but by age 6, mutual exploration with a peer of either sex is common, often in "doctor games." Exploration consists of insertion of objects into body orifices, insertion of the penis into the vagina, direct observation of the anatomy, manual exploration, oral contacts, exhibitionism, and comparing masculine prowess in the toilet.

HOMOSEXUAL PLAY
As a means of satisfying curiosity, play with members of the same sex is more common than heterosexual play. Homosexual play mainly involves exploration of the genitals.

MASTURBATION
By handling and playing with their sex organs, children learn that this produces pleasurable sensations. This they may learn by trial and error, by watching other children masturbate, or by being taught to masturbate by older children.

TALKING TO FRIENDS ABOUT SEX
Children pass on the information they get from parents and other sources to their friends, either as statements of fact or in smutty stories and jokes.

LOOKING AT PICTURES
Pictures of adults in amorous poses in sex comics and of sex organs, reproduction, and childbirth in sex education books provide children with facts that they do not fully understand when verbal explanations are given.

READING BOOKS
There are many books for home and school use written for children of different ages to explain facts about sex, which are known, from studies of children's interests in and comprehension of sex, to be able to meet their needs. These are carefully illustrated with drawings and pictures to make the text material meaningful to the reader.

SEX EDUCATION
Special classes, designed to give children accurate and comprehensible facts about sex, are offered on a noncompulsory basis by schools, camps, and churches. The approach may be constructive, preventive, or both. *Constructive* education concentrates on giving facts and explaining the meaning of sexual behavior. *Preventive* education gives facts but concentrates on teaching children what to avoid in sexual behavior and relationships.

the causes and meanings of these changes. With the appearance of changes on the surface of the body—the secondary sex characteristics—there are changes in the sex organs—the primary sex characteristics. These changes produce new sensations that focus children's attention on what these sensations mean, such as why they now feel differently about themselves and members of the other sex than they did when they were younger. Although interest in the different aspects of sex that preoccupied them when they were younger still persists, pubescent children now shift the focus of their interest to puberty changes. The addition of these interests to their old interests is primarily responsible for children's preoccupation with sex at this age (8, 78).

In this normal pattern of interest in sex throughout the childhood years, it is important to realize that at all ages this interest is mainly objective until children reach puberty. Then interest becomes mainly subjective. Interest in the origin of babies, in differences between the sexes, and in the relationships of the two sexes, for example, is *objective*. Children are interested in what is happening to other people rather than what is happening to them. The shift to *subjective* interest comes with the puberty changes which affect them, their friends, and age-mates, not just age groups older or younger than they are.

Ways of Expressing Interest in Sex

Since it is known from studies of children's interest in sex that this interest normally increases throughout childhood and reaches a peak at puberty, overt expressions of this interest indicate that the reverse is true. Older children, for example, ask fewer questions than younger, and there are fewer overt manifestations of homosexual and heterosexual play among older than among younger children.

The explanation for this apparent contradiction as children grow older is that their interest is not overtly expressed because of social pressures to inhibit these expressions, and fear of social disapproval and punishment if they fail to do so. Children have learned from past experiences, for example, that if they want to masturbate they must do so in private. They discover that if they cloak their questions in apparently scientific interest that they will have a better chance of getting answers to these questions than if the questions suggest morbid curiosity on the child's part.

This cloaking of interest does not mean a waning of interest. Instead, it means that interest is strong but is expressed in ways that are more likely to bring the information desired than the methods used when children were younger.

Box 15–8 describes the many ways children try to satisfy their interest in sex. Almost all children use all these methods at some time or other during the childhood years. However, some give children greater satisfaction when they are young and others, more satisfaction as they grow older. Young children, for example, get more satisfaction from asking questions about sex, and older children get more satisfaction from reading books or from sex education courses in school (8, 13, 27, 58, 78).

Interest in School

Studies of children's interests in school have revealed two very important facts: interest in school follows a pattern that is almost universal in today's American culture, and interest in school becomes more selective as children grow older.

In the *predictable pattern* of interest in school, there is a tendency for interest to wane and to be replaced by boredom or actual dislike of school. To young children, going to school means "growing up." From early preschool days, they look forward eagerly to the time when they will be known to members of the social group as "school children." Going to school is thus a status symbol for them.

As children progress through the grades, however, interest in things that are distinctly a part of school and in scholarship declines and interest in things that go along with life outside school, such as recess, sports, and play, increases. By the time children approach the end of elementary school, with the onset of puberty, they often claim that they "hate" school, they rebel against doing schoolwork, and they talk about how anxious they are to leave school as soon as the law permits them to do so.

This change in attitude toward school is, by no means, universal. However, it is widespread enough to be considered "characteristic." Many children who actually like school claim that they do not like it because it is the thing to do. They do not want to be regarded by peers as "squares" by having interests that are different from those of the group with which they are identified (18, 57, 80, 82).

There are many conditions that are responsible for changes in interest in school as childhood progresses. These changes are, for the most part, in the form of decline rather than increase in interest. What they are and how they lessen children's interests in school are explained in Box 15-9 (5, 6, 24, 38, 67).

The second important fact about children's interests in school is that their interests become *more selective* as they grow older. Instead of liking everything in school, as most children do at first, older children select certain things that they like and do not like about school. Some children, for example, are primarily interested in academic activities, but for others, the extracurricular activities are the focal point of their inter-est. Since the major part of the school day is spent in academic activities, children who fail to find academic activities interesting tend to develop an unfavorable attitude toward school in general.

There is also a selective interest within these two areas of school life. Children tend to be interested in the school subjects they find relevant to their needs, sex appropriate, easy, and in which they get good grades. On the other hand, they tend to lack interest in school subjects they regard as irrelevant, sex inappropriate, difficult, boring, badly taught or taught in a

---

BOX 15-9

CONDITIONS RESPONSIBLE FOR CHILDREN'S INTEREST IN SCHOOL

EARLY SCHOOL EXPERIENCES
Children who are physically and intellectually ready for first grade have more favorable attitudes toward school than children who are unready for school. Nursery school and kindergarten experience facilitate adjustment and make early school experiences more pleasant.

PARENTAL INFLUENCES
Parents influence children's attitudes toward school in general and also their attitudes toward the importance of education, toward studying, toward different school sub jects, and toward their teachers.

SIBLING ATTITUDES
Older siblings have much the same influence on children's attitudes toward school as do parents. By contrast, the attitudes of younger siblings are relatively unimportant.

PEER ATTITUDES
Interest in and attitudes toward school in general and toward different school activities is peer-instigated. To ensure acceptance by the peer group, children learn that they must accept the group's interests and values. If classmates verbalize their dislikes of school, children must do likewise or risk being called a "brain" or "teacher's pet."

ACCEPTANCE BY THE PEER GROUP
Because the favorite parts of the school day center around extracurricular activities with peers, good relationships with teachers and good marks cannot compensate for lack of peer acceptance.

ACADEMIC SUCCESS
How great an influence academic success will have on children's attitudes toward school will depend on how much value the peer group places on it. If it is a status symbol, it will enhance the achiever's status in the peer group. Academic failure is ego-deflating to all children and leads to a dislike of the situation in which this failure occurs. If academic failure means loss of promotion, it further increases children's dislike of school and weakens their interest in school.

ATTITUDE TOWARD WORK
Children brought up in homes where parents believe that childhood should be a happy, carefree time of life, usually develop a dislike for any activity that resembles work. So long as school is primarily play, they like it. But, as they advance through the grades, it requires more and more effort to do the work and this leads to a dislike for school.

TEACHER-PUPIL RELATIONSHIPS
How much or how little interest children have in school is influenced by their attitudes toward their teachers. When children bring to school an unfavorable concept of "teacher" based on what their parents or older siblings say and based on mass media portrayals of teachers, or when they have unfavorable personal experiences with teachers, their attitudes toward all teachers tend to be unfavorable.

EMOTIONAL CLIMATE OF THE SCHOOL
The emotional climate of the school is influenced by teacher attitudes and type of discipline used. Teachers who have good rapport with pupils and use democratic discipline encourage more favorable attitudes on the part of pupils than teachers who have "pets," who are bored with their jobs, who teach in a dull manner, and who are either too authoritarian or too permissive in their control of the classroom situation.

SOME COMMON CHILDHOOD INTERESTS

"boring" way by teachers they dislike, and in which they get poor grades.

Since enjoyment of extracurricular activities depends on peer acceptance, children who are well accepted find them more interesting than those who are marginally or poorly accepted. Children whose play skills are below those of their age-mates, for example, are not included in the games their classmates play during recess and before and after school. As a result, they feel left out of the fun their classmates are having. This has a great impact on how they feel about school in general.

Effects of Interests on Behavior in School

When children are interested in school and the academic and extracurricular activities connected with it, they enjoy the time spent in school, have good relationships with their teachers and classmates, do the work assigned to them to the best of their abilities, and are good "school citizens" in the sense that they try to obey the rules and regulations and avoid trouble-making. Because of their favorable attitudes and behavior, they are liked by their teachers and classmates. This further increases their liking for and interest in school (69).

On the other hand, children who are bored with school or actually dislike it show it by behavior that annoys their teachers and classmates and increases their dislike for school. Figure 15–6 shows some of the conditions that give rise to school boredom and how widespread its effects are on children's attitudes and behavior in the school situation.

There are many ways in which children show their attitudes toward school, the most common and most serious of which are discussed below.

SCHOOL PHOBIA   School phobia is a total or partial aversion to school and is expressed in such physical symptoms as nausea, anorexia, and a slight fever. The child may go to school and then complain of some somatic problem, such as upset stomach or headache. On the surface, the child's fear of school appears to stem from some aspect of the school situation, as shown by heightened anxiety when it is time to go to school. There is little evidence, however, that such is the case. Instead, the fear is part of a generalized anxiety resulting from fear of being away from the mother, a strong dependency on the mother or a mother substitute, and inability to establish autonomy (7, 57, 77).

While school phobia sometimes develops among older children, it is most common during kindergarten and the first four grades. Older children discover that fear of school is considered "babyish." Therefore, they usually project the blame on someone or something in the school situation. They maintain, for example, that they do not want to go to school because they are unprepared for a test, that the teacher does not like them, or that their classmates are always teasing them or refusing to play with them. Not recognizing that school phobias are "homegrown," some parents and schools try putting the child into another class or another school. This rarely works because the trouble lies not with the school but with the child.

TRUANCY   There are two kinds of truancy. In the first kind, children absent themselves from school *without* a lawful cause and without the permission of parents or school authorities. They go where they can do as they please without being seen by parents, neighbors, or law-enforcing officers. They may leave school during the day, complaining that they are "not feeling well" or that their parents want them to come home early. As there is always the possibility that parents will be notified if a child leaves school during the school day, the truant usually skips school for the entire day.

In the second kind of truancy, a child skips school *with* parental knowledge and consent. This is often true of children of the lower socioeconomic groups whose parents place little value on education or who want them to help at home or to leave school and take jobs as soon as they can get work papers. They contribute heavily to the school dropouts (76).

DISRUPTIVE BEHAVIOR   Children who are bored with school tend to become mischievious and trouble-makers. Having little or no interest in learning or in the different school or extracurricular activities, they spend the time their classmates are spending on learning in doing things to disturb them and to make the teacher's job difficult. As was stressed in the discussion of childhood misdemeanors (see Chapter 14), they are not ignorant of school rules but willfully break them in retaliation for lack of peer acceptance and unfavorable teacher attitudes toward them (33, 44, 68, 74).

UNDERACHIEVEMENT   Underachievers are individuals who work below their known capacities. Their capacities can be assessed either by standard tests or by

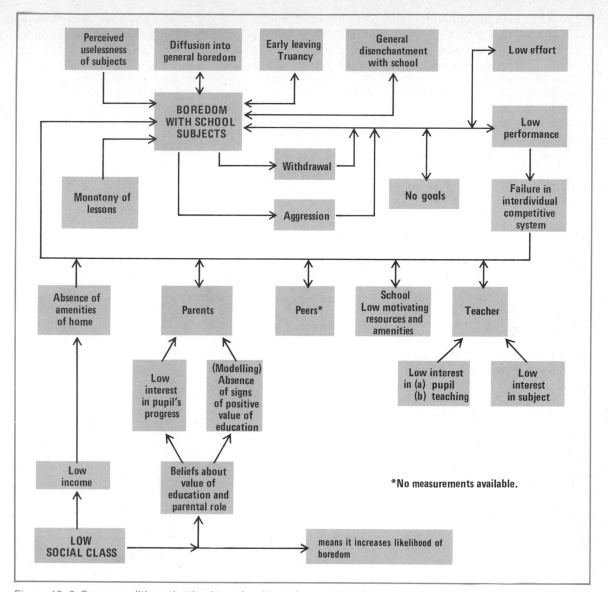

Figure 15–6. Some conditions that lead to school boredom and its widespread effects. (*Adapted from W. P. Robinson: Boredom in school.* British Journal of Educational Psychology, *1975, 45, 141–152. Used by permission.*)

objective evidence of what they are capable of when they are highly motivated.

School underachievers are students whose academic work falls below their academic ability as measured by standard tests of intelligence. Underachievers in school may be regarded as "intellectual delinquents." There are two kinds of underachievers:

long-term underachievers who show, over a period of time, that they are working below their capacities and *situational* underachievers who work below their capacities because of some traumatic experience, such as the death of a family member, a change to another school, or some other emotion-producing experience. The situational underachiever may become a long-term underachiever or the underachievement may last only until the individual has adjusted to the situation that gave rise to the underachievement.

Some students are *general* underachievers, working below their capacities in all school subjects; some are *specific* underachievers, working below their capacities in certain subjects only. However, unless the cause of underachievement is corrected, a specific underachiever is likely to develop into a general underachiever.

When children are underachievers, it is usual to blame the school. People claim that the teachers do not know how to teach or are too disinterested in their jobs to do them properly. Others blame parents for being too permissive and not requiring their children to study at home or pay attention at school. One area of parental permissiveness that has come under repeated attack is that of children's television watching.

Studies of the causes of underachievement have shown that the primary cause is within the child, although indirectly the home and school may be involved. The primary cause is rebellion and hostility against studying. This may be because of parental pressures to get good grades or poor teacher-pupil relationships stemming from boredom in a situation unfitted to the child's needs or interests. Most very bright children, for example, are underachievers because of boredom with schoolwork planned for children of average intelligence. Underachievement is also common when peer attitudes toward education are negative. Children who want to be accepted by agemates must conform to their behavior patterns. If doing just enough work to pass is the accepted practice, that is the standard pattern for other children to follow.

How important a role these conditions play in underachievement is shown by the fact that the onset of underachievement begins just about the time children's interest in school begins to wane and their interest in peer acceptance begins to grow stronger and stronger. This may begin as early as the second or third grade or it may occur slightly later. Figure 15-7 shows the pattern of underachievement as compared with the pattern of achievement of children who continue to work up to their capacities throughout the school years (2, 4, 66, 73, 79).

OVERACHIEVEMENT   Overachievement means achievement above the individual's known capacities. As in the case of underachievement, the individual's known capacities can be determined by tests or by objective evidence of what the individual is capable of when strongly motivated.

In the school situation, overachievers are students whose academic achievement is above their tested abilities. Children who are overachievers do better academic work that one can expect or hope from them. Like underachievement, overachievement may be long-term or it may be situational, such as during threat of failure. It, likewise, may be general or specific.

There is little evidence that overachievers are made such by good teaching or educational opportunities per se. Instead, there is evidence that if academic success is highly valued by parents, teachers, and members of the peer group, children who feel inadequate or who are hostile because they have not won the acceptance they crave may become overachievers to "show others." To achieve academic success, they may devote proportionally too much time to their studies, they may get help from parents or teachers, they may try to win teacher approval by "polishing the apple," or they may cheat. Whatever method they use to achieve the goal they hope will increase their acceptance, there is no evidence that their interest is in academic work per se, but rather it is in the prestige that this can bring. Because overachievement is a less common method of showing interest—or lack of interest—in school than is underachievement, studies of when it starts have been limited in number. There is, however, some evidence that it begins early in the school grades, as does underachievement, at the time when craving for peer acceptance is growing and when the initial enthusiasm for school has started to wear off (4, 42, 66, 79).

Interest in Future Vocations

Even before children enter school, they begin to show an interest in their future vocations—what they want to do when they are grown up. This interest is aroused by people's asking them what they want to do when they grow up and by what they hear and see about different vocations. As children read books about how people earn a living, for example, as they see in movies and television how people carry out exciting and adventuresome jobs in glamorous settings, and as they hear family members and neighbors talk about their jobs, they not only increase their interest in their own future vocations but they begin to make vocational

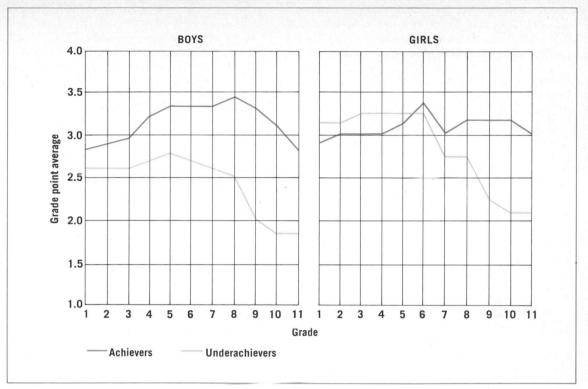

BOYS　　　　　　GIRLS

— Achievers　　　— Underachievers

Figure 15–7. The onset of underachievement in boys and girls. (*Adapted from M. C. Shaw and J. T. McCuen: The onset of academic underachievement in bright children.* Journal of Educational Psychology, *1960*, 51, *103–105. Used by permission.*)

choices—they want to do this when they grow up and they do not want to do that.

After children enter school, their interest in their future vocations increases. They hear age-mates talk about their future vocational plans, and they learn about more and more possible vocational opportunities from classroom discussions about different jobs, from mass media, and from school visits to different community business and industrial organizations.

There are many conditions that affect children's interests in, and attitudes toward, different vocations. The most common and most important of these conditions are given and explained in Box 15–10.

Early Vocational Choice

Asking children what they want to do or be when they are grown up encourages them to make vocational choices when they are too young and too inexperi-

enced to make wise choices. These choices are usually made on the basis of a whim, not an interest.

Even when children have been told, in school or in the home, about different vocational opportunities, they still do not know just what training, abilities, and interests these vocations require. Consequently, the choice is usually based on what is important to them *at that time:* the work of a person the child hero-worships or something important to the child (51, 52). See Figure 15–8.

Throughout the major part of childhood, children are in what is described as a "period of fantasy vocational choices." This period lasts until children approach puberty, around 11 or 12 years of age. Their choices are guided more by what they would like to do than by what they are capable of doing. Under such conditions, it is not surprising that their vocational choices change as their interests change and that they may make many choices within a period of a year.

FACTORS INFLUENCING CHILDREN'S VOCATIONAL ATTITUDES AND INTERESTS

PARENTAL ATTITUDES

Parental attitudes affect children's vocational attitudes in two ways. First, parents urge children to be interested in vocations they regard as desirable and prestigious, regardless of children's interests and aptitudes, and, second, they advise children to avoid certain vocations because they regard them as undesirable.

PRESTIGE OF VOCATIONS

Very early, children discover that different vocations have different degrees of prestige associated with them. White-collar jobs, for example, have far greater prestige than blue-collar or overall jobs.

ADMIRED PEOPLE

Children develop favorable attitudes toward the vocations of the people they admire or hero-worship— teachers, community or national leaders, or people in the mass media. There is a tendency to develop unfavorable attitudes toward the vocations of people they dislike.

ABILITIES AND INTERESTS

Children's physical and intellectual abilities, their interests, and their personalities play important roles in their attitudes toward different vocations. Unadventuresome children, for example, have favorable attitudes toward "safe jobs" while those who are more aggressive and daring regard such jobs as "boring" and want "exciting jobs."

SEX APPROPRIATENESS

Even though the sex barriers between jobs are rapidly breaking down, some jobs are still regarded as "men's work" and others as "women's work." Boys, as a group, are pressured by parents and peers to be interested in jobs regarded as appropriate for their sex, and girls, to have more favorable attitudes toward jobs considered "women's work" than toward those regarded as "men's work."

OPPORTUNITIES FOR INDEPENDENCE

Each year, as children become increasingly frustrated by adult restrictions, independence becomes increasingly important to them. Any jobs that offer some autonomy, such as the professions, are more favorably viewed by them than those they regard as "regimented," such as office and factory jobs.

CULTURAL STEREOTYPES

As children learn about different vocations, they learn the cultural stereotypes associated with these vocations. Unfavorable stereotypes—"old-maid school teachers" —lead to unfavorable attitudes toward teaching while favorable stereotypes—"athletic hero" or "war hero" —lead to favorable attitudes toward professional sports or military careers.

PERSONAL EXPERIENCES

Personal experiences with people in different vocations color children's attitudes toward those vocations. A child who regards the policeman at the school crossing as a "great guy" develops a favorable attitude toward a police career. By contrast, children who have unpleasant experiences with doctors and dentists claim they would "rather starve" than earn their livings as doctors or dentists.

The vocational choices of older children gradually become more stable as children increase their knowledge about vocational opportunities and as they become more aware of their abilities and limitations. However, there is no stability of vocational choice even during the adolescent years. Only when there is evidence of interests based on marked abilities in certain areas is there likely to be any degree of stability in vocational choice until the person is ready to enter the work world. Even then, shifts to different occupations and to different areas of work are far from uncommon (39, 41, 63).

Hazards in the Development of Interests

Because interests play such an important role in determining children's behavior and in the development of their aspirations and self-concepts, the types of interests they develop and the way in which they express these interests are very important. Consequently, any condition that interferes with the development of wholesome interests and with the expression of these interests in socially approved patterns of behavior will

Drawing by Charles Schulz ©1968 United Feature Syndicate, Inc.

Figure 15–8. The child's vocational choice is based on what is important to the child at that time. (*Adapted from Charles Schulz, "Peanuts," United Features Syndicate, 1970. Used by permission.*)

be hazardous to children's personal and social adjustments.

In almost every important area of interest development there are certain hazards. However, because many of these hazards overlap, the following discussion will center around certain hazards common to several areas of interest. These areas will be used to illustrate the serious consequences from these hazards.

Interpreting Whims as Interests

Many adults, teachers as well as parents, make the mistake of interpreting childish whims as interests. When children show strong enthusiasm for doing something, adults assume that the children have a strong enough interest in it to justify providing them with opportunities to acquire the skills needed for these activities.

Or, if children spend proportionally more of their time on an activity than seems reasonable to adults, adults may interpret this to mean that the children have strong interests in it. In reality, the interest may not be strong at all. The time spent on the activity may be due to the fact that children have nothing more interesting to do to occupy their time or they may engage in the activity because it is "the thing to do" and they want to follow the crowd in the hopes of increasing their social acceptance.

In no area is failure to distinguish between whims and interests more hazardous to the personal and social adjustments of children than in vocational interests, as shown by their statements of vocational choice. If parents accept these statements as indications of interests based on abilities, they are likely to inform relatives and family friends of these choices. This tends to reinforce the whims by suggesting to children that their choices have the stamp of parental approval or that their parents believe that they have the abilities necessary to succeed in the vocations they have chosen. At the same time, acceptance of a whim as an indication of a real interest leads to narrowing down children's opportunities to explore other voca-

447

SOME COMMON CHILDHOOD INTERESTS

tional opportunities to see if they might meet their needs better than their original choices.

The hazards to children from adult failure to distinguish between vocational whims and vocational interests are innumerable; three of them are especially common. *First,* children tend to cling to an original choice because they feel their parents expect them to do the work they said they wanted to do and because their parents have often made personal sacrifices to give them the training needed for this work. *Second,* children may hesitate to say they are no longer interested in the work they earlier claimed they wanted to do because they are afraid they will be judged as unstable and immature. *Third,* if children cling to vocational choices, even after they have lost interest in them, they may find, as they grow up, that they are locked into a line of work they find boring and frustrating or for which they lack the ability to carry out successfully.

Peer Influences on Interests

All children discover that one condition that contributes heavily to social acceptance is having interests in common with members of the peer group. If, for example, members of the peer group are interested in playing ball games, a child who wants to be an accepted member of the group must be willing to show an interest in these games by learning to play well enough to be an accepted member of the team. If peers verbalize their boredom about an activity, other children must do likewise or run the risk of facing peer disapproval. As was pointed out earlier, many school underachievers are the product of the influence of their peers. To avoid peer disapproval, they must claim that school "bores" them as it bores their peers. To make their claims of boredom ring true, they must work below their capacities and verbalize their boredom to convince others that they mean what they say.

Hazards from acceptance of peer interests as their own are threefold. *First,* children may develop interests unsuited to their abilities. As a result, these interests do not meet their needs. *Second,* permitting peers to influence their interests results in children's developing unfavorable attitudes toward interests that are better suited to their abilities and that would meet their needs better. *Third,* developing interests unsuited to their abilities because of peer influences means that children will do less well than they would if they de-

voted their time and energies to activities in which they were interested. This leads to unfavorable social and self-judgments, conditions that lead to poor social and personal adjustments.

Interests That Deviate from Peer Interests

Just as interests that are similar to peer interests facilitate peer acceptance, so interests that deviate from peer interests jeopardize peer acceptance. Being different is regarded as inferior. This makes peer acceptance difficult if not impossible.

Interests that deviate from peer interests may be of three kinds—those that are stronger, those that are weaker, and those that are different. When children have greater interests in appearance, in clothes, in health, or in status symbols than their peers, they are out of step with them and are apt to be judged as "squares." A child who constantly talks about health, for example, tends to be regarded as a "baby"—a label that is damaging to a favorable reputation and social acceptance.

Greater interest in schoolwork than that of the peer group, as shown in overachievers, results in their being among the least popular members of the class. Their classmates regard them as "curve raisers" who lead to teacher expectations that the rest of the class should do good work also. To maintain their status as good students, many overachievers become nervous, tense, and highly sensitive to social disapproval—characteristics that militate against peer acceptance. Overachievers feel guilty if they take time out to play and, as a result, they do not learn the play skills of their age-mates. Furthermore, to achieve success, they must be highly competitive, often playing up to the teacher to win favor or refusing to help a classmate with an assignment. Such behavior is hazardous to good personal or social adjustments.

When children *lack* interest in what the peer group considers important, such as sports or status symbols, it is just as hazardous as too obsessive an interest. Perhaps even more hazardous is an interest so *different* from the interests of the peer group that it makes a child conspicuous. A child with a musical talent, for example, may be more interested in playing a musical instrument than in playing games and sports with age-mates.

Any deviant interest makes children different and being different, to children, means being inferior. Realizing that they are regarded as inferior by their age-mates is always hazardous to the personal and social adjustments of children—especially when they reach the gang age.

Interests Based on Unrealistic Concepts

When interests are based on unrealistic concepts, they are always a source of potential hazard to good adjustments. The reason for this is that, sooner or later, as children's cognitive development increases and as their experiences broaden, they will realize that their interests are built on faulty foundations. What formerly was a source of satisfaction then becomes a source of dissatisfaction, disappointment, or disillusionment.

As was pointed out earlier, one of the common causes of waning interest in school can be traced to unrealistic concepts of what going to school means—a place where there will be plenty of playmates, where there will be opportunities to learn interesting things, and where there will be teachers to teach them things their parents either cannot or do not have the time to teach them.

When children discover how unrealistic their concepts of school have been—learning interesting things, for example, means work, not play as they anticipated—their interest not only wanes but tends to be colored by unfavorable attitudes in place of the favorable ones that formerly existed. As a result of this waning of interest comes boredom, underachievement, truancy, disruptive classroom behavior, and other expressions of disenchantment with school.

The same kind of hazard occurs when children's religious beliefs are built on unrealistic concepts. Much of their interest in religious observances, such as prayer and different holiday celebrations, is built on the concept that these observances will benefit them personally. When their prayers for material possessions or help in meeting a difficult task successfully go unanswered, they become skeptical about prayer. When they discover that there is no Santa Claus or Easter Bunny, their interest in celebrating Christmas and Easter wanes.

Once doubting starts in one area, it tends to spread to other areas of religious beliefs. Each year, as children grow older, they discover more and more unrealistic foundations in their religious beliefs—life after death, angels, and the Devil, for example. When religious doubting becomes widespread, as it tends to

when children approach adolescence, it weakens their interest in religion. With this weakening of religious interest comes a loss of the feeling of security religion formerly gave them. For children who relied on religion for a feeling of security, doubting becomes a serious personal hazard.

Unfavorable Emotional Weighting of Interests

Of all hazards in the development of interests, an unfavorable emotional weighting of the interest is most serious because its effect on behavior is most persistent. As was pointed out in the beginning of the chapter, as interests develop, attitudes toward these interests are associated with them and this gives the interests their emotional weighting—the *affective aspect* of the interests. Several examples of important childhood interests will serve to illustrate the hazardous nature of unfavorable emotional weighting of interests. Because *names* are a source of interest to all children, any disliked name becomes a hazard to their personal and social adjustments. That dislike for a name affects children unfavorably is seen by the way children react to a disliked name. Some children, for example, may beg family members not to use a disliked pet name in front of age-mates. Others may shun social situations as much as possible to avoid the embarrassment and irritation of hearing themselves being called by disliked names. Still others may try to persuade parents or peers to call them by a middle name or some nickname of their choosing.

Interest in *sex* is usually weighted with favorable or unfavorable attitudes. As children satisfy their curiosity about sex, they acquire attitudes that determine the quality of their behavior. These attitudes are acquired from the significant people in the child's life. As these significant people change from parents to teachers, to peers of the same sex—and in adolescence, to peers of the opposite sex—the child's attitudes likewise change. However, the basic attitude, established in the home, dominates later attitudes.

A number of factors influence children's attitudes toward sex, the two most important of which are the methods used to give sex information and the source from which children receive it. The amount and accuracy of the information about sex children receive are not as important in shaping their attitudes as the *method* used to give this information. Children may, for example, forget most or all the information given in answer to the question, "Where do babies come from?" but they are not likely to forget the way in which the question was answered—the expression on the face of the person who answered it or the ease or difficulty the person had in talking about this matter. These behavior symbols convey to children how that person feels about sex. Should these symbols suggest that sex is something to be talked about in whispers or that it is embarrassing and not "nice," children will adopt similar attitudes.

The *source* from which children receive their sex information likewise has a profound effect on their attitudes toward sex. Parents who surround sex with mystery and taboo or who establish a "conspiracy of silence"—warning children not to talk about sex to anyone outside the home—not only encourage the development of unfavorable attitudes but they also whet children's curiosity. Children then turn to friends or classmates for further information. This is often given in whispers, with demands "never to tell" where they got this information, and is often accompanied by giggles and other symbols of embarrassment. Under such conditions, it would be hard for children to develop wholesome attitudes toward sex.

The damaging consequences of unfavorable attitudes are not limited to sexual behavior. If children learn to think of the sex organs as something to talk about only in a whisper, if they think touching the sex organs is wicked and depraved, and if they learn to think of the marital relationship as something to be "endured" only for the sake of having children, their feelings about many aspects of life will be affected. Although this may not matter very much while children are still young, it can and often does affect their personal and social adjustments when they are adolescents or adults.

The long-term serious consequences of unfavorable emotional weighting of interests is also seen in children's early *vocational choices*. When children have highly glamorized concepts of some occupations, their concepts can be corrected by letting them see these people at work and by informing them about what is needed in the way of abilities, training, and personal sacrifices to carry out these occupations.

On the other hand, changing the emotional weighting of these unrealistic concepts is not so easy. And, because vocational choice is greatly influenced by the affective aspect of this interest, it can play havoc with later vocational adjustment if the choice made during childhood is unsuited to the individual's abilities and more mature interests. The seriousness of this hazard has been stressed by Nuckols and Banducci when they said, "Vital decisions which may potentially affect an entire life time are predicated upon the occupational images to which one subscribes" (63).

Chapter Highlights

1 Interests differ from whims not in strength or ability to motivate action but in persistence. Boredom is the opposite of interest.

2 Interests play important roles in children's lives as sources of motivation to learn of aspirations, of enjoyment, and of achievement.

3 There are many ways to discover children's interests, the most accurate of which are: observations of their activities, analysis of their questions and wishes, listening to the topics of their conversations, studying what they read or draw spontaneously, and their own reports of their interests.

4 All interests have two aspects, the cognitive and the affective, or the "emotionally weighted" aspect. They develop by three common forms of learning—trial and error, identification, and learning through guidance and direction.

5 Interest in the human body follows a predictable pattern with interest in the exterior of the body preceding interest in the interior of the body. Interest in health normally does not develop until children approach puberty.

6 Interest in appearance and clothes develops as children discover the role they play in social acceptance.

7 Of the many possible names children have—first names, surnames, middle names, nicknames, pet names, and kinship names—children's interests tend to be focused on first names, nicknames and pet names. This interest is stronger when names are disliked by their bearers than when they are liked.

8 Interest in status symbols in childhood is concen-

trated on those which have prestige in the eyes of the peer group at that age.

9 Interest in religious observances usually precedes interest in religious beliefs. Both interests wane as childhood progresses and as doubting begins.

10 Interest in sex in childhood is expressed in asking questions, exploration of the sex organs, homosexual play, masturbation, talking to friends about sex, looking at pictures in books and comics, reading books, and attending sex-education classes in school.

11 Interest in school follows a predictable pattern in which interest in all aspects of school precedes interest in selective areas within the academic and extracurricular programs of the school. Waning interest in school is expressed in school phobias, truancy, under- and overachievement, and disruptive behavior.

12 Children's interests in their future vocations develop early and are influenced by parental attitudes, the prestige of different vocations, the vocations of admired people, children's abilities and interests, the opportunity different occupations offer for independence, cultural stereotypes, and personal experiences with people in different occupations.

13 The most common hazards in the development of interests include interpreting whims as interests, peer influences on interests, interests that deviate from peer interests, interests based on unrealistic concepts, and the unfavorable emotional weighting of interests.

14 When adults interpret childish whims as interests, children are faced with the dilemma of clinging to an interest that no longer meets their needs or changing to another interest and being regarded as unstable.

15 Of all hazards in the development of interests, the unfavorable emotional weighting of interests is most serious because it tends to be persistent and thus have a long-lasting effect on the child's personal and social adjustments.

Bibliography

1 Albott, W. L., and J. L. Bruning. Given names: A neglected social variable. *Psychological Record*, 1970, *20*, 527–533.

2 Allen, D. A. Underachievement is many-sided. *Personnel and Guidance Journal*, 1971, *49*, 529–532.

3 Amatora, Sister M. Interests of pre-adolescent boys and girls. *Genetic Psychology Monographs*, 1960, *61*, 77–113.

4 Asbury, C. A. Selected factors influencing over and under achievement in young school age children. *Review of Educational Research*, 1974, *44*, 409–428.

5 Barry, A., and R. J. Barry. Easing the child's entry into kindergarten. *Perceptual and Motor Skills*, 1974, *38*, 762.

6 Beelick, D. B. Sources of student satisfaction and dissatisfaction. *Journal of Educational Research*, 1973, *67*, 19–22, 28.

7 Berecz, J. M. Phobias of childhood: Etiology and treatment. *Psychological Bulletin*, 1968, *70*, 694–720.

8 Bernstein, A. C. How children learn about sex and birth. *Psychology Today*, 1976, *9* (8), 31–35, 66.

9 Boshier, R. Attitudes toward self and one's proper names. *Journal of Individual Psychology*, 1968, *24*, 63–66.

10 Buchanan, B. A., and J. L. Bruning. Connotative meanings of first names and nicknames on three dimensions. *Journal of Social Psychology*, 1971, *85*, 143–144.

11 Busse, T. V., and C. Love. The effect of first names on conflicted decisions: An experimental study. *Journal of Psychology*, 1973, *84*, 253–256.

12 Busse, T. V., and J. Helfrich. Changes in first name popularity across grades. *Journal of Psychology*, 1975, *89*, 281–283.

13 Calderone, M. S. Sex education and the roles of school and church. *Annals of the American Academy of Political and Social Sciences*, 1968, *376*, 53–60.

14 Calderone, M. S. Eroticism as a norm. *Family Coordinator*, 1974, *23*, 337–341.

15 Caplan, P. J., and M. Kinsbourne. Sex differences in response to school failure. *Journal of Learning Disabilities*, 1974, *7*, 232–235.

16 Carey, R. G. Influence of peers in shaping religious behavior. *Journal for the Scientific Study of Religion*, 1971, *10*, 157–159.

17 Chase, J. A. Differential behavioral characteristics of nonpromoted children. *Genetic Psychology Monographs*, 1972, *86*, 219–277.

18 Clifford, M. M. Physical attractiveness and academic performance. *Child Study Journal*, 1975, *5*, 201–209.

19 Cummins, S., E. Garns, and L. Zusne. Another note on Santa Claus. *Perceptual and Motor Skills*, 1971, *32*, 510.

20 Davison, J. Mothers buy clothes: Boys make costumes. *The New York Times*, March 14, 1976.

21 Dion, K. K. Young children's stereotyping of facial attractiveness. *Developmental Psychology*, 1973, *9*, 183–188.

22 Engel, D. E. Education and identity: The function of questions in religious education. *Religious Education*, 1968, *63*, 371–375.

23 Engel, M., G. Marsden, and S. Woodaman. Orientation to work in children. *American Journal of Orthopsychiatry*, 1968, *38*, 137–143.

24 Fagon, B. I. Influence of teacher behavior in the preschool. *Developmental Psychology*, 1973, *9*, 198–206.

25 Flanders, N. A., B. M. Morrison, and E. L. Brode. Changes in pupil attitudes during the school year.

Journal of Educational Psychology, 1968, *59*, 334–338.

26 Formanek, R. When children ask about death. *Elementary School Journal*, 1974, *75*, 92–97.

27 Gagnon, J. H., and W. Simon. They're going to learn in the streets anyway. *Psychology Today*, 1969, *3* (2), 46–47, 71.

28 Gellert, E. Children's conceptions of the content and function of the human body. *Genetic Psychology Monographs*, 1962, *65*, 293–405.

29 Gellert, E., J. S. Girgus, and J. Cohen. Children's awareness of their bodily appearance: A developmental study of factors associated with the body percept. *Genetic Psychology Monographs*, 1971, *84*, 109–174.

30 Good, T. L., J. N. Sikes, and J. E. Brophy. Effects of teacher sex and student sex on classroom interaction. *Journal of Educational Psychology*, 1973, *65*, 74–87.

31 Haley, E. G., and N. J. Hendrickson. Children's preferences for clothing and hair styles. *Home Economics Research Journal*, 1974, *2* (3), 176–193.

32 Harari, H., and J. W. McDavid. Name stereotypes and teachers' expectations. *Journal of Educational Psychology*, 1973, *65*, 222–225.

33 Hartlage, L. C., and J. Schlagel. Teacher characteristics associated with student classroom behaviors. *Journal of Psychology*, 1974, *86*, 191–195.

34 Havighurst, R. J. *Developmental tasks and education*, 3d ed. New York: McKay, 1972.

35 Hewitt, L. S. Age and sex differences in the vocational aspirations of elementary school children. *Journal of Social Psychology*, 1975, *96*, 173–177.

36 Hirt, N., W. D. Ross, R. Kurtz, and G. C. Gleser. Attitudes to body products among normal subjects. *Journal of Abnormal Psychology*, 1969, *74*, 486–489.

37 Horrocks, J. E., and N. C. Mussman. Developmental trends in wishes, confidence, and the sense of personal control from childhood to middle maturity. *Journal of Psychology*, 1973, *84*, 241–252.

38 Huberty, C. J., and W. W. Swan. Preschool classroom experience and first-grade achievement. *Journal of Educational Research*, 1974, *67*, 311–316.

39 Isaacs, A. F. Giftedness and careers.

Gifted Child Quarterly, 1973, *17*, 57–59.

40 Jackson, P. W., and H. M. Lahaderne. Scholastic success and attitude toward school in a population of sixth graders. *Journal of Educational Psychology*, 1967, *58*, 15–18.

41 Jacobsen, R. B. An exploration of parental encouragement as an intervening variable in occupational-educational learning of children. *Journal of Marriage and the Family*, 1971, *33*, 174–182.

42 Johnson, C. D., and J. Gormley. Academic cheating: The contribution of sex, personality and situational variables. *Developmental Psychology*, 1972, *6*, 320–325.

43 Johnson, P. A., and J. R. Staffieri. Stereotypic affective properties of personal names and somatotypes in children. *Developmental Psychology*, 1971, *5*, 176.

44 Jones, F. H., and W. H. Miller. The effective use of negative attention for reducing group disruption in special elementary school classrooms. *Psychological Record*, 1974, *24*, 435–448.

45 Koocher, G. P. Childhood, death, and cognitive development. *Developmental Psychology*, 1973, *9*, 369–375.

46 Krebs, D., and A. A. Adinolfi. Physical attractiveness, social relations, and personality style. *Journal of Personality and Social Psychology*, 1975, *31*, 245–253.

47 Lerner, R. M., and C. Schroeder. Physique identification, preference and aversion in kindergarten children. *Developmental Psychology*, 1971, *5*, 538.

48 Lerner, R. M., J. Venning, and J. R. Knapp. Age and sex effects on personal space schemata toward body build in late childhood. *Developmental Psychology*, 1975, *11*, 855–856.

49 Levitin, T. E., and J. D. Chananie. Responses of female primary school teachers to sex typed behavior in male and female children. *Child Development*, 1972, *43*, 1309–1316.

50 Long, D., D. Elkind, and B. Spilka. The child's conception of prayer. *Journal for the Scientific Study of Religion*, 1967, *6*, 101–109.

51 Looft, W. R. Sex differences in the expression of vocational aspirations by elementary school children. *Developmental Psychology*, 1971, *5*, 366.

52 Looft, W. R. Vocational aspirations of second grade girls. *Psychological Reports*, 1971, *28*, 241–242.

53 Ludwig, D. J., T. Weber, and D. Iben. Letters to God: A study of children's religious concepts. *Journal of Psychology and Theology*, 1974, *2*, 31–35.

54 Macmillan, D. L., S. R. Forness, and B. M. Trumball. The role of punishment in the classroom. *Exceptional Children*, 1973, *40*, 85–96.

55 Mathes, E. W., and A. Kahn. Physical attractiveness, happiness, neuroticism and self-esteem. *Journal of Psychology*, 1975, *90*, 27–29.

56 McKinney, J. D. Teacher perception of the classroom behavior of reflective and impulsive children. *Psychology in the Schools*, 1975, *12*, 348–352.

57 Morris, L. W., C. S. Finkelstein, and W. R. Fisher. Components of school anxiety: Developmental trends and sex differences. *Journal of Genetic Psychology*, 1976, *128*, 49–57.

58 Mussen, P. H., J. J. Conger, and J. Kagan. *Child development and personality*, 4th ed. New York: Harper & Row, 1974.

59 Nash, H. Recognition of body surface regions. *Genetic Psychology Monographs*, 1969, *79*, 297–340.

60 Neidhart, W. What the Bible means to children and adolescents. *Religious Education*, 1968, *63*, 112–119.

61 Nelson, M. A. The concept of God and feelings toward parents. *Journal of Individual Psychology*, 1971, *27*, 46–49.

62 Nordberg, R. B. Developing the idea of God in children. *Religious Education*, 1971, *66*, 376–379.

63 Nuckols, T. E. and R. Banducci. Knowledge of occupations—is it important in occupational choice? *Journal of Counseling Psychology*, 1974, *21*, 191–195.

64 Packard, V. *The status seekers*. New York: Pocket Books, 1961.

65 Pitcher, E. G. The Bible for young children. *Religious Education*, 1963, *58*, 384–387.

66 Primavera, L. B., W. S. Simon, and A. M. Primavera. The relationship between self-esteem and academic achievement: An investigation of sex differences. *Psychology in the Schools*, 1971, *11*, 213–216.

67 Radin, N. Three degrees of maternal involvement in a preschool program:

Impact on mothers and children. *Child Development*, 1972, *43*, 1355–1364.

68 Redl, F. Disruptive behavior in the classroom. *School Review*, 1975, *83*, 569–594.

69 Robinson, W. P. Boredom at school. *British Journal of Educational Psychology*, 1975, *45*, 141–152.

70 Ryan, M. S. *Clothing: A study in human behavior*. New York: Holt, 1966.

71 Schonberg, W. B., and M. Murphy. The relationship between the uniqueness of a given name and personality. *Journal of Social Psychology*, 1974, *93*, 147–148.

72 Shane, H. G. Children's interests. *NEA Journal*, 1957, *46*, 237–239.

73 Simons, R. H., and J. J. Bibb.

Achievement motivation, test anxiety, and underachievement in the elementary school. *Journal of Educational Research*, 1974, *67*, 366–369.

74 Stott, D. H. Classification of behavior disturbance among school-age children: Principles, epidemiology and syndromes. *Psychology in the Schools*, 1971, *8*, 232–239.

75 Telegdy, G. A. The relationship between sociometric status and school readiness. *Psychology in the Schools*, 1974, *11*, 351–356.

76 Thomas, W. D. Maturation age: Another dropout factor? *Canadian Counsellor*, 1972, *6*, 275–277.

77 Thompson, B. Adjustment to school. *Educational Research*, 1975, *17*, 128–136.

78 Thornburg, H. D. Educating the pre-adolescents about sex. *Family Coordinator*, 1974, *23*, 35–39.

79 Thorndike, R. L. *The concept of over- and underachievement*. New York: Teachers College, Columbia, 1963.

80 Veldman, D. J., and J. E. Brophy. Measuring teacher effects on pupil achievement. *Journal of Educational Psychology*, 1974, *66*, 319–324.

81 Williams, R. Theory of God-concept readiness: From the Piagetian theories of child artificialism and the origin of religious feelings in children. *Religious Education*, 1971, *66*, 62–66.

82 Willis, S., and J. E. Brophy. Origin of teachers' attitudes toward young children. *Journal of Educational Psychology*, 1974, *66*, 520–529.

CHAPTER 16

SEX-ROLE DEVELOPMENT

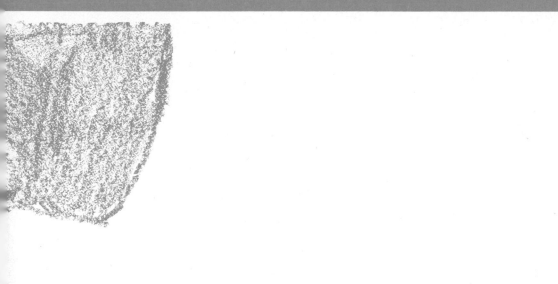

There was a time when learning to play sex roles was so much a part of growing up that no one regarded it as a problem. There were culturally approved and prescribed ways for boys and girls to think, to act, to look, and to feel. There were also culturally approved and prescribed ways for them to be prepared for the patterns of their adult lives.

As children passed from babyhood to childhood, to adolescence, and finally to adulthood, they learned to play these prescribed roles as well as everything else that was considered necessary for successful adjustment to the pattern of life for their age levels. By the time they reached adulthood, they knew exactly what the pattern of life for them would be and they knew they were prepared to carry it out with success. Because there had never been any alternatives open to them, they had learned to accept their sex roles, even though they might have wished that they had been born members of the other sex.

Now all of this is changing. With changes in the pattern of life for people of all ages brought about by the change from hand labor to mechanization, from rural to urban or suburban living, and from individual enterprise to large corporations, it was inevitable that sex roles would change.

Just as other changes have not been universal in today's American culture—individual enterprise still exists side by side with large corporations and hand labor goes on side by side with mechanization—so the old patterns of approved behavior for members of the two sexes persist side by side with the new patterns.

If and when the transition that is now taking place in the pattern of American life becomes complete and if there is an approved pattern of behavior for people in all areas of the nation, there will also be an approved pattern of sex roles. However, until this happens, sex-role development becomes one of the major adjustment problems American children must face in the process of growing up.

While this transition is taking place, it has attracted widespread interest among anthropologists, sociologists, and psychologists. From their research has come a rapidly expanding fund of information about the effects of changes in sex roles on the individual as well as on the social group. This interest has been spurred by the Women's Liberation Movement, the Equal Rights Amendment, and pressures by HEW on business, the professions, and industry to treat women as equals of men in the business, professional, and industrial segments of the American economy.

In this chapter, what is known to date about sex roles and their effects on the personal and social adjustments of children will be briefly summarized and interpreted. Within a few years, new evidence may appear to refute some of this information, or it may substantiate it. In either case, it will add to what is now known and fill in some of the gaps in present-day information.

Meaning of Sex Roles

Used in a general way, the term "sex roles" means the patterns of behavior for members of the two sexes approved and accepted by the social group with which the individual is identified. Block has defined a sex role more specifically as "a constellation of qualities an individual understands to characterize males and females in his culture" (9). Ward has amplified on this definition by saying, "A culturally defined sex role reflects those behaviors and attitudes that are generally agreed upon within a culture as being either masculine or feminine" (109).

The qualities that determine the approved patterns of behavior for members of the two sexes within a culture depend upon what is valued by that culture. If high value is placed on status symbols, for example, it is believed that men are better equipped, both physically and intellectually, to earn the money essential to get these status symbols than women. Consequently, the social group expects men to be wage earners and women to devote their time to pursuits that will free men to give their undivided attention and efforts to earning the money necessary for these valued status symbols.

In time, stereotypes develop about sex roles. Included in these stereotypes of male and female roles are specific concepts about approved appearance—including body build, facial features, and clothes—approved patterns of behavior, approved speech, approved ways to express feelings and emotions, approved ways to earn a living, and many other qualities.

Once formed, these stereotypes act as standards by which each individual is judged by members of the social group to be sex appropriate or sex inappropriate. The individual is then treated in accordance with these judgments. Stereotypes also serve as standards for self-evaluation. People judge themselves to be sex appropriate or sex inappropriate by how their qualities rate in terms of the standards set up in the stereotype.

456

Stereotypes also act as guidelines for the training of children. Children are taught, from earliest childhood, to look, to think, to feel, and to act in accordance with the standards set by the stereotype for their sex group. "Sex-role typing" thus means learning to conform to the approved stereotype for one's sex. One of the important developmental tasks of childhood is centered on this learning (41). Refer to Havighurst's list of developmental tasks, page 39.

As is true of all stereotypes, sex-role stereotypes have three aspects—cognitive, affective, and conative. What these are and what role they play in sex-role typing have been explained by Naffziger and Naffziger and are highlighted in Box 16–1 (83). As they have pointed out, all aspects of a stereotype combine to create a rigid judgmental and distancing attitude toward individuals who do not conform to a stereotyped pattern. In the case of sex-role stereotypes, these rigid judgmental and distancing attitudes are directed against members of the opposite sex.

Origin of Sex-role Stereotypes

There is no documented evidence about how, when, where, or under what conditions sex-role stereotypes first came into existence. Therefore, one can only *speculate* about this matter. Historical records indicate that sex-role stereotypes existed as far back as tribal life and that they were well developed during the ancient civilizations of Greece, Rome, Egypt, and many other cultures in that part of the world, as well as in the cultures of China, Japan, and other eastern nations.

Speculation about the origin of sex-role stereotypes can be based on anthropological studies of tribal life, on sociological studies of patterns of family life as far back as there are records available, on medical studies of physical and physiological differences between the sexes dating back centuries B.C., and on traditional beliefs dating back too far to know when and under what conditions they originated.

Some of the most important facts believed true, even if not proved true, on which stereotypes of sex roles were developed, are given in Box 16–2 (31, 60, 68, 73, 90, 108). Note that all these beliefs stress differences between the sexes, a fact on which was developed the belief that members of the two sexes should play different roles. What roles members of the two sexes were assigned to play were determined by these differences.

BOX 16–1

ASPECTS OF SEX-ROLE STEREOTYPES

COGNITIVE ASPECT
The cognitive aspect includes the perceptions, the beliefs, and the expectations people hold with regard to the male and female sex groups. These beliefs, perceptions, and expectations are simple, often inadequately grounded, and sometimes partially inaccurate. However, they are held with considerable assurance by a number of people.

AFFECTIVE ASPECT
The affective aspect includes both a general friendliness or unfriendliness toward the object of the attitude and the various specific feelings that give the attitude its emotional coloring. These feelings may be of admiration and sympathy or they may be of contempt, envy, and fear.

CONATIVE ASPECT
The conative aspect of all stereotypes includes beliefs about what should be done with regard to the group in question and with the specific members of that group. In the case of sex-role stereotypes, there are beliefs that members of the male sex should assume responsibilities that require physical strength, and that members of the female sex should be protected against any responsibilities that might prove damaging to their weaker physical condition.

Beliefs about Superior and Inferior Roles

At no time in recorded history was there the belief that sex roles were equal. Instead, there was the belief that the role assigned to members of one sex was superior to the role assigned to members of the opposite sex. In few cases was the female role regarded as superior to the male role, though anthropologists report that in some tribes this was true.

What was used to determine the superiority of one role over the other role was which role could contribute more to the welfare of the members of the group. In days when the pattern of life was centered around fighting, hunting, and fishing, it was believed that the male role could contribute more to the social group than the female role. Hence the male role was regarded as the superior role.

As group activities turned from warlike pursuits to

SOME FACTS ON WHICH SEX ROLE STEREOTYPES WERE BASED

PHYSICAL DIFFERENCES

Males have larger bodies, heavier muscles, and greater muscular strength. Females have smaller bodies, smaller muscles, and less strength. Males are therefore capable of doing things requiring greater strength, and females of doing things that require greater skills resulting from better muscle coordination.

PHYSIOLOGICAL DIFFERENCES

Females are capable of producing children and are subject to periodic discomforts at their menstrual periods. When menopause occurs, women lose one of their major physiological functions and, with it, a decline in the sex drive. By contrast, men have no periodic discomforts, they do not experience a decline in the sex drive, the ability to procreate persists, and their only role in procreation does not interfere with their normal pattern of living.

DIFFERENCES IN INSTINCTS

When it was believed that a person's life was controlled by instincts or hereditary driving forces, the maternal instinct was believed to motivate women to want to be mothers and to devote their time to caring for children. The paternal instinct acted only as a driving force to protect the young so long as they were incapable of protecting themselves.

INTELLECTUAL DIFFERENCES

Until the turn of the present century, it was believed that size of brain and level of intelligence were closely correlated. Because males, at every age, had larger brains than females, it was assumed that they had a higher level of intelligence.

ACHIEVEMENT DIFFERENCES

Throughout history, the greatest achievements in art, music, literature, science, etc. have come from males. It was assumed that their superior strength and intellectual abilities made these greater achievements possible.

EMOTIONAL DIFFERENCES

Because of the periodic disturbances that accompany menstruation in women, it was taken for granted that these physiological disturbances would lead to emotional disturbances, thus causing women to be emotionally unstable. By contrast, males were believed to be emotionally stable, just as they were physiologically stable.

HEALTH DIFFERENCES

The label "weaker sex" was applied to women because it was believed that they experienced more physical disturbances and illnesses than men. This weaker physical condition was attributed to their smaller and weaker bodies and to the periodic menstrual discharges and childbearing.

MORTALITY DIFFERENCES

Early mortality in women was attributed to natural causes—a physical weakness that made them incapable of withstanding the rigors of childbirth—but in men early mortality was attributed to their more hazardous life, not to natural causes. The greater longevity of females was explained by their more protected and easier lives, owing to protection by males, and men died earlier because they worked harder and were subjected to more hazards than women.

BIBLICAL TEACHINGS

Throughout the Bible, there are many references to the superiority of men over women and the superiority of the male role. For example, in I Corinthians it is stated, "For a man . . . is the image and glory of God: but the woman is the glory of the man. . . . Neither was the man created for the woman; but the woman for the man." Acceptance of the teachings of the Bible has reinforced the stereotype of masculine superiority.

peaceful activities and as survival depended not on hunting and fishing but on growing food or earning money to buy it, it was believed that members of the male sex were better equipped to fill this role than members of the female sex. Dissatisfaction with the established pattern of life gave rise to demands for improvement. Once again, it was believed that members of the male sex, because of their superior intellectual abilities, could meet these demands better than members of the female sex through inventions and achievements that would make the "better life" possible.

Superiority always leads to prestige. It soon became customary to add to the stereotype of the male role the label of "prestige." The male role was accepted as the more prestigious of the two sex roles. All members of the group that bore this label then lived in its reflected glory and became known as members of the "superior sex." Thus the custom of regarding males as superior to females came into existence.

Evolution of Sex-role Stereotypes

As is true of all stereotypes, sex-role stereotypes were not built up over night. As new facts were added to the stereotypes, based on what members of the social group believed to be true about differences between the sexes, beliefs about the approved patterns of behavior for members of the two sexes covered more and more aspects of their lives. Today, sex-role stereotypes literally cover every important aspect of a person's life. So widespread is this coverage that approved patterns for members of the two sexes leave few opportunities for them to be similar and require that they be different if they are to win the approval of the group.

In the area of *appearance,* there are approved patterns for grooming, hair styles, and clothing for the two sexes. Clothes that symbolize ability to do things are regarded as appropriate for males and those that symbolize dependency—inability to walk long distances because of high heels or to engage in hard work because of fragile clothes—are approved for females.

From earliest babyhood, *play* materials and play activities are different for the two sexes. There are boys' toys and girls' toys, boys' books and girls' books, boys' games and girls' games, etc. This distinction does not end with childhood. As adults, the recreational interests and activities approved for the two sexes are just as different as they are throughout the childhood years.

Even when children of both sexes are educated in the same schools, certain *school subjects* are regarded as more appropriate for one sex than for the other. Boys, for example, are encouraged to concentrate on science and mathematics and girls on English, different languages, and art.

In the area of *emotions,* it is assumed that girls are more emotional than boys. According to the stereotype of males, there is greater emotional control than among females. Males likewise are believed to have stronger unpleasant emotions—anger and fear, for example—and the dominant female emotions are

stereotyped as the pleasant emotions—joy in its different forms and affection.

In no area of sex-role stereotypes is the difference between the sexes more pronounced than in *personality traits.* The typical feminine personality pattern, for example, is characterized by dependency, passivity, and compliance. By contrast, the typical masculine personality pattern is that of a dominant, aggressive, and active person.

Because there are certain *vocations* that are regarded as appropriate for males and others for females, from earliest childhood children are encouraged and pressured to choose and prepare for vocations that will fit into this stereotype. Boys, for example, are expected to go into leadership roles in business, industry, and the professions. If girls want to enter these typically masculine areas of work, they are expected to play subordinate roles. To conform more closely to the stereotyped pattern, girls are encouraged to go into "women's work"— teaching, nursing, domestic service, and areas where their work will contribute to the welfare of others (67, 68, 96, 110).

Persistence of Stereotypes of Sex Roles

Once stereotypes of approved sex roles are developed, they tend to become persistent. This persistence lasts as long as the behavior of members of the two sex groups fills the needs of the members of the social group and as long as the members of the sex groups are satisfied to play the roles assigned to them.

So long as males can provide members of the social group with what the group regards as important to its welfare—a "good life" for the majority of the group members—they are permitted and encouraged to continue to play the dominant role. Should males not fulfill group expectations, their dominant role would then be shifted to members of the female sex. To date, this has not happened.

Because playing a dominant role is always satisfying to those who play this role, males are willing to play it. Even if they do not derive as much satisfaction from the male role as from the female role, they continue to play it, knowing that shifting to the female role would bring disapproval from the social group and thus weaken the satisfaction they otherwise would derive from playing the female role.

So long as playing the female role resulted in a

pleasant life for women, most women were willing to play it. They derived satisfaction from being spared the rigors of the work world, from having homes and children of their own, and from feelings of security about their futures. Because conditions are now changing in the cultures in which many women live, the satisfaction they formerly derived from the female role is less than it formerly was. As a result, they are beginning to revolt against playing the role the social group assigned to them and are demanding an opportunity to play a new role they feel is better suited to their needs.

Persistence of sex-role stereotypes is achieved by teaching children, from earliest childhood, to play roles regarded as appropriate for members of their sex and by denying them the opportunities to learn to play roles regarded as inappropriate. Because this child training begins early in life, often during babyhood, children tend to accept the roles they are expected to play without question. Only as they grow older and find that the roles they were taught to play do not always bring them the satisfaction such roles are supposed to bring do they rebel and demand an opportunity to play roles that will meet their needs better. This, in part, has been responsible for the change in sex roles that is taking place in many cultures today (36, 110, 116).

Causes of Changes in Stereotypes of Sex Roles

Since the turn of the present century, but especially since World War II, there has been a gradual shift away from the stereotypes of approved sex roles, stereotypes that have persisted through the centuries, to a new kind of stereotype in which there is emphasis on similarity rather than difference between members of the two sexes.

This shifting from the old stereotypes to the new has gained momentum since the 1960s with government pressure and laws to prohibit discrimination against women in schooling, in employment, and in inheritance. However, like any change, changes in stereotypes that have persisted for a long time are slow. As a result, there is no evidence that there has been a widespread acceptance of new stereotypes to replace the old stereotypes or that men and women in large numbers have given up the old stereotypes in favor of the new.

There are many conditions in the American culture

that have given rise to changes in the accepted stereotypes of approved sex roles. Some of those that have had the greatest impact on these changes are listed in Box 16–3 (15, 67, 68, 84). Many of these changes are similar to those in other cultures throughout the world where sex-role stereotypes are also changing and where the differences in male and female roles are gradually being replaced by similarities.

Even when changes do occur in the traditional stereotypes of sex roles, they do not occur in all areas simultaneously. With evidence, for example, that the differences in intellectual abilities that were formerly believed to exist are only slight, there are changes in the concept of masculine intellectual superiority. On the other hand, there has been little or no change in the concept of masculine physical superiority. Most people still cling to the belief that females are the "weaker sex."

As more and more evidence accumulates about qualities and abilities that make up the sex-role stereotypes, these stereotypes are bound to change. How soon this change will occur will depend upon the amount and accuracy of the evidence that is accumulated from research studies.

To date, changes in sex-role stereotypes have not covered all areas of the stereotypes. Where changes occur first will depend on how much and how accurate the information there is that contradicts the traditional beliefs in those areas. When, for example, there was adequate information from intelligence tests to show that female intelligence is not below that of male intelligence, the element of the stereotype related to intellectual differences has gradually changed to a concept of intellectual similarities. Similarly, undisputed evidence from mortality and health statistics has changed the traditional concept of the "weaker sex." Shortage of manpower during periods of war, when it was essential to employ women in occupations formerly stereotyped as "men's work," showed that women could do the work as well as men with no greater hazards to their health than men experienced.

Kinds of Sex Roles

From the beginning of recorded history of civilized cultures, there was only one approved pattern of sex roles—the kind that is now know as the "traditional role"—a well-developed stereotype of what males and females can and should be and do. This is still widely

SOME REASONS FOR CHANGES IN SEX-ROLE STEREOTYPES

CHANGES IN LIFE STYLES

When a culture changes from a rural to an urban or suburban culture, strength is less important than skills. There is far less difference between males and females in skills than in physical strength.

THE INTELLIGENCE TESTING MOVEMENT

Beginning with the work of Binet at the turn of the present century, intelligence testing has become so widespread for all age levels that there is little doubt today that the belief of masculine intellectual superiority has been replaced with evidence of intellectual equality.

THE HEREDITY VERSUS ENVIRONMENT CONTROVERSY

Although this controversy is far from settled, there is ample evidence that environmental influences are far greater than was originally believed. From cross-cultural studies, where environmental influences are different, there is evidence that the differences between the sexes are due more to training than to heredity.

SIMILAR EDUCATION

As similar education, from nursery school through graduate school, has replaced "boys' education" and "girls' education," it has become apparent that, when given equal educational opportunities, girls can do the same academic work as boys and equally as successfully.

MOBILITY

When geographic mobility, to achieve vocational advancement, takes families away from relatives, women can no longer call on female relatives for help in emergencies. Through necessity, many men must carry out work that was formerly regarded as "women's work." This has contributed to the breakdown of the stereotype of sex-related work.

TREND TOWARD SMALLER FAMILIES

The trend toward earlier marriage, smaller families, and longer life spans for members of both sexes has encouraged women to turn from their traditional roles as wives and mothers when their children no longer need their care to roles in the work world.

IMPORTANCE OF STATUS SYMBOLS

To achieve upward social mobility—a widespread aspiration in today's culture—money for status symbols and for higher education for children has become a problem that male wage earners alone cannot always solve. Entrance into the labor force by female family members has helped solve this problem.

HIGHER EDUCATION FOR WOMEN

With the opening up of opportunities for higher education to women in all areas, even those that were formerly closed to them, women were no longer willing to devote their lives to the traditional vocational roles of their sex. Instead, they are entering the world of work and achieving success in it, which in the past would have been impossible because of the barriers placed in their paths.

EQUAL VOCATIONAL OPPORTUNITIES

Changes in laws and pressures from the federal government to open up vocational opportunities to women has made it possible for women to play roles in the work world, especially in the higher levels in business, industry, and the professions.

HEALTH AND MORTALITY STATISTICS

Health and mortality statistics have been revealing over the past 50 or more years that females have no more illnesses, age for age, than have males, and that females, as a group, live longer than males. These statistics have helped to break down the stereotype of females as the "weaker sex."

FEMALE ACHIEVEMENTS

When given equal training, equal opportunity to use their training, and encouragement to do so, females at every age from kindergarten to retirement achieve as great success as males with comparable training and opportunities. Academically as well as in extracurricular activities in school and college, females equal or surpass males. Barriers to advancement of women in business, industry, and the professions have limited their achievements in the adult areas, but, when these barriers are removed, female achievements have been found to be on a par with those of males. Figure 16–1 shows how female achievements are helping to debunk the traditional belief about inferiority.

Figure 16–1. Female achievements are gradually debunking the traditional belief about female inferiority. (*Adapted from Morris Turner: "Wee Pals."* King
Features Syndicate, *Aug. 6, 1975. Used by permission.*)

held throughout the world, even though there are some modifications and changes in the traditional stereotypes for both males and females.

In cultures where there have been rapid and radical changes in patterns of living, as in America and other highly industrialized nations, a new stereotype of sex roles has been evolving. This has been given many labels—"developmental," "equalitarian," and "egalitarian." Today, the most widely accepted label is "egalitarian" sex roles. As the term implies, the fundamental belief is that the sexes are equal rather than different and, as a result, should play similar rather than different roles.

Traditional Sex Roles

The stereotypes on which traditional male and female sex roles are based embody the fundamental principle of differences between the two sexes. Not only are the two sexes different but they are also different in areas that are important to the welfare and progress of the social group with which they are identified. In addition, this difference is in favor of the male sex.

Because of their alleged superiority, it has been an accepted belief that males can and should make different contributions to the social group than females and that their contributions are superior to those of females. To be able to make the contributions of which they are capable, members of both sexes must learn to play rigidly prescribed roles, regardless of personal interests and abilities. To play these roles successfully, members of both sexes must present an image of having the qualities approved for their sexes, they

must shun any behavior that is inappropriate for members of their sex, even though it is appropriate for members of the other sex, and they must show an intolerance and scorn for those who do not conform to their approved sex roles, as a way to motivate them to do so.

Egalitarian Sex Roles

The stereotype of egalitarian sex roles is based on the fundamental principle that differences between the sexes are far less than was formerly believed and that what differences do exist are not important in a culture where technology has replaced the role formerly played by physical strength.

Because the pattern of life has become more complex than it formerly was, the cultural group needs contributions of a more varied kind than was needed when the pattern of life was simpler. As a result, both sexes can contribute to the welfare and progress of the group. Even though their contributions are different, those of the two sexes are of value with little or no evidence that the male group makes more valuable contributions than the female group or vice versa. It is through these different contributions that progress is made possible.

To make the contributions to the group that members of both sexes can and should make, they should not be molded into a prescribed pattern. Instead, each individual should be free to develop individual interests and abilities, without being regarded as sex inappropriate. Furthermore, because members of both sexes can contribute to the welfare and

BOX 16–4

IMPORTANT ELEMENTS OF SEX-ROLE STEREOTYPES

TRADITIONAL SEX-ROLE STEREOTYPES

Male Sex-role Stereotype
- Dominance in all situations as shown by aggressive and assertive behavior
- Self-fulfillment only by own achievements
- Control of emotions at all times to show strength
- Self-oriented, considering self first in all situations
- Because superior, expects to be waited on by females
- As wage earner, makes all major decisions
- Only role at home is advising and disciplining children and serving as role model for sons
- Work in home and outside more dangerous, difficult, and taxing of strength than work by females and therefore carries greater prestige
- Custodian of family money, whether earned or inherited
- Tendency to derogate all females and female achievements
- Upward social mobility through own achievements

Female Sex-role Stereotype
- Subservience in all situations as shown by willingness to comply with male wishes and wait on males
- Satisfaction by "proxy"—through achievements of male family members
- Expression of emotions, thus giving warmth to social relationships in the home and outside
- Other-oriented, considering others before self
- Major role is caretaker of home and family
- Willing to let major decisions be made by males
- Works outside home only when necessary and then only in occupations regarded as "women's work"
- Turns over management of money—earned or inherited—to males
- Work inside and outside the home less demanding and difficult, therefore it carries little prestige and is paid less
- Serves in community affairs in roles inferior to those of males
- Feels guilt if considering own interests above those of others
- Upward social mobility through marriage to higher-status male

EGALITARIAN SEX-ROLE STEREOTYPES

Male Sex-role Stereotype
- Feels superior only when achievements are superior, not because of sex
- Feels free to satisfy interests and abilities in behavior of his choice without fear of being considered sex inappropriate
- Less self- than other-oriented
- Works on a companionship basis with females and does not feel sex inappropriate when working under females
- Shares home responsibilities and care of children
- Includes family members in decision making
- Proud of achievements of female family members, even if superior to his
- Does not feel it necessary to impress others with masculine superiority by dangerous and overtaxing activities
- Does not feel sex inappropriate when doing work regarded as "women's work" inside or outside the home

Female Sex-role Stereotype
- Actualizes own potentials regardless of activity
- More self- than other-oriented
- Expects others to help her instead of waiting on them
- Does not feel guilty about using her abilities to give her satisfaction
- Expects equal opportunities, equal treatment, and equal pay for work
- Does not feel unfeminine if achievements surpass those of males
- Willing to assume leadership roles in work or community affairs
- Does not feel sex inappropriate doing work in "men's" fields
- Does not feel guilt if work of own choosing gives her greater satisfaction than "women's work"
- Insists upon making decisions that affect her own life and interests
- Upward social mobility through own achievements

progress of the group, they should be given equal opportunities to contribute what they are capable of. They should also be given the training needed for their contributions, regardless of what sex group they are identified with.

In general, the egalitarian stereotypes of sex roles eliminate the emphasis on extreme differences between the sexes which is characteristic of the stereotypes of traditional sex roles. They are modified in such a way that the female role is slanted in the direction of the male role and the male role, in turn, is slanted toward the female role. As a result, they meet in the middle with more elements in each stereotype similar to those in the stereotype for the opposite sex role than different.

Because stereotypes of sex roles contain many elements, it would be impossible to list and explain the concepts of these elements. Only the most important and most widely accepted of these concepts have been selected from the complex interweaving of these elements to show what the major elements of each are. They are briefly summarized in Box 16–4. Note that in the listing of elements of the traditional sex-role stereotype for males the elements are almost the opposite of these in the female stereotype. On the other hand, note how similar the elements of the stereotypes for the male and female sex roles are in the case of egalitarian roles.

Learning the Meaning of Sex-role Stereotypes

Before children can learn to play the sex roles approved for the members of their sexes, they must learn the meaning of these stereotypes. And, because these stereotypes contain many elements, the learning takes time and opportunities to learn.

Whether children will learn the meaning of traditional or egalitarian stereotypes first will depend on the kind of sex roles played within their families. In a home where the mother works outside the home, children learn the meaning of egalitarian sex-role stereotypes unless there is a mother substitute taking care of them as a nonworking mother would.

As children broaden their social horizons to include people outside the home, and as they spend more and more of their playtime in amusements through the mass media, they learn that there are two kinds of sex-role stereotypes, the one that is accepted in their

homes and another that is accepted by some people outside the home.

Before childhood has come to an end, it is questionable that many children in the American culture today do not know the meanings of both the traditional and egalitarian sex-role stereotypes. It is also questionable whether they do not have a preference for one of the stereotypes. This preference is likely to be highly emotionally weighted. As such, it will have an influence on which type of sex role they will choose to play when they are free to make the choice.

A girl, for example, who has been expected to play the role of mother substitute for younger siblings while the mother is working outside the home, may decide that she does not want to play the traditional female role when she is grown up. Even though obstacles are put in her way to learning how to play an egalitarian role—a role which she discovers is more to her liking and offers her more opportunities to use her interests and abilities than the traditional female role—she may readily take the matter in her own hands and get the training she needs for her chosen role in spite of parental objections and obstacles.

On the other hand, preference for a role other than those children have learned to play may be blocked by environmental obstacles or obstacles within the children themselves. Under such conditions, they will be forced to play roles that meet neither their interests nor their abilities. Should a boy, for example, have a father who regards all artistic pursuits as sex inappropriate, the boy may be ridiculed and shamed into accepting the traditional role of business as his chosen career and be forced to select school subjects not to his liking to prepare him for this vocation. How hazardous to good personal and social adjustments it is to be forced to play roles not to one's liking will be explained in the section of this chapter dealing with hazards in sex-role development.

Pattern of Learning Meanings of Sex-role Stereotypes

Because sex-role stereotypes contain so many elements, it is impossible for children to learn all the elements at one time. Studies of how they learn these elements have revealed that the learning follows a predictable pattern. Although this pattern may vary somewhat from child to child, the general pattern is much the same for all children, because it depends on the child's cognitive development, on the opportunities the child is given to learn these elements, and on the social pressures placed on the child by different people to learn them.

In general, the pattern of learning the meaning of sex-role stereotypes contains five stages, each of which follows the other at relatively predictable ages. There is likely to be more variation in the ages at which the learning takes place than in the pattern of learning because of the role played by cognitive development in this learning. Even when opportunities to learn are given, the learning cannot take place unless the child is able to understand the meaning of what these opportunities provide.

In the *first* stage of learning meanings of sex-role stereotypes, children learn that males and females are different in appearance, wear different clothes, and have different hair styles. These differences are more apparent in older children, adolescents, and adults than in babies and preschoolers. However, at every age level, even in babyhood, children discover that there are physical differences even if there are not differences in clothing and hair styles.

Shortly after children learn there are sex differences in appearance, they enter the *second* stage of learning, in which they discover that members of the two sexes do different things. In toy play, boys and girls have different toys; in games and sports, boys and girls play differently, and in adulthood, men do things that are different from what women do. The males of the family work outside the home, and the females work inside the home. A girl who acts as baby-sitter to earn spending money works with children in a neighbor's home, and a boy earns spending money by delivering newspapers, clerking in a store, or doing some other work outside the home.

In the *third* stage of learning meanings of sex-role stereotypes, children learn that males and females have different abilities and show these abilities in different achievements. Whether these differences in achievement are due to innate differences in ability or opportunities to develop their abilities is of little concern to children. They know from their own experiences that these differences do exist.

At school, for example, they discover that girls are better readers, age for age, than boys. In ball play, the reverse is true. At home, the father can fix broken toys and household objects better than the mother, but the mother's cooking is superior to the father's.

Even before children enter school, they enter the *fourth* stage of learning the meanings of sex-role

stereotypes. In this stage, they discover that the social group judges certain patterns of appearance, speech, and behavior as sex appropriate and other patterns as sex inappropriate. Along with these discoveries, they learn that anything that is regarded as sex appropriate is more favorably judged than anything that is regarded as sex inappropriate. These discoveries are based on the type of reaction members of the social group have toward the things they judge as sex appropriate and those they judge as sex inappropriate.

A boy who is well groomed, for example, is labeled a "sissy" by members of the gang, but a girl who is well groomed is admired and envied by female age-mates. Parents and peers react very differently to the use of slang and swear words by males as compared with females. This is true also of bragging, boasting, and other forms of unsocial speech. A boy is regarded as a "regular boy" and, hence, sex appropriate, for such speech, but a girl is more likely to be criticized or punished for not being "ladylike" when she uses the same forms of speech.

In the *fifth* stage of learning meanings of sex-role stereotypes, children learn that different degrees of prestige are associated with different characteristics and patterns of behavior. They discover, for example, that working outside the home is more prestigious than working in the home because the worker is paid for the work outside the home but not for work in the home. Wearing dress-up clothes to work gives greater prestige to the job than wearing overalls. Because prestige means "superior" to children, the person who has prestige symbols is regarded as a superior person.

By the time children enter first grade in school, they have learned enough of the elements of sex-role stereotypes to have definite concepts of how members of the social group rate members of the two sexes and their achievements. It has been reported that by this time children's attitudes are "sexist" toward home roles and vocations as well as toward other important areas of their lives (9, 19, 34, 45, 49).

Sources of Meanings of Sex-role Stereotypes

The meanings associated with the appearance, behavior, and attitudes of members of the two sexes come from many sources. The most important of these sources are given in Box 16–5 (13, 51, 94, 100, 105, 112).

BOX 16–5

SOME COMMON SOURCES OF MEANINGS ABOUT SEX ROLES

OBSERVATIONS OF BEHAVIOR

How members of the two sexes behave in the same situation gives children clues about what is regarded as appropriate for them. If the father sits down at the table while the mother brings in food, the child logically concludes that females are supposed to wait on males.

CLOTHES WORN BY TWO SEXES

The type of clothes worn gives clues about the prestige and the difficulty of the play and work of members of the two sexes. The sturdier clothes of boys suggests rougher play than the less sturdy clothes of girls. Aprons for housework indicate easier work than overalls or clothes made of heavier materials. Uniforms suggest prestigious jobs.

ANSWERS TO QUESTIONS

From answers to their questions, children get clues about what members of the social group regard as sex appropriate, how much prestige they associate with different sex roles, and how they rate the players of the roles. When told in answer to the question why girls do not play football that girls are not strong enough to do so, girls logically conclude that boys are stronger and capable of playing more prestigious sports than girls.

PLAY EQUIPMENT

Toys, equipment for games and sports, and amusement opportunities for reading, watching television and movies, and looking at comics are so sex-typed that boys and girls not only learn that they are meant to play differently but also learn that boys' play is more exciting, more adventuresome, and more interesting that girls' play.

TREATMENT BY OTHERS

How children are treated by parents, teachers, and peers of the other sex conveys important meanings to them about what is appropriate for their sex. Girls are encouraged by parents to be dependent and boys to be independent. Boys are reproved less for poor schoolwork and disruptive behavior by teachers than are girls. Boys exclude girls from their gangs and ridicule girls' play as "sissy play."

OPPORTUNITIES FOR LEARNING

In the home, school, and playground, boys are encouraged to learn things regarded as appropriate for boys, and girls are denied these learning opportunities and expected to learn things considered appropriate for them. See Figure 16–2. Girls, for example, are discouraged from taking manual-skills training in school and encouraged to take courses in home economics.

DISCIPLINE

Even though home and school rules are usually the same for boys and girls, enforcement of these rules is less strict for boys than for girls and punishment for breaking rules is more lenient for boys than for girls.

SEX EDUCATION

Whether information about sex is given in the home or school, it emphasizes that the roles of members of the two sexes are very different in courtship, marriage, procreation, and child care.

MASS MEDIA

Because of the amount of time and interest children devote to different mass-media amusements and because of their belief that anything printed in books or shown on the screen must be correct, comics, storybooks, textbooks, movies, and television programs have a tremendous influence on contributing information about sex-role stereotypes.

Different sources give children meanings about different elements of the sex-role stereotypes. All meanings are, by no means, derived from one source. When the meanings from several different sources are similar, they reinforce each other. When, on the other hand, they are different, they result in confusion and a blurred meaning.

When, for example, children see their mothers working in the home, doing the traditional things associated with homemaking—child care, cooking, cleaning, etc.—the meaning of the adult female role acquired from their observations is reinforced by seeing the mothers of their age-mates playing a similar role, by television commercials showing women using different advertised products to clean, cook, and wash clothes, by comics, storybooks, and other mass media that depict women in the traditional female role, and by sex education classes in which they learn what the roles of males and females are in reproduction and child care.

When meanings from different sources conflict, on the other hand, meanings are blurred and children are unsure of what the approved stereotype is. This is far more likely to happen in meanings associated with female sex-role stereotypes than with male stereotypes. It is difficult, for example, for children to have clear concepts of the female role if they observe their mothers working outside the home or doing "men's work" in the home, such as washing cars, raking leaves, or fixing broken household appliances, than when their mothers play roles in keeping with the stereotyped activities as depicted in the mass media or carried out by the mothers of their age-mates.

How definite and specific children's sex-role stereotypes are has been shown by a study Hartley did in which boys and girls, between the ages of 7 and 11 years, explained what the approved sex roles for members of the two sexes meant to them (40). Boys in this group, for example, gave the following description of what they considered appropriate for boys:

They must be able to fight in case a bully comes along; they have to be athletic; they have to be able to run fast; they must be able to play rough games; . . . they need to be smart; they need to be able to take care of themselves; they should know what girls don't know—how to climb, how to make a fire, how to carry things; they should have more ability than girls; they need to know arithmetic and spelling more than girls do.

Boys also have a definite concept of the stereotype of the sex role considered appropriate for girls. According to this stereotype:

They have to stay close to the house; they are expected to play quietly and be gentler than boys; they must not be rough; they have to keep clean; they cry when they are scared and hurt; they are afraid to go to rough places like rooftops and empty lots; . . . they need to know how to cook, sew and take care of children, but spelling and arithmetic are not as important for them as for boys.

Learning the meaning of sex roles depends upon the ability of children to understand the meaning as it is presented to them. Anything in pictorial form, such as comics and pictures in storybooks or school textbooks

"It's not fair! You always play at the deep end and put me in the shallow part!"

Figure 16–2. Acceptance of the traditional belief of female weakness causes many girls to be deprived of opportunities to learn to do what boys are given opportunities to learn. (*Adapted from Bil Keane: "The Family Circus."* Register and Tribune Syndicate, *March 5, 1974. Used by permission.*)

is more meaningful than if presented verbally. Children, for example, learn more about the traditional stereotype of women as inferior to men by comics showing them calling on males for help in a predicament or doing things to win male admiration and attention than from jokes, such as those about "henpecked" husbands or "bossy" wives (102).

The more prestige there is to the source from which information comes, the greater its contribution to the child's learning of sex-role stereotypes. Television announcers for commercials carry a voice of authority which children accept without questioning. If the announcer tells the audience that a certain food will give all the needed nutrients for good health and growth, children ask their parents to buy this food for them. Because the announcers are usually sex-typed—women doing or talking about the traditional tasks of the home, and men, the traditional tasks in the world outside the home, this carries the meaning to children that these are the approved roles for males and females (17, 30, 69).

Just as few children would hesitate to question what

their school textbooks tell them, so they would hesitate to question the implications that females play a less exciting, less prestigious, and less dangerous role in life than males (65). Their history books, for example, say little about women and their contributions to civilization through the ages but much about the contributions of males. Even the readers for the early grades are sex-typed, showing girls and women playing the traditional female role and boys and men, traditional male role. This is true also of storybooks used as a form of amusement. These books are about people playing traditional sex roles, with boys' books emphasizing the exciting adventures of men and girls' books concentrating on the less exciting activities of females in the home (45, 85, 104).

Acceptance of Sex-role Stereotypes

Learning the meaning of sex-role stereotypes and accepting them as guidelines for behavior are separate and distinct. Just because children know what the male and female sex roles are does not automatically result in their acceptance of these roles. Only if they can see how the roles they have learned as appropriate for their sex will be of personal benefit to them will they be willing to accept the stereotypes for these roles as guidelines for their behavior.

There is no statistical evidence to show what acceptance there is of the two kinds of sex-role stereotypes that exist at present. There is, however, evidence that, within some communities, both stereotypes are accepted, though one may enjoy greater acceptance than the others.

On the other hand, there is some evidence that *males* are more favorable to the traditional sex-role stereotypes than to the egalitarian and are more willing to accept them. The reverse is true of females. There are *age* differences in attitudes toward these two kinds of sex-role stereotypes. Young children are willing to accept either traditional or egalitarian stereotypes, depending on which they find their parents accept. As social horizons include peers outside the home, acceptance of stereotypes is greatly influenced by members of the *peer group*. Male peer groups are far less receptive to egalitarian stereotypes than female peer groups.

Children whose parents have come from *foreign countries* accept their parents' sex-role stereotypes and these are usually the traditional ones. *Religious*

training in the home or outside the home has a marked influence on whether children are more favorable to traditional or egalitarian sex-role stereotypes. Except for Protestant training, the tendency is to favor traditional stereotypes. In households where the *mother works* outside the home, children learn to accept the egalitarian sex-role concepts from earliest childhood. As they grow older and are influenced by peers, they may shift their preference to traditional concepts even if they are forced to play egalitarian roles in their homes.

Learning to Play Sex Roles

One of the important developmental tasks of the latter years of childhood is learning to play sex roles approved by the social group. Like other developmental tasks, learning to play approved sex roles is regarded as essential to good personal and social adjustments. Its inclusion in the list of developmental tasks (see page 39 for a list of developmental tasks) is justified by the knowledge of its importance to every child's adjustments. It is also justified by knowledge of how failure to master this task leads to unfavorable social reactions which, in turn, affect the child's self-concept unfavorably.

Learning to play approved sex roles is usually called "sex-role typing." It means not only acting in the socially approved way for members of the sex group with which the individual is identified but also accepting the values, attitudes, and beliefs of the stereotype, of which the approved pattern of behavior is only the outward manifestation. A boy, for example, may act like a boy but prefer to be a girl. Similarly, a girl may act like a girl but inwardly rebel against some of the beliefs and attitudes of the sex-role stereotype for her sex (23, 27).

Sex-role typing is easier for boys than for girls. There are several reasons for this. *First,* from earliest childhood, boys have been made aware of what the social group regards as appropriate for their sex group and have been encouraged, prodded, or even shamed into behaving in a way that is regarded as appropriate for them. By contrast, girls often have a blurred concept of what the approved sex role for females is because, unlike boys, there has not been pressure placed on them to behave in a prescribed way. Often, they are permitted or even encouraged to do what boys do until they approach the adolescent years.

The *second* reason why girls experience more diffi-

468

CHAPTER 16

culties in sex-role typing than boys is that they discover that the female sex role carries less prestige and more restrictions on behavior than the male role. There are even more restrictions on girls' behavior than there were in the earlier years of childhood. Through social disapproval, girls may learn to behave in a way that is approved for their sex group, but they are not completely sex-role typed because they do not accept the beliefs and attitudes that constitute a major part of every sex-role stereotype.

This is in direct contrast to boys. With each passing year, boys discover that the male sex role is more prestigious than the female sex role and carries with it more freedom from social restrictions. Consequently, accepting the beliefs and attitudes of the male sex-role stereotype is not difficult. Even if a boy might have interests and abilities better suited to self-fulfillment in behavior that is regarded as feminine, he shuns such behavior because he realizes the social handicap its acceptance would be.

When Sex-role Typing Begins

Even though learning to play socially approved sex roles is a developmental task for late childhood, few parents wait until then to begin the typing process. Realization of how important a role sex-role typing plays in children's social adjustments, many parents begin the typing process right after babies are born. This they do by identifying babies with one sex or the other by their clothes, toys, and nursery furnishings. Boy babies, for example, are dressed in blue wrappers, sweaters, and buntings, and girls in pink. Sex-appropriate toys are given to the baby to play with and the decorations of the nursery proclaim that it is a "boy's" or a "girl's" room.

Parental preferences for the sex of the baby also contribute to early sex-role typing. If the parents' preference was for a male child and if the baby turns out to be a male, parental treatment will be more favorable than if the baby were female. This treatment, when associated with knowledge of what sex he is, lays the foundation for the belief that he is favored because of his sex (66).

The actual process of sex-role typing does not begin until babies are capable of doing things. Pressures are then put on them to do the things they are learning to do in a sex-appropriate way, by approval, and to avoid doing them, through the force of disapproval, in a sex-inappropriate way. In addition, they are denied opportunities to learn to do things in a sex-inappropriate way. In toy play, for example, babies are given toys appropriate for their sexes and shown how to use them in the approved way. Even if they show preferences for toys appropriate for members of the other sex, they are told that "boys don't play with dolls" or the dolls are taken away from them and they are made to feel ashamed of being seen playing with a sex-inappropriate toy.

Each year, as children's comprehension and skills increase, new aspects of the sex-role concept for their sexes are learned. By the time they are old enough to play with children outside the home, they have a fairly clear concept of what is approved and what is disapproved, not only in behavior but also in beliefs and attitudes. Although sex-role typing will continue as children grow older, the foundations for it are laid in the home and the parents are primarily responsible for the form this sex-role typing takes.

Pattern of Sex-role Typing

Because the foundations for sex-role typing are learned during the early years of life, whether these foundations will conform to the traditional or egalitarian concepts of sex roles will depend on the pattern of family life. When the mother works outside the home, or if the home is a one-parent home with the mother or father in charge of the children, the chances are that the life pattern of the home will be egalitarian. All family members, regardless of sex, will be expected to make some contribution to family life. Even when the children are living in a home with only the father, he will have to call on the children, whether boys or girls, to help with the tasks traditionally performed by females.

On the other hand, if both parents are living in the home and the mother plays the traditional role of homemaker, the chances are that both parents have accepted the traditional stereotypes of sex roles. Under such conditions, children will have role models in the form of parents to imitate.

Furthermore, if parents who play traditional sex roles believe that their children will be happier and make better adjustments to life if they learn traditional rather than egalitarian sex roles, they will see to it that their children learn to play these roles and they will teach them the meanings of traditional sex-role stereotypes. This will be done by the child-training method they use.

However, just because the stereotype of one sex-role type is learned at home during the early years of life, that does not guarantee that it will be persistent. Nor is there evidence that playing these roles will be persistent. They may and they may not be.

Changes may come from two sources: the child's dissatisfaction with the role learned in the home, and pressures from members of the peer group to play another role. A girl, for example, who has been trained to conform to the traditional female stereotype may get *little satisfaction* from this role and rebel against playing it. If, for example, she finds doll play "boring" and girls' books "silly," she will insist on playing with toys that are traditionally labeled "boy's toys" and will want to have traditional "boys' books" read to her. Later, she will rebel against preparing for a career in the traditional female occupations and will use her time and energies to prepare for a career in the traditional area of masculine careers.

Even when a boy finds that playing egalitarian sex role conforms to his interests and abilities, he may shift to the traditional male role because of criticism and ridicule from older siblings or age-mates. Rather than be called a "sissy," the boy learns to be a "regular boy"—acting as members of the peer group think boys should act. He may, however, retain many of the elements of the egalitarian sex-role stereotype—feeling that girls are as bright as boys, having an aspiration to be an artist rather than a businessman or showing respect for members of the female sex instead of derogating their achievements as prescribed by the traditional male sex-role stereotype.

The second common cause for changes in early sex-role typing is *peer pressure*. As childhood draws to a close, girls who have been permitted to play egalitarian roles in their play and schooling discover that they are often confronted with social disapproval and loss of social acceptance by peers. They must then decide whether playing a role suited to their needs is more important than acceptance by the peer group. When interest in social activities with boys begins to develop, peer pressures are especially strong to play the traditional role. Many girls succumb to these pressures and learn to play the traditional female sex role. Boys, having been subjected to peer pressures even before entering first grade, have made the change to the traditional sex role long before they reach the age where social contacts with members of the other sex begin.

When conflicts arise between playing the role they learned at home and playing the role members of the peer group they think they should play, children are faced with two dilemmas. The *first* is confusion about which is the approved sex role—the one favored by parents or the one favored by peers. This gives them a blurred concept of what they should learn. If they have been satisfied with the role they learned to play at home, they are far less willing to change their concepts about what they should do than they would be had they derived little satisfaction from their roles at home. This adds to their confusion.

The *second* dilemma children face when sex-role typing is changed is social disapproval. If they accept the approved sex-role stereotype of one group they will likely win disapproval of the other group. Their decision is then usually made on the basis of which group is more important to them at that time—the family or the peer group.

People Responsible for Sex-role Typing during Childhood

There are three kinds of people primarily responsible for the sex-role typing of children—parents, teachers, and peers. Studies of the influence of these three kinds of people have shown that all influence children's learning of sex-role stereotypes and their learning to play sex roles. However, their influence is in different degrees and at different ages. There are also differences in the type of sex role—traditional or egalitarian—they are most likely to favor and transmit to children.

PARENTS Although both parents play important roles in the sex-role typing of children, their roles are different for children of the two sexes and at different ages. Because the mother assumes more responsibility for the care of children during the early years of life than the father, sex-role typing is done more by the mother than the father at that time. How much influence the father will have later on the sex-role typing of children will depend partly on the relationship of the father with the children and partly on their sex.

During the early years of life, mothers tend to be more interested in and more nurturant of children than fathers. As a result, their relationships with children are more favorable. This encourages children to be more influenced by their mothers than by their fathers. This is true of both boys and girls. How children react to their parents also affects the influence of the parents on children's sex-role typing. When, for example, children—whether boys or girls—show a dependency on parents, parents tend to encourage this dependency. Because mothers, as a group, encourage dependency more than fathers, both boys and girls tend to become dependent rather than independent and aggressive—a sex-appropriate trait for girls but inappropriate for boys, according to the traditional sex-role stereotype (70).

As children grow older and their social horizons broaden, they discover that the father's role is regarded as more prestigious than the mother's. Consequently, the father begins to have an increasingly important influence on the sex-role typing of children, both boys and girls. For boys, the father acts as a role model and, for girls, as a source of approval or disapproval for their sex-typed behavior. Should a father, for example, like feminine women, he will encourage his daughters to conform to the traditional stereotype of the female role and reward them with his approval when they do conform.

Even at the age when children learn the prestige associated with the male role, the father's influence on their sex-role stereotyping will depend on the kind of relationship the father has with the children. A relationship characterized by interest and warmth will encourage greater influence on sex-role typing than a relationship characterized by lack of interest or a punitive, rejectant attitude toward the children (13, 49, 66, 70, 79, 93).

TEACHERS As is true of parents, how much influence teachers have on the sex-role typing of children depends on the kind of relationship there is between teachers and pupils and on the prestige associated with teachers. As was explained in the preceding chapter, in the discussion of children's interests in school, one of the causes of deterioration of interest in school is a decline in relationships between pupils and teachers.

During the preschool years, nursery school and kindergarten teachers play the parent-surrogate role. In this role, there is a warmth in the pupil-teacher relationship similar to that in the parent-child relationship. This pleasant relationship encourages children to want to imitate their teachers and to learn what their teachers teach them, whether it be play skills or how to get along with age-mates.

Decline in pupil-teacher relationships parallels decline in interest in school. By the second grade, many children begin to find school boring, or they actually dislike it. Their dislike for school spreads to their teachers. As a result, the former warm, close relationship gives way to a strained and often antagonistic relationship. Under such conditions, the teacher's influence on sex-role typing declines.

Part of this strained, antagonistic relationship can be traced to the loss of prestige teachers have in the eyes of their pupils. Because of the low prestige children discover that is associated with teaching as a vocation and the low prestige associated with women as a group—an attitude that comes with learning the meanings of sex-role stereotypes—it is understandable that a poor pupil-teacher relationship would develop. This is especially likely to happen among boys who tend to regard both teaching and women unfavorably.

Today, there is a slow but gradual increase in the number of male teachers in preschools and elementary schools. They carry greater prestige in the minds of children, both male and female, than female teachers. For boys, they serve as role models and, for girls, reinforcers of the traditional female sex role.

Whether teachers will encourage traditional or egalitarian sex-role typing will depend partly on their own attitudes toward these types of sex roles, but mainly on what they believe the parents of their pupils want them to encourage. This, to some extent, depends on the community in which the school is located. In a community where many of the mothers work outside the home, there is reason to believe that parents would not be as concerned about having their children learn egalitarian sex-role stereotypes as in communities where the pattern of life is controlled by traditional sex roles (20, 32, 37, 39, 62, 89).

Although few studies have been made to date to see if teachers of both sexes are consistent in teaching children to conform to one type of sex role, there is limited evidence that male teachers emphasize the traditional roles, and that female teachers make some attempt to modify the strict traditional sex-role concept and slant their teaching in the direction of egalitarian sex-role stereotypes.

There are two ways in which teachers carry out sex-role typing. *First,* by encouraging children to learn what is regarded as appropriate for their sexes, using the criteria in either the traditional or egalitarian sex-role stereotypes and, *second,* by denying children the opportunity to learn what they regard as inappropriate for their sex. A teacher who wants to encourage children to learn egalitarian sex roles will permit boys and girls to play with toys of their own choosing, regardless of their sexes. If a boy wants to play with dolls and a girl with trains and mechanical toys, for example, neither will be criticized or shamed for being sex inappropriate. Instead, the teacher will help them to learn how to play with the chosen toys so as to get the maximum enjoyment from the play activities. By contrast, a teacher who wants to encourage children to learn traditional sex-role stereotypes will make a boy who prefers girls' toys feel guilty and ashamed and may even take away the toy he has selected to play with, replacing it with one that conforms to the approved pattern for boys' toys (21, 22, 49, 58, 108).

PEERS Members of the peer group, as was pointed out earlier, do not begin to have an influence on the sex-role typing of children until there is interaction between children and their peers. In early peer interrelationships, little interaction occurs. Children play side by side with other children in parallel or associative play but with little cooperation. There is likewise little communication. When children talk, they usually talk about what they are doing but make no attempt to communicate with the other children who are with them.

As early childhood draws to a close, play interactions appear and communication takes place between playmates. When this happens, peers begin to influence children's sex-role typing. This influence may come from imitation on the part of one child of the playmate's behavior, or it may come from identification with that playmate. When, for example, a warm, close relationship exists between a child and a playmate, each child wants to be like the other child. If both have been sex-role typed in the home by the same form of sex-role stereotype—traditional or egalitarian—the interaction of the child with the playmate will reinforce the sex-role typing begun in the home. If, on the other hand, they have been subjected to different sex-role typing in their homes, which child will serve as the pattern for peer influence will depend on which one is dominant in the playmate relationship. Should it be a child brought up in a home where emphasis was placed on traditional sex role typing, for example, the less dominant child will become less egalitarian in behavior and conform more to the stereotype of the traditional sex role.

As children reach the gang age, peer influence becomes stronger than parent or teacher influence. Because most boys prefer the traditional sex role which emphasizes their superiority, their influence on their peers will be in favor of traditional sex-role typing. Until girls reach the latter part of childhood and become interested in social contacts with boys, their influence on their female peers will likely be in favor of egalitarian sex-role typing. Later, this may and often does change. When this happens, girls show scorn and tend to reject girls who cling to the egalitarian sex-role stereotype.

Motivation to Become Sex-role Typed

In all learning, motivation plays an important role. When children recognize the personal advantages to them of learning to conform to an approved sex-role stereotype, they are motivated to learn to play this approved sex role. When, on the other hand, they can see no personal advantage from doing so, their motivation is weak.

Just knowing what the approved sex-role stereotype is does not provide motivation. Only when children recognize the benefits they will derive from playing the role do they put forth the effort needed to learn to play the role. Boys, as a group, recognize the advantages of the traditional sex role to members of the male sex. Consequently, they want to learn to be sex appropriate as defined by the stereotype of the traditional sex role. By contrast, the egalitarian sex role is less favorable to boys than the traditional. This weakens their motivation to learn to play this role. The reverse is true of girls. The egalitarian role is more favorable to them than the traditional. This gives them the necessary motivation to learn to play this role and weakens their motivation to learn to play the traditional role. See Figure 16–3.

Whether the individual will learn to play any approved sex role, either traditional or egalitarian, will depend on the strength of motivation. The strength of motivation, in turn, will depend upon three conditions.

First, how strong the motivation is to learn to play an approved sex role will vary according to the ability to see the relationship between playing that role and social acceptance. Only when children are aware of the fact that playing a sex role approved by the group with which they wish to be identified will increase their chances of acceptance by that group will their motivation be strong enough to make them willing to put the effort into learning a role that fails to meet their needs and interests as much as another role would. When, for example, girls feel that their acceptance by members of their own sex group as well as by boys will be jeopardized if they fail to conform to the approved sex-role pattern of the group, it will provide the motivation needed to learn to play the role.

Second, the strength of the child's motivation to learn to play a group-approved sex role will depend upon the strength of the child's desire to be accepted by the group. Children who are well accepted want to retain their favorable status in the group. Those who are social climbers or neglectees want to improve their status and thus want to learn to conform to group-approved standards in the hopes of improving their status. An involuntary isolate, unless there are chances of improving the present status, has little motivation to learn to conform. Because voluntary isolates are satisfied with their status, they conform to a sex-role stereotype of their choosing, ignoring the group-approved stereotype.

Third, when a choice must be made between sex roles that meet children's needs and those that conform to group standards but fail to meet their needs, children will then have to decide which brings them the greater advantage. If the decision is in favor of self-fulfillment, the motivation to conform to a group-approved sex-role stereotype will be weak. By contrast, a decision in favor of group approval and acceptance will provide the necessary motivation to learn the group-approved sex-role stereotype and to learn to play the role associated with that stereotype.

Methods of Learning to Play Sex Roles

There are three common methods of sex-role typing of children. What these methods are and the characteristics of each are explained in Box 16–6.

When children learn to play sex roles by *imitation,* they may or they may not learn a sex-role stereotype that meets their needs. It depends on whether the stereotype they imitate is suited to their interests and abilities. On the one hand, it conforms to social expectations because it is patterned along the lines approved by the group if the person imitated is an accepted member of the group. If, on the other hand, the person imitated is regarded as sex inappropriate and, consequently, is not accepted by the group, the child learns a pattern of behavior that will jeopardize acceptance.

Sex-role typing by *identification* tends to produce better results because the person admired by the child

"... And don't bring me anything that requires me to act out traditional female roles."

Figure 16–3. Very early, girls learn that the traditional female role is less favorable to them than the male role and this weakens their motivation to play this role. (*Adapted from George Lichty and Fred Wagner: "Grin and Bear It."* Field Newspaper Syndicate, *Dec. 19, 1974. Used by permission.*)

is likely to be regarded favorably by the group—one of the major reasons for the child to select that person for identification. However, during the early childhood years, when the object of identification is a family member, usually a person of the child's own sex, there is no guarantee that the person will be favorably viewed by the social group. A father, for example, may be a hero in the mind of a small boy but not in the minds of people outside the home.

A serious problem arising from sex-role typing by identification is that children change their ideals frequently and, by so doing, change the object of identification. A girl may, one week, regard a teacher as her ideal and want to be exactly like the teacher. Next week, she may shift her ideal to a glamorous female on the screen or a heroine in the sports world. Unless these two objects of identification conform to a similar sex-role stereotype, it will be confusing to the girl to know which patterns of behavior to imitate and, even more seriously, which values and interests to accept as her own.

COMMON METHODS OF SEX-ROLE TYPING

IMITATION

When children learn to play sex roles by imitation, they do so by copying the speech, behavior, and personality characteristics as well as the interests and values of the person they are imitating. This method of learning is especially common during the early childhood years when children tend to imitate anyone in authority with whom they are frequently associated. The usual models for imitation are parents, older siblings, or such caretakers as nursery-school or kindergarten teachers.

IDENTIFICATION

Instead of imitating anyone with whom they have frequent contacts, children select from those available the ones they especially admire or for whom they have strong affection as their models. At first, the model may be a parent of either sex or an older sibling who has been kind to the child. Later, their models are more likely to come from outside the home—especially a person in the mass media, a community or national leader, or a hero in the world of sports.

CHILD TRAINING

In sex-role typing by child training, children learn to act, think, and feel as they are expected to by the person in authority. They may be given reasons for doing so or they may be expected to obey blindly. Sometimes rewards are given for compliance with the expectation of the person in authority and sometimes it is taken for granted that they will comply. Punishment in the form of disapproval is widely used for noncompliance. In most child training, more emphasis is placed on the negative aspect of sex roles than the positive. Boys, for example, are told that "boys don't cry" but they are not told what boys should do when they are hurt, frustrated, or disappointed.

sports hero will lead to disappointments and frustrations.

If the person who is responsible for using *child training* to type the child takes into consideration the child's interests and abilities, the results will be good. On the other hand, forcing stereotyped sex roles on children that are unsuited to their abilities or interests will lead to dissatisfactions and frustrations. This is especially likely to happen if the sex-role stereotypes children are expected to learn differ radically from those used as guidelines for their playmates' sex-role typing.

Of the three common methods of child training, the best for sex-role typing is democratic. In this type of child training, children not only learn what they are expected to do but they are also given explanations of why they should do it. If it is pointed out to them that acceptance of a sex-role stereotype will be to their personal advantage, they will be far more willing to accept it and will be more strongly motivated to learn to think and act in accordance with this stereotype than if an explanation were not given, as is true of authoritarian child training.

Because permissive child training gives little guidance, children who are sex-role typed by permissive parents or teachers tend to fall back on imitation or identification as ways of becoming sex-role typed. By so doing, they encounter the problems these methods give rise to.

Effects of Sex-role Typing on Behavior

Sex-role typing has profound and far-reaching effects on children's behavior. These effects are different for boys and girls. They are also different for children who have received egalitarian sex-role typing and those whose sex-role typing has followed the traditional pattern. These differences will be pointed out in the discussion of the following important areas of behavior.

Sex Cleavages

Young children play together happily with no more than the usual fights for their age levels. Boys enjoy playing with girls' toys and girls with boys' toys. They cooperate in dramatic play, in constructions, and in

Another problem arising from sex-role typing by identification is that the pattern learned may not fit the child's interests and abilities. Studies of hero-worshipping in childhood, as was explained earlier, have shown that children more often select as their ideals people who have characteristics they admire and wish they had than people who are similar to them. A boy whose body build makes success in the sport world difficult or impossible may find trying to pattern his sex-role development along the lines of a

games. Sometimes girls play leadership roles in these play activities and sometimes boys.

Should they go to nursery school or kindergarten, or be in a child-care center, this is likely to change. Many teachers begin to put pressures on children to play with what has traditionally been regarded as "boys' toys" and "girls' toys." Although there is less pressure on girls than on boys to play with sex-appropriate toys, girls are often denied opportunities to use boys' toys and are often not encouraged or shown how to play the traditional boys' games.

By the time children enter the first grade, cleavages between the two sexes are well developed. These cleavages are primarily the result of pressures put on boys by fathers and older male siblings to shun girls and girls' play in favor of boys and boys' play.

As boys begin to withdraw from their former female playmates to play with other boys, girls have no alternative but to play with girls. At the same time, pressures are put on them, by parents, teachers, and older siblings of their sex, to play like girls and to behave in other ways considered appropriate for girls. They are also denied opportunities to learn many of the things boys of their age are encouraged to learn, whether play activities, school subjects, or about possible future vocations that might meet their needs better than the vocations they are expected to learn about.

Each year, as children grow older, the cleavage between the sexes grows deeper. The less boys and girls have in common, the less congenial they will be and the less they will be able to communicate with one another. Consequently, the less enjoyment they will get from their interactions. Their greatest enjoyment comes from interaction with members of their own sex in gang activities.

In the schoolroom, where boys and girls sit side by side, interaction is limited. The same is true in the home where there are boys and girls. Although children get more enjoyment from interactions with members of their own sex than from those of the other sex, sibling interactions are far less enjoyable than peer interactions because of the age and level-of-development differences between siblings of the same sex. This is one of the causes of deterioration in sibling relationships, as will be pointed out in the next chapter.

When sex-role typing follows the egalitarian pattern, there are fewer and less pronounced cleavages between the sexes than when the traditional pattern is followed. However, as children grow older and be-

come members of gangs, they will be influenced by the pattern of behavior accepted by the majority of the gang members. If most of them have been sex-role typed according to the traditional stereotypes, children whose sex-role typing has conformed to the egalitarian stereotype will be misfits unless they are willing to accept the pattern favored by the group as a whole. This they are likely to do to ensure acceptance by the gang.

It is of little importance whether or not girls have been sex-role typed by one stereotype or another because they are rarely responsible for sex cleavages. However, girls whose training has been along egalitarian lines are more likely to be psychologically damaged by sex cleavages than those whose training has been according to the traditional pattern. This damage is shown mainly by resentments at rejection by former playmates and at attempts to make them feel inferior and inadequate because they are girls.

Sex Antagonism

Accompanying cleavages between the sexes there develops an antagonism toward members of the opposite sex. Boys and girls belittle one another's interests, appearance, skills, and activities; they make jokes at the expense of members of the other sex; they refuse to associate with one another, even at parties; and they are constantly bickering, name calling, and quarreling. This usually starts in the gang and spreads into the home. Within the home, any harmonious relationship that formerly existed between siblings of the two sexes is likely to be replaced by antagonism (69, 72).

Although antagonism between the sexes usually starts in the peer group, it spreads to all age levels—younger siblings, adolescent siblings, parents, and relatives. It is not uncommon, for example, for boys who formerly had a relationship with mothers that closely approximated hero-worship to begin to derogate their mothers and their mothers' achievements just as they derogate girls of their own age and their achievements. See Figure 16–4.

As is true of sex cleavages, boys are, for the most part, the aggressors in this battle of the sexes. It is they who usually start the name calling, ridiculing, and other forms of derogation and belittlement. Girls then retaliate by refusing to associate with boys and by returning in kind the treatment they have received.

There is no evidence that sex antagonism comes from physical changes or physical differences

Figure 16–4. When sex antagonism develops, it spreads to all age levels and even parents of the opposite sex are not spared. (*Adapted from Bil Keane: "The Family Circus." Register and Tribune Syndicate, July 14, 1975. Used by permission.*)

between boys and girls or from the maturation of any mental ability. Instead, all evidence points to *cultural* influences. As sex-role typing occurs, during the preschool years, pressures are put on children of both sexes to develop what is traditionally considered appropriate behavior and attitudes for members of the two sexes. The male sex, for example, is presented as superior and the female sex as inferior. This pressure, which is stronger on boys than on girls, comes from parents, other siblings of the same sex, peers, and other adults.

As boys accept these traditional attitudes about their superiority, they display their feelings about girls in overt behavior. This is the starting point of the battle between the sexes.

Children who have been brought up by egalitarian sex-role typing learn to think of boys and girls as different but not as superior and inferior. However, when they come in contact with peers who have learned traditional attitudes about members of the two sexes, they often assimilate these attitudes and act in accordance with them. This they do to guarantee social acceptance. Although they may not accept all the ele-

ments of the traditional sex-role stereotype, they usually accept the overt expressions of this stereotype.

Discrimination against Sex-inappropriate Children

When antagonism between the sexes develops, so does the tendency to discriminate against members of the same sex who are regarded as sex inappropriate in attitudes, interests, values, appearance, or behavior. This derogation is stronger among boys than among girls. One of the worst stigmas that can be attached to a boy is the label "sissy." It suggests to others that the boy is not sex appropriate and, as such, is inferior to other members of the male sex.

Although girls who are not sex appropriate may be regarded with more tolerance than boys, tolerance does not win social approval. Instead, it may ward off social rejection temporarily, but as girls approach adolescence, this tolerance gives way to the same strong disapproval that boys experience when they are regarded as sex inappropriate.

Once children are familiar with the socially approved stereotype of sex appropriateness for members of the two sexes—usually before they enter first grade—they regard anyone who deviates in any way from this stereotype as "funny." They express their attitudes about the deviant person by criticism, name calling, nicknames, jokes, and other forms of derogation (72). Later, they refuse to play with or be seen with those whom they regard as sex inappropriate. As a result, children who are regarded by their age-mates as sex inappropriate are either rejected or neglected and forced to play the role of involuntary isolates.

Even when children do not regard differentness as inappropriateness, they often follow the crowd that does. They then discriminate against those whom their age-mates discriminate against to avoid being classed as one of the sex inappropriates because of their association with a child who has been so labeled.

Sex Typing of Behavior and Objects

As children learn what the social group regards as sex appropriate for members of the two sexes and as they learn the favorable attitudes toward what is regarded as sex appropriate, they accept these as their own and label objects and behavior as "boys'" or "girls'." This has a profound effect on their own attitudes toward different patterns of behavior and different objects.

As young children, certain *toys* are labeled "boys'" toys and others "girls'" toys. *Colors* and *clothing* styles are also labeled in this way. When children go to school, *school subjects* and *extracurricular activities* are quickly sex-typed. In the area of *behavior,* sex typing is just as widespread as in the area of objects. Crying, for example, is regarded as all right for girls but all wrong for boys. Fighting and other aggressive acts, such as teasing, bullying, and name calling are regarded as signs of masculinity while being docile, dependent, cooperative, kind, and sympathetic are regarded as signs of femininity.

At all times and under all circumstances, judgments of self and others are more favorable when associated with objects and behavior typed as appropriate for the individual's sex. Even when a boy derives more enjoyment from playing with girls' play equipment than with boys', much of his enjoyment is negated by feelings of guilt about preferring it to equipment regarded as appropriate for boys and by shame, if seen playing with this equipment by others, especially by members of the male sex (10, 26, 28, 63, 80, 116).

Levels of Aspiration

After years of exposure to sex-role typing, to discrimination and to antagonism, it is understandable that this would have some effect on the kinds of aspiration children set for themselves and how high or low these aspirations would be. Believing that their abilities are superior to those of girls, boys as a group tend to aspire higher than girls. Many develop the habit of aspiring unrealistically high for their abilities.

By contrast, having been indoctrinated with the belief of their inferiority since earliest childhood, many girls develop the habit of aspiring lower than their abilities justify. Indoctrination of their inferiority has its greatest effect on aspirations in areas which are traditionally regarded as "masculine." In areas that are traditionally regarded as "feminine," there is less social pressure from adults and peers on girls to set their aspirations below their abilities than there is in areas traditionally sex-typed as "masculine" (34, 92).

As children grow older and think about future vocations, sex-role typing plays an especially strong role. Not only do girls aspire to vocations in what are traditionally regarded as "women's work" but they also aspire to vocations on a lower rung on the vocational ladder than do boys. Because the social group—adult as well as peer—expects them to aspire in this way, it

has a marked influence on their levels of aspiration as well as on the type of aspiration they set for themselves.

Achievement Striving

Before children become sex-role typed to the point where they accept the belief that success is more approved for males than for females, girls strive for success in whatever they do, just as boys do. They enjoy the ego satisfaction of success and are willing to put effort into the activity needed to achieve this success.

As sex-role typing progresses, an attitudinal barrier to striving for success begins to develop in girls. Not only do they begin to aspire to goals below their abilities, but they learn to believe that their achievements will be on a lower level than male achievements in the same areas. Acceptance of this sex-typed belief weakens their achievement striving and they begin to be underachievers, working below their capacities and achieving far less success than they are capable of. Accompanying this are attitudes typical of underachievers—frustrations, resentments, feelings of guilt and shame, and a tendency to blame others for their lack of success (4, 53, 99).

Just the opposite is true of boys. As their sex-role typing progresses, boys accept the belief that males are capable of greater success than females in the same areas and that an insignia of masculinity is success above that of females in these areas. Boys whose abilities make superior success possible learn to work up to their capacities to maintain their status of male superiority—a status that becomes progressively easier for them to maintain as girls' achievement striving is weakened by acceptance of the belief that their abilities are inferior to those of boys and, hence, their chances of success are less than boys' (92).

Boys whose abilities are limited are faced with the dilemma of showing superiority in achievements as a symbol of their masculinity at any cost or of being less successful than girls and winning the reputation of being sex inappropriate because they allow girls to outdo them. This encourages the typical attitudes and behavior of overachievers as described in the preceding chapter—attempts to be successful at any cost, whether by help from others, playing up to the person who judges their success, or cheating, and by an attitude colored by guilt if they take time from the activities in which they are striving for superiority to do

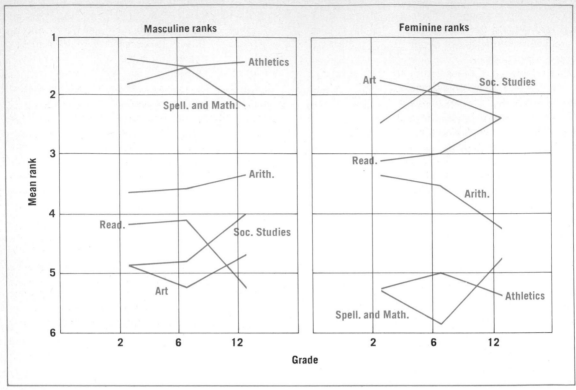

Figure 16–5. How boys and girls rank achievement in different areas of schoolwork and extracurricular activities. (*Adapted from A. H. Stein and J. Smithells: Age and sex differences in children's sex-role standards about achievement.* Developmental Psychology, *1969, 1, 252–259. Used by permission.*)

things more to their liking and by shame if they are outstripped by the achievements of others, especially females.

Achievements in different areas of the child's life begin to have different degrees of prestige associated with them as sex typing of activities progresses. In schoolwork and in extracurricular activities, for example, children learn that different degrees of prestige are associated with them by the social group and they accept these ratings as their own. Figure 16–5 shows how boys and girls rank achievement in different areas. Note that these rankings change as children enter adolescence and accept the values of the adult group rather than those of the peer group (12, 43, 99).

Regardless of whether children are subjected to egalitarian or traditional sex-role typing in the home, when their social horizons broaden the influence of

traditional sex-role typing begins to be dominant. As a result, the achievement striving of boys and girls starts to follow the pattern considered appropriate by standards set down in the traditional stereotype. Girls who formerly worked up to capacity now tend to slip in their achievement striving, while boys tend to increase their achievement striving in the hopes of showing their masculine superiority. By the time childhood ends, these patterns of achievement striving are likely to have become firmly rooted habits (6, 25, 86).

Hazards in Sex-role Development

There are many serious hazards in the area of sex-role development. The reason for this is that, even in cultures where patterns of living for all people are changing rapidly and radically, changes in sex roles tend to lag behind other changes. This lag may be explained, in part at least, by the reluctance on the part of males to relinquish the status of superiority they have enjoyed for centuries.

This reluctance is intensified by the realization that superiority gained by achievement can sometimes be held by members of the sex traditionally believed to be inferior. Sharing a status taken for granted as theirs or relinquishing it to those regarded as inferior is always an ego-deflating experience.

Whenever change occurs, a period of ambiguity about the approved pattern of behavior occurs. This adds to the problems of adjustment that normally are present. Until the social group accepts a consistent pattern of sex-role typing for its children as a guideline for those who are responsible for the training, children will pay the penalty in having to face more problems in their personal and social adjustments than they would if greater consistency in the approved pattern of sex-role typing prevailed.

Because sex-role typing presents so many hazards to the personal and social adjustments of children, it would be impossible to cover them all. Therefore, in the brief discussion to follow only those that are known to be hazardous, through extensive studies of these problems, will be touched on. As research in the area of sex-role typing continues, unquestionably more and perhaps more serious hazards will be reported.

Widespread Effects of Sex-role Typing

Unlike most other areas of development in childhood where the common hazards affect the children alone, the hazards in the present uncertainty about the approved pattern of sex-role typing and sex-role playing affects many segments of the social group. Parents and teachers are at a loss to know how best to sex-role type the children under their care for a future pattern of living that may be radically different from the present pattern. Producers of mass media are uncertain about what type of sex-role stereotype they should present to children—egalitarian or traditional. If they present a stereotype not in keeping with the stereotype held by the majority of the group—especially the adult members of the group—they will be blamed for maladjustments of the children that their stereotypes are claimed to have caused. Should they, for example,

present in pictorial and other media girls playing a role similar to boys in excitement, venturesomeness, and risk taking, the producers will be blamed for making girls dissatisfied and discontented with the role they are expected to play in real life.

Perhaps the most important way in which sex-role typing influences the social group as a whole is in the number of maladjusted people it contributes to the group. Children who are forced to learn roles not suited to their abilities and interests and are prevented from playing roles that do meet their needs contribute heavily to the malcontents and troublemakers of a social group. If they later assume a role of responsibility for the training of the young, they will pass on their dissatisfaction to those under their care, thus increasing the number of maladjusted people in the social group.

Another way the social group is affected by sex-role typing is through the barriers it erects to the contibutions of a segment of the group that has, for centuries, been regarded as inferior. By closing doors of opportunity for training and achievements to the female sex, the social group deprives itself of contributions that may equal or surpass those of the male group.

Confusion about Approved Sex-role Stereotypes

Before sex-role typing can be carried out successfully, those in charge of the typing must know two things: *first,* the essential elements of the stereotype—the beliefs, attitudes, and behavior patterns associated with it—and, *second,* which is the more widely approved and accepted stereotype. In American culture today, the sex-role stereotypes, whether traditional or egalitarian, are more clearly defined for boys than for girls. On the other hand, there is no clear-cut evidence that the traditional or the egalitarian sex roles are so widely approved and accepted that it is possible to say which is the "right" stereotype.

Children as well as those who are responsible for seeing to it that they learn the approved sex-role stereotypes and conform to them are confused about how children should think, feel, and act if they are to learn to be sex appropriate. In the home, children may learn the elements of one pattern of sex roles and, later, when they go out into the neighborhood and school, they may discover that the stereotype they learned at home is different from what their peers have learned. They may also find contradictions between the home-learned stereotype and what their books—either school textbooks or books read just for fun—present, what they see on the screen, and how members of the two sexes are depicted in the comics. When they visit in the homes of age-mates, they may discover that the parents of their age-mates play markedly different roles from those their parents play. Should they be geographically mobile, moving to a new neighborhood or community, their confusion may be increased by finding different approved sex-role stereotypes accepted there than in the neighborhood or community from which they have come.

Confusion is hazardous to sex-role typing because it slows down the learning process and weakens the child's motivation to learn. Until children know exactly what they are expected to learn—and this will be greatly influenced by how certain those who are responsible for their sex-role typing are that they are teaching them the socially approved stereotypes—their learning will be slow and the end results poor.

Because the social group expects children to be sex-role typed by the time they enter first grade in school, slowness in being typed leads to unfavorable social judgments. These, in turn, lead to unfavorable self-judgments. The slower the learning of this important developmental task, the more sex inappropriate the child will be judged to be—a judgment that is hazardous to good personal as well as social judgments.

Confusion about Sex-role Typing

When those who are responsible for the sex-role typing of children are confused about what to teach them, they add to the confusion children are already experiencing from conflicting observations and experiences with patterns that appear to be radically different. This is serious because children must have a stable model and confidence that those who are teaching them the model are convinced that it is the right one.

Confusion on the part of those responsible for sex-role typing of children raises many questions, four of which are very common. *First,* what type of sex-role stereotype will best fit the needs and interests of a particular child? For example, parents may question whether a small, delicate boy should be sex-role typed to conform to the traditional stereotype of the "regular American boy" or whether learning a more egalitarian role might not be better for that child.

Second, if parents hope and plan to improve their so-

cial and vocational status, will the sex-role typing of their children at the present time be right for the social group they aspire to be identified with as they climb the ladder? Should they, for example, plan to move to the suburbs from an urban area, will the sex roles their children are now learning in the urban area be approved when they live in the suburbs?

Third, with the rapid and radical changes taking place in American life today—as well as in many other cultures around the world—will the approved sex-role stereotype of today be the approved sex-role stereotype when their children reach adolescence and, later, adulthood? They may be appropriately sex-role typed for the present but that does not guarantee that they will be appropriately sex-role typed for the future.

Fourth, because approved patterns of sex-role behavior vary greatly from one community to another and from one area of the country to another, will children who are appropriately sex-role typed for where their families now live be appropriately sex-role typed for the area their future vocations may take them? If a girl, for example, should learn to play the traditional female role that is approved where her family now lives, will she be prepared for good adjustments to her adult environment should marriage or a job take her to another part of the country or even to a foreign country?

To play safe and to anticipate the future, Hartley has offered the suggestion that training children, especially boys, according to the egalitarian sex-role stereotype is better than using the traditional model. This suggestion is based on studies of how children, from 8 to 11 years, perceive the roles of girls and boys in today's culture. As Hartley has concluded (40):

These data suggest that the more egalitarian and less sex-separated culture offers the boy, as well as the girl, a superior opportunity to feel consistently wanted and worthwhile. They also suggest that the stance of defensive superiority will be less and less necessary for the male in the egalitarian culture.

Should the pendulum swing from the present trend toward a more egalitarian culture to one controlled by traditional stereotypes of sex appropriateness, will children sex-role typed as Hartley has suggested be able to adjust successfully to a world where traditional sex-role stereotypes dominate the pattern of life? This is one of the major problems those responsible for sex-role typing of children must face because their choice will determine whether the training they give to children will prove to be beneficial or hazardous to children's personal and social adjustments.

Difficulties in Accepting Approved Sex-role Stereotypes

Even when parents and teachers are convinced that they are sex-role typing children in a way that will lead to good personal and social adjustments, there is no guarantee that children will act in accordance with the stereotype they have learned. Knowing the meaning of a stereotype and accepting it as a model for behavior are two separate and distinct things.

As a group, boys are more willing to accept the traditional sex-role stereotypes than the egalitarian, and the reverse is true for girls as a group. The traditional stereotype is more favorable to boys and the egalitarian to girls.

However, within both sex groups, there are children who are unwilling or unable to accept the approved stereotypes they have learned. A boy, for example, who lacks the physique or strength to be a "regular boy," according to the traditional stereotype, or who has some special ability that is satisfied in activities that are traditionally regarded as "feminine," may reject the traditional male role. A girl whose interests are centered mainly on traditional feminine activities— homemaking and child care—may prefer the traditional female role and reject the egalitarian role.

Following a pattern suited to the child's interests and abilities may contribute to good personal adjustments but it may, at the same time, be hazardous to good social adjustments. How hazardous it will be will depend largely on the attitudes of the majority of the members of the social group with which the child is identified. If the majority of boys with whom the boy with feminine interests and attitudes comes in contact are traditionally masculine sex-role typed, the boy will be judged a "sissy"—a judgment that will be hazardous to social acceptance.

Similarly, a girl who prefers the traditional female sex role may be constantly associated in school and in the neighborhood with girls whose mothers have encouraged them to learn the egalitarian sex-role stereotype. She will then be regarded by her age-mates as an "odd ball" or accused of "living in the dark ages."

When children are unwilling or unable to accept the sex-role stereotype they have learned as the approved type for the group with which they are associated, they are faced with a dilemma. They may do what meets their needs best, thus making good personal but poor social adjustments, or they may do what the group expects them to do, thus making good social but poor personal adjustments. If the desire for social approval and acceptance is strong, they will accept a sex-role stereotype that is approved by the group and put up a front of being sex appropriate. The satisfaction they get from social acceptance may compensate for the personal dissatisfaction of thinking, feeling, and acting in opposition to their interests and beliefs. When, on the other hand, they prefer the role of voluntary isolate, they can satisfy their personal needs and be personally well adjusted without being disturbed or unhappy about social adjustments that are of little interest or concern to them.

Influence of Mass Media

The influence of the different forms of mass media on sex-role typing in childhood is hazardous to the good personal and social adjustments of children for two reasons. *First,* because the different forms of mass media usually stress the traditional sex-role stereotypes, it is confusing to children who are learning at home or in the school roles that more closely approximate those of the egalitarian stereotype. As was stressed above, when confusion occurs, it slows down learning and weakens the learner's motivation to learn.

Second, the prestige children associate with the mass media encourages an uncritical acceptance of what the different mass media present, whether humor, stories, pictures, or educational material. Furthermore, because of the time children spend on mass media, either in school or as favorite forms of amusement, there is constant reinforcement of what children are learning from this source. This adds to the confusion children experience.

To avoid confusing children about what sex-role stereotype to accept as the socially approved stereotype—that learned from the mass media or that learned from other sources—an attempt has been made to convince the producers of different forms of mass media to abandon their emphasis on the traditional sex-role stereotypes and to put more emphasis on egalitarian stereotypes. This, to date, has met with limited success.

The major reason for this is that producers of mass

media have been faced with certain dilemmas which they find difficult to resolve. Several of these are serious enough to justify pointing out.

First, do parents of today's children want their children to get a sex-role stereotype from the mass media that differs radically from the stereotype they are attempting to teach them in the home or do they want the mass media to reinforce the home teaching? Stated in another way, how will it affect the market for their products if producers stress the egalitarian sex-role concept instead of the traditional concept?

Second, which will have a broader appeal—and hence bigger sales—media that stress the egalitarian or the traditional sex-role stereotypes? If there were conclusive evidence that egalitarian sex-role typing is more widespread than traditional, it would be good business to shift to this form of typing in books, comics, television programs, and other forms of mass media. At the present time, there is no conclusive evidence that either egalitarian or traditional typing is universal, though there is some evidence that the egalitarian is less widely used than the traditional.

Third, any mass media that makes use of the comic as a source of appeal to children—comic books, comic strips, humorous television programs, etc.—relies heavily on the battle of the sexes and on the frailties of the female sex as a source of humor. If producers wanted to stress the egalitarian role stereotype, what could they substitute as a source of humor that would be as effective as the old and tried source based on the theme of sex differences?

Fourth, what can be done about the classics in different areas, especially children's books, which stress the traditional sex-role stereotype? Should producers, for example, stop making books based on the writings of the famous tellers of fairy tales and other stories that have come down through the generations; should producers of television programs abandon all themes from these classics because of their "sexist" approach; and should illustrators of classic themes eliminate all suggestions of traditional sex roles in favor of egalitarian roles? (83)

Effects on Personality

Sex-role typing affects personality through the effect it has on the self-concept. When children see themselves favorably through the treatment they receive from others, especially those who are most important to them, it will have a favorable effect on the personality and, as such, lead to good personal and social adjustments. The reverse will be true if the self-concept is unfavorable owing to unfavorable treatment from others. Children who are judged as sex appropriate, it has been reported, make better personal and social adjustments than those who are judged as sex inappropriate. The former are favorably judged by the social group and the latter unfavorably judged (40, 52).

The effect of sex-role typing is especially hazardous to personal and social adjustments when it conforms to the *traditional sex-role stereotype.* In the case of boys, it leads to an unwarranted feeling of superiority—a superiority complex based on the belief that all who are male are automatically superior to all who are female. In girls, it leads to an unwarranted feeling of inferiority—an inferiority complex based on the traditional belief that all females are inferior to all males, regardless of abilities and achievements. In neither case do children see themselves realistically. The wider the gap between their real selves and their idealized selves, the greater the chance that maladjustments will develop. This will be discussed in more detail in the chapter on personality (10, 33, 67, 76).

SOME EFFECTS OF EARLY SEX-ROLE TYPING ON ADULTS

ON MEN

- High, often unrealistically high, levels of aspiration to conform to the masculine stereotype of superiority.
- Overtaxing strength to prove masculine physical superiority.
- Unnecessary risk taking which contributes to physical defects and mortality.
- Tendency to underrate female achievements at home and at work.
- Resentment against or refusal to be subservient to women at home or at work.
- Intolerance of all who are sex inappropriate according to the traditional stereotype.
- Self-oriented as expressed in the assumption that females in the home and outside the home will wait on them.
- Expectations of playing leadership roles in the home, in the community, and at work.
- Compulsive in work to maintain belief that male achievements are always superior to female achievements in the same areas.
- Acceptance of cultural belief of personal superiority because of being male.

ON WOMEN

- Resentment against blocks in way of personal fulfillment.
- Other-oriented which makes fulfillment of own interests and abilities impossible.
- Feeling of inadequacy which encourages level of aspiration below abilities.
- Tendency to underrate own and overrate masculine achievements.
- Underachievement stemming from feelings of inferiority and inadequacy.
- "Fear of success" or motive to avoid success to avoid being judged "unfeminine."
- Willingness to accept roles below abilities, especially in traditionally male activities.
- Acceptance of cultural stereotype as inferior to men.
- Noncompetitive in any activity in which men are involved.
- Resentment at playing subordinate roles in the home and vocation after playing egalitarian or near-egalitarian roles in school and college.
- Resentment against work overload, especially when necessity makes it imperative that work outside the home be added to home responsibilities, as compared with the workload carried by males.
- Resentment against lack of cooperation from males in home duties, except in extreme emergencies.
- Resentment at having to pull up roots when husband's climb up the vocational ladder necessitates geographic mobility.
- Resentment at having to give up opportunities for vocational advancement because of husband's refusal to share home responsibilities or to move to another area where vocational advancement is offered.
- Hesitancy to be creative for fear of being regarded as sex inappropriate.

Traditional sex-role typing almost always leads to sex cleavages. When they develop, the effects on personality are similar to those that result from discrimination due to racial, religious, or other differences. Those who are responsible for the cleavages—in this case, usually members of the male sex—develop feelings of superiority and treat those whom they discriminate against as inferiors, unworthy of their time and attention. Feelings of superiority or inferiority, fostered by sex cleavages, reinforce the feelings of superiority or inferiority that come from acceptance of the traditional belief of the inherent superiority of the male and the inherent inferiority of the female.

When sex cleavages develop, sex antagonism almost always follows. Sex antagonism affects children who belittle members of the opposite sex just as it affects the victims of the belittling. This means that boys are unfavorably affected, just as girls are, but in a different way. Box 16–7 lists some of the important effects of antagonism and shows how hazardous they are to good personal and social adjustments on the part of *all* children who are involved in sex antagonism, either as agents or victims of it.

Egalitarian sex-role typing is not without its hazards to good personal and social adjustments. These hazards are far greater in the case of boys than girls, though members of both sexes are often unfavorably affected. If boys are made to feel sex inappropriate by adults or peers, it affects their self-judgments unfavorably and is reflected in poor personal as well as social adjustments. Girls who are judged unfavorably because they do not conform to the widely held traditional stereotype of femininity are affected in much the same way. These unfavorable social judgments discourage a desire to accept and play the egalitarian roles and encourage a shift to the traditional roles.

Persistent Effects of Sex-role Typing

Unquestionably the most serious hazard in sex-role typing is its persistent effect on the personal and social adjustments of children, effects that carry into adult life. These effects come primarily from the beliefs and attitudes developed during the typing process.

Changing patterns of behavior, once formed, can be done without too much difficulty if it becomes apparent that they are hazardous to good adjustments. Changing beliefs and attitudes, on the other hand, is difficult and rarely more than partially successful. The reason for this is that beliefs and attitudes are heavily weighted emotionally. This makes them resistant to change.

Furthermore, because sex-role typing begins early in life when the child's experiences are limited, when children are greatly influenced by pressures from adults in authority as well as by peers, when their undeveloped reasoning ability makes them less critical of what they are expected to learn than they will be later, and when the influence of the mass media is at its peak, sex-role stereotypes are so well learned that changing them later is difficult or almost impossible. They have served as guidelines for behavior for so long that learning new guidelines is strongly resisted.

One essential to change is motivation. This is weak when it comes to changing sex-role stereotypes. Boys discover, as they grow older, that being sex-typed according to the traditional male stereotype is to their personal advantage. This weakens any motivation they might otherwise have to change. Even though girls may find, as they grow older, that the traditional sex role for females does not meet their needs, they feel inadequate to play any other role because they have been totally unprepared to do so. This weakens their motivation just as lack of desire to change weakens the motivation of males.

Studies of the persistent effects of sex-role typing are of recent origin, dating back to the pioneer study of Horner in the late 1960s. Most of the studies made to date have been based on the effects of childhood sex-role typing on women (48). Only a few scattered studies have been reported of the effects on men.

Because sex-role typing followed the traditional pattern almost exclusively when the adults of today were children, these early studies have, of necessity, concentrated on the persistent effects of traditional sex-role typing. It will be another decade or more before the persistent effects of egalitarian sex-role typing can be known. If the present trend toward substituting egalitarian for traditional sex-role typing continues, when today's children become adults, there will be evidence of the effects it has on their personal and social adjustments to adult life as well on their adjustments during the childhood years.

Limited as the material now available is, it is worth summarizing to show why persistence of sex-role typing may be regarded as a serious hazard to personal and social adjustments. Some of the reported effects of traditional sex-role typing on adults—effects that may be regarded as just as hazardous to good adjustments in adult life as in childhood—are summarized in Box 16–8 (2, 11, 21, 25, 46, 48, 55, 74, 77).

Chapter Highlights

1 Sex roles are patterns of behavior for members of the two sexes that are approved and accepted by the group with which the individual is identified.

2 The stereotype of approved behavior which serves as the foundation for sex roles contains three elements—the cognitive, the affective, and the conative.

3 Sex-role stereotypes are based on the fundamental belief that males are superior to females because of their physical and physiological superiority. This belief spreads to all other areas of their capacities and abilities.

4 Cultural changes since the turn of the present century are gradually causing changes in sex-role stereotypes that have persisted through the centuries.

5 Today, there are two widely accepted patterns of

sex-role stereotypes—the *traditional,* based on the fundamental principle of masculine superiority and the *egalitarian,* based on the fundamental principle that differences between the sexes are smaller than was formerly believed and that these differences are of relatively little importance in the present culture where technology has replaced the need for physical strength.

6   Children learn the meanings of sex-role stereotypes in a predictable pattern that contains five stages, paralleling their cognitive development. By the time children enter first grade, their sex-role concepts are so well developed that they can be regarded as "sexist."

7   Meanings of sex-role stereotypes come from many sources, the most important of which are observations of behavior, clothes worn by members of the two sexes, answers to questions, play equipment, treatment by others, opportunities for learning, discipline, sex education, and the mass media.

8   Acceptance of sex-role stereotypes as guidelines for behavior does not automatically occur when children learn the meaning of these stereotypes. Only when children can see the personal advantage of accepting them have they the necessary motivation to do so.

9   Children learn to play sex roles—sex-role typing—early. This learning follows a predictable pattern in which parents, teachers, and peers play dominant roles.

10   Sex-role typing comes from three common methods of learning—imitation, identification, and child training.

11   The effects of sex-role typing are widespread and include such areas of behavior as sex cleavages, sex antagonism, discrimination against sex-inappropriate children, sex typing of objects and behavior, levels of aspiration, and achievement striving.

12   Of all effects of sex-role typing, the most important are the effects on levels of aspiration and patterns of achievement striving because they are persistent in their effects while the other effects are, for the most part, transient.

13   Because studies of sex-role typing are of recent origin, only a limited number of hazards in this area have been studied extensively enough to have documented evidence about their serious and far-reaching effects. What evidence is available today suggests that their seriousness comes from the fact that the effects are persistent and, as a result, affect the individual's lifetime personal and social adjustments.

14   Among the important hazards to personal and social adjustments resulting from sex-role typing that have been investigated are the following: the widespread effects of sex-role typing on the social group, confusion about approved sex-role stereotypes and about sex-role typing, difficulties in accepting approved sex-role stereotypes, the influence of the mass media on sex-role stereotypes, the effects on personality, and the persistence of the effects of sex-role typing.

15   Limited as they have been to date, studies of sex-role typing have shown that, once it occurs, it tends to become persistent and to have serious effects on adult achievements as well as on adult personality patterns.

Bibliography

1   Aldous, J. The making of family roles and family change. *Family Coordinator,* 1974, *23,* 231–235.

2   Bachtold, L. M. Women, eminence, and career-value relationships. *Journal of Social Psychology,* 1974, *95,* 187–192.

3   Bacon, C., and R. M. Lerner. Effects of maternal employment status on the development of vocational-role perception in females. *Journal of Genetic Psychology,* 1975, *126,* 187–193.

4   Barnett, R. C. Sex differences and age trends in occupational preference and occupational prestige. *Journal of Counseling Psychology,* 1975, *22,* 35–38.

5   Bem, S. L. Sex role adaptability: One consequence of psychological androgyny. *Journal of Personality and Social Psychology,* 1975, *31,* 634–643.

6   Berens, A. E. Sex-role stereotypes and the development of achievement motivation. *Ontario Psychologist,* 1973, *5,* 30–35.

7   Bernstein, J. The elementary school: Training ground for sex role stereotypes. *Personnel and Guidance Journal,* 1972, *51,* 97–103.

8   Beuf, A. Doctor, lawyer, household drudge. *Journal of Communication,* 1974, *24*(2), 142–145.

9   Block, J. H. Conceptions of sex role: Some cross-cultural and longitudinal perspectives. *American Psychologist,* 1973, *28,* 512–526.

10   Bohan, J. S. Age and sex differences in self-concept. *Adolescence,* 1973, *8,* 379–384.

11   Breedlove, C. J., and V. C. Cirirell.

Women's fear of success in relation to personal characteristics and type of occupation. *Journal of Psychology*, 1974, *86*, 181–190.

12 Bruce, P. Reactions of preadolescent girls to science tasks. *Journal of Psychology*, 1974, *86*, 303–308.

13 Burstyn, J. W., and R. R. Corrigan. Images of women in textbooks: 1880–1920. *Teachers College Record*, 1975, *76*, 431–440.

14 Chasen, B. Sex-role stereotyping and prekindergarten teachers. *Elementary School Journal*, 1974, *74*, 220–235.

15 Church, J. *Understanding your child from birth to three: A psychological guide for parents.* New York: Random House, 1973.

16 Constantinople, A. Masculinity-feminity: An exception to a famous dictum? *Psychological Bulletin*, 1973, *80*, 389–407.

17 Courtney, A. E., and T. W. Whipple. Women in TV commercials. *Journal of Communication*, 1974, *24* (2), 110–118.

18 Dempewolff, J. A. Some correlates of feminism. *Psychological Reports*, 1974, *34*, 671–676.

19 Domash, L., and L. Balter. Sex and psychological differentiation in preschoolers. *Journal of Genetic Psychology*, 1976, *128*, 77–84.

20 Etaugh, C. Effects of maternal employment on children: A review of recent research. *Merrill-Palmer Quarterly*, 1974, *20*, 71–98.

21 Etaugh, C., G. Collins, and A. Gerson. Reinforcement of sex-typed behavior of two-year-old children in a nursery school setting. *Developmental Psychology*, 1975, *11*, 255.

22 Etaugh, C., and V. Hughes. Teachers' evaluations of sex typed behaviors in children: The role of teacher sex and school setting. *Developmental Psychology*, 1975, *11*, 394–395.

23 Fagot, B. I. Sex differences in toddlers, behavior and parental reaction. *Developmental Psychology*, 1974, *10*, 554–558.

24 Fagot, B. I., and I. Littman. Stability of sex role and play interests from preschool to elementary school. *Journal of Psychology*, 1975, *89*, 285–292.

25 Featherman, D. L., and R. M. Hauser. Sexual inequalities and socioeconomic achievement in the U.S.: 1962–1973. *American Sociological Review*, 1976, *41*, 462–483.

26 Fein, G., D. Johnson, N. Kosson, L. Stork, and L. Wasserman. Sex stereotypes and preferences in the toy choices of 20-month-old boys and girls. *Developmental Psychology*, 1975, *11*, 527–528.

27 Feinman, S. Approval of cross-sex-role behavior. *Psychological Reports*, 1974, *35*, 634–648.

28 Fling, S., and M. Manosevitz. Sex typing in nursery school children's play interests. *Developmental Psychology*, 1972, 7, 146–152.

29 Frankel, P. M. Sex-role attitudes and the development of achievement need in women. *Journal of College Student Personnel*, 1974, *15*, 114–119.

30 Franzwa, H. H. Working women in fact and fiction. *Journal of Communication*, 1974, *24*, (2), 104.

31 Garai, J. E., and A. Scheinfeld. Sex differences in mental and behavioral traits. *Genetic Psychology Monographs*, 1968, *77*, 169–299.

32 Gold, A. R., and M. C. St. Ange. Development of sex role stereotypes in black and white elementary school girls. *Developmental Psychology*, 1974, *10*, 461.

33 Gordon, F. E., and D. T. Hall. Self image and stereotype of femininity: Their relationship to women's role conflicts and coping. *Journal of Applied Psychology*, 1974, *59*, 241–243.

34 Halas, C. M. Sex role stereotypes: Perceived childhood socialization experiences and the attitudes and behavior of adult women. *Journal of Psychology*, 1974, *88*, 261–275.

35 Haley, E. G., and N. J. Hendrickson. Children's preference for clothing and hair style. *Home Economics Research Journal*, 1974, *2*, 179–193.

36 Hansen, L. S. We are furious (female) but we can shape our own development. *Personnel and Guidance Journal*, 1972, *51*, 87–93.

37 Harris, M. B. Sex role stereotypes and teacher evaluation. *Journal of Educational Psychology*, 1975, *67*, 751–756.

38 Harris, S. R. Sex typing in girls' career choices: A challenge to counselors. *Vocational Guidance Quarterly*, 1974, *23*, 128–133.

39 Harrison, B. G. Education and sex-role stereotypes. *The New York Times*, Nov. 23, 1975.

40 Hartley, R. E. Children's perceptions of sex preferences in four culture groups. *Journal of Marriage and the Family*, 1969, *31*, 380–387.

41 Havighurst, R. J. *Developmental tasks and education*, 3d ed. New York: McKay, 1972.

42 Herson, P. F. Biasing effects of diagnostic labels and sex of pupil on teachers' views of pupils' mental health. *Journal of Educational Psychology*, 1974, *66*, 117–122.

43 Hill, C. E., M. A. Hubbs, and C. Verble. A developmental analysis of the sex-role identification of school related objects. *Journal of Educational Research*, 1974, *67*, 205–206.

44 Hillman, J. S. An analysis of male and female roles in two periods of children's literature. *Journal of Educational Research*, 1974, *68*, 85–88.

45 Hirsch, G. T. Non-sexist child rearing: Demythifying normative data. *Family Coordinator*, 1974, *23*, 165–170.

46 Hjelle, L. A., and R. Butterfield. Self-actualization and women's attitudes toward their roles in contemporary society. *Journal of Psychology*, 1974, *87*, 225–230.

47 Hoffman, L. W. Effects of maternal employment on the child: A review of the research. *Developmental Psychology*, 1974, *10*, 204–228.

48 Horner, M. S. Toward an understanding of achievement-related conflicts in women. *Journal of Social Issues*, 1972 28(2), 157–175.

49 Howe, F. Sexual stereotypes start early. *Saturday Review*, Oct. 16, 1971, pp. 76–82, 92–94.

50 Humphrey, F. G. Changing roles for women: Implications for marriage counselors. *Journal of Marriage and Family Counseling*, 1975, *1*, 219–227.

51 Hutton, S. S. Sex role illustrations in junior high school home economics textbooks. *Journal of Home Economics*, 1976, *68*(2), 27–30.

52 Inselberg, R. M., and L. Burke. Social and psychological correlates of masculinity in young boys. *Merrill-Palmer Quarterly*, 1973, *19*, 41–47.

53 Jackaway, R. Sex differences in the development of fear of success. *Child Study Journal*, 1974, *4*, 71–79.

54 Jennings, S. A. Effects of sex typing in children's stories on preference and recall. *Child Development*, 1975, *46*, 220–223.

55 Joesting, J. The influence of sex roles on creativity in women. *Gifted Child Quarterly*, 1975, *19*, 336–339.

56 Klemmack, D. L., and J. N. Edwards. Women's acquisition of stereotyped occupational aspirations. *Sociology and Social Research*, 1973, *57*, 510–525.

57 Laosa, L. M., and J. E. Brophy. Effects of sex and birth order on sex-role development and intelligence among kindergarten children. *Developmental Psychology*, 1972, *6*, 409–415.

58 Loo, P. C. Male and female teachers in elementary schools: An ecological analysis. *Teachers College Record*, 1974, *75*, 79–98.

59 Lee, P. C., and N. B. Gropper. Sex role culture and educational practice. *Harvard Educational Review*, 1974, *44*, 369–410.

60 Lerner, H. E. Early origins of envy and devaluation of women: Implications for sex role stereotypes. *Bulletin of the Menninger Clinic*, 1974, *38*, 538–553.

61 Levine, A., and J. Crumrine. Women and the fear of success: A problem in replication. *American Journal of Sociology*, 1975, *80*, 964–974.

62 Levitin, T. E., and J. D. Chananie. Responses of female primary school teachers to sex-typed behaviors in male and female children. *Child Development*, 1972, *43*, 1309–1316.

63 Liebert, R. M., R. B. McCall, and M. A. Hanratty. Effects of sex-typed information on children's toy preferences. *Journal of Genetic Psychology*, 1971, *119*, 133–136.

64 Losco, J., and S. Epstein. Humor preference as a subtle measure of attitudes toward the same and the opposite sex. *Journal of Personality*, 1975, *43*, 321–334.

65 Lynch, J. Equal opportunity or lip service? Sex-role stereotyping in the schools. *Elementary School Journal*, 1975, *76*, 20–23.

66 Lynn, D. B., and A. DeP. Cross. Parent preference of preschool children. *Journal of Marriage and the Family*, 1974, *36*, 555–559.

67 Maccoby, E. E., and C. N. Jacklin. Myth, reality and shades of gray: What we know and don't know about sex differences. *Psychology Today*, 1974, *8*(7), 109–112.

68 Maccoby, E. E., and C. N. Jacklin. *The psychology of sex differences*. Stanford, Calif.: Stanford University Press, 1974.

69 Manes, A. L., and P. Melnyk. Televised models of female achievement. *Journal of Applied Social Psychology*, 1974, *4*, 365–374.

70 Marcus, R. E. The child as elicitor of parental sanctions for independent and dependent behavior: A simulation of parent-child interaction. *Developmental Psychology*, 1975, *11*, 443–452.

71 McArthur, L. Z., and B. G. Resko. The portrayal of men and women in American television commercials. *Journal of Social Psychology*, 1975, *97*, 209–220.

72 McGhee, P. E., and P. Grodzitsky. Sex-role identification and humor among preschool children. *Journal of Psychology*, 1973, *84*, 189–193.

73 Mead, M. *Male and female*. New York: Morrow, 1975.

74 Midgley, N., and M. S. Abrams. Fear of success and locus of control in young women. *Journal of Consulting and Clinical Psychology*, 1974, *42*, 737.

75 Miller, S. M. Effects of maternal employment on sex role perception, interests, and self-esteem in kindergarten girls. *Developmental Psychology*, 1975, *11*, 405–406.

76 Miller, T. W. Male self-esteem and attitudes toward women's roles. *Journal of College Student Personnel*, 1973, *14*, 402–406.

77 Mischel, H. N. Sex bias and the evaluation of professional achievement. *Journal of Educational Psychology*, 1974, *66*, 157–166.

78 Mischel, W. Sex-typing and socialization. In P. H. Mussen (ed.), *Carmichael's manual of child psychology*, 3d ed. New York: Wiley, 1970. Vol. 2, pp. 3–72.

79 Mitchell, E. The learning of sex roles through toys and books: A woman's view. *Young Children*, 1973, *28*, 226–231.

80 Montemayer, R. Children's performance in a game and their attraction to it as a function of sex-typed labels. *Child Development*, 1974, *45*, 152–156.

81 Mueller, R. J., and A. H. Frerichs. Changing sex roles: The views of major authorities. *Thresholds in Secondary Education*, 1975, *1*, 3–9.

82 Nadelman, L. Sex identity in American children: Memory, knowledge, and preference tests. *Developmental Psychology*, 1974, *10*, 413–417.

83 Naffziger, C. C., and K. Naffziger. Development of sex role stereotypes. *Family Coordinator*, 1974, *23*, 251–258.

84 Norman, R. D. Sex differences in preference for sex of children: A replication after 20 years. *Journal of Psychology*, 1974, *88*, 229–239.

85 Oliver, L. Women in aprons: The female stereotype in children's readers. *Elementary School Journal*, 1974, *74*, 253–259.

86 Oliver, L. W. Counseling implications of recent research on women. *Personnel and Guidance Journal*, 1975, *53*, 436–437.

87 Ramsdell, M. L. The trauma of TV's troubled soap families. *Family Coordinator*, 1973, *22*, 299–304.

88 Rapoport, R., and R. N. Rapoport. Early and later experiences as determinants of adult behavior: Married women's family and career patterns. *British Journal of Sociology*, 1971, *22*, 16–30.

89 Reha, R. K., and A. T. Nappi. Are your sex stereotypes showing? *Elementary School Journal*, 1975, *76*, 70–74.

90 Rheingold, H. L., and K. V. Cook. The contents of boys' and girls' rooms as an index of parents' behavior. *Child Development*, 1975, *46*, 459–463.

91 Ribal, J. E. *Learning sex roles: American and Scandinavian contrasts*. San Francisco: Canfield, 1973.

92 Romer, N. The motive to avoid success and its effect on performance in school-age males and females. *Developmental Psychology*, 1975, *11*, 689–699.

93 Rosen, A. C., and J. Teague. Case studies in development of masculinity and femininity in male children. *Psychological Reports*, 1974, *34*, 971–983.

94 Saario, T. N., C. N. Jacklin, and C. K. Tittle. Sex-role stereotyping in the public schools. *Harvard Educational Review*, 1973, *43*, 386–416.

95 Sandridge, S., and S. J. Friedland.

Sex-role-typing and aggressive behavior in children. *Journal of Genetic Psychology*, 1975, *126*, 227–231.

96 Shields, S. A. Functionalism, Darwinism, and the psychology of women: A study in social myth. *American Psychologist*, 1975, *30*, 739–754.

97 Spence, J. T., R. Helmreich, and J. Stapp. Ratings of self and peers on sex-role attributes and their relation to self-esteem and conceptions of masculinity and femininity. *Journal of Personality and Social Psychology*, 1975, *32*, 29–39.

98 Stein, A. H., and M. M. Bailey. The socialization of achievement orientation in females. *Psychological Bulletin*, 1973, *80*, 345–366.

99 Stein, A. H., and J. Smithells. Age and sex differences in children's sex-role standards about achievements. *Developmental Psychology*, 1969, *1*, 252–259.

100 Steinmann, A., and A. P. Jurich. The effects of a sex education course on the sex role perceptions of junior high school students. *Family Coordinator*, 1975, *24*, 27–31.

101 Sternglanz, S. H., and L. A. Serbin. Sex role stereotyping in children's television programs. *Developmental Psychology*, 1974, *10*, 710–715.

102 Streicher, H. W. The girls in the cartoons. *Journal of Communication*, 1974, *24* (2), 125–129.

103 Taylor, P. A., and N. D. Glenn. The utility of education and attractiveness for females' status attainment through marriage. *American Sociological Review*, 1976, *41*, 484–498.

104 Tibbetts, S-L. Children's literature—a feminist viewpoint. *California Journal of Educational Research*, 1975, *26*, 1–5.

105 Tibbetts, S-L. Sex-role stereotyping in the lower grades: Part of the solution. *Journal of Vocational Behavior*, 1975, *6*, 255–261.

106 Vanck, J. Time spent in housework. *Scientific American*, 1974, *231* (3), 116–120.

107 Van Dusen, R. A., and E. B. Sheldon. The changing status of American women: A life cycle perspective. *American Psychologist*, 1976, *31*, 106–116.

108 Vroegh, K. Masculinity and femininity in the elementary and junior high school years. *Developmental Psychology*, 1971, *4*, 254–261.

109 Ward, W. D. Patterns of culturally defined sex-role preference and parental imitation. *Journal of Genetic Psychology*, 1973, *122*, 337–343.

110 Whiting, B., and C. P. Edwards. A cross-cultural analysis of sex differences in the behavior of children aged three through 11. *Journal of Social Psychology*, 1973, *91*, 171–188.

111 Wilkinson, M. Romantic love: The great equalizer? Sexism in popular music. *Family Coordinator*, 1976, *25*, 161–166.

112 Will, J. A., P. A. Self, and N. Dafan. Maternal behavior and perceived sex of infant. *American Journal of Orthopsychiatry*, 1976, *46*, 135–139.

113 Williams, J. E., S. M. Bennett, and D. L. Best. Awareness and expression of sex stereotypes in young children. *Developmental Psychology*, 1975, *11*, 635–642.

114 Winchel, R., D. Fenner, and P. Shaver. Impact of coeducation on "Fear of Success" imagery expressed by male and female high school students. *Journal of Educational Psychology*, 1974, *66*, 726–730.

115 Wolf, T. M. Effects of live modeled sex-inappropriate play behavior in a naturalistic setting. *Developmental Psychology*, 1973, *9*, 120–123.

116 Wolf, T. M. Response consequences of televised modeled sex-inappropriate play behavior. *Journal of Genetic Psychology*, 1975, *127*, 35–44.

CHAPTER 17

FAMILY RELATIONSHIPS

Early interest in the study of the family was concentrated mainly in the works of anthropologists and sociologists. These studies were designed primarily to find out what the patterns of family life were in different cultures, the roles played by different family members, and the child-training methods in common use in these cultures.

Early psychological interest in the family was concentrated mainly on the effects of the family on the child's development. This interest was spurred on by studies of psychoanalysts who have, for many years, stressed the importance of early family experiences on children's attitudes and behavior. According to Freud, the pioneer in this area of research in family relationships, "neuropathic parents who overprotect children and smother them in affection awaken in them a disposition for neurotic diseases" (38). The emphasis on "momism" since the mid-1940s has stressed the psychological damages caused by maternal dominance and overprotection.

More recently, studies of maternal deprivation—where the babies were separated from their mothers and institutionalized—have revealed how important a role early family relationships play in the child's development. While some of the detrimental effects of maternal deprivation may be counteracted if a satisfactory mother substitute is provided, even this partial solution is often not possible, principally because a satisfactory substitute is not always available.

Today, with the radical changes in the pattern of family life that have been taking place since the turn of the present century, but especially since World War II, psychological interest has been heightened by a desire to know how these changes influence the child's development and how persistent these influences are. As a result of this new interest, studies of family relationships have increased greatly in number and in breadth of areas covered.

Changes in the American Family Pattern

Changes in American culture have brought about changes in all areas of family life and have fundamentally affected the status of women in the home, the relationships between husbands and wives, and between parents and children. As a result, the pattern of family life today is radically different from the pattern that existed before these cultural changes took place.

Of the many changes that have taken place since the turn of the present century, those that have had the greatest impact on children and their development are as follows: families are smaller; ties with relatives are weaker and there are fewer contacts with them; less work is done in the home and it is done mainly with the aid of labor-saving machines and prepared foods; children spend more time outside the home than in the home; recreation has shifted outside the home; the major family recreation is television watching; many mothers work outside the home; divorce, separation, and remarriage are on the increase; child-training methods are more democratic than in the past; fathers play a greater role in child care; caretakers other than parents are frequent; social and vocational mobility has increased; status symbols are increasingly important; homes are shifting from urban and rural areas to the suburbs; parents are more ambitious for their children and are willing to make personal sacrifices for education to prepare them for their futures; and there is more interaction with outsiders than with family members (10, 11, 17, 27, 57, 96, 109).

Reasons for Change in the American Family Pattern

The change in the American family pattern may be traced to a number of causes. *First,* as the nation has gradually shifted from a rural to an urban economy, the family has been changed from a closely knit, interdependent unit to a loosely knit unit. *Second,* with the rapid shift from small to large business, the mobility of workers has broken or weakened family ties. *Third,* as the number of people from different countries has grown, the different cultural influences have produced a variety of patterns of family life, not a typically American pattern. See Box 17–1. *Fourth,* a new philosophy regarding the child's status in the family has resulted in child-centered families as compared with adult-centered families of past generations. *Fifth,* a swing from authoritarian to more permissive child training and from adult control of the child's behavior has placed more responsibility for control on the child (17, 23, 27, 33, 36, 96, 100, 110).

Effects of Changes on Family Relationships

Changes in the pattern of family living inevitably bring changes in the relationships of different family members. The rapid rate of change in America means that today's children have many experiences which

SOME COMMON FAMILY PATTERNS IN AMERICA TODAY

NUCLEAR FAMILIES

The nuclear family—consisting of parents and children—has largely replaced the elongated family—a nuclear family plus relatives who live under the same roof.

SMALL FAMILIES

Small families, with three or less children are more numerous than large families, with six or more children.

CHILDLESS FAMILIES

Through choice, childless families are becoming increasingly more popular among highly educated men and women who are often more career-oriented than family-oriented.

YOUNG-PARENT FAMILIES

Families with parents under 30 when the last child is born are more common than families with parents over 30 at the time of the last child's birth.

FAMILIES WITH WORKING MOTHERS

Families where mothers work outside the home and turn over the home and children to caretakers are increasing in all socioeconomic groups.

SINGLE-PARENT FAMILIES

In a single-parent family, the parent may be either the mother or the father who assumes the responsibility for the children after death or divorce or the birth of an illegitimate child.

RECONSTITUTED FAMILIES

In a reconstituted family, following death or divorce, one parent is the real parent and the other, a stepparent.

FOSTER-PARENT FAMILIES

Foster parents are paid, usually by the government, to play the role of real parents except that they have no legal responsibilities for the support of the children nor do the children bear their names.

COMMUNAL FAMILIES

Several nuclear families band together and share responsibilities for the care of the home and the children.

ADOPTIVE FAMILIES

In an adoptive family, some or all the children have no blood ties with their parents though the parents have a legal responsibility for them and give them the family name, as in the case of natural children.

INTERRACIAL FAMILIES

The father and mother, in an interracial family, come from different racial groups.

INTERRELIGIOUS FAMILIES

In an interreligious family, the two parents come from different religious groups though they may and often do come from the same racial group.

---

their parents never had and are often unable or unwilling to understand. Young parents, as a rule, understand their children better than older parents because the smaller the age gap between parent and child, the less change there will have been in cultural values and patterns of living.

Television teaches children much more about many subjects than their parents could possibly have known at their ages. Children learn from television, for example, how other people live. This often makes them critical of their parents and the pattern of their family life.

Child training methods in America have undergone an almost revolutionary change in the last 50 years, and parents are often confused about the proper way to bring up children. This is in direct contrast to many other cultures in which family life follows a traditional pattern with a set, rigid program for child training.

It is also in direct contrast to the *continuous* patterns of child training in cultures which prepare the child for adult roles by starting with simple learning experiences and progressing to more complex learning experiences of a similar nature as the child grows older.

Our training of the child is characterized by *discontinuities* in the sense that the training in childhood has little or no relationship to the pattern of life in adulthood. This kind of training adds to the difficulties the child encounters and increases tension in the family.

That many American parents feel inadequate for their role is apparent in the frequency with which they seek advice from relatives, friends, or child-guidance experts. When parents feel inadequate, the tensions they build up are reflected in the parent-child relationship. Conflicts between parents about the best way to train the child increase family friction and add to the feeling of inadequacy both parents experience (12).

Influence of the Family on Children

In spite of the radical changes that have taken place in the pattern of American life in recent decades, the family is still the most important part of the child's "social network." This is because the members of the family constitute the child's first environment and are the most significant people during the early, formative years.

From contacts with family members, children lay the foundations for attitudes toward people, things, and life in general. They also lay the foundations for patterns of adjustment and learn to think of themselves as the members of their family think of them. As a result, they learn to adjust to life on the basis of the foundations laid when the environment was limited largely to the home.

As social horizons broaden and children come in contact with peers and adults outside the home, these early foundations, laid in the home, may be changed and modified, though they are never completely eradicated. Instead, they influence later attitudes and behavior patterns.

What the Family Contributes to Children

How widespread the influence of the family is on children and on their development cannot be fully appreciated until one realizes what family members contribute to the child. Some of the contributions that are most common and most important are given in Box 17–2 (18, 19, 42, 54, 74, 111).

Not every kind of family makes all these contributions nor does every family member. However, regardless of the kind of family, most of the important contributions given in this box are made at some time or other in the childhood years. When this happens, the child grows up to be a well-adjusted person. By contrast, a home that fails to make these important contributions leads to poor personal and social adjustments in the child, some of which can be and often are overcome by outside influences as the child grows older.

Differences in Family Influence

How much influence and what form this influence will take in the child's development will depend upon two conditions: the kind of family pattern, and the different members of the family group.

The *kind of family* in which children grow up affects their development by determining the kind of relationship they have with different family members. In a father-absent home, for example, a boy's relationship with the mother will be very different from that of a boy who grows up in a family where the father is not only present but also plays an active and dominant role in family life. When mothers work outside the home and children are cared for by relatives, neighbors, or in child-care centers, the relationship of the children with the mother will be very different from that of children

---

BOX 17–2

CONTRIBUTIONS OF THE FAMILY
TO THE DEVELOPMENT OF CHILDREN

- Feelings of security from being a member of a stable group.
- People children can rely on to meet their needs—physical and psychological.
- Sources of affection and acceptance, regardless of what they do.
- Models of approved patterns of behavior for learning to be social.
- Guidance in the development of socially approved patterns of behavior.
- People they can turn to for help in solving the problems every child faces in adjustment to life.
- Guidance and help in learning skills—motor, verbal, and social—needed for adjustment.
- Stimulation of their abilities to achieve success in school and in social life.
- Aid in setting aspirations suited to their interests and abilities.
- Sources of companionship until old enough to find companions outside the home or when outside companionship is unavailable.

brought up in a home with a homemaking-oriented mother (13, 17, 96).

Not all *members of the family group* exert equal influence on children. How much influence a family member exerts depends largely upon the emotional relationship that exists between the child and the family member. Even though a father normally exerts less influence on children than the mother, especially during the early years of childhood, an autocratic father can cause maladjustive development in children as readily as a permissive father whose discipline is ineffectual.

In sibling relationships, children are influenced more by older siblings than by younger siblings. They are also influenced more by siblings of their own sex than by siblings of the opposite sex. This is because they can identify more readily with the former than with the latter. When grandparents or other relatives live in the home, their influence on children is greater than when they see the children only occasionally. The influence they exert is also determined by how children react to relatives and the closeness of the emotional tie between them and the children (18, 78, 111, 112).

How children will react to home influences and how family relationships will affect them will depend on two conditions: what kind of individual the child is, and the child's age. The quiet child, for example, will react differently from the aggressive child; the introvert will react differently from the extrovert. The second condition, the child's age, is also important. The younger the child, the more influence the family and the different family members have. As children grow older, peers and other outsiders have increasingly more influence, and family members increasingly less.

How the Family Contributes to Children's Development

The contributions of the family to children's development come from the type of relationships children have with different family members. These relationships, in turn, are influenced by the pattern of family life as well as by the attitudes and behavior of different family members toward the children of the family.

Children, for example, whose parents believe that they should sacrifice personal interests and activities to devote their time and attention to their children, produce a child-centered home in which the child is treated as the most important member of the family. By contrast, parents who believe that children "should be seen but not heard," produce an adult-centered home where the adults are the most important members and the children are expected to play subservient roles.

There are many conditions in family life that affect family relationships and, in turn, the child's development. Why these conditions affect family relationships and how, in turn, they affect the development of children will be discussed in detail in the following sections of this chapter.

Influence of Parental Attitudes on Family Relationships

Parental attitudes influence the way parents treat their children and their treatment of the children, in turn, influences their children's attitudes toward them and the way they behave. Fundamentally, therefore, the parent-child relationship is dependent on the parents' attitudes.

If parental attitudes are favorable, the relationship of parents and children will be far better than when parental attitudes are unfavorable. Many cases of maladjustment in children as well as in adults can be traced to unfavorable early parent-child relationships which developed because parental attitudes, even though cloaked in behavior that suggested favorable attitudes, were actually unfavorable. Feeling guilty about not being satisfied with a daughter when they wanted a son, for example, may make parents appear to be very acceptant of the daughter, because they are indulgent in their treatment of her.

The importance of parental attitudes on family relationships comes from the fact that, once formed, they tend to be persistent (31). If these attitudes are favorable, all to the good. But, if they are unfavorable, they will tend to persist, even when in a cloaked form, and affect the relationships the parents have with their children even into the adult years. Refer to the discussion of persistence of early parental attitudes in Chapter 3 for a further explanation of why they are persistent and the seriousness of this to children's personal and social adjustments.

Sources of Parental Attitudes

Like all attitudes, the attitudes of parents toward their children are a product of learning. Many factors help to determine what attitudes will be learned, the most common of these are as follows:

First, the "dream child" concept, formed before a

child's birth, which is highly romanticized and based on what parents would like their child to be. When the child falls short of parental expectations, parents are disappointed and this encourages the development of a rejectant attitude.

Second, early experiences with children color parental attitudes toward their own children. A parent who, as a member of a large family, was expected to assume responsibilities for the care of younger siblings will likely have a far less favorable attitude toward all children, including the parent's own child, than a parent who, as a child, had happy experiences with siblings.

Figure 17–1. Adults must make a radical change in the pattern of living as they go from an ego-centered childhood to parenthood. (*Adapted from S. Clavan: The family process: A sociological model.* Family Coordinator, *1968,* 17, *312–317. Used by permission.*)

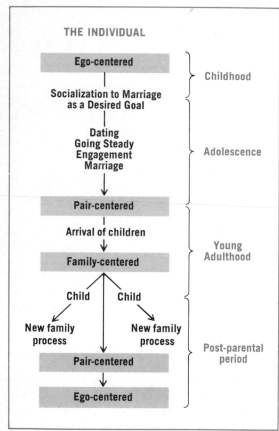

THE INDIVIDUAL

Ego-centered — Childhood

Socialization to Marriage as a Desired Goal

Dating
Going Steady
Engagement
Marriage — Adolescence

Pair-centered

Arrival of children

Family-centered — Young Adulthood

Child   Child

New family process   New family process

Pair-centered — Post-parental period

Ego-centered

Third, cultural values about the best way to treat children, whether in an authoritarian, democratic, or permissive way, will influence parents' attitudes toward and treatment of their own children.

Fourth, parents who enjoy the parental role and are happy and well adjusted to marriage, reflect their favorable attitudes in their attitudes toward their children.

Fifth, when parents feel adequate for the parental role, their attitudes toward their children and their children's behavior are far more favorable than when they feel inadequate and unsure of how to bring up their children.

Sixth, parents who are satisfied with the sex, number, and characteristics of their children have more favorable attitudes than parents who are dissatisfied.

Seventh, the ability and willingness to adjust to a family-centered pattern of living after years of enjoying an ego-centered pattern will determine how favorable parental attitudes are toward the children who have made this shift in roles essential. Figure 17–1 shows the shifts that must be made to parenthood.

Eighth, if parents' reason for having a child was to hold together a faltering marriage and if this did not work, the attitude toward the child will be far less favorable than if parents wanted the child to add to the satisfaction of their marriage.

Ninth, how children react to parents influences the parents' attitudes toward them. If children show affection for and dependence on their parents, parents react to them very differently than they do when their children are independent and more attached to outsiders than to them (26, 45, 68, 81, 102, 104).

Typical Parental Attitudes

Because of the many conditions responsible for the development of attitudes, it is to be expected that there would be a wide variety of different parental attitudes, not a uniform attitude. Box 17–3 lists the most common and most frequent of these attitudes, together with a brief statement about how they affect children's behavior and, in turn, family relationships.

In general, attitudes of young parents tend to be more liberal than those of older parents. However, this is not always true. Some young parents tend to be dominating and some older parents tend to be permissive. Regardless of the age of the parent, it is the attitude of the parent toward the child, not the age of the

SOME TYPICAL PARENTAL ATTITUDES

OVERPROTECTIVENESS

Parental overprotectiveness consists of excessive care and control over the child. This fosters overdependency in children, dependency on all people, not parents alone, lack of self-confidence, and frustrations.

PERMISSIVENESS

Parental permissiveness is shown by the parents' willingness to permit children to do things much as they wish, with few restraints. This leads to a "child-centered home." If permissiveness is reasonable, it encourages children to be resourceful, self-reliant, and well adjusted socially. It also encourages self-confidence, creativity, and poise.

INDULGENCE

Excessive permissiveness—indulgence—makes children selfish, demanding, and often tyrannical. They demand attention and service from others—behavior that leads to poor social adjustments in the home and outside.

REJECTION

Rejection may be expressed by unconcern for the child's welfare or by excessive demands on the child and open hostility. This leads to resentment, feelings of helplessness, frustrations, nervous mannerisms, and hostility to others, especially those who are smaller and weaker.

ACCEPTANCE

Parental acceptance is characterized by a keen interest in and love for the child. The accepting parent provides for the development of the child's abilities and takes into account the child's interests. The accepted child is gen-

erally well socialized, cooperative, friendly, loyal, emotionally stable, and cheerful.

DOMINATION

The child who is dominated by one or both parents is honest, polite, and careful but tends to be shy, docile, easily influenced by others, submissive, and overly sensitive. Dominated children often develop inferiority complexes and feel martyred.

SUBMISSION TO CHILD

Parents who submit to their children permit the children to dominate them and the home. Children boss their parents and show them little consideration, respect, or loyalty. They learn to defy all authority and try to boss people outside the home.

FAVORITISM

In spite of claims that they love all their children equally, most parents have their favorites. This makes them more indulgent and loving to the favorites than to the other children of the family. Favored children tend to play up to their parents but are aggressive and dominating in sibling relationships.

PARENTAL AMBITIONS

Almost all parents have ambitions for their children—often unrealistically high. These are often influenced by thwarted parental ambitions and parental desires to have their children rise on the social ladder. When children cannot live up to parental ambitions, they tend to become resentful, irresponsible underachievers. In addition, they develop feelings of inadequacy often colored by feelings of martyrdom stemming from parental criticism for their lack of achievements.

---

parent, that determines the effect of the attitude on family relationships.

Effects of Parental Attitudes on Family Relationships

Parental attitudes have a strong impact not only on family relationships but also on the attitudes and behavior of children. Most of those who become successful as they grow older come from homes where parental attitudes toward them were favorable and

where a wholesome relationship existed between them and their parents. Such a relationship will produce happy, friendly children who are appealing to others, relatively free from anxieties, and constructive, interdependent members of the group.

Poorly adjusted children, by contrast, are usually the product of unfavorable parent-child relationships. Children who are deprived of attention and affection from parents are hungry for affection; they are afraid of being left out. Furthermore, they are *overwilling* to please and to do things for others. All this is a form of compensation and an attempt to buy affection at any cost.

The effects of parental attitudes are not limited to the parents' relationships with their children; they affect sibling relationships and the kind of relationship the child has with grandparents and other relatives. These, likewise, affect family relationships.

When parents show preference for one child, for example, this causes resentments and hostilities among siblings. There is a tendency for those who are not favored to band together in open hostility against the child who is favored. When parents are dominating, children gang together against their parents, showing little affection or respect for them.

How the child is treated by the parents affects the child's attitudes toward the parent and the kind of relationship that develops between them. The child, rather than the parent, is the instigator in this relationship.

When, for example, parents are submissive to their children or indulgent in their attitudes and treatment of the children, children have little respect for the parents. Instead, they do as they please and show little or no consideration for the rights of other family members. This leads to bad family relationships and a home climate marked by constant frictions between family members. In addition, indulgent parents who are dominated by their children develop feelings of antagonism because they sense that their children have little respect or affection for them. This colors their attitudes toward the children unfavorably and contributes further to the already-existing bad family relationships (8, 22, 60, 68, 85, 86).

Influence of Child-training Methods on Family Relationships

Whether parents use authoritarian, permissive, or democratic child-training methods will depend partly on their own upbringing and partly on what they have found, from personal experience or the experience of their friends, will produce the results they desire in their own children. This subject was discussed in detail in Chapter 14.

The parent-child relationship is also greatly influenced by the way children perceive the training they receive and the interpretation they place on the parents' motivation for punishment. The more authoritarian the child training, the more resentful the child and the more likely the child is to be defiant and willfully disobedient. Defiant behavior contributes heavily

to the characteristic deterioration of parent-child relationships as the child grows older.

If children feel that their parents do not agree on the proper method of training or disciplining, they begin to lose respect for their parents. If the mother is blamed by the father for not bringing up the children properly, children have less respect for the mother, but may also resent the father's criticism of the mother.

Although sibling relationships are often strained, siblings generally rally to the defense of a sibling who they feel has been unfairly treated, and they put up a united front against the offending parent. This, too, threatens good family relationships (5, 9, 21, 32).

Influence of Family Size on Family Relationships

Family size, per se, is not alone responsible for the kinds of relationships that develop among family members. Instead, they depend upon a number of factors, four of which are especially important.

First, the number of interactional systems in a family must be considered. A specific example will serve to show how much more complex the interactional systems become with the arrival of each new family member. At first, there are two family members, husband and wife. There is 1 interactional system. With the arrival of the first baby, there are 3 interactional systems. When a new sibling arrives, there will be 6. Then, if there is another baby, making three children, there will be 10. Should the grandmother come to live with the family, the number of interactional systems will jump to 15. This is shown in Figure 17–2.

The larger the family, the greater the number of interactional systems and, normally, the greater the friction in the home. However, friction is often counteracted by the authoritarian discipline of the parents. To avoid the unhealthy home climate that friction gives rise to and to enable each family member to live in harmony with other family members, parents of large families more often use authoritarian child-training methods than do parents of smaller ones.

Second, the composition of the family affects the relationships. When the family is composed of more female than male members, as is likely to be true in elongated families, friction tends to be greater. Females are in the home more than males and, as a result, have closer and more continuous relationships with one another—a condition that tends to lead to friction.

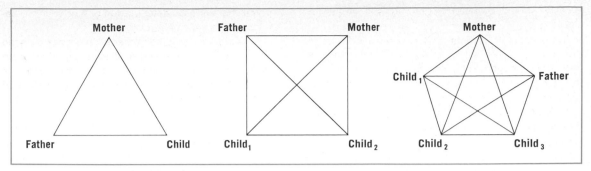

Figure 17–2. Family relationships in different-sized families. Note that the number of interactional systems in the family increases with the addition of each new family member. In the one-child family, for example, there are only three interactional systems, whereas in the three-child family there are 10 such systems.

Third, family relationships are affected by parental attitudes toward family size. Parents who want a large family and have such a family will create a favorable emotional climate in the home because they are happy in their parental roles and willing to make the personal and financial sacrifices demanded by a large family. When, on the other hand, parents wanted a small family, but have a large one, their attitudes toward *all* their children will tend to be unhealthy. They will resent having to make sacrifices in time, effort, and money, and they will often blame each other for the larger-than-hoped-for family. Their resentment will lead to poor marital relationships and have unfavorable effects on family relationships.

Fourth, the spacing of the arrival of children affects family relationships, depending on how it coincides with parental desires. Parents may want to have children close together, for example, so that the interruption in the mother's career will be shortened or so that the children will be companionable. If the arrival of children coincides with these desires, parents' attitudes will be favorable.

Influence of Different-sized Families on Family Relationships

It is customary among sociologists and psychologists to divide families into four general categories: the one-child family, the small family, the medium-sized family, and the large family.

In the *one-child family,* the nuclear family consists of one child in addition to the two parents. This kind of family is more likely to become elongated by the addition of boarders or relatives living under the same roof than are families with several children where extra space is less readily available.

The *small family* is one in which there are two or three children; the *medium-sized family* has three, four, or five children; and the *large family* has six or more children. In medium-sized families with three or four children, the pattern approximates that of the small family; when there are five children, it more closely approximates the large family in its effects on family relationships. Small, medium-sized, and large families are more likely to be nuclear than elongated because of the lack of space and money to take care of outsiders.

Each family category is, of necessity, subject to different influences and these will result in different home climates and different kinds of family relationships. Box 17–4 lists the major factors that influence relationships in each size of family (1, 14, 37, 72, 82, 83).

A careful study of the factors that influence family relationships in each family category will reveal that each has some conditions that are likely to lead to good relationships as well as some that are likely to lead to poor relationships. Therefore, it is impossible to say which category is the *best* from the point of view of the effect it has on family relationships; nor is it possible to rank the categories in order of merit. However, it is generally agreed by sociologists who have made extensive studies of the effects of family size that, all things considered, the medium-sized family—

BOX 17–4

FACTORS INFLUENCING FAMILY RELATION-
SHIPS IN DIFFERENT-SIZED FAMILIES

ONE-CHILD FAMILIES
- Often smaller than parental desires
- Close parent-child relationship results in child's maturity of behavior, which contributes to good peer relationships
- Overprotection by parents
- Democratic or permissive child training
- Minimum family friction due to absence of sibling jealousy and rivalry
- Parental willingness and ability to give child advantages and status symbols
- Parental pressures for academic, athletic, and social achievement
- Child encouraged to play role of own choosing

MEDIUM-SIZED FAMILIES
- Usually planned and, therefore, meet parental desires in size and spacing
- Less democratic and more authoritarian control as family size increases
- Role assignments by parents common
- Children often denied outside companionship because they are needed to help at home
- Parental pressures for achievement usually concentrate on firstborn
- Frequent and intense sibling rivalries and jealousies are common
- Limited parental ability to provide advantages and status symbols
- Tendency of parents to compare child's achievements with those of siblings

SMALL FAMILIES
- Usually planned and, therefore, consistent with parental desires in size and spacing

- Parents able to devote adequate time and attention to each child
- Commonly employ democratic control of child behavior
- Frequent sibling rivalry and jealousy
- Tendency of parents to compare child's achievements with those of siblings
- Parental willingness and ability to give each child equal advantages and status symbols
- Parental pressures for academic, athletic, and social achievement
- Role assignment by parents common

LARGE FAMILIES
- Often unplanned and, therefore, foster parental resentment
- Marital friction due to necessity for personal and financial sacrifices
- Role assignment by parents essential to family harmony and efficiency
- Authoritarian control essential to avoid confusion or anarchy
- Children often denied outside companionship because their help is needed at home or because of lack of money for peer activities
- Sibling rivalry and friction kept to minimum by strict parental control but expressed indirectly in teasing, bullying, and name calling
- Frequent parental inability to give children advantages and status symbols their peers have
- Little parental pressure for achievement except on firstborn
- Little overprotection except for firstborn

especially that with three or four children—is *probably* the best from the point of view of healthy family relationships, and the large family is *probably* the worst.

Influence of Sibling Relations on Family Relationships

In a child-centered home, sibling relationships have a greater impact on the home climate and on all family members than in an adult-centered home. Because American families today tend to be child-centered, sibling relationships have a greater influence on family relationships than they did in the past.

When sibling relationships are favorable, the home climate is pleasant and relatively free from friction. When, on the other hand, sibling relationships are frictional and marked by jealousies, antagonisms, and other forms of disharmony, they play havoc with other family relationships and with the home climate. By so doing, they are hazardous to the personal and social adjustments of all family members, adults as well as

500

children. This is one of the causes of deterioration in family relationships, so common in today's families, which will be discussed later.

Conditions Influencing Sibling Relationships

There are many conditions responsible for the kind of relationships that exists between siblings. Some of these are controllable and others could be prevented. However, with the trend toward permissiveness in many homes today, control or prevention of unfavorable relationships is more difficult than if different child-training methods were used.

Not one of the conditions discussed below is totally responsible for either good or poor sibling relationships. In most cases, several of them operate at the same time. It is this combination of conditions that makes control of sibling relationships that are proving to be damaging to good family relationships so difficult.

PARENTAL ATTITUDES The attitudes of parents toward their children are influenced by how closely the children conform to parental desires and expectations. Parental attitudes are also influenced by the children's attitudes and behavior toward one another and toward their parents. When sibling rivalry and animosity exist, parental attitudes toward *all* the children in the family are less favorable than when siblings get along reasonably well with one another.

Firstborn children, as a result of their early training and close association with their parents, tend to conform more to parental expectations than do later-born children. Thus, parents often show a preference for them. Middle children, on the other hand, often feel neglected in favor of the first- and lastborn children. They feel that their parents play favorites and they resent their siblings. Such attitudes, whether justified or not, lead to jealousies and animosities that affect sibling relationships unfavorably. They, in turn, affect family relationships unfavorably.

ORDINAL POSITION In all except one-child families, all children are assigned roles according to the order of their birth and they are expected to carry out these assigned roles. If children like the roles assigned them, all will be well. But, the very fact that the roles were assigned and not voluntarily selected is likely to lead to friction. An older daughter, for example, may bitterly resent her role as "mother's helper" and feel that her younger sisters should share some of the responsibilities thrust on her. This can lead to deterioration in the parent-child as well as in sibling relationships.

SEX OF SIBLINGS Boys and girls react very differently to brothers and sisters. In a girl-girl combination, for example, there is more jealousy than in a boy-girl or a boy-boy combination. An older sister is likely to be more bossy in her relationship with a younger sister than with a younger brother. Boys fight more with their brothers than with their sisters, partly because parents will not permit as much aggressiveness against sisters as against brothers.

Throughout the gang age of late childhood, antagonism between the sexes, which often develops in the gang and spreads to the home, leads to more or less constant conflicts between brothers and sisters. The relationships between siblings of the two sexes usually reaches a low point at this time. This can and often does have a devastating effect on family relationships, especially when parents step in and try to put an end to the battles between the sexes. Parents are then accused of playing favorites—an accusation that further damages family relationships.

AGE DIFFERENCE The age difference between siblings influences their reactions toward one another and the way in which their parents treat them. When the age difference between siblings is large, whether the children are of the same or the opposite sex, a more friendly, cooperative, and affectionate relationship exists than when they are close together in age. Figure 17–3 shows some characteristic sibling relationships according to the siblings' age and sex. A small age difference between siblings, regardless of their sex, tends to increase friction between them.

If the age difference between siblings is large, there is an entirely different relationship between parent and child than when the age difference between siblings is small. When children are close together in age, parents tend to treat them in much the same way. But parents tend to expect older children to set good models and they criticize them when they fail to do so. The younger child, in turn, is expected to imitate the older children and obey them. These parental expectations contribute to poor sibling relationships.

Sibling relationships are best when no age difference exists between siblings, as in the case of twins and other multiple births. In a study of young twins it has been reported that they show more affection for each other and are less aggressive than singletons.

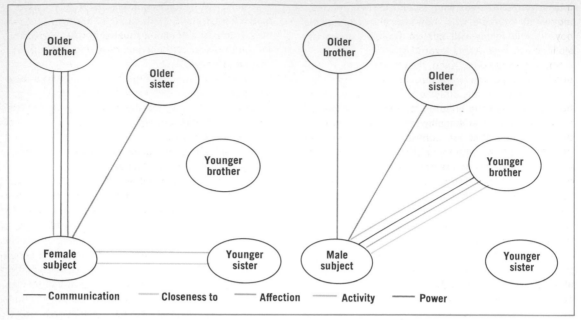

Figure 17–3. Typical relations of older adolescents with siblings of both sexes. (*Adapted from A. Yourglich: Explorations in sociological study of sibling systems. Family Life Coordinator, 1964, 13, 91–94. Used by permission.*)

Although the actual difference between singletons and twins may not be great, it is great enough to result in a better sibling relationship (59).

NUMBER OF SIBLINGS   A small number of siblings tends to lead to a more frictional relationship than a large number. There are two reasons for this. *First,* when there are only two or three children in a family, they are likely to be thrown together more than when there are larger numbers. Because the age difference is also likely to be small, parents expect them to play together and to do things together. This sets the stage for potential friction. With the age differences that come when there are many children, contacts between siblings are less frequent.

Second, when there are many children in the family, disciplinary control tends to be authoritarian. Even if antagonisms and resentments are present, there is strict control over their overt expression. This is not usually true when there are few children in the family. The more relaxed, permissive parental control over their behavior permits these antagonisms and resentments to express themselves openly, thus leading to a frictional emotional climate in the home.

TYPE OF DISCIPLINE   Overtly, sibling relationships are far pleasanter in homes where authoritarian discipline is used than when discipline follows the permissive pattern. When children are permitted to do much as they please, sibling relationships often become chaotic. Democratic discipline helps to control some of the chaos that occurs when permissive discipline is used but not to the extent that authoritarian discipline does. However, in the long run democratic discipline leads to pleasanter and more wholesome sibling relationships than authoritarian. In the former, children learn why they should give and take on a cooperative basis; in authoritarian, they are forced to do so and this they bitterly resent.

INFLUENCE OF OUTSIDERS   There are three ways in which people outside the immediate family influence sibling relationships: the presence of outsiders in the home, pressures from outsiders on family members, and comparison by outsiders of children with their siblings. When relatives or guests are in the home, for visits or as permanent members of the family—as in the elongated family—the number of interactional systems is increased. This is likely to give rise to or intensify an already-existing sibling friction. A grandmother, for example, who shows favoritism toward the boys in the family will stir up trouble among the siblings who resent this favoritism.

Should, on the other hand, the grandmother not live under the roof of the family but, through frequent contacts with the parents, criticize and advise them about how to bring up the children, she is likely to stir up trouble among the siblings by recommending ways to deal with them that are contrary to the ways their parents have dealt with them. If, for example, parents have given their daughters privileges that are equal to those of their sons, the grandmother may warn that this will cause trouble for the girls and urge the parents to insist upon more limitations. This the girls will bitterly resent and it will play havoc with a formerly pleasant brother-sister relationship.

Outsiders—whether family members, friends of the parents, or teachers—can stir up or intensify already-existing friction between siblings by comparing one child in the family with the other children. Should the comparison be favorable to the child, it will cause resentments on the part of the other siblings toward that child. Should, on the other hand, the comparison be unfavorable to the child, it is likely to lead to resentments on the child's part toward the sibling who is more favorably judged.

Typical Sibling Relationships

There is a more or less universal pattern of sibling relationships among American children of all socioeconomic and intellectual levels. Friction increases as childhood progresses, but at every age, some favorable as well as some unfavorable sibling relationships exist. When the favorable predominate, they contribute to good family relationships, and when the unfavorable predominate, they affect *all* family relationships adversely. See Box 17–5 for a list of important sibling relationships and their effects on the family (24, 37, 51, 63, 89, 106).

Significance of Sibling Relationships

The seriousness of unfavorable sibling relationships is that they affect the relationships of all family members and even relationships with outsiders. When one parent accuses the other parent of permitting friction between siblings to develop or to persist, it is likely to lead to resentments on the part of the accused parent. This leads to a frictional husband-wife relationship. Parents then tend to become disenchanted with marriage and parenthood.

Parent-child relationships become strained when sibling friction occurs. Parents blame one child for causing the trouble and the other children are then likely to gang together against the parents in defense of the accused child.

Unquestionably one of the most serious aspects of sibling friction is that it often becomes a pattern of social relationships that children are likely to carry outside the home and apply in their relationships with peers. Habitual quarreling, name calling, bullying, and teasing do not contribute to children's chances of acceptance in the peer group. Also, sibling friction weakens motivation to form relationships with people outside the home. When children have unpleasant relationships with their siblings, they have little motivation to extend their social contacts further.

Not all sibling relationships are frictional nor do those that are frictional remain so all the time. In every family where there are several children, friction between siblings is common and its effects outweigh the effects of pleasant relationships. Unquestionably one of the greatest hazards to good family relationships, as will be stressed in the discussion of hazards

---

BOX 17–5

HOW SIBLING RELATIONSHIPS AFFECT FAMILY RELATIONSHIPS

FOSTER GOOD FAMILY RELATIONSHIPS
- Affection for sibling
- Willingness to play with sibling
- Willingness to share with sibling
- Willingness to help sibling
- Hero-worship of sibling

FOSTER POOR FAMILY RELATIONSHIPS
- Unwillingness to help sibling
- Unwillingness to share with sibling
- Unwillingness to play with or care for sibling unless forced
- Aggressive attacks on sibling
- Tattling on sibling
- Destruction of sibling's possessions

in family relationships, comes from frictional sibling relationships.

Influence of Home Setting on Family Relationships

Relationships with family members are greatly influenced by the home setting—the pattern of life in the home, the kind of people who make up the group living in the home, the economic and social status of the family in the community and other conditions that give the home a distinctive character. Some of these conditions contribute to good family relationships, and others lead to poor family relationships. Each of the important conditions, discussed below, will emphasize the role they play in family relationships.

Social Status of Family

The pattern of family life differs from one social group to another. There are differences in home management; in husband-wife relations; in concepts of the roles of parents, children, and relatives; in family values; in the use of money; in social conformity; in child training and attitudes toward discipline; and in attitudes toward family life.

When children are old enough to recognize the social status of their families, it has a marked effect on their attitudes toward their parents, especially toward the father who is the family breadwinner. If their families' social status is at least equal to that of their peers, children are proud of their fathers. When they recognize it to be inferior, they are ashamed of their fathers and hypercritical of them. Upward social mobility, as was explained in Chapter 10, often worsens family relationships. In the new situation, children may be ashamed of parents and relatives whose behavior is different from that of new neighbors or friends. In downward mobility, children resent the father, who is regarded as responsible for the family's downhill slide.

Parental Occupations

The *father's* occupation is important to a young child only insofar as it has a direct bearing on the child's welfare. For the older child, however, the father's occupation has a cultural significance in that it affects the child's social prestige.

Elementary school children stratify people on the basis of jobs and accept the adult attitudes and values concerning different jobs. When a child is ashamed of the father's occupation, because of the level of work done or the kind of clothes demanded by the work, the child's attitude will be adversely affected.

The father's occupation affects the child indirectly in that it influences the father's standards for the child. From his experiences in work, the father knows what attitudes, skills, and qualities are essential to success. He then tries to foster these in the child. Thus, standards of the occupational world "infect" the home and influence the father's role.

The effect of the *mother's* working on the mother-child relationship depends to a great extent on the child's age at the time the mother starts to work. If she begins working before the child becomes accustomed to spending most of the time with her—before any definite relationship has been established—the effect will be minimal. If strong attachments have been formed, however, the child will suffer from maternal deprivation unless a satisfactory mother substitute is provided—a substitute whom the child likes and whose methods of child training will not cause confusion or resentment on the child's part.

How older children feel about the mother's working depends partly upon how seriously her working interferes with the pattern of family life, partly upon what their friends' mothers do, partly upon the stereotype they have learned of "mother," and many other factors. When mothers work outside the home, opportunities for social life and recreation with the family are usually limited, and each child must assume more home duties than otherwise. If everything in the home must be run like clockwork and if the child is constantly pressed to do things in a businesslike way, reactions to the mother and her work will be less favorable than they would be if she left her principles of efficiency behind in the office (7, 35, 45, 99, 107).

Outsiders in the Home

Although the nuclear family is the cultural standard in the United States, many families are extended or elongated. This is done by having outsiders live under the same roof as the nuclear family for varying lengths of time. The three most common kinds of outsiders are elderly relatives, guests of the parents, and paid domestic workers.

504

ELDERLY RELATIVES Grandparents and other elderly relatives spend varying lengths of time with the nuclear family, either as guests or as permanent members. How they will affect family relationships will depend partly on how long they remain with the nuclear family and partly on the roles they play in the family.

To date, studies of elderly relatives have been limited to grandparents, mainly grandmothers. However, what effects they have on family relationships are probably similar to those of elderly uncles and aunts or other relatives.

The role the grandparents play in the pattern of family life is the most important determinant of the effect they will have on family relationships. In Box 17–6 are given the five most common grandparenting roles in the American home today, as described by Neugarten and Weinstein (72). Of these roles, the fun-seeking and reservoir-of-family-wisdom roles will, unquestionably, have the most favorable effects on child-grandparent relationships; the formal, surrogate-parent and distant-figure roles will contribute to deteriorations in family relationships. Of these three, the surrogate-parent role is likely to be the most damaging to family relationships.

Studies show that children's reactions to grandparents change as children grow older. The baby and preschool child like indulgent grandparents and welcome them in the home. The reactions of school-age children depend on two conditions. *First,* if grandparents have any authority over them and if they are stricter than the parents, children will resent their presence in the home. On the other hand, if the grandparents are mainly interested in fun-sharing activities, they will be welcome members of the family. *Second,* when grandparents are good listeners in the sense that they are willing to let children talk to them about their problems or their pleasures—something that far too many parents of older children have neither the time nor the patience to do—children will have a favorable relationship with the grandparents.

As childhood draws to a close and as children become peer-oriented, their relationships with grandparents usually deteriorate, as they do with parents. This grandparents often resent, as parents do, and this adds further to the deterioration that sets in in the child-grandparent relationship (72, 76).

The most hazardous three-generation household, as far as family relationships are concerned, is the one in

BOX 17–6

COMMON ROLES PLAYED BY GRANDPARENTS

THE FORMAL ROLE
Grandparents do what they regard as the proper and prescribed things. This role includes giving special treats and gifts and assuming a "hands-off" policy in child training.

THE FUN-SEEKING ROLE
This role is characterized by an informal relationship in which grandparents enjoy playing with the grandchild.

THE SURROGATE-PARENT ROLE
The grandparent substitutes for the parent and assumes both the care and the discipline of the child. This role is played mainly by grandmothers.

THE RESERVOIR-OF-FAMILY-WISDOM ROLE
This role, played mainly by grandfathers, concentrates on teaching the child special skills and knowledge. It differs from the traditional patriarchal or matriarchal role which concentrated on control of the child's behavior.

THE DISTANT-FIGURE ROLE
In this role, grandparents come in contact with the child only on special occasions. The contacts are short, infrequent, and fairly formal.

which the elderly relatives are *female*. Having a maternal grandmother in the home, for example, often creates a situation that is unsatisfactory for the father as well as the children. Children suffer because of the contradictory demands made on them by the mother and the grandmother.

GUESTS Guests of the parents are usually in the home for only short periods of time, an evening or perhaps a weekend. While they are there, however, they have an effect on family relationships.

They provide children with a perspective from which to assess their parents, the family status, and the pattern of family living. From listening to what guests say and observing what they do, children often learn new social roles and skills and acquire new information and new interests.

However, the effects on family relationships are

often less than favorable. Children tend to resent having guests in the home because it means extra work for every family member, a disruption of children's play plans, and changes in the usual routine of family life. Most serious of all, guests often create tensions between children and their parents who are constantly prodding the children to behave in such a way that they will make "good impressions" on the guests or criticizing them for doing things parents fear will make "bad impressions."

PAID DOMESTIC WORKERS Paid domestic workers play roles similar to some of those of grandparents as described in Box 17–6—the fun-seeking role, the surrogate-parent role, and the reservoir-of-wisdom role. Which it will be will depend on the reason for being in the home. Baby-sitters, for example, are there mainly to keep children happy and safe for the short times their parents are out of the home. A working mother, on the other hand, who employs a housekeeper during the days she is at work, turns over the discipline as well as the care of the children to the housekeeper, who plays the role of a surrogate mother.

How paid domestic workers influence family relationships depends upon two conditions: how much time they spend with the children, and how the children react to them. If children have outside caretakers for only a short time, and if their role is primarily to keep the children safe and happy, there will be little effect on family relationships. Children may wonder why and complain if their parents do not play with them as much as a baby-sitter does, but, otherwise, their impact on family relationships will be slight.

By contrast, a housekeeper for a working mother may have great impact on family relationships. Should this surrogate mother use different child-training methods than the parents or should the children feel neglected when the surrogate parent is in charge, they will resent the mother's turning over their care to an outsider.

When children like the person who takes care of them, the only effect it may have on family relationships is to make the mother temporarily jealous of the surrogate mother. A dislike for the surrogate mother, on the other hand, can play havoc with family relationships by causing resentments on the part of children toward the mother for turning over their care to a disliked person. This leads to a bad mother-child relationship and a frictional home climate.

Defective Children

Family relationships can be damaged by the presence in the home of a child who is either maladjusted or physically or mentally defective. Although all young children require more of the parents' time, attention, and energy than older children, defective children continue to need the parents long after they have reached the age when they should be more independent. Often their need increases as they grow older.

Just as all children normally resent the time and attention parents must give to a younger sibling, so they resent it when their parents continue, year after year, to give proportionally more time to a defective sibling. Even though they may sympathize with the defective sibling and understand why the child needs attention, they feel sorry for themselves. This feeling of martyrdom is intensified when they compare themselves with their peers.

Older children are often expected to assume some responsibility for the care of a defective sibling. They resent this even more than the care of a normal younger sibling because the defective child requires more time and attention and can do little to reciprocate. Instead of showing gratitude, the defective child is likely to complain or to criticize the care received.

One of the most serious aspects of having a defective child in the home is that the attitudes of members of the peer group toward such a child, toward the siblings, and toward the family may affect family relationships. Attitudes of peers may range from pity and sympathy to ridicule and scorn. Since children are sensitive to peer attitudes, their own attitudes toward the defective child are affected (39).

Since a physically or mentally defective child can put such a severe strain on family relationships, many parents institutionalize the child. While this reduces many of the stresses in the family environment, it does not eliminate them. Two factors continue to militate against good family relationships: *first,* feelings of guilt or resentment or both on the part of the parents, and *second,* financial burdens which deprive other children of the family of many of the things they otherwise might have and which they resent not having.

If, on the other hand, defective children are kept in the home, they can play havoc with family relationships. This is because they are often troublemakers. If, for example, they are aggressive, they will tease, bully, and tattle and they often destroy their siblings' possessions. If they are introverted, they will be self-bound and selfish, making few contributions to the family but expecting others to do things for them. This other family members bitterly resent.

Adopted Children

There are four potential sources of friction in a family where there are adopted children. The *first* comes from the attitudes of adopted children toward their parents. If, as they grow older, children learn from relatives or outsiders that they are adopted and that the people they call their parents are not their real parents, they may develop an obsessive desire to know who their real parents are and express a desire to live with them. The adoptive parents may and often do resent this. Indirectly, these parental attitudes may be expressed in a rejectant attitude toward the adopted children—an attitude that is damaging to their relationships with their adopted children.

The *second* potential source of friction in a family where there are adopted children comes when the real children of the family outshine the adopted child in appearance, achievement, and affection. The parents may regret having adopted a child. Indirectly these feelings will be reflected in a rejectant attitude toward the child, an attitude which the child senses and reacts to unfavorably.

The *third* potential source of threat to good family relationships in a family where there are adopted children comes from the attitudes of the real children toward their adopted siblings. Although sibling relationships are never wholly harmonious, frictional relationships are more common with adopted children. Many real children feel that adopted children are not their siblings and do not belong to the family. They then treat their adopted siblings in much the same way as they treat members of the peer group whom they do not include in their gangs (9).

The *fourth* potential source of friction in a family where there are adopted children comes from the attitudes of relatives and outsiders toward these children. It is not uncommon for members of the older generation to disapprove of adoption on the ground that "if God wanted a couple to have children, He would give them children of their own." Although the typical American family of today is a nuclear family, relatives play an important enough part in family relationships for their attitudes to be a source of disturbance. Similarly, attitudes of outsiders cannot be dismissed. At no time are these sources of disturbance greater than in interreligious or interracial adoptions. While members of the family may wholeheartedly accept a child of a different religious or racial background, outsiders often do not. This affects the adopted child as well as parents and siblings.

On the other hand, adoption can improve family relationships by providing a childless couple with children. It can also provide an only child with a playmate and can lessen the overprotectiveness and overconcern that parents of only children often manifest.

Influence of Broken Homes on Family Relationships

The effects of broken homes on family relationships depend on many factors, the most important of which are the causes of the break, when it occurs, and whether it is temporary or permanent. When a break in the home is caused by *death* and when children realize that the parent will never return, they mourn the loss and transfer their affection to the remaining parent, hoping in this way to regain the security they formerly had. Should the remaining parent be preoccupied with grief and the practical problems a broken home gives rise to, children feel rebuffed and unwanted. This will lead to resentments that seriously damage family relationships.

In early life, loss of the mother is more damaging than loss of the father. The reason for this is that care of young children must, under the circumstances, be turned over to relatives or paid housekeepers whose child-training techniques may differ from those used by the mothers and who rarely can give children the attention and affection they formerly received from their mothers.

As children grow older, loss of the father is often more serious than loss of the mother, especially for boys. The mother may have to go to work, and with the double burden of homemaking and outside work, the mother may lack the time or energy to give children the care they need. Consequently, they feel neglected and become resentful. If mothers are unable to provide the recreational opportunities and status symbols children's peers have, this will add to their resentment. For older boys, loss of the father means that they have no source for identification as their friends have, and they resent petticoat rule in the home as they do in the school.

Should children lose both parents, the effects are

missing parent is or why they have a new parent to replace the missing parent, they become embarrassed and ashamed. Furthermore, they may feel guilty if they enjoy the time they spend with the missing parent or if they prefer living with the missing parent to living with the parent who is taking care of them (16, 80, 98).

Temporary breaks are even more hazardous to family relationships than permanent breaks. These occur when the mother or father is away for a relatively short time. The absence of the father is usually due to a vocation that takes him away from home, while the absence of the mother is usually due to illness which necessitates hospitalization. Such temporary breaks create stressful situations both for the child and for the parent and lead to a deterioration in family relationships. First, the family must adjust to the break, and then it must readjust to being reunited.

Temporary absence of the mother deprives young children of the stable source of care they have been accustomed to and is equally damaging for boys and girls. Among older children, it has been reported, the temporary absence of the father is more damaging for boys than for girls. Chapter 7 has a more complete discussion of deprivation during the mother's temporary absence from the home (6, 30).

Influence of Reconstituted Homes on Family Relationships

Remarriage is often considered a good solution to the problems of the broken home. This is because home life is restored to its former pattern, with two parents sharing the responsibility for the care and training of the children.

However, reconstituting a home broken by death or divorce brings with it its own problems and necessitates difficult adjustments for all, not for the children of the family alone. Although remarriage may eliminate some of the financial problems of the broken home and thus prevent radical changes in the standard of living of the family, the interpersonal problems created by bringing a new person into the family in the role of stepparent are often so difficult that they counteract the favorable effects.

Problems created by having a stepparent come into the home to replace the missing parent arise partly from the attitudes and behavior of the stepparent, partly from those of the children of the family, and partly from those of the real parent. Some of the

doubly serious. Besides having to make radical changes in the pattern of their lives, children will have to adjust to the care of another person, often a person unknown to them (14, 53).

A home broken by *divorce* can be even more damaging to children and to family relationships than a home broken by death. There are two reasons for this. First, the period of adjustment to the divorce is longer and more difficult for children than the period of adjustment following the death of a parent. Hozman and Froiland have found that most children go through five phases in this adjustment: denial of the divorce, anger which strikes out at those involved in the situation, bargaining in an attempt to bring the parents back together, depression, and finally acceptance of the divorce (50).

Second, breaks caused by divorce are serious because they tend to make children "different" in the eyes of the peer group. If children are asked where the

child's and the stepparent's contributions to the new family relationships in a reconstituted family are given in Box 17–7.

Poor stepparent-child relationships inevitably affect the relationship of the parents. This, in turn, affects all family relationships. Unlike in their first marriages, the parents have no opportunity to establish a wholesome relationship between themselves *before* the stepparent role is assumed. If there were an interval during which the two parents could be alone together, the strains and stresses brought about by the stepparent-child relationship might more easily be met and, as a result, their impact on the family would be lessened.

In general, the home climate is better when the stepparent is the father. There are two major reasons: *First,* a stepfather's financial contribution to the home makes it possible for the family to live more comfortably than it did when the mother had to live on her alimony or inheritance or had to go out of the home to work. Usually, a stepmother's financial contribution is not this significant. *Second,* stepfathers usually assume less responsibility for the care of children than the real fathers. Instead, they limit their contacts mainly to "fun" experiences. Stepmothers, on the other hand, usually assume the child-training and disciplinary roles of the real mothers (105).

Many men do not find the role of stepparent satisfying. They resent having to support another man's children and they resent hearing the children express a preference for their real father. In addition, the presence of the stepchildren in the home is an ever-present reminder of the wife's first marriage and her love for the children's father. This arouses jealousies that can be a threat to wholesome marital adjustments (14, 66, 105).

Influence of Concepts of Family Roles on Family Relationships

In spite of the changes that have taken place in family life and in spite of the many different patterns of family life, there are certain concepts of certain family roles that are so widely held by children in American culture today that they may be regarded as "typical." Many of these concepts are influenced by different forms of the mass media. This tends to make the roles more glamorized than they are in real life—a potential source of danger for real-life relationships (3, 47).

In some respects, children's and adults' concepts of

a given role are quite different and, in other respects, they are similar. An examination of these concepts will help to explain the part they play in changes in family relationships as children grow older.

Since most children are egocentric, it is not surprising that their concepts of "parents" are based mainly on how their parents treat them, especially in the areas of discipline, nurturance, and recreation. Parents are "good," for example, if they help the children, but "bad" if they frustrate them. In Box 17–8 are given some of the major elements in children's concepts of "good" and "bad" parents.

BOX 17–8

CHILDREN'S CONCEPTS OF PARENTS

CONCEPT OF "GOOD" PARENT

- Does things for the child
- Can be depended on by the child
- Is reasonably permissive and giving
- Is fair in discipline
- Respects the child's individuality
- Inspires love, not fear
- Sets a good example
- Is companionable and does things with the child
- Is good-natured most of the time
- Shows the child affection
- Is sympathetic when the child is hurt or in trouble
- Encourages the child to bring friends to the home
- Is interested in making a happy home
- Grants independence appropriate for the child's age
- Does not expect unreasonable achievements

CONCEPT OF "BAD" PARENT

- Punishes harshly, frequently, and unfairly
- Interferes with child's interests and activities
- Tries to mold the child into a pattern
- Sets a poor example
- Is peevish and cross
- Shows little affection for the child
- Scolds when the child has an accident
- Shows little interest in the child or the child's activities
- Forbids or does not encourage visits by peers
- Is "mean" to the child's friends
- Discourages or forbids the child's playing with friends
- Tries to "tie apron strings" to the child
- Has unrealistic expectations for the child
- Criticizes or blames the child for failures
- Makes home a stressful and unpleasant place for all

"Mrs. Tippit must be a good mommy 'cause
she smiles a lot."

Figure 17–4. The young child's concept of "mother"
puts emphasis on being happy and tolerant of childish behavior. (*Adapted from Bil Keane: "The Family
Circus."* Register and Tribune Syndicate, *March 19,
1976. Used by permission.*)

Figure 17–5. How boys and girls perceive parental
power in mothers and fathers. (*Adapted from W. Emmerich: Variations in the parent role as a function of
the parent's sex and the child's sex and age.* Merrill-
Palmer Quarterly, *1962, 8, 3–11. Used by permission.*)

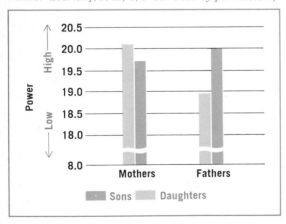

Young children usually think of "mother" as a
person who does things for them, who takes care of
their physical needs, who gives them affection and
attention, who is almost always happy and in good
humor, who tolerates a great deal of childish mischief,
and who comes to their aid in times of trouble. See
Figure 17–4. They perceive mothers as having greater
authority over them than fathers.

Older children also think of "mother" primarily in
terms of what she does for them. But, they recognize
that the authority and prestige of the mother in the
eyes of the world are not so great as they once
thought. The influence of the mass media, especially
movies and television, has been largely responsible for
giving children the traditional cultural stereotype of
the housewife-mother role as inferior to the father role.
This has had a great impact on older children's attitudes toward their mothers. As their attitudes change,
with changes in their concepts of the mother role, they
become less respectful and loving and more
critical—a condition that has a strong impact on
mother-child relationships.

Most children have a fairly definite concept of
"father," which differs greatly from their concept of
"mother." According to this concept, the father is
away from home more than the mother; he punishes
more and harder than the mother; he knows more
and is, in general, more important than the mother
because he earns the money, owns more, and is the
head of the family, the "boss." The tendency to perceive the father's role in the family as more powerful
is especially likely in the case of boys, as Figure 17–5
shows.

The concept of the role of "children," as held by
many children, is greatly influenced by parental concepts. If parents think of children as dependents, children will learn to think of this as the child's role; if parents wait on their children, children will believe that a
child should be waited on by parents. Regardless of
socioeconomic class, most children hold the concept, based on their moral and religious training in the
home, the school, and Sunday school, that a "good"
child honors and respects parents and is obedient,
cooperative, and never a troublemaker in the home.

Since "relatives" usually play a minor role in the life
of the child, concepts of them are built on fewer personal experiences and are likely to include meanings
acquired from peers' comments and from stories,
movies, television, and comics. A child whose most intimate friend has a grandmother living in the home, for

example, may hear things about her that will influence his developing concept of "grandmother."

If "grandparents" are depicted favorably in stories or on the screen, the child will be likely to develop a favorable concept of "grandmother" or "grandfather." However, in American culture today, elderly people are usually stereotyped as unattractive in appearance, rigid and punitive in their attitudes, quarrelsome and hard to live with, and old-fashioned in their dress, their manner of doing things, and their values. It is not surprising, therefore, that children incorporate this stereotype into their own concepts of elderly people.

Because young children have not had opportunities to learn the cultural stereotype of the "wicked stepmother" from fairy tales, stories, movies, or comments by others, they react to their stepmothers on the basis of the way their stepmothers treat them. As children grow older, their concept of "stepmother" often becomes unfavorable. From the mass media, they build up a concept of the "wicked stepmother" and this influences their reactions to their own stepmothers. Stepfathers do not appear in fairy tales, though they occasionally appear in modern fiction, in movies, and on TV. In general they are depicted so favorably that any concept children may develop of "stepfather" is likely to be more favorable than their concepts of stepmothers.

Effects of Concepts of Family Roles on Family Relationships

Concepts of the roles of different family members have an important bearing on family relationships. If parents think they are "good parents" but their children think they are not, there will be a poor parent-child relationship. A mother who believes that doing things for her children makes her a "good mother," for example, may discover that her children regard her as cold, uninterested, and even rejecting. If their concepts of a "good mother" include demonstrations of affection and permissiveness, they will perceive her far less favorably than she perceives herself, and this will lead to poor mother-child relationships. *Thus, it is not the relationship of parent and child, per se, that is important, but how the child and parent perceive it.*

Far too often, concepts of family roles are so romanticized that they fail to coincide with reality. The result is that few family members, whether they are parents, children, grandparents, or siblings can hope to come up to the expectations of other family members. Few

parents, for example, can approach the romanticized concept of the "ideal" parent presented in the stereotypes of parents in books, comics, and movies. Children who judge their parents by these concepts are likely to become highly critical of them and to feel that their parents are inferior to the parents of their friends.

Patterns of behavior in social relationships tend to persist, and so an unfavorable concept about any family member can damage the relationship with that member and lead to a deterioration in the relationships with other family members. A child who gets along badly with a grandmother because of a poor concept of "grandmother," for example, often stirs up enough trouble in the family to lead to general family friction. The child who dislikes a stepmother because of a concept of her based on fairy tales can cause enough trouble in the home to precipitate a separation or divorce.

Influence of Preference for One Parent on Family Relationships

A child's slight preference for one parent may be accepted with good humor, or it may lead to hurt feelings and friction. When a close bond develops between a child and the preferred parent, on the other hand, it often causes the other parent to feel like the third member of a triangle.

A preference for one parent is usually based on reasons that, *at that time,* are very important to children. Of the many factors that determine how children perceive their parents and interpret what their parents mean to them, the most important are explained in Box 17–9 (8, 20, 28, 43, 65, 103).

Children's Ways of Showing Preferences

Even before children can verbalize their preferences for one parent, they can show it by their behavior. During the first year of life, for example, babies show their preference by wanting to touch and to be near the preferred parent. This is illustrated in Figure 17–6.

After they can speak, young children show their likes and dislikes in easily recognized ways. Thus, parents have little difficulty in knowing whether or not they are the preferred parents. Four very common clues indicate where children's preferences lie.

FACTORS INFLUENCING THE CHILD'S PREFERENCE FOR ONE PARENT

TIME SPENT WITH THE CHILD

The more a parent is absent, the greater the child's preference for the other.

PLAY WITH THE CHILD

Mothers have more opportunity to play with children than fathers. As children grow older, fathers play more with their sons than with their daughters.

CARE OF THE CHILD

Mothers must, of necessity, assume most of the care of children's physical needs because fathers are unavailable to do so.

EXPRESSION OF AFFECTION

Fathers often fail to show their affection in ways the child can understand because they feel that such expressions of affection are unmasculine.

DISCIPLINE

As mothers are more tolerant and use corporal punishment less than fathers, they are usually preferred. Children turn toward the parent who "lets me" and away from the parent who "won't let me."

PARENTAL EXPECTATIONS

The parent who expects too much of the child and who is critical when the child does not live up to expectations is less favored.

PARENTAL FAVORITISM

The child who is the parent's favorite usually prefers that parent; the child who is not the favorite prefers the other parent. That is why boys generally prefer their mothers, and girls, as they grow older, prefer their fathers.

STATUS OF PARENTS

Since the mother is the important parent in early childhood, she is usually the favorite. As children grow older, they discover that the father's role is more highly valued by the social group. This encourages them to shift their preference to the father.

CONCEPTS OF IDEAL PARENT

As ideal concepts change, the parent who more closely fits the child's ideal of what a parent should be *at that time* will be the favorite parent.

First, children want the preferred parent to do things for them most of the time.

Second, when both parents are readily available, the child elects to be with the preferred parent.

Third, children identify with and imitate the preferred parent. If a child says, "I want to be just like Mommy when I grow up," the child is saying, "I prefer Mommy to Daddy."

Fourth, the term of address the child uses for a favored parent has a warmth to it that is lacking in the term used for a less favored parent. This warmth may not be in the label itself, but in the way the child says it.

Even as children grow older and learn, from social contacts outside the home, how to be more tactful in their interpersonal relationships, their ways of showing preferences for parents are still far from subtle. A very mature parent will accept childish preferences in a philosophical and sometimes a good-natured way. Unfortunately, few parents are so mature, and the child's preferences are a source of potential trouble in the family.

Effects of Childish Preferences on Family Relationships

How childish preferences for one parent will affect family relationships will depend on how the parent reacts to the preferences and to the child who shows the preference.

If the child shows a readily interpreted preference for the mother, for example, the mother will feel so loved and appreciated that she will want to reciprocate. She will do more for the child than she otherwise would and will show her love more frequently and more warmly. Thus, the influence is circular, with the child affecting the parent and the parent, in turn, affecting the child. It is from this interaction that the effect on family relationships is felt.

Just as a child resents parental favoritism toward one sibling, so does a parent resent a child's preference for the other parent. Fathers, for example, who discover that their children prefer to be with their mothers and to have their mothers do things for them have less warm and affectionate feelings toward their children than fathers who feel that they are the preferred parents. It is flattering to adults to feel that they are important people in the eyes of their children and it is ego-deflating to feel that they are regarded as unimportant.

As children approach adolescence, many boys

begin to shift their preference from the mother to the father. When this happens, there is often a split between the sexes, with the father and sons on one side and mother and daughters on the other. Any split in family relationships, no matter how slight it may be, is likely to lead to friction. Thus, as preferences shift from one parent to the other, they continue to play an important role in the deterioration of family relationships. Were there no other causes of deterioration, the shifting of preferences alone would be enough to bring it about.

Hazards in Family Relationships

Because the home provides children with feelings of security and stability—feelings that are essential to good personal as well as social adjustments—anything that interferes with these feelings can be regarded as hazardous for children. Just feeling, for example, that the patterns of their home lives are different enough from the patterns of home life of their playmates and friends can take away the feeling of security children should derive from their homes.

Unlike hazards in most other areas of the child's development, hazards in family relationships affect not the child alone but other family members as well. As other family members are affected by the changes these hazards bring in family relationships, the child will be indirectly affected. When, for example, husband-wife relationships are frictional, this frictional home climate and the possibility of a broken home will affect the child.

Because family relationships involve all family members, not just the relationships between parents and children, opportunities for hazardous relationships that will lead to poor personal and social adjustments are myriad. The important hazards will be categorized into two major areas: hazards that lead to deterioration in family relationships, and the effects of deviant family patterns.

Deterioration in Family Relationships

Relationships with people, inside or outside the home, rarely remain static. The reason for this is that, as people change in their interests and values, their relationships with one another also change.

This is true of family relationships. Unfortunately for

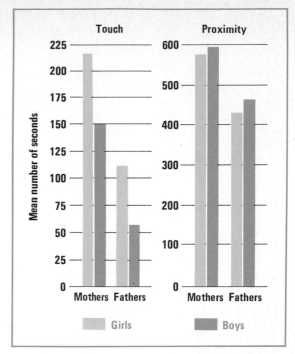

Figure 17–6. Babies, during the first year of life, show a preference for the mother by wanting to be near the mother and to touch the mother more often than the father. (*Adapted from P. L. Ban and M. Lewis: Mothers and fathers, girls and boys: Attachment behavior in the one-year-old.* Merrill-Palmer Quarterly, *1974, 20, 195–204. Used by permission.*)

all family members, not for children alone, family relationships tend to change for the worse. This deterioration usually begins, for husbands and wives, during the first year of marriage. Although it may not lead to a divorce or separation, there is evidence that the disenchantment with marriage—often due to a romanticized concept of it—leads to a deterioration in husband-wife relationships (95).

Deterioration in the parent-child relationship generally begins during the latter part of the child's first year of life and is readily apparent early in the second year. It is shown by a decrease in parental warmth toward the child and an increase in restrictiveness and punitiveness.

Although parent-child relationships may improve somewhat when the child first goes to school—whether it is nursery school, kindergarten, or the first grade—they usually do not. Adjusting to school is

BOX 17–10

COMMON CAUSES OF DETERIORATION IN FAMILY RELATIONSHIPS

HUSBAND-WIFE RELATIONSHIPS
Should either husband or wife become disenchanted with the parental role, because of radical changes in their lives which they had not anticipated, husband-wife friction develops. The disenchanted parent then becomes highly critical of the other parent and of the children. When both husband and wife become disenchanted, the frictional relationship will be intensified.

PARENT-CHILD RELATIONSHIPS
When children no longer need to depend so much on their parents as they did earlier and are no longer so demonstrative in their affection, consideration, and respect, they often treat their parents in such a way that the parents feel rejected. Even when children are not critical and rebellious, their changed behavior toward their parents cannot fail to contribute to a deterioration in parent-child relationships. Parents add to this deterioration by being more critical and punitive in their attitudes and treatment of the children than they were when the children were younger.

SIBLING RELATIONSHIPS
The older sibling who regarded a younger sibling as an "adorable doll" when the younger sibling was a baby may come to consider the younger sibling a "brat" when expected to act as an unpaid baby-sitter. The younger sibling, who formerly regarded the older sibling as an idol, may find that the idol has lost some of its glamor when the older sibling is critical and refuses to play with the younger.

RELATIONSHIPS WITH RELATIVES
The doting grandmother who "spoiled" her grandchildren when they were babies may turn into a strict disciplinarian as they grow older. As they grow older, children often accept the cultural stereotypes of old people and of grandparents. They may then develop an antagonistic attitude toward grandparents and all elderly relatives.

CHANGES IN THE FAMILY PATTERN
Whenever there is a change in the accustomed pattern of family life, the homeostasis of the family life will be upset and trouble will ensue unless changes are made in their role playing by *all* family members. The arrival of a new baby in the home usually upsets all family members, as does the arrival of an elderly relative as a permanent member of the household.

always accompanied by emotional tension, and this is expressed in an increase in the number of behavior problems or in the intensity and frequency of those which already exist.

As the child spends more and more time with people outside the home, new interests and values give rise to increasing friction with family members. In the closing years of childhood, parent-child relationships usually deteriorate steadily, reaching a low point as puberty changes occur. Friction then becomes the dominant aspect of the relationship.

CAUSES OF DETERIORATION IN FAMILY RELATIONSHIPS Deteriorations in family relationships do not come from one cause alone but from many. That is why deterioration, once it begins, is difficult to stop. It also explains why, once deterioration begins in one area of family relationships—husband-wife or parent-child—it affects the home climate and spreads to other areas of family relationships, such as relationships with siblings or with relatives.

Box 17–10 gives some of the most common causes of deterioration in family relationships. Note that, with the exception of changes in the family pattern, all come from relationships of different family members. Even change in the family pattern is indirectly related to family relationships because it means that new patterns of relationships between different family members must be established (17, 18, 58, 70, 82, 97).

EFFECTS OF DETERIORATION IN FAMILY RELATIONSHIPS Once poor relationships develop, they tend to persist and grow worse rather than better. This is partly because people develop the habit of reacting to one another in a frictional way and partly because there is less and less communication between them and, hence, less understanding.

Studies of the way mothers treat their children reveal that treatment during infancy is significantly related to later treatment. Changes usually occur in *quantity* of treatment rather than in *quality;* indulgent parents tend to become more indulgent, and rejective parents more rejective. Consequently, small frictions in early childhood are likely to become major disruptions in late childhood (18, 29, 90, 92, 94).

When children misinterpret parental behavior and believe that their parents are rejecting them or love them less than they formerly did, they become anxious, insecure, and rebellious. Parents, not understanding what is behind this childish behavior, feel unappreciated and rejected. In time, parents reject their children because of the mutual hostility that is generated. This vicious cycle may begin at any time, but it is most likely to begin early in childhood. At this time children find it difficult to understand the behavior of others unless the reasons for their behavior are spelled out in words children can comprehend. That is why, as was stressed earlier, democratic discipline which puts emphasis on telling children why their behavior is wrong and why they are being punished for intentional misbehavior is so superior to authoritarian discipline which ignores any explanation on the parent's part. Once misunderstandings begin, they are likely to gain momentum and the "vicious cycle" of parent-child relationships, as shown in Figure 17–7, is thrown into motion.

How serious this vicious cycle of bad parent-child relationships is has been shown in case of *child abuse.* Studies of child abuse have all revealed that it does not develop overnight. Instead, there is ample evidence that when children are beaten and otherwise mistreated by their parents, there is a history of bad parent-child relationships that have become progressively worse as time passes. Whether the abused child is a baby, a toddler, or an older child, there is a mutual feeling of rejection and an open hostility. Because parents are in control of the home, they then become the aggressors in venting their growing hostilities by overt attacks on their children. How intense their hostilities are is shown by the intensity of their attacks on their children (4, 17, 40, 87).

When deterioration in family relationships becomes persistent, it weakens the emotional bonds between family members. As a result, family members have little interest in and affection for other family members. Hostility between brothers and sisters during the time when sex antagonism in the gang is at its height will likely result in an antagonistic attitude that will persist long after this antagonism has subsided. However, the damage has been done. As brothers and sisters grow older, the chances are that they will grow further apart. By the time they reach adulthood, they will establish patterns of life that will not include their brothers and sisters.

The same is true with other family members. Once an antagonistic relationship develops, whether between parent and child, sister and sister, or child and grandparent, the emotional tie between them is broken and each drifts away from the other. By the time they reach adulthood, the solidarity of the family and the loyalty and affection for family members that

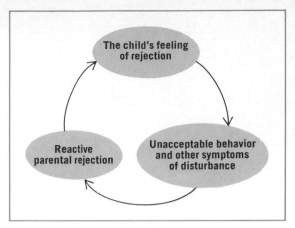

Figure 17–7. The "vicious cycle" of parent-child relationships. (*Adapted from D. Hallowitz and B. Stulberg: The vicious cycle of parent-child relationship breakdown.* Social Casework, *1959,* 40, *268–275. Used by permission.*)

should be present has deteriorated to the point where the family unit has disintegrated.

Children who grow up in a home marked by frictional family relationships often develop personality maladjustments that persist into adult life (29). This matter will be discussed in more detail in the following chapter. Furthermore, they often develop unhealthy attitudes about marriage and parenthood which, if they persist, will color their adult attitudes unfavorably. See Figure 17–8.

A pattern of life, marked by deteriorating relationships with family members, may readily be carried from the home into relationships with people outside the home. That is why, as was pointed out in the earlier discussions of conditions contributing to social acceptance, children who have a deteriorating relationship with family members often use this as a model for their relationships with peers. As a result, they are far more likely to be rejected and neglected by peers than are children whose home life has provided a more favorable model of relationships to carry into their peer relationships.

Some families, recognizing the damaging effects to all family members that come from deteriorating family relationships try to cope with the problem by separation. If there is friction between the parents, one may go away for a time and hope that, on the return, the situation will improve. When friction occurs between parents and children, parents may leave them under

Figure 17–8. Deteriorating family relations often color children's attitudes toward marriage and parenthood unfavorably. (*Adapted from Ernie Bushmiller: "Nancy."* United Features Syndicate, *Nov. 10, 1975. Used by permission.*)

the care of a relative while they take a vacation, or the children may be sent to camp or to visit relatives. This rarely solves the problem. Unless attitudes that have given rise to the behavior responsible for the deterioration are changed, the frictional relationship that gave rise to the deterioration will likely be resumed. Should, for example, the friction come from parental overprotectiveness of children, the only solution to the deteriorating family relationship problem is for the parents to recognize that their children are capable of doing things for themselves and that they want the opportunity to do them. Changing from waiting on their children to guiding and helping them learn to become independent may bring about a changed and healthier family relationship.

Deviant Family Patterns

In the American culture today, there is no standard pattern of family living. In the same community there are nuclear and elongated families, small and large families, families broken by death or divorce and families reconstituted by bringing in a stepparent to replace the missing parent, families where one parent, either mother or father, lives alone with the children, and families with very young or overage parents. Refer to Box 17–1 for a list of family-life patterns in America today.

Because different family patterns are common, no one pattern can be called "deviant." However, for children, a "deviant family pattern" means one that is different from the patterns that are common among the children with whom they associate. And, because of this difference, the children feel that they are conspicuous. Children, for example, whose parents are conspicuously older than the parents of age-mates or children who have stepparents while the other children they play with have their natural parents interpret this to mean that they are "different."

WHY DEVIANT FAMILY PATTERNS ARE HAZARDOUS
The reason that deviant family patterns are hazardous to good personal and social adjustments, as has been explained before, is that children tend to judge "difference" as being synonymous with "inferiority." Anyone who is different from them is, by this standard, regarded as "inferior" to them.

When children are judged inferior by the peer group, it has an unfavorable effect on their self-concepts. They think of themselves as inferior to their peers. Unfavorable social judgments also affect the degree of social acceptance children are able to achieve in the peer group. Just as children who are discriminated against because they belong to a racial, religious, or socioeconomic group regarded as inferior by their peers are psychologically damaged, so are those who are discriminated against because their patterns of family living are different from those of the members of the peer group.

How hazardous deviant family patterns are to children's personal and social adjustments will depend upon three conditions. *First,* the prevailing social attitude toward a certain deviant pattern of family living will have a strong impact on peer attitudes. These social attitudes children learn from their parents and other adults and accept as their own. The social attitude, for example, toward a one-parent family where the mother lives alone with an illegitimate child is, in most communities, far less favorable than toward a one-parent family where the parent is living alone with children because of the death of a spouse (49). Similarly, reconstituted families following the death of a parent are usually more favorably viewed than those following divorce.

Second, there are variations according to the social group that make the judgments. In interreligious marriages, for example, the social group that is most strongly opposed to the marriage and makes the most unfavorable judgments about it is most often the family group and friends. By contrast, in interracial marriages, the social group of the community tends to make more unfavorable judgments than the family group, though unfavorable judgments by the family group are common. Members of the peer group judge overage parents far less favorably than do members of the adult group.

Third, how conspicuous the deviant family pattern makes the child influences its effects on the child's adjustments. Children with stepfathers are made more conspicuous because their names differ from those of their parents than are children with stepmothers whose parents' names are the same as theirs. Children from interracial families are conspicuous because of the difference in appearance between their parents and their relatives.

EFFECTS ON FAMILY RELATIONSHIPS   As children become aware of social attitudes toward their family-life pattern because it differs from that of most of their peers, it affects their relationships with members of their families. Because children, as was stressed above, regard being different as a sign of inferiority, the effect on family relationships tends to contribute to a deterioration. Children who, when young, welcomed stepparents because of the security and stability the stepparents brought into their lives, may develop a frictional relationship with the stepparents when they become aware of how their age-mates feel about stepparents and when their own attitudes are colored by the mass-media stereotypes of stepmothers.

When the hazards that come from deteriorating family relationships are added to the hazards that come from unfavorable judgments that have such a profound influence on children's personal and social adjustments, it becomes apparent that deviant family patterns rank even above deterioration in family relationships as a major hazard in family life. The greater the deviation from the accustomed pattern in the group with which the child is identified, the greater its hazardous influence will be.

Chapter Highlights

1   Changes in the traditional pattern of the American family have resulted in marked changes in family relationships for all family members.

2   Regardless of changes in the American family pattern, all types of families play important roles in the development of children, though the influence of different family members varies as does the age of the child.

3   There are many parental attitudes toward children—overprotective, permissive, indulgent, rejectant, acceptant, domineering, submissive, favoring one child, and ambitious for the child—each of which has its own characteristic effect on family relationships.

4   The type of child-training method used in the home influences relationships of children with different family members, not with the parents alone.

5   The larger the number of children in a family, the more frictional the relationships with different family members will be unless strict, authoritarian child-training methods are used to prevent overt expression of frictional attitudes.

6   Sibling relationships, which are influenced by parental attitudes toward the different children in the family, ordinal position and sex of children, number of siblings, type of discipline used by parents, and the influence of outsiders on children and their parents, more often lead to friction than to pleasant family relationships.

7   There are many conditions in the family setting that affect family relationships, the most important of which are the socioeconomic status of the family, the occupations of the father and the mother, outsiders in the home, whether guests, elderly relatives, or paid domestic workers, and defective and adopted children.

8   How broken homes affect family relationships depends on whether the break is due to death of one parent or divorce and on whether the break is permanent or temporary.

9   Families reconstituted by remarriage tend to be damaging to children's personal and social adjustments because the relationships between children and

their stepparents are more often unfavorable than favorable. This frictional relationship is more pronounced when the stepparent replaces a missing mother than when a missing father is replaced by a stepfather.

10 From personal experiences, mass media, and other sources, children build up specific concepts of different family roles—the role of parent, of mother, of father, of children, and of relatives. When their concepts differ from those of their parents or other family members, a frictional family relationship invariably develops.

11 When children show a preference for one parent, the other parent usually resents this and reacts unfavorably both to the child and to the preferred parent, thus causing a frictional home climate.

12 Deterioration in family relationships is hazardous to children's personal and social adjustments because it results in a frictional home climate. Once this deterioration starts, it weakens the bonds between family members and, unless corrected, this in time leads to a breakdown in family solidarity.

13 Deterioration in family relationships comes mainly from unfavorable relationships with different family members—husband-wife relationships, parent-child relationships, sibling relationships, and relationships with relatives—though it may come from changes in the family pattern, should this, indirectly, cause unfavorable interpersonal relationships in the home.

14 A deviant family pattern is hazardous to good personal and social adjustments in children because children tend to judge a child whose pattern of family life deviates from theirs as "different" and, to most children "different" is synonymous with "inferior."

15 Because there is no single standard of family living in American culture today, deviant patterns of family living are judged on the basis of what is the prevailing pattern in the environment in which the child lives. Consequently, what is common and accepted in one environment may be considered "deviant" in another environment.

Bibliography

1 Adams, R. L., and B. N. Phillips. Motivational and achievement differences among children of various ordinal birth positions. *Child Development,* 1972, *43,* 155–164.

2 Ainsworth, M. D. S., S. M. Bell, and D. J. Stayton. Individual differences in the development of some attachment behaviors. *Merrill-Palmer Quarterly,* 1972, *18,* 123–143.

3 Aldous, J. The making of family roles and family change. *Family Coordinator,* 1974, *23,* 231–235.

4 Alvy, K. T. Preventing child abuse. *American Psychologist,* 1975, *30,* 921–928.

5 Armentrout, J. A., and G. K. Burger. Children's reports of parental child-rearing behavior at five grade levels. *Developmental Psychology,* 1972, *7,* 44–48.

6 Atkinson, B. R., and D. G. Ogston. The effect of family absence on male children in the home and school. *Journal of School Psychology,* 1974, *12,* 213–221.

7 Bacon, C., and R. M. Lerner. Effects of maternal employment on the development of vocational role perception in females. *Journal of Genetic Psychology,* 1975, *126,* 187–193.

8 Ban, P. L. Mothers and fathers, boys and girls: Attachment behavior in the one-year-old. *Merrill-Palmer Quarterly,* 1974, *20,* 195–204.

9 Barton, K., T. E. Dielman, and R. B. Cattell. Child rearing practices and achievement in school. *Journal of Genetic Psychology,* 1974, *124,* 155–165.

10 Beels, C. C. Whatever happened to father? *The New York Times,* Aug. 25, 1974.

11 Bernard, J. Note on changing lifestyles, 1970–1974. *Journal of Marriage and the Family,* 1975, *37,* 582–593.

12 Bigner, J. J. Parent education in popular literature: 1950 to 1970. *Family Coordinator,* 1972, *21,* 313–319.

13 Biller, H. B. The mother-child relationship and the father-absent boy's personality development. *Merrill-Palmer Quarterly,* 1971, *17,* 227–241.

14 Bossard, J. H. S., and E. S. Boll. *The sociology of child development,* 4th ed. New York: Harper & Row, 1966.

15 Bowlby, J. A. Guide to the perplexed parent. *The New York Times,* March 2, 1974.

16 Brandwein, R. A., C. A. Brown, and E. M. Fox. Women and children last: The social situation of divorced mothers and their families. *Journal of Marriage and the Family,* 1974, *36,* 498–514.

17 Bronfenbrenner, U. The origins of alienation. *Scientific American,* 1974, *231* (2), 53–61.

18 Bronson, W. C. Mother-toddler interaction: A perspective on studying the development of competence. *Merrill-Palmer Quarterly,* 1974, *20,* 275–301.

19 Brook, J. S., M. Whiteman, E. Peisach, and M. Deutsch. Aspiration levels of and for children: Age, sex, race, and socioeconomic correlates. *Journal of Genetic Psychology,* 1974, *124,* 3–16.

20 Brooks, J., and M. Lewis. Attachment behavior in thirteen-month-old, opposite-sex twins. *Child Development,* 1974, *45,* 243–247.

21 Burger, G. K., R. E. Lamp, and D. Rogers. Developmental trends in children's perceptions of parental child-rearing behavior. *Developmental Psychology*, 1975, *11*, 391.

22 Campbell, S. B. Mother-child interaction in reflective, impulsive and hyperactive children. *Developmental Psychology*, 1973, *8*, 341–349.

23 Chang, T. S. The self-concept of children of ethnically different marriages. *California Journal of Educational Research*, 1974, *25*, 245–252.

24 Cicirelli, V. G. Effects of sibling structure and interaction on children's categorization style. *Developmental Psychology*, 1973, *9*, 132–139.

25 Clarke-Stewart, K. A. Interactions between mothers and their young children: Characteristics and consequences. *Monographs of the Society for Research in Child Development*, 1973, *38*, 1–109.

26 Clavan, S. The family process: A sociological model. *Family Coordinator*, 1968, *17*, 312–317.

27 Cogswell, B. E. Variant family forms and life styles: Rejection of the traditional nuclear family. *Family Coordinator*, 1975, *24*, 391–406.

28 Cohen, L. J., and J. J. Campos. Father, mother, and stranger as elicitors of attachment behaviors in infancy. *Developmental Psychology*, 1974, *10*, 146–154.

29 Cross, H. J., and G. L. Davis. College students' adjustment and memories of parents. *Journal of Genetic Psychology*, 1976, *128*, 145–146.

30 Crumley, F. E., and R. S. Blumenthal. Children's reactions to temporary loss of the father. *American Journal of Psychiatry*, 1973, *130*, 778–782.

31 Davids, A., and R. H. Holden. Consistency of maternal attitudes and personality from pregnancy to eight months following childbirth. *Developmental Psychology*, 1970, *2*, 364–366.

32 Dielman, T. E., K. Barton, and R. B. Cattell. Cross-validational evidence on the structure of parental reports of child rearing practices. *Journal of Social Psychology*, 1973, *90*, 243–250.

33 Eiduson, B. T., J. Cohen, and J. Alexander. Alternatives to child rearing in the 1970s. *American Journal of Orthopsychiatry*, 1973, *43*, 720–731.

34 Emmerich, W. The parental role: A functional-cognitive approach. *Monographs of the Society for Research in Child Development*, 1969, *34* (8).

35 Etaugh, C. Effects of maternal employment on children: A review of recent research. *Merrill-Palmer Quarterly*, 1974, *20*, 71–98.

36 Feldberg, R., and J. Kohen. Family life in an anti-family setting: A critique of marriage and divorce. *Family Coordinator*, 1976, *25*, 151–159.

37 Forer, L. *The birth order factor*. New York: McKay, 1976.

38 Freud, S. *The standard edition of the complete psychological works of Sigmund Freud*. London: Hogarth Press, 1953–1962. 21 vols.

39 Gath, A. Sibling reactions to mental handicap: A comparison of brothers and sisters of mongol children. *Journal of Child Psychology and Psychiatry*, 1974, *15*, 187–198.

40 Gil, D. G. Violence against children. *Journal of Marriage and the Family*, 1971, *33*, 637–648.

41 Gilbert, S. J. Self disclosure, intimacy and communication in families. *Family Coordinator*, 1976, *25*, 221–231.

42 Graves, D., J. Walters, and N. Stinnett. Relationship between perceptions of family life and attitudes concerning father-son interaction. *Journal of Genetic Psychology*, 1974, *124*, 303–310.

43 Greenberg, M., and N. Morris. Engrossment: The newborn's impact upon the father. *American Journal of Orthopsychiatry*, 1974, *44*, 520–531.

44 Haney, C. A., R. Michielutte, C. M. Cochrane, and C. E. Vincent. Some consequences of illegitimacy in a sample of black women. *Journal of Marriage and the Family*, 1975, *37*, 359–366.

45 Harrell, J. E., and C. A. Ridley. Substitute child care, maternal employment, and the quality of mother-child interaction. *Journal of Marriage and the Family*, 1975, *37*, 556–564.

46 Helson, R. Effects of sibling characteristics and parental values on creative interest and achievement. *Journal of Personality*, 1968, *36*, 589–607.

47 Hendrickson, N., D. Perkins, S. White, and T. Buck. Parent-daughter relationships in fiction. *Family Coordinator*, 1975, *24*, 257–265.

48 Hoffman, L. W. Effects of maternal employment on the child: A review of research. *Developmental Psychology*, 1974, *10*, 204–228.

49 Howell, M. C. Employed mothers and their families (1). *Pediatrics*, 1973, *52*, 252–263.

50 Hozman, T. L., and D. J. Froiland. Families in divorce: A proposed model for counseling the children. *Family Coordinator*, 1976, *25*, 271–276.

51 Jacobs, B. S., and H. A. Moss. Birth order and sex of siblings as determinants of mother-infant interaction. *Child Development*, 1976, *47*, 315–322.

52 Jacobsen, R. B. An exploration of parental encouragement as an intervening variable in occupational-educational living in children. *Journal of Marriage and the Family*, 1971, *33*, 174–182.

53 Jones, A. P., and R. G. Demaree. Family disruption: Social indices and problem behavior: A preliminary study. *Journal of Marriage and the Family*, 1975, *37*, 497–502.

54 Jones, P. A. Home environment and verbal ability. *Child Development*, 1972, *43*, 1081–1086.

55 Kahana, B., and E. Kahana. Grandparenthood from the perspective of the developing grandchild. *Developmental Psychology*, 1970, *3*, 98–105.

56 Kaplan, H. B., and A. D. Pokorny. Self-derogation and childhood broken home. *Journal of Marriage and the Family*, 1971, *33*, 328–337.

57 Kempler, H. L. Extended kinship ties and some modern alternatives. *Family Coordinator*, 1976, *25*, 143–149.

58 Kennell, J. H., R. Jerauld, H. Wolfe, D. Chesler, W. C. Kreger, W. McAlpine, M. Steffa, and M. H. Klaus. Maternal behavior one year after early and extended post-partum contact. *Developmental Medicine and Child Neurology*, 1974, *16*, 172–179.

59 Kim, C. C., R. J. Dales, R. Connor, J. Walters, and R. Witherspoon. Social interaction of like-sex twins

and singletons in relation to intelligence, language, and physical environment. *Journal of Genetic Psychology,* 1969, *114,* 203–214.

60 Klein, M. M., R. Plutchik, and H. R. Conte. Parental dominance-passivity and behavior problems of children. *Journal of Consulting and Clinical Psychology,* 1973, *40,* 416–425.

61 Korner, A. F. Individual differences at birth: Implications for early experience and later development. *American Journal of Orthopsychiatry,* 1971, *41,* 608–619.

62 Leichter, H. J. Some perspectives on the family as educator. *Teachers College Record,* 1974, *76,* 175–217.

63 Longstreth, L. E., G. V. Longstreth, C. Ramirez, and G. Fernandex. The ubiquity of big brother. *Child Development,* 1975, *46,* 769–772.

64 Lott, B. E. Who wants the children? Some relationships among attitudes toward children, parents, and the liberation of women. *American Psychologist,* 1973, *28,* 573–582.

65 Lynn, D. B., and A. deP. Cass. Parent preference of preschool children. *Journal of Marriage and the Family,* 1974, *36,* 555–559.

66 Maddox, B. Neither witch nor good fairy. *The New York Times,* Aug. 8, 1976.

67 Manen, G. C. The validity of parent-child socialization measures: A comparison of the use of assumed and real parent-child similarity with criterion variability. *Genetic Psychology Monographs,* 1973, *88,* 201–227.

68 Marcus, R. F. The child as elicitor of parental sanctions for independent and dependent behavior: A simulation of parent-child interaction. *Developmental Psychology,* 1975, *11,* 443–452.

69 McIntyre, W. G., and D. C. Payne. The relationship of family functioning to school achievement. *Family Coordinator,* 1971, *20,* 265–268.

70 Mead, M. Grandparents as educators. *Teachers College Record,* 1974, *76,* 240–249.

71 Mnookin, R. H. Foster care—in whose best interest? *Harvard Educational Review,* 1973, *43,* 599–638.

72 Neugarten, B. L., and K. K. Weinstein. The changing American grandparent. *Marriage and Family Living,* 1964, *26,* 199–204.

73 Nevill, D., and S. Damico. Family size and role conflict in women. *Journal of Psychology,* 1975, *89,* 267–270.

74 Norman, R. D. Sex differences in preferences for sex of children: A replication after 20 years. *Journal of Psychology,* 1974, *88,* 229–239.

75 Osofsky, J. D., and E. G. O'Connell. Parent-child interaction: Daughters' effects upon mothers' and fathers' behavior. *Developmental Psychology,* 1972, *7,* 157–168.

76 Pieper, E. Grandparents can help. *Exceptional Parent,* 1976, *6* (2), 6–10.

77 Radin, N. Father-child interaction and the intellectual functioning of four-year-old boys. *Developmental Psychology,* 1972, *6,* 353–361.

78 Rebelsky, F., and C. Hanks. Fathers' verbal interaction with infants in the first three months of life. *Child Development,* 1971, *42,* 63–68.

79 Rheingold, H. L. To rear a child. *American Psychologist,* 1973, *28,* 42–46.

80 Rose, V. L., and S. Price-Bonham. Divorce adjustment: A woman's problem? *Family Coordinator,* 1973, *22,* 291–297.

81 Rosenblatt, P. C. Behavior in public places: Comparison of couples accompanied and unaccompanied by children. *Journal of Marriage and the Family,* 1974, *36,* 750–755.

82 Russell, C. S. Transition to parenthood: Problems and gratifications. *Journal of Marriage and the Family,* 1974, *36,* 294–301.

83 Scheck, D. C., and R. Emerlck. A young male adolescent's perception of early child-rearing behavior: The differential effects of socioeconomic status and family size. *Sociometry,* 1976, *39,* 39–52.

84 Schooler, C. Childhood family structure and adult characteristics. *Sociometry,* 1972, *35,* 255–269.

85 Seitz, S., and S. Marcus. Mother-child interactions: A foundation for language development. *Exceptional Children,* 1976, *42,* 445–449.

86 Slater, P. E. Parental behavior and the personality of the child. *Journal of Genetic Psychology,* 1962, *101,* 53–68.

87 Spinetta, J. J., and D. Bigler. The child-abusing parent: A psychological review. *Psychological Bulletin,* 1972, *77,* 296–304.

88 Sutton-Smith, B., and B. G. Rosenberg. *The sibling.* New York: Holt, Rinehart & Winston, 1970.

89 Sweetser, D. A. The structure of sibling relationships. *American Journal of Sociology,* 1970, *76,* 47–58.

90 Thompson, S. K., and P. M. Bentler. A developmental study of gender constancy and parent preference. *Archives of Sexual Behavior,* 1973, *2,* 379–385.

91 Tizard, B., and J. Rees. A comparison of the effects of adoption, restoration of the natural mother, and continued institutionalization on the cognitive development of four-year-old children. *Child Development,* 1974, *45,* 92–99.

92 Troll, L. E. Is parent-child conflict what we mean by the generation gap? *Family Coordinator,* 1972, *21,* 347–349.

93 Tulkin, S. R., and B. J. Cohler. Child-rearing attitudes and mother-child interaction in the first year of life. *Merrill-Palmer Quarterly,* 1973, *19,* 95–106.

94 Tulkin, S. R., and J. Kagan. Mother-child interaction in the first year of life. *Child Development,* 1972, *43,* 31–41.

95 *U.S. News & World Report:* Who stays married longer? Oct. 30, 1972, 39.

96 *U.S. News & World Report* The American family: Can it survive today's shocks? Oct. 27, 1975, pp. 30–46.

97 Veevers, J. E. The social meanings of parenthood. *Psychiatry,* 1973, *36,* 291–310.

98 Wallerstein, J. S., and J. B. Kelly. The effects of parental divorce: Experiences of the preschool child. *Journal of the American Academy of Child Psychiatry,* 1975, *14,* 600–616.

99 Wallston, B. The effects of maternal employment on children. *Journal of Child Psychology and Psychiatry and Allied Disciplines,* 1973, *14,* 81–95.

100 Wexler, J. G. The family: Nuclear and human. *Journal of Home Economics,* 1973, *65* (6), 23–24.

101 Whiting, B. E. Folk wisdom and child rearing. *Merrill-Palmer Quarterly,* 1974, *20,* 9–19.

102 Will, J. A., P. A. Self, and N. Dafan. Maternal behavior and perceived sex of infant. *American Journal of Orthopsychiatry,* 1976, *46,* 135–139.

103 Willemsen, E., D. Flaherty, C. Heaton, and G. Ritchey. Attachment behavior of one-year-olds as a function of mother vs. father, sex of child, session and toys. *Genetic Psychology Monographs,* 1974, *90,* 305–324.

104 Williams, T. M. Child-rearing practices of young mothers: What we know, how it matters, why it's so little. *American Journal of Orthopsychiatry,* 1974, *41,* 70–75.

105 Wilson, K. L., L. A. Zurcher, D. C. McAdams, and R. L. Curtis. Stepfathers and stepchildren: An exploratory analysis from two national surveys. *Journal of Marriage and the Family,* 1975, *37,* 526–536.

106 Wohlford, P., J. W. Santrock, S. E. Berger, and D. Liberman. Older brothers' influence on sex-typed, aggressive, and dependent behavior in father-absent children. *Developmental Psychology,* 1971, *4,* 124–134.

107 Woods, M. B. The unsupervised child of the working mother. *Developmental Psychology,* 1972, *6,* 14–25.

108 Wright, J. D., and S. R. Wright. Social class and parental values for children: A partial replication and extension of the Kohn thesis. *American Sociological Review,* 1976, *41,* 527–537.

109 Yorburg, B. *The changing family.* New York: Columbia University Press, 1973.

110 Yost, E. D., and R. J. Adamek. Parent-child interaction and changing family values: A multivariate analysis. *Journal of Marriage and the Family,* 1974, *36,* 115–121.

111 Zern, D. The relationship between mother-infant contact and later differentiation of the social environment: *Journal of Genetic Psychology,* 1972, *121,* 107–117.

112 Zuger, B. The role of familial factors in persistent effeminate behavior in boys. *American Journal of Orthopsychiatry,* 1970, *126,* 1167–1170.

CHAPTER 18

PERSONALITY DEVELOPMENT

Popular recognition of the role personality plays in successful adjustments to modern life has given strong impetus to the scientific study of personality. In simple cultures, personality is of secondary importance in social relationships, but in cultures where social life is complex, personality is of major importance. Today's parents and teachers put great emphasis on developing personality patterns in children which will help them to make satisfactory adjustments both in the present and in the future.

A second impetus to the scientific study of personality has come from the growing evidence that learning, rather than heredity, largely determines what one's personality will be like. This recognition has had two effects. *First,* it has emphasized that people can no longer blame a poor hereditary endowment or environment for their unfavorable personality characteristics but rather must blame themselves for developing such personality patterns. See Figure 18–1. *Second,* because personality, like so many other areas of development, is controllable, children can, with guidance and help, develop personality patterns that will make successful adjustment to life possible.

The *third* and, in many respects, the greatest impetus to the scientific study of personality is the realization that, since personality development can be controlled, the personality pattern can also be changed and modified in ways that lead to improved personal and social adjustments. Although there is no evidence of a deadline after which learning cannot bring about modifications in an undesirable trait or an undesirable self-concept, there is evidence that the early years of life are the "critical" years in personality development and that, with each passing year, changes are more difficult to accomplish.

Meaning of Personality

The term "personality" comes from the Latin word *persona,* meaning "mask." Among the ancient Greeks, the actors wore masks to hide their identity and to enable them to represent the characters they were depicting in the play. This dramatic technique was later adopted by the Romans, and from them we get our modern term personality.

To the Romans, *persona* meant "as one appears to others," not as one actually is. The actor was creating, in the minds of the audience, an impression of the character depicted on the stage, not an impression of what the actor was. From this connotation of the word *persona,* our popular idea of personality as the effect one has on others has been derived. What a person thinks, feels, and is are included in that person's whole psychological makeup and are, to a great extent, revealed through behavior. Personality, then, is not one definite, specific attribute; rather, it is the quality of the person's total behavior.

There are many definitions of the term "personality," most of which have been modeled along the lines of Allport's definition because it is one of the most inclusive. According to his definition, personality is the *dynamic organization within the individual of those psychophysical systems that determine the individual's unique adjustments to the environment* (3). The term "dynamic" points up the changing nature of personality; it emphasizes that changes can occur in the quality of a person's behavior. "Organization" implies that personality is not made up of a number of different

Figure 18–1. Evidence that learning plays a dominant role in personality development makes it impossible for individuals to blame heredity or environment alone for an undesirable personality characteristic. (*Adapted from George Lichty: "Grin and Bear It."* Field Newspaper Syndicate, *Oct. 13, 1973. Used by permission.*)

"Some authorities would blame your behavior on your genes, others on your home environment! . . . BUT I BLAME YOU, OTIS, plain and simple!"

traits, one simply added to the others, but that they are interrelated. The interrelationship changes, with some traits becoming more dominant and others less so, with changes in the child and in the environment.

The "psychophysical systems" are the habits, attitudes, values, beliefs, emotional states, sentiments, and motives which are psychological in nature but which have a physical basis in the child's neural, glandular, and general bodily states. These systems are not the product of heredity, though they are based on hereditary foundations; they have been developed through learning as a result of the child's various experiences.

The psychophysical systems are the *motivating forces* which determine what kind of adjustment the child will make. Since each child has different learning experiences, the kind of adjustment the child makes is "unique" in the sense that no other child, even an identical twin, will react in exactly the same manner. Furthermore, as the psychophysical systems are the product of learning, the traditional belief that personality traits are inherited is refuted.

The Personality Pattern

The term "pattern" means a design or configuration. In the case of the personality pattern, the different psychophysical systems that make up the individual's personality are interrelated, with one influencing the others. The two major components of the personality pattern are the *core*—the "concept of self"—and the spokes of the wheel—the "traits" which are held together and influenced by the core. A description of each of these components is given in Box 18–1.

The degree of stability of the self-concept plays an important role in the degree of organization of the personality pattern. Lack of stability in the self-concept may come from many sources, the two most important of which are, *first*, conflicting self-concepts from the ways children are treated by significant people in their lives. If, for example, parents treat them one way and peers another way, it is hard for children to develop stable concepts of themselves. *Second*, instability may occur when there is a marked discrepancy between children's real self-concepts and their ideal self-concepts. When children see themselves as others see them and also as they would like to be, it is difficult for them to maintain a stable self-concept.

Because the self-concept is the core of the personal-

ity pattern, it influences the form the different traits will take. When the self-concept is positive, children develop such traits as self-confidence, self-esteem, and the ability to see themselves realistically. They can then assess their relationships with others accurately and this leads to good social adjustments. When, on the other hand, the self-concept is negative, children develop feelings of inadequacy and inferiority. They are uncertain and lack self-confidence. This leads to poor personal as well as social adjustments (14).

Development of the Personality Pattern

It was formerly believed that the personality pattern was the product of heredity and that the child was a "chip off the old block." Today, there is ample evidence that the personality pattern is a product of both heredity and environmental influences. As Thomas et al. have said, "Personality is shaped by the constant interplay of temperament and environment." They explain further that "if the two influences are harmonized, one can expect healthy development of the child: if they are dissonant, behavioral problems are almost sure to ensue" (93).

Studies of the development of the personality pattern have revealed that three factors are responsible for its development; hereditary endowment, early experiences within the family, and events in later life. The pattern is closely associated with the maturation of the physical and mental characteristics which constitute the individual's *hereditary endowment*. These characteristics provide the foundations on which the structure of the personality pattern is built through learning experiences.

Through *learning*, attitudes toward self and characteristic methods of responding to people and situations—the traits of personality—are acquired through repetition and the satisfaction they give. The early learning experiences are mainly in the home, and later learning experiences are in the different environments children come in contact with outside the home.

Children, for example, who learn to think of themselves as inferior, owing to the treatment they receive in the home or outside the home, develop characteristic methods of adjusting. These methods differ markedly from those of children who develop more favorable concepts of themselves as a result of more favorable treatment from members of the family, the peer group, and outsiders. Figure 18–2 shows some of the ways children learn to think of themselves as a result of the way they believe significant people in their lives think of them. If, for example, they think of themselves as "show-offs," as "imps," or as "featherbrains," their characteristic patterns of behaving and adjusting to life will be very different than they would be if they learned to think of themselves as "leaders," "loyal friends," and "scholars" (85).

Social pressures in the home, the school, and the peer group likewise influence the form the traits will take. When aggressiveness is encouraged because it is considered a sex-appropriate trait for boys, the boy will try to learn to behave in an aggressive manner.

Since the self-concept and the traits are developed differently, they will be discussed separately. It is necessary to keep in mind, however, that the three factors discussed above—hereditary endowment, early home experiences, and events in later life—all help to deter-

Figure 18–2. The concept of self determines the characteristic role the child learns to play. (*Adapted from H. G. Shane: Social experiences and selfhood. Childhood Education, 1957, 33, 297–298. Used by permission.*)

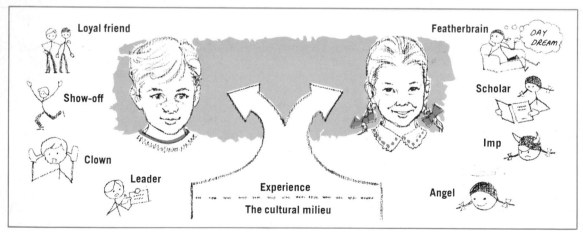

mine the pattern of development of both the self-concept and the traits.

DEVELOPMENT OF THE SELF-CONCEPT   Concepts of self, as was explained in Chapter 13, came from the contacts children have with people, how they treat children, what they say to and about children, and what status children have in the group with which they are identified. At first, the most significant people in children's lives are family members. As a result, their influence on the developing self-concept is dominant. Later, as peers and teachers become significant, their influence on the self-concept becomes greater and greater.

The role of the hereditary endowment in the development of the self-concept comes from the way children interpret the treatment they receive from others. As was explained in Chapter 9, social insight is greatly influenced by the individual's level of intelligence. Age for age, bright children can interpret better how people feel about them from what they say or do than can children who are less bright. Their interpretations of the feelings of others, in turn, determine whether they will develop favorable or unfavorable self-concepts (33, 52, 74).

By adolescence, the self-concept is firmly established, though it often is revised later as children have new personal and social experiences. Children, for example, who have developed concepts of themselves as outstanding athletes because they could play better than the other members of their gangs may have to revise their concepts radically when they reach high school and find that their sports skills are so inferior to those of their age-mates that they cannot make the athletic teams.

DEVELOPMENT OF TRAITS   Traits are a product of learning, though they are based on a hereditary foundation. They are molded mainly by child training in the home and school and by imitating a person with whom the child identifies. A child, for example, who identifies with the father will imitate the father's characteristic methods of reacting to people and situations to the point where it appears that the child has inherited these characteristics—that the child is, indeed, a "chip off the old block." Later, the child will imitate the traits of members of the peer group, developing the characteristic methods of adjustment accepted and approved by the peer group.

Some personality traits are learned by trial and error. If, for example, children learn more by chance than by imitation or direct teaching that aggressiveness in frustrating situations wins approval from the peer group and satisfies their needs, they will repeat the aggressive behavior whenever similar situations arise. In time, this will develop into their characteristic method of adjusting to frustration and they will be known as "aggressive children."

Not only do children develop personality traits that serve their needs but they also try to develop traits that are admired by members of the social group with which they are identified. They discover that people who have admired traits are more likely to win social approval and acceptance than those who have unadmired traits—traits that lead to criticism, scorn, and rejection.

Furthermore, children discover, as they grow older, that not all people value traits in the same way. Parents, teachers, and other adults, they discover, value certain traits more highly than members of the peer group and vice versa. They also discover that there are sex-approved and social-class-approved traits. In spite of these variations, children learn that certain basic traits are admired by all cultural groups. Honesty, respect for the rights of others, respect for authority, and a sense of appreciation, they discover, are universally approved.

As children grow older, their values change. As a result, the traits they admired when they were younger are often less admired as they approach adolescence and, later, adulthood (25). Figure 18-3 shows changes in values as children go from the early grades in elementary school into the adolescent years. Note that some traits that are highly valued by children are less highly valued by adolescents and vice versa.

As traits develop, they begin to organize into clusters, forming *syndromes*. Children who are subjected to strict authoritarian child training, for example, usually develop a rigidity in their characteristic pattern of adjustment or "authoritarian personality syndromes." They are inhibited, overcontrolled, introverted, withdrawn, conservative, and conventional. As a result of these characteristics, they are intolerant of change, irregularity, and things that are not clearly defined. They tend to be submissive to authority figures but aggressive toward all who are weaker than they are. Characteristically, they are anxious, guilt-prone, worry-prone, compulsively doubtful, insecure, rigidly

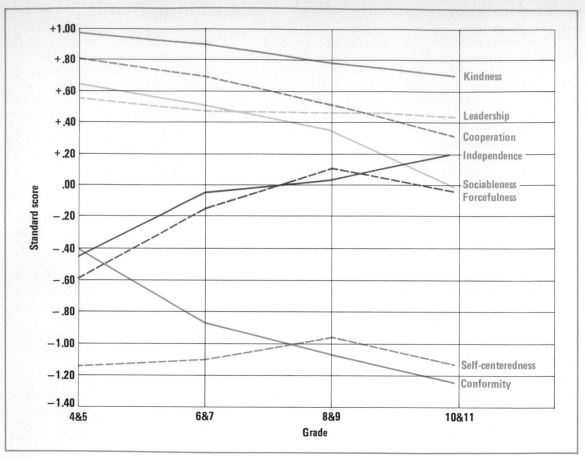

Figure 18–3. Changes in values as children grow older affect the traits they admire in others. (*Adapted from W. Emmerich: Developmental trends in evaluations of single traits.* Child Development, *1974, 45, 172–193. Used by permission.*)

Individuality

moral, and plagued by feelings of inadequacy and inferiority. These characteristics color all of their adjustments to life.

Each personality pattern is *unique* in that it varies in the combination and organization of the traits that constitute the pattern, in the strength of the different traits, and in the core of the pattern, the self-concept. Allport has referred to individuality as a "never-repeated phenomenon" and has emphasized that the "outstanding characteristic of man is his individuality" (3).

Individuality in personality means differences in *kind*, rather than differences in amount. Within the personality pattern are not only differences in the core but also differences in traits. Some traits may be *common* to large groups of people, such as truthfulness, generosity, and sociability, because they have been developed by similar child-training methods and similar environmental influences. Others are *unique* in that they are not found in others; they have developed from unusual combinations of hereditary qualities, personal experiences, and social environments.

Even common traits contain a unique element. As a result, *no two people have exactly the same trait in exactly the same degree.* Children, for example, may be generous because generosity is a highly valued trait in the culture in which they grow up. Nevertheless, they will express their generosity in their own individual ways and their expressions of it will be influenced by their uniquely developed self-concepts. To some children, generosity may be "good business"—a way to "buy popularity"—and to others it may be motivated by feelings that they owe society something and they are repaying their debt by helping those less fortunate than they are (31, 32).

Causes of Individuality

Recognition of individuality goes back at least as far as the ancient Greeks. Hippocrates referred to four different personality "types": The *sanguine,* or quick, active persons; the *choleric,* or strong and easily aroused persons; the *phlegmatic,* or slow and stolid type; and the *melancholic,* or sad and pessimistic individuals. The cause of the differences in personality patterns which gave each type an individuality, according to Hippocrates, was a difference in the strength of the body humors. Thus, according to him, individuality had a physical cause, though there is no evidence that Hippocrates considered this to be due to differences in heredity.

It is now believed that the foundation of personality comes from the maturation of hereditary traits but that these are influenced partly by learning in connection with direct social contacts and partly by conditioning. Because no two children, even identical twins, have exactly the same physical and mental endowments and the same environmental experiences, no two children will develop identical personality patterns. Instead, each child will be an individual.

Once a trait has been developed through environmental influences, it affects behavior as well as interests and attitudes. The trait is thus strengthened and made more resistant to change. However, in spite of environmental influences, each personality pattern has a tough core of traits. Because this gives an inner resistance, children react in their own individual manner to people and things in the environment. This increases their individuality.

Early Appearance of Individuality

Even at birth there is a clearly discernible individuality in the infant's characteristic adjustment to the new environment. This individuality is shown in responses to food, in motor activities, and in crying (23). Although individual responses may be due in part to hereditary differences, there is evidence that a disturbed prenatal environment, resulting from the mother's metabolic or emotional processes, may modify the infant's behavior patterns. The influence of the prenatal environment was discussed in detail in Chapter 3.

There is also evidence that parental attitudes toward the newborn infant affect their treatment of the infant. If, for example, parents are disappointed in the sex, the appearance, or the behavior of the infant, their reactions will be far less favorable than if their attitudes had been more acceptant. This leaves its mark on the infant's personality. Refer to Chapter 4 for a more complete discussion of parental attitudes on infant behavior.

When the infant's behavior, influenced by the conditions in the prenatal environment and parental attitudes, interferes with good postnatal adjustment on the infant's part, the infant will seem less "desirable" in the eyes of the parents. This will further influence their attitudes toward, and treatment of, the infant, thus reinforcing the unfavorable personality pattern the infant is starting to develop (2, 32). As Erikson has pointed out, this is the time when basic trust or distrust develops. Which is developed will determine how the infant will react to people and situations not only then but throughout life (26).

By the time babies are several months old, they begin to respond to people. How these people treat them will have a profound influence on the self-concepts they are developing and their characteristic ways of adjusting to people (37, 81, 99).

Since no two individuals have the same social environments, even if they have the same physical environments, they tend to exhibit increasingly different personality patterns as they grow older. As the social environment expands as children grow older, there are more influences that produce differences in their personality patterns, thus increasing their individuality.

Among young children, Thomas et al. have identified three common personality syndromes, and within each they found individual differences. These syndromes they labeled "easy children," those who are well adjusted both physically and psychologically; "difficult children," those who are irregular in bodily functions, intense in their reactions, and slow to adapt to change; and "slow-to-warm-up children," those who have a low activity level and are slow in their ability to adapt to new situations (93). Among first graders, it has been reported, various personality types can be distinguished. Some children are helpers who can look out for other children; some are leaders who have sufficient initiative to make suggestions and attract followers; some are maternal; some are despotic; some like to joke and make fun of others; some are inveterate show-offs; some are much-loved favorites; and some are solitary and withdrawn (89).

Persistence in Personality

The term *persistence* means "enduring" and "constantly recurring"; *it does not mean that no change occurs*. It does mean, however, that there is a tendency for certain traits to remain in an unchanged, or relatively unchanged, form, even when training and social pressure have been operative. As Allport has stressed, the "important fact about personality is its relatively enduring and unique organization" (3).

For example, children who, as infants, showed irritability will show the same trait as they grow older, even though their irritability may be somewhat modified and toned down as a result of environmental pressures. Children who have been waited on by parents and other family members often develop a weak achievement-striving drive. As a result, they develop the habit of working below their capacities and become underachievers in whatever they do. Unless environmental conditions or personal pride provide them with the necessary motivation to make the most of their innate potentials, their tendency to underachieve will become persistent.

The reason for persistence in the personality pattern is that the core of the pattern—the self-concept—remains fundamentally the same. This preserves the balance of traits within the pattern. Once the core of the pattern is fixed, it does not change unless radical steps are taken to produce such a change.

In young children, the core of personality is not well established. It can therefore be changed without disturbing the total personality balance. But the personality becomes less flexible as the person grows older, because of the larger and more fixed core of habits and attitudes, and any change will require a great deal of effort and pressure. Also, care will have to be taken to avoid disturbing the personality balance.

Figure 18–4. A girl who learns to be bossy as a result of playing the surrogate-parent role in childhood tends to develop into a bossy woman.

Causes of Persistence

According to popular beliefs, based on the assumption that personality is largely a hereditary characteristic, the personality pattern persists in a relatively unchanged form throughout life. Any change that does occur, it was believed, was the result of physical changes, especially at the time of puberty and in old age. Today, with the acceptance of evidence that environment plays an important role in determining what the personality pattern will be, environmental conditions are believed to be mainly responsible for persistence.

Many conditions are responsible for persistence in the personality pattern. It is important to know what they are, not only to understand why persistence is so common, but from a practical view, to understand why changing the personality becomes increasingly difficult. Some of the conditions contributing to persistence in the personality pattern are shown in Box 18-2.

Evidence of Persistence

Mention of persistence of personality traits was made in some early baby biographies. In recent years, genetic studies of groups of children over a period have emphasized the persistence of personality patterns and have shown under what conditions changes occur. They have shown that although traits vary from year to year within a narrow range, they remain fairly consistent. There is also evidence from these studies that no child remains *absolutely* consistent with respect to predominant forms of behavior; nor are there any revolutionary changes. On the other hand, shifts are almost always in the direction of behavior that has been evident earlier, though not necessarily in a pronounced form (6, 12, 49, 58, 71).

Studies of Terman's gifted group, in a follow-up 50 years after the study was inaugurated, have shown a tendency toward persistence in the characteristic methods of adjusting to life by the members of this group (65). As was stressed in the chapter on sex-role development, the personality patterns developed in the process of sex-role typing in childhood persist into the adult years and influence the way men and women adjust to life in adulthood just as they influence their adjustments during the childhood years.

Because of the traditional belief that marked personality changes occur when the puberty changes take place, it is important to determine whether they actu-

---

BOX 18-2

CONDITIONS CONTRIBUTING TO PERSONALITY PERSISTENCE

HEREDITY
A trait that is related, either directly or indirectly, to the child's hereditary endowment will be more stable than a trait that has little relationship to heredity.

CHILD TRAINING
The method of child training and the attitudes of the person who uses it remain relatively stable; this reinforces the developing self-concept and the child's characteristic pattern of adjustment.

PARENTAL VALUES
Personality traits that parents value highly are reinforced by parental rewards, while traits that are not valued are extinguished by punishment or lack of reward.

ROLE PLAYING
The role children learn to play in the home influences their self-concepts. Because this role playing tends to be persistent during the childhood years, the effect on the self-concept will be persistent. See Figure 18-4.

SOCIAL ENVIRONMENT
Since children see themselves as others see them, this reinforces the developing self-concept and the characteristic method of adjustment. Later changes in the social environment may not be adequate to change the personality pattern.

SELECTION IN THE SOCIAL ENVIRONMENT
The child's personality or some dominant trait in it determines the selection of the social environment. Through constant association with people in that environment, the child's self-concept and characteristic patterns of adjustment will be reinforced.

---

ally do occur or not. Genetic studies have shown that, even in late adolescence and early adulthood, some fluctuations in traits do occur but, for the most part, early patterns are maintained. In general, undesirable traits tend to be less undesirable because of the adolescent's strong desire to conform to socially approved patterns (66).

When changes do occur in the personality pattern as a result of environmental conditions, they tend to be persistent. Studies of early- and late-maturing boys show that the personality patterns, influenced by the treatment the boys received from adults and peers because of their physical status at puberty, persisted into the early thirties. Those who matured early were, as young men, responsible, enterprising, sociable, warm, persistent in working toward a goal, self-controlled, dominant, and able to create confidence in others. These characteristics were similar to those they had shown in adolescence. By contrast, the men who matured late were touchy, rebellious, impulsive, self-indulgent, and assertive; they sought encouragement and help until a fuss was made over them whenever they were hurt. In general, their behavior was a carry-over of the "little-boy behavior" of their adolescent years (47).

Studies of maladjusted people reveal that unusual behavior in childhood is often a precursor of personality disturbances in adulthood. Records of patients in mental hospitals show that the personality characteristics of psychotic patients have been stable since childhood. Those who are excitable as adults have been excitable since childhood, and those who are schizophrenic have been apathetic since they were young children. In short, childhood schizophrenics tend to grow up to be adult schizophrenics, although the clinical manifestations and their intensity may change (35, 66).

Children who are problem children often grow up to be juvenile delinquents and adult criminals. Those who are so poorly adjusted that they are problems in school and in the home contribute a disproportionate share to such serious social problems as crime, homicide, and suicide (36).

Significance of Persistence

Difficult as it is to determine how persistent the personality pattern is and when, how, or how much it can be changed, an understanding of persistence is needed for several practical reasons. The four most significant are described below.

First, if the personality pattern is persistent, good foundations which can guarantee reasonably good adjustment throughout life must be laid early. This can best be achieved by guidance to ensure that a favorable self-concept will be developed and that socially acceptable methods of adjusting to people and situations will be learned and reinforced through repeated experiences.

Second, symptoms of maladjustment can be recognized and the maladjustments corrected as soon as they appear. Since there is little evidence that changes occur of their own accord or that they will be changes for the better, the sooner they are made, the easier they are and the more likely they are to persist.

Third, the personality pattern influences the kind of adjustment the child makes rather than vice versa. There is substantial evidence that the children who make good adjustments have well-integrated personality patterns in which the core is a stable, realistic self-concept, while those who make poor adjustments have poorly integrated personalities with unstable and unrealistic self-concepts.

Fourth, since the personality pattern becomes increasingly stable with the passage of time, it is possible to predict early in childhood what sort of person the child will be in adolescence and adulthood.

Change in Personality

To "change" means to "alter" or to "vary"; it does not necessarily mean that the alteration or change will be complete. There is evidence that both the self-concept and traits do change. However, in the case of traits, the changes may be qualitative or quantitative. In qualitative changes, a socially undesirable trait may be replaced by one that is socially admired. In quantitative changes, there is a strengthening or weakening of an already present trait. Quantitative changes, for the most part, are more common than qualitative changes. As Thomas et al. have explained, "A child's temperament is not immutable. In the course of his development, the environmental circumstances may heighten, diminish or otherwise modify his reactions and behavior" (93).

Changes in the characteristic method of adjusting to people and situations may suggest that greater changes in the personality pattern have occurred than is actually true. These may be only "fronts." Children, for example, may modify their behavior in response to social pressures in the hopes of winning greater social approval and of avoiding social disapproval. But, when the social pressures are not present, they may revert to their former patterns of behavior. It is not unusual, for example, for aggressive children to curb their aggressiveness when it becomes apparent to them that their aggressiveness is leading to unfavorable social reactions. But, in circumstances where social disapproval is not present, they often revert to their former aggressiveness (1, 24).

The core of the personality pattern, the self-concept, is relatively stable and changes only when children perceive changes in the attitudes and treatment of people who are significant to them. An increase in skills that are important to members of the peer group, for example, may lead to more favorable social attitudes and acceptance (57).

Changes in personality—whether in traits or in the self-concept—are more frequent and more pronounced in younger children than in older children and adolescents, and very much more frequent than in adults. The reason for this is that, as time goes on, the core of the personality pattern becomes less and less flexible. Changing the self-concept in older children is more difficult than it is when they are younger. Unless this is done, there can be no real change in the personality pattern.

Causes of Change

According to tradition, changes in personality are due to physical changes. At puberty, for example, there is the change from a childish to an adult body. Because this physical change is regarded as an improvement, the traditional belief maintains that there will be an improvement in personality also. By contrast, the physical changes occurring at the time of the climacteric and with advancing age are regarded as forms of deterioration. The personality changes that are believed to accompany these physical changes are assumed to be changes for the worse.

When these traditional beliefs are accepted, parents and other adults who are responsible for the training of children believe that changes for the better will automatically occur as children grow older. Children who are selfish, or aggressive, or shy, for example, will, it is assumed, outgrow these undesirable traits at puberty. Consequently, they do little or nothing to change these traits which are proving to be stumbling blocks to social adjustments.

It is now recognized that changes in personality do *not* occur spontaneously. Instead, they are the result of advancing maturity, experience, pressures from the social and cultural environment, and factors within the individual, such as emotional pressures or identification with another person. If the desire for social acceptance is strong enough, the child will try to replace undesirable traits with those that are more likely to lead

BOX 18–3

CONDITIONS CONTRIBUTING TO
PERSONALITY CHANGE

PHYSICAL CHANGES
Physical changes, resulting from maturation, structural disturbances in the brain, organic disorders, endocrine disorders, injuries, malnutrition, drugs, or illness, are often accompanied by personality changes. The effects are mainly on the child's self-concept.

ENVIRONMENTAL CHANGES
When changes in the environment improve the child's status in the peer group, it has a favorable effect on the self-concept. The effect comes not from environmental changes per se but from the effect the change has on the child.

SOCIAL PRESSURES
The stronger the drive for social acceptance, the more the child will try to develop personality traits that conform to socially approved patterns.

INCREASE IN COMPETENCE
Increase in competence, either in motor or mental skills, has a favorable effect on the self-concept because of the social recognition this increase in competence brings. It helps the child to change from feelings of inadequacy to feelings of adequacy and even of superiority.

ROLE CHANGES
Change from a subordinate to an egalitarian or leadership role in the home, school, or neighborhood will improve the child's self-concept. A change in the reverse order will damage it.

PROFESSIONAL HELP
Psychotherapy helps children to develop more favorable self-concepts by helping them to gain insight into the causes of their unfavorable self-concepts and by helping them to change these unfavorable self-concepts to those that are more favorable.

to social approval and acceptance. This is done by learning, not by maturation.

When changes in the personality pattern do occur, they are usually not due to one factor or one condition. Instead, they are usually brought about by the interaction of two or more factors. In Box 18–3 are given the most important conditions that are known to contribute to personality change (3, 9, 47, 49, 57, 71).

Cautions in Personality Change

From a practical as well as from a theoretical angle, it is important to know just how much change there actually is and when the changes can best be made, should it become apparent that they are needed to improve a child's personal and social adjustments. Studies of personality changes have given some clues about this matter.

There is evidence that in every personality pattern there is a point of fixity beyond which changes cannot be made without upsetting the balance of the entire pattern. These limits of change may vary from one person to another and from one age to another in the same person, but the limit exists and must be recognized if disturbance to the entire pattern is to be avoided. Furthermore, some areas of the personality are more easily changed than others, and some may be so rigid that change is impossible. These differences in flexibility come partly as a result of life experiences.

Some children are more susceptible to guidance and more responsive to efforts to change their personality patterns than others. Children who are voluntary isolates, for example, may prefer to be so because they have not found congeniality in the children available for them to play with. Unless they can see the advantages to them, personally, of becoming social, they will resist the change.

Changing one or two personality traits that are distinct social handicaps to a child is one thing, but trying to revamp the entire personality pattern is quite a different matter. Trying to revamp the personality pattern can be done only when there is a radical change in the core of the pattern, the self-concept.

Equally serious is any attempt to bring about quick changes in the personality pattern. Sudden changes in personality are one of the criteria used to diagnose mental illness. They are not characteristically found in normal people. Any attempt to revamp the personality pattern too quickly may result in emotional disturbances that will be reflected in personality maladjustments. By contrast, slow and gradual changes can be made without the danger of bringing about maladjustments, provided the emphasis is on change in the self-concept rather than the different traits of the personality pattern (3, 71, 91).

Some Important Personality Determinants

Some of the determinants of personality have their greatest effect on the core of the personality pattern, the self-concept, and some of the traits related to the core. No determinant, however, affects just one part of the personality pattern. For example, a physical defect affects not only the child's characteristic pattern of adjustment to life but also the core of the personality pattern; it influences the child's concept of self as a person in comparison with other members of the peer group.

How much influence different factors will have on personality development will depend to a large extent upon children's ability to understand the significance of the factors in relation to themselves. If, for example, their appearance is such that others admire it, appearance will be a favorable factor in personality development. If, on the other hand, children are aware that others do not admire their looks, appearance will be a liability to personality development.

The analysis of the determinants of personality in the following pages covers only those which most commonly affect American children today. Figure 18–5 shows some of the determinants that influence the child's self-concept and, through it, the child's characteristic pattern of adjustment.

Early Experiences

The importance of early experiences to personality development was first stressed by Freud, who found that many of his adult patients had had unhappy childhood experiences (29). Following in Freud's footsteps, Rank claimed that the "birth trauma," or the psychological shock that results when the infant is separated from the mother, has a lasting effect on personality by making the individual feel insecure (77).

Studies of the effects of early experiences have shown that these experiences and the memories of them, even though vague, are highly influential because they leave an indelible impression on the child's self-concept. There is, however, no convincing evidence that the individual's personality reflects the kind of care given during babyhood. That is, there is no definite evidence that breast feeding or late toilet training is better than bottle feeding or early toilet training so far as the personality pattern is concerned. Nor is there

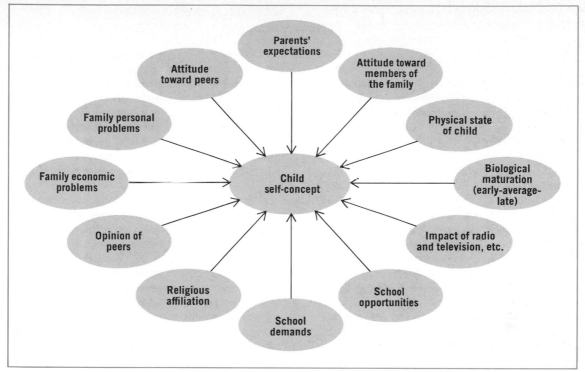

Figure 18–5. The impact of environmental influences on the developing self-concept in childhood. (*Adapted from L. D. Crow and A. Crow:* Child development and adjustment. *Macmillan, 1962, Used by permission.*)

any definite evidence that the effects of these early experiences carry into the adult years.

On the other hand, there is ample evidence that the attitude and emotional reactions of parents, the total cultural context of the environment in which the child grows up, and other factors in the child's total experience are of great importance in determining the pattern of personality. Only when parents' attitudes make the child feel anxious and guilty in relation to training or eating will there be any real effect on the child's personality (4, 6).

Cultural Influences

It has been said that you can take children away from their culture but you cannot take the culture away from children. In every culture, children are subjected to pressure to develop a personality pattern that will conform to the standards set by the culture.

The cultural group to which children's parents belong sets the model for the approved personality pattern. Through child training in the home and school, children are expected to adopt this pattern as a model for their own personalities. The way children are brought up, thus, is responsible for the kind of personality patterns they develop. As they grow older, pressures from the peer group and from the adult social group outside the home supplement family and school pressures. From all these, children learn to behave in a way that is socially approved in their culture.

In a cultural group, for example, that puts strong pressures on children to conform to approved stereotypes of sex appropriateness, how closely they conform to these cultural expectations will influence their self-concepts and, in turn, their patterns of adjustment. As Inselberg and Burke have pointed out, as early as the late preschool years, "appropriate sex-role identification in boys is associated with favorable personality characteristics" (44).

In many cultures in foreign countries, children are

trained to be family-oriented. As a result, they develop personality patterns characterized by loyalty, cooperation, self-sacrifice, and often unrealistic concepts of themselves and their roles in life. In cultures that are more individual-oriented, as is true of American culture today, children become more egocentric, more concerned about their independence and rights, and more anxious to help themselves than others.

Physique

Physique, or body build, influences personality both directly and indirectly. *Directly,* it determines what children can and cannot do. *Indirectly,* it determines how children feel about their bodies. This, in turn, is influenced by how significant people in their lives feel about them (61).

Children who are markedly overweight, for example, are not affected by their obesity until they become aware of the fact that people regard overweight as ugly (60, 73, 96). When children become aware of the respect and prestige associated with being tall, it affects the self-concepts of those who are taller than their age-mates favorably (40).

Every cultural group has its own standards of what is "right" or appropriate for boys and girls. Extremes are regarded as "wrong." If a short, frail boy is in a group of children of his own size and build, size will have no effect on his concept of self. Only when the variation from the *norm of his own group* is great enough to be noticed by others will it affect him.

At an early age, children become aware of any marked deviation from the group norm because of the effect it has on their social relationships. Nicknames that imply physical differences, such as "Fatty," "Skinny," or "Skyscraper," show how other children feel about these differences. Because being different makes children feel inferior, it affects their personalities.

Children who are markedly different from their age-mates in physique often develop some compensatory behavior, such as clowning and showing off. This leads to unfavorable social reactions that reinforce the unfavorable social reactions to their physiques.

Even when the deviation from the group norm is only temporary—fat children may lose weight or tall children may find that age-mates catch up to them when they begin their puberty growth spurts—the unfavorable effects on their personalities may persist long after these deviations have disappeared. As a re-

sult, the poor personal and social adjustments caused by an unfavorable self-concept will persist because the unfavorable self-concept, once developed, has become persistent.

Physical Condition

There are two aspects of children's physical conditions that affect their personalities—general health and physical defects. Not only does good *health* enable children to engage in the normal activities of their age groups but it also has a favorable effect on their personalities. The attitude of the family and of the social group is much more favorable toward healthy children than toward those who are sickly. This is certain to influence their self-concepts favorably. Furthermore, children who are delicate and sickly come to expect the consideration from other people that they have been accustomed to at home and they react unfavorably when they do not receive it. In addition, because they cannot engage in the activities of their healthier age-mates, they develop feelings of inferiority and martyrdom (69). How the most common physical conditions of children affect their personalities is shown in Box 18-4.

How *physical defects* affect personality depends on two conditions: the activities children can engage in, and the attitudes of others toward them because of their defects. The more different the defects make children from their age-mates, the greater will be their beliefs of their inferiority, inadequacy, and martyrdom.

Normally, as children grow older, they have a more sympathetic attitude toward those with physical defects than they had when they were younger. This more favorable attitude is reflected in a more favorable attitude toward those with defects. However, if the defect is serious enough to necessitate the removal of children from the regular school classroom and putting them in special classes for the handicapped, the more favorable treatment of their peers may be counteracted by feelings of inferiority on the part of the handicapped children (78).

Attractiveness

At all ages, social attitudes are more favorable toward people who are judged "attractive" than toward those who are judged unattractive or actually ugly. These judgments may be based on physical features, body build, clothing that is stylish and becoming, or becoming hair styles. Furthermore, it is assumed that those who are attractive have more desirable personality characteristics than those who are unattractive. This reinforces favorable social attitudes toward them (16, 53, 96).

Favorable social attitudes toward attractive children are not limited to one segment of the social group but they permeate all segments. In the home, parents and other relatives tend to react more favorably toward children who are attractive than toward those who are less attractive and are more lenient toward them when they misbehave. The same is true of teachers. It has been reported that teachers not only give better grades to attractive children than they actually deserve but they are, like parents, more lenient in their attitudes toward them when they misbehave (16). Among peers, attractive children are more popular than unattractive, and they are more often selected for leadership roles.

At an early age, attractive children sense these favorable social attitudes toward them and this influences their self-concepts favorably. As a result, they are more self-confident, more relaxed, and more friendly and gracious than are children who are less attractive (22).

However, just because attractiveness of appearance leads to favorable personality characteristics, it does not mean that the more attractive children are the more favorable their personalities will be. Too attractive children may and often are the targets of envy and jealousy among their peers. This is true both in the home and outside the home. When this happens, they are treated with discrimination and sometimes even rejection by their peers. This unfavorable social treatment is increased if attractive children become conceited and show it by their attitudes toward, and treatment of, their peers. Because peer acceptance means so much to children, those who are rejected or neglected, regardless of the cause, develop unfavorable self-concepts that are reflected in unfavorable patterns of behavior (19).

Intelligence

Except when there is a marked deviation from the norm, young children are not aware of what their intellectual level is. The bright, for example, do not realize how bright they are, the dull are unaware of their dullness, and the average take their intelligence for granted. After they enter school, children measure

<hr>

BOX 18–4

PHYSICAL CONDITIONS
AFFECTING PERSONALITY

FATIGUE
Fatigue causes the child to be irritable and quarrelsome, thus affecting reactions to people and theirs to the child.

MALNUTRITION
Malnutrition results in a low energy level which is shown in shyness, irritability, depression, and unsocial behavior.

IRRITATING PHYSICAL CONDITION
A physical irritation, such as hives or eczema, leads to emotional overreactions.

CHRONIC DISEASE
Such chronic diseases as allergies and diabetes cause emotional instability, strong negative emotions, and emotional dependence on family members.

ENDOCRINE GLANDS
Of all the glands in the endocrine system, the thyroids have the greatest effect on personality. A hyperthyroid condition makes the child nervous, excited, jumpy, restless, and overactive. A hypothyroid condition makes a child lethargic, unresponsive, depressed, dissatisfied, and distrustful.

<hr>

their level of intellectual development by the kind of adjustment they make to schoolwork.

How a child feels about being intellectually different is greatly influenced by social attitudes, especially those of parents, teachers, and members of the peer group. Attitudes toward *brightness,* for example, differ from one school to another and, within a school, according to whether the bright children are popular or unpopular. The more superior the intelligence of the child, the less favorable the social attitudes tend to be.

Adults—both parents and teachers—often have unrealistically high expectations for very bright children. When children accept these expectations as their own, they feel inadequate when they do not live up to them. Furthermore, they are often regarded as "threats" by their peers. The reason for this is that they may raise the standard of work in the class and make teachers expect more of all students. This tends to make very bright children unpopular with their class-mates. If, in addition, they become conceited about their brightness, this further increases their unpopu-larity. As a result, many very bright children develop unfavorable self-concepts (7, 95).

Another condition that increases very bright chil-dren's poor social acceptance is the fact that children of average intelligence often feel uncomfortable when they are with very bright children because they seem "stupid" by comparison. And, as the cultural stereo-type maintains that very bright people are "odd," there is a tendency to be hypercritical or suspicious of every-thing very bright children say or do. This unfavorable social attitude has an unfavorable effect on these chil-dren's self-concepts.

Furthermore, awareness of the fact that they are considered "different"—which is usually interpreted by children to mean "inferior"—tends to make very bright children uneasy in the presence of members of the peer group. This, in turn, makes them feel inade-quate in social relationships and reinforces the popu-lar belief that they are "different" if not "inferior."

Children whose intelligence is definitely *below* that of other children of the same age usually find them-selves as outsiders in the peer group. Their interests as well as their abilities are different from those of their age-mates and this leads to feelings of inadequacy. Because of their narrow social experiences, owing to lack of social acceptance by peers, dull children tend to have poor social insight. This further impairs their social adjustments and adds to their social rejection. Fortunately, dullness does not damage the personality pattern as much as one might anticipate. The reason for this is that most dull children lack the social in-sight to realize how unfavorable social attitudes toward them are (38).

Emotions

Frequent, intense, and apparently unjustified emo-tional outbursts lead others to judge the individual as "immature." Suppression of emotional expressions results in moodiness, which tends to make the individ-ual rude, uncooperative, and preoccupied with self. Heightened emotionality, even when the expressions are controlled, tends to make one nervous and ill at ease; it is often accompanied by specific mannerisms, such as nail-biting or giggling, which create the impression that the person is silly or immature. Height-ened emotionality is especially common among prepu-bescent girls at the time of the menstrual period (55).

People tend to judge children favorably when they keep their emotions under control. They also consider some forms of emotional expression more acceptable than others. "Picking on others," for example, is usually more acceptable than moodiness, just as gen-eral jitteriness tends to be less readily tolerated than nervous mannerisms.

How children's emotions affect their self-concepts is greatly influenced by how they affect the judgments others make of them. This is an *indirect* effect of emo-tions on personality. The *direct* effect, though often less noticeable than the indirect effect, is too great to go unnoticed. When emotions are so strong that behavior becomes disorganized, they will adversely af-fect children's characteristic patterns of adjustment. By so doing, they have a profound effect on their per-sonalities by leading to unfavorable self-concepts (1, 24).

Names

A name, per se, has little effect on the self-concept. Its influence is felt only when children realize how it af-fects significant people in their lives. When children start to play with other children, around the third year, they begin to realize how important their names are. Each year thereafter, their names have an increasingly greater influence on their self-concepts.

The names by which children are called color the first judgments others make of them. This is usually the first or given name. If this name elicits pleasant associations in the minds of others, they will treat the bearers of these names well and this will have a favor-able effect on their self-concepts. The reverse is true when a name elicits unpleasant associations.

The effect of names does not end with first associa-tions. In fact, the effect may and often does become greater with repetition. As a result, names have a marked influence on children's social relationships, especially with members of the peer group.

As was pointed out in Chapter 15, in the discussion of children's interest in names, children have reasons for liking or disliking their names. Their reactions to their names are emotionally weighted because they re-flect how others feel about their names. If others like their names—or if children *believe* that others like their names—it will have a favorable effect on their self-concepts. On the other hand, if they suspect or have reason to believe that others react unfavorably to their names, it will have a damaging effect on their self-concepts.

Nicknames and pet names, which often are used as frequently as given names in addressing children, also have a profound effect on their personalities. In fact, because nicknames are often forms of ridicule, their effect on the self-concept is even greater than the given names. So long as pet names are reserved for home use, their effect is more likely to be favorable than unfavorable. They suggest to the bearers that they are loved and accepted by family members. But, if used in front of members of the peer group, or if members of the peer group pick up these pet names and use them as a form of ridicule, their effects on children's self-concepts will be very damaging.

Only as children grow older and are called by family names will these names begin to have an effect on their personalities. Should family names be associated with religious or racial groups against which there is prejudice, peer reactions to them will be unfavorable. As such, their effects on children's self-concepts will be unfavorable. Another way in which family names can be a source of unfavorable effect on the self-concept is when children's family names differ from those of their parents. As was pointed out in the discussion of reconstituted families, the child whose mother remarries after the death or divorce of the child's father is often embarrassed about a family name that differs from that of the parents.

Success and Failure

The self-concept is greatly influenced by whether children regard themselves as successes or failures. They may be "successes" in the eyes of others but "failures" in their own eyes. This means that a person who is *objectively* a success can be, *subjectively*, a failure. This is because the person's achievements have come up to the expectations of others but have fallen short of the person's own expectations.

How children react to what they regard as their successes and failures influences their personal and social adjustments. This, in turn, has a marked effect on their self-concepts. Although different children react differently to success and failure, it has been reported that there are certain common reactions among all children. These are shown in Box 18–5 (30, 47, 57, 70, 83). In general, reactions to failure are more varied than reactions to success.

Failure not only damages the self-concept but it encourages the development of patterns of behavior that are harmful to personal and social adjustments. These harmful effects come from children's realization

---

BOX 18–5

EFFECTS OF SUCCESS AND FAILURE ON PERSONALITY

SUCCESS
- Makes children proud and self-satisfied
- If too easy and too frequent, makes children conceited and arrogant
- Makes children satisfied with their achievements
- Increases children's motivation and efforts for future successes
- If too easy and too frequent, decreases motivation and effort
- Makes children willing to help others
- Encourages children to seek new challenges
- Encourages children to be boastful
- Encourages children to be independent of help
- Helps to build up self-confidence
- If too easy and too frequent, leads to overconfidence and inability to face stiff competition later
- Makes children cheerful and happy

FAILURE
- Encourages children to lower their aspirations to realistic levels
- Makes children unsure of their abilities
- Contributes to feelings of inadequacy and inferiority
- If frequent or severe, leads to a "failure complex"
- Makes impulsive children more cautious
- Makes children embarrassed and self-conscious
- Encourages children to seek advice and help
- Encourages children to shun future threat situations
- Weakens children's motivation and willingness to expend effort
- Encourages children to rationalize the cause of their failures
- Encourages children to project the cause of failure on others.
- Is often expressed in angry outbursts and destruction of property.
- Makes children gloomy, depressed, and unhappy

---

of the unfavorable evaluations of others as well as from their own self-evaluations.

By contrast, *success* leads to favorable self-concepts which, in turn, lead to good personal adjustments and favorable social evaluations. These contribute heavily to good future adjustments. As Isen et al. have explained, "The warm glow generated by success increases our optimism in general and our affection for others, such that we are more willing to give them more of our prized possessions" (45).

However, it cannot be assumed that the more successes children have, the more favorable the effects on their personalities. Too many successes can and often do make children conceited and cocky in their attitudes as well as intolerant toward those who are less successful than they are. In time, this will lead to unfavorable social evaluations which will have a damaging effect on the self-concepts of those who normally would receive favorable social evaluations because of their successes.

As pointed out in Box 18–5, if success is too easy and too frequent, the good effects which harder-won success brings will be lost. For that reason, the child's environment should be controlled so that this will not happen. Control of the environment should take two forms. *First,* failure should be avoided, if possible, in the early years while the self-concept is in the formative stage. If children do experience failure at this time, control of the environment should make it possible for them to achieve several successes immediately after the failure so as to wipe out some of its psychological damage before it undermines their self-confidence. *Second,* severe failures that undermine self-confidence should be avoided. When this is impossible, some of the psychological damage of the failure can be counteracted by explaining to children why they failed, by avoiding all suggestions that they are to blame for the failure, and by following the failure as quickly as possible with successes great enough to convince the children that they are not "failures."

Social Acceptance

Social acceptance influences every child's desire to develop socially approved personality *traits* and it affects the self-concept favorably. Since young children are anxious to have the approval of their parents, they try to develop personality traits that will please them. After they enter school, the approval of the peer group becomes even more important than parental approval. Children then try to develop personality traits which their peers admire, even though they may not be admired by their parents.

Social acceptance plays a large role in the development of the *self-concept.* Children who are accepted in the social group or who, from time to time, fill positions of leadership develop self-confidence and poise. Children who are friendly and self-confident, in turn, win more friends; as their popularity increases, their poise, self-assurance, and leadership qualities also grow stronger.

By contrast, unpopular children feel inferior; they are envious of their more popular age-mates; they resent being left out of the play activities their age-mates enjoy; and they are sullen, irritable, and ready to fly off the handle at the slightest provocation. Many feel that they are being martyred by their age-mates. These reactions, naturally, do not help them to develop the personality traits that will improve their acceptance.

Children who enjoy marginal acceptance, the "fringers," or those who hope to improve their acceptance, the "climbers," show a degree of tension and often seem awed. They acquiesce to the popular children, try to impress them by showing off or boasting, or they agree impetuously with whatever they suggest. Children who are overlooked or ignored by age-mates, the "neglectees," resent the treatment they receive, feel martyred, and often develop a resentful attitude not only toward those who neglect them but also toward people in general. In addition, they often withdraw from social contacts and develop the shut-in characteristics of introverts (15, 17, 68, 79, 80, 82). Refer to Chapter 10 for a more detailed discussion of levels of social acceptance and their effects on children's personal and social adjustments.

Status Symbols

Before status symbols can affect the personality through their effect on the self-concept, children must become aware of the symbols that are valued by the social group with which they are identified and must realize that they are judged in terms of the status symbols they and their families possess. This realization begins to occur when children spend more time with members of the peer group than with the family group and when they become members of a gang.

Of all the status symbols that are of interest to children (refer to Chapter 15 for a discussion of status symbols), none has a more important effect on personality than clothes. As Bickman has pointed out, although clothes "may seem to be superficial qualities, they are important determinants of one person's reaction to another" (10).

The reason that clothes, of all status symbols, have such a profound effect on personality is that they are an ever-present manifestation of their status. Not only do clothes tell, indirectly, the socioeconomic status of the family, but they tell, directly, the status of children in the peer group (42, 59, 95).

Children whose families are able to provide the clothes and material possessions that give them prestige in the peer group usually develop better self-concepts and thus more wholesome personalities than children whose parents cannot make such provisions for them. If children fail to gain social acceptance, they are likely to project the blame on their parents who have not provided the status symbols that the peer group values. They complain about their own lot, envy the lot of others, and tell others how lucky they are. Self-pity makes children unpopular because it makes others uncomfortable and it makes the children themselves unhappy. It is thus a handicap to good personal and social adjustments.

Some children, when deprived of the status symbols that their age-mates have, defensively criticize or ridi-cule these status symbols. Children who use this defense mechanism develop unwholesome self-concepts and behave in a manner that will ensure poor social acceptance. By doing so, they damage their personalities both directly and indirectly.

School Influences

The school influences the child's developing personality both in the area of traits and in formation of the self-concept. A careful study of the major areas of influence, given in Box 18–6, will reveal the direct and indirect influence of teachers. Their influence on the child's personality is second only to that of the parents, just as the influence of the schoolroom is second only to that of the home.

Because of the profound influence teachers have on personality development, teachers' personalities are

---

BOX 18–6

SCHOOL INFLUENCES ON PERSONALITY

EMOTIONAL CLIMATE OF THE CLASSROOM
A healthy emotional climate makes the child relaxed, cooperative, happy, and motivated to study and to conform to rules. An unhealthy emotional climate makes the child tense, nervous, irritable, quarrelsome, hypercritical, disinterested in studying, and prone to troublesome behavior. The emotional climate is due mainly to the attitude of teachers toward their work and their pupils, the kind of discipline used, and the efforts of teachers to make schoolwork interesting and stimulating.

TEACHERS
Directly, teachers affect children's self-concepts by their attitudes toward academic work and school behavior and their interest in their pupils. Indirectly, their influence comes from helping children to develop socially approved patterns of adjustment.

DISCIPLINE
The discipline used in the school affects the child's attitudes and behavior. Authoritarian discipline makes the child tense, nervous, resentful, and antagonistic; permissive discipline leads to lack of responsibility, lack of respect for authority, and egocentrism; democratic discipline gives children a feeling of self-worth and encour-ages them to be happy, relaxed, cooperative, trustworthy, and fair.

TRANSMITTER OF CULTURAL VALUES
The school is more important than the home in seeing to it that the child accepts the cultural values as a price for social acceptance.

FAVORITISM
The teacher's favorite becomes conceited, arrogant, and self-centered. Nonfavorites become resentful, antagonistic, troublesome, hypercritical of school, and plagued by feelings of martyrdom.

ACADEMIC ACHIEVEMENT
Grade placement—whether in a "slow" or "fast" section—promotion, and marks are the criteria by which children assess their academic achievement. Success is ego-inflating; failure is ego-deflating.

SOCIAL ACHIEVEMENT
The child measures social achievement in terms of social acceptance and the holding of leadership roles. The more value the school places on extracurricular achievements, the more influence these criteria of achievement have on the child's self-concept.

more important than their knowledge or teaching skills. Well-adjusted teachers, for example, are usually warm and acceptant in their attitudes toward their pupils. As a result, they not only motivate them to do good work and to conform to the rules and regulations of the school but they also help them to develop both favorable and realistic self-concepts.

Poorly adjusted teachers, by contrast, set a model of poorly adjusted behavior which many pupils imitate. They also deal with the school situation and with pupils in such a way that the pupils feel inadequate, resentful, and antagonistic not only toward their teachers but also, in time, toward all in authority. Under the influence of such teachers, any undesirable "home-grown" personality traits are likely to become more pronounced and persistent.

Because success and failure play such an important role in the development of the self-concept, as explained above, academic achievement as revealed by grades and promotion is an important factor in children's personality development through the effect on their self-concepts. Good grades mean "success" to children just as poor grades mean "failure." Lack of promotion is especially damaging to the self-concept because it means both "failure" and lack of social acceptance by their former classmates who no longer consider them a part of the group when they are in a class of younger children (51).

Family Influences

Of all personality determinants, the family is the most important. There are a number of reasons why: The family is the first social group with which the child is identified; the child spends more time with the family group than with any other social group; family members are the most significant people in the child's life during the years when the foundations of personality are being laid; and the areas of family influence are broader than those of any other personality determinant, even the school. How great an influence the family has on the personality development of the child has been expressed in the following way by an anonymous writer:

- If a child lives with criticism, he learns to condemn.
- If he lives with hostility, he learns to fight.
- If he lives with fear, he learns to be apprehensive.
- If he lives with pity, he learns to feel sorry for himself.
- If he lives with tolerance, he learns to be patient.
- If he lives with jealousy, he learns to feel guilty.
- If he lives with ridicule, he learns to be shy.
- If he lives with shame, he learns to be ashamed of himself.
- If he lives with encouragement, he learns to be confident.
- If he lives with praise, he learns to be appreciative.
- If he lives with acceptance, he learns to love.
- If he lives with approval, he learns to like himself.
- If he lives with recognition, he learns to have a goal.
- If he lives with fairness, he learns to value justice.
- If he lives with honesty, he learns to value truth.
- If he lives with security, he learns to have faith in himself and others.

The influence of the family on the developing personality depends to some extent upon the kind of child. A child who is nervous and tense, for example, will be more upset by the attention given to a new baby in the family than a child of a more phlegmatic disposition. Similarly, a healthy child will react very differently to parental overprotectiveness and pampering than will a delicate, sickly child.

Level of Adjustment

The term "adjustment" refers to the extent to which an individual's personality functions efficiently in the world of people. There are certain patterns of behavior that are characteristically associated with well-adjusted children and others with poorly adjusted children.

Well-adjusted children enjoy a kind of inner harmony, in the sense that they are satisfied with themselves. Regardless of occasional setbacks and disappointments, they continue to strive for their goals. If they find these goals are unrealistically high, they are willing to modify them to fit their capacities.

In addition to making good personal adjustments, well-adjusted children have harmonious relationships with the people with whom they are associated. Lawton has proposed twenty characteristics which can be used to describe and assess well-adjusted people—characteristics that are as important in childhood as in adulthood (59). These characteristics, which vary according to age and ability, are given in Box 18–7.

Role of Self-acceptance in Adjustment

Children who are self-acceptant accept themselves just as they accept as friends others whom they like. When they like themselves reasonably well, they behave in a manner that leads to social acceptance. The more others like and accept them, the better children like themselves and the more self-acceptant they become. This leads to good personal and social adjustments.

At certain times in life, self-acceptance is easy for children but, at others, it is almost impossible. It is easy, for example, for babies to be self-acceptant because the significant people in their lives show them love and attention. However, as they become older, harsh, critical words, frowns, and slaps often replace the demonstrations of love they formerly had. As a result, young children begin to accept themselves less and reject themselves more.

The low point in family and social relationships, as was explained earlier, comes at puberty. Self-acceptance, likewise, reaches its low point then. Self-evaluations of children, as they grow older, are, as a result of unfavorable social attitudes, less favorable than they were earlier. These less favorable self-evaluations come partly from the way children are treated by the people who are significant to them and partly from the discrepancy between what they would like to be—their ideal self-concepts—and what they perceive themselves to be—their real self-concepts—as based on the opinions of others.

Because of the importance of self-acceptance to good personal and social adjustments, attempts have been made to find out what can be done to counteract the decline in self-acceptance that is so common among children as they grow older. These studies have revealed that self-acceptance is aided by a number of factors which help children to develop satisfactory self-concepts and to close the gap between their real and ideal self-concepts. Some of the most important aids that have been suggested are briefly explained in Box 18–8 (8, 43, 59, 63).

Role of Adjustment in Happiness

To be happy, children must make good personal as well as social adjustments. Because of the high social value placed on social acceptance in American culture today, children cannot be happy unless they are rea-

---

BOX 18–7

CHARACTERISTICS OF WELL-ADJUSTED PEOPLE

- Able and willing to assume responsibilities appropriate to their age
- Participate with pleasure in experiences belonging to each successive age level
- Willingly accept the responsibilities pertaining to their roles in life
- Attack problems that require solution
- Enjoy attacking and eliminating obstacles to happiness
- Make decisions with a minimum of worry, conflict, and advice-seeking
- Abide by a choice they make until convinced it is a wrong choice
- Get major satisfactions from real rather than imaginary accomplishments
- Can use thinking as a blueprint for action, not as a device for delaying or escaping action
- Learn from defeats instead of finding excuses for them
- Do not magnify successes or apply them to unrelated areas
- Know how to work when working and to play when playing
- Can say "No" to situations harmful to their best interests
- Can say "Yes" to situations that will ultimately aid them
- Can show anger directly when injured or when rights are violated
- Can show affection directly and appropriate in kind and amount
- Can endure pain and emotional frustration when necessary
- Can compromise when they encounter difficulties
- Can concentrate their energies on a goal that is important to them
- Accept the fact that life is an endless struggle

---

sonably well accepted by the people in their lives who are significant to them. Although acceptance and affection normally go hand in hand, if affection is to add to children's happiness it must, as was pointed out in Chapter 2 in the discussion of the three A's of happiness, be in a form that is developmentally appropriate for the child. How important a role affection from others plays in a child's level of adjustment has been shown when children lack love. As Horn has said, "Someone who experiences a shortage of love in

AIDS TO SELF-ACCEPTANCE

REALISTIC ASPIRATIONS

Children, to be self acceptant, must be realistic about themselves and not aim for the impossible. This does not mean that they should lack ambition or set goals below their capacities. Instead, it means setting goals within their potentials even though their potentials are lower than they would like them to be.

SUCCESSES

If goals are realistic, the chances for success are greatly increased. In addition, children, to be self-acceptant, must develop success factors if they are to make the most of their potentials. These success factors include taking the initiative instead of waiting to be told what to do, being accurate and painstaking in whatever they do, being cooperative and willing to do more than their share.

SELF-INSIGHT

Being able and willing to appraise themselves realistically, and recognizing and accepting their weaknesses as well as their strengths, increase self-acceptance. Each year, as they grow older and have broader social experiences, children should be able to appraise themselves more accurately.

SOCIAL INSIGHT

Being able to see themselves as others see them acts as a guide to behavior that enables children to conform to social expectations. By contrast, a marked discrepancy between the opinions others have of them and the opinions children have of themselves leads to behavior that antagonizes others and lowers the opinions others have of them.

STABLE SELF-CONCEPTS

When children see themselves one way at one time and another way at another time—sometimes favorably and sometimes unfavorably—they become ambivalent about themselves. To achieve stable as well as favorable self-concepts, significant people in their lives must regard children favorably most of the time. Their views form the basis of the mirror images children have of themselves.

childhood is unhappy then, and also develops values that perpetuate unhappiness in later life" (41).

In addition to acceptance and affection, if children are to be happy they must have enough achievements that are important to them at that time so that they can be self-acceptant. However, if they are to have the achievements that will contribute to their happiness, children must set goals for their achievements realistically so that their chances of reaching these goals are reasonably good. As Shaver and Freedman have pointed out, "Happiness has a lot to do with accepting and enjoying what one is and what one has, maintaining a balance between expectations and achievements" (87).

There are two important aids to achieving the good adjustment that is essential to happiness. The *first* is guidance to help children learn to be realistic about themselves and their abilities. This will eliminate much of the temptation to use defense mechanisms which lead to poor personal as well as social adjustments. Children who are realistic about themselves do not expect more of themselves than they are capable of. Consequently, they do not have to justify their behavior if it falls short of perfection.

The *second* aid to achieving the level of adjustment that will lead to happiness in childhood is guidance in learning how to behave in a manner that will facilitate social acceptance and affection from others. Children discover early in their social relationships that they must fit into the socially approved pattern of the group if they are to be accepted members of it. If they develop self-concepts or patterns of behavior that are unfavorable to social acceptance, their chances are slim of becoming accepted members of the group. That is why they need guidance and help in developing patterns of adjustment that will conform to the patterns approved by the group.

Hazards in Personality Development

The high social value placed on personality in American culture today makes anything that interferes with the development of a well-adjusted child a serious hazard. In few areas of the child's development are the hazards to good personal and social adjustments more serious and more far-reaching than in the area of personality development.

Prevention of unfavorable personality development has, for years, been greatly handicapped by the acceptance of traditional beliefs about personality. Acceptance of the belief that personality is a hereditary trait—expressed in the old saying, "He is a chip off the old block"—has led to the belief that there is little one can do to improve a child's personality. Consequently parents and teachers who accept this belief make little or no effort to change undesirable personality characteristics. Acceptance of the traditional belief that changes in personality accompany physical changes has likewise prevented remedial steps to counteract unfavorable personality characteristics. The belief that children will "outgrow" undesirable personality characteristics when their bodies change from those of children to those of adults has led to a hands-off policy. As a result, undesirable personality characteristics are permitted to persist and become deeply rooted habits that are increasingly difficult to change with each passing year.

Studies of personality persistence have highlighted the hazardous nature of accepting these traditional beliefs. There is ample evidence, as was explained earlier in this chapter, that once unfavorable personality characteristics develop, the chances that they will persist are greater than that they will change. Furthermore, these studies have shown that when changes do occur they are more likely to be quantitative than qualitative. For example, an unfavorable self-concept developed when children's environments are limited almost exclusively to the home may improve as children grow older and have more and more contacts with people outside the home where the opinions of outsiders may be more favorable toward them than the opinions of family members. Although this may modify their unfavorable homegrown self-concepts, there is little likelihood that favorable self-concepts will completely replace the unfavorable ones developed in the home.

In the following pages, some of the most common hazards in personality development will be discussed and an attempt will be made to show how these hazards affect the personal and social adjustments children make.

Unfavorable Self-concepts

Many children develop unfavorable self-concepts. As a result, they have difficulty in accepting themselves and often become self-rejectant to the point where they make poor personal and social adjustments.

Unfortunately, many parents, teachers, and others responsible for the guidance and control of children's behavior either do not realize that children are developing unfavorable self-concepts or, if they do realize it, they feel that this is just a "passing phase" and that the unfavorable self-concepts will correct themselves. In fact, they tend to grow worse as children grow older, unless steps are taken to improve them.

CAUSES OF UNFAVORABLE SELF-CONCEPTS   The foundations of unfavorable self-concepts are usually laid in the home. Because self-concepts are mirror images of what children believe the significant people in their lives think of them, as family relationships deteriorate, so do children's self-concepts. Whether these family relationships involve parents, siblings, or relatives, the effect of deterioration in these relationships on children's self-concepts is to make them unfavorable. Children think of themselves as these significant people think of them—as "nuisances," as "naughty," as "careless," or as "selfish."

When children's social horizons broaden and they come more and more in contact with people outside the home, the attitudes of those who are especially significant to them—members of the peer group and teachers—begin to have an effect on their self-concepts. Should they find that they are rejected or neglected by members of the peer group because they belong to a minority religious or racial group, because they are physically handicapped and cannot participate in the games of their peers, because the pattern of their family lives deviates from that of other group members, or for some other reason, they begin to develop feelings of inferiority or even of martyrdom (19, 68, 72, 82).

How teachers' attitudes and treatment will affect children's self-concepts will depend largely on how children behave in the school. If their behavior conforms to school standards, if they are conscientious about their work and if they are good "school citizens," they will see themselves through their teachers's eyes in a favorable way. If, by contrast, they are poor students and disruptive in the classroom, from teachers' remarks, grades, and punishments for misbehavior, the mirror image they form of themselves is that of a "nuisance" or "a dull child."

Sometimes the mirror image children get of themselves from the home environment is more favorable than that from the outside environment, and, at other times, the reverse is true. When this happens, the group that has the greater effect on their self-concepts will be the group that is more significant to them.

When children are young, the family group is usually more significant than the group outside the home. As childhood progresses, the reverse is true.

EFFECTS OF UNFAVORABLE SELF-CONCEPTS When children have poor opinions of themselves, they become self-rejectant. They then behave in a way that others regard as unsocial or immature. If, for example, they feel unloved and unwanted by parents, they may become resentful, rebellious, negativistic, and aggressive toward siblings whom they regard as the cause of parental rejection. Or, they may become withdrawn or overdependent on parents, hoping to regain the love and affection their parents gave them when they were younger. Deterioration in relationships with siblings often leads to such unsocial behavior as name calling, tattling, and aggressive attacks. Regardless of what form of behavior comes from unfavorable self-concepts, it influences the attitudes of family members toward them unfavorably and this leads to a vicious circle of poor relationships and poor opinions, which reinforce children's unfavorable self-concept.

Patterns of unsocial or immature behavior resulting from unfavorable self-concepts developed from family relationships extend outside the home and affect children's relationships with people there. Children who develop aggressive reactions to others antagonize them, and those who become withdrawn are overlooked and neglected. In either case, their unfavorable behavior reinforces the unfavorable opinions others have of them and this, in turn, reinforces the unfavorable concepts they have of themselves.

Egocentrism

Egocentrism means concern about self rather than about others. Egocentric children are self-bound in the sense their interests are centered mainly in themselves. They think and talk more about themselves than about others and their acts are designed mainly to bring benefit to them (80).

Because helplessness in the early years of life necessitates care from others, all babies and young children tend to be egocentric. However, as their helplessness decreases with the development of skills and the ability to communicate, egocentrism should normally wane. Children are then expected to become decreasingly egocentric and increasingly social.

Not all children, however, make this shift. Some continue to be egocentric long beyond the time when their age-mates have become social. As a result of their failure to learn to behave in a social way, they are regarded unfavorably by members of the social group—adults as well as peers. Because unfavorable social judgments lead to unfavorable self-judgments, egocentric children make poor personal as well as social adjustments. That is why egocentrism may be regarded as one of the major hazards in personality development.

FORMS OF EGOCENTRISM It is popularly assumed that all egocentric people have favorable opinions of themselves and, as a result, their concentration of interest in and concern about self comes from a feeling of superiority. This is not necessarily true. Some egocentric people, it is true, feel superior and, consequently, have favorable self-concepts. However, there are others who have unfavorable self-concepts which express themselves in two common forms: feelings of inferiority, and feelings of martyrdom. If these self-concepts persist and are constantly reinforced by environmental influences, they are likely to develop into complexes—constellations of beliefs that express themselves in behavior related to these beliefs.

Egocentrism based on feelings of *superiority* is characterized by interest in and concern about self as a superior person. Children whose egocentrism is of this type expect others to wait on them, to applaud their every act, to give them leadership roles and submerge their interests in favor of them. They become egotistical, bossy, inconsiderate of others, selfish, uncooperative, and show a tendency to engage in unsocial forms of speech—boasting about themselves, their achievements, and their possessions and making derogatory, critical comments about the possessions and achievements of others (80).

When egocentrism is based on feelings of *inferiority*, individuals turn inward and concentrate on self in the belief that they have nothing of worth to contribute to the group. Children whose egocentrism is characterized by feelings of inferiority are highly suggestible, easily led by others, and apologetic in their reactions to others. Because they feel they have little to contribute to the group, they tend to be overlooked and neglected. Although they may not be disliked, as is often true of children whose egocentrism is based on feelings of superiority, they have so little to contribute to others that they are not included in the activities of the group. This reinforces their belief in their inferiority.

Egocentrism based on feelings of *martyrdom* affects children in much the same way as feelings of inferiority. Believing that they are unfairly treated makes them angry and resentful against all people. As a result, they have little desire to make a contribution to the group and the group then tends to neglect and overlook them. Should they show their resentments overtly in aggressive acts or speech, they will be rejected by the group instead of merely being overlooked and neglected.

CAUSES OF EGOCENTRISM   The foundations of egocentrism can be traced to early conditions in the home. These come mainly from parental attitudes toward, and treatment of, children while they are young. Some of the conditions in the home environment that contribute to egocentrism and prolong the egocentrism characteristic of all babies and very young children are explained in Box 18–9.

As children grow older, their own attitudes and behavior tend to reinforce the foundations of egocentrism laid during the early years. Children, for example, who are encouraged to develop unrealistically high aspirations for themselves as a result of constant exposure to the unrealistically high aspirations their parents have for them, concentrate their interests on reaching these goals. Their concern is mainly in doing things that will help them to reach their goals rather than doing things for others. If they fail to reach the goals they have set for themselves, they will become preoccupied with thoughts about their failures. Successful achievement of their goals, on the other hand, will encourage preoccupation with thoughts of their successes. Whichever form their achievements take,

---

BOX 18–9

SOME CONDITIONS CONTRIBUTING TO EGOCENTRISM

OVERPROTECTIVENESS
Children who are waited on by others and protected from the environmental experiences their age-mates have, develop an expectancy to have others do things for them instead of making the effort to do them for themselves. This stifles cooperativeness and other qualities that characterize those who are social and outer-bound in their attitudes and behavior.

PARENTAL FAVORITISM
Parents who show favoritism toward their children encourage those who are favored to develop feelings of self-importance while those who are not favored develop feelings of inferiority or martyrdom. In both cases, it encourages the children to become self-bound instead of outer-bound in their attitudes.

PARENTAL ASPIRATIONS
Strong parental aspirations for children encourage them to become egocentric in their striving for these goals. Success in reaching the goals encourages superiority complexes and failure encourages inferiority or martyr complexes.

PARENTAL AGE
Young parents tend to be more concerned about their own affairs than about their children's affairs and, as a result, do not usually encourage egocentrism in children.

Overage parents, by contrast, often become child-oriented and this encourages their children to be egocentric.

FOCUS OF INTEREST IN HOME
A child-centered home encourages egocentrism colored by feelings of superiority in children. An adult-centered home makes children feel rejected and neglected, thus encouraging egocentrism colored by feelings of martyrdom.

ORDINAL POSITION
Firstborns and lastborns of a large family often become egocentric because they are the focal points of attention from all family members.

FAMILY SIZE
The smaller the family, the more likely the child is to become egocentric. Only children tend to be far more often egocentric than are children from larger families.

SEX OF CHILD
Among young children, boys tend to be parental favorites and this encourages them to be egocentric. Among older children, encouragement of boys to be independent and socially oriented curbs their egocentrism. By contrast, older girls are encouraged to be dependent and this increases their tendency to be egocentric.

success or failure, it will encourage egocentrism rather than interest in or concern for others.

Some members of the social group outside the home encourage egocentrism in children and others discourage it. Because during the gang age most of the play of childhood is cooperative, children are encouraged by their peers to curb their egocentricity and to contribute their share to the activities of the group. The same is true of communications. Members of the peer group encourage cooperation in conversation just as they encourage cooperation in play. Children who fail to contribute their share quickly discover that the penalty for egocentrism is social rejection and neglect. To avoid paying this penalty, many children are motivated to curb the egocentrism developed earlier in the home.

In the school, many teachers unwittingly encourage egocentrism in children and reinforce the egocentrism developed in the home. Emphasis on the importance of grades, on striving to do better and better work, on not giving aid to classmates who may be having difficulties in their studies because it is "cheating," on talking and writing compositions of what they did or thought about a certain experience, and encouragement to do something original in their artwork all encourage egocentrism. Although some schools emphasize cooperative efforts in the classroom and most do so in their athletic programs, the actual work of American schools today encourages egocentrism in children rather than the cooperation that is characteristic of a social person.

EFFECTS OF EGOCENTRISM   Egocentrism affects both the behavior and the personality pattern of the child unfavorably. That is why it is such a serious hazard to good personal and social adjustments.

Egocentric children *behave* in a way that antagonizes and alienates others. They are selfish, demanding, and uncooperative. Instead of contributing to the group, they expect the group to do things for them. This is true also of their speech. They contribute little to a conversation and what they do contribute more often than not is concentrated on derogation of others, boasting about themselves, or complaining about being unfairly treated (80).

Because their behavior creates an unfavorable impression on others, people—whether adults or peers—tend to reject or neglect them. Seeing themselves through the eyes of others, they get unfavorable *mirror images* of themselves. As a result, they develop

unfavorable self-concepts and this encourages self-rejection. Self-rejection, in turn, leads to personal and social maladjustments.

Lack of Social Recognition of Individuality

Even babies want to be recognized and treated as individuals. Each year, as children grow older, the desire to be recognized as individuals grows increasingly stronger, reaching its peak during the adolescent years. As Erikson has explained, the search for identity—a sense of being able to function as a separate person but with a close relationship to others—reaches a "crisis stage" in adolescence. To be happy and well adjusted, children must have an inner assurance of their ability to function independently. Until they get this feeling of assurance, they are insecure, trying to cut parental apron strings and associate themselves emotionally with their peers (27).

Although all children want to be different from their age-mates, they do not want to be so different that they will be conspicuous. On the other hand, they want to be different enough so that they will not only not be overlooked but so that they also will be noticed favorably by others.

Failure to be recognized as individuals is hazardous to good personal and social adjustments. People, regardless of age, who feel that their individuality is not recognized by others are likely to interpret this to mean that they have so little to offer that they are overlooked. This leads to feelings of inadequacy and inferiority. These feelings in children are intensified when they see their age-mates in the center of attention in the peer group and they become jealous of the status their age-mates have been able to attain.

CAUSES OF LACK OF RECOGNITION OF INDIVIDUALITY   There are six common symbols of self by which children are judged by others. Acceptance of the judgments by others as a basis for self-judgments forms the basis on which children judge their individuality or lack of it. When children feel that these symbols of self lack distinctiveness and, as a result, they will be unnoticed and overlooked by others, it has a damaging effect on their self-concepts.

The *first* symbol of self that contributes to individuality is appearance. Children who are neither attractive nor unattractive, neither tall nor short, fat or thin are likely to go unnoticed. They are so inconspicuous in appearance that they lack individuality.

Second, clothes that are nondescript or that have been worn by an older sibling make children feel that one of the important ways of making others notice them is denied them. Rebellion against wearing hand-me-down clothes from an older sibling and interest in ornamentation and newness as attention-getters show how important children regard clothes as symbols of their individuality.

Third, when children realize the important symbolic roles of names, they begin to feel that they lack individuality when their names are so common that several of their classmates have the same names as they do or when their names are the same as those of the parent of their sex. A girl whose name is the same as her mother's or a boy who is named for his father lack the feeling of individuality that siblings with their own names have.

Being called by different names by different people likewise causes a child to feel a lack of individuality. Confusion of identity is well expressed in the old rhyme:

Mother calls me William
Auntie calls me Will
Sister calls me Willie
But Dad calls me Bill.

This confusion of identity, which leads to feelings of lack of individuality, is illustrated in Figure 18–6.

Fourth, behavior patterns that conform strictly to social expectations may lead to social approval but, like inconspicuous clothing, they make the child seem nondescript. By contrast, doing something to attract attention, even if it is unfavorable attention, children soon discover puts them in the limelight of attention. The pleasure they derive from this attention makes them feel that they are individuals, even though the attention they get may not be favorable.

Fifth, like behavior, speech is a symbol of self. Much of the unconventional speech of children, whether it be slang, swearing, boasting, or derogatory comments, has attention value and gives children a feeling that they are individuals who are noticed and recognized as such.

Sixth, lack of originality or creativity leads to a lack of feeling of individuality. Children discover early in their play that if they make something that is different it attracts attention to them, but if they make some-

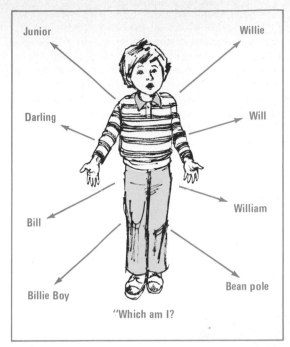

Figure 18–6. A common cause of feeling of lack of individuality is being called different names by different people.

thing like a model, it goes unnoticed. Even when the attention their creations attract are unfavorable, it is more satisfying to children than being unnoticed.

EFFECTS OF LACK OF RECOGNITION OF INDIVIDUALITY Lack of social recognition of individuality affects children's behavior and their personalities. In both cases, the effects tend to be more unfavorable than favorable. The reason for this is that because few children know, without guidance and help from others, how to achieve the recognition of individuality and the favorable social judgments they crave, they more often than not use techniques which they have discovered, by trial and error, put them in the limelight of attention and, momentarily at least, give them feelings of being individuals, not just unnoticed parts of the group.

Children who feel that they are overlooked because they lack individuality often *behave* in a way that guarantees the attention that makes them stand out from the group. They, for example, do foolhardy things in play, they cut up in class at school, they talk in an unconventional way, using slang and swear words which they have discovered from past experience have great attention value, they boast about their possessions and achievements, they wear their conventional clothes in unconventional ways, and they do countless other things that attract attention to themselves. These, they hope, will compensate for the lack of recognition of their individuality. However, although they give children momentary satisfaction, in the long run they are damaging to good personal and social adjustments because of unfavorable social judgments of their behavior.

Because of unfavorable social reactions to children who lack individuality, such children develop unfavorable *self-concepts* which, in turn, tends to make them self-rejectant. They dislike themselves because they feel that others must dislike them if they ignore and overlook them. This is one of the common contributing factors to personality maladjustments in childhood, the hazard to personality development to be discussed in the following section of this chapter.

Personality Maladjustments

Children who make poor personal and social adjustments are labeled "maladjusted." They are frequently called "problem children." There are two major kinds of personality maladjustments. The *first* involves behavior which is satisfying to the child but is socially unacceptable. The *second* involves behavior which is socially acceptable but is a source of continuous, excessive, and disturbing conflict to the child.

CAUSES OF MALADJUSTMENT   One of the major causes of maladjustment is self-rejection. Children who have a self-rejectant attitude dislike themselves. Just as children reject as playmates or friends those whom they dislike, so they reject themselves when they feel that they are not what they want to be.

No one, at any age, is consistently self-rejectant. Self-rejection, like self-acceptance, is greatly influenced by the environment and by the attitudes of significant people. It is, therefore, logical that the degree of self-rejection the child experiences would vary from time to time. Just as there must be a consistency in self-acceptance if children are to make good social adjustments, so there must be a degree of consistency in self-rejection if they are to become self-rejectant and make poor personal and social adjustments.

There are two common but very serious obstacles to

self-acceptance. These are primarily responsible for the self-rejection that is back of personality maladjustments.

The *first* is the tendency for almost all children to develop ideal self-concepts that are unrealistic for their capacities. As was explained in the discussion of ideal self-concepts in Chapter 12, this is often encouraged by parents and teachers who believe that ideal self-concepts serve as a source of motivation.

Children, for example, who are encouraged to picture themselves as leaders in the peer group or at the top of the class academically, will be bitterly disappointed when they are not chosen for leadership roles or when their grades put them far below the top of the class. The larger the gap between the ideal self-concept and the real self-concept, the harder it is to be self-acceptant and the more likely the child is to become self-rejectant.

With each passing year, as children become increasingly personality-conscious, they become more anxious to be like their ideal selves and less satisfied with their real selves. As a result, the tendency to be self-rejectant increases (15, 35).

The *second* major obstacle to self-acceptance comes from the dissatisfaction that results when children compare themselves with their age-mates or when parents and teachers compare them unfavorably with siblings or classmates. If, for example, parents constantly tell younger siblings that they should "act their age" like their older siblings, or that they should be neat and orderly about their possessions as their older siblings are, younger siblings cannot help feeling inferior—feelings that encourage self-rejection.

DANGER SIGNALS OF MALADJUSTMENTS   A number of personality traits of an undesirable sort appear in mild form in all children. At first, they appear to be harmless and are frequently allowed to persist, without any real effort to overcome them. No single trait is enough to cause alarm when viewed by itself. When several are observable in the same child, however, and when they seem to fit into a maladjustive "personality picture," or syndrome, they are significant and may be regarded as "danger signals" of future trouble. Most children, for example, fidget. Only if their fidgeting is accompanied by other symptoms of maladjustment, however, such as inability to concentrate, impatience, impulsivity, clowning, or unruliness—the "hyperactive-child syndrome"—is it symptomatic of poor personal and social adjustment. Figure 18–7 shows some of the characteristic traits on the hyper-active-child syndrome.

In Box 18–10 are given some of the most common and most serious danger signals of maladjustment in childhood (5, 8, 37, 46, 76, 84, 92, 97). Although one trait is not necessarily a symptom of trouble, it should not be overlooked; nor should one assume that the child will automatically outgrow it. Instead, it should be regarded as a fever when otherwise a child seems to be well. It means that unless remedial steps are taken, trouble may break out into the open.

Two specific examples—accident-proneness and threat of suicide—will suffice to illustrate the danger of ignoring *any* signal of maladjustment. Studies of *accident-prone* children reveal that they frequently suffer from repeated and severe frustrations and turn their aggressions outward, thus becoming overactive, impulsive, adventuresome, and anxious for attention and approval. They often feel insecure and this prompts them to bid for attention by doing foolhardy things which often lead to an accident. Boys who suffer from feelings of inadequacy because they are sex inappropriate in appearance are so anxious to prove their sex appropriateness by "stunting" and other bids for attention that they throw caution to the wind and have accidents (67).

Accident-proneness should not be ignored, not only because an accident may leave a permanent physical scar or even lead to death, but also, as was explained in an earlier discussion of accident-proneness, because an accident may leave a serious psychological scar. Children who have repeated accidents begin to question their adequacy, and this intensifies an already-existing feeling of incompetence and inferiority. Inferiority complexes are often intensified by accident-proneness.

While young children may *threaten to commit suicide* when they are angry at parents who refuse to permit them to do what they want to do, older children are often impulsive enough to try to commit suicide in the hope of frightening their parents and gaining a means of manipulating them in the future. If children found,

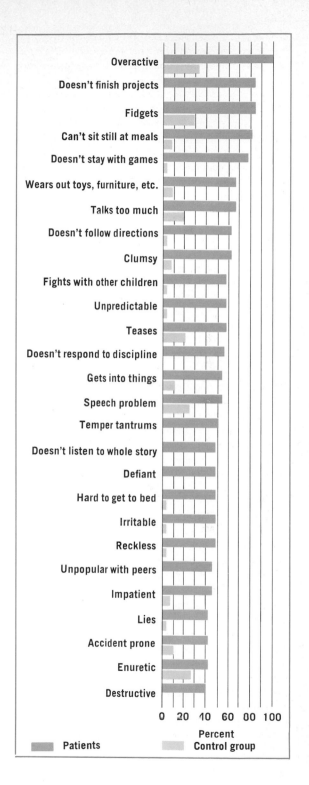

Figure 18–7. Some of the characteristic traits of the hyperactive-child syndrome. (*Adapted from M. A. Stewart: Hyperactive children. Scientific American, 1970, 222 (4), 94–98. Copyright 1970 by Scientific American, Inc. All rights reserved. Used by permission.*)

COMMON DANGER SIGNALS
OF MALADJUSTMENT

- Flying into a rage on the slightest provocation
- Showing signs of excessive worry and anxiety
- Frequently appearing depressed and rarely smiling or joking
- Repeated stealing of small articles, despite severe punishment
- Frequently appearing to be lost in daydreams
- Showing very sensitive reactions to real or imagined slights
- Excessive cruelty to younger or smaller children or animals
- Abnormal anxiety about achieving perfection
- Frequent expression of the idea that the child is punished more than others
- Inability to avoid misbehavior even when repeatedly warned and punished
- Excessive concern with physical appearance.
- Habitual lying to suit some purpose
- Extreme indecisiveness in making relatively minor choices
- Hostility toward any kind of authority
- Accident-proneness
- Finicky appetite and food fads
- Enuresis
- Running away
- Hypercritical and self-righteous
- Diffuse hyperactivity
- Talking about or attempting suicide
- Repeated acts of destruction
- Teasing and bullying others when feeling rejected
- Homesickness when away from familiar people and places
- Clowning to attract attention
- Projecting blame on others and rationalizing acts when criticized
- Tattling on others to win adult attention and approval
- Sour-grapes attitude—covering up disappointment by minimizing the value of unattainable things

when they were younger, that threats "worked" but are now losing their effectiveness, they may take a bold step and actually try to commit suicide. This is the real danger of ignoring suicide threats and of failing to recognize how serious a sign of maladjustment it is (84).

PERSISTENCE OF MALADJUSTMENTS Once a pattern of maladjustive behavior appears, it is likely to persist. Unless minor disturbances are detected and remedial steps are taken to correct them before they become serious problems in maladjustments, they are likely to persist and develop into handicapping disorders.

Children can be helped to prevent this from happening and to improve their adjustments by gaining better insight into themselves and a more realistic concept of their abilities. But improvement is far from easy as long as they remain in the environment that has fostered their unrealistic self-concepts or maladjustive patterns of behavior.

If the teacher condones cheating and clowning, for example, the child will regard these as approved patterns of behavior and will repeat them until they become habitual. Similarly, when parents condone aggressive attacks on siblings or overlook lies, these will become the child's characteristic way of adjusting. It is thus apparent that the environment helps to determine whether the child learns approved or deviant behavior patterns and whether the child will become well adjusted or maladjusted.

EFFECTS OF MALADJUSTMENTS ON HAPPINESS No child who is self-rejectant can hope to make good personal and social adjustments. And, no child who makes poor personal and social adjustments can hope to be happy. That is why maladjustments are such a serious hazard in childhood.

To become well-adjusted people, all children should have a reasonably happy childhood. Because childhood is the age when the foundations are laid for later life, if children lay foundations that guarantee happiness in childhood, they will know how to behave so that they can achieve happiness during the remaining years of their lives. By developing realistic self-concepts and patterns of behavior that conform to social expectations, this happiness can be achieved. For their own sakes as well as for the good of the social group with which they are identified, it is essential that children be well-adjusted individuals.

Chapter Highlights

1 The meanings of the terms "personality" and "personality pattern" put emphasis on the important role played by learning in the development of the hereditary potentials that form the foundations for personality.

2 The two major elements of the personality pattern are the self-concept and traits. The self-concept is the core of the pattern and, as such, influences the form the traits take.

Individuality, which is apparent at birth, is caused by hereditary differences and by differences in learning experiences.

4 Genetic studies of children over varying lengths of time have emphasized the persistence of the two elements of the personality pattern: the self concept and traits.

5 The important conditions contributing to personality persistence include heredity, child training, parental values, role playing, the social environment, and selection of people in the environment.

6 Changes in the personality pattern, which are more often quantitative than qualitative, are due to a number of causes, the most important of which are physical and environmental changes, social pressures, increase in competence, role changes, and professional help.

7 There are many personal and environmental conditions that are responsible for the development of the self-concept and the different traits in the personality pattern. How great an influence they will have on the developing personality pattern will depend on children's ability to understand the significance of these conditions in relation to themselves.

8 The most important personality determinants include early experiences, cultural influences, physique, physical condition, physical attractiveness, intelligence, emotions, names, success and failure, social acceptance, status symbols, and school and family influences.

9 The level of adjustment children achieve is greatly influenced by the social acceptance they receive from people—adults and peers—who play significant roles in their lives.

10 Happiness in childhood is greatly influenced by how self-acceptant children are. Their self-acceptance, in turn, is influenced by social acceptance by people who are significant to them and by whether their achievements and the affection they receive from others come up to their expectations.

11 Because of the high social value placed on personality, anything that interferes with the development of a favorable self-concept is hazardous to the child's personal and social adjustments because of the effects of an unfavorable self-concept on the quality of the child's behavior.

12 Egocentrism, which is a serious hazard to good personal and social adjustments, is caused by parental overprotectiveness, parental favoritism, and parental aspirations for the child, among other factors. It is especially common in child-centered homes, in families where parents are overage, among first- and lastborn children, and in small families.

13 Lack of social recognition of individuality is especially serious in late childhood because, at this age, children normally want to establish their identity as individuals.

14 There are two major kinds of personality maladjustment. The first involves behavior that is satisfactory to the child but unacceptable to the group and the second involves behavior acceptable to the group but not satisfactory to the child's needs. The second form is more readily spotted than the first and, as a result, is believed to be more common.

15 Danger signals of personality maladjustment are often overlooked or ignored because many parents and teachers believe that children will outgrow their unsocial patterns of behavior and develop more favorable self-concepts as their bodies change to those of adults during puberty.

Bibliography

1 Alland, A. Anger and Aggression. *Humanitas*, 1976, *12*, 221–237.

2 Allen, M. G., W. Pollin, and A. Hoffer. Parental, birth, and infancy factors in infant twin development. *American Journal of Psychiatry*, 1971, *127*, 1597–1604.

3 Allport, G. W. *Pattern and growth in personality*. New York: Holt, 1961.

4 Baumrind, D. Child care practices anteceding three patterns of preschool behavior. *Genetic Psychology Monographs*, 1967, *75*, 43–88.

5 Bax, M. The active and the overactive school child. *Developmental Medicine and Child Neurology*, 1972, *14*, 83–86.

6 Bayley, N. Behavioral correlates of mental growth: Birth to twenty-six years. *American Psychologist*, 1968, *23*, 1–17.

7 Belmont, L., and F. A. Margolla. Birth order, family size, and intelligence. *Science*, 1973, *182*, 1096–1101.

8 Bennett, S. N., and M. B. Youngman. Personality and behavior in school. *British Journal of Educational Psychology*, 1973, *43*, 228–233.

9 Berscheid, E., E. Walster, and G. Bohrnstedt. The happy American body: A survey report. *Psychology Today*, 1973, 7 (6), 119–131.

10 Bickman, L. Social roles and uniforms: Clothes make the person. *Psychology Today*, 1974, 7 (11), 48–51.

11 Birns, B., and M. Golden. Prediction of intellectual performance at 3 years from infant tests and personality measures, *Merrill-Palmer Quarterly*, 1972, *18*, 53–58.

12 Busk, P. L., R. C. Ford, and J. L. Schulman. Stability of sociometric responses in classrooms. *Journal of Genetic Psychology*, 1973, *123*, 69–84.

13 Carpenter, T. R., and T. V. Busse. Development of self concept in Negro and white welfare children. *Child Development*, 1969, *40*, 935–939.

14 Cattell, R. B., and R. M. Dreger. Personality structure as revealed in questionnaire responses at the preschool level. *Child Development*, 1974, *45*, 49–54.

15 Chang, T. S. The self-concept of children in ethnic groups: Black American and Korean American. *Elementary School Journal*, 1975, *76*, 52–58.

16 Clifford, M. M., and E. Walster. The effect of physical attractiveness on teacher expectations. *Sociology of Education*, 1973, *46*, 248–258.

17 Condry, J., and M. L. Siman. Characteristics of peer- and adult-oriented children. *Journal of Marriage and the Family*, 1974, *36*, 543–554.

18 Conners, C. K. Symptom patterns in hyperkinetic, neurotic and normal children. *Child Development*, 1970, *41*, 667–682.

19 Dermer, M., and D. C. Thiel. When beauty may fail. *Journal of Personality and Social Psychology*, 1975, *31*, 1168–1176.

20 Dion, K. K. Children's physical attractiveness and sex as determinants of adult punitiveness. *Developmental Psychology*, 1974, *10*, 772–778.

21 Dion, K. K., and E. Berscheid. Physical attractiveness and peer perception among children. *Sociometry*, 1974, *37*, 1–12.

22 Dion, K. K., E. Berscheid, and E. Walster. What is beautiful is good. *Journal of Personality and Social Psychology*, 1972, *24*, 285–290.

23 Dittrichová, J., K. Paul, and J. Vondráček. Individual differences in infants' sleep. *Developmental Medicine and Child Neurology*, 1976, *18*, 182–188.

24 Ellis, A. Healthy and unhealthy aggression. *Humanitas*, 1976, *12*, 239–254.

25 Emmerich, W. Developmental trends in evaluations of single traits. *Child Development*, 1974, *45*, 172–183.

26 Erikson, E. H. *Childhood and society*, rev. ed. New York: Norton, 1964.

27 Erikson, E. H. *Identity: Youth and crisis*. New York: Norton, 1968.

28 Forer, L. *The birth order factor*. New York: McKay, 1976.

29 Freud, S. *The standard edition of the complete psychological works of Sigmund Freud*. London: Hogarth Press, 1952–1963. 21 vols.

30 Friend, R. M., and J. M. Neale. Children's perceptions of success and failure: An attitudinal analysis of the effects of race and social class. *Developmental Psychology*, 1972, 7, 124–128.

31 Garai, G. E., and A. Scheinfeld. Sex differences in mental and behavioral traits. *Genetic Psychology Monographs*, 1968, 77, 169–299.

32 Gardner, R. W. Individuality in development. In W. R. Looft (ed.), *Developmental psychology: A book of readings*. Hinsdale, Ill.: Dryden Press, 1972. Pp. 402–414.

33 Gecas, V., J. M. Calonico, and D. L. Thomas. The development of self-concept in the child: Mirror theory versus model theory. *Journal of Social Psychology*, 1974, *92*, 67–76.

34 Gibbins, K., and T. K. Gwynn. A new theory of fashion change: A test of some predictions. *British Journal of Social and Clinical Psychology*, 1975, *14*, 1–9.

35 Glavin, J. P. Persistence of behavior disorders in children. *Exceptional Children*, 1972, *38*, 367–376.

36 Glueck, E. T. A more discriminative instrument for the identification of potential delinquents at school entrance. *Journal of Criminal Law, Criminology, and Police Science*, 1966, *57*, 27–30.

37 Goggin, J. E. Sex differences in the activity level of preschool children as a possible precursor of hyperactivity. *Journal of Genetic Psychology*, 1975, *127*, 75–81.

38 Gottlieb, J. Attitudes toward retarded children: Effects of labeling and behavior aggressiveness. *Journal of Educational Psychology*, 1975, *67*, 581–585.

39 Gove, W. R., and T. R. Herb. Stress and mental illness among the young: A comparison of the sexes. *Social Forces*, 1974, *53*, 256–265.

40 Hartnett, J. J., R. G. Bailey, and C. S. Hartley. Body height, position and sex as determinants of personal scale. *Journal of Psychology*, 1974, *87*, 129–136.

41 Horn, J. Love: The most important ingredient of happiness. *Psychology Today*, 1976, *10* (2), 98–102.

42 Hurlock, E. B. *The psychology of dress*. New York: Blum, 1973.

43 Illingsworth, R. S. How to help a young child to achieve his best. *Journal of Pediatrics*, 1968, *73*, 61–68.

44 Inselberg, R. M., and L. Burke. Social and psychological correlates of masculinity in young boys. *Merrill-*

Palmer Quarterly, 1973, *19,* 41–47.

45 Isen, A. M., N. Horn, and D. L. Rosenhan. Effects of success and failure on children's generosity. *Journal of Personality and Social Psychology,* 1973, *27,* 239–274.

46 Jenkins, R. L. Classification of behavior problems of children. *American Journal of Psychiatry,* 1969, *125,* 1032–1039.

47 Jones, M. C. Psychological correlates of somatic development. *Child Development,* 1965, *36,* 899–911.

48 Kagan, J. Body build and conceptual impulsivity in children. *Journal of Personality,* 1966, *34,* 118–128.

49 Kagan, J., and H. A. Moss. *Birth to maturity: A study in psychological development.* New York: Wiley, 1962.

50 Karabenick, S. A. On the relation between personality and birth order. *Psychological Reports,* 1971, *28,* 258.

51 Katz, I., O. J. Cole, and R. M. Baron. Self-evaluation, social reinforcement and academic achievement of black and white school children. *Child Development,* 1976, *47,* 368–374,

52 Kirchner, E. P., and S. I. Vondráček. Perceived sources of esteem in early childhood. *Journal of Genetic Psychology,* 1975, *126,* 169–176.

53 Kleck, R. E., S. A. Richardson, and L. Ronald. Physical appearance cues and interpersonal attraction in children. *Child Development,* 1974, *45,* 305–310.

54 Knapper, C. K. The relationship between personality and style of dress. *Dissertation Abstracts International,* 1973, *34* (2–8), 856.

55 Koeske, R. K., and G. F. Koeske. An attributional approach to moods and the menstrual cycle. *Journal of Personality and Social Psychology,* 1975, *31,* 473–478.

56 Kokens, B. Grade level differences in factors of self-esteem. *Developmental Psychology,* 1974, *10,* 954–958.

57 Koocher, G. P. Swimming, competence and personality change. *Journal of Personality and Social Psychology,* 1971, *18,* 275–278.

58 Labouvie, E. W., and E. W. Schaie. Personality structure as a function of behavioral stability in children.

Child Development, 1974, *45,* 252–255.

59 Lawton, G. *Aging successfully.* New York: Columbia University Press, 1951.

60 Lerner, R. M., S. A. Karabenick, and M. Meisels. Effects of age and sex on the development of personal space schemata towards body build. *Journal of Genetic Psychology,* 1975, *125,* 92–101.

61 Lester, D. *A physiological basis for personality traits: A new theory of personality.* Springfield, Ill.; Charles C Thomas, 1974.

62 Loewenthal, K. Handwriting and self-presentation. *Journal of Social Psychology,* 1975, *96,* 267–270.

63 Lombardo, J. P., S. C. Fantasia, and G. Solheim. The relationship of internality-externality, self-acceptance, and self-ideal discrepancies. *Journal of Genetic Psychology,* 1975, *126,* 281–288.

64 MacDonald, A. P. Birth order and personality, *Journal of Consulting and Clinical Psychology,* 1971, *36,* 171–176.

65 Maeroff, G. A rare look at the gifted. *The New York Times,* Nov. 7, 1975.

66 Mahrer, A. R. Childhood determinants of adult functioning: Strategies in the clinical research use of the personal-psychological history. *Psychological Reports,* 1969, *19,* 39–46.

67 Manheimer, D. L., and G. D. Mellinger. Personality characteristics of the child accident repeater. *Child Development,* 1967, *38,* 491–513.

68 Matthews, L. B. Improving the self-image of the socially disabled. *Journal of Home Economics,* 1975, *67* (3), 9–11.

69 Mattsson, A. Long-term physical illness in childhood: A challenge to psychological adaptation. *Pediatrics,* 1972, *50,* 801–811.

70 McReynolds, P. The motives to attain success and to avoid failure: Historical note. *Journal of Individual Psychology,* 1968, *24,* 157–161.

71 Mischel, W. Continuity and change in personality. *American Psychologist,* 1969, *24,* 1012–1018.

72 Morin, S. F., and R. L. Jones. Social comparison of abilities in blind children and adolescents. *Journal of Psychology,* 1974, *87,* 237–243.

73 Nathan, S. Body image in chroni-

cally obese children as reflected in figure drawings. *Journal of Personality Assessment,* 1973, *37,* 456–463.

74 Paponsěk, H., and M. Paponsěk. Mirror image and self recognition in young human infants: 1. A new method of experimental analysis. *Developmental Psychology,* 1974, *7,* 149–157.

75 Peck, R. F., and R. J. Havighurst. *The psychology of character development.* New York: Wiley, 1962.

76 Phillips, B. N. Problem behavior in the elementary school. *Child Development,* 1968, *39,* 859–903.

77 Rank, O. *The trauma of birth.* New York: Harcourt, Brace, 1929.

78 Rapier, J., R. Adelson, R. Carey, and K. Croke. Changes in children's attitudes toward the physically handicapped. *Exceptional Children,* 1972, *39,* 219–224.

79 Roff, M., S. B. Sells, and M. M. Golden. *Social adjustment and personality development in children.* Minneapolis, Minn.: University of Minnesota Press, 1972.

80 Rubin, K. H. Relationship between egocentric communication and popularity among peers. *Developmental Psychology,* 1972, *7,* 364.

81 Rubin, K. H. Egocentrism in childhood: A unitary construct? *Child Development,* 1973, *44,* 102–110.

82 Sailor, P., and W. Crumley. Self-image: How do the poor see themselves? *Journal of Home Economics,* 1975, *67* (3), 4–8.

83 Schneider, D. J. Tactical self-presentation after success and failure. *Journal of Personality and Social Psychology,* 1969, *13,* 262–268.

84 Shaffer, D. Suicide in childhood and early adolescence. *Journal of Child Psychology and Psychiatry and Allied Disciplines,* 1974, *15,* 279–291.

85 Shane, H. G. Social experiences and selfhood. *Childhood Education,* 1957, *33,* 297–298.

86 Shannon, B. E. The impact of racism on personality development. *Social Casework,* 1973, *54,* 519–525.

87 Shaver, B., and J. Freedman. The pursuit of happiness. *Psychology Today,* 1976, *10* (3), 26–32, 75.

88 Shinn, M. W. *Notes on the development of a child.* Berkeley, Calif.: University of California Press, 1909.

89 Sontag, L. W. Implications of fetal behavior and environment for adult personalities. *Annals of the New York Academy of Sciences,* 1966, *132,* 782–786.

90 Sontag, L. W. Somatopsychics of personality and body function. In D. C. Charles and W. R. Looft (eds.), *Readings in psychological development through life.* New York: Holt, Rinehart & Winston, 1973. Pp. 91–99.

91 Stagner, R. *Psychology of personality,* 4th ed. New York: McGraw-Hill, 1974.

92 Stewart, M. A. Hyperactive children. *Scientific American,* 1970, *222* (4), 94–98.

93 Thomas, A., S. Chess, and H. G. Birch. The origin of personality. *Scientific American,* 1970, *223* (2), 102–109.

94 Thomas, L. E. Clothing and counter culture: An empirical study. *Adolescence,* 1973, *8,* 93–112.

95 Trowbridge, N. Self concept and IQ in elementary school children. *California Journal of Educational Research,* 1974, *25,* 37–49.

96 *U.S. News & World Report:* When an authority looks into the problem of ugliness. Aug. 23, 1976, pp. 51–52.

97 Werry, J. S., and H. C. Quay. The prevalence of behavior symptoms in younger elementary school children. *American Journal of Orthopsychiatry,* 1971, *41,* 136–143.

98 Wilcox, A. H., and B. R. Fritz. Actual-ideal discrepancies and adjustment. *Journal of Counseling Psychology,* 1971, *18,* 166–169.

99 Willerman, L. Activity level and hyperactivity in twins. *Child Development,* 1973, *44,* 288–293.

100 Woolley, H. T. Agnes: A dominant personality in the making. *Journal of Genetic Psychology,* 1925, *32,* 569–598.

INDEX